> Endorsements for *Java Web Services Architecture*

A wonderfully clear and concise guide to using XML to interconnect your network services.

James Gosling
Sun Microsystems

Java Web Services Architecture *really is one of the nicest technical books I have seen in a long time, combining a basic introduction to the subject with a systematic coverage of a very technical set of specifications. I can't imagine anyone is going to write anything better than this for a software developer or architect that wants to design Java Web services applications.*

Java Web Services Architecture *is a nearly perfect guide book to what Web services are and to all aspects of the Java approach to Web services development. In a domain filled with vague generalities, this book is precise and practical. I really like the way it defines everything, one step at a time, to ensure you know exactly how all the confusing acronyms fit together to architect useful systems. The authors are Sun Java specialists and software architects from Hartford Financial Services and the combination of technical precision and business pragmatics works perfectly. The book assumes a basic knowledge of Java and UML and proceeds from there. If you are an architect or a Java developer and want to learn about Java Web services, this is the book to get.*

Paul Harmon, Senior Consultant
Distributed Architecture Service, Cutter Consortium

Web services aims to solve the challenges of linking enterprise software in a heterogeneous computing environment. Therefore, it is critical that every IT professional understand the technology and benefits of this evolution in distributed computing. This comprehensive book will provide you with the know-how to take advantage of the value created from loosely-coupled, reusable components in a service-oriented architecture.

Graham Glass
Chairman, Chief Architect and Founder, The Mind Electric

Appropriate use of service oriented architecture (SOA) is critical to the successful application of Web services technologies, and Java is one of the most important development languages for implementing Web services. This book contains an excellent introduction to SOA and cutting-edge information on the Java Web Services Development Pack (WSDP). Anyone developing Web services in Java will find this book of tremendous value.

Eric Newcomer
CTO, Iona

Java Web Services Architecture

> **James McGovern**

> **Sameer Tyagi**

> **Michael E. Stevens**

> **Sunil Mathew**

MORGAN KAUFMANN PUBLISHERS

AN IMPRINT OF ELSEVIER SCIENCE

SAN FRANCISCO   SAN DIEGO   NEW YORK   BOSTON
LONDON   SYDNEY   TOKYO

Senior Editor Lothlórien Homet
Editorial Assistant Corina Derman
Publishing Services Manager Simon Crump
Senior Project Manager Julio Esperas
Production Services Graphic World Publishing Services
Design Rebecca Evans and Associates
Composition Rebecca Evans and Associates
Illustration Technologies 'N Typography
Cover Design Frances Baca Design
Printer The Maple-Vail Book Manufacturing Group
Cover Image Great Rotunda Stone, Solomon R. Guggenheim Museum, New York;
Paul Edmondson, Getty Images

Morgan Kaufmann Publishers
An imprint of Elsevier Science
340 Pine Street, Sixth Floor
San Francisco, CA 94104–3205
www.mkp.com

Printed in the United States of America

07 06 05 04 03 5 4 3 2

Library of Congress Control Number: 2002117799

ISBN: 1–55860–900–8

This book is printed on acid-free paper.

Contents

Foreword   xi

Preface   xiii

Acknowledgments   xxi

Part {One}   The Foundation   1

Chapter 1   Web Services Overview   3

What Are Web Services?   4
History   4
Web Services Technology   14
Other Concerns   17
Java and Web Services   20
Application Scenarios   21
Implementation Scenarios   25
Benefits of Web Services   28
A Word about Standards   30
Summary   33
References   34

Chapter 2   Service-Oriented Architecture   35

SOA Entities   37
SOA Characteristics   40
Summary   61
References   62

Chapter 3   Component-Based Service Development   65

Development Lifecycle   66
Design   80

	Verification and Validation	91
	Maintenance	94
	Summary	95
	References	96
Chapter 4	**SOAP**	**97**
	The Case for SOAP	97
	What Does SOAP Define?	101
	SOAP Message Structure	102
	SOAP Message Elements	103
	SOAP Processing Model	112
	SOAP Encoding	119
	SAAJ	125
	Summary	131
Chapter 5	**WSDL**	**133**
	Describing a Web Service	134
	Describing Functional Characteristics of Services	135
	WSDL 1.2	174
	Summary	176
	References	176
Chapter 6	**UDDI**	**177**
	Discovering Web Services	178
	Categorizing Services	192
	Identifiers	196
	Business Entity Relationships	198
	UDDI's SOAP Interfaces	199
	UDDI and SOAP/WSDL Relationships	202
	Publishing WSDL Service Interfaces in UDDI	213
	Internationalization and Multiple Languages	216
	Extending a UDDI Registry	219
	UDDI4J	221
	Private UDDI Registries	227
	UDDI Futures	231
	Summary	233
Chapter 7	**ebXML**	**235**
	Architectural Overview of ebXML	237
	Putting It All Together	261
	Summary	262

Part
{Two} **The JAX APIs**   **265**

   Chapter 8 **Java Web Service Developer Pack**   **267**

      Setting Up Java WSDP   268
      Java WSDP Components   268
      Summary   276

   Chapter 9 **JAXP**   **277**

      JAXP Architecture   278
      SAX   278
      DOM   287
      When to Use SAX   292
      When to Use DOM   292
      When Not to Use Either   293
      JAXP and XML Schemas   293
      XSLT   298
      XSLTc   307
      JDOM   308
      JAXP RI   311
      Summary   311
      References   312

   Chapter 10 **JAX-RPC**   **313**

      JAX-RPC Service Model   314
      Data Types and Serialization   315
      JAX-RPC Development   336
      Advanced JAX-RPC   367
      JAX-RPC Interoperability   393
      JAX-RPC and J2EE   398
      Summary   402

   Chapter 11 **JAXM**   **405**

      Messaging and MOM   405
      Messaging and Web Services   410
      Messaging in Java   411
      JAXM Architecture   428
      Designing with JAXM   434
      Developing with JAXM   439
      What Is Right for Me—JAXM or JAX-RPC?   472
      Summary   476

Chapter 12	**JAXR**	**479**
	Registries and Repositories	479
	JAXR Architecture	480
	The JAXR Information Model	483
	The JAXR API	491
	JAXR to UDDI Mapping	531
	JAXR and ebXML Registry	533
	Summary	544

Chapter 13	**JAXB**	**545**
	The Need for Binding and JAXB	545
	When to Use JAXB	549
	JAXB Architecture	550
	Developing with JAXB	551
	XML-to-Java Mapping	555
	The JAXB API	559
	Validation with JAXB	566
	Customizing JAXB	567
	When to Use Custom Declarations	579
	Summary	580

Part {Three}	**Advanced Topics**	**581**

Chapter 14	**Transaction Management**	**583**
	Concepts	583
	A Transaction Model for Web Services	593
	New Transaction Specifications	597
	JSRs for Web Service Transaction Support	618
	Summary	619

Chapter 15	**Security**	**621**
	Security Considerations for Web Services	621
	Web Services Security Initiatives	626
	Canonical XML	634
	XML Digital Signatures	635
	Apache XML Security	639
	XML Encryption	648
	Security Assertions Markup Language	650

Web Services Security Assertions   658
XML Access Control Markup Language   658
XML Key Management Specification   659
WS-I Specifications   660
SOAP and Firewalls   668
Security and J2EE   669
Java Cryptography Extensions   672
Implementation Scenarios   676
Identity Management   680
Liberty Alliance   682
SourceID   685
Summary   688

Chapter 16   **Practical Considerations**   **689**

Systems Management   689
Interoperability   690
Pricing Models   693
XMLPay Specification   696
Service Level Agreements   697
Testing Web Services   699
Performance   703
High Availability   707
Scalability   713
Clustering   715
Fault Tolerance   718
Grid Computing   720
Enabling Services   722
Final Checklist   724
Summary   725

Chapter 17   **Future Standards**   **727**

Web Service Composition   728
Summary   742

Appendix A   **XML Schema**   **743**

Document Type Definition   745
XML Schema   747
Bringing It All Together   760
Advanced Topics   762
Summary   770

Appendix B **JSTL**   **771**

    Expression Languages   771
    Using JSTL   773
    XML Support Tags in JSTL   774
    Putting It Together   781

Appendix C **The Software Architect's Role**   **785**

    The Architect Manages Stakeholder Expectations   785
    The Architect Designs the System   787
    The Architect Implements the Baseline Architecture   788

    Index   **789**

    About the Authors   **829**

    About the CD   **831**

Foreword

> An Agile Foreword

I wish I had written this book. You really need to read it if you're building or using Web services with Java.

> A Prescriptive Foreword

I started programming in the early 1980s writing Fortran on cards. Technology has clearly improved since then and now I develop large-scale, mission-critical applications using multi-tiered J2EE and Web services. Not only have technologies improved in this time, so have methodologies. In the past I preferred a prescriptive approach to development, one that was documentation heavy and which required large teams of professionals to build complex systems. As I gained greater experience I came to realize that the overhead of prescriptive processes made them inappropriate for most modern efforts. I came to realize that a more streamlined approach, one that focuses on doing just the minimum required to get the job done, was much more effective. In other words I have learned that an agile approach is often superior to a prescriptive approach.

So what does that have to do with this book? This book is the equivalent of my "agile foreword"—it focuses on exactly what you need to get the job done without going into needless fluff. Each chapter covers a single concept that is critical to your success developing and/or using Web services in Java. The chapters are well written, and more importantly they are written by developers with real-world experience. Each chapter concisely covers the concepts that would be found in a specialized book ten times as long. Yet each chapter isn't simply an overview; instead it is a thorough discussion that describes everything you need to know to be effective. This book is really well done.

For the most part this book focuses on technology. Because the true focus of agile software development is on people, my agile analogy doesn't quite work. That's okay; the important thing is that I came up with a new approach to writing a foreword that has not to my knowledge been tried before. I guess I'll just have to learn to live with the guilt.

Part One describes the foundations of Web services, covering the basics that every developer needs to understand. This section could very easily have been a book on its own. Part Two does an incredible job of covering the Java technologies—JWSDP, JAXP, JAX-RPC, JAXM, JAXR, and JAXB—for Web services. Part Three and the Appendices cover topics critical to your success. In short, you want to read this book cover to cover. I could go into greater detail but the reality is that it's easier for you to simply read through the Table of Contents. Really. Go do it. Now. Don't worry, I'll wait for you.

<Pause>

Dum de dum de dum . . .

</Pause>

See what I mean? Pretty impressive. Although this book is large it covers everything you need to become an effective Web services developer. I can safely say that you would need to purchase several books to obtain material equivalent to what is contained here. So stop reading this foreword and read the book already!

Scott W. Ambler

Senior Consultant, Ronin International, Inc. (www.ronin-intl.com)

Coauthor of *Mastering EJB 2/e* and *The Elements of Java Style*

Preface

In many organizations, applications can be grouped into two broad categories: (1) outward-facing front-office or Web applications that involve user interaction and (2) back-office applications based on enterprise information resources (EIS) that are oriented toward running the core business. Web services hold the promise to provide a solution that will allow interoperability between the two approaches.

From the Fortune 500 to the Internet startup, each IT department has a guiding set of principles that include eliminating application silos, sharing critical information between applications, using open standards to eliminate vendor lock-in, and relying on proven, stable technologies to maximize return on investment and reduce total cost of ownership.

Web services are modular business process applications, based on open Internet standards, that are able to describe their own functionality and locate and dynamically interact with other Web services. They provide a method for different organizations to conduct dynamic e-business across the Internet, regardless of the application or the language in which the service was implemented.

The biggest benefit Web services provide is application interoperability. Traditional approaches required that two applications work together creating lots of work and even more planning. To be successful, users had to agree on standard mechanisms for data passing, the platforms to be used, and so on. The key to a cost-effective, agile integration is to convert these tightly coupled applications into loosely coupled distributed applications, by separating business logic from the data layer. Web services using Java and XML technologies are the key to making this possible.

The Web services approach uses WSDL (to describe), UDDI (to advertise), and SOAP (to communicate). Web services will be the approach used in the future to extend an organization's value chain. Many prominent book and magazine authors of Web services have used the technology to create hype and have even convinced many it is the Holy Grail that will solve their integration woes. While no technology can live up to its hype, the real power of Web services in the immediate future may be to allow legacy systems to communicate with each other. Large corporations face problems extending their old mainframe systems and have tried using messaging oriented middleware, with lots of effort expended but marginal success. Web services will enable both two-hundred-year-old Fortune 500 organizations and Internet startups to be successful in extending their systems and services to trading partners, customers, and other third parties.

Over the next couple of years, Web services will become the de facto method for communication between information systems. For those ready for the journey, this book is a guide to the best approach to architecting scalable, robust, extensible Web services in Java.

> Audience

There is no doubt that Web services are a hot topic. The term is strewn throughout the software development industry and across the media. Without a doubt, many publishers will provide books on each component in Web services architecture, with tons of code scattered across multiple pages.

This isn't one of those books. The author team—not only as writers but as purchasers of books themselves—wanted to write a book that allows architects and developers alike to understand what it takes to be successful in the architecture and implementation of Web services using Java. Our goal is to provide a broad overview of the major J2EE technologies and how they will help you succeed in a Web services paradigm. Java and J2EE technologies provide you with parts that can be joined to create the perfect solution for your organization. Each of the J2EE components used to build a Web service exploits another. It is equally important to show how each of the J2EE technologies works together.

If you are a chief technology officer, architect, developer, or even a manager and appreciate a no-frills introduction to Java and Web services, this is the book for you. The author team has diligently tried to create the ultimate guide that explains the architecture of a Java Web service. We strive to provide enough detail to satisfy our audience, to provide leading-edge but practical examples to illustrate how Web services can be applied to existing business and technology initiatives. Where additional detail is required, we provide the stepping-stone and point out other sources of information.

> Contents of This Book

Web services is the convergence of a suite of technologies into a cohesive whole. It unifies approaches that we as an industry have been doing in a standalone manner for many years. Java is a powerful technology that has contributed to the successful development of many large, mission-critical enterprise applications yet on its own is relatively powerless. When an enterprise combines Java with other industry principles such as XML, UML, object orientation, design patterns, and a good software development process, it can create meaningful services with strong value propositions: the key to Web services and this book.

We recommend that the chapters in this book, or at least in each part, be read in order, as each chapter builds on the previous one.

- Part I provides an overview of the motivation behind the creation of Web services and their usage. It briefly covers how to start designing a Web service and some of the infrastructure and other basic components used in Web service construction. It jumps into the standards and technologies used in all Web services, regardless of the language implemented. Here you will learn about Simple Object Access Protocol (SOAP), Web Services Description Language (WSDL), and Universal Description, Discovery and Integration (UDDI).

- Part II covers all the JAX APIs that are the foundation of Web services within Java. You'll learn about the basic usage of the APIs and some advanced techniques.

- Part III explores advanced topics that are not directly related to Java but are things to think about when architecting a Java-based Web service. It includes checklists, tips, and additional resources.

This book assumes you understand Java and have had real-world experience with the language. Its coverage of Java is limited to the APIs needed to deploy a Web service. All the examples use Java, but an understanding of another object-oriented language is sufficient. We also assume you have basic familiarity with XML and its syntax.

We have intentionally avoided presenting any formal software development process for Web services. The only processes mentioned in this regard are those that are time-tested and proven to lead you to success.

UML notation is expansive. This book limits its examples and usage of UML to use cases, class diagrams, and sequence diagrams, as these are the most useful in the development lifecycle. Within each of these types, we limit our diagrams' complexity to the level typically covered in an introductory book.

Because design patterns are used extensively in this book, we hope you have some familiarity with the topic. We assume you have a basic understanding of some of the most frequently used patterns with J2EE, such as Proxy, Adapter, Composite, Chain of Responsibility, Observer, and Bridge. If you are unfamiliar with this topic, we suggest the immediate purchase of *Core J2EE Patterns* and *Design Patterns*.

> Miscellaneous Ramblings

Authors and readers alike have their own religions when it comes to the best way to explain a given topic. In this book, most of the examples do not contain a blow-by-blow description of what the code is doing. This is intentional. Long lists of code are hard for readers to follow and provide no long-term benefit. Readers spend time learning the variable naming conventions and aspects, which distracts them from learning about the topic at hand.

We have also decided against printing out Javadocs, which are freely available for download from the *www.java.sun.com* site.

We have also avoided writing a book that contains highly speculative information on specifications not even close to release. While we are early adopters of many technologies used to create Web services, we have decided to create a book that has a longer shelf life and provides more for your money.

The momentum of Java and Web services will help revolutionize information technology. The author team has debated countless hours over the "best" way to help others build solutions that are extremely scalable, highly available, and easily maintainable. Many late nights have resulted in, we hope, the right mix of architectural advice and implementation details.

> Conventions Used in This Book

Text and Code

We observe code guidelines described in Scott Ambler's naming convention *(www.ambysoft.com)*. Where elements are subject to interpretation, we have left the choice up to each author.

To avoid ambiguity, we employ full method signatures throughout the book, including empty parentheses after the name of a no-argument method. The sole exception to this practice is for overloaded methods, such as println.

The vocabulary in this book conforms to the Java, UML, and design patterns usage. Where appropriate, we use nonstandard Java terminology (after first alerting the reader), coin a new term, or take exception to the official definition.

The terms *application server, server,* and *J2EE application server* are used interchangeably. Unless otherwise noted, these terms all refer to a J2EE application server.

For additional information on UML, we recommend *UML Distilled* and *Unified Modeling Language User Guide.*

Graphics

The graphical conventions used here are based on the Unified Modeling Language (UML) standard. UML is a modeling language for object-oriented and component-based development. Only subsets of the UML diagrams are used. The three primary UML diagrams used and of interest to our readers are use cases, sequence diagrams, and class diagrams. Use cases show interactions, class diagrams depict the static structure of classes, and sequence diagrams show dynamic object interaction. Because different notations can be used to represent the same model, Figures P.1 through P.3 illustrate how we use these UML conventions.

Figure P.1 illustrates the connectors, arrows, and other elements in a standard UML class diagram, along with different types of associations.

Figure P.2 illustrates the connectors and other elements used in a standard UML sequence diagram.

Figure P.3 illustrates the connectors and other elements used in a standard UML use case diagram.

Figure P.1
UML Class
Diagram

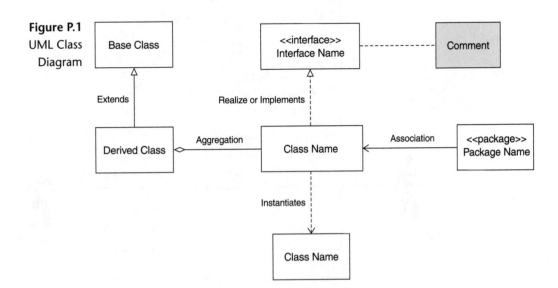

Figure P.2
UML Sequence
Diagram

Figure P.3
UML Use Case
Diagram

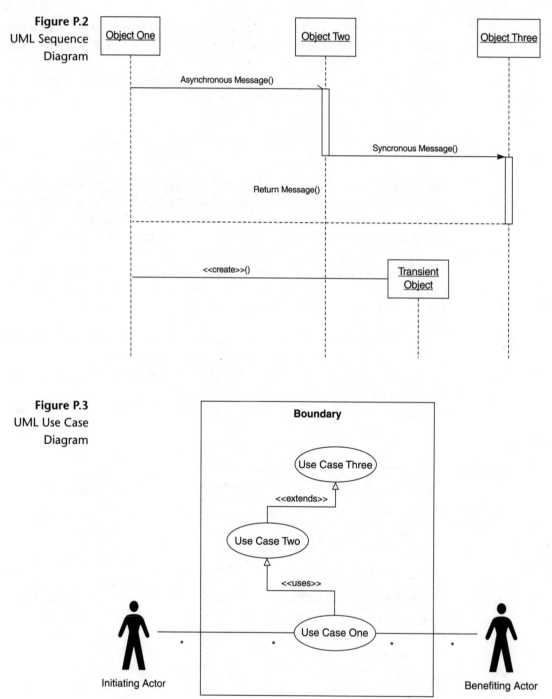

Code terms are indicated by a monospaced font, including interfaces, methods, variables, deployment descriptor elements, and programming language keywords (e.g., "uses a ServiceFactory object," "invokes the getServiceConfig method").

> More Information

The first source of additional information on Web services and Java is the J2EE Web site, *http://java.sun.com/j2ee*. The following are related to Web services and the Java J2EE platform and are of particular interest:

Books

Alur, D., Crupi, J., and Malks, D. *Core J2EE Patterns.* Prentice Hall, 2001.

Booch, G., Rumbaugh, J., and Jacobson, I. *The Unified Modeling Language User Guide.* Addison-Wesley, 1999.

Fowler, M., and Scott, K. *UML Distilled,* 2nd edition. Addison-Wesley, 2000.

Gamma E., Helm R., Johnson R., and Vlissides, J. *Design Patterns: Elements of Reusable Object-Oriented Software.* Addison-Wesley, 1994.

Kassem, N., et al. *Designing Enterprise Applications with the Java 2 Platform, Enterprise Edition.* Addison-Wesley, 2000.

Matena, V., and Stearns, B. *Applying* Enterprise JavaBeans: Component-Based Development for the J2EE Platform. Addison-Wesley, 2000.

Reed, P. *Developing Applications with Java and UML.* Addison-Wesley, 2002.

Web Sites

Java Community Process. *www.jcp.org.*

Sun Microsystems. Enterprise JavaBeans specification. *http://java.sun.com/j2ee/docs.html.*

——. Java API for XML Binding (JAXB) specification. *http://java.sun.com/xml/jaxb/index.html.*

——. Java API for XML Messaging (JAXM) specification. *http://java.sun.com/xml/jaxm/index.html.*

———. Java API for XML Processing (JAXP) specification. *http://java.sun.com/xml/ jaxp/index.html.*

———. Java API for XML Registries (JAXR) specification. *http://java.sun.com/xml/ jaxr/index.html.*

———. Java API for XML Remote Procedure Calls (JAX-RPC) specification. *http:// java.sun.com/xml/jaxrpc/index.html.*

———. Java API for XML Transactions (JAXTX) specification. *http://java.sun.com/ xml/jaxtx/index.html.*

———. Java Authentication and Authorization Service (JAAS). *http://java.sun.com/ security/jaas/doc.*

———. Java Authentication and Authorization Service specification. *http:// java.sun.com/products/jaas.*

———. JavaBeans Activation Framework Specification. *http://java.sun.com/prod-ucts/javabeans/glasgow/jaf.html.*

———. Java Naming and Directory Interface specification. *http://java.sun.com/ products/jndi.*

Organization for the Advancement of Structured Information Standards (OASIS). Universal Description, Discovery and Integration (UDDI) specification. *www.uddi.org.*

World Wide Web Consortium (W3C). Simple Object Access Protocol (SOAP) specification. *www.w3.org/TR/SOAP.*

———. Web Services Description Language (WSDL) specification. *www.w3.org/ TR/wsdl.*

Disclaimer

The source code used in this book is available on the accompanying CD. The code is free and may be used as your heart desires, with the sole restriction that you may not claim to be the author. Neither the publisher, the authors, nor their respective employers provide any form of warranty on the code or guarantee its usefulness for any particular purpose.

The author team and editors have worked hard to bring you an easy-to-understand, accurate guide to Java Web services architecture. If you find any mistakes, we would appreciate your contacting us at our email addresses given at the end of the book. We equally appreciate any comments, suggestions, and praise.

This book uses for its examples a fictitious online financial services organization named Flute Bank. Any example companies, organizations, products, domain names, email addresses, people, places, and events depicted herein are fictitious. No association with any real company, organization, product, domain name, email address, person, place, or event is intended or should be inferred.

Acknowledgments

This book is the result of many people's efforts. We would first like to thank our acquisitions editor, Lothlórien Homet, for providing insight into the publishing industry in general and allowing us to focus on writing a good book instead of simply following a publishing formula.

For a book to be successful requires the input and feedback of many people. We would like to acknowledge the reviewers who read our early work: the EBC team at Hartford Financial Services, Madhu Siddalingaiah, Casey Kochmer, Jason Bloomberg, Mitchell Smith, Brian Kernighan, and Anne Thomas Manes. We also gratefully acknowledge the reviewers: Dave Hollander, Jim Webber, Peter Herzum, Sang Shin, and Jeff Ryan.

Special acknowledgement goes to SOAP specialist Benjamin Navarez, who participated in the planning stages of the book but was unable to join the writing team.

James McGovern

I would like to thank my wife, Sherry; my mom and dad, Mattie and James; my mother-in-law, Soogia; and my late father-in-law, Sylvester, for their love, encouragement, and everlasting support. I would also like to thank my coworkers at Hartford Financial Services for providing the right balance of challenge and support. I would like to acknowledge past coworkers at Enherent and Command Systems for providing motivation, suggestions, and constructive criticism throughout my career. Finally, I would like to praise God for his blessings and mercy. I, James Jr., dedicate this book to my perfect son, Little James (a.k.a. James III).

Sameer Tyagi

I would like to dedicate this book to the people who taught me the things I like to do; to Steve Ahlfield and Caroline Goldman, for helping me make my first skydives; everyone at Executive Fliers and John Hannah, for helping me with my first flying lessons; Steve Burrows, who taught me my first note on the guitar; Bob Patz, who taught me to drive on the right side of the road; and Richard Bach, for his writings that made me think when I needed to; and Nadine Pelletier, for reminding me what a jerk I can be at times.

Michael E. Stevens

My life has been touched by many souls. I owe my life and my happiness to my wife, Rhonda, and my daughter, Katie, without whom I could not exist. To my father, Ed, and my mother, Doris, I would not be the person I am today without your love and support. To my sisters, Lori and Lisa, thank you for lifelong bonds that I cherish. To my niece and nephew, Cody and Jessica, you bring me joy. To my little angel, Christine, you are with me always.

Sunil Mathew

I am indebted to Stu Stern, whose inspiration, guidance, and advice shaped my career. My contributions to this book are, to a large extent, a direct result of knowledge gained while working at Sun. A special thanks to my friends Chris Steel and Shaun Terry for reviewing the initial drafts of my chapters. I acknowledge the help and support received from my colleagues at the Sun Java center in Boston and Somerset. Of course, this endeavor would not have been possible without the support and encouragement from my parents, Verghis and Sally Mathew, and from Sajan, Sheila, Sumith, and Amita.

Part {One}

The Foundation

In this section, we will provide an overview on the motivation behind the creation of Web services and their usage. This section briefly and succinctly covers initiating the design of a Web service and some of the infrastructure and other basic components that are used in its construction. It also covers the four standards that are used in Web services: Simple Object Access Protocol (SOAP), Web Services Description Language (WSDL), and Universal Description, Discovery and Integration (UDDI).

Chapter One *Web Services Overview*

The goal of Web services is to allow normally incompatible applications to interoperate over the Web regardless of language, platform, or operating system. Web services allow for business processes to be made available over the Internet.

Chapter Two *Service-Oriented Architecture*

Service-oriented architectures allow for business logic to be invoked across a network and can be discovered and used dynamically. A service is a behavior that is provided by a component for use by any other component-based service using only the interface contract. It stresses interoperability and may be dynamically discovered and used.

Chapter Three *Component-Based Service Development*

Component-based services allow applications to be assembled from components from a variety of sources. The components themselves may be written using different programming languages.

Chapter Four *SOAP*

SOAP is an XML-based protocol for accessing remote objects over networks.

Chapter Five *WSDL*

WSDL is an XML-based protocol for describing Web services and their functions, parameters, and return values.

Chapter Six *UDDI*

UDDI allows organizations to describe their business and services, to discover other businesses that offer desired services, and to integrate with these other businesses.

Chapter Seven *ebXML*

ebXML is a joint initiative between OASIS and UN/CEFACT to apply XML to electronic business using a common technical framework.

Chapter

Web Services Overview

The most significant aspect of Web services is that every software and hardware company in the world has positioned itself around these technologies for interoperability. No single technological advancement will have as great an impact on the way systems are developed as Web services.

Web services allow systems to communicate with each other using standard Internet technologies. Systems that have to communicate with other systems use communication protocols and the data formats that both systems understand. Developers use technologies such as CORBA, RMI, or DCOM most often. The principal problem with these communication technologies is that not every platform supports them. Developers must create gateways to convert an unsupported protocol and data format into one that the target platform understands.

The emergence of the Internet has forced vendors to support standards such as HTTP and XML. Over the past few years, vendors and their customers quickly realized that programs that communicate with each other could also use the technologies that run the Internet. Web services use Internet technology for system interoperability. The advantage that Web services have over previous interoperability attempts, such as CORBA, is that they build on the existing infrastructure of the Internet and are supported by virtually every technology vendor in existence. As a result of the ubiquitousness of the technologies they use, Web services are platform-independent. This means that whether the Web service is built using .NET or J2EE, the client uses the service in the exact same way. ▷

This platform independence is also evident on the World Wide Web itself. A Web site uses HTTP and HTML to pass data to a user's browser–this is the only requirement the site must support. A Web site may be developed using a large number of languages and platforms, but the platform is irrelevant as long as the

▷ "Ubiquitous computing" was first described in its current form by Mark Weiser at Xerox PARC. For more, see *http://www.ubiq.com/hypertext/weiser /UbiHome.html*.

data is ultimately provided to the browser using HTTP and HTML. These same principles apply to Web services.

Web services are fast becoming the single interoperability standard for program-to-program communication. This chapter answers the following questions:

What are Web services?

What is the history of computing in terms of its physical and logical evolutions?

What are the technologies involved in Web services?

How does Java support Web services?

What kinds of Web services are there?

What kind of benefits can be realized by implementing Web services?

▶ What Are Web Services?

"A Web service is a software application identified by a URI, whose interface and bindings are capable of being identified, described and discovered by XML artifacts and supports direct interactions with other software applications using XML based messages via Internet-based protocols."

(World Wide Web Consortium)

A Web service is simply an application that exposes a function that is accessible using standard Web technology and that adheres to Web services standards. This is significant because Web services are developed for and deployed onto any platform using any programming language. There is nothing revolutionary or exceptional about the technology of Web services. The technology is simple. In fact, you use and probably have developed applications already that incorporate most of the technologies of Web services.

▶ History

Before getting into the details of Web services, it is important to understand the history of computing systems and how they have evolved. Computer hardware has become more powerful, and more complex software is being built to take advantage of that power. However, the most striking aspect of the physical evolution of computing systems has been the advent of networking.

In the past, applications were initially limited to execution on one or a few interconnected machines. As networking grew, so did application size, complexity, and power. Today, vast interconnected computing resources on the Internet are available for applications to exploit. Yet the only way to do so is to develop new logical models for application development.

Traditionally, the main technique for managing program complexity has been to create more modular programs. Functions, objects, components, and services have allowed software developers to build units of reusable code whose implementations (data, behavior, and structure) are increasingly hidden from the consumer.

Another driving factor in this evolution is the business consumer's expectation that a company will provide more online access to information and a means for conducting business electronically. To satisfy this expectation, businesses have broadened the scope of their applications from small departments to the enterprise to the Internet. For instance, a company's inventory system became online procurement, and brochures became Web pages. Today, companies find themselves integrating enterprise applications to provide a single online experience for users.

Physical Evolution: The Evolution in Computer System Deployment

Historically, the physical evolution of systems has centered on the use of networking. Figure 1.1 and Table 1.1 show how faster and more available networks

Figure 1.1
The transformation in computer system deployment.

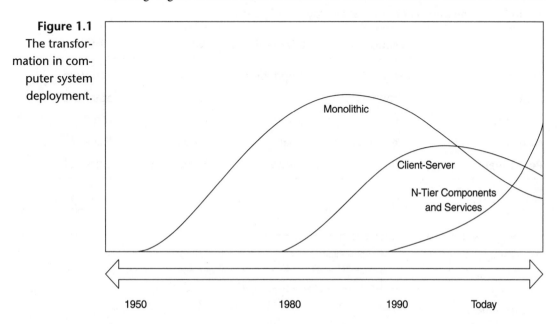

Monolithic

Client-Server

N-Tier Components and Services

1950   1980   1990   Today

have changed the way applications are written. Networks connect multiple dispa-rate computers into a distributed computing resource for a single application. In the early days, monolithic programs were written to run on a single machine. As departmental networks became popular, client-server and *n*-tier development became the standard. Now, the Internet has connected millions of computers into a vast sea of computing resources. Web services take advantage of this.

Monolithic

From the 1950s through the 1980s, programmers developed systems mostly on closed, monolithic mainframe systems, using languages such as COBOL and FORTRAN. These procedural methods for systems development, represented in Figure 1.2, required that all parts of a software system run on the same machine and that the program have direct access to the data upon which it was acting. The software was developed in a handful of languages and required an intricate knowledge of the physical storage of the data.

Software designers and programmers quickly realized that system and soft-ware decomposition were necessary to deal with software complexity and change. They implemented structured programs and shared libraries of code to separate software systems into different modules. These modules still had many dependencies with each other, and change was still difficult to manage.

Table 1.1   Comparison of Physical Deployment Types

	Monolithic	**Client-server**	**N-tier**	**WWW**
Data formats	Proprietary	Proprietary	Open	Standard
Protocols	Proprietary	Proprietary	Open	Standard
Scalability	Low	Low	Medium	High
Number of nodes	Very small	Small	Medium	Huge
Pervasiveness	Not	Somewhat	Somewhat	Extremely

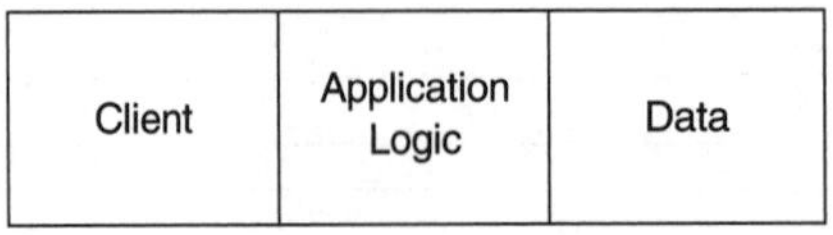

Figure 1.2
The monolithic
approach
to software
development.

Client	Application Logic	Data

Client-Server

In the 1980s, client-server computing fostered a leap forward in the decomposition of system components. As Figure 1.3 shows, client-server developers separated the processor of the data (client) from the keeper of the data (server). This separation was both logical and physical. The client process retrieved the data from a server across a network connection. This enhanced flexibility, because the data was encapsulated into a database server. Database designers and administrators wrapped the data in referential integrity constraints and stored procedures to ensure that no client program could corrupt the data. The relational database also insulated the client from having to know the physical layout of the data.

However, the layers of the application that presented the data to the user were usually intermingled with the layers of the application that acted on the data in the database. More separation of the presentation from the data manipulation logic was necessary. *N*-tier development attempted to do this.

N-*Tier Development*

N-tier development, which started in the early 1990s, reduced the coupling between the client and the business logic. As Figure 1.4 shows, developers created a business-logic layer that was responsible for accessing data and providing application logic for the client. This additional layer also allowed multiple clients to access the business logic. The clients converse with the business logic tier in less interoperable protocols, such as DCOM.

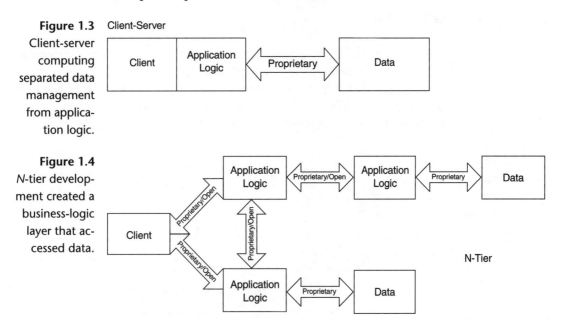

Figure 1.3 Client-server computing separated data management from application logic.

Figure 1.4 *N*-tier development created a business-logic layer that accessed data.

CORBA was and still is a technology that made client interaction with the application layer more open and flexible. However, CORBA did not allow clients across the Internet to easily access internal application logic. The CORBA protocol is not firewall-friendly. CORBA also has not produced a large enough following to make it a universal standard for interoperability.

World Wide Web

With the introduction of the World Wide Web, *n*-tier development has been taken a step further. As Figure 1.5 shows, developers create independent services accessible through the firewall. Services are modules that support one discrete function. For instance, a checking account service supports all the functions of managing checking accounts, and no other function. Clients interact with services using open technologies. Services are built from standard technologies, such as the ones used by the Internet. Applications are assemblies of services. Services do not "know" into which applications they are assembled.

The Internet itself has evolved and matured. Initially, it began as a way to publish scientific papers and was essentially static. The static system evolved into dynamic HTML, generated through CGI programs. Eventually, the dot-com era of the late 1990s brought a tremendous explosion of new technologies for creating full, robust Internet applications, including application servers such as J2EE and .NET.

Logical Evolution

Since its inception, software development has gone through several different logical models. Each development method shift, shown in Table 1.2, occurs in part to manage greater levels of software complexity. That complexity has been managed by continuously inventing coarser-grained software constructs, such as functions, classes, and components. These constructs are software "black boxes."

Figure 1.5
Services use open protocols that can be accessed through the Internet.

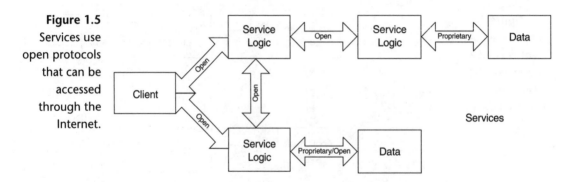

Table 1.2　Comparison of Logical Design Methods

	Structured development	Object-oriented development	Component-based development	Service-based development
Granularity	Very fine	Fine	Medium	Coarse
Contract	Defined	Private/public	Public	Published
Reusability	Low	Low	Medium	High
Coupling	Tight	Tight	Loose	Very Loose
Dependencies	Compile-time	Compile-time	Compile-time	Runtime
Communication scope	Intra-application	Intra-application	Interapplication	Interenterprise

Through an interface, a software black box hides its implementation by providing controlled access to its behavior and data. For example, objects hide behavior and data at a fine level of granularity. Components hide behavior and data at a coarser level of granularity.

Structured Design

Structured design and development (Yourdon and Constantine 1975), diagrammed in Figure 1.6, involves decomposing larger processes into smaller ones. Designers break down larger processes into smaller ones to reduce complexity and increase reusability. Structured design addresses the behavior portion of a software system separately from the data portion. Breaking down a program's structure helps develop more complex applications, but managing data within the application is difficult, because different functions act on much of the same data.

Structured development helps hide information about a program's structure and processes but does not hide details of the data within the program. A standard design principle known as *information hiding* (Parnas 1972) involves limiting the knowledge one part of a program has about another part. This includes data, data formats, internal structures, and internal processes. Object-oriented development allows developers to hide program behavior and data inside objects.

Object-Oriented Development

Object-oriented development (Booch 1990), represented by Figure 1.7, allows software designers and developers to encapsulate both data and behavior into classes and objects. This places the data near the code that acts on the data and reduces

Figure 1.6
Structured
design involves
decomposing
larger pro-
cesses into
smaller ones.

Structured Development

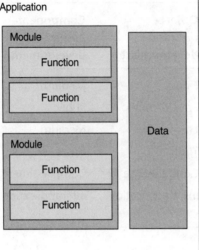

Figure 1.7
Object-
oriented
development
encapsulates
both data and
behavior into
classes and
objects.

Object Based Development

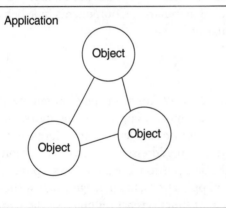

the dependencies between objects. An additional benefit to object orientation is that software structures more easily map to real-world entities. Object-based development advances the information-hiding principles of software design by providing more support for hiding behavior and data.

However, a large number of interconnected objects create dependencies that can be difficult to manage. In a large system, objects tend to know a lot about each other's structures and internal states. Objects are relatively fine-grained. Although interfaces control access to object internals, a large number of fine-grained objects make dependencies difficult to control in large applications. Component-based development helps construct large object-oriented applications.

Component-Based Development

Components are larger and coarser grained than objects and do not allow programs to access private data, structure, or state. *Component-based development* allows developers to create more complex, high-quality systems faster than ever before, because it is a better means of managing complexities and dependencies within an application.

Szyperski (1998) defines a software component as "a unit of composition with contractually specified interfaces and explicit context dependencies only. A software component can be deployed independently and is subject to composition by third parties." A component is a small group of objects with a contractually specified interface, working together to provide an application function, as shown in Figure 1.8. For example, a claim, automobile, and claimant object can work together in a claims component to provide the claim function for a large insurance application. The claim and automobile objects are not accessible to any

Figure 1.8
Component-based development involves a small group of objects with a contractually specified interface, working together to provide an application function.

Component-Based Development

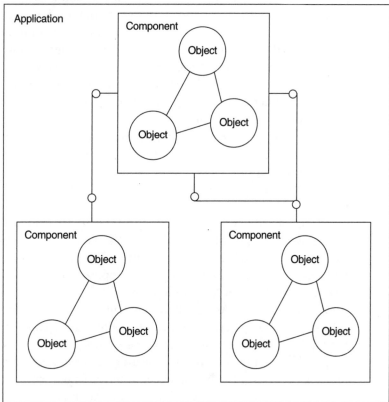

other part of the system except the claim component. This means that no other part of the system can become dependent on these objects, since they are completely hidden.

The protocols used to access components cannot easily pass through a firewall, making these protocols less interoperable. In addition, components are composed into applications at the time the developer compiles the program (compile time). An application that uses a component must have the interface definition at compile time, so the interface can be bound to and executed at runtime. Service-based development helps solve these problems.

Service-Based Development

With *service-based development,* represented in Figure 1.9, services are usually components wrapped in a service layer. A service tends to aggregate multiple components into a single interface and is thus coarser-grained. Also, the consumer of a service does not know the location or the interface of the service until runtime. This is called "late binding." The consumer finds the location of the service at runtime by looking it up in a registry, which also contains a pointer to the service contract. The contract describes the interface for the service and how to invoke it.

The service contract is discovered dynamically at runtime, bound to, and then executed. This feature of service-based development allows the consumer to perform real-time contract negotiation with several services in a dynamic fashion. For example, if several credit-card authorization services are available, the service consumer may use the service that offers the best rate for the transaction at the moment of execution.

While pure runtime binding is possible, it is important to note that many service consumers use the service contract to generate a proxy class at compile time that is used at runtime. When service consumers use this method to invoke a service, the service consumers are technically bound to the service contract at compile time.

Service-based development has solved the interoperability issue by adopting Web-based interoperability standards. Web services use the HTTP protocol to transfer data and XML for the data format. This allows service requests to easily pass through firewalls. Service-based development has been enabled through the advent of the Internet, the World Wide Web, and the ubiquitous technologies they have promoted. As we will see in Chapter 2, services have also realized true information hiding between parts of the application. This is done by separating the service's interface from its implementation.

In addition, the potential for reusing services in applications has greatly increased, because of the use of standard technologies, which have also enabled

Figure 1.9
In service-
based develop-
ment, services
are usually
components
wrapped in a
service layer.

Service-Based Development

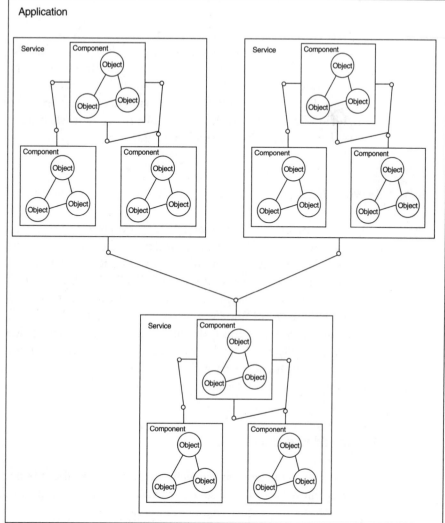

broader interorganization service use. Standards bodies have formed to develop definitions for XML messaging within trading partner communities, to external- ize the semantics of services. Trading partners adopt these messaging standards rather than creating their own. The data formats are standardized by external bodies, which reduces idiosyncrasies in the way an organization's services must be used. This allows organizations to use each other's services more freely.

▷ Web Services Technology

The Web services stack (adapted from Kreger 2001), shown in Figure 1.10, categorizes the technology of Web services into a layered model. The stack starts at the bottom with the basic technologies that allow data to transfer from one machine to another. Each layer builds on the lower layers and adds higher-level abstractions. The upper layers of the stack do not necessarily depend on the lower layers and in some ways are orthogonal concerns. They are shown in this format simply to demonstrate a higher level of abstraction.

Service Transport

The main function of the service transport layer is to transfer data from one machine to another. This is the protocol for the transmission of data for Web services. Web services use multiple transports to transfer data from service to service—including, but not limited to, HTTP, SMTP, and FTP.

The most popular protocol by far for use in Web services is HTTP. The Internet and the World Wide Web use HTTP to transmit data. HTTP is not blocked by most firewalls and thus is the standard for interoperable systems. HTTP 1.0 is a connectionless and stateless protocol. This means that each request and response a client sends and receives from a server is independent and not in the overall context of a conversation.

Service Messaging

The messaging layer of the technology stack describes the data formats used to transmit data from one service to another over the transport. XML is the base

Figure 1.10
Web services
technology
stack.

Web Services Technology Stack

Layer Description	Implementation(s)	Other Concerns			
Standard Messaging	Electronic Business XML Initiative (ebXML)				
Service Composition	Business Process Execution Service for Web Services (BPEL4WS)				
Service Registry	Universal Description, Discovery and Integration (UDDI) ebXML Registries	Quality of Service	Management	Security	Service Development
Service Description	Web Services Description Language (WSDL)				
Service Messaging	Simple Object Access Protocol (SOAP)/Extensible Markup Language (XML)				
Service Transport	Hypertext Transfer Protocol (HTTP) Simple Mail Transfer Protocol (SMTP) File Transfer Protocol (FTP)				

format used for Web services. XML is a text-based protocol whose data is represented as characters in a character set. The XML data is structured as a tree with elements, and the entire tree structure is called a document. XML has no data description separate from the data itself, unlike fixed or delimited data formats. The messages are self-describing. The data has specially formatted tags around it that give the data a name as well as a position in the document's tree structure.

Simple Object Access Protocol (SOAP) is a specification that tells a service consumer and a service provider how to format and read a specially formatted XML message for use in a service. A SOAP message has three sections: the envelope, the header, and the body.

The envelope is the top element of the XML message. It indicates that the message is a SOAP message, and it has instructions for processing the message.

The SOAP header contains application context information and directives. The header information is usually read and processed by the server, not the service. For instance, if an application needs entries for authentication or transaction management, the header will contain data for these features. SOAP messages can be passed along through multiple intermediaries between the service consumer and the service provider. Each intermediary reads the header information and uses it for routing, logging, and other system functions.

The SOAP body contains the application data. Web services support multiple message exchange patterns. A SOAP message may be sent in a document-oriented format or an RPC style format. In a document-oriented message exchange, the service consumer and provider exchange XML documents. In the RPC-style message exchange, data is passed as arguments. SOAP messages are by nature one-way transmissions from a sender to a receiver but are usually combined to implement a request/response model.

For an extensive look at the SOAP protocol, please refer to Chapter 4.

Service Description

The service description specifies three aspects of the service:

- Operations the service has made available
- Messages the service will accept
- The protocol to which the consumer must bind to access the service

Web services uses the Web Services Description Language (WSDL) to specify a service contract. The service contract is a description of a set of endpoints that operate on messages and the specification for how an XML document should be formatted when it is sent to the endpoints. An endpoint is a network address that accepts a message formatted to the specification defined in the WSDL. WSDL uses the term *port* to describe a service endpoint for a message. WSDL describes the contract for a service as a collection of ports the service has made available.

The service consumer uses the service description in one of two ways. At development time, the consumer can generate a service stub by using the service description. The service stub is a class that has an API that matches the service description. The service consumer binds to the stub at compile time. This is called "early binding." Web services also support the concept of "late binding," a runtime-only binding between the consumer and the producer. This is done by using a dynamic proxy configured dynamically at runtime by using the WSDL description of the service.

Chapter 5 discusses WSDL in depth.

Service Registry

Web services support the concept of dynamic discovery of services. A consumer of a service uses a service registry to find the services it is interested in using. Universal Description, Discovery and Integration (UDDI) is a Web service itself that supports a standard set of services that allow a Web service consumer to dynamically discover and locate the description for a Web service. UDDI registries are themselves Web services that expose an API as a set of well-defined SOAP messages. The Web service provider and Web service consumer use SOAP and HTTP to publish and retrieve information about services in the registry. Public UDDI registries contain a Web services contact, business owner, and technical information about the Web service. UDDI supports two types of conversations:

- The service provider uses the UDDI directory to publish information about the Web services it supports.

- The Web service consumer sends SOAP-formatted XML messages over HTTP to the UDDI directory, to retrieve a listing of Web services that match its criteria.

- For more on UDDI, please refer to Chapter 6.

Service Composition

Service composition, an emerging topic in Web services, refers to the ability to combine Web services into a business process. This is also referred to as *service orchestration* or *service choreography*. Service composition is the ability to sequence and manage conversations between Web services into a larger transaction. For example, a transaction that adds a customer to a bank account service might also create several accounts along with adding the customer information to the customer service. All of these requests are managed in the context of a larger business process flow that either succeeds or fails as a whole.

There are a number of proposed languages for specifying business process flows; the two most popular are WSFL and XLANG. Recently, IBM, Microsoft, and BEA combined both specifications into a single specification called Business Process Execution Language for Web Services (BPEL4WS).

> Other Concerns

Besides the technology concerns of building Web services, several issues are related to the creation, management, security, and development of Web services.

Quality of Service

When deploying a Web service for use by applications, it is not necessarily good enough to specify just the Web service interface and location . If the Web service takes longer to execute than the caller expects, the service will still fail. The specification for the amount of time it takes the service to return a result is part of the service's quality of service (QoS) specification. The QoS specification also contains some of the following information (Mani and Nagarajan 2002):

Availability: Availability is the quality aspect of whether the Web service is present or ready for immediate use. Availability represents the probability that a service is available. Larger values represent that the service is always ready to use while smaller values indicate unpredictability of whether the service will be available at a particular time. Also associated with availability is time-to-repair (TTR). TTR represents the time it takes to repair a service that has failed. Ideally smaller values of TTR are desirable.

Accessibility: Accessibility is the quality aspect of a service that represents the degree it is capable of serving a Web service request. It may be expressed as a probability measure denoting the success rate or chance of a successful service instantiation at a point in time. There could be situations when a Web service is available but not accessible. High accessibility of Web services ca be achieved by building highly scalable systems. Scalability refers to the abililty to consistently serve the requests despite variations in the volume of requests.

Integrity: Integrity is the quality aspect of how the Web service maintains the correctness of the interaction in respect to the source. Proper execution of Web service transactions will provide the correctness of interaction. A transaction refers to a sequence of activities to be treated as a single unit of work. All the activities have to be completed to make the transaction successful. When a transaction does not complete, all the changes made are rolled back.

Performance: Performance is the quality aspect of Web service, which is measured in terms of throughput and latency. Higher throughput and lower latency values represent good performance of a Web service. Throughput represents the number of Web service requests served at a given time period. Latency is the round-trip time between sending a request and receiving the response.

Reliability: Reliability is the quality aspect of a Web service that represents the degree of being capable of maintaining the service and service quality. The number of failures per month or year represents a measure of reliability of a Web service. In another sense, reliability refers to the assured and ordered delvery for messages being sent and received by service requestors and service providers.

Regulatory: Regulatory is the quality aspect of the Web service in conformance with the rules, the law, compliance with standards, and the established service level agreement. Web services use a lot of standards such as SOAP, UDDI, and WSDL. Strict adherence to correct versions of standards (for example, SOAP version 1.2) by service providers is necessary for proper invocation of Web services by service requestors.

Security: Security is the quality aspect of the Web service of providing confidentiality and nonrepudiation by authenticating the parties involved, encrypting messages, and providing access control. Security has added importance because Web service invocation occurs over the public Internet. The service provider can have different approaches and levels of providing security depending on the service requestor.

These are also called the service's *nonfunctional aspects*. Web services do not currently have a way to specifiy QoS parameters. The UDDI registry is the logical place to store this information; however, the fact that the registry is not capable of doing so is one of the inadequacies of the current UDDI specification (Tarak 2002). Even without direct UDDI support, a known service consumer and a service producer should agree on a service level agreement (SLA) for the services provided.

Management

An organization that implements Web services must be concerned with the management of their services. A service will require changes from time to time. The messages a service accepts, the routing of messages from one service to another, and the usage of the service will change over time. Tools for managing these changes involve

- Monitoring the execution of Web services
- Chargeback of Web service usage
- Metering service usage
- Evolution of Web services from machine to machine
- Management of Web services versioning
- Routing messages
- Transformation of messages

These capabilities involve both reporting and changing the configuration parameters for a service. The reporting capabilities are necessary to find out what applications are using the service at a given point in time. Reporting also involves monitoring service usage over a period of time. This is necessary to understand the growing or shrinking demand on the service for capacity planning and to provide information about service utilization so that users can be charged accordingly.

When the requirements of the service change, such as a new argument, the configuration parameters for the service must also change. A flexible service allows a service administrator to update its behavior by changing configuration parameters and not by changing program code.

Service management is an important aspect to Web services. The Web services an organization develops should also consider the effort required to manage those services once they are placed into production.

Security

The security requirements for a service vary. Security standards are still emerging for services that must be secure over an Internet connection. The issues involved with securing Web services include

Authenticating that users or applications are who they say they are

Authorizing users or applications for access to the service

Making sure that the data is not intercepted

These issues are solved by providing mechanisms for creating digital signatures that validate that service consumers are who they say they are. In addition, the set of credentials or claims service consumers present service providers are necessary for them to obtain authorization. Finally, the transport itself must use encryption to ensure that messages cannot be intercepted and read by an unauthorized third party.

These are only some of the issues involved with security. The task of securing Web services is difficult. The details of the current and future means of doing so are vast. For complete coverage of this topic, please refer to Chapter 15.

Service Development

Organizations that create services must be concerned with the tools and techniques they use to develop those services. An organization that develops services must choose the set of frameworks, integrated development environments, XML editors, and other tools that enable the creation of high-quality services quickly. In addition, implementation of each service an organization creates should follow a common architecture, which enhances the service's maintainability and reusability. A common service architecture can also provide common management features for all services that plug into a management toolset for administrators. Common tools and architecture are essential components to addressing the issues related to developing Web services.

> Java and Web Services

Web services are platform-independent. This means that a Web service may be developed in a large number of languages to run on many platforms. The Java language and Java 2 Enterprise Edition (J2EE) platform provide features for building and deploying Web services. The benefits of the Java language and the J2EE platform are vendor independence and application portability. Applications built on the J2EE platform may be deployed on J2EE implementations from a large number of vendors. Using Java to develop Web services gives you the benefit of vendor independence in addition to the inherent platform independence of Web services.

Java has support for Web services through the Java Web Services Developer Pack (JWSDP). JWSDP contains libraries for generating XML and SOAP, processing XML, accessing service registries, and calling RPC-based Web services. JWSDP and the libraries it contains constitute the bulk of this book, so we won't go into detail here.

▷ Application Scenarios

A case can be made for using Web services in many types of applications, ranging from home appliances to video games, because Web services can be implemented to solve many different types of problems. However, Web services are getting the most attention from organizations building business-to-business and enterprise application integration (EAI) applications.

Business-to-Business

The most widely talked-about use for Web services is business-to-business transactions. Web services enables business-to-business communication across the Internet or on private networks. Businesses are forming and joining "trusted partner" organizations, in which members agree on external semantic standards for messaging. Web services are a set of specifications that provide interoperability for these trading communities. Organizations such as OASIS *(www.oasis-open.org)* are creating standards for electronic commerce. ebXML *(www.ebxml.org)*, a set of specifications for XML messages in electronic commerce, is jointly sponsored by OASIS and UN/CEFACT. RosettaNet is another consortium of companies that provide XML specifications for electronic commerce.

Prior to the ebXML and RosettaNet specifications, electronic data interchange (EDI) was the standard for electronic business. EDI was expensive to implement and is still a fairly closed system. The networks were usually private, and the data formats were mostly proprietary, specific to an industry, and sometimes particular to a pair of trading partners. The conventions used by standards such as ebXML allow developers to build applications based on common structures and syntax for messaging across all industries.

Many industries form consortiums to define messaging formats specific to their industry. For example, the ACORD group provides specifications for messaging related to the insurance industry. IFX provides standards related to the banking industry. Hundreds of consortiums, some active and some not, set standards for nearly any industry imaginable.

Web services do not by themselves provide business-process collaboration capabilities. Standards such as ebXML provide a basis for complex message interactions between organizations, enabling trading partners to participate in open and complex business processes. Also, the ebXML group has standardized common services, such as exceptions, security, and notification of failure. These larger infrastructure requirements would not be possible without new external and independent semantic standards for managing them.

Through the convergence of the Internet, Web services, and messaging standards, organizations can conduct electronic business in a standard and open way. They can leverage existing applications by placing Web service façades for those applications on the Internet to perform electronic business. However, because of a concern for security and a slow standards process, progress in this area is slow.

Enterprise Application Integration

The more likely short-term candidate for Web services use is in the enterprise application integration (EAI) space. EAI is a solution to the problem of getting applications within an organization to communicate with each other. It converts the protocols and data formats that internal applications use. In many ways, this is the same problem Web services solve.

Vendors have created EAI products to solve the problem of communication between applications within an organization. These EAI product suites strive to solve three problems:

- Wire protocol conversion
- Data format transformation
- Routing messages between systems

Typical EAI products deliver tools that adapt one protocol to another or that provide a single standard for interoperability. The typical EAI solution, shown in Figure 1.11, follows a "hub-and-spoke" model for application integration. That

Figure 1.11
The enterprise
application
integration
hub-and-spoke
topology.

EAI Hub and Spoke

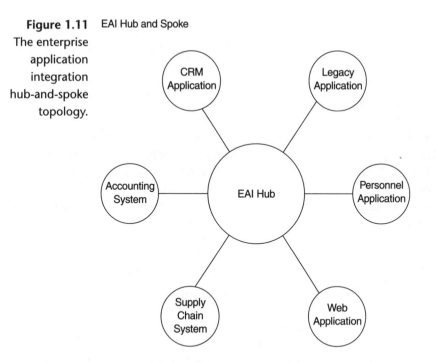

is, each application that needs to communicate with another must first send the message to the EAI hub, which transforms and routes the message to the recipient on behalf of the sender.

Some products allow the sender and receiver to use different protocols. For instance, upon purchasing a customer relationship management (CRM) system, an organization needs to populate data for that system from legacy COBOL applications that reside on the mainframe. The CRM application can use a standard middleware protocol, such as IBM's MQSeries, to communicate with the EAI hub, or it may choose a different protocol, such as HTTP. The EAI hub will accept the message over multiple protocol types, transform the message into a format that a COBOL application understands, and route the message to the host system. All viable EAI vendors are adding Web services support to their products. This will allow the EAI products to route Web services messages to other data formats and protocols.

EAI solutions have several drawbacks. They are expensive, and they externalize many business rules outside the application. Typical EAI products have specialized languages to describe the rules for data transformation and routing. The rules for data transformation use data tables and have specific knowledge about the data formats. Some EAI products, if not managed correctly, can house a major part of the business rules for an application. The hub-and-spoke model for communication makes integration and management of an EAI solution easier, but it introduces a single point of failure that leaves many systems vulnerable. The single-point-of-failure problem has been mitigated in EAI products by providing hot backup and clustering features. However, a rule corruption problem, a bad version upgrade, or some other catastrophe could bring down an entire enterprise that relies on the EAI solution.

Web services solve some of these problems. The business logic is not externalized. The logic for transforming the data into a format the service understands is close to the service. Finally, Web services do not follow the hub-and-spoke model. Each connection from Web service consumer to Web service producer is a direct connection, with no third-party involvement. Therefore, problems are localized to individual services, which allows other services to function normally.

In addition, instead of using EAI solutions for protocol and data format translations, systems communicate directly with each other over Web services, as shown in Figure 1.12. Instead of having a single point of failure using hub-and-spoke topology, Web services form a semi-lattice topology for application communication.

Newer vendor products are emerging to manage Web services in an enterprise. These products provide message routing, orchestration, and service management. Some of these products implement a "service bus" paradigm similar to the EAI model.

Figure 1.12
The enterprise application integration Web services topology.

EAI Direct

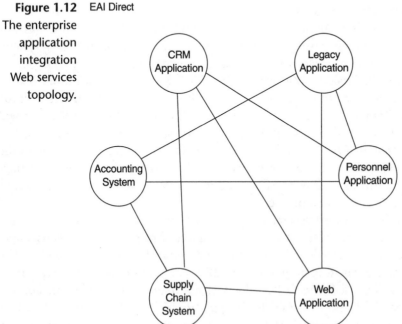

> **Implementation Scenarios**

Since a Web service can be developed on many different types of platforms, it can follow many different implementation models. The implementation model it uses depends on the problem it needs to solve and the platforms available to create it. The model for Web service implementations can be grouped into four types: simple service, composite service, middleware service, and service bus.

Simple Service

A *simple service,* shown in Figure 1.13, is a service-enabled component or servlet that accesses a database or other resource directly. For instance, if a company has a stateless session bean that handles credit-card validation, JAX-RPC can be used to provide a Web service interface. This is an example of a simple Web service. Simple services are most common for green-field development of a small, discrete function.

Composite Service

A *composite service,* shown in Figure 1.14, fronts other simple or composite services. The composite service does this to create a coarser-grained behavior. For instance, an order-entry service would be a composite service that uses a credit-card authorization service, a customer service, and an order-entry component. The combination of these three functions into a composite service also gives the service consumer the ability to use each service separately or together through the order-entry service.

Figure 1.13
A simple
Web service
scenario.

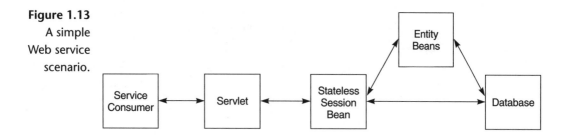

Middleware Service

A Web service that places requests onto a middleware bus is an example of *middleware service* implementation, shown in Figure 1.15. Many organizations have existing messaging oriented middleware (MOM) systems installed. A MOM system provides third-party binding from the message sender to the message receiver. A message sender places a message on a queue, which is mapped to an endpoint. The sender is not aware of the physical location or implementation of that endpoint.

Service Bus

The *service bus,* shown in Figure 1.16, is similar to the EAI solution for enterprise application integration. It lets Web services communicate with each other through a third party.

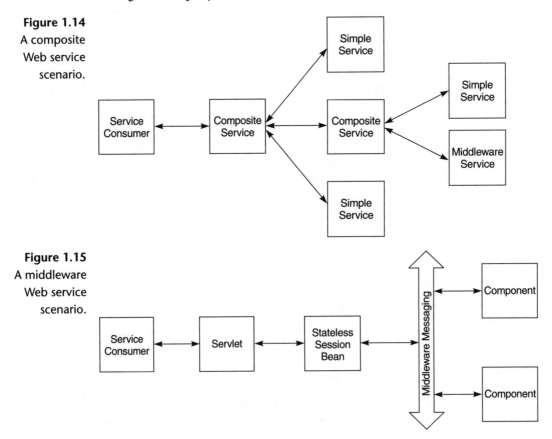

Figure 1.14
A composite
Web service
scenario.

Figure 1.15
A middleware
Web service
scenario.

For example, consider a banking application that consists of a banking graphical user interface (GUI) and an account service for processing deposit requests. Upon system startup, the account service registers its interest in deposit requests with a service bus. Let's assume that a banking GUI accepts a deposit request from a user. Rather than a banking GUI communicating with the account service directly, the banking GUI places the request onto the service bus. Because the account service registered its interest in deposit requests, the service bus forwards the request to the account service on the requester's behalf. The account service receives the deposit request from the service bus, processes the request, and places the results back onto the service bus. Then, on behalf of the account service, the service bus forwards the results to the banking GUI for display.

This method of routing messages between Web services is powerful. Not only can the account service get a notification that a message has been placed on the bus it is interested in, but other services can register their interest as well. If a logging service or a customer relationship management service were also interested in deposit to account requests that appeared on the bus, they, too, could register their interest in these transactions. This is a multi-cast method of communication,

Figure 1.16
A service bus.

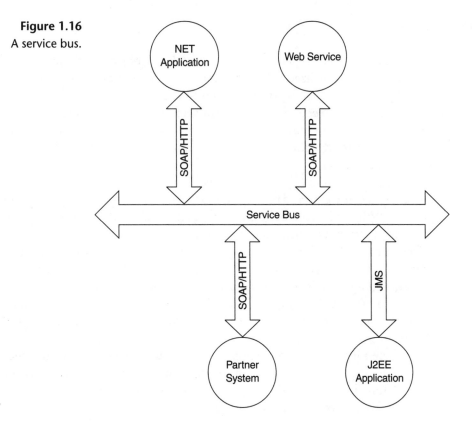

where a single requester can send messages to multiple services simultaneously. The requester also has no knowledge of what other services are consuming its request. The service bus management software configures the routing of these messages. The service bus also provides many other capabilities of an EAI solution such as transforming requests from one format to another. In all these scenarios, there are distinct benefits to using Web services. The following section explores many of them.

> Benefits of Web Services

For any new idea to be adopted by industry, it must have distinct benefits over other solutions. So far in this chapter, we have explored the evolution to Web services and some of the ways to implement a Web service. Many of the benefits have been implied, but now we lay them out explicitly (Stevens 2002).

Reusability

The promise of reusable legacy applications, databases, objects, and components have been largely unrealized. Web services can play a significant role in improving software reusability within organizations. Web services can wrap legacy applications, databases, objects, and components and expose them as reusable services. The likelihood of reusability depends on several factors that Web services improve on: interoperability, modularity, central registry, and reduced compile-time dependencies.

Interoperable technology improves reuse. For instance, if it is difficult for an application to connect to and use a component, it is unlikely the component will be reused. Web services are built on open, interoperable, and ubiquitous standards, which maximizes their potential for reuse.

The creation of a robust service layer improves reusability, which leads to a better return on the investment. Services map to distinct business domains. For example, a company might create an inventory service that has all the methods necessary to manage the company's inventory. Placing the logic into a separate layer allows the layer to exist well beyond the lifetime of any system into which it is composed.

Developers have two options when they create functionality. They can either develop the functionality as part of the application that needs it or as a separate service. A function developed as a separate component and used as a service is more likely to outlive the original application.

Location Transparency

A service environment achieves location transparency, because the location is stored in a registry. A client finds and binds to a service and does not care where the service is located. Therefore, an organization has the flexibility to move services to different machines or to move a service to an external provider.

It is also possible to move code from one platform to another. Service-oriented architecture requires that the service support the published contract. The way the service is implemented is irrelevant. Therefore, if it becomes necessary to move a service from a J2EE platform to a .NET platform, no changes to the clients should be necessary.

"Wrap and replace" is a powerful pattern in a service-oriented environment. It gives an organization the flexibility to service-enable current legacy systems without losing the ability to sunset the systems later. A service-enabled legacy system can be replaced with a new component or system without requiring changes to the clients who use the service.

Composition

Developers assemble applications from a preexisting catalog of reusable services. Services do not depend on the applications into which they are composed. Because services are independent, developers will logically reuse these services in many applications. The interface design process promotes the design of interfaces that are modular and independent from the application for which they are designed. Properly designed interfaces and the creation of independent components will also maximize these items' potential for composition into other applications.

Developers by nature want to reuse software unless it is more difficult to reuse than to build from scratch. One of the greatest impediments to reuse is determining the software available for reuse. The registry in a service-oriented architecture provides this single place to store service descriptions.

Scalability and Availability

A system is scalable if the overhead required to add more computing power is less than the benefit the additional power provides. Because service clients know only about the service interface and not its implementation, changing the implementation to be more scalable and available requires little overhead. Typical Java implementations of Web services are deployed into a clustered environment, where the servlets and entity beans that implement the service logic are replicated, and requests are dynamically routed to instances of each, based on load.

Even without a clustered execution environment, a Web service that receives a request may route that request to multiple endpoints for execution. The logic for routing may be based on the identity of the requestor. For instance, the Web service may route VIP customer requests to a high-speed server and other customer requests to a lower-powered server. A request-dispatcher Web service can forward requests to different servers, because one of the requirements of service-oriented architecture is location transparency. This feature promotes scalability, because a load balancer may forward requests to multiple service instances without the knowledge of the service client.

Maintaining Investment in Legacy Applications

Services help maintain investments in legacy applications because they specify only the method of interaction, not the method of implementation. Legacy systems can be wrapped in a service façade. This method of creating services has the advantage of allowing organizations to replace legacy applications without changing the way that consumers access the service.

Reduced Vendor Dependence

As long as the platform used to build the application supports Web services standards, it is irrelevant to the consumer of the service. Web services allow organizations to make decisions about which platform to use based on the merits of the platform rather than vendor lock-in. Web services represent a major shift in power from the software and hardware vendor to the software and hardware consumer.

> A Word about Standards

Web services are a collection of technologies driven by standards. Standards are extremely important for the adoption of Web services to be successful. The interoperability of different vendors' Web service implementations rests on the standards process. A vague specification will ultimately mean that different vendor implementations will not work together.

Today, Web services consist of specifications that are not quite standards yet. This is because it takes a long time for a specification to ultimately mature to a standard. Typically, once a specification is available in a working draft, vendors will build products that implement the specification. In fact, many specifications become de facto standards before the are ultimately approved as standards by the organization that proposes them.

Several organizations manage Web service specifications. These organizations are consortiums of companies, universities, and individuals, each of which is responsible for one or more of the specifications. Table 1.3 shows which group owns what specification.

Each group has a slightly different process for creating a standard. Many standards bodies follow a process similar to that of the World Wide Web Consortium (W3C), which is as follows (W3C 2002):

- A need is identified that is in the domain of the standards body.

- A working group is formed that analyzes the need and creates a working draft of a specification document that addresses the need.

- The working group creates a last-call working draft that the working group feels is complete. Thise draft goes to other W3C groups and members as well as to the general public for review.

- Once all issues and objections the reviewers raise have been answered, the draft becomes a candidate recommendation.

- The candidate recommendation is used in software implementations. If it can be shown that all objections have been answered and if two or more of the implementations of the candidate recommendation are shown to be interoperable, the candidate recommendation can become a proposed recommendation.

- If progress on the adoption of the proposed recommendation continues within the W3C and the public, the proposed recommendation becomes a recommendation. The recommendation is the highest level of maturity within the W3C. The recommendation stays at recommendation level indefinitely. At this point, the recommendation can also be submitted to other standards bodies for approval.

If at any level the proper entrance criteria are not met, the specification will not progress through the other levels of approval. It is also possible that the recommendation may fall back to a previous level if sufficient objections or issues are raised.

Table 1.3 Web Services Standards Bodies

Organization	Web site	Description	Standard
World Wide Web Consortium (W3C)	*www.w3c.org*	The W3C is a consortium of over 500 member organizations that sets standards for the Internet.	XML, SOAP, HTTP
Web Services Interoperability Organization (WS-I)	*www.ws-i.org*	WS-I is a consortium of mostly vendor companies focusing on Web services standards.	BPEL4WS WS-Security WS-Transaction WS-Coordination WS-Attachments WS-Inspection WS-Referral WS-Routing
Organization for the Advancement of Structured Information Standards (OASIS)	*www.oasis-open.org, www.uddi.org*	OASIS is an consortium that focuses on the development of e-business standards.	UDDI
UN/CEFACT (United Nations Centre for Trade Facilitation)	*www.unece.org/cefact*	The UN/CEFACT and OASIS are joint committees on the ebXML standard. UN/CEFACT is sponsored by the UN and focuses on standards for trade.	ebXML
The Internet Engineering Task Force (IETF)	*www.ietf.org*	IETF is a consortium of vendors, universities and individuals. It handles mostly low-level Internet protocol standards.	DIME

The WS-I organization is taking the lead in Web services standards. This body was formed primarily by IBM, Microsoft, and BEA. Sun has also joined this body. An important aspect to the WS-I process, in addition to the creation of specifications, is the creation of test suites. The test suites make sure an implementation of the specification conforms to the specification. In addition, WS-I also requires sample applications, built in many languages and run on many platforms, that implement the proposed specification. These applications are also used to validate the correctness of the test suites. Vendors who implement the specifications can self-certify their implementations by running the test suites and the sample applications.

The standards process involves several organizations responsible for pieces of the Web services specifications. WS-I is attempting to coordinate the efforts of various standards bodies involved in Web services standards. Also, when a standard is required, WS-I is taking the lead in creating and promoting it. Because the major benefit to Web services is interoperability, the success or failure of Web services rests largely on the efforts of these groups.

> ## Summary

Service-oriented development is finally realizing the promise of component-based development. The additional layers of abstraction, the registry concept, and the implementation of standards are paying off. Rather than settling on a single product and platform for application development, organizations can choose best of breed with much less risk.

Web services have been touted as the method for providing application-to-application communication for electronic business. However, crucial to the adoption of e-business are efforts such as RosettaNet, ebXML, and other consortium efforts that provide the necessary message semantics for an industry. In the short term, the intraorganization need for application integration can be met through Web services. EAI vendor and application providers are adding direct Web services support to their products, and organizations can easily service-enable existing legacy applications with these new tools.

Service development is not a one-size-fits-all endeavor. Some organizations will develop simple services and composite services on application servers such as J2EE. When existing applications must be integrated, messaging-oriented middleware platforms play a significant role. An organization beginning the transformation to a services-based environment must focus on several areas. It must understand its current environment and its desired future state. It must then build a platform for service execution, management, and development customized for its needs.

J2EE is the ideal platform for implementing Web services. Web services provide interoperability, and Java and J2EE provide portability. Combining these two technologies can optimize flexibility, which greatly enhances an organization's ability to respond to change.

The computer software and hardware industries have never rallied around a single set of technologies for interoperability before Web services. It is difficult to predict how successful their efforts will be. However, it is clear that Web services will have a significant impact on the future of computing.

> References

Booch, G. *Object Oriented Design with Applications,* Benjamin-Cummings Publishing Co., 1990.

Kreger, H. *Web Services Conceptual Architecture (WSCA 1.0),* IBM, May 2001, *www-3.ibm.com/software/solutions/webservices/pdf/WSCA.pdf.*

Mani, A., and Nagarajan, A. *Understanding Quality of Service for Web Services.* IBM DeveloperWorks, January 2002, *www-106.ibm.com/developerworks/webservices /library/ws-quality.html?dwzone=webservices,* accessed October 2002.

Parnas, D. *On the Criteria to Be Used in Decomposing Systems into Modules.* Communications of the ACM, 15(12):1053–58, December 1972. Reprint: *www.acm.org /classics/may96.*

Stevens, M. *The Benefits of a Service-Oriented Architecture.* Developer.com, *http:// softwaredev.earthweb.com/msnet/article/0,,10839_1041191,00.html,* accessed October 2002.

Szyperski, C. *Component Software: Beyond Object-Oriented Programming.* Addison-Wesley, 1998.

Tarak, M. *WSIL: Do We Need Another Web Services Specification?* Web Services Architect, January 2002, *www.webservicesarchitect.com/content/articles/modi01.asp.*

World Wide Web Consortium (W3C). *W3C Process Document: 5 Technical Reports .www.w3.org/Consortium/Process-20010719/tr.html,* accessed October 2002.

Yourdon, E., and Constantine, L. *Structured Design.* Prentice Hall, 1975.

Service-Oriented Architecture

As we explored in the previous chapter, Web services promote an environment for systems that is loosely coupled and interoperable. Many of the concepts for Web services come from a conceptual architecture called service-oriented architecture (SOA). SOA configures entities (services, registries, contracts, and proxies) to maximize loose coupling and reuse. This chapter describes these entities and their configuration in an abstract way. Although you will probably use Web services to implement your service-oriented architecture, this chapter explains SOA without much mention of a particular implementation technology. This is done so that in subsequent chapters, you can see the areas in which Web services achieve some aspects of a true SOA and other areas in which Web services fall short. Although Web services are a good start toward service-oriented architecture, this chapter will discuss what a fully implemented SOA entails. We will examine the following issues:

What is SOA? What are its entities?

What are the properties of SOA?

How do I design an interface for a service?

Before we analyze the details of SOA, it is important to first explore the concept of software architecture, which consists of the software's coarse-grained structures. Software architecture describes the system's components and the way they interact at a high level.

These components are not necessarily entity beans or distributed objects. They are abstract modules of software deployed as a unit onto a server with other components. The interactions between components are called *connectors*. The configuration of components and connectors describes the way a system is structured and behaves, as shown in Figure 2.1. Rather than creating a formal definition for software architecture in this chapter, we will adopt this classic definition: "The software architecture of a program or computing system is the structure or structures of the system, which comprise software components, the externally

Figure 2.1
Software
architecture
describes a
system's com-
ponents and
connectors.

visible properties of those components, and the relationships among them."
(Bass, Clements, and Kazman 1997)

Service-oriented architecture is a special kind of software architecture that has several unique characteristics. It is important for service designers and developers to understand the concepts of SOA, so that they can make the most effective use of Web services in their environment.

SOA is a relatively new term, but the term "service" as it relates to a software service has been around since at least the early 1990s, when it was used in Tuxedo to describe "services" and "service processes" (Herzum 2002). Sun defined SOA more rigorously in the late 1990s to describe Jini, a lightweight environment for dynamically discovering and using services on a network. The technology is used mostly in reference to allowing "network plug and play" for devices. It allows devices such as printers to dynamically connect to and download drivers from the network and register their services as being available.

The goal in developing Jini was to create a dynamically networked environment for devices, services, and applications. In this environment, services and devices could be added to and removed from the network dynamically (Sun Microsystems, *Jini Network Technology, www.sun.com/jini*). There is more interest lately in the software development community about the concepts behind SOA because of the arrival of Web services.

Figure 2.2 shows that other technologies can be used to implement service-oriented architecture. Web services are simply one set of technologies that can be used to implement it successfully.

The most important aspect of service-oriented architecture is that it separates the service's implementation from its interface. In other words, it separates the "what" from the "how." Service consumers view a service simply as an endpoint that supports a particular request format or contract. Service consumers are not concerned with how the service goes about executing their requests; they expect only that it will.

Consumers also expect that their interaction with the service will follow a contract, an agreed-upon interaction between two parties. The way the service executes tasks given to it by service consumers is irrelevant. The service might fulfill the request by executing a servlet, a mainframe application, or a Visual Basic application. The only requirement is that the service send the response back to the consumer in the agreed-upon format.

> SOA Entities

The "find, bind, and execute" paradigm as shown in Figure 2.3 (Talking Blocks 2001) allows the consumer of a service to ask a third-party registry for the service that matches its criteria. If the registry has such a service, it gives the consumer a contract and an endpoint address for the service. SOA consists of the following six entities configured together to support the find, bind, and execute paradigm.

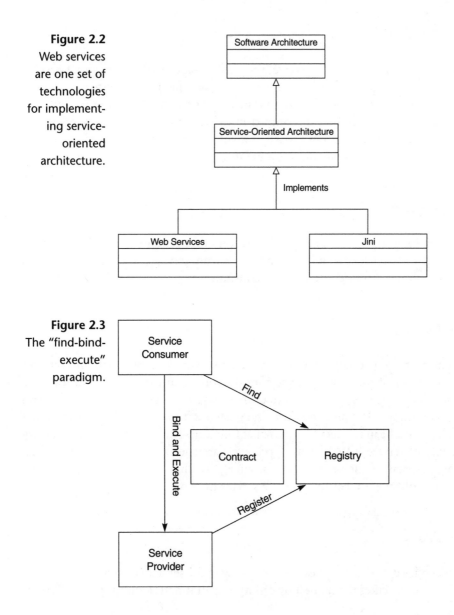

Figure 2.2
Web services are one set of technologies for implementing service-oriented architecture.

Figure 2.3
The "find-bind-execute" paradigm.

Service Consumer

The service consumer is an application, service, or some other type of software module that requires a service. It is the entity that initiates the locating of the service in the registry, binding to the service over a transport, and executing the service function. The service consumer executes the service by sending it a request formatted according to the contract.

Service Provider

The service provider is the service, the network-addressable entity that accepts and executes requests from consumers. It can be a mainframe system, a component, or some other type of software system that executes the service request. The service provider publishes its contract in the registry for access by service consumers. Chapter 3 describes the issues involved with creating a service provider by using component-based development techniques.

Service Registry

A service registry is a network-based directory that contains available services. It is an entity that accepts and stores contracts from service providers and provides those contracts to interested service consumers.

Service Contract

A contract is a specification of the way a consumer of a service will interact with the provider of the service. It specifies the format of the request and response from the service. A service contract may require a set of preconditions and postconditions. The preconditions and postconditions specify the state that the service must be in to execute a particular function. The contract may also specify quality of service (QoS) levels. QoS levels are specifications for the nonfunctional aspects of the service. For instance, a quality of service attribute is the amount of time it takes to execute a service method.

Service Proxy

The service provider supplies a service proxy to the service consumer. The service consumer executes the request by calling an API function on the proxy. The service proxy, shown in Figure 2.4, finds a contract and a reference to the service provider in the registry. It then formats the request message and executes the request on behalf of the consumer. The service proxy is a convenience entity for the service consumer. It is not required; the service consumer developer could write the necessary software for accessing the service directly.

The service proxy can enhance performance by caching remote references and data. When a proxy caches a remote reference, subsequent service calls will not require additional registry calls. By storing service contracts locally, the consumer reduces the number of network hops required to execute the service.

In addition, proxies can improve performance by eliminating network calls altogether by performing some functions locally. For service methods that do not require service data, the entire method can be implemented locally in the proxy. Methods such as currency conversion, tip calculators, and so on, can be implemented entirely in the proxy. If a method requires some small amount of service data, the proxy could download the small amount of data once and use it for subsequent method calls. The fact that the method is executed in the proxy rather than being sent to the service for execution is transparent to the service consumer. However, when using this technique it is important that the proxy support only methods the service itself provides. The proxy design pattern (Gamma et al. 2002) states that the proxy is simply a local reference to a remote object. If the proxy in any way changes the interface of the remote service, then technically, it is no longer a proxy.

A service provider will provide proxies for many different environments. A service proxy is written in the native language of the service consumer. For instance, a service provider may distribute proxies for Java, Visual Basic, and Delphi if those are the most likely platforms for service consumers. Although the service proxy is not required, it can greatly improve both convenience and performance for service consumers.

Figure 2.4
A service
proxy.

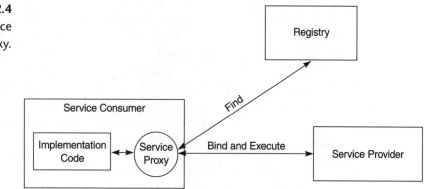

Service Lease

The service lease, which the registry grants the service consumer, specifies the amount of time the contract is valid: only from the time the consumer requests it from the registry to the time specified by the lease (Sun Microsystems, *Jini Technology Core Specification,* 2001). When the lease runs out, the consumer must request a new lease from the registry.

The lease is necessary for services that need to maintain state information about the binding between the consumer and provider. The lease defines the time for which the state may be maintained. It also further reduces the coupling between the service consumer and the service provider, by limiting the amount of time consumers and providers may be bound. Without the notion of a lease, a consumer could bind to a service forever and never rebind to its contract again. This would have the effect of a much tighter coupling between the service consumer and the service provider.

With a service lease, if a producer needs to somehow change its implementation, it may do so when the leases held by the services consumers expire. The implementation can change without affecting the execution of the service consumers, because those consumers must request a new contract and lease. When the new contract and lease are obtained, they are not guaranteed to be identical to the previous ones. They might have changed, and it is the service consumer's responsibility to understand and handle this change. ▷

▷ SOA Characteristics

Each system's software architecture reflects the different principles and set of tradeoffs used by the designers. Service-oriented software architecture has these

> ▷   While Web services provide support for many of the concepts of SOA, they do not implement all of them. They do not currently support the notion of a contract lease. Also, no official specification provides QoS levels for a service. An organization cannot implement a complete service-oriented architecture given these limitations with Web services. In addition, service consumers can execute Web services directly if they know the service's address and contract. They do not have to go to the registry to obtain this information. Today, in fact, most organizations implement Web services without a registry. Consequently, the extent to which an organization implements an SOA with Web service varies greatly.

characteristics Bieber and Carpenter 2001, Stevens, *Service-Oriented*, 2002, Sun Microsystems, *Jini Technology Architectural Overview* 2001):

- Services are discoverable and dynamically bound.
- Services are self-contained and modular.
- Services stress interoperability.
- Services are loosely coupled.
- Services have a network-addressable interface.
- Services have coarse-grained interfaces.
- Services are location-transparent.
- Services are composable.
- Service-oriented architecture supports self-healing.

Discoverable and Dynamically Bound

SOA supports the concept of service discovery. A service consumer that needs a service discovers what service to use based on a set of criteria at runtime. The service consumer asks a registry for a service that fulfills its need. The best way to explain dynamic binding and discover is to use an example. For example, a banking application (consumer) asks a registry for all services that perform credit-card validation. The registry returns all entries that support this. The entries also contain information about the service, including transaction fees. The consumer selects the service (provider) from the list based on the lowest transaction fee.

Using a pointer from the registry entry, the consumer then binds to the provider of the credit card service. The description of the service consists of all the arguments necessary to execute the service. The consumer formats a request message with the data, based on the description provided by the directory pointer.

The consumer then binds the message to a transport type that the service expects and sends the service the request message over the transport. The service provider executes the credit-card validation and returns a message, whose format is also specified by the service description. The only dependency between producer and consumer is the contract, which the third-party registry provides. The dependency is a runtime dependency and not a compile-time dependency. All the information the consumer needs about the service is obtained and used at runtime.

This example shows how consumers execute services dynamically. Clients do not need any compile-time information about the service. The service interfaces are discovered dynamically, and messages are constructed dynamically. The removal of compile-time dependencies improves maintainability, because consumers do not need a new interface binding every time the interface changes.

This method of service execution is powerful. The service consumer does not know the format of the request message or response message or the location of the service until the service is actually needed. If the transaction fees for the credit-card validation services changed from minute to minute, consumers could still ensure that they received the best price.

Self-Contained and Modular

Services are self-contained and modular. One of the most important aspects of SOA is the concept of modularity. A service supports a set of interfaces. These interfaces should be cohesive, meaning that they should all relate to each other in the context of a module. The principles of modularity should be adhered to in designing the services that support an application so that services can easily be aggregated into an application with a few well-known dependencies. Since this is such an important concept when creating services, we will explain some of the principles of modularity and, in particular, how they apply to the creation of services. Bertrand Meyer (Meyer 1997) outlined the following five criteria for determining whether a component is sufficiently modular. These criteria apply equally well when determining whether a service is sufficiently modular.

Modular Decomposability

The *modular decomposability* of a service refers to the breaking of an application into many smaller modules. Each module is responsible for a single, distinct function within an application. This is sometimes referred to as "top-down design," in which the bigger problems are iteratively decomposed into smaller problems. For instance, a banking application is broken down into a savings account service, checking account service, and customer service. The main goal of decomposability is reusability. The goal for service design is to identify the smallest unit of software that can be reused in different contexts. For instance, a customer call-center application may need only the customer's telephone number and thus need access only the customer service to retrieve it.

Modular Composability

The *modular composability* of a service refers to the production of software services that may be freely combined as a whole with other services to produce new systems. Service designers should create services sufficiently independent to reuse in entirely different applications from the ones for which they were originally intended. This is sometimes referred to as *bottom-up design*. Sometimes, the composability and decomposability approaches to service design can create two different designs. The bottom-up approach is more focused on the application functions. The top-down design tends to be more focused on the business problem. It is important to use both methods to find the right interface for a service.

The typical design process starts as a decomposition exercise. When the designers get to a point at which they have exhausted the top-down design, performing a bottom-up analysis should validate the design. The bottom-up analysis starts by defining the significant scenarios that the modules need to support. For instance, in a banking application, a scenario is "deposit money into checking account." The significant scenarios will cover the important functional aspects of the modular design.

Once designers define the scenarios, they create sequence diagrams to illustrate the messages that flow between modules to satisfy the scenarios. Once the scenarios are satisfied, the designer can perform additional iterations of bottom-up and top-down analysis to tune the design of the modules.

Modular Understandability

The *modular understandability* of a service is the ability of a person to understand the function of the service without having any knowledge of other services. For instance, if a banking application implements a checking account service that does not implement a deposit function but instead relies on the client to use a separate deposit service, this would detract from the service's modular understandability. The modular understandability of a service can also be limited if the service supports more than one distinct business concept. For example, a service called *CustomerCheckingAccount* that mixes the semantics of both a customer service and a checking account service also limits modular understandability. The modular understandability is especially important for services, because any unknown consumer can find and use a service at any time. If the service is not understandable from a functional perspective, the person deciding whether to use the service will have a difficult time making a decision.

Modular Continuity

The *modular continuity* of a service refers to the impact of a change in one service requiring a change in other services or in the consumers of the service. An interface that does not sufficiently hide the implementation details of the service creates a domino effect when changes are needed. It will require changes to other services and applications that use the service when the internal implementation of the service changes. Every service must hide information about its internal design. A service that exposes this information will limit its modular continuity, because an internal design decision is exposed through the interface.

Modular Protection

The *modular protection* of a service is sufficient if an abnormal condition in the service does not cascade to other services or consumers. For instance, if an error in the checking account service causes invalid data to be stored on a database, this could impact the operation of other services using the same tables for their data. Faults in the operation of a service must not impact the operation of a client or other service or the state of their internal data or otherwise break the contract with service consumers. Therefore, we must ensure that faults do not cascade from the service to other services or consumers.

In addition to the above criteria for modularity, two rules ensure that a service's modularity and independence are not compromised: Direct mapping and contracts and information hiding.

Direct Mapping

A service should map to a distinct problem domain function. During the process of understanding the problem domain and creating a solution, the designer should create boundaries around service interfaces that map to a distinct area of the problem domain. This is important so that the designer creates a self-contained and independent module. For instance, interfaces that deposit, withdraw, and transfer from a checking account should map to the checking account service. This sounds simplistic, but it is easy to accidentally pollute a service's interface with functions that

- Logically belong in another existing service
- Belong in a new service
- Span multiple services and require a new composite service
- Are really internal knowledge that should not be exposed through an interface

To directly map a service's interfaces to a distinct business concept in the problem domain, the service designer needs a good understanding of the problem domain. Creating a conceptual service model provides this understanding.

Conceptual Service Model The conceptual service model consists of a model of the problem domain. Techniques for defining module interfaces assume that the problem domain is known a priori. In other words, the application's problem domain is known when the designers and developers create or enhance an application. With service-based development, this is not always the case. Services may be assembled into applications in the future that the service designer had no knowledge of when the service was designed. Therefore, designers must estimate service interfaces based on the service's expected use.

The conceptual model of the business, sometimes referred to as the *business architecture* (Fowler 1997), helps drive the expected use of the services. A conceptual model is one created without regard for any application or technology. It typically consists of a structural model derived from a set of use cases that illustrate how the business works. For instance, a bank manages checking accounts, savings accounts, and customer information. A conceptual service model for this domain might look similar to Figure 2.5, although it would be illustrated in much more detail.

This logical model of the business provides the basis for creating and managing service interfaces. Each entity in the logical model is either a stateful entity or

Figure 2.5
A conceptual
service model.

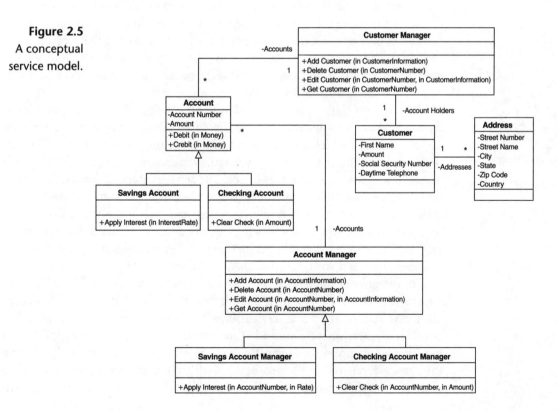

a stateless entity. The manager classes are stateless entities, and the other classes are stateful entities. For example, the account entity contains attributes that contain the state of a single account; namely, account number and amount. The savings account, checking account, customer, and address entities also maintain state and are also stateful entities. These entities can be translated into software as entity beans and/or rows in databases. Each stateful entity also has a key that uniquely identifies it within the system.

The entity classes are not directly accessible to the service consumer in SOA. However, in component-based systems, a component consumer accesses an entity component by obtaining a handle to the component. The handle maintains a stateful connection to an entity that has a unique key to identify it. In service-oriented architecture, service consumers cannot access these entities. The service consumer accesses them indirectly by going through the manager interfaces. In SOA, these manager interfaces are implemented as service interfaces.

The manager classes in Figure 2.5 are stateless classes that manage entities of a particular class. They are the classes that perform create, read, update, and delete (CRUD) operations on the entities they manage. Because the manager classes do not represent a single entity but manage multiple entities, the interfaces for the manager classes require that a unique key be passed in. The unique key identifies the entity for which the action is to be performed. For instance, the *ApplyInterest* method of *SavingsAccountManager* requires the rate as well as the account number to identify the entity for executing *ApplyInterest* behavior. The *ApplyInterest* method on the *SavingsAccount* entity does not need a unique key, because it represents a single savings account instance.

The manager classes comprise the basis of the design of the service layer interfaces. The manager interfaces may be converted directly into service interfaces, and the stateful entities may be converted directly into persistent state. The persistent state may be an Enterprise JavaBean, a database row, or both. Stateful entities are not exposed outside the service. The service interface is a stateless interface. Services manipulate stateful entities on behalf of consumers, based on the method consumers call when requesting an operation to perform. Consumers pass in the unique key of the entity they are manipulating and the data for the operation. The service locates the entity that matches the unique key and performs the operation on it with the data.

The integrity of the service layer interfaces will be maintained only if the interfaces map directly to the logical model for the business. Because different applications will use the same services, the logical model must cross application boundaries. Developers should add functionality to services as new applications need those functions. The logical model provides the city plan for developing the service layer. As developers build applications, the software will support more of the logical model's functionality. It is difficult to maintain services' integrity over time, because new applications need to interact with services in different ways. The more closely this conceptual model maps to the overall structure of the business it supports, the longer-lived the service layer will be.

Direct mapping is only the first rule we need to implement for modularity. Contracts and information hiding is the second.

Contracts and Information Hiding

An interface contract is a published agreement between a service provider and a service consumer. The contract specifies not only the arguments and return values a service supplies but also the service's preconditions and postconditions. The preconditions are those that must be satisfied before calling the service, to allow the service to function properly. For instance, consider a credit-card validation service that is a two-step process. In the first step, the application sends the account number and amount information to the service. The service responds with an OK. However, for the transaction to go through, the consumer must send a confirmation message to the service. The precondition of the confirmation function is that the information for the confirmation has previously been sent.

The postcondition is the system's state after a function has been executed. The postcondition of the initial submission of information is that the information has been stored for a subsequent commit request.

Parnas and Clements best describe the principles of information hiding:

> *Our module structure is based on the decomposition criterion known as information hiding [IH]. According to this principle, system details that are likely to change independently should be the secrets of separate modules; the only assumptions that should appear in the interfaces between modules are those that are considered unlikely to change. Each data structure is used in only one module; one or more programs within the module may directly access it. Any other program that requires information stored in a module's data structures must obtain it by calling access programs belonging to that module.*

(Parnas and Clements 1984)

This statement assumes that the software executes in a single machine. With service-oriented architecture, we take this principle a little further. The service should never expose its internal data structures. Even the smallest amount of internal information known outside the service will cause unnecessary dependencies between the service and its consumers. Although the information stored in the data structures is necessarily exposed, that information must be transformed from the internal storage structure into an external structure. In other words, the internal data semantics must be mapped into the external semantics of an independent contract. The contract depends only on the interface's problem domain, not on any implementation details.

Exposing internal implementation details is easy to do by creating an interface design with arguments that map to the service's implementation aspects rather than to its functional aspects. For instance, consider a credit-card validation service. The service requires that a credit-card validation request contain the account number, amount, and a special system code. The service uses the system code to determine in which internal database to find the account. The special system code is exposed through the interface, and it exposes information about the internal structure of the service.

There is no functional reason to expose the system code outside the service, because the service should identify the database itself based on the functional data passed in to it. This information is necessary strictly for implementation. Service maintainability is severely affected when designers implement designs such as this. If the internal structure of the service changes, clients of this service are likely to require changes also. If a third internal system is added, for example, clients will have to be updated, even though the interface contract has not changed. This design is generally not consistent with the principles of information hiding and modular design.

The principle of separating the service's interface from its implementation is relevant to the topic of modular software design. It is often thought that service-oriented architecture enforces this principle, which is not strictly true. Service-oriented architecture promotes the idea of separation, but as the previous example illustrates, implementation details can pollute a service's interface.

These techniques and concepts help create modular services. Services also stress interoperability, or the ability of different types of systems to use a service.

Interoperability

Service-oriented architecture stresses interoperability, the ability of systems using different platforms and languages to communicate with each other. Each service provides an interface that can be invoked through a connector type. An interoperable connector consists of a protocol and a data format that each of the *potential* clients of the service understands. Interoperability is achieved by supporting the protocol and data formats of the service's current and potential clients.

Techniques for supporting standard protocol and data formats consist of mapping each platform's characteristics and language to a mediating specification. The mediating specification maps between the formats of the interoperable data format to the platform-specific data formats. Sometimes this requires mapping character sets such as ASCII to EBCDIC as well as mapping data types. For instance, Web services is a mediating specification for communicating between systems. JAX-RPC and JAXM map Java data types to SOAP. Other platforms that support Web services mediate between Web service specifications and their own internal specifications for character sets and data types.

Loose Coupling

Coupling refers to the number of dependencies between modules. There are two types of coupling: loose and tight. Loosely coupled modules have a few well-known dependencies. Tightly coupled modules have many unknown dependencies. Every software architecture strives to achieve loose coupling between modules. Service-oriented architecture promotes loose coupling between service consumers and service providers and the idea of a few well-known dependencies between consumers and providers.

A system's degree of coupling directly affects its modifiability. The more tightly coupled a system is, the more a change in a service will require changes in service consumers. Coupling is increased when service consumers require a large amount of information about the service provider to use the service. In other words, if a service consumer knows the location and detailed data format for a service provider, the consumer and provider are more tightly coupled. If the consumer of the service does not need detailed knowledge of the service before invoking it, the consumer and provider are more loosely coupled.

SOA accomplishes loose coupling through the use of contracts and bindings. A consumer asks a third-party registry for information about the type of service it wishes to use. The registry returns all the services it has available that match the consumer's criteria. The consumer chooses which service to use, binds to it over a transport, and executes the method on it, based on the description of the service provided by the registry. The consumer does not depend directly on the service's implementation but only on the contract the service supports. Since a service may be both a consumer and a provider of some services, the dependency on only the contract enforces the notion of loose coupling in service-oriented architecture.

Although coupling between service consumers and service producers is loose, implementation of the service can be tightly coupled with implementation of other services. For instance, if a set of services shares a framework, a database, or otherwise has information about each other's implementation, they may be tightly coupled. In many instances, coupling cannot be avoided, and it sometimes contradicts the goal of code reusability.

Network-Addressable Interface

The role of the network is central to the concept of SOA. A service must have a network-addressable interface. A consumer on a network must be able to invoke a service across the network. The network allows services to be reused by any consumer at any time. The ability for an application to assemble a set of reusable services on different machines is possible only if the services support a network interface. The network also allows the service to be location–independent, meaning that its physical location is irrelevant.

It is possible to access a service through a local interface and not through the network, but only if both the consumer and service provider are on the same machine. This is done mainly to enhance performance. Although a service may be configured for access from a consumer on the same machine, the service must also simultaneously support a request from across the network.

Because of this requirement, service interface design is focused to a large extent on performance. In a pure object-based system design, data and behavior are encapsulated into objects. This design works well for objects in the same machine. However, when those objects are distributed across a network, performance degrades quickly because of the "chatter" that occurs between fine-grained objects. Because we can assume that services will be distributed, it is possible to design service interfaces to be more coarse-grained and, as a result, enhance network performance.

Coarse-Grained Interfaces

The concept of granularity applies to services in two ways. First, it is applied to the scope of the domain the entire service implements. Second, it is applied to the scope of the domain that each method within the interface implements.

The levels of granularity are relative to each other. For instance, if a service implements all the functions of a banking system, then we consider it coarse-grained. If it supports just credit-card validation, we consider it fine-grained. In addition, if a method for inquiring about a customer returns all customer information, including address, this method would be coarser-grained than a method that does not return the customer's address.

The appropriate level of granularity for a service and its methods is relatively coarse. A service generally supports a single distinct business concept or process. It contains software that implements the business concept so that it can be reused in multiple large, distributed systems.

Before components and services, distributed systems were centered on the idea of distributed objects (Object Management Group 2002). Distributed object-based systems consist of many fine-grained networked objects communicating with each other across a network. Each object has dependencies with many other objects in the system. Since accessing an object requires a network hop and thus does not perform well, the design principles for distributed object-based systems quickly moved toward coarser-grained interfaces.

Figure 2.6 illustrates a distributed object-based system. The number of connections between objects is great. As system size and complexity grows, these dependencies become difficult to manage. Performance suffers because of the large number of network hops. Maintainability also suffers because of the large number of dependencies between objects. Since any object can connect to and use any other object, it becomes difficult to know what dependencies exist. When the developer makes a necessary change to an interface, it might affect a large number of other distributed objects. The developer must then compile and deploy together all the changed objects and the objects that depend on them.

A service-based system controls the network access to the objects within the service through a set of coarse-grained interfaces, as shown in Figure 2.7. A service may still be implemented as a set of fine-grained objects, but the objects themselves are not accessible over a network connection. A service implemented as objects has one or more coarse-grained objects that act as distributed façades. These objects are accessible over the network and provide access to the internal object state from external consumers of the service. However, objects internal to the service communicate directly with each other within a single machine, not

Figure 2.6
Fine-grained distributed objects.

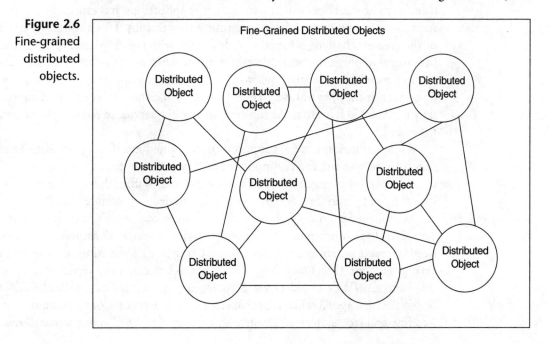

Figure 2.7
Coarse-grained
services.

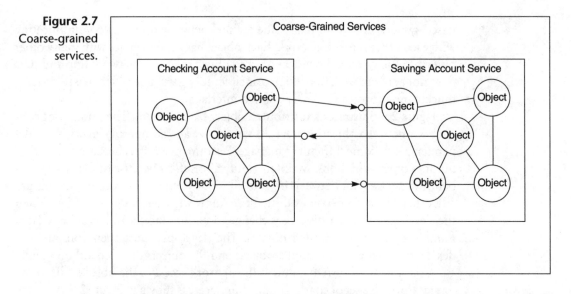

across a network connection. All service interfaces are relatively coarse–grained compared with distributed object interfaces. However, within the range of coarse, there are options. It is important to understand these options for interface design.

One of the benefits of service-oriented architecture is service composition. Developers compose services into applications. Unfortunately, one cannot always know how services will be used in these applications. It is especially difficult to predict how services will be used in future applications. This uncertainty is one of the greatest challenges for service designers, who typically attempt to anticipate future applications when determining the structure of an interface. Because services are executed across a network, it is especially important for interfaces to be correct. If they are not, service consumers will either receive more data than they need or will have to make multiple trips to the service to retrieve all the data they need.

While services in general support coarser-grained interfaces than distributed object-based systems and component-based systems do, the range of coarse still contains degrees of granularity, as Figure 2.8 shows. Within the range of granularity expected for services, designers still need to decide interface coarseness.

As explained previously, the service itself can be coarse-grained or fine-grained. This refers to how much functionality the service covers. Let's assume developers need to create an application for manipulating both a checking account and a savings account. Developers have two choices when creating a service to support this function. They could create a coarse-grained service called *BankAccountService* that manipulates both checking and savings accounts, or they could create two fine-grained services—a *SavingsAccountService* and a *CheckingAccountService*.

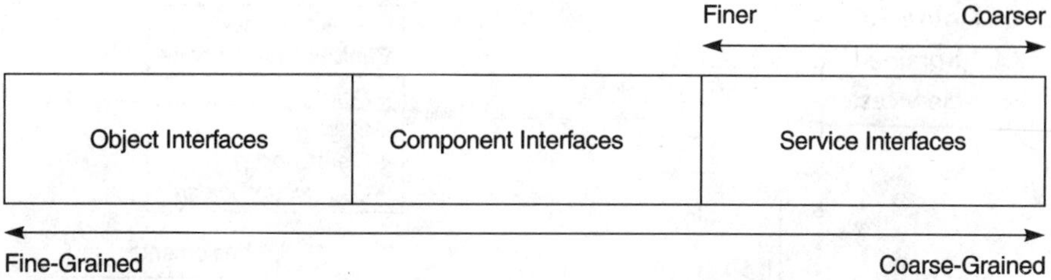

Figure 2.8
Degrees of
granularity.

Finer	Coarser

Object Interfaces	Component Interfaces	Service Interfaces

Fine-Grained   Coarse-Grained

Because *BankAccountService* supports the functionality of both checking and savings, it is coarser-grained.

Granularity also applies to the way developers implement service methods. Suppose *BankAccountService* contains a method called *GetAccountHolder.* A coarse-grained implementation of this function would return the account holder's name and address. A fine-grained version would return just the name. A separate method, called *GetAccountHoldersAddress,* would return the address. A service method that returns more data is a coarse-grained method. A service method that returns less, more specific, data is a fine-grained method. Sometimes service consumers need both fine-grained and coarse-grained methods for a similar function. This is the concept of multi-grained services.

Multi-Grained Services

Because services will be used in ways the designers cannot fully anticipate when designing them, the decision about granularity does not have to be absolute. Services do not have to be coarse-grained or fine-grained; they can be coarse-grained and fine-grained, or *multi-grained* (Stevens 2002). In other words, *BankAccountService, SavingsAccountService,* and *CheckingAccountService* can exist simultaneously, as in Figure 2.9. If service consumers needs access only to a customer's savings account, they should use *SavingsAccountService.* There is no need for them to know anything about checking accounts. If, on the other hand, they need to know about both checking accounts and savings accounts, they should use *BankAccountService.*

Why is it necessary to create a composite *BankAccountService* if there is already a *SavingsAccountService* and *CheckingAccountService*? The reason is that services should be as easy as possible to use, and they should meet the expectations of the consumers that use them. It is logical that a consumer would more often than not want access to both checking and savings accounts. Implementing both interfaces is best, because it provides all service consumers with the interfaces that best suit their needs.

Service designers create multi-grained service interfaces by first creating fine-grained services and then wrapping them in coarse-grained façades. It is also pos-

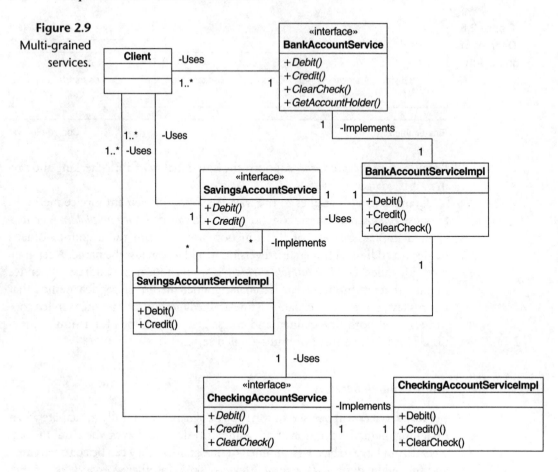

Figure 2.9
Multi-grained
services.

sible to create fine-grained façades that access coarse-grained services. However, it is better to create finer-grained base services, because developers will have more flexibility when deploying them. It is difficult to break up a larger service and deploy it onto multiple machines. However, it is easy to deploy a large number of small-grained services to multiple machines.

The granularity of the service is a crucial design decision. If it is incorrectly predicted, consumers will have access to more functionality than they need. This can be a problem for security at the service level. It might not be possible to restrict a consumer from some methods and not others, only to the entire service. If this is the case, the entire service might have to be opened up to consumers. Developers can do this if they design services at the appropriate level of granularity.

The service interfaces constitute an established contract between the services and the clients. One of the tradeoffs of creating multiple interfaces is that each interface is essentially a published contract. Additional interfaces make managing these contracts between clients and services more difficult, because a change to a functional requirement will affect multiple interfaces. Although it is important to provide the best possible interfaces to consumers, it is also important not to substantially compromise the service's maintainability.

Multi-Grained Methods

The granularity of the methods within a service is of equal or greater importance than the granularity of the service itself. Using the previous bank account example, consider the retrieval of account holder information from the bank account service. There are several ways to implement this interface:

- A method in *BankAccountService* called *GetAccountHolder* that returns only account-holder information and not the address
- Two methods in *BankAccountService,* called *GetAccountHolder* and *GetAccountHolderAddress; GetAccountHolder* would not return address information
- A method in *BankAccountService* called *GetAccountHolder* that could return both the name and address of the account holder
- A method in *BankAccountService* called *GetAccountHolder* that could have a switch that tells the service whether to return address information as well as account-holder information
- A method in *BankAccountService* called *GetAccountHolder* that could accept a list of attributes it wants the service to return; the consumer can choose to get the address by adding the address attributes to the attribute list it passes in to the service

Let's examine these options and their consequences. As Figure 2.10 shows, *BankAccountService* returns just account-holder information.

Figure 2.10
A method that returns only account-holder information.

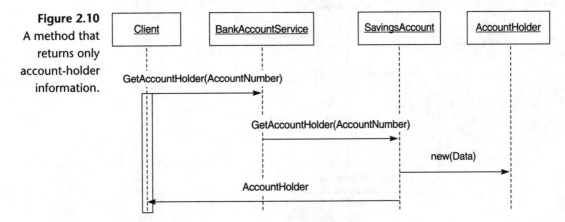

This scenario works well if the consumer needs only account-holder information. But a consumer who needs address information as well is out of luck. The address information could be retrieved from the service by adding a *GetAccountHolderAddress* method, as illustrated in Figure 2.11.

This solves the problem of retrieving address information, but if most of the consumers need address information, more trips are necessary. Having the *GetAccountHolder* method return both account-holder information and address information in one call would improve performance and reduce the work necessary for the consumer to assemble the two results.

Figure 2.12 illustrates this scenario.

This solution works well for consumers who always retrieve address information, but if they almost never need this information, more data than necessary will travel across the network. It will also take longer for service consumers to extract the account-holder data they need from the larger message.

Another solution is to pass in an argument that directs the service whether to return address information. A *BankAccountService* would have only one *GetAccountHolder* method. The developer would add an additional argument to the method, to instruct the service whether to return address information as well.

Figure 2.11
A method that returns both the account-holder's information and address.

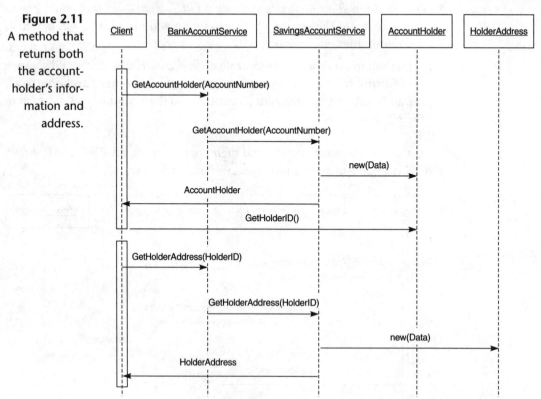

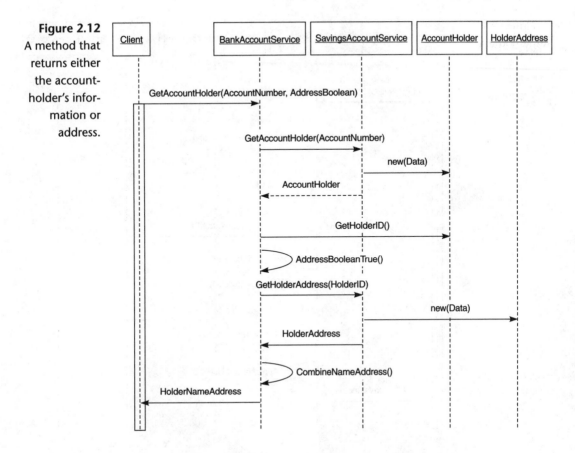

Figure 2.12
A method that returns either the account-holder's information or address.

Consumers who need only account-holder information could pass in the proper switch to retrieve it. Users who need address information as well could pass in the proper switch to retrieve both.

But what if consumers need only zip codes for all account holders? They would have to retrieve both account-holder information and address information and extract zip codes from a very large message. What if consumers pass in the list of attributes in which they're interested?

This sophisticated alternative implements an interface that accepts a list of attributes to return to the consumer. Instead of sending the account number and an address indicator, consumers submit a list of all of the attributes to return. The list may contain just first and last names or may include all or portions of the address data, such as city and street address. The service would interpret this list and construct the response to consumers to include only the data requested. This solution minimizes both the number of trips consumers make to the service and the amount of data that must travel the network for each request. Figure 2.13 illustrates this option.

Figure 2.13
A method that
returns just the
attributes
requested.

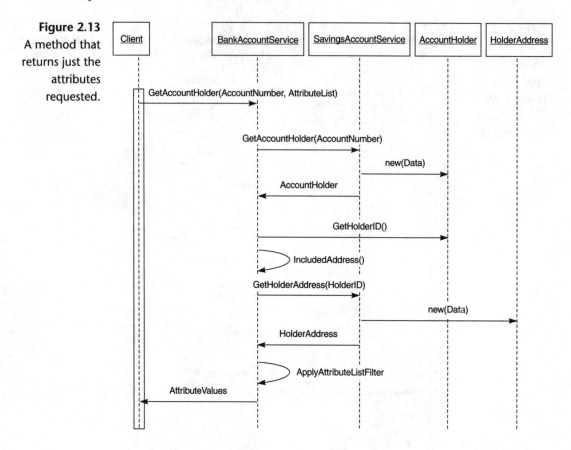

This approach has two downsides. The first is that the request message will be larger than any of the previous solutions, because the consumer must send the request data as well as the data map on each request. If all service consumers need the exact same data from the service, this solution would perform worse than the previously discussed alternatives.

Second, this solution is also more complex to implement for service developers, and service consumers might find the interface more difficult to understand and use. To alleviate this problem, a service proxy could wrap the complexities of the service interface and provide a simple interface for consumers. A consumer would use multiple distinct and simple service methods on the proxy. The methods map to the way the consumer wants to use the service. The proxy would internally map these multiple methods into a single service-request interface format that accepts a map of data to return. The advantage of this technique is that it allows the service to support any granularity, while providing specific granularities to consumers based on their domain understanding.

If these implementations are not possible, it is always better to return more data, to minimize network round trips, because future clients are likely to need the data. It is also possible to implement several of these options, to solve the needs of multiple consumers. However, this increases the effort to maintain the service and also detracts somewhat from the service's modular understandability.

A service's ability to have multi-grained methods that return the appropriate amount of data is important to reduce network traffic. Extra network traffic is due either to excessive unnecessary data or to a large number of requests to get data.

Granularity is a difficult problem to reconcile when designing service interfaces. It is important to understand the options and implement the most appropriate interface. In the past, arguments surrounding service interfaces have focused mainly on determining the right granularity. Services actually require the designer to find the right granularities for service consumers.

Location Transparency

Location transparency is a key characteristic of service-oriented architecture. Consumers of a service do not know a service's location until they locate it in the registry. The lookup and dynamic binding to a service at runtime allows the service implementation to move from location to location without the client's knowledge. The ability to move services improves service availability and performance. By employing a load balancer that forwards requests to multiple service instances without the service client's knowledge, we can achieve greater availability and performance.

As mentioned earlier, a central design principle in object-oriented systems is separation of implementation from interface. This means that an object's interface and its implementation may vary independently. The primary motivation for this principle is to control dependencies between objects by enforcing the interface contract as their only means of interaction.

Service-oriented architecture takes this principle one step further, by reducing the consumer's dependency on the contract itself. This reduced dependency through the use of dynamic binding also has the effect of making the service's location irrelevant. Because the service consumer has no direct dependency on the service contract, the contract's implementation can move from location to location.

Composability

A service's composability is related to its modular structure. Modular structure enables services to be assembled into applications the developer had no notion of when designing the service. Using preexisting, tested services greatly enhances a system's quality and improves its return on investment because of the ease of reuse.

A service may be composed in three ways: application composition, service federations, and service orchestration.

An *application* is typically an assembly of services, components, and application logic that binds these functions together for a specific purpose. *Service federations* are collections of services managed together in a larger service domain. For example, a checking account service, savings account service, and customer service may be composed into a larger banking-account service. *Service orchestration* is the execution of a single transaction that impacts one or more services in an organization. It is sometimes called a *business process*. It consists of multiple steps, each of which is a service invocation. If any of the service invocations fails, the entire transaction should be rolled back to the state that existed before execution of the transaction.

For a service to be composed into a transactional application, federation, or orchestration, the service methods themselves should be *subtransactional*. That is, they must not perform data commits themselves. The orchestration of the transaction is performed by a third-party entity that manages all the steps. It detects when a service method fails and asks all the services that have already executed to roll back to the state that existed before the request. If the services have already committed the state of their data, it is more difficult for the method to be composed into a larger transactional context.

If the service cannot be subtransactional, it should be *undoable*. Especially when dealing with legacy systems, it is sometimes impossible to execute a function within the context of a transaction. For instance, consider an older system that manages checking accounts. The service is a façade for the legacy application. When the service receives a request to deposit money into a checking account, it puts the request into a queue. The legacy system reads the request from the queue and executes it. It is difficult to make this request subtransactional, but it can be undoable. If the deposit transaction is composed into a larger transaction and another step in the larger transaction fails, the checking account deposit transaction can be undone by withdrawing the same amount from the checking account. While to a developer this makes perfect sense, a customer would probably see the deposit and withdrawal transactions on his or her statement at the end of the month, so it should be used with care.

Self-Healing

With the size and complexity of modern distributed applications, a system's ability to recover from error is becoming more important. A *self-healing* system is one that has the ability to recover from errors without human intervention during execution.

Reliability measures how well a system performs in the presence of disturbances. In service-oriented architecture, services will be up and down from time to time. This is especially true for applications assembled from services from multiple organizations across the Internet. The extent to which a system is self-healing depends on several factors.

Reliability depends on the hardware's ability to recover from failure. The network must also allow for the dynamic connection to different systems at runtime. Modern Internet networking protocols inherently provide this capability.

Another aspect of self-healing is the architecture from which the application is built. Architecture that supports dynamic binding and execution of components at runtime will be more self-healing than one that does not. For instance, service-based systems are self-healing to a greater degree than previous architectures, because services are bound to and executed dynamically at runtime. If a service fails, the client may find, bind, and execute a different service, as long as the other service provides the same or a similar interface contract.

In addition, because service-based systems require that the interface be separate from the implementation, implementations may vary. For instance, a service implementation may run in a clustered environment. If a single service implementation fails, another instance can complete the transaction for the client without the client's knowledge. This capability is possible only if the client interacts with the services interface and not its implementation. This property is fundamental to all service-oriented architectures.

▶ Summary

Software architecture has been emerging as a discipline over the last decade (Garlan 2000). A system's software architecture describes its coarse-grained structures and its properties at a high level. As long as the technology supports those structures and properties, the technology can be considered to implement the architecture. For instance, Jini is a technology that supports service-oriented architecture, because it supports the properties of SOA.

It is important to apply the concepts of software architecture to any new technology to take full advantage of it. Service-oriented architecture is implemented by technologies other than Web services, but the term and concepts have gained popularity recently because of Web services. For instance, the computer industry has used the term *service* for about two decades to describe various platforms.

Some of the characteristics of service-oriented architecture are supported better by certain technologies than by others. For instance, CORBA and Jini are less interoperable than Web services, but Jini excels in other properties (though this is arguable), such as discovery.

Interface design is perhaps the most difficult part of designing services in service-oriented architecture. The modularization techniques practiced for decades still apply to services. Service design is even more difficult, because the domain a service supports is not limited to a single application. Therefore, it is best to perform modularization starting with a conceptual model of the business rather than of a single application. If the interface design is done well, the services are more likely to be reusable in other applications, and organizations will realize a higher return on their investment.

Web services are refocusing organizations on the concepts of service-oriented architecture. Although highly reusable, loosely coupled architectures have been a goal for many organizations. Web services are fostering interest in and providing the technology to implement service-oriented architectures that enable them to realize their vision.

> References

Bass, L., Clements, P., and Kazman, R. *Software Architecture in Practice.* Addison-Wesley, 1997.

Bieber, G., and Carpenter, J. *Introduction to Service-Oriented Programming (Rev 2.1).* www.openwings.org/download/specs/ServiceOrientedIntroduction.pdf, accessed October 2002.

Fowler, M. *UML Distilled: Applying the Standard Object Modeling Language.* Addison-Wesley, 1997.

Gamma, E., Helm, R., Johnson, R., and Vlissides, J. *Design Patterns: Elements of Reusable Object-Oriented Software.* Addison-Wesley, 1994.

Garlan, D. *Software Architecture: A Roadmap.* ACM Press, 2000.

Herzum, P. *Web Services and Service-Oriented Architectures.* Executive Report, vol. 4, no. 10. Cutter Distributed Enterprise Architecture Advisory Service, 2002.

Meyer, B. *Object Oriented Software Construction.* Prentice Hall, 1997, pp. 39–48.

Object Management Group (OMG). *CORBA Basics.* www.omg.org/gettingstarted/corbafaq.htm, accessed October 2002.

Parnas, D., and Clements, P. *The Modular Structure of Complex Systems.* IEEE, 1984.

Potts, M. *Find Bind and Execute: Requirements for Web Service Lookup and Discovery.* www.talkingblocks.com/resources.htm#, accessed January 2003.

Stevens, M. *Service-Oriented Architecture Introduction, Part 2.* Developer.com, *http:/ /softwaredev.earthweb.com/msnet/article/0,,10527_1014371,00.html,* accessed October 2002.

——. *Multi-grained Services.* Developer.com, *http://softwaredev.earthweb.com/java/ sdjjavaee/article/0,,12396_1142661,00.html,* accessed October 2002.

Sun Microsystems. *Jini Network Technology, www.sun.com/jini.*

——. *Jini Technology Architectural Overview, http://wwws.sun.com/software/jini/ whitepapers/architecture.html,* accessed October 2002.

——. *Jini Technology Core Specification: LE-Distributed Leasing. http://wwws.sun.com /software/jini/specs/jini1.2html/lease-spec.html,* accessed October 2002.

Chapter 3

Component-Based Service Development

In the previous chapter, we discussed service-oriented architecture, which specifies service interfaces and the way service consumers, services, and registries interact. However, it does not specify how a service is implemented. Organizations that want to use service-oriented architecture for new development need to know how to develop the service implementations as well.

A basic tenet of software design is to separate a software module's interface from its implementation. SOA describes the interface. Now we will discuss implementation using component-based development. Service-based development is simply an extension of this. *Component-based service* (CBS) development describes a service that uses components and component-based development practices for its implementation.

The word *component* is applied to many different software constructs. It is used to describe user interface components, such as Java beans, and server-side logic, such as entity beans. It is also used to describe an entire functional system, such as for billing or order entry. In all cases, a component is a software package with one or more well-defined interfaces. In addition, a component executes on a component execution environment. For instance, a robust execution environment, such as a J2EE container, provides functions all components need, such as transaction management and database connection pooling. Another feature of a component is that it is packaged and deployed as an independent software entity into an execution environment. A classic definition of a software component states, "In general, software components are binary units of possibly independent production, acquisition and deployment that interact to form a functioning system" (Szyperski 1998).

In this chapter, we will discuss the component development lifecycle, from requirements-gathering through maintenance. However, we will highlight the special aspects of developing component-based services and will focus our discussion on component design principles. Each principle will be related to the effect it has on the overall system's quality attributes.

▷ Development Lifecycle

The development lifecycle of a component-based service, shown in Figure 3.1, is similar to the lifecycle of any software system. It goes through the following phases: requirements analysis, design, implementation, quality assurance, and maintenance.

Requirements Analysis

During the requirements analysis phase of component-based service development, an entire system's functional and nonfunctional requirements are defined. The functional requirements relate to the way the component-based service will fulfill the business need. Credit-card validation is an example of a functional requirement. Nonfunctional requirements are technical in nature. A requirement that states that a response must be returned to the consumer within two seconds is an example of a nonfunctional requirement. Techniques such as looking at existing documentation and conducting user interviews are used to construct a set of artifacts that constitute the requirements for the system.

Figure 3.1
Development lifecycle of a component-based service.

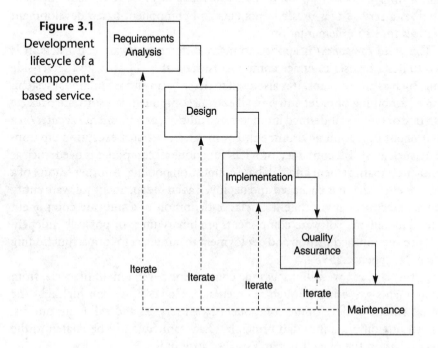

Functional Requirements

Developing the functional requirements for a service is different from developing functional requirements for a single application. Services support multiple applications. Therefore, services designed and developed for a single application are not likely to meet the needs of other applications that require the same or similar functions.

How do we design services when we don't know what applications will use them? The answer is to develop a business architecture—a description of the business the organization performs—which consists of documents and models. To a service developer, the most valuable part of the business architecture is the functional decomposition of the business into different subject areas. Each subject area describes a single part of the organization and the functions the area contains. For example, a bank has checking-account, savings-account, and customer functions.

Services are coarse-grained structures that should map not to a single application but to the functional areas of the business. This mapping increases the services' reusability, because a service that maps to the business rather than an application is more likely to support the requirements of multiple applications. When designing a service, it's tempting to map services to existing legacy systems.

For instance, if a banking system performs both checking and savings-account functions, many service designers will implement a banking-system service. This is wrong for two reasons. First, the banking system performs two logical functions that should be split into two services, one each for checking and savings. Also, the service is named for a system, not for the functional area the service supports. The advantage of this is that each service uses the banking system as a resource for executing service requests, but if the banking system is ever replaced, service consumers may not have to be updated, because the services map to a function, not a system.

Once the business architecture is created, a conceptual service model is derived from it. Designing services is usually not a green-field exercise. The conceptual service model contains areas of the business implemented in services. It also focuses more on implementation aspects of the services but does not assume a particular implementation technology. The conceptual service model provides the basis for designing service boundaries and interfaces.

However, in true green-field development, a set of artifacts should be created to identify the functionality a service should support. Service development is usually performed within the context of an application, which drives the parts of the conceptual service model to be implemented. Some of the interfaces will be needed and others will not (yet). The application requirements drive the implementation of small pieces of the component service model within the enterprise vision of a services layer.

To identify application requirements, the requirements analyst creates a set of artifacts from existing documentation and user interviews that describes the application to be built. As Figure 3.2 shows, these artifacts include a feature list, use cases, quality scenarios, and an object model.

The feature list contains all the features the system must support. The use cases define the ways users will exercise those features. The object model describes the structure of the business process. The techniques used to elicit the functional requirements for an application are necessary and are well documented elsewhere and thus are not detailed here.

Along with the functional requirements for a system, the nonfunctional aspects must also be defined, to determine the technical level of service the system will support.

Nonfunctional Requirements

A system's nonfunctional requirements are defined in the quality scenarios. Just as it is necessary to make the functional requirements concrete by developing use cases, it is necessary to make the quality requirements concrete. It is not sufficient for a quality scenario to state that the system should be "highly reusable." A specific reusability requirement would state that the "credit-card validation service will be reused by system X." Another example is when a performance requirement is stated in reference to an overall latency requirement but not in terms of usage patterns, scalability, or the impact on system usability (Clements and Northrop 2002).

Figure 3.2
The requirements analyst creates a set of artifacts that describes the application.

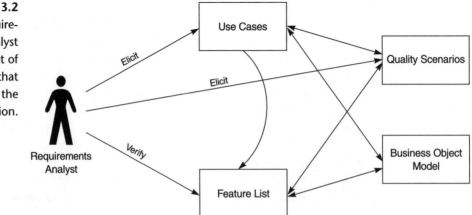

Another term for the set of nonfunctional requirements a service supports at runtime is *quality of service* (QoS). Other nonfunctional requirements not evident at runtime, such as maintainability and reusability, are not part of QoS. Each component-based service in service-oriented architecture supports a specific quality of service (QoS) level. Simply defining the service's functional requirements may not make the service usable if it does not support the quality attributes necessary to deliver a fully functioning system.

Although it can be difficult to estimate the a system's quality requirements, the exercise will greatly enhance the designer's knowledge of expectations for the system. Defining the quality requirements as rigorously as possible greatly reduces the risk that the system will not satisfy them (Clements and Northrop 2002).

In modern component-based development, it is especially necessary to pay attention to nonfunctional requirements such as performance, security, modifiability, reusability, integrability, testability, availability, reliability, and portability.

Once the nonfunctional quality of service attributes have been identified, they can be described using Web Services Endpoint Language (WSEL). WSEL allows a service provider to describe things such as QoS and security characteristics.

Performance

The performance-quality attribute requirement must be defined during the requirements analysis phase. Performance is the responsiveness of the system, measured in the time required to execute some function. Some of the questions that must be answered to design the system correctly include

- What is the expected response time for each use case?
- Will bad performance dramatically affect usability?
- How must the system perform?
- What is the synchronous response time?
- What is the asynchronous response time?
- What is the batch execution time?
- Can the time differ dramatically based on the time of day or system load?
- What is the expected growth of the system load?

A component-based system uses the network to communicate between components. Any performance requirement must be looked at closely to determine if the system can meet it. When a performance requirement cannot be met, the designer should consider several strategies:

- Make the request asynchronous.
- Take advantage of scalable component execution environments.
- Cache data in the proxy.
- Execute the request in the proxy.

If actual performance will not meet the requirement for a service request, it might be possible to make the request asynchronous. An asynchronous request returns control immediately to the service consumer after the consumer sends the request to the provider. The consumer continues processing and does not wait for the request to return. The consumer gets the results of the request in one of two ways: by checking periodically to see if the request has executed or by being notified when the results are ready.

If a consumer needs to know immediately when the results are ready, the service provider will interrupt the consumer and give the consumer the results of the service request. Making a request asynchronous is appropriate especially if the service consumer does not require a response. For instance, a consumer who calls the *AddCustomer* method in a customer service might not require the add customer to happen immediately. The information could be passed in, and control could be immediately given back to the consumer. The add customer transaction would happen at a later time, and the consumer could optionally check the status of the transaction periodically to see if it has executed. In general, to improve consumer performance, any requests that do not return a response should execute asynchronously.

Scalability is also related to the system's ability to respond to increasing load. All components execute in a component execution environment such as J2EE. The design should take full advantage of the component execution environment (CEE) (Herzum 1998), most of which support clustering. This allows the component execution environment to create components on multiple machines, to load-balance their requests across multiple component instances.

As discussed in the previous chapter, a proxy can cache service data, such as reference tables. Robust proxy implementations can cache service results so that subsequent service requests to the proxy can return data cached in the proxy rather than making a network call. In addition, a proxy can execute methods that do not require the state of the service. Rather than incurring a network call, methods such as standard calculations can be made in a local proxy. This approach is problematic, because new proxies need to be redistributed every time the service changes. The best way to implement a proxy is to make it dynamically download-able. In other words, when a consumer needs to access a service, it downloads a new proxy from a server. The proxy should also have a lease attached to it, such that when the lease expires, the service consumer must download another proxy from the server. This eliminates the problems that occur when services change and proxies are out of date.

When it comes to performance, the best strategy is "Make it run, make it right, make it fast, make it small" (Coplien and Beck 1996). The techniques outlined in this chapter and other performance-enhancing techniques should not cause the designer to sacrifice other quality attributes of the system in the name of improving performance.

Security

The security quality attribute must also be defined during this phase. Some of the questions that must be answered to design the system correctly as it relates to security include

- How critical is the system?
- What is the expected impact of a security failure?
- If there have already been security failures, what was their impact?
- Are there any known vulnerabilities?

If the system is highly critical, such as electronic control, security is of high concern. Even if the system is not critical but a security breach would cost a large amount of money, time, or resources, it is also of high concern. Creating or adopting specialized components for authorization, using secure transports, and implementing sound security policy can address security. For more on security, see Chapter 13.

Modifiability

A system's modifiability refers to its receptiveness to change. These questions will help identify how modifiable a system should be:

- How often is it expected that a system change will be required?
- What is the usual extent of the change?

- Who is expected to make the changes?
- Is it necessary for the system to use current platform versions?

The cost of system development is not the only important factor. This cost is low compared to the cost of the system over its lifetime. In many organizations, the budget for application maintenance is larger than for software development. Unless the system has a short lifecycle, building modifiability into it should be a top priority, to reduce the cost of maintenance. Several factors determine modifiability:

- The extent to which the system is modular and loosely coupled determines to a large degree its modifiability. The determination as to how modifiable the system needs to be will in many ways answer the question as to how modular it should be.

- The use of layering within components to reduce intracomponent coupling is a technique for increasing component modifiability. Layering within the component separates the component's different technical responsibilities. Functions such as networking, business logic, and data access should be split into separate layers so that they can be maintained as units and reused in other component-based services.

- As shown in Figure 3.3, systems that are declarative and configurable will be more modifiable. The role expected to make system changes is also a factor in modifiability. It must be determined whether a developer, a business user, an analyst, or some combination of these is responsible. If the system is expected to have frequent business-related changes, a design that is declarative and

Figure 3.3
Degrees of
modifiability.

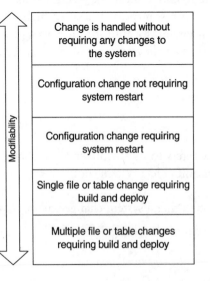

configurable will respond better to those changes. A developer designing such a system should also consider making it modifiable by businesspeople. For instance, an engine that executes business rules and works from configuration metadata may allow a business user to change the system's behavior. In addition, if these rules change frequently, and changes in the rules do not require the system to be rebuilt or restarted, the system will be more modifiable.

Reusability

Reusability is the ability of a software asset to be used in a different application context without modification. A system's reusability must be determined, because a highly reusable system is more expensive to build and will necessarily be more generic and cover more functionality than necessary for the specific application. Some questions to ask in relation to the system's reusability:

- Is this the start of a new product line? In other words, will more systems be built that more or less match the design of the system under consideration?
- Will any other systems use the components, libraries, and frameworks built for this system?
- Will this system use existing components?
- What existing framework and other code assets are available to reuse?
- Will other applications use the frameworks and other code assets created for this application?
- What technical infrastructure is in place that can be reused?
- Will other applications reuse the technical infrastructure created for this application?
- What are the associated costs, risks, and benefits of building reusable components?

An organization can take the following steps to increase reusability.

Establish a Product Line for Building Services

A product line (Clements and Northrop 2002) consists of a set of assets that supports the creation of a specific type of software artifact. Product lines within an organization consist of software assets, execution platforms, processes, and organizations centered on creating a particular class of software system. A product line for reusing component-based services should be considered, due to the large return on investment when multiple services use the same core assets. By establishing a product line, not only will the services themselves be reused, but core assets for building component-based services are reused as well.

To build the services product line, the commonalities and variations between services must be identified. The product line assets are implemented based on the commonalities between services and must support all variations between services. In other words, they must be able to support all the functional and nonfunctional requirements of the services built using the product line's core assets.

Creating of a product line involves mining, buying, and building assets for creating new services. The common core assets for creating component-based services are reused by each new service built using those assets, greatly improving overall reusability. For instance, if a product line's core assets consist of a persistence framework, an event framework, a set of project management templates, and a J2EE execution platform, those assets are reused by every component-based service built on that product line.

Implementating new services on the product line will also identify requirements it does not support and must be upgraded to support. A downside to upgrading product lines is that it may be necessary to refactor older component-based services to run on the new product line.

Not only will the product line share reusable core assets, it will support a common set of nonfunctional quality attributes for all services. Each service developed using the product line's core assets inherits its level of security, modifiability, and so on. By instituting a product line for services, an organization can realize many benefits, including better productivity, improved time to market, increased project predictability, better quality, and better return on investment.

When initiating a product line for service development, the organization should identify common assets for inclusion in the product line. These common assets include

- Infrastructure
  - Application servers
  - Database servers
  - Security servers
  - Networks, machines
  - Software tools
    Modeling
    Traceability
    Compilers and code generators
    Editors

      Prototyping tools
Integrated development environments
Version control software
Test generators
Test execution software
Performance analysis software
Code inspection and static analysis software
Configuration management software
Defect tracking software
Release management and versioning software
Project planning and measurement software

- Frameworks and libraries
  - Frameworks and libraries are necessary to obtain a level of code reuse. For instance, frameworks and libraries for persistence, transactions, and business rules execution can provide a robust platform for creating component-based services.

- Patterns, styles, and blueprints
  - The product line is developed according to a set of principles outlined in patterns, styles, and blueprints. For instance, the J2EE patterns, the J2EE blueprints, and a layered architecture are principles that feed into the development of the product line. A product line may also have a custom set of patterns and styles. The proper use of these patterns and styles is demonstrated in the blueprints developed for the component-based services product line.

- Process
  - The process for using the product line to create usable services must be identified. Iterative and incremental practices for service development should be considered. The process is customized to include project templates specific to the activities that must occur to produce component-based services using the product line. As experience with the product line increases, these processes can be tuned to increase predictibility and reduce project risk for each subsequent project.

- Organization
  - The organization that develops functional code and the organization that develops product line assets must be determined. Some organizations separate the development of core assets from functional development. Some develop core assets along with a project and then harvest those assets for use on other projects. Each organization needs to figure out which is best for it. In smaller organizations, a single group may both create services and

manage core assets. In larger organizations, these functions can be split up and performed by two different organizations. If a single group performs both functions, there is a risk that the separation between core asset and functional code will not be clear. If two distinct organizations are involved, there is a risk that the requirements for the component-based services will not be well understood by the core asset developers and the core assets will not meet those requirements.

There are two additional ways to improve reusability in services: by improving modularity and modifiability.

Improve Modularity

In addition to the reusability of the assets for building services, the services themselves are obvious candidates for reuse. Therefore, the modularity and interface definitions of the component-based services are critical to their potential for reuse. In other words, the more modular a component-based services is, the more likely it will be reused.

In addition to reusing the service in its entirety, individual layers can be reused within other services. For instance, if a service uses a data access layer for accessing a legacy system, this can be designed for reuse in other services that access the same legacy system.

Improve Modifiability

A service's modifiability is also important to determine its reusability. If reusing a component requires it to undergo change, the magnitude of the effort to change the component must be small. The original service designer cannot fully predict all possible requirements for future applications. Therefore, the service will need to be updated from time to time. To reuse the service effectively, the effort involved in modifying the service must be less than the effort involved in writing a new service.

The modifiability of the core assets themselves is also of critical importance. They will support the system's current set of functional and nonfunctional requirements. When those requirements change, the core assets are likely to change as well. Therefore, they must be highly modifiable. The downside is that when the core asset changes, the changes ripple through each service built using that asset. Therefore, core assets must be built such that changes and improvements to them do not have devastating consequences for other component-based services that use them.

Integrability

A component's integrability is its ability to communicate with other systems. By definition, service-oriented architecture consists of highly interoperable services. Some questions to ask during requirements analysis include

- Should we use highly interoperable technologies?
- Are the component interfaces consistent and understandable?
- How do we version component interfaces?

To improve integrability:

- Make sure the interfaces are consistent and understandable. The extent to which a component-based service's interfaces are consistent and understandable will determine its integrability. A versioning strategy is also necessary so that as new interfaces are developed, old ones may be easily maintained and eventually retired.
- Adapt the service for different environments. Although a component-based service supports a service-based interface, the component is also likely to be used in non-service-based environments. Therefore, it is better to separate the layer that participates in the service environment (service façade) from the layers that implement the component. That way, if a legacy system needs to access the service, assuming it supports only a legacy communication standard and not a new service-based integration standard, the legacy client will be able to use the component outside the service environment. This is accomplished by building a legacy protocol adapter that adapts the legacy protocol to the protocol used by the native component. The component can then be used by both service consumers and legacy consumers at the same time, as Figure 3.4 shows. This ability is also related to reusability. If a system cannot connect to and use the service, it will obviously not be reused.

Testability

A service's testability relates directly to its overall quality. A service that is not easily tested will be a low-quality service. The requirements for testability are

- What kind of process should be in place to certify a component-based service's correctness?

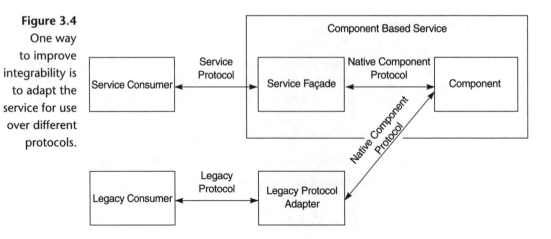

Figure 3.4
One way
to improve
integrability is
to adapt the
service for use
over different
protocols.

- Are tools, processes, and techniques in place to test language classes, components, and services?

- Are tools, processes, and techniques in place to test service federations?

- What kind of features does the architecture need to test component-based services?

The architecture should support a level of testability that allows the component-based service to be certified for use. This is especially difficult in service-oriented environments, because the organization that certifies the service may not have access to the service consumer. For instance, the consumer could be on the other side of the Internet and not part of the organization that developed the service. Therefore, the testability of the service contract, the objects that make up the service, and the testing of component interfaces are extremely important. Also, even though services are certified individually, they may require retesting when assembled into service federations that support some orchestrated business process.

One of the downsides of a reusable product line for service creation is that a change in a core asset, such as a framework, may require all the services built using that framework to be regression tested and recertified. The extent of reusable code can sometimes have a negative impact on the effort required to test the impact of this change. However, it is almost always preferable to leverage existing assets than to build new ones from scratch.

Availability

A system's availability must be established. Availability measures the time between failures and how quickly the system is able to resume operation after a failure (Bass 1998). In addition to system failures that produce downtime, we also include normal maintenance operations that require downtime. Some questions to ask about availability include

- What are the expected hours of operation?
- What is the maximum expected downtime per month?
- How available is the current system?

A system's batch cycles, upgrades, and configuration changes must support the availability expectation. If a batch cycle requires two hours to run but the system is expected to be available 23 hours per day, either the requirement must be changed or the batch process must perform better. If a configuration change is made to the service, does it require restarting the service? If the service is currently in the middle of an orchestrated process, how will the change affect processes that are running? A robust architecture will allow runtime configuration changes and mitigate the impact of those changes on processes currently being executed.

Another aspect to availability is the way service consumers are notified that the service is not available. Do your service consumers simply time out, or will you provide a "Not Available" message? In some implementations, an endpoint description can provide QoS information, such as availability. The QoS description of the endpoint provides a proactive way to inform consumers about the service's availability.

Reliability

The system's reliability must be established. Reliability has to do with the system's capability to maintain a level of performance for a stated period. Questions related to determining reliability include

- What is the impact of a hardware or software failure?
- How quickly must the system become operational after a system failure?
- When will performance impact reliability?
- What is the impact of a failure on the business?

Reliability is related to several factors that include the architecture, design, and implementation. Reliability can be enhanced through the configuration of component-based services for rollover in case of hardware failures. In the event of a software or hardware failure, can the system be easily recovered? Does a failure result in an incorrect system state? A highly reliable and correct system will not only guard against system failure but will be easily recoverable when a failure does occur.

Portability

A system's portability relates to its ability to run on multiple platforms. Several questions to ask related to how portable to make the system include

- Do the benefits of a proprietary platform outweigh the drawbacks?
- Should the expense of creating a separation layer be incurred?
- At what level should system portability be provided—application, application server, or operating system?

To enhance an application's portability, a separation layer can be developed to create an interface for the service to use, rather than making the interface a feature of the service platform. This is accomplished by creating an adapter that adapts the generic interface the service expects to the particular implementation of the feature the platform provides. For instance, consider the creation of a logging adapter that provides a generic interface for logging to the service and logs messages using the Log4J library. If the library of choice changes to a newer version or a completely different implementation, the service will not change—only the adapter must change.

Another factor affecting system portability is the component execution environment. Some commercial component-execution environments are built to be more portable than others. For instance, a component built for the Microsoft .NET platform can run only on a .NET platform provided by Microsoft. A component built using the J2EE platform can run on J2EE platforms provided by a large number of vendors.

▷ Design

After the requirements analysis is complete, the design phase can begin. You do not have to wait until all the requirements have been documented before beginning the design phase. During design, you will identify areas where the requirements are incomplete and where more information is needed. Requirements, design, and implementation should be done in small increments to create the service. In each phase, new information will require a change to previous phases. During the design phase for an application,

- The services that make up the application must be designed.
- The design of the services in the service layer must support QoS requirements identified during requirements analysis.
- The design must also support the functional requirements that were identified.
- The design must support the feature list and use cases.
- The design must map to the business architecture and the conceptual service model.
- Existing services that can be reused must be identified.

Architecture

Organizations that set up a services product line establish a set of core assets for building services. For purposes of discussion, we group those assets into three distinct architectural viewpoints, shown in Figure 3.5: application architecture, technical architecture, and process architecture. Each architectural viewpoint consists of artifacts that address that particular concern.

Figure 3.5 Architecture refers to core assets grouped into three viewpoints.

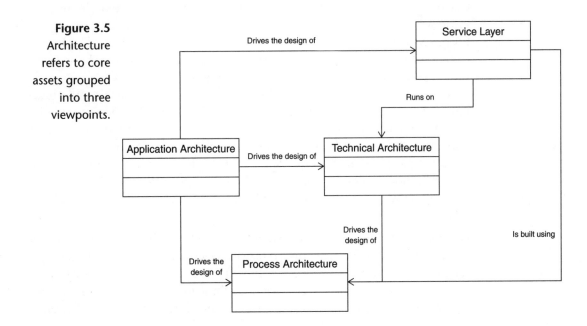

Application Architecture

Application architecture for the component-based services layer consists of the artifacts that guide and provide the vision for the design and implementation of services. Some of these artifacts include conceptual architecture, frameworks and libraries, baseline architecture, developer guides, and blueprints. These artifacts determine the software architecture of the services in the service layer. The conceptual architecture provides a description and diagrams of the various layers within a component-based service and how those layers collaborate to provide a functioning service.

When an organization sets out to develop a services layer for applications, it usually creates a set of frameworks to help developers create services. These frameworks implement the conceptual architecture. The frameworks give the service developer plug points to provide functional code in each layer of the service. They also dictate the way messages pass between layers. The framework provides additional features that separate the functional developer from many platform details, so a developer who writes functional code does not need to worry about too many technical details of the execution environment. A good services framework will let the functional service developer focus on implementing the solution to the business problem rather than creating solutions to technical problems.

Once the framework is complete, the architect selects a set of "architecturally significant" use cases to implement the baseline architecture. The use cases should be sufficient to eliminate technical risks from the project. They should be selected to demonstrate that the nonfunctional requirements could be met. In most cases, only a few use cases will be selected, and the baseline architecture will fully implement them. They should demonstrate a thread through all layers and tiers of the architecture and provide enough of a demonstration of the architecture to permit successful development of the system.

In addition to conceptual architecture, frameworks, and architecture baseline, the architecture should also include detailed developer documentation. This documentation gives functional developers the information they need to implement the rest of the use cases for the component-based services. Also, in a typical product line, a set of blueprints should be developed that contains a sample application for developing services. These blueprints show the best practices for using the frameworks to develop services using the product line assets provided.

Layered Architecture A conceptual architecture for a services layer is a model that depicts a layered architectural style. Each layer in a layered architectural style is a package of software that has a well-defined interface and a few well-known dependencies with other layers. Each layer implements one technical function within the service. For instance, a data access layer is responsible for encapsulating the technical means for accessing a database. All data access requests to a database go through the data access layer for that database. The data access layer has the responsibility of hiding the data access mechanism from upstream layers.

In a closed layer system, a layer may only access adjacent layers. In an open layer system, layers may access any other layer in the system, not just the ones they are adjacent to. We recommend the open layered architectural style for J2EE service development. This gives developers the ability to interchange layers, which greatly improves the service's maintainability. If one layer changes, and the new layer supports the same interface contract as the one it is replacing, adjacent layers don't necessarily need to change. The layered architectural style also facilitates parallelism in development. Once the contracts have been defined for each layer, multiple development teams can implement each layer independently. As long as the contract for each layer is not broken, an integration task at the end of the project is all that is necessary to complete development. The conceptual architecture for a typical component-based service consists of six layers, shown in Figure 3.6.

Proxy Layer The proxy layer follows the classic proxy design pattern from the Gang of Four book (Gamma et al. 1994). The J2EE patterns book (Alur, Crupi, and Malks 2001) calls this layer the "Business Delegate." The proxy layer consists of local objects that the consumer of the service uses to access the service. The proxy abstracts all the details of looking up the service and invoking the remote method. It provides a strongly typed interface for the service client, which will not allow the client to send incorrectly typed data. If a service requires an integer and a string, the proxy will ensure that the client uses those data types.

The client uses local native method invocation on a local object. For instance, a bank account service proxy will have a method called debit account with a bank account number *String* and a *BigDecimal* amount argument. The proxy looks up the URL of the bank account service in a registry, translates the arguments into a SOAP XML message, and posts it to the service. The service proxy handles all the complexities of registry lookup–SOAP, XML, and URL connections. The service developer creates proxies for any client who wishes to use the service. For

Figure 3.6
The conceptual architecture for a typical component-based service consists of six layers.

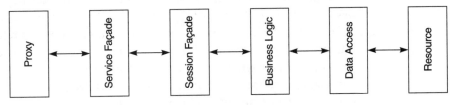

instance, if a Java client, Visual Basic client, and Perl script all need to access the service, the developer provides a proxy for each one, to make accessing the service as easy as possible.

An alternative to creating a different proxy for each service is to use a dynamic proxy. A dynamic proxy uses a WSDL contract specification to dynamically provide strongly typed methods that match the WSDL specification. It uses reflection to create methods that match the specification in the WSDL document. This technique allows the developer and consumer to use a single proxy for all available services.

Service Façade The service façade receives the service request, transforms it into a native method call, and invokes the proper method on the component. It adapts the component for use in a service-based environment. For instance, JAX-RPC is itself a service façade layer. It accepts a SOAP message and calls a stateless session bean with the arguments from the SOAP message. It also formats the results from the call to the stateless session bean into SOAP and returns it to the proxy. The service façade understands the protocol and data format of the services environment in a Web services environment; this is typically SOAP and HTTP. The service may have multiple service façades for each protocol type the service supports. For instance, a service might use both JAX-RPC to expose services via HTTP as well as a message-driven bean that accepts a SOAP message over JMS. The service façade layer may also translate the SOAP message into a *ValueObject* passed to the session façade for execution.

Session Façade The session façade layer implements the distributed interface for the component. For instance, a stateless session bean that executes the logic for a bank account service has a session façade. It supports Remote Method Invocation (RMI) for the component interface. The session façade does not implement the business logic itself. Instead, the session façade dispatches the request to the business logic layer for execution. The session façade understands the native protocol and data format for the component.

Business Logic The business logic layer contains objects that execute the business functions. The Command pattern should be considered to implement these objects. With the Command pattern, each use case in the requirements document is implemented as a separate command or set of commands executed in the business logic layer. Each command object implements a command interface. The command interface has a simple execute (*ValueObject*) method. A value object contains just data, no business logic, and is meant to transfer data from one tier or layer to another. It has simple attributes and getters and setters. It is built from the SOAP message passed in to the session façade layer.

Figure 3.7
A typical
session façade
and business
logic layer.

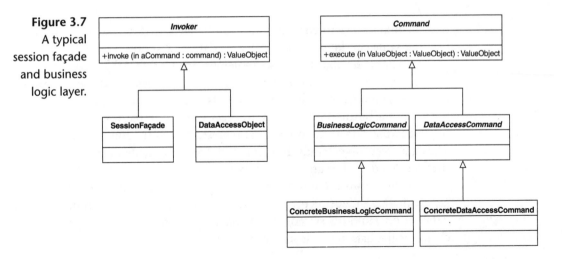

Each command object has business logic in its execute method. The value object argument for the execute method contains the request data required for executing the use case command. The typical execute method performs functions such as accessing the data access layer, executing the business logic, and returning a value object that contains the results of the use case to the session façade.

Figure 3.7 is a typical UML diagram for a session façade and business logic layer. Here, the business logic commands are executed by the session façade, which implements a *CommandInvoker* interface. Command invokers are responsible for creating the correct command, executing it, and returning the results to the upstream layer.

Data Access Layer The business logic layer commands do not access resource systems directly. They do so via the data access layer, which contains data access objects. Each data access object wraps a single data resource. The object is responsible for encapsulating the data access mechanism from the resource's clients. The objects map their interfaces directly to a system, but they do not expose any of the details of the data access mechanism to their clients.

For example, a savings account database has a corresponding savings-account data-access object that wraps the database with a set of methods for manipulating the database, such as update account, add account, and delete account.

The data access object can be used by a service's business logic or any data access client that needs to access the resource. For instance, if time is at a premium and it is not possible to create a full-scale checking account service but a checking account database exists, a checking-account-database data-access object could be created. A servlet could use the checking-account-database data-access object directly to manipulate checking account data. When the schedule permits, this design could be refactored to provide a full-fledged checking account service that uses the same checking-account-database data–access object directly.

The data access object can also implement the Command pattern, and if so, it also implements the *CommandInvoker* interface. The object creates and executes a data access command to fulfill the requests of the business logic layer.

When the business logic needs to access a data resource, it sends a *ValueObject* request to the data access object that represents the function it needs to access. The data access object finds the command that will execute the request, executes the command, and returns the results as a *ValueObject*.

By splitting up the responsibilities of business logic and data access, each layer can vary independently. For instance, if a system moves from an Oracle database on a mid-tier system to DB2 on a host system, the only layer that must change is the data access layer, not the business logic.

Resource Layer   The resource layer is the "system of record" for the data. It might be a database accessed via JDBC and entity beans. It might be a legacy mainframe system accessed via MQSeries or a packaged application such as Seibel or Peoplesoft. The data access objects encapsulate the resource, so if the implementation of the resource changes, only the data access layer must change, not the business logic, session façades, or service façades, and especially not the service's clients.

Technical Architecture

The technical architecture for the services layer is the runtime environment for service execution. It is the J2EE application server, the database servers, the directory servers and any other machines, networks, and operating systems that enable the service layer to run. The technical architecture impacts the application architecture in terms of the versions and configuration of the servers. For instance, if clustering is used, that has an impact on the way the frameworks must use the technical environment. The frameworks can't hold on to bean references, because the reference may switch from one server to another if the server goes down. The software versions also have an impact on application architecture. The frameworks and libraries will use a specific version of the J2EE environment. If the application servers are upgraded, then so must the frameworks that run on them.

Although application architecture has a major impact on the modifiability, reusability, integrability, and testability of the services layer, the technical architecture in large part impacts the performance, security, availability, reliability, and portability of services. Performance, availability, and reliability are to a large extent a result of the technical architecture's scalability. A robust technical architecture makes it easy to add application and database server nodes to a cluster and hubs to the network. If a node fails, the ability to dynamically move the processes on that node to another node is essential to the service layer's reliability. If the technical architecture does not perform well and batch cycles take hours, this will degrade the availability of the system. If processes cannot be allocated dynamically to multiple nodes for execution, performance will be impacted.

The application architecture and technical architecture must have a cohesive design to fulfill all the QoS requirements for the service built on the architecture. As shown in Figure 3.8, there are two classes of services: functional services and technical services.

Technical Services A technical service is a full-fledged service which, when coupled with a vendor platform, makes up the full execution environment for services. Common services include those for logging, transformation, configuration data, transaction management, reference data, and so on. These common services are used by other services and applications to perform specific technical functions. Although a business service might implement the functions of a bank account, a technical service implements functions around a technical problem domain.

Technical services use all the same assets of the services product line. They are built using the same frameworks, libraries, and platforms as business services. The technical services and frameworks also serve as "separation layers" between the business services and specific aspects of the platform. For instance, a logging service publishes an interface used by business services. The interface supports the requirements of the business services and has no relation to the particular technology used to implement the logging service. Internally, the logging service might use Log4J to log messages. Externally, this is not known by any of the busi-

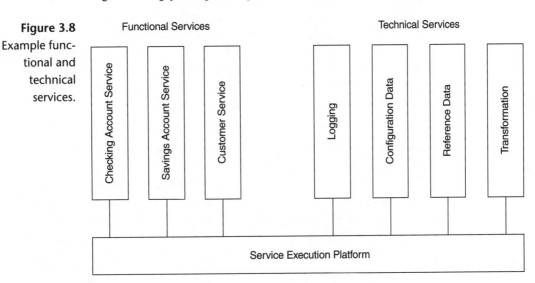

Figure 3.8 Example functional and technical services.

ness services. If the implementation of the logging service changes, as long as it supports the same interface contract, none of the services needs to know about the change.

Technical services are accessed like any other service across a network. However, it is possible, for performance reasons, to implement all of the technical service in the proxy. Therefore, a logging service proxy could log to a local file. If a more robust implementation is necessary, the file could be swept periodically and dumped into a database for reporting. If performance becomes less of an issue and real-time logging is necessary, the proxy could be exchanged for one that performs real-time logging to a logging service. In each case, the interface to the business service remains the same.

To make this design even more flexible, the proxy could be retrieved from a proxy factory. The proxy factory is configured in the runtime environment to return a proxy of a particular type that implements the same logging proxy interface. The runtime configuration for the service might one day return a proxy that implements a file-based scheme and the next day return a proxy that logs across the network. This can be accomplished without changing any code, only a configuration file.

Process

Entire books are available that describe the processes by which applications and architectures are built. Although we won't go into detail for any one process, it is important to note the distinction between creating and maintaining the business services themselves and creating and maintaining the architecture for the services. Building services is one part of building an application. The steps necessary to gather requirements for, design, code, and maintain a service are similar to those of any application. Processes such as the Rational Unified Process and OPEN and more agile methods such as XP and SCRUM are appropriate for the development of services. However, architecture has a different lifecycle and thus requires a different process. The product line process provides a means of developing and maintaining core assets for services.

Product Line Process The architecture for service design and execution has a more iterative lifecycle and therefore requires a different process. The product line process from the Software Engineering Institute is a method for maintaining core assets for service development. The development of a functional service has a discernible inception-through-deployment lifecycle. When developing an architecture, the tasks are much more iterative and do not have a discernible endpoint. Architectures need to be carefully maintained to minimize the impact on existing services while still taking advantage of updates to vendor platforms and new design techniques.

Core assets—machines, licenses, frameworks, libraries, and so on—are harvested from an organization's inventory of assets. The gaps that remain in the platform must be filled in. For instance, if there is no solution for logging, one must be built. Or if there is a solution but it does not perfectly fit the needs of the service platform, it must be adapted.

Technical and business changes drive iterations of the architecture. An event such as a platform upgrade will cause an update to the architecture in terms of frameworks and libraries. A new business process not supported by the platform will necessitate a change to the architecture. A new quality requirement, such as 24/7 availability, will require an update. The service platform is a product line in which all elements of the service share the same core assets. This improves return on investment. However, any business or technical change to the architecture affects all services built on that product line. Because of this risk and the potential to disrupt a large number of services, it is important to have a sound process to manage this change.

Design Issues

Interface Definition

Designing interfaces for services is critical to successful service development. The service supports a distinct business function, a clear and autonomous business concept. For instance, services such as a credit-card validation service, savings account service, and stock ticker service all support this concept. The modularity and interface definition of a modular service was discussed in the previous chapter. The process of defining the interface and attributes of the interfaces that must be captured is best addressed through the principles of the "design by contract" method from Bertrand Meyer (1997) and expanded upon by Richard Mitchell and Jim McKim (2001).

Design by Contract The design by contract method of interface contract design was developed for designing the interfaces of classes, but the principles fit service interface design equally well, although with a different slant. Design by contract for interface design is based on six principles:

1. **Separate basic queries from derived queries.** Derived queries can be specified in terms of basic queries. A derived query is a query that uses other queries to obtain an ultimate answer. A basic query goes directly after the data source

to get the data. Consider a bank account service that supports all the account activity for a bank, including checking and savings accounts. If a client needs to get the balance of the account, it calls the *GetBalance* service. This method inquires about the account holder's checking and savings account balances, sums them, and returns the result. If all the client needs is the total balance, there would never be a problem. If, however, a client needs just the checking account balance, the service will not fulfill this need. Therefore, it is necessary to separate the "basic" queries of *GetBalance* for savings and checking accounts from the composite derived query for both accounts. A correct design would consist of three service interfaces: *GetBalance* on a checking account service, on a savings account service, and on a composite *BankAccount* service. The composite derived service method would use the basic queries to derive the data on the client's behalf.

2. **For each command, write a postcondition that specifies the value of every basic query.** A postcondition specifies the effect of calling a feature of the service. For instance, a *Withdraw* command on a checking account service will guarantee that if the method succeeds, the *GetBalance* query will return the previous balance minus the withdrawal amount.

3. **For every query command, decide on a suitable precondition.** For methods that require multiple steps, specify the preconditions necessary for the multiple steps to succeed. For instance, consider a credit-card validation sequence where the first step is a validation that the cardholder has not exceeded his or her credit limit for the transaction. The second method actually confirms the transaction. The precondition for the confirm transaction has with it a precondition that the validate transaction has already occurred.

4. **For each derived query, write a postcondition that specifies what result will be returned in terms of one or more basic queries.** If we know the values of the basic queries, we will know the values of the derived queries. For instance, in the previous example, the postcondition for the *GetBalance* method on the derived *BankAccount* service specifies that the result is the sum of the *GetBalance* method on the checking account service and that on the savings account service.

5. **Separate queries from commands.** The first principle of writing interface contracts is to separate queries from commands. A query inspects the state of the service, and a command updates the state of a service. For example, consider a bank account service. A *GetBalance* query retrieves the state of the bank account service. The command *Withdraw* updates the state of the balance in the account. A bad design would return the new balance in the account when *Withdraw* was called. This would combine the query with the command. The

reason this is undesirable is that a user will be tempted to call the *Withdraw* method to query the balance of the account and thus inadvertently cause the state of the service to change. The *Withdraw* method should return only the result of the service call, such as "OK" or "Fail."

6. **Write invariants to define unchanging properties of objects.** For instance, the account balance in the savings account service can never be less than zero. Having these invariants specified somewhere helps define all possible states of the service, so proper error handling can be built.

Transactions

When implementing a service, each service method must be subtransactional, which means that it should not perform a commit on the data. One of the benefits of services is their composability, their ability to be assembled into a new composite service. As indicated in Chapter 2, this is sometimes called service "orchestration."

Consider our checking-account service example. Suppose a customer wanted to pay a credit card bill directly from his or her checking account. This requires two methods to execute: a "pay credit card" transaction and a "debit checking account" transaction. If either transaction fails, the other must be rolled back. If either is written such that as soon as it occurs, the transaction is committed, the transaction cannot be rolled back if the other transaction fails.

Sometimes it is not possible to make a method subtransactional. This is true where a service wraps a legacy system. Sometimes, the technology used to access the resource does not have transactional capabilities. In this case, the service should have "compensating" transactions, which reverse the effect of a transaction. For instance, on a checking account service, a deposit request would have a compensating *undoDeposit* request. The logical compensating transaction for deposit would be withdrawal. However, a withdraw request would be a logged request on the customer's account. An *undoDeposit* request would not log the transaction on the customer's account. In addition, the *undoDeposit* request would probably need the transaction ID for a previous deposit request.

▷ **Verification and Validation**

The concepts behind testing a service are basically the same as those behind testing components, except that an organization typically does not have visibility across the entire application. Interorganizational access to services requires that the service itself be certified without knowing how it is actually used by clients. This means that validation and verification of services is even more difficult and important, because it is used across organizations.

Testing the entire system is especially difficult for interorganizational systems, especially since a published service executes commands that change state. For instance, it is impossible to test the production version of the *Withdraw* method of the checking account service without actually removing money from an account. The service provider must supply test versions of the service to validate client access to the service.

Testing the QoS of a service is also important. A simple unit or regression test might not find that the service that once took two seconds to execute is now taking 20 seconds to execute. Even though the service is returning the correct result, the consumer might still time out because the request took too long. In addition, the service might work fine with one or two simultaneous requests, but when 20 simultaneous requests are made, the requests may fail the stated QoS for performance.

To thoroughly test services, functional testing, regression testing, load testing, and code inspections are necessary.

Unit Testing

Unit testing verifies all the objects within the service. A unit test is written before or during construction of the class and is used to validate that the class works correctly. Unit testing is usually performed with the support of testing and debugging tools such as JUnit. The same programmers who write the code for the classes write the unit tests.

Functional Testing

Functional testing, sometimes referred to as *black box* testing, tests the service interfaces, to ensure that they perform as expected. Functional tests test every possible state of a transaction. Invalid data is sent to the service, such as low limits (zero and negative numbers) and high limits. As with the unit test, the goal of the functional test is to provide maximum code coverage, executing all the code in the service.

Functional testing occurs on services that are new or have undergone change. If the functional tests are not time-consuming, they can be placed into the regression test suite in their entirety. Otherwise, a portion of them can be placed into the suite.

Regression Testing

Regression testing, a subset of functional testing, shows that previously passed tests still pass. These tests are performed on all services before the release of any change to any service in the service layer. Full functional testing is performed on services that have changed. Regression testing is performed on those that have not changed but that might be affected by changes in other services.

QoS Testing

QoS testing tests scalability, performance, and reliability. Load testing, one component of the QoS test suite, executes multiple requests of the same type at the same time, to guarantee a basic level of service under a specific system load. Performance testing finds the time it takes to execute a single service request. Reliability testing finds any correctness problems that might occur. For instance, these tests identify a potential for file corruption because two threads update a file at the same time. Reliability testing also verifies that the system can recover after a disaster.

Service Federation Testing

Service federation testing tests that multiple services work correctly together in a federation. For instance, consider a request that requires both the checking account service and customer service. The request requires that both these services communicate with each other and that both can roll back in the event of failure. Tests built to check for service-to-service coordination and communication are service federation tests.

System Tests

System tests include the clients in the testing process. This is the most difficult type of testing to perform in a service-oriented architecture, because the organization that provides the services is usually not the organization that consumes them. This means that multiple organizations must coordinate their testing efforts, to ensure that the service's clients can access it. If the consumer organization is not willing to participate in the tests or if the number of clients is too vast to perform full system tests, the service must go through a much more rigorous certification testing prior to release to ensure that it works correctly.

Inspections

Code inspections are good at finding defects of maintainability, reliability, and functionality. A code inspection checklist can find simple errors of omission and commission. An *omission defect* is when functionality is missing from the code that should have been there. A *commission defect* is when the code performs a function incorrectly. A *maintainability defect* is one that obviously negatively impacts the service's maintainability. This might be a defect in which a hard-coded value would be better stored in a file and read at runtime.

A reliability defect is one that might affect the running of the system. Reliability defects are best found by code inspections. A functionality defect is one in which the behavior of the service does not meet the requirements for the service. For example, if a service method was stubbed out during development and never implemented, it could pass all the functional tests, because it returns correct data, but it always returns the same data. Defects of this type are identified easily by code inspections.

> Maintenance

Maintenance of service development is the last phase in the software lifecycle. The maintenance phase deals with changes that need to be made to the service over its lifetime because of new or changed requirements.

Dealing with change is particularly difficult in service-oriented architecture, because the interface contract initially agreed upon by the service producer and the consumer must be maintained throughout the service's life. Unless both producer and consumer agree to a contract revision, the contract is in force. It is necessary to provide new features and interfaces for new clients while maintaining previous contracts. A change may require a change to the request message. If this is necessary, the service must support a new contract for the slightly different service call.

Sometimes the request does not require a change, but the response is different. If this is the case, the service must sometimes use information about the caller of the service to determine which response to deliver. The best way to handle interface changes is to include the version of the interface the caller is requesting in the request message. In either case, handling interface changes is difficult.

The goal of managing these changes is to support new requirements for the service while maintaining the service's integrity. Making a change to a service is the same as for any software artifact. The process is described in the IEEE Maintenance Process Activities diagram, shown in Figure 3.9 (SWEBOK 2002).

Figure 3.9
The IEEE
Maintenance
Process
Activities
diagram.

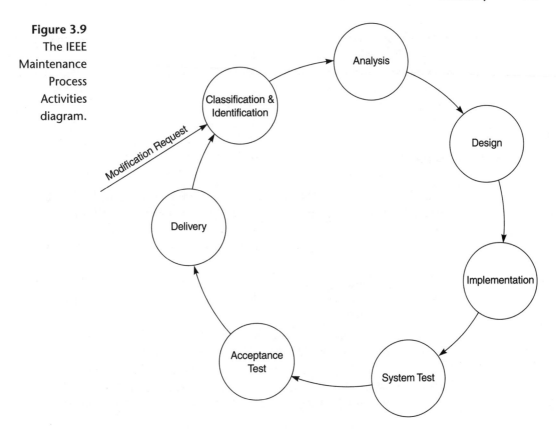

Over the life of a service, the cost of maintenance will greatly outpace the cost of initial implementation. Therefore, it is necessary to have a process to ensure that the service's integrity is not compromised and that new requirements are supported in a timely fashion.

> Summary

The concept of a component is central to the development of a service. Component-based development has been around since the early 1990s. The principles behind component-based development have evolved and matured since then. Service-oriented architecture depends on the same principles of component-based development. A service's development lifecycle is identical to a component's lifecycle. The only difference is the addition of a services layer on top of the component. A service also adds complexity, because the service's clients are sometimes outside the organization that created the service. These special considerations of a service-oriented architecture must be kept in mind, and the principles of component-based development that address the particular concerns of services, such as interface definition and testing, should be highlighted by the service development process.

> References

Alur, D., Crupi, J., and Malks, D. *Core J2EE Patterns.* Prentice Hall, 2001.

Bass, L., Clements, P., and Kazman, R. *Software Architecture in Practice.* Addison-Wesley, 1997.

Clements, P., Kazman, R., and Klein, M. *Evaluating Software Architectures.* Addison-Wesley, 2002.

Clements, P., and Northrop, L. *Software Product Lines.* Addison-Wesley, 2002.

Coplien, J., and Beck, K. "After all, We Can't Ignore Efficiency—Part 2." *C++ Report,* July 1996, p. 72.

Gamma, E., Helm, R., Johnson, R., and Vlissides, J. *Design Patterns: Elements of Reusable Object-Oriented Software.* Addison-Wesley, 1994.

Herzum, P., and Sims, O. *Business Component Factory.* Wiley, 1998.

Meyer, B. *Object-Oriented Software Construction,* 2nd edition. Prentice Hall, 1997.

Mitchell, R., and McKim, J. *Design by Contract, by Example.* Addison-Wesley, 2002.

Software Engineering Institute. *www.sei.cmu.edu/plp/plp_init.html.*

SWEBOK [IEEE 121.9]. *IEEE Standard for Software Maintenance.* 1992.

Szyperski, C. *Component Software: Beyond Object-Oriented Programming.* Addison-Wesley, 1998.

Chapter 4

SOAP

Like every other distributed computing platform, the Web services platform has also settled on a standard, well-known protocol for communication between distributed components of a system. For CORBA, the protocol was IIOP; for RMI, first JRMP and later IIOP; in Microsoft environments, DCOM.

For Web service architectures, the de facto standard for the basic protocol for communication between two parties is the Simple Object Access Protocol (SOAP). Because SOAP is the basic messaging protocol for Web services, other specifications build on top of the SOAP specification or have "bindings" to it. In this chapter, we discuss the role SOAP plays in Web services and how service nodes process SOAP messages. At the end of the chapter, you will have an understanding of a SOAP message construct and how SOAP can be extended to provide for more complex communication patterns between Web services.

> The Case for SOAP

To understand the value of an XML-based protocol for information exchange, we need to understand the doors it has opened. The fundamental shift in distributed computing SOAP has introduced is the ability to communicate effectively between distributed systems that rely on heterogeneous software and hardware stacks. Before SOAP, organizations had two main options to communicate between two geographically or physically distributed points, as Figure 4.1 shows.

The first approach takes the network for granted and concentrates on defining how parties communicate. This involved building wide-area networks and allowing the parties to plug into them. Often, these parties were valued business partners. This was the approach adopted by Electronic Data Interchange (EDI). EDI defined message constructs and how those messages were exchanged but left the network details to the parties involved. This was an acceptable solution for large corporations that had established relationships with their partners, and it

Figure 4.1
SOAP and the
enterprise

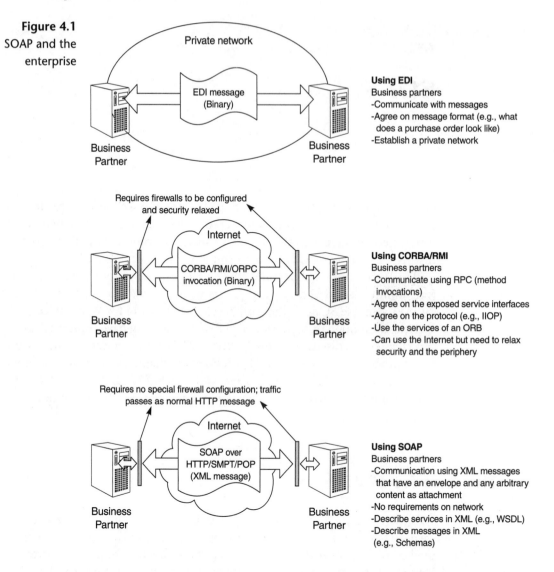

Private network

EDI message
(Binary)

Business
Partner

Business
Partner

Using EDI
Business partners
-Communicate with messages
-Agree on message format (e.g., what
  does a purchase order look like)
-Establish a private network

Requires firewalls to be configured
and security relaxed

Internet

CORBA/RMI/ORPC
invocation (Binary)

Business
Partner

Business
Partner

Using CORBA/RMI
Business partners
-Communicate using RPC (method
  invocations)
-Agree on the exposed service interfaces
-Agree on the protocol (e.g., IIOP)
-Use the services of an ORB
-Can use the Internet but need to relax
  security and the periphery

Requires no special firewall configuration; traffic
passes as normal HTTP message

Internet

SOAP over
HTTP/SMPT/POP
(XML message)

Business
Partner

Business
Partner

Using SOAP
Business partners
-Communication using XML messages
  that have an envelope and any arbitrary
  content as attachment
-No requirements on network
-Describe services in XML (e.g., WSDL)
-Describe messages in XML
  (e.g., Schemas)

was, in fact, quite successful. However, it resulted in collections of networks that
were not only expensive but that also locked the parties into using proprietary
products and solutions. For example, if Flute Bank decided to communicate with
Pipe Bank, both would need to buy expensive software that implemented EDI's
data and messaging specification and pay for a wide area network and data transfer.

The second approach started with standardizing the communication protocol and involved building distributed computing infrastructures that could run
on an open network. This was the route taken by CORBA, RMI, and DCOM. Each
developed its own protocol (IIOP, JRMP, and ORPC, respectively) that was positioned on top of TCP/IP and allowed two distributed objects to communicate.

While this approach reduced the need for private networks, the problem still remained: CORBA implementations could communicate with CORBA, RMI with RMI (with RMI-IIOP in J2SE 1.2 RMI and CORBA), and DCOM with DCOM. Though CORBA promoted platform independence by allowing objects to be written in any language, it still required both parties to use underlying object request broker (ORB) software, which usually had to be from the same vendor, because of the fragmentation in vendor implementations when it came to interoperability.

It is from this background that SOAP has been developed. SOAP decouples the data format and the underlying protocol, by leveraging a platform-independent language such as XML to describe the data and allowing for the use of well-established protocols such as HTTP to transport that data across the network. Some aspects that contribute to the simplicity of the SOAP protocol come from the fact that SOAP does not need to support features found in its predecessors, IIOP and JRMP, nor does it require the use of any broker software. For example, SOAP does not support distributed garbage collection, nor does it support the RMI/CORBA concept of servant activation.

SOAP was initially designed with HTTP in mind. HTTP by itself is very simple, in that a client makes a GET/POST request with some data and gets back a file or error response. It makes no requirements on the data, the way the client processes the data, or the underlying network infrastructure. It requires only the ability to establish a TCP/IP connection between the two endpoints. ▷

SOAP is the evolution of a movement to define an XML-based RPC standard on top of HTTP that would leverage this simplicity. Userland Software initiated the process in 1998. In 1999, Microsoft and Develop Mentor joined the effort and soon thereafter jointly published the SOAP 0.9 specification, which was not readily accepted. Only with the publication of the SOAP 1.1 specification and the SOAP with Attachment capability did the industry at large move to accept SOAP as the de facto standard for a Web services communication protocol. SOAP 1.1 with Attachments is covered in this chapter. ▷▷

▷ Tim Berners-Lee is credited with authoring the first HTTP-HTML implementation and a browser called "WorldWideWeb." He later founded the World Wide Web Consortium (W3C) (source: *www.w3.org/People/Berners-Lee/*).

▷▷ As of this writing, SOAP 1.2 became a candidate recommendation by the W3C *(www.w3.org/TR/SOAP/)*. This chapter examines SOAP with respect to version 1.1, but wherever appropriate, the changes proposed in version 1.2 are noted.

By itself, SOAP addresses only the basic needs of how disparate applications in different address spaces communicate. As different industry consortiums continue to define standards for various essential aspects of a distributed system (security, transactions, messaging patterns, etc.), SOAP is capable of extending itself to accommodate such emerging and, in some cases, established standards. Figure 4.2 shows how different value-added services can be layered on top of SOAP and how SOAP takes advantage of lower layers in the communication stack. SOAP can be extended in two important ways:

- Allowing it to be "bound" to a number of lower-level communication protocols. Nothing in the specification requires parties exchanging SOAP messages to use any particular protocol to transport those messages. For instance, the parties could send a SOAP message using HTTP, email (SMTP/POP), raw sockets, text files, or even the United States Postal Service.

- Accommodating the addition of robust, enterprise-class messaging capabilities, such as reliable messaging, transactions, and secure messaging, to the basic SOAP message. Several specifications (e.g., for transactions and security) detail how such value-added features and protocols can be added. SOAP accommodates these additions by defining a processing model for messages in which intermediate SOAP nodes process a message based on instructions in

Figure 4.2
The Web services communication stack

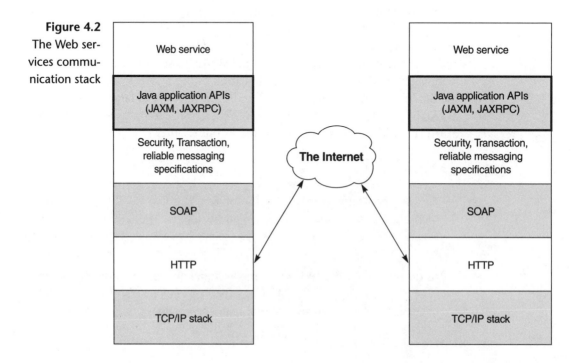

the SOAP message header. Many of these extensions also take advantage of a related specification, SOAP with Attachments.

> What Does SOAP Define?

SOAP defines four basic pieces of information, which we will look at in turn:

- The way the XML message is structured
- The conventions representing a remote procedure call in that XML message
- A binding to HTTP, to ensure that the XML message is transported correctly
- The conventions for representing an error back to the sender

SOAP does not define an object model or language bindings. It provides only the overall framework for an XML message to be communicated between a sender and a receiver, generically called SOAP processing *nodes* (Figure 4.3). A node may be a sender, a receiver, or both. This one-way message between nodes is often combined to implement request-response, asynchronous messaging, and notification type interactions. For example, a client may send a SOAP message within an HTTP request. The server processes that message and returns the SOAP response with the HTTP response.

Figure 4.3
SOAP nodes

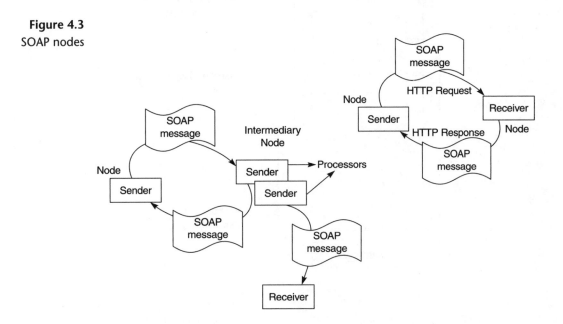

▶ SOAP Message Structure

A SOAP message is a well-formed XML document that contains an Envelope element, an optional Header element, and a mandatory Body element, as Figure 4.4 shows.

The Envelope element serves as a container for the Body and Header elements and also as an indicator to the processing node that the XML is a SOAP message. The key use of the envelope is to indicate the start and end of the message to the receiver. Once the receiver comes across the </Envelope> tag, it knows the message has ended and can start processing it (or picking up the attachments, if any). The envelope is essentially just a packaging structure.

The Header element is optional, but if present, it should be the first immediate child element of the Envelope element. SOAP does not define any individual header entries or XML elements in the header block. This is a key feature that many other specifications exploit by standardizing on the entries. This means that to add some functionality, the new specifications can define headers the

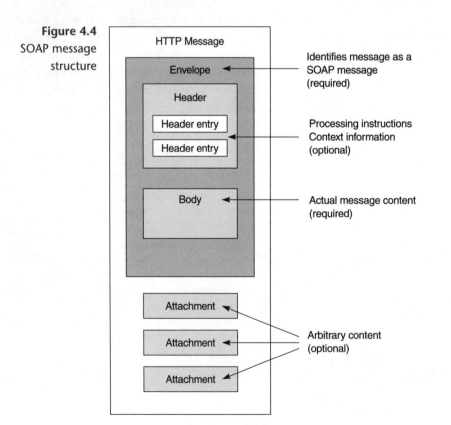

Figure 4.4
SOAP message
structure

SOAP message will carry and that vendor implementations of that specification can use in a standard manner. For example, the header may also contain metadata entries that help describe or augment the main content of the SOAP message, or information on how to route the message to different paths, add security, and so on.

The Body contains the actual, mandatory message intended for the final recipient. This may be XML elements that describe a procedure invocation—for example, describing arguments and parameters along with a procedure name—or other XML content, such as a complete purchase order. These two different techniques are generically called RPC-style and document-style SOAP messaging, respectively. ▷

As Figure 4.2 shows, a SOAP message has to be layered on top of a transport protocol. The rules that pertain to how a SOAP message is to be sent over a particular protocol are called the SOAP *binding* to that protocol. While the header elements may determine how a SOAP node processes the message, the protocol binding framework determines how a message travels *between* processing nodes.

▷ SOAP Message Elements

The details of the XML elements in the SOAP message are best explained with an example. We will use Flute Bank's bill payment service as an example and examine how one of its operations may be invoked using SOAP. The online bill payment service is offered to Flute's customers as a value-added service. In keeping with this chapter's goal of focusing on SOAP, the bill payment service illustrated is deliberately kept simple. The service assumes that payees or merchants have been registered with the bank and that Flute Bank's customers may only schedule new payments or view scheduled payments.

To illustrate the structure and content of a SOAP message, Listing 4.1a shows the SOAP message sent from a service consumer to the Web service in an HTTP request for the operation "getLastPayment." The service processes this message and returns a response with the last payment amount information. Listing 4.1b shows the corresponding response message sent by the service. Figure 4.5 maps Listing 4.1a to elements of the SOAP message structure.

> ▷ The body of the SOAP message can contain any arbitrary XML content as the message payload.

Figure 4.5
Mapping of
Listing 4.1a to
elements of the
SOAP message
structure

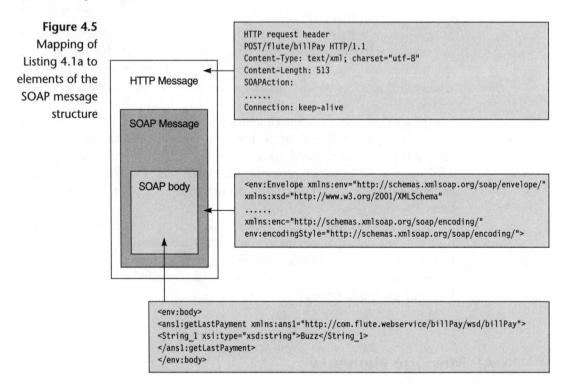

Listing 4.1a SOAP request corresponding to RPC style *getLastPayment* method invocation over http

```
HTTP request header
POST /flute/billPay HTTP/1.1
Content-Type: text/xml; charset="utf-8"
Content-Length: 513
SOAPAction:
User-Agent: Java1.3.1_04
Host: localhost:8080
Accept: text/html, image/gif, image/jpeg, *; q=.2, */*; q=.2
Connection: keep-alive

<?xml version="1.0" encoding="UTF-8"?>
<env:Envelope env:encodingStyle="http://schemas.xmlsoap.org/soap/encoding/"
            xmlns:env="http://schemas.xmlsoap.org/soap/envelope/"
            xmlns:xsd="http://www.w3.org/2001/XMLSchema"
            xmlns:xsi="http://www.w3.org/2001/XMLSchema-instance"
            xmlns:enc="http://schemas.xmlsoap.org/soap/encoding/"
            xmlns:ns0="http://www.flutebank.com/xml">
```

```
<env:Body>
   <ns0:getLastPayment>
      <String_1 xsi:type="xsd:string">my cable tv provider</String_1>
   </ns0:getLastPayment>
</env:Body>
</env:Envelope>
```

Listing 4.1b SOAP response corresponding to RPC style *getLastPayment* method invocation over http

```
HTTP/1.1 200 OK
Content-Type: text/xml; charset="utf-8"
SOAPAction: ""
Transfer-Encoding: chunked
Date: Thu, 03 Oct 2002 17:52:05 GMT
Server: Apache Coyote HTTP/1.1 Connector [1.0]
<?xml version="1.0" encoding="UTF-8"?>
<env:Envelope xmlns:env="http://schemas.xmlsoap.org/soap/envelope/"
              xmlns:xsd="http://www.w3.org/2001/XMLSchema"
              xmlns:xsi="http://www.w3.org/2001/XMLSchema-instance"
              xmlns:enc="http://schemas.xmlsoap.org/soap/encoding/"
              xmlns:ns0="http://www.flutebank.com/xml"
env:encodingStyle="http://schemas.xmlsoap.org/soap/encoding/">
   <env:Body>
     <ns0:getLastPaymentResponse>
     <result xsi:type="xsd:double">829.0</result>
     </ns0:getLastPaymentResponse>
   </env:Body>
</env:Envelope>
```

Envelope

The SOAP Envelope element identifies to the processing node that the message is a SOAP message. The namespace is used in place of versioning numbers as a means for the processing node to handle versioning. This is quite different from the approach taken by protocols such as HTTP, in which it is possible to derive a meaning from the version number—that is, HTTP 1.1 is a newer version than HTTP 1.0. In the case of SOAP versioning, no such numeric meaning can be inferred.

SOAP messages rely heavily on XML namespaces. Because the message can contain any XML elements, the SOAP elements must be scoped in some manner, to avoid conflicts with the elements of the message. For example, the message may contain a user-defined Envelope tag, which will break the well-formed structure and validity of the message itself. Namespace usage is analogous to the way Java uses package names for classes. ▷

A SOAP node may support one or more SOAP versions. If the node receives a message with a version it does not understand, the SOAP specification requires that it discard the message or, in a request-response scenario, return a Version-Mismatch "fault." We will talk about faults soon.

Header

The SOAP Header provides a container to add metadata to the content of the SOAP body and a facility to influence the processing of the SOAP message. Listings 4.1a and 4.1b contain no header element, because it is optional.

Headers are a key mechanism of vertical extensibility in SOAP. By adding appropriate entries in the header, context information relating to areas such as authentication, authorization, transitions, and routing may be included with the message. ▷▷

As an example of a SOAP header in use, consider how the Business Transaction Protocol (BTP) specification covered in Chapter 14 extends SOAP by defining the XML elements that can be contained in the header block. The header in Listing 4.2 shows how a transaction coordinator passes the context of the transaction from one service to another by adding header entries.

▷   The *Namespaces in XML Recommendation* can be found at *www.w3.org/TR/REC-xml-names* and is explained further in Appendix A.

SOAP 1.1 specifies the namespace for the Envelope as http://schemas.xmlsoap.org/soap/envelope/.

SOAP 1.2 specifies the namespace as http://www.w3c.org/2001/12/soap-envelope.

SOAP 1.1 and 1.2 processors will generate a version mismatch fault if the envelope does not contain their respective namespaces.

▷▷ Vertical extensibility refers to the ability to add information to a SOAP message without affecting applications that cannot process that information. SOAP messages achieve this with headers.

Listing 4.2 A transaction coordinator passes the context of the transaction from one service to another by adding header entries

```
<?xml version="1.0" encoding="UTF-8"?>
<env:Envelope xmlns:env="http://schemas.xmlsoap.org/soap/envelope/"
              xmlns:xsd="http://www.w3.org/2001/XMLSchema"
              xmlns:xsi="http://www.w3.org/2001/XMLSchema-instance"
              xmlns:enc="http://schemas.xmlsoap.org/soap/encoding/"
              env:encodingStyle="">
    <env:Header>
        <btp:messages
            xmlns:btp="urn:oasis:names:tc:BTP:1.0:core"
                env:mustUnderstand="1">
            <btp:context>
                <btp:superior-address>
                    <btp:binding>soap-http-1</btp:binding>
                    <btp:binding-address>
                            http://www.flute.com/btpengine
                    </btp:binding-address>
                </btp:superior-address>

                <btp:superior-identifier>
                    http://www.flute.com/btp01
                </btp:superior-identifier>

                <btp:qualifiers>
                    <btpq:transaction-timelimit>
            xmlns:btpq="urn:oasis:names:tc:BTP:1.0:qualifiers">
                    <btpq:timelimit>500</btpq:timelimit>
                    </btpq:transaction-timelimit>
                </btp:qualifiers>
            </btp:context>
        </btp:messages>
    </env:Header>
<env:Body>
<!--some XML content here-->
</env:Body>
</env:Envelope>
```

Sometimes the meta-information included in the headers may be critical to the message exchange. For example, in Listing 4.2, if the message recipient does not process the headers, the entire transaction processing model comes unhinged.

This is where the mustUnderstand attribute comes in. A sender can indicate the header entries the recipient must process by setting the mustUnderstand attribute to true (i.e., mustUnderstand="1"). If the recipient does not know what to do with this mandatory header, it will generate a well-defined fault. This ensures a robust processing model. ▷

Body

The Body element contains the message sent from consumer to provider, or vice versa. This message can be RPC style, in which it describes details about the procedure and the parameters, using an encoding style. In Listing 4.3a, the getLastPayment element indicates the procedure to invoke on the receiver. It consists of one parameter that describes the name of the account for which the last payment is to be returned.

Listing 4.3a   An RPC-style Body element

```
<env:Body>
    <ans1:getLastPayment xmlns:ans1="http://com.flute.webservice/billPay/wsdl/billPay">
    <String_1 xsi:type="xsd:string">Buzz</String_1>
    </ans1:getLastPayment>
</env:Body>
```

Alternatively the Body element can include a complete XML document, such as a purchase order, as in Listing 4.3b.

Listing 4.3b   A Body element that consists of an XML document

```
<env:Body>
<purchaseorder xmlns="http://www.flutebank.com/schema"
xmlns:xsi="http://www.w3.org/2001/XMLSchema-instance"
xmlns:po="http://www.flutebank.com/schema"
xsi:schemaLocation="http://www.flutebank.com/schema purchaseorder.xsd">
    <identifier>87 6784365876JHITRYUE</identifier>
    <date>29 October 2002</date>
    <billingaddress>
        <name>John Malkovich</name>
```

> ▷   A header optionally includes one or more of three attributes: actor, encodingStyle, and mustUnderstand.

```
        <street>256 Eight Bit Lane</street>
        <city>Burlington</city>
        <state>MA</state>
        <zip>01803–6326</zip>
    </billingaddress>
    <items>
        <item>
            <quantity>3</quantity>
            <productnumber>229AXH</productnumber>
            <description>High speed photocopier machine with automatic sensors
                                                    </description>
            <unitcost>1939.99</unitcost>
        </item>
        <item>
            <quantity>1</quantity>
            <productnumber>1632</productnumber>
            <description>One box of color toner cartridges</description>
            <unitcost>43.95</unitcost>
        </item>
    </items>
</purchaseorder>
</env:Body>
```

In both cases, the SOAP message is still well-formed and valid XML data from the sender to the receiver. What is different is the way the recipient uses the *encoding scheme*. We will see this later in the chapter. ▷

Handling Errors: The Fault *Element*

Earlier in this chapter, we used the term *fault,* which requires some elaboration. By embedding a well-defined XML Fault element in the body, a SOAP node indicates it had a problem processing the message. Such a message is generically termed a *SOAP fault.* The processing error could arise from any number of causes, from application-specific (e.g., account not found) to system issues (e.g., problem resolving a host name or finding a class in Java).

> ▷   Another way to look at the SOAP body is to think of it as a special case of a header block with a mustUnderstand="1" attribute, indicating that it must be processed.

Listing 4.4 shows a SOAP fault message sent by a message receiver in the HTTP response to the client. The message was generated as a result of an unchecked RuntimeException in the Java code.

Listing 4.4   A SOAP fault message sent by a receiver to the client

```
HTTP/1.1 500 Internal Server Error
Content-Type: text/xml; charset="utf-8"
SOAPAction: ""
Transfer-Encoding: chunked
Date: Wed, 18 Sep 2002 18:10:34 GMT
Server: Apache Coyote HTTP/1.1 Connector [1.0]
<?xml version="1.0" encoding="UTF-8"?>
<env:Envelope xmlns:env=http://schemas.xmlsoap.org/soap/envelope/
    xmlns:xsd=http://www.w3.org/2001/XMLSchema xmlns:xsi="http://www.w3.org/2001/
                                                        XMLSchema-instance"
    xmlns:enc="http://schemas.xmlsoap.org/soap/encoding/"
    xmlns:ns0="http://com.flute.webservice/billPay/types/billPay"
    env:encodingStyle="http://schemas.xmlsoap.org/soap/encoding/">

    <env:Body>
        <env:Fault>
            <faultcode>env:Server</faultcode>
            <faultstring>
                Internal Server Error (caught exception while handling request:
                            java.lang.RuntimeException: Demo of SOAP runtime Fault)
            </faultstring>
        </env:Fault>
    </env:Body>
</env:Envelope>
```

The SOAP body contains the single Fault element, which has the following subelements: ▷

- A mandatory faultcode element, which indicates the general class of errors.

- A mandatory faultstring element, which provides a human-readable explanation of the error.

> ▷   The SOAP fault is generated by a *node* which could be sending the message or receiving it. It is not uncommon for faults to be generated in a SOAP client because it couldn't dispatch the request in the first place.

- An optional `faultactor` element, which indicates the URI of the fault source. This element is mandatory if a SOAP intermediary reports the error.

- An optional `detail` element. If the fault is generated because of the request in the SOAP request body, the `detail` element must provide details for the processing error. If the fault is generated because of a processing error in the SOAP request header, this element must not be present—that is, the presence of this element indicates that the fault occurred in processing the SOAP request body. The `detail` element can have subelements, and the content of the detail element can be encoded.

The `faultcode` format provides an extensible mechanism to report the type of error that occurred. Fault codes are XML-qualified names. The dot (".") is used as a separator to indicate that the code to the left of it is a more generic `faultcode` (e.g., `client.Authentication`). The `faultcode` element can have the following four possible classes of values:

- `versionMismatch`. The processing node does not support SOAP message with the version reflected in the namespace. As discussed earlier, SOAP does not handle versioning through the use of version numbers. The `Envelope` namespace is used instead, and a SOAP processing node should throw this fault if it cannot handle the `Envelope` namespace.

- `mustUnderstand`. This fault is returned if a processing node cannot understand the semantics of a mandatory SOAP header element targeted at that node.

- `client`. This value signifies that the fault occurred because of some error within the client itself. It could be that the client did not provide sufficient/ and or correct information (such as authentication credentials) or that the request itself was not formed correctly. The fault is assumed to have originated at the client that composed the message and is an indication that retrying the message without making the appropriate correction will result in the same error.

- `server`. An error occurred at the server. Based on the error, the client may decide to retry. All Java exceptions that occur on the service provider's side (both application-thrown and runtime exceptions) are reported under this fault code. ▷

▷   In SOAP 1.2, when a SOAP node generates a `mustUnderstand` fault, it is required to identify by its qualified name the header block that caused the error to be generated.

When using HTTP, the server returns all SOAP fault messages with the HTTP response code of 500–(Internal Server Error).

▷ SOAP Processing Model

Earlier, we mentioned how a node may send, receive, or do both with a SOAP message. The mechanics of how a node handles these SOAP messages are called the *processing model*. In addition to the sending and receiving nodes, a SOAP intermediary may sit between the message originator and the ultimate destination (Figure 4.6), playing both a receiver and a sender role, adding to SOAP's horizontal extensibility. Intermediaries receive a SOAP message from the originator or another SOAP intermediary and pass the message on to the intended destination or another intermediary. ▷

SOAP messages can target specific headers at individual nodes, to ensure en route processing as the message goes hop by hop. The SOAP node for which a header element is intended may be the ultimate recipient of the message or an intermediary. Each header entry can identify which node must *act* on that header by specifying an actor attribute, like this:▷▷

```
<env:Header>
  <x:someheader someattribute="somevalue"
            soap:actor="http://www.flutebank.com/accountcheck ">
</env:Header>
```

The model of the SOAP actor attribute is intended to be quite simple and is based on two assumptions:

- All SOAP nodes are identified by a unique URI.
- This URI can target one or more header entries at the node.

Figure 4.6
SOAP nodes and
intermediaries

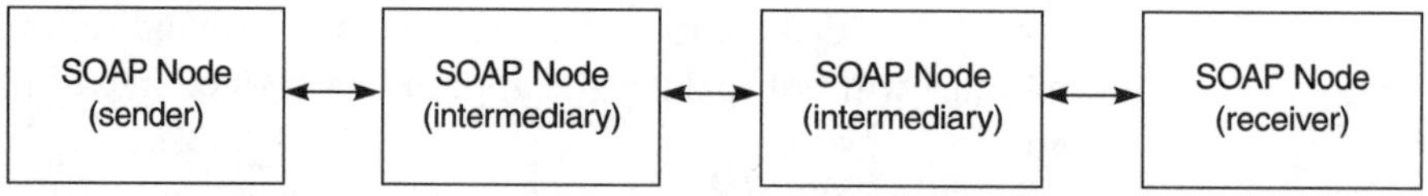

| SOAP Node (sender) | ↔ | SOAP Node (intermediary) | ↔ | SOAP Node (intermediary) | ↔ | SOAP Node (receiver) |

▷   Horizontal extensibility refers to the ability to target different parts of a SOAP message at different recipients along the processing path and is achieved using intermediaries.

▷▷   An intermediary can modify only the headers in a SOAP message, not the message body. The intermediary first processes, then removes header entries intended for it. An intermediary can also add headers targeted at other nodes.

The URI is only a logical identification criterion. The actor http://www.flutebank.com/accountcheck in the preceding example does not need to point to a physical URL but only identifies the actor responsible for validating an account number and balance. SOAP defines two special cases for the actor attribute:

- A special SOAP actor URI of http://schemas.xmlsoap.org/soap/actor/next indicates that the header block is to be processed by the node that has received the message.

- If no actor is specified, the node assumes it is the ultimate message recipient.

These two cases are specified because these actors are so commonly used, and it is useful to specify these details independently of where the message is going or how it gets there. For example, an intermediary may route a message dynamically between a set of "next" actors or when a node redirects the message to another node. Either way, there is no need to change the message.

The act of inserting a header entry into a message is like establishing a contract between the party responsible for the message and the party receiving it. An intermediary that inserts a header entry can be thought of as acting on behalf of the initial sender, because the receiver views the message as coming from the intermediary, not the sender. It also means that an intermediary cannot take a block out if the block is not intended for it. It is worth nothing that nothing prevents it from looking at blocks not intended for it. ▷

With the combination of the actor and mustUnderstand attributes, it is possible to route a message along a path with several different processing nodes. This model of distributing message processing across nodes makes for very scalable architecture, with each node providing value-added features to the request.

As an example, one value-added feature is caching responses to frequent or unchanging requests. If special caching servers are identified as actors with a particular URI, upon receiving the SOAP message with the appropriate header, a cache server can determine if the data within the message body is to be cached on the server. The header block shown below identifies the intended actor with the URI http://www.flute.com/cache. Any node acting in that capacity may choose to interpret and act upon the block. In this example, the header indicates whether the data in the body is cacheable.

▷   In SOAP, all parties in a message path are identified by URI, not just the final destination.

```
<env:Header>
    <c:cache xmlns:m="http://www.flute.com/BillPay/"
            soap:actor="http://www.flute.com/cache">
      <m:cachable>1</m:cacheable>
    </c:cache>
</env:Header>
```

In general, a SOAP node follows the following steps in processing a message:

1. Verify that the message is a SOAP message.
2. Identify and process header blocks targeted at the node. The node must understand each mandatory header block (header with mustAttribute set to "1"). If it cannot process a mandatory block, it must generate the SOAP fault of type mustUnderstand.
3. If the node is an intermediary, forward the request.
4. If the node is the ultimate recipient, process the SOAP body. ▷

Though SOAP defines this processing model using actors and headers, it does not define any message routing protocol. The ebXML specifications define the

---

▷   In SOAP 1.2, SOAP nodes take on different roles in processing a message and can act in more than one role. Each header block can be targeted for nodes in a particular role by tagging the header block with the name of the role. This is a refinement of the SOAP 1.1 notion of a SOAP actor and provides for a better processing model. The 1.2 version defines the following special SOAP roles:

- Header blocks with the role http://www.w3.org/2002/06/soap-envelope/role/next are intended for each SOAP intermediary and the ultimate SOAP receiver.

- Blocks with the role http://www.w3.org/2002/06/soap-envelope/role/none are forwarded without any processing, along with the message, to the ultimate SOAP receiver.

- Blocks with role http://www.w3.org/2002/06/soap-envelope/role/ultimateReceiver are meant for the ultimate SOAP receiver, which must act upon the block.

Messaging Service, and IBM-Microsoft have defined the WS-Routing protocol. These are covered in Chapters 7 and 17, respectively.

SOAP Bindings

As mentioned earlier, a SOAP message essentially provides the capability of sending a one-way message. Any real-world application will require more sophisticated message exchange patterns. For example, request-response, notification, one-way with acknowledgment, asynchronous communication, and reliable messaging are richer patterns needed for enterprise applications.

The binding mechanism, which defines how SOAP messages are processed *between* SOAP nodes, is one way to extend SOAP functionality SOAP relies on the underlying protocol to provide much of this functionality. In some cases (e.g., reliable messaging and secure messaging), additional specifications are needed to implement it. In either case, a SOAP message must be layered on top of, or bound to, an underlying protocol, which the various message-exchange patterns rely on for the added functionality. The SOAP 1.1 specification provides bindings for HTTP and defines how a request-response messaging model is to work over HTTP. Using SOAP over HTTPS also may satisfy some, but not all, of your security needs.

Although not advisable, it is entirely possible to create a custom implementation of a new binding—say, SOAP over raw TCP sockets. In case you are considering a new custom binding, you must recognize the disadvantages of such an approach, the biggest of which is that those services will not be able to interoperate with external Web services. Nor will you be able to take advantage of popular SOAP processing engines, such as Apache AXIS or Java WSDP. If you define your own SOAP headers to provide the context information for the message, you will also need to build the engine to process that information. Of course, building your own security and transactional functionality will be an enormous challenge as well.

HTTP Binding

The SOAP specification defines how the SOAP message is bound to the HTTP POST request mechanism. Figure 4.5 showed how the SOAP message is wrapped in such a request.

A formal definition by the specification of a binding mechanism to HTTP ensures that a SOAP message enjoys the features built previously to handle HTTP messages. For HTTP nodes capable of handling SOAP messages, the binding mechanism provides rules for uniformly processing a SOAP message wrapped in an HTTP request. For example, nodes can take advantage of HTTP response codes to determine the outcome of a request such as the HTTP 500 response when a fault occurs. ▷

The HTTP SOAPAction header indicates the type of action or the intent of the SOAP message. In Listing 4.1, no value was specified, because in a typical RPC style invocation, the intent of the message can be conveyed using other means (such as the location URL /flute/billPay), and this can be used by the processing SOAP node to identify the service to which the request is to be dispatched. ▷▷

In data-oriented or document-style messaging, the meaning of the data (or the action to be taken) can be embedded in the data itself. To interpret the data, the processing node must parse the data content and extract the intent. Besides being slow, this approach violates a good design principle, wherein data and its metadata are kept separate. In such a scenario, the SOAPAction field may be used to convey the intent of the request. Because this field is part of the lower layer protocol, it can be parsed relatively quickly. This design also satisfies the guideline to keep the metadata (intent of the request) separate from the data sent within the SOAP body. The SOAPAction field may also be used by firewalls to filter SOAP messages by quickly (relatively speaking) parsing incoming traffic.

By using the HTTP response, a SOAP-based Web service can implement a request-response message exchange pattern. Although not specified by the SOAP specifications, it is conceivable that in the future, other HTTP mechanisms like HTTP PUT may be used to implement a one-way with acknowledgment message-exchange pattern.

The following additional rules apply to this binding:

- The HTTP response code of 2XX indicates that the processing was successful.

- In case of application-defined errors, the SOAP Fault element should be used to indicate the application error.

▷   The SOAP request must be sent in a HTTP POST request and the HTTP request content type must be text/xml.

▷▷   The "intent" of the SOAPAction header was to provide any intercepting party (even hardware) a peek at what the message was about, without the need to parse the whole message. The party could look at this URI and possibly make a better routing decision. This has not been realized, because traditional URL filtering is adequate in most cases.

- If a request cannot be processed, the SOAP node must return an HTTP 500 internal server error code. ▷

SMTP-POP Binding

We saw how single SOAP messages that represent a complete unit of work can be combined into request-response-style communication by binding to HTTP. By using email protocols such as SMTP and POP, applications can take the advantage of the asynchronous store and forward messaging capabilities of the mail systems to provide a one-way transport for SOAP. This allows SOAP to be used in a number of scenarios where a protocol such as HTTP may not be suitable.

While the SOAP 1.1 specifications do not directly address these bindings, it is easy to see how the SOAP message and its attachment may be included in an email message. Listing 4.5 shows a SOAP message containing an XML document (a purchase order) as an attachment in an email message.

Listing 4.5 An email containing a SOAP message, with an XML document as an attachment

```
Return-Path: <flutebank@localhost>
Received: from 127.0.0.1 ([127.0.0.1])
        by BYTECODE (JAMES SMTP Server 2.0a3-cvs) with SMTP ID 155 for
                                                    <javaws@localhost>;
        Wed, 11 Sep 2002 15:03:18 -0400
Message-ID:  6123606.1031770997849.JavaMail.Administrator@BYTECODE
Date: Wed, 11 Sep 2002 15:03:16 -0400 (EDT)
From: flutebank@localhost
To: officemin@localhost
Subject: PurchaseOrder
Mime-Version: 1.0
Content-Type: multipart/mixed; boundary="-----=_Part_0_4944979.1031770996528"
```

▷ Several free tools can help intercept and dump a SOAP message. Apache provides the TcpMon Java utility, and Pocketsoap.com provides the TCP-trace windows executable. These utilities act as proxies, by listening to a configurable port and redirecting traffic to another configurable port. To dump the SOAP message, have these utilities listen to a port (say, 8080), have the SOAP server listen to another (9090), and configure the utility to redirect all traffic from port 8080 to 9090. These tools provide a graphical user interface and automatically show all traffic in the GUI.

```
X-Mozilla-Status: 8001
X-Mozilla-Status2: 00000000
X-UIDL: Mail1031770998410-7
------=_Part_0_4944979.1031770996528
Content-Type: text/plain; charset=us-ascii
Content-Transfer-Encoding: 7bit
<?xml version="1.0" encoding="UTF-8"?>
<soap-env:Envelope xmlns:soap-
          env="http://schemas.xmlsoap.org/soap/envelope/">
   <soap-env:Header/>
 <soap-env:Body>
   <po:PurchaseOrder xmlns:po="http://www.flutebank.com/schema">
     <senderid>myuserid@Mon Aug 19 23:55:28 EDT 2002</senderid>
    </po:PurchaseOrder>
  </soap-env:Body>
</soap-env:Envelope>
------=_Part_0_4944979.1031770996528
Content-Type: application/octet-stream; name=purchaseorder.xml
Content-Transfer-Encoding: 7bit
Content-Disposition: attachment; filename=purchaseorder.xml

<?xml version="1.0" encoding="UTF-8"?>
<purchaseorder xmlns="http://www.flutebank.com/schema"
        xmlns:xsi="http://www.w3.org/2001/XMLSchema-instance"
       xsi:schemaLocation="http://www.flutebank.com/schema purchaseorder.xsd">
  <identifier>87 6784365876JHITRYUE</identifier>
  <date>29 October 2002</date>
  <billingaddress>
       <name>John Malkovich</name>
       <street>256 Eight Bit Lane</street>
       <city>Burlington</city>
       <state>MA</state>
       <zip>01803</zip>
 </billingaddress>

<!--other XML from purchase order here, not shown-->

</purchaseorder>

------=_Part_0_4944979.1031770996528--
```

In Chapter 11, we will look at how SOAP can be combined with the JavaMail API to build asynchronous messaging systems. ▷

> SOAP Encoding

In any distributed computing protocol, object or application state will frequently be exchanged across communicating nodes. This requires state to be sent across the wire enclosed in the agreed-upon communication protocol. In the case of Web services, it means that within a SOAP message, the XML representing the object state must be represented in a standardized format, so that both parties can understand and interpret that state information. Encoding refers to the rules for serializing and deserializing specific elements in the SOAP message. It is sometimes called "Section 5" encoding, because it is defined in Section 5 of the SOAP specifications.

Because Web services can be implemented in any number of programming languages, the application-defined data structures must be represented as XML on the wire. This is derived from the language bindings for that platform—for example, Java to XML and XML to Java, C++ to XML and XML to C++. However, once data is capable of being represented as XML, the SOAP message can carry that data in the body in two ways:

- Based on an agreed upon schema that defines the contents of the XML. This is often referred to as literal encoding. For example, in Listing 4.5, both parties know that the `billingaddress` contains a `city`, `state`, and `zip`. The city and state are of type `string`, and the zip is an `integer`. The types are not specific to any language but refer to the primitive types defined in the XML Schema specification.

- Based on a predetermined set of rules defined by some standard schema. This is the part played by SOAP encoding—which, however, is completely optional. Section 5 encoding rules are available essentially as a convenience that allows nodes to exchange information without any prior knowledge about the type of information. ▷▷

▷ SOAP 1.2 specifies the email bindings for SOAP at *www.w3.org/TR/2002/ NOTE-soap12-email-20020626.*

▷▷ Java-XML bindings are described by JAX-RPC and JAXB, covered in Chapters 10 and 13, respectively.

In both cases, the sender and receiver have to use the same serialization format on the wire to correctly process the message. Both parties also have to agree on schemas for

- The overall SOAP message
- The encoding mechanism used
- Headers in use
- Application-specific XML documents in the body or attachment. Though not required, this is good practice if the content is XML. For example, to process a purchase order sent as an attachment, the receiver must know what that purchase order looks like.

SOAP defines an encoding scheme. The value of the `encodingStyle` attribute, a URI, provides the receiving SOAP node a pointer to the rules used for encoding and decoding the data. In Listing 4.4, we saw that the `Envelope` element had an attribute `encodingStyle="http://schemas.xmlsoap.org/soap/encoding/"`. This `encodingStyle` is used to encode messages within the SOAP body and SOAP header elements, unless individual elements override this with an `encodingStyle` attribute of their own.

Although the SOAP specification defines, through a schema, a set of encoding rules that map well to programming constructs, it does not specify any default encoding. This means that if the `encodingStyle` attribute does not appear in the message or appears with the `encodingStyle=""` attribute, the receiver cannot make any assumptions about how data will be represented in the message and will have to try to figure out how to deserialize that information on its own. Let us now look at these encoding rules defined by SOAP. ▷

Simple Data Types

Loosely speaking, a simple type is any XML element that represents a single data unit and is represented as a single element in the body. From the SOAP messages shown earlier, the identifier and date elements in the purchase order are simple data types:

> ▷   SOAP 1.1 encoding is indicated by the `encodingStyle` namespace of `"http://schemas.xmlsoap.org/soap/encoding/"`.
>   SOAP 1.2 specifies the namespace `http://www.w3c.org/2001/12/ soap-encoding`. The schemas are also available at these locations.

```
<identifier>87 6784365876JHITRYUE</identifier>
<date>29 October 2002</date>
```

SOAP encoding exposes all the simple types built into the XML Schema specifications (see Appendix A) and provides two alternate syntaxes for expressing instances of these data types, as shown for the `<identifier>` element in this SOAP message:

```
<?xml version="1.0" encoding="UTF-8"?>
<env:Envelope xmlns:env="http://schemas.xmlsoap.org/soap/envelope/"
    xmlns:xsd="http://www.w3.org/2001/XMLSchema"
    xmlns:xsi="http://www.w3.org/2001/XMLSchema-instance"
    xmlns:enc="http://schemas.xmlsoap.org/soap/encoding/"
    env:encodingStyle="http://schemas.xmlsoap.org/soap/encoding/">
<env:Body>
    <identifier xsi:type="xsd:string">87 6784365876JHITRYUE</identifier>
    <identifier xsi:type="enc:xsd:string">87 6784365876JHITRYUE</identifier>
</env:Body>
</env:Envelope>
```

Of the over three dozen types in the specification, those commonly used are `string`, `integer`, `byte`, `short`, `int`, `long`, `decimal`, `float`, `double`, `Boolean`, `date`, and `base64Binary` (to represent binary content).

It may seem confusing that Java WSDP uses the enc prefix, although other documentation and toolkits use the prefix `SOAP-ENC` or `ENC`, and so on. Keep in mind that these are just namespace prefixes that can be anything—the XML parsers will resolve them. What matters is the namespace they point to, which in this case is the SOAP encoding schema at `http://schemas.xmlsoap.org/soap/encoding/`, which will be the same for any and all toolkits that use this encoding.

More on the *xsi:type*

Type information can be associated with an element in two different ways:

- Using the type information directly with the element, as we just saw:

  ```
  <identifier xsi:type="xsd:string">87 6784365876JHITRYUE</identifier>
  ```

- Referencing a schema directly, as in the purchase order in the attachment from Listing 4.5:

```
<purchaseorder xmlns="http://www.flutebank.com/schema"
       xmlns:xsi="http://www.w3.org/2001/XMLSchema-instance"
       xsi:schemaLocation="http://www.flutebank.com/schema
                                       purchaseorder.xsd">
    <identifier>87 6784365876JHITRYUE</identifier>
</purchaseorder>
```

- This was the cause for earlier issues of interoperabilty between different toolkit implementations. Apache and other Java toolkits expected the former, whereas Microsoft adopted the latter. This has now been resolved though a community effort, such as the SoapBuilders community. We will talk about this and other interoperability issues in Chapter 10.

Compound Data Types

A compound type represents two or more simple types grouped under a single element. For example, the billing address in Listing 4.5 is a compound type:

```
<billingaddress>
    <name>John Malkovich</name>
    <street>256 Eight Bit Lane</street>
    <city>Burlington</city>
    <state>MA</state>
    <zip>01803</zip>
 </billingaddress>
```

A compound data type can be either a *struct* or an *array*. A struct is an element that contains disparate child elements. The billing address above is an example of a struct. Compound structs use the same xsi:type attribute to specify type information about individual elements.

An array, on the other hand, is a compound type that contains elements of the same name—for example, a group of email addresses:

```
<emailaddresses>
    <email> "mailto:John.Malkovich@flutebank.com </email>
    <email> "mailto:J.Malkovich@home.com" </email>
</emailaddresses>
```

Arrays are encoded as elements of type enc:Array and take an additional attribute, enc:arrayType, to describe their content. This declaration takes the form type[size], which is similar to the way arrays are declared in Java. Let us look at an example of a SOAP message that encodes the above array:

```
<?xml version="1.0" encoding="UTF-8"?>
<env:Envelope xmlns:env="http://schemas.xmlsoap.org/soap/envelope/"
            xmlns:xsd="http://www.w3.org/2001/XMLSchema"
            xmlns:xsi="http://www.w3.org/2001/XMLSchema-instance"
            xmlns:enc=http://schemas.xmlsoap.org/soap/encoding/
            xmlns:ns0="http://www.flutebank.com/xml"
          env:encodingStyle="http://schemas.xmlsoap.org/soap/encoding/">
<env:Body>
   <ns0:emailaddresses xsi:type="enc:Array" enc:arrayType="xsd:String[2]" >
       <email xsi:type="xsd:string"> John.Malkovich@flutebank.com </email>
       <email xsi:type="xsd:string"> J.Malkovich@home.com </email>
   </ns0:emailaddresses>
 </soap-env:Body>
</soap-env:Envelope>
```

An array is not limited to simple types and can contain other compound types. The SOAP-encoded message below shows an array of two addresses. Note that the compound type must be specified in the schema associated with its namespace prefix (ns0 in the example below):

```
<?xml version="1.0" encoding="UTF-8"?>
<env:Envelope xmlns:env="http://schemas.xmlsoap.org/soap/envelope/"
            xmlns:xsd="http://www.w3.org/2001/XMLSchema"
            xmlns:xsi="http://www.w3.org/2001/XMLSchema-instance"
            xmlns:enc=http://schemas.xmlsoap.org/soap/encoding/
            xmlns:ns0="http://www.flutebank.com/xml"
          env:encodingStyle="http://schemas.xmlsoap.org/soap/encoding/">
<env:Body>
   <ns0:addresses xsi:type="enc:Array" enc:arrayType="ns0:BillingAddresses[2]" >
   <billingaddress>
       <name xsi:type="xsd:string"> John Malkovich</name>
       <street xsi:type="xsd:string">256 Eight Bit Lane</street>
       <city xsi:type="xsd:string">Burlington</city>
       <state xsi:type="xsd:string">MA</state>
       <zip xsi:type="xsd:string">01803</zip>
    <billingaddress>
   <billingaddress>
       <name xsi:type="xsd:string"> John Malkovich</name>
```

```
        <street xsi:type="xsd:string">256 64 Bit Street</street>
        <city xsi:type="xsd:string">Unix Town</city>
        <state xsi:type="xsd:string">MA</state>
        <zip xsi:type="xsd:string">01803</zip>
    <billingaddress>
   </ns0:addresses>
</soap-env:Body>
</soap-env:Envelope>
```

To support multidimensional arrays, SOAP uses *references,* which are analogous to local anchors in an HTML page. A reference is specified with the href attribute, which points to an element identified with an id attribute.

Let us look at this further with an example. The SOAP message below shows how a service returns an array of compound types. The message is in response to an invocation of a Java method with the signature public PaymentDetail[] listScheduledPayments();

```
<?xml version="1.0" encoding="UTF-8"?>
<env:Envelope xmlns:env="http://schemas.xmlsoap.org/soap/envelope/"
            xmlns:xsd="http://www.w3.org/2001/XMLSchema"
            xmlns:xsi="http://www.w3.org/2001/XMLSchema-instance"
            xmlns:enc="http://schemas.xmlsoap.org/soap/encoding/"
            xmlns:ns0="http://www.flutebank.com/xml"
            env:encodingStyle="http://schemas.xmlsoap.org/soap/encoding/">
    <env:Body>
        <ns0:listScheduledPaymentsResponse>
            <result href="#ID1"/>
        </ns0:listScheduledPaymentsResponse>
        <ns0:ArrayOfPaymentDetail id="ID1" xsi:type="enc:Array"
                                    enc:arrayType="ns0:PaymentDetail[2]">
            <item href="#ID2"/>
            <item href="#ID3"/>
        </ns0:ArrayOfPaymentDetail>
        <ns0:PaymentDetail id="ID2" xsi:type="ns0:PaymentDetail">
            <date xsi:type="xsd:dateTime">2002-10-05T00:12:18.269Z</date>
            <account xsi:type="xsd:string">Credit</account>
            <payeeName xsi:type="xsd:string">Digital Credit Union</payeeName>
            <amt xsi:type="xsd:double">2000.0</amt>
        </ns0:PaymentDetail>
        <ns0:PaymentDetail id="ID3" xsi:type="ns0:PaymentDetail">
            <date xsi:type="xsd:dateTime">2002-10-05T00:12:18.269Z</date>
```

```
            <account xsi:type="xsd:string">Credit</account>
            <payeeName xsi:type="xsd:string">AAA Club</payeeName>
            <amt xsi:type="xsd:double">180.0</amt>
        </ns0:PaymentDetail>
    </env:Body>
</env:Envelope>
```

The body contains a compound type listScheduledPaymentsResponse, which refers to an array. The array contains two elements of compound type Payment-Detail, which are referred to as individual items.

In all the above examples, we have specified the encodingStyle attribute for the entire envelope. Sometimes it may be desirable to have different encoding schemes defined within a single message. SOAP accomodates this requirement by providing the ability to specify an encodingStyle at the element level. The general rule is that child elements inherit the encoding style of the parent elements, unless they override the parent's encoding style with one of their own. ▷

▷ SAAJ

SOAP with Attachments API for Java (SAAJ) is defined to enable applications to take advantage of the SOAP protocol. It defines a Java API for producing, consuming, and manipulating SOAP messages that conform to the SOAP 1.1 specification and SOAP with Attachments note. SAAJ was created as part of the Java API for XML messaging (JAXM) under JSR-67 but was refactored into its own specification, because all the other JAX APIs used it. It made sense to have this common API stand on its own. Let us now take a closer look at SAAJ.

SAAJ provides a level of abstraction that insulates developers from low-level manipulation of angle brackets. Developers create and work with Java classes in the javax.xml.soap package that model different XML elements in a SOAP message and the semantics of connecting and sending SOAP messages.

The API relevant to modeling the SOAP message is shown in Figure 4.7 and explained in Table 4.1.

Each part of the SOAP message discussed in this chapter is modeled in SAAJ as a Java class or interface developers can work with in their code. Though Figure 4.7 is self-explanatory, there are two other classes in SAAJ are important. Like the

▷   The mapping of SOAP-encoded types to Java is defined by the JAX-RPC specifications and is covered in Chapter 10.

Figure 4.7
The SAAJ
object model

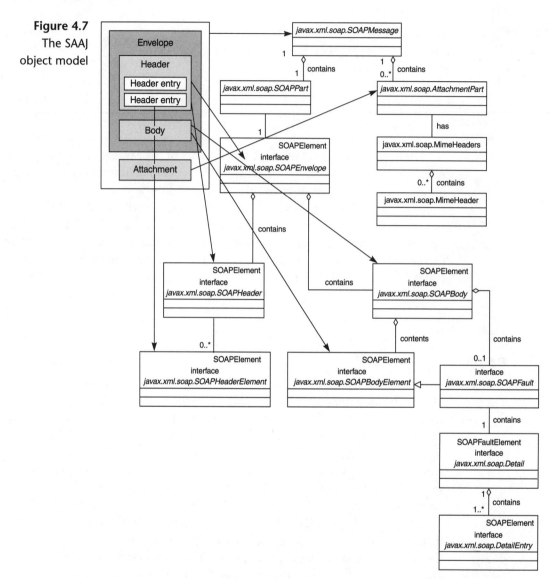

rest of the API that abstracts the SOAP message, these classes abstract the semantics relating to a request-response–based transmission of the message:

- MessageFactory. This class is responsible for creating empty SOAPMessage objects.

- SOAPConnection. This class abstracts a connection between two nodes. A SOAP client can create a SOAPConnection object from a SOAPConnection-Factory and dispatch the SOAPMessage using the call() method, which takes

Table 4.1   The Object Representation of a SOAP Message in SAAJ

AttachmentPart	Models the attachment in a SOAP message.
MimeHeader	An object that stores a MIME header name and its value.
MimeHeaders	A container for MimeHeader objects, which represent the MIME headers present in a MIME part of a message.
Node	The base interface that represents an XML element. Though it is analogous to the Node in the W3C DOM discussed in Chapter 9, it is not the same.
SOAPBody	Models the body from a SOAP message.
SOAPBodyElement	Represents the contents in a SOAPBody object.
SOAPElement	Subclasses Node to provide the base functionality for all classes that represent SOAP objects defined in the SOAP specification.
SOAPEnvelope	Models the envelope in a SOAP message.
SOAPFault	Models a fault and is contained in a SOAPBody object.
SOAPFaultElement	A representation of the contents in a SOAPFault object.
SOAPHeader	Models the header element of the SOAP message
SOAPHeaderElement	Models individual header elements in a SOAPHeader.
SOAPMessage	The root class for all SOAP messages.
SOAPPart	The container for the SOAP-specific portion of a SOAPMessage object.

two arguments: the SOAPMessage to send and a destination for the message. The destination is abstracted by the javax.xml.messaging.URLEndpoint class.

- SOAPConnectionFactory: This is a factory for creating SOAPConnection objects.

To understand how SAAJ works, let us put everything together with an example of this API in action. The BillPay service exposes a Java method with the following syntax:

```
PaymentConfirmation schedulePayment( Date date, String nickName, doubleamount);
```

Listing 4.6 shows the SOAP request this Web service expects. We will put aside the part about how the service is implemented until Chapter 11. Listing 4.7

shows the SAAJ code, and Listing 4.8 shows the SOAP response that the service returns. The client code takes the following sequence:

1. Instantiate the `MessageFactory`.

2. Create an empty `SOAPMessage` from the factory.

3. Access the `SOAPEnvelope` from the message.

4. Access the `SOAPBody` from the envelope.

5. Create the elements in the body and save the changes to the message.

6. Create a `SOAPConnection` object from a `SOAPConnectionFactory`.

7. Send the `SOAPMessage` to the endpoint, using the connection.

Listing 4.6   The SOAP request message

```
<?xml version="1.0" encoding="UTF-8"?>
    <env:Envelope xmlns:env="http://schemas.xmlsoap.org/soap/envelope/"
    xmlns:xsd="http://www.w3.org/2001/XMLSchema"
    xmlns:xsi="http://www.w3.org/2001/XMLSchema-instance"
    xmlns:enc="http://schemas.xmlsoap.org/soap/encoding/"
    xmlns:ns0="http://www.flutebank.com/xml"
    env:encodingStyle="http://schemas.xmlsoap.org/soap/encoding/">
    <env:Body>
        <ns0:schedulePayment>
            <Date_1 xsi:type="xsd:dateTime">2002-10-05T04:49:26.769Z</Date_1>
            <String_2 xsi:type="xsd:string">my account at sprint</String_2>
            <double_3 xsi:type="xsd:double">190.0</double_3>
        </ns0:schedulePayment>
    </env:Body>
</env:Envelope>
```

Listing 4.7   A SAAJ client for constructing and sending a SOAP message

```
import javax.xml.soap.*;
import java.util.Iterator;
import java.util.Date;
import java.text.SimpleDateFormat;
import javax.xml.messaging.URLEndpoint;

public class SAAJClient{
```

```
/** Class to demonstrate how to send a soap message synchronously with SAAJ API. */
    public static void main(String args[]) throws Exception {
        String url = "http://127.0.0.1:9090/billpayservice/jaxrpc/BillPay";
        if (args.length > 0)
            url = args[0];

// Construct a default SOAP message factory.
        MessageFactory mfactory = MessageFactory.newInstance();
// Create an empty message
        SOAPMessage message = mfactory.createMessage();
        SOAPPart soap = message.getSOAPPart();
// Access the envelope
        SOAPEnvelope envelope = soap.getEnvelope();
        envelope.addNamespaceDeclaration("xmlns:xsd","http://www.w3.org/2001/
                                                          XMLSchema");
    envelope.addNamespaceDeclaration("xmlns:xsi",
                                    "http://www.w3.org/2001/XMLSchema-instance" );
        envelope.addNamespaceDeclaration("xmlns:ns0","http://www.flutebank.com/xml" );
    envelope.setEncodingStyle("http://schemas.xmlsoap.org/soap/encoding/");
// Access the body
        SOAPBody body = envelope.getBody();
        Name name = envelope.createName("schedulePayment", "ns0",
                                                "http://www.flutebank.com/xml");
        SOAPBodyElement element = body.addBodyElement(name);
// create a name for the attribute name that can be reused
        Name xsitype = envelope.createName("xsi:type");
// create the Date_1 element
        Name dateelement = envelope.createName("Date_1");
        SOAPElement date = element.addChildElement(dateelement);
    date.addAttribute(xsitype,"xsd:dateTime");
// Format the Java Date object in the syntax that is compliant with the XML schema
    SimpleDateFormat  dateFormatter
                            new SimpleDateFormat("yyyy-MM-dd'T'HH:mm:ss.SSS'Z'");
        String xmldate=dateFormatter.format(new Date()).toString();
        date.addTextNode(xmldate);
// create the String_2 element
    Name strelement = envelope.createName("String_2");
    SOAPElement str = element.addChildElement(strelement);
    str.addAttribute(xsitype,"xsd:string");
    str.addTextNode("my account at string");
```

```
// create the double_3 element
    name dblelement = envelope.createName("double_3");
        SOAPElement dbl = element.addChildElement(dblelement);
    dbl.addAttribute(xsitype,"xsd:double");
        dbl.addTextNode("190.0");
// save changes to the message
        message.saveChanges();
 // Construct a default SOAP connection factory.
        SOAPConnectionFactory factory = SOAPConnectionFactory.newInstance();
 // Get SOAP connection.
        SOAPConnection connection = factory.createConnection();
 // Construct endpoint object.
        URLEndpoint endpoint = new URLEndpoint(url);
// Send SOAP message.
        SOAPMessage response = connection.call(message, endpoint);
// process the return message
        SOAPPart sp = response.getSOAPPart();
        SOAPEnvelope se = sp.getEnvelope();
        SOAPBody sb = se.getBody();
        Iterator it = sb.getChildElements();
        while (it.hasNext()) {
            SOAPBodyElement bodyElement = (SOAPBodyElement)it.next();
            System.out.println(bodyElement.getElementName().getQualifiedName() + "
                            namepace uri=" +bodyElement.getElementName().getURI());
            Iterator it2 = bodyElement.getChildElements();
            while (it2.hasNext()) {
                SOAPElement element2 = (SOAPElement)it2.next();
                System.out.print(element2.getElementName().getQualifiedName() +" = ");
                System.out.println(element2.getValue());
            }
        }
 //Debug method, Print response to the std output
        System.out.println("\n\n\n Dumping complete message \n\n--------------\n\n");
        response.writeTo(System.out);
 // close the connection
        connection.close();
    }
}
```

Listing 4.8   The SOAP response from the service

```
<?xml version="1.0" encoding="UTF-8"?>
<env:Envelope xmlns:env="http://schemas.xmlsoap.org/soap/envelope/"
              xmlns:xsd="http://www.w3.org/2001/XMLSchema"
              xmlns:xsi="http://www.w3.org/2001/XMLSchema-instance"
              xmlns:enc="http://schemas.xmlsoap.org/soap/encoding/"
              xmlns:ns0="http://www.flutebank.com/xml"
              env:encodingStyle="http://schemas.xmlsoap.org/soap/encoding/">
    <env:Body>
        <ns0:schedulePaymentResponse>
            <result href="#ID1"/>
        </ns0:schedulePaymentResponse>
        <ns0:PaymentConfirmation id="ID1" xsi:type="ns0:PaymentConfirmation">
            <confirmationNum xsi:type="xsd:int">81263767</confirmationNum>
            <payee xsi:type="xsd:string">Sprint PCS</payee>
            <amt xsi:type="xsd:double">190.0</amt>
        </ns0:PaymentConfirmation>
    </env:Body>
</env:Envelope>
```

Though we have seen how a SOAP request and response can be constructed and sent using SAAJ, the preceding example was meant more as an insight into the workings of SAAJ. We don't envision direct use of this API by developers, because it is unlikely visual inspection of a SOAP request would be necessary. Other APIs, such as JAXM and JAX-RPC, abstract away this usage with higher-level constructs and with tools to interpret the SOAP service descriptions in a WSDL file. SAAJ is more likely to form the underpinnings of these high-level constructs in different vendor implementations. We will talk more about SAAJ and this type of request-response communication in Chapter 11.

> Summary

In this chapter we started by taking a look at the role SOAP plays in a Web services architecture. We looked at what a SOAP message is and how it can be used to wrap XML content for transportation between two parties. The content is separated from the underlying transport, and the parties processing that message can be written in any programming language. SOAP represents a simple yet powerful abstraction for realizing a cross-platform and loosely coupled architecture.

An enterprise-level application requires more sophisticated features that those offered by SOAP alone. In subsequent chapters, we examine how to exploit SOAP's extensible nature to address these needs. In Chapter 7, we discuss a more complex business collaboration scheme offered by ebXML, using SOAP. In Chapter 14, we look at how transactions can be layered on top of SOAP messages. In Chapter 15, we deal with security issues and discuss how SOAP can be extended to address these concerns.

In this chapter, we have intentionally not covered every minor detail surrounding SOAP. Our intention was to present the reader with just enough depth to establish the fundamental concepts. In subsequent chapters, we discuss pertinent details where the concepts are applicable. For example, Chapter 10 covers the pros and cons of RPC- versus document-style communication, and Chapter 11 covers messaging with SOAP.

WSDL

Previous chapters introduced the concept of service-oriented architecture (SOA), where consumers discover and invoke services published to service registries. Once a service is discovered,

- How does a service consumer know what the service offers?
- How does the service consumer know how to invoke the service?
- How can the service consumer differentiate between similar services offered by different service providers?

To answer these questions, we have to first understand the different elements of Web service description. The Web services technology stack in Chapter 1 introduced the notions of the service description layer and the service composition layer. These two layers are related, in that the service composition layer builds on the service description layer. In this chapter, we describe in detail the Web Services Description Language (WSDL). The WSDL specification addresses the service description layer but not service composition and collaboration (both of which are also forms of service description).

> WSDL is an XML format for describing network services as a set of endpoints operating on messages containing either document-oriented or procedure-oriented information. The operations and messages are described abstractly, and then bound to a concrete network protocol and message format to define an endpoint. Related concrete endpoints are combined into abstract endpoints (services). WSDL is extensible to allow description of endpoints and their messages regardless of what message formats or network protocols are used to communicate, however, the only bindings described in this document describe how to use WSDL in conjunction with SOAP 1.1, HTTP GET/POST, and MIME. (World Wide Web Consortium)

▶ Describing a Web Service

To make a Web service useful, a service consumer who has discovered a set of useful services must be able to determine

1. How to invoke the service.
    - What is the service interface; that is, what are its methods, method signatures, and return values?
    - Where is the service located?
    - What protocol does the service understand?

2. Which service offers superior quality of service (QoS) when multiple services advertise similar functional capabilities.
    - Is one service more secure than the others?
    - Does a particular provider guarantee a faster response or a more scalable and available service?
    - What legal agreements need to be in place for collaborating business partners?

3. In what order should related services and their operations be invoked?
    - How can services be combined to create a macro service (often referred to as service orchestration)?

Although these three forms of description provide complete information regarding a service, a consumer may not require all three every time the service is used. It is quite probable, for example, that a consumer invoking a standalone service is uninterested in how the service is to be orchestrated or combined with other services. Also, where only one provider exists for a service, the nonfunctional characteristics (response performance, scalability, etc.), although important, may serve no useful purpose. ▷

> ▷ Only the first form of description, the functional (the "how to invoke") is always required before a service can be invoked. In this chapter, the focus is on explaining the most common, accepted form for functional description of Web services: WSDL. The WSDL specification is a submission to the World Wide Web Consortium (W3C) that addresses the first of these three forms and is the focus of this chapter. The latter two forms are discussed in Chapters 6 and 7, respectively.

> **Describing Functional Characteristics of Services**

Functional characteristics of a Web service pertain to the service interface (the "how") and its deployment information (the "where"), which together provide the requisite information for invoking the service. Service-oriented architectures are not a new concept, and consequently, published services have in the past had their functional characteristics described using different standards. Readers who have worked with CORBA and COM will remember respective interface definition languages that described the methods and method signatures of CORBA and COM components. EJB and RMI programmers may know that a Java remote interface served a similar purpose in distributed Java computing environments. WSDL serves a similar function for Web services. A WSDL service description is the XML grammar and vocabulary to describe a Web service. The WSDL specification was submitted to the W3C in the fall of 2000. The entire WSDL note is available at *www.w3.org/TR/wsdl.*

WSDL Document Overview

Minimally, the consumer will need to know the service's signature (what goes in and what comes out), its location, and the wire protocol to be used to send the invocation message. A WSDL document provides this information. The information is organized in two logical sections, shown in Figure 5.1: abstract descriptions and concrete descriptions.

Abstract Descriptions

Consider a Java object with just one public method. When another object interacts with it by invoking its public method, the interaction can be characterized as a series of message exchanges. The object accepts the incoming message, may return an outgoing message, and may throw an exception message. Each type of message can be described further by listing the data types and the order of its parameters.

Now consider a Java object with multiple methods, each of which defines one possible interaction with the object. In each interaction, up to three messages may be exchanged. Each message can be further described by describing the data types exchanged. When the object has multiple methods, it is possible that some methods exchange the same messages (two methods could have the same return value; i.e., the same "output" message) and that some data types are common

Figure 5.1
WSDL
document:
a conceptual
representation

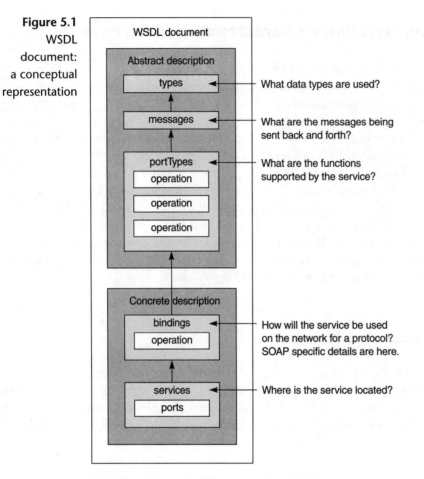

WSDL document

Abstract description

types — What data types are used?

messages — What are the messages being sent back and forth?

portTypes — What are the functions supported by the service?
operation
operation
operation

Concrete description

bindings — How will the service be used on the network for a protocol? SOAP specific details are here.
operation

services — Where is the service located?
ports

Note: Arrows represent a reference relationship between elements and the boxes represent a containment relationship.

across messages. To represent the information about the object without duplicating information (normalized form), one would

1. Describe all the data types used in all messages.
2. List all messages that can be exchanged and represent the message as a set of data types.
3. Describe each method (interaction with the object) as a collection of input, output, and exception type messages.
4. Describe what the object does as a collection of possible interactions.

For a Web service, these descriptions would need to be captured in a platform- and language-independent manner, which is the way a WSDL document organizes information. In WSDL, each of these four abstract descriptions is an element in the XML. The four elements are listed here and are covered in detail later in this chapter.

1. `types`: contain the platform- and language-independent data type definitions

2. `messages`: contain input and output parameters for the service and describe different messages the service exchanges

3. `operations`: represents a particular interaction with the service and describes the input, output, and exception messages possible during that interaction

4. `portTypes`: uses the messages section to describe function signatures (operation name, input and output parameters) and represents a set of operations supported by the service

Concrete Descriptions

Each Web service or "endpoint" runs on a network address. The Web service also understands a particular protocol, or format, in which messages and data are sent to it . These aspects of the service description are specific to the implementation of the service and are thus logically grouped into one category. In short, the concrete descriptions define the implementation-specific descriptions for the Web service. Two significant elements in the WSDL XML fall into this category, each of which is covered in detail later in this chapter.

1. `bindings`: specifies binding of each operation in the `portTypes` section.

   It associates the abstract descriptions of a `portType` (i.e., a `portType`'s operations, messages, and data types) with a network protocol.

2. `services`: In addition to protocol-specific information, the WSDL document should also describe where the service is deployed. The association between a binding and the network address at which it can be found is defined by a port. The `service` element is a collection of `ports`, and a port describes a network `location` for a `binding`.

The logical separation of abstract information (such as methods, parameters, and error messages) from information that changes with implementation type (such as transport protocols) allows reuse of abstract definitions of the service across different implementations of the service. As an example, the same service may be exposed as an HTTP service and an SMTP service. In both cases, the service performs the same function, so the abstract description of the service and its methods can be reused, and only the concrete, implementation-specific information needs to be changed across the two instances of the service.

WSDL and Dynamic Interactions

A practical way to understand the role of the seven key elements in a WSDL document is to keep in mind the service consumer's interaction with the service. This is illustrated in Figure 5.2.

A Web service exposes groups of business operations for service consumers to use. Operations are grouped to form portTypes. To perform an operation, consumers send an input message containing input data. They receive an output message containing the data that results from processing the input or a fault message in case of any problem in processing. The input and output messages may have multiple data items in them; each is called a part.

The wire protocol used for the invocation and the format of the input and output messages on the wire for that protocol are specified in a binding. The service exposes itself to the consumers though one or more ports, where each port

Figure 5.2
Dynamic
interaction of
a service and
its consumer

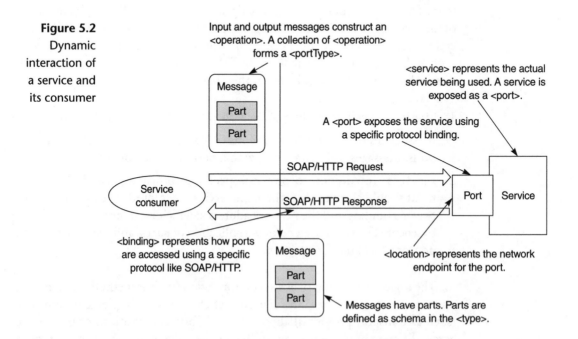

specifies a network address giving the service's location. and the binding to XML Schema use with that port. A service may render itself though several ports, where each port has a different binding (e.g., the same service may expose itself via SOAP/HTTP and SOAP/SMTP).

Figure 5.3 is a logical class diagram that shows the relationship among the seven key elements that make up the abstract and concrete descriptions. Each binding references a portType, the operations in that portType, and the messages that constitute the operation. Each portType contains zero or more operations, each with an input and output message. Each message has zero or more parts, and each part is of some data type. The data type could be an inbuilt type in the standard (e.g., xsd:string) or a custom type defined in the types definition.

Although the above overview of a WSDL document's elements may be confusing to the first-time reader, the following section, which explains WSDL document organization using a Java example, should help clarify the document's structure and form. A comforting thought for Java developers is that WSDL documents are well-formed XML documents, so a majority of the programmatic tasks associated with WSDL are tool driven. For example, tools automatically generate WSDL given a Java interface, and vice versa.

Figure 5.3
A logical class
diagram of the
key WSDL
elements

Abstract definitions

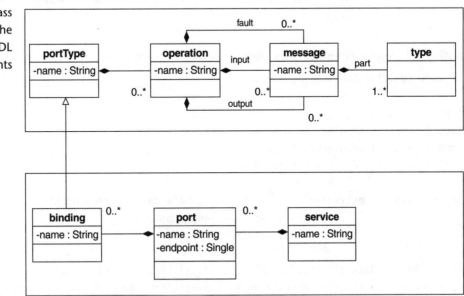

Concrete definitions

Elements of a WSDL Document

This section examines the WSDL document specification in greater detail. A Web service provided by Flute Bank is used to illustrate the different elements of a WSDL document.

Flute Bank, beyond providing simple account-related services, also has the infrastructure to support online bill payments. The online bill payment system is offered to Flute's customers as a value-added service and is also available to other banks and financial institutions. In keeping with this chapter's goal of focusing on WSDL, the bill payment service illustrated is deliberately kept simple. The service assumes that payees or merchants have been registered with the bank and that Flute Bank's customers may only schedule new payments or view scheduled payments.

If you were to write a Java RMI object for this service, it would look similar to Listing 5.1. The interface contains three methods:

- The schedulePayment method returns a confirmation number and throws an exception if the payment cannot be scheduled.

- The getLastPayment method return the amount last paid to a payee.

- The listScheduledPayments method returns an array of PaymentDetail instances.

Listing 5.1   Flute Bank's bill payment service illustrated as Java Interface

```
package com.fluteblank.billpayservice;

import java.util.*;
import java.rmi.Remote;
import java.rmi.RemoteException;
public interface BillPay extends Remote {

public PaymentConfirmation schedulePayment( Date date, String nickName, double amount)
                throws ScheduleFailedException,
                        RemoteException;

public PaymentDetail[] listScheduledPayments() throws RemoteException;
public double getLastPayment(String nickname) throws RemoteException;
}
```

Listing 5.2 shows the WSDL document that describes the same service. It also shows the mapping of `BillPay` interface elements to the corresponding WSDL elements.

Listing 5.2 Flute Bank's bill payment service WSDL document

```
<?xml version="1.0" encoding="UTF-8"?>
<definitions name="billpayservice"
targetNamespace="http://www.flutebank.com/xml"
xmlns:tns="http://www.flutebank.com/xml"
xmlns="http://schemas.xmlsoap.org/wsdl/"
xmlns:xsd="http://www.w3.org/2001/XMLSchema"
xmlns:soap="http://schemas.xmlsoap.org/wsdl/soap/">
  <types>
    <schema targetNamespace="http://www.flutebank.com/xml"
xmlns:wsdl="http://schemas.xmlsoap.org/wsdl/"
xmlns:tns="http://www.flutebank.com/xml"
xmlns:xsi="http://www.w3.org/2001/XMLSchema-instance"
xmlns:soap-enc="http://schemas.xmlsoap.org/soap/encoding/"
xmlns="http://www.w3.org/2001/XMLSchema">

      <import namespace="http://schemas.xmlsoap.org/soap/encoding/"/>

    <complexType name="ArrayOfPaymentDetail">
      <complexContent>
        <restriction base="soap-enc:Array">
          <attribute ref="soap-enc:arrayType"
                                    wsdl:arrayType="tns:PaymentDetail[]"/>
        </restriction>
      </complexContent>
    </complexType>
    <complexType name="PaymentDetail">
      <sequence>
        <element name="date" type="dateTime"/>
        <element name="account" type="string"/>
        <element name="payeeName" type="string"/>
        <element name="amt" type="double"/>
      </sequence>
    </complexType>
```

```xml
      <complexType name="PaymentConfirmation">
        <sequence>
          <element name="confirmationNum" type="int"/>
          <element name="payee" type="string"/>
          <element name="amt" type="double"/>
        </sequence>
      </complexType>
      <complexType name="ScheduleFailedException">
        <sequence>
          <element name="message" type="string"/>
          <element name="localizedMessage" type="string"/>
        </sequence>
      </complexType>
</schema>
</types>

  <message name="BillPay_getLastPayment">
    <part name="String_1" type="xsd:string"/>
  </message>

  <message name="BillPay_getLastPaymentResponse">
    <part name="result" type="xsd:double"/>
  </message>

  <message name="BillPay_listScheduledPayments"/>

  <message name="BillPay_listScheduledPaymentsResponse">
    <part name="result" type="tns:ArrayOfPaymentDetail"/>
  </message>

  <message name="BillPay_schedulePayment">
    <part name="Date_1" type="xsd:dateTime"/>
    <part name="String_2" type="xsd:string"/>
    <part name="double_3" type="xsd:double"/>
  </message>

  <message name="BillPay_schedulePaymentResponse">
    <part name="result" type="tns:PaymentConfirmation"/>
  </message>
```

```
  <message name="ScheduleFailedException">
    <part name="ScheduleFailedException" type="tns:ScheduleFailedException"/>
  </message>

<portType name="BillPay">
    <operation name="getLastPayment" parameterOrder="String_1">
      <input message="tns:BillPay_getLastPayment"/>
      <output message="tns:BillPay_getLastPaymentResponse"/>
    </operation>

    <operation name="listScheduledPayments" parameterOrder="">
      <input message="tns:BillPay_listScheduledPayments"/>
      <output message="tns:BillPay_listScheduledPaymentsResponse"/>
    </operation>

    <operation name="schedulePayment"
                  parameterOrder="Date_1 String_2 double_3">
      <input message="tns:BillPay_schedulePayment"/>
      <output message="tns:BillPay_schedulePaymentResponse"/>
      <fault name="ScheduleFailedException"
            message="tns:ScheduleFailedException"/>
    </operation>
</portType>

  <binding name="BillPayBinding" type="tns:BillPay">
    <soap:binding transport="http://schemas.xmlsoap.org/soap/http"
                  style="rpc"/>
    <operation name="getLastPayment">
      <input>
        <soap:body encodingStyle="http://schemas.xmlsoap.org/soap/encoding/"
                  use="encoded" namespace="http://www.flutebank.com/xml"/>
      </input>
      <output>
        <soap:body encodingStyle="http://schemas.xmlsoap.org/soap/encoding/"
                  use="encoded" namespace="http://www.flutebank.com/xml"/>
      </output>
      <soap:operation soapAction=""/>
    </operation>>
```

```
    <operation name="listScheduledPayments">
     <input>
       <soap:body encodingStyle="http://schemas.xmlsoap.org/soap/encoding/"
                  use="encoded" namespace="http://www.flutebank.com/xml"/>
     </input>
     <output>
       <soap:body encodingStyle="http://schemas.xmlsoap.org/soap/encoding/"
                  use="encoded" namespace="http://www.flutebank.com/xml"/>
     </output>
     <soap:operation soapAction=""/>
  </operation>

    <operation name="schedulePayment">
     <input>
       <soap:body encodingStyle="http://schemas.xmlsoap.org/soap/encoding/"
                  use="encoded" namespace="http://www.flutebank.com/xml"/>
     </input>
      <output>
       <soap:body encodingStyle="http://schemas.xmlsoap.org/soap/encoding/"
                  use="encoded" namespace="http://www.flutebank.com/xml"/>
      </output>
      <fault name="ScheduleFailedException">
        <soap:fault encodingStyle="http://schemas.xmlsoap.org/soap/encoding/"
                    use="encoded" namespace="http://www.flutebank.com/xml"/>
     </fault>
      <soap:operation soapAction=""/>
   </operation>
</binding>

  <service name="Billpayservice">
   <port name="BillPayPort" binding="tns:BillPayBinding">
     <soap:address location="http://www.flutebank.com:0090/billpayservice/services/
                                                              BillPay"/>
     </port>
   </service>
</definitions>
```

XML Schema

Java mappings to WSDL and vice versa are prescribed by the JAX-RPC specifications and are covered in detail in Chapter 10. Figure 5.4 provides an overview of how the different elements of the BillPay service WSDL correspond to the conceptual WSDL model introduced earlier.

The root element of a WSDL document is a definitions element, under which the rest of the XML elements are defined. The definitions element contains the relevant namespace declarations like http://schemas.xmlsoap.org/wsdl/, which describe the schemas being used for the document. Figure 5.5 shows the with the first level of elements under the root element of definitions. The following sections examine these individual elements in detail.

Figure 5.4
BillPayservice
service WSDL
mapped to the
WSDL concep-
tual model

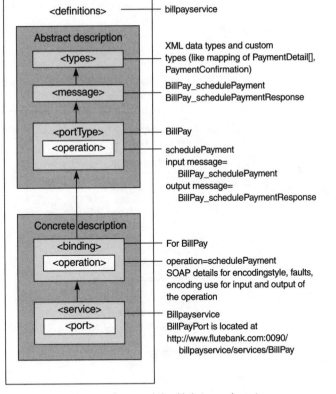

Note: Arrows represent a reference relationship between elements.

Defining the Data Types for the Service: The types Element

The types element, shown in Figure 5.6, lists all user-defined data types used by the service. Although this example uses XML Schema definition (XSD), it is possible to use some other type system in a WSDL document. The WSDL specification recognizes that a single type system may not be able to describe all message formats and makes it possible to use other type definition languages via an extensibility mechanism. For all practical purposes, the types element can be thought of as the location where the schemas used are defined and referenced. XSD is also the canonical type system in a WSDL document. XSD is introduced in Appendix A, and the full XML Schema specification can be found at *www.w3.org/ XML/Schema.*

The bill payment service contains two complex types, PaymentDetail and PaymentConfirmation. As an example, the schema definition for Payment-Confirmation user-defined is shown again on the following page:

Figure 5.5
The definitions element

Figure 5.6
The types element

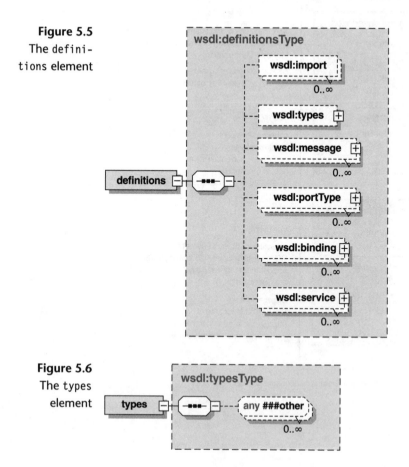

```
<complexType name="PaymentDetail">
    <sequence>
        <element name="date" type="dateTime"/>
        <element name="account" type="string"/>
        <element name="payeeName" type="string"/>
        <element name="amt" type="double"/>
    </sequence>
</complexType>
```

This corresponds to a Java bean:

```
package com.flute.webservice;

import java.util.*;

public class PaymentDetail extends Exception {
private String payeeName;
    private String account;
    private double amt;
    private Date date;
public PaymentDetail() {
}
public PaymentDetail(String payeeName, String account, double amt, Date date) {
    this.payeeName = payeeName;
    this.amt = amt;
    this.account = account;
    this.date = date;
}
public String getAccount() {
    return account;
}
...
other getters and setters for bean properties.
```

Like the Java-WSDL mappings, the exact semantics of mapping the XML to Java and vice versa are also prescribed by the JAX-RPC specification and are covered in detail in Chapter 10.

The WSDL specification does specify the special handling of arrays, which are described using the SOAP encoding *(http://schemas.xmlsoap.org/soap/encoding)*. As of the time of writing the WSDL 1.1 specification, the XSD specification did not describe the mechanism to provide default values to array types, so

WSDL introduces the arrayType attribute. Details of WSDL handling of array types can be found in the WSDL and XSD specifications.

Describing the Exchange: The message Element

When a Flute Bank customer invokes a method on the Flute Bank bill payment service, a series of messages is exchanged between the consumer and the service. For example, when the listScheduledPayments method is invoked, a message is sent from the consumer to the service; then the service may return an exception or a message with an array of scheduled payments.

An interaction between a service consumer and the service usually entails a set of messages sent back and forth. All possible messages that can be exchanged between the service consumer and the service are listed in the WSDL document using message elements. A message element contains the abstract definition of the message content.

The content of a message depends on the nature of the interaction between the consumer and the service. For example, in an RPC style interaction, a message sent by a consumer of a service may consist of zero or more parameters, so the message can be described by listing its parameters. An asynchronous message may consist of name-value pairs. In general, a message may be thought of as consisting of one or more logical parts. As Figure 5.7 shows each part can be associated with a type, listed in the types element. ▷

In the example that follows, SchedulePaymentResponse represents a message sent by the bill payment service to a service consumer, to indicate the result of scheduling a payment. (This is the result of the service's having received a SchedulePayment message.) The message has only one part, named result. The type associated with that part is defined as an XSD complex type, Payment-Confirmation, in the types element of this document.

```
<message name="schedulePaymentResponse">
  <part name="result" type="ns2:PaymentConfirmation"/>
</message>
```

Each message has a name attribute that should provide a unique name to each message in the enclosing WSDL. Each message element has zero or more *part* elements. The part element has a name attribute to provide a unique name to each

> ▷   The WSDL wsdl:input, wsdl:output, and their corresponding wsdl:message elements map to Java arguments and method return values.

Figure 5.7
The message
element

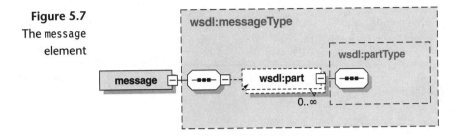

part and a type element, which associates the part with an XSD type (complex type or simple type).

CORBA developers may recall the concept of in, out, and inout parameters. Like IDL, operations in WSDL may take out or inout parameters as well as in parameters. An out type is a variable that is initialized and set in the service and sent back to the client. An inout type is initialized in the client and set but possibly reset in the service and sent back. In other words, if an operation receives a parameter expected to change as a result of the operation, it is termed an inout parameter. As a general rule in WSDL, if a part name appears in

- Both the input and output messages, it is an inout parameter
- Only the input message, it is an in parameter
- Only the output message, it is an out parameter ▷

In many cases, the service will expect the parameters in a certain order, which consumers need to know. For this reason, the operation node described later in the port has an attribute called parameterOrder—a comma-separated list of parameters in the order in which they occur in the method signature. The fragment below is an example of how this is done.

```
<message name="BillPay_schedulePayment">
    <part name="Date_1" type="xsd:dateTime"/>
    <part name="String_2" type="xsd:string"/>
    <part name="double_3" type="xsd:double"/>
</message>
```

▷   The concept of in, out, and inout parameters is tied to holder classes. Holder classes and these parameter types are covered in detail in Chapter 10.

```
// other code ...
   <portType name="BillPay">
      <operation name="schedulePayment" parameterOrder="Date_1 String_2
                                                           double_3">
// other code ...

      </operation>
   </portType>
```

Describing Service Interactions: The operation *Element*

An operation defines an interaction (resulting in the exchange of one or messages) between a service consumer and a service in the abstract. The operation element is a container for all abstract messages that can be exchanged for a particular interaction with the service. ▷

An operation contains an input, an output, and one or more fault elements that reference the message elements described earlier. The fault elements represent the abstract message format for any errors or exceptional messages that may result as output of the operation. ▷▷

```
<operation name="schedulePayment" parameterOrder="Date_1 String_2 double_3">
    <input message="tns:BillPay_schedulePayment"/>
    <output message="tns:BillPay_schedulePaymentResponse"/>
    <fault name="ScheduleFailedException"
                  message="tns:ScheduleFailedException"/>
</operation>
```

As mentioned earlier, a service consumer and the service can have different types of interactions. Figure 5.8 shows the schema for the operation element and the four different types of abstract operations.

> ▷ The WSDL operation element is analogous to and maps to a Java method declaration.
>
> ▷▷ The WSDL fault element is analogous to and maps to Java exceptions in a method declaration.

Figure 5.8
The schema
for the opera-
tions element

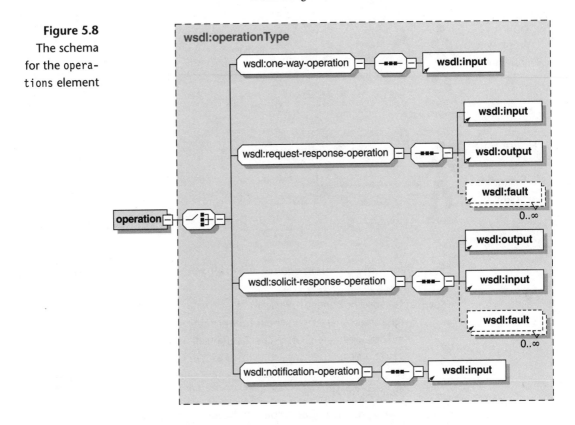

- **One-way.** A one-way operation is one in which a message is sent to the service but no response is generated in return. A one-way message is useful to model "fire and forget" type messages, where the work done by the consumer of the message is asynchronous to the sender. In WSDL, a one-way operation does not have an output element. Figure 5.9 shows the grammar for a one-way message. Note that this example is not a part of the bill payment service WSDL.

```
<operation name="onewayOp">
    <input message="tns:logActivity"/>
</operation>
```

- **Request-response.** In a request-response type interaction, shown in Figure 5.10, the consumer sends a message to the service and waits for a response. The service may respond to the waiting requestor with a return message signifying the result of the request or with a fault message signifying that something went wrong.

Figure 5.9
A one-way
operation

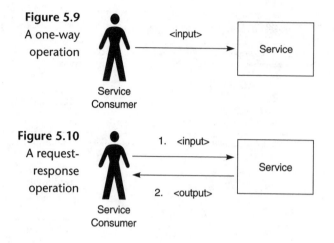

Figure 5.10
A request-
response
operation

- Flute Bank's bill payment service WSDL has the following operation:

```
<operation name="schedulePayment">
    <input message="tns:schedulePayment"/>
    <output message="tns:schedulePaymentResponse"/>
    <fault  message="tns:scheduleFailedException"
                          name="scheduleFailedExceptionMessage" />
    </operation>
```

The *input* and *output* elements specify the abstract message that correspond to the request and the response respectively. The *fault* element specifies any error or exception messages that may result.

- **Solicit-response.** A solicit-response-style operation, shown in Figure 5.11, has the reverse message flow of a request-response operation. The Web service sends a message to the client (output message) and receives a message from the client in response (input message). The grammar for this type of operation is similar to that of the request-response, except that the *output* element comes before the *input* element.

```
<operation name="fictitiousSR">
        <output message="tns:schedulePaymentResponse"/>
        <input message="tns:schedulePayment"/>
        <fault  message="tns:scheduleFailedException"
                          name="scheduleFailedExceptionMessage"/>
    </operation>
```

- **Notification.** In a notification-style operation, shown in Figure 5.12, the Web service notifies a client when an event occurs in which the client has registered interest. In such an interaction, from the viewpoint of the Web service,

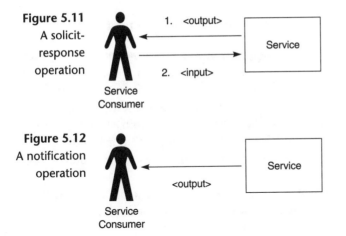

Figure 5.11
A solicit-
response
operation

1. <output>
2. <input>

Service Consumer

Service

Figure 5.12
A notification
operation

Service Consumer

Service

there is no input message, just an output message. As Flute Bank does not offer any notifications in the bill payment service, the grammar for a notification operation shown below is not a part of the bill payment service WSDL example. ▷

```
<operation name="notifyOp">
    <output message="tns:stockUpdate"/>
</operation>
```

▷ WSDL provides the mechanism to describe different types of operations but does not define how, for example, solicit-response and notification messages are to be *implemented* in a Web service architecture. One approach might be to indicate, in the WSDL describing the service, how a service consumer is to handle these types of operations (e.g, explicitly describe how a callback or notification message can be correlated to the request).

A better approach is to describe, in a separate specification, the different message exchange patterns that can be used in a Web service architecture—that is, describe message exchange patterns in the abstract. Protocol specifications like SOAP can then specify how that particular protocol supports all or some of the abstract message exchange patterns (i.e., how it provides a concrete implementation for each abstract message exchange pattern). WSDL operation bindings can then simply refer to the particular concrete pattern the protocol describes.

SOAP 1.2 and WSDL 1.2 specifications propose a somewhat similar solution. More information on the future of message exchange patterns can be found at *www.w3.org/2002/ws/cg/2/07/meps.html*.

Describing Groups of Operations: The portType *Element*

The portType element combines all the abstract information that together describes what the service offers—its abstract interface. So the portType element is a container for operations, which in turn is a container for messages. Although a WSDL document can contain one or more portType elements, it is good practice to have just one occurrence of the portType element within a WSDL document—that is, to describe only one Web service interface within a WSDL document (this practice is similar to the practice of keeping only one Java interface definition in a physical class file).

The name attribute of the portType element must be unique within the WSDL document. As Figure 5.13 shows, each port type contains a set of operations, and each operation describes the messages exchanged between the service and the service consumer. ▷

Implementation Details: The binding *Element*

All the WSDL document elements described thus far have described the abstract nature of the service. Before a consumer can interact with a service, some details of the service's implementation have to be known. Operations of the service with a list of messages exchanged during the operation only partly describe the service. The wire protocol and invocation style the service implementation understands affect how data is marshaled and unmarshaled over the wire. As Figure 5.14 shows, *binding* associates the concrete implementation information about messages, data types, and operations to the corresponding abstract notions.

Each portType can have one or more binding elements that associate the portType to specific protocols for invoking the service. SOAP over HTTP may be the most popular protocol today for implementing RPC-style Web services, but it's not the only one. One could implement a Web service that understands SOAP over SMTP or HTTP/GET, and so on. The important thing is that the list of protocols the Web service community may support is not finite.

So, how do we bind an abstract service definition to a concrete protocol in WSDL and accommodate all possible protocol bindings without having to change the WSDL standards every time a new binding is supported? WSDL provides a mechanism to incorporate protocol-specific information using the extensibility elements, which provide the concrete grammar for each message within every operation. The WSDL specification currently defines binding extension endpoints that understand SOAP over HTTP, HTTP GET/POST, and MIME.

▷   The WSDL portType is analogous to a Java interface declaration.

Figure 5.13
The portType
element

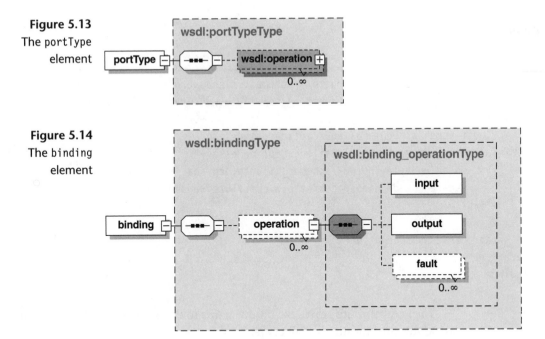

Figure 5.14
The binding
element

In the example below (a fragment of Listing 5.2), the bill payment service port type is bound to SOAP over HTTP.

```
<binding name="BillPayBinding" type="tns:BillPay">
 <soap:binding transport="http://schemas.xmlsoap.org/soap/http" style="rpc"/>
    <operation name="listScheduledPayments">
       <input>
          <soap:body encodingStyle="http://schemas.xmlsoap.org/soap/encoding/"
              use="encoded" namespace="http://com.flute.webservice/billPay"/>
       </input>

       <output>
         <soap:body encodingStyle="http://schemas.xmlsoap.org/soap/encoding/"
              use="encoded" namespace="http://com.flute.webservice/billPay"/>
       </output>
       <soap:operation soapAction=""/>
    </operation>
     <operation name="schedulePayment">
      <input>
        <soap:body encodingStyle="http://schemas.xmlsoap.org/soap/encoding/"
                use="encoded"
```

```
namespace="http://com.flute.webservice/billPay"/>
    </input>
     <output>
       <soap:body encodingStyle="http://schemas.xmlsoap.org/soap/encoding/"
          use="encoded" namespace="http://com.flute.webservice/billPay"/>
      </output>
       <fault name="scheduleFailedExceptionMessage">
       <soap:fault name="scheduleFailedExceptionMessage"
           encodingStyle="http://schemas.xmlsoap.org/soap/encoding/"
           use="encoded" namespace="http://com.flute.webservice/billPay"/>
       </fault>

      <soap:operation soapAction=""/>
</operation>
</binding>
```

The name attribute provides a unique name to the binding. The type attribute associates the binding to a portType.

WSDL defines three bindings that describe how a service that exposes itself physically using one of these bindings can be invoked:

- **SOAP bindings** describe how a service can be consumed using SOAP messages.

- **MIME bindings** describe how a service can be consumed by sending MIME messages.

- **HTTP bindings** describe how a service can be consumed by sending HTTP GET requests and POST messages.

SOAP Binding WSDL 1.1 has built-in facilities that allow SOAP-specific details to be specified in the WSDL document itself. These SOAP-specific elements are collectively referred to as *SOAP binding extensions,* because they are specified using the WSDL extension mechanism, covered later in the chapter.

- soap:binding. The soap:binding element signifies that the binding is for SOAP protocol format. This element should be present if using the SOAP binding.

```
<binding name="BillPayBinding" type="tns:BillPay">
    <soap:binding transport="http://schemas.xmlsoap.org/soap/http" style="rpc"/>
<!--other elements>
</binding>
```

The style attribute indicates the style of operations to follow: rpc style or document style. An RPC style invocation signifies that operations take input parameters and return an output result. A document-centric style signifies document-oriented messages, where entire XML documents are passed as input and output to the service.

The transport attribute indicates the underlying transport protocol to be used for SOAP–that is, the value http://schemas.xmlsoap.org/soap/http indicates HTTP transport; http://schemas.xmlsoap.org/soap/smtp indicates SMTP transport.

- soap:operation. The soap:operation extension's soapAction attribute specifies the value to be put in the SoapAction header.

```
<soap:operation soapAction=""/>
```

A SOAP message header may contain a SOAPAction field, as a way to inform the SOAP processing node of the intent of the SOAP message. The SOAPAction element is required for SOAP over HTTP and must be specified, even if the value of SOAPAction is an empty string (""), as in this example. This is not uncommon; for most SOAP requests sent over HTTP, HTTP Request-URI already provides the intent of the SOAP message to the SOAP processing node, so the SOAPAction attribute is left empty. The SOAPAction attribute, explained in detail in Chapter 4, must *not* be specified for any other binding.

- soap:body. The soap:body element specifies how message parts are to be assembled in the SOAP body element. soap:body elements are used to map the abstract input and output messages to their SOAP-protocol-specific implementations. Error messages are handled differently–see the soap:fault extension description.

Within the soap:body element, the *use* attribute determines whether the data is encoded (use="encoded") using an encodingStyle ("http://schemas.xmlsoap .org/soap/encoding") or whether the XML can be validated using a schema (use= "literal").

In Listing 5.2, the operations of the BillPayservice are described as RPCs, and the message parts of the operations are encoded using the SOAP encoding rules. That is, the BillPayservice methods take in typed parameters, and the service understands how to serialize and deserialize these message parts using the SOAP encoding rules.

Typically, operations that are document style will not have the data encoded; rather, it is sent as a literal, so the XML can be validated against a schema. So the most common forms are document style with no encoding (doc/literal) and RPC style with encoding (rpc/encoded). It is uncommon, but not impossible, to have an operation with the other allowed combinations of style and use (rpc/literal and doc/encoded). The style and use attributes are explained in detail in a later section.

- soap:header. Any headers to be transmitted as part of the SOAP header are defined in the soap:header element. The optional headerfault element, shown in Figure 5.15, is used to transmit error information corresponding to the message defined in soap:header. The SOAP specification requires that errors pertaining to headers be returned in the header section, not in the body of the SOAP message.

- soap:fault. What happens when a Java service method throws an exception? How is that to be handled and transmitted over the wire to the service consumer? The soap:fault extension element is used to describe the fault message. As the example shows, the soap:fault extension has the same attributes as a soap:body.

```
<fault name="scheduleFailedExceptionMessage">
     <soap:fault name="scheduleFailedExceptionMessage"
     encodingStyle="http://schemas.xmlsoap.org/soap/encoding/" use="encoded"
     namespace="http://com.flute.webservice/billPay"/>
</fault>
```

MIME Binding WSDL also provides a way to bind abstract messages to MIME types. Specifically, WSDL supports the following MIME types:

- Multipart/related
- Application/x-www-form-urlencoded
- Text/xml

In the BillPayservice example, the only data types used for input and output were simple or complex types. If the services wanted to return some binary data (e.g., a GIF/JPEG image), the message would contain a binary part. The following WSDL fragments represent a new BillPay service method, getFluteLogo, that returns a string and a GIF image logo.

Figure 5.15
The SOAP
header

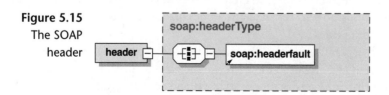

```
<message name= "getFluteLogo">
    <part name="fluteName" type="xsd:string"/>
    <part name="logo" type="xsd:binary"/>
</message>
```

In the binding element, the following operation would also have to be added:

```
<operation name="getFluteLogo">
  <soap:operation soapAction=""/>
    <output>
    <mime:multipartRelated>
        <mime:part>
        <soap:body use="encoded" namespace="http://www.flute.com/billPay"
                encodingStyle="http://schemas.xmlsoap.org/soap/encoding/"/>
        </mime:part>
        <mime:part>
            <mime:content part="logo" type="image/gif/"/>
        </mime:part>
    </mime:multipartRelated>
    </output>
</operation>
```

The `multipartRelated` element, shown in Figure 5.16, consists of individual part elements. Therefore, in the code example above, the MIME binding appears as multiple parts: one is the image, and the other is the returned `String` in the soap body.

HTTP Bindings Thus far we have discussed how WSDL can be used to describe SOAP-based Web services. WSDL also defines a binding for invoking operations using only HTTP GET or POST requests. This is a rarely used aspect but is useful when exposing only parts of a Web service that typically accept limited parameters and return read-only results. For example, a free `StockQuote` service provided by Flute Bank on its Web site may require only the ticker symbol as the input. Simply sending an HTTP GET or POST request to the service should return the

Figure 5.16
The `multipart-`
`Related` element

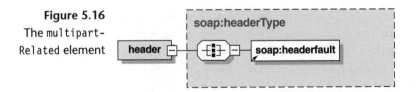

appropriate response. That is, pointing to `http://www.flutebank.com/services/` `stockquote/getQuote.jsp?ticker=FLUT` will return a response like this:

```
<?xml version="1.0" encoding="UTF-8"?>
<stockquote xmlns:tns="http://www.flutebank.com/xml">
<symbol>FLUT</symbol>
<high>36.98</high>
<low>22.00</low>
<currentask>35.00</currentask>
<tick>up</tick>
<marginable>yes</marginable>
<lasttrade>
    <number>2888</number>
    <price>34.99</price>
</lasttrade>
</stockquote>
```

These HTTP bindings in WSDL are more for backward compatibility with the early generation of Web services, which used this approach. We recommend using SOAP bindings rather than plain HTTP bindings.

Bindings and Style/Use

A Web service can expose its operations as *RPC* style operations or as *document* style operations. For a SOAP message, the style of invocation affects the body of the message. In RPC style (Figure 5.17a), the client invokes a method on the server by sending all the information necessary for that method execution in the body of the SOAP message. The client receives a response message in the same fashion. In document style (Figure 5.17b), the client and server communicate using XML documents. The client sends an XML document, such as a purchase order. The server processes the document and returns another XML document, say an invoice, as a result. The document represents a complete unit of information and may be completely self-describing.

Encoding refers to how data is serialized and sent over the wire. The parties can agree on a predefined encoding scheme or use an XML schema directly in the data to define the data types. The message with the former notation is said to be an *encoded* message; the latter is said to be a *literal* message.

For encoded messages, the rules to encode and interpret a SOAP body are in a URL specified by the `encodingStyle` attribute. A literal message indicates that the rules to encode and interpret the SOAP body are specified by a XML schema. Thus there are four combinations of style and encoding:

Figure 5.17
(a) RPC and
(b) document
styles

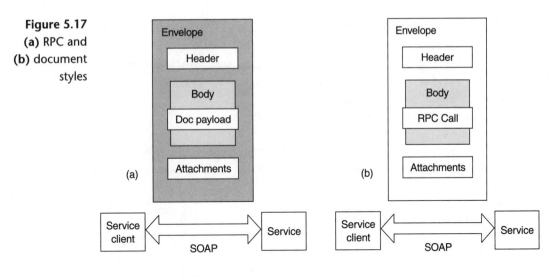

- RPC/encoded

- RPC/literal

- Document/encoded

- Document/literal

The `style` attribute of the `soap:binding` element and use attribute of the `soap:body` element in the WSDL file can be used to describe these four combinations of invocation mentioned previously, as shown in Listings 5.3 through 5.6.

Listing 5.3   WSDL for RPC/encoded style

```
<binding name="BillPayBinding" type="tns:BillPay">
    <soap:binding transport="http://schemas.xmlsoap.org/soap/http"
            style="rpc"/>
  <operation name="listScheduledPayments">
  <soap:operation soapAction=""/>
    <input>
      <soap:body encodingStyle="http://schemas.xmlsoap.org/soap/encoding/"
            use="encoded" namespace="http://com.flute.webservice/billPay"/>
    </input>
    <output>
      <soap:body encodingStyle="http://schemas.xmlsoap.org/soap/encoding/"
            use="encoded" namespace="http://com.flute.webservice/billPay"/>
    </output>
</operation>
</binding>
```

Listing 5.4   WSDL for RPC/literal style

```
<binding name="BillPayBinding" type="tns:BillPay">
    <soap:binding transport="http://schemas.xmlsoap.org/soap/http"
            style="rpc"/>
  <operation name="getMonthlyReport">
   <soap:operation soapAction="" style="rpc"/>
     <input>
       <soap:body use="encoded" namespace="http://com.flute.webservice/billPay"
                 encodingStyle="http://schemas.xmlsoap.org/soap/encoding"/>
     </input>
     <output>
       <soap:body use="literal"
                    namespace="http://com.flute.webservice/types/output.xsd"/>
     </output>
   </operation>

<operation name="getWeeklyReport ">
  <soap:operation soapAction="" style="rpc"/>
  <input>
     <soap:body use="encoded" namespace="http://com.flute.webservice/billPay"
            encodingStyle="http://schemas.xmlsoap.org/soap/encoding" />
  </input>
  <output>
     <soap:body use="literal"
                   namespace="http://com.flute.webservice/types/output.xsd"/>
  </output>
  </operation>
</binding>
```

Listing 5.5   WSDL for document/encoded style

```
<binding name="BillPayBinding" type="tns:BillPay">
    <soap:binding transport="http://schemas.xmlsoap.org/soap/http"
            style="document"/>
  <operation name="listScheduledPayments">
  <soap:operation soapAction=""/>
    <input>
      <soap:body encodingStyle="http://com.flute.webservice/encoding/"
            use="encoded" namespace="http://com.flute.webservice/billPay"/>
    </input>
```

```
    <output>
      <soap:body encodingStyle="http://com.flute.webservice/encoding/"
            use="encoded" namespace="http://com.flute.webservice/billPay"/>
    </output>
</operation>
</binding>
```

Listing 5.6 WSDL for document/literal style

```
package com.flutebank.billpayservice;
<binding name="BillPayBinding" type="tns:BillPay">
<soap:binding transport="http://schemas.xmlsoap.org/soap/http"
            style="document"/>
<operation name="listScheduledPayments">
  <soap:operation soapAction=""/>
    <input>
            <soap:body use="literal"
                    namespace="http://com.flute.webservice/types/input.xsd"/>
    </input>
    <output>
            <soap:body use="literal"
                    namespace="http://com.flute.webservice/types/output.xsd"/>
      </output>
  </operation>
</binding>
```

Chapter 10 examines invocation and encoding styles in greater detail and discusses the implications for selecting one combination over another, best practices, and implementation techniques.

Describing the Physical Service: The **port** and **service** Elements

As mentioned earlier, a porttype—that is, an abstraction of the service—can be bound to multiple protocol-specific implementations, with each implementation running on a specific network address. The *port* specifies the location that processes a particular encoding scheme—in short, the port element identifies the network address of the endpoint. There is one port element for each *binding* element.

```
<service name="BillPayservice">
  <port name="BillPayPort" binding="tns:BillPayBinding">
    <soap:address location="www.localhost:8080"/>
  </port>
</service
```

In a WSDL document, a *service* element acts as a container for one or more ports, as Figure 5.18 shows. The notion of a service as a collection of ports is useful, because the same service could be implemented using different protocols. In such a case, there would be one portType element, multiple binding elements, one port for each binding, and one service element to combine all the ports in the WSDL document. Although a WSDL document can contain more than one service element, it is not recommended or terribly useful.

Referencing Other Descriptions: The import *Element*

Within a WSDL document, a service's interface is described using the types, messages, portTypes, and binding elements, and the service's implementation details are described using the port, address, and service elements. It is possible, and desirable, to author a WSDL description by separating the service's interface description from its implementation description. The service implementation WSDL document should refer to (or import) the reusable service interface description document. The WSDL import element provides a means to refer to one WSDL document from another. The *import* element is used to associate a namespace with a document location.

Figure 5.18
The service
element

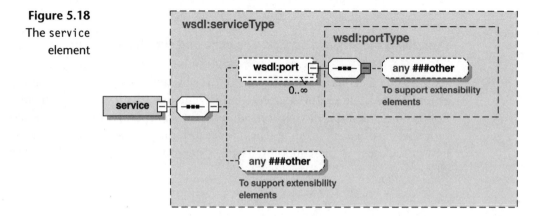

```
<import namespace="uri" location="uri"/>
```

Separation of the interface definition from deployment information is particularly important when registering Web services in a registry, such as Universal Description, Discovery and Integration (UDDI), which allows software to be categorized by function. Typically, industry consortiums will devise common service definitions for that industry and make them publicly available, by registering these service definitions as UDDI tModels. Service creators access the UDDI registry for service interface definitions, then create and deploy Web services conforming to the interface definition. The WSDL document describing the implemented Web service will *import* the service interface definition to which it was built. Detailed information on UDDI appears in Chapter 6. ▷

Extending WSDL

We briefly touched upon the concept of extensibility while discussing types and bindings. Let us look at this in further detail. The WSDL specification allows the WSDL defined elements to be extended. In fact, the SOAP-specific elements discussed earlier, such as soap:header, soap:body, and soap:fault are examples of this mechanism, where the WSDL binding element has been extended to include SOAP protocol-specific information. Such elements that extend the WSDL specified elements are called WSDL extensibility elements. The specification defines specific elements of the WSDL document under which such elements may be added; these are listed in Table 5.1. For example, the port element can be extended by protocol-specific elements, which allows additional location information to be specified. soap:address does exactly this.

Architects can add their own extensibility elements to a WSDL document describing value-added features, but they should be aware that not all service consumers will know how to interpret these nonstandard extensions, which have to be explained to them manually. Moreover, general-purpose WSDL tools and utilities will not know how to make use of these nonstandard extensions—which are, however, useful in providing extra information to service consumers. As an example, the WSDL document fragment below shows that the BillPay service operation listScheduledPayments may include additional information about the hours of the day between which a financial service will be available or the minimum time a particular operation takes to execute, and so on.

▷   The WSDL import element is analogous to the import statement in Java.

Table 5.1 WSDL Elements that May Be Extended

Location	Examples of extensibility
definitions	Introduce additional information or definitions that apply to the entire WSDL structure
types	Specify the data types in a format other than schemas
service	Introduce additional information or definitions for the service
port	Specify protocol-specific details about the address for the port
binding	Introduce information that applies to all operations in the portType being bound, such as quality of service details
operation	Provide protocol-specific information that applies to both the input and output messages, e.g., soap:operation
input	Introduce information about the input message, e.g., the soap:body with its use attribute
output	Introduce information about the output message, e.g., the soap:body with its use attribute
fault	Introduce additional information for the fault message, e.g., soap:fault

```
<definitions name="billpayservice"
            xmlns:ext="" ... >
<binding name="BillPayBinding" type="tns:BillPay">
    <operation name="listScheduledPayments">
        <ext:responseTime min="100" average="150" maximum="250"/>
        <ext:operationAvailability starttime="800" endtime="2300"/>
        <soap:operation soapAction=""/>
         <input>
            <soap:body use="encoded"
                    namespace="http://www.flutebank.com/xml"/
                encodingStyle="http://schemas.xmlsoap.org/soap/encoding/">
        </input>
        <output>
            <soap:body use="encoded"
                    namespace="http://www.flutebank.com/xml"/
                encodingStyle="http://schemas.xmlsoap.org/soap/encoding/">
        </output>
    </operation>
</definitions>
```

WSDL Usage Patterns

So far, we have examined the structure and content of a WSDL document. This section explains how such a document can be used in a Web services application. Applications that use WSDL fall into two broad categories: service consumers and service providers.

Service Consumers

As in RMI or EJB environments, before clients can invoke a method exposed by an RPC-style Web service, they must know the following:

- The location of the service
- The protocol the service understands (so the request can be marshaled correctly)
- The service's methods and method signatures

A WSDL document describing the service contains this information. The physical WSDL file can be obtained either from a reference in the UDDI registry where the service is registered, from a well-known URL, or by any other mechanism previously agreed upon by the service producer and consumer (such as email).

Service Producers

A service producer is responsible for implementing and exposing the service on the network. A service producer may

- Take an existing implementation and expose it as a Web service by implementing a layer of SOAP interfaces. Examples of this scenario are exposing existing Java applications with a layer of SOAP interfaces.
- Import a WSDL describing the interface to which the service must conform, generate the outline code from it, fill in the appropriate pieces of implementation, and deploy the service.
- On both the producer and consumer sides, vendor tools associated with the vendor's runtime environment play a significant role. Figure 5.19 indicates this relationship.

The vendor's tools are responsible for importing the WSDL and creating the specific language bindings (e.g., Java, C#, C++, VB, etc.) that are then deployed in the language-specific container (e.g., Java servlet, ASP, Perl, etc.) Compliance with standards and specifications such as JAX-RPC should be an important factor in deciding on vendors, because tools play a critical part in generating the bindings, as Figure 5.20 shows. For example, the tools parse the WSDL and generate the appropriate Java data types in the types element as well as in the method signatures, parameters, and returns from the operations and bindings. If the data type mapping is not compliant with that specified in JAX-RPC, the application will not be portable or vendor-neutral.

Some of the things to check for compliance to standards when a vendor tool imports WSDL are

- Mapping parameter to data types; for example, XML Schema namespace to Java package name, XML Schema data type to Java types

- Mapping portTypes to interfaces and classes

- Generating bindings based on the style and use elements (RPC/encoded, RPC/literal, document/encoded, document/literal)

- Importing endpoint information for use by generated client proxies

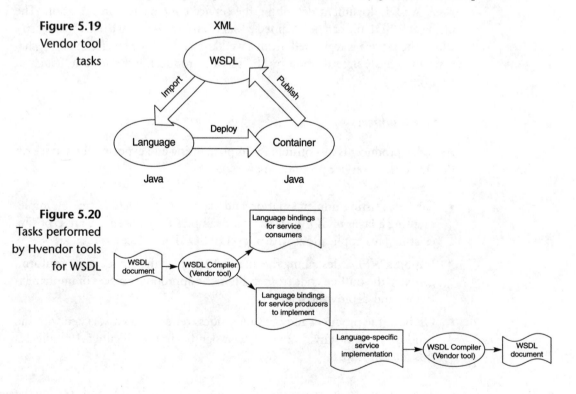

Figure 5.19
Vendor tool
tasks

Figure 5.20
Tasks performed
by Hvendor tools
for WSDL

The same is true for service providers. The tools must be capable of crossing the language implementation-to-specification bridge transparently, using the information outlined above to generate a WSDL-compliant document. In short, architects should choose the vendor runtime and implementations with care. ▷

Early or Late Binding

In Chapter 2, we introduced the concept of early and late binding. This describes the time at which consumers discover type information and other details of the service they want to interact with. Once the WSDL document that contains this information is available, consumers can use a few architectural patterns based around the concept of binding when invoking the service.

Early Binding

For service consumers who intend to use a Web service, one alternative is to import the WSDL into the development environment, where vendor-provided tools generate artifacts that the consumer can use (we just looked at the critical role vendor tools play in this step). Consumers can then directly use these artifacts (stubs, data type mappings, generated code, etc.) for all subsequent interactions with the service, eliminating the need for inspecting WSDL each time the service is invoked. Such an approach is termed *early binding*. This approach is best suited for services whose location and functional interface are not volatile.

An example of early binding is the consumption of RPC style services described by WSDL. WSDL can generate the necessary client-side stub proxy classes. The exact mechanism for this generation is specific to the vendor's runtime implementation. For example, the XML RPC compiler (xrpcc) tool of the JAX-RPC reference implementation reads an XML configuration file to generate the client-side code, as Figure 5.21 shows. The configuration file is an XML file that provides xrpcc with information regarding the package name to be used

▷   JWSDL JSR-110, *Java API for WSDL*, proposes that a standard API be defined for programmatic creation, manipulation, and parsing of WSDL documents. JWSDL will be useful for creating tools to manipulate (generate/edit) WSDL and possibly for future tools that generate stubs for invoking services on the fly.

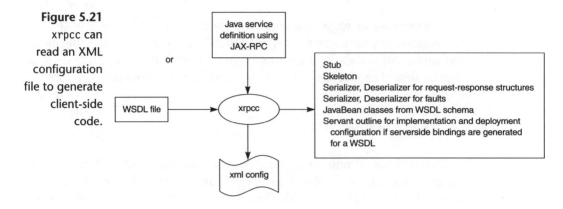

Figure 5.21
xrpcc can
read an XML
configuration
file to generate
client-side
code.

for the generated classes and the location of the WSDL document. xrpcc is covered in detail in Chapter 8. ▷

```
xrpcc -client -d <destination directory–s <source directory> <configuration file>
<?xml version="1.0" encoding="UTF-8"?>
    <configuration xmlns="http://java.sun.com/xml/ns/jax-rpc/ri/config">
        <wsdl location=
                packageName="com.flute.webservice">
        </wsdl>
</configuration>
```

Early binding has essentially the following three variations, based on *when* the abstract and concrete definitions described in the WSDL are used by the consumer. Keep in mind that the portType defines the functional signature of the service.

- **Static compile-time binding.** Both the abstract and concrete descriptions in WSDL are known, and the concrete descriptions are used directly. For example, port, portType, and the location are known and set at compile time. Typically, the consumer is developed using stubs. The client code is generated using vendor tools based on the WSDL portType, and the location is set in

> ▷ Service consumers can be designed using three approaches: client-side stubs, dynamic invocation interface (DII), or dynamic proxies. The programming model, architecture, and usage scenarios for these modes can be found in Chapter 10. You are encouraged to follow up the reading of the subsequent Late Binding section below with the Service Consumers section in Chapter 10.

the stub by the same tools or by the service consumer For example, Flute Bank always buys office supplies from OfficeMin, because of a long-term contract, and the portType is standardized as part of the service level agreement with OfficeMin.

- **Static deploy-time binding.** This is similar to static compile-time binding, with the difference that though the functional signature (portType) of the service is known at development time, the location is not set until the service is deployed. This means that at deployment, the consumer or an administrator for the consumer looks up the WSDL, selects a port, and gets a location from it. Typically, the consumer is developed using stubs generated at compile time. For example, Flute Bank develops a client to order office supplies from Office-Min's Web service that it distributes to all its branches. The branches can then set the location to point to the closest store location during deployment.

- **Static runtime binding.** The functional signature (portType) is known and set at development time; however, the consumer doesn't know the service's location. This means that during deployment or at runtime, the consumer looks up the WSDL, selects a port, and obtains its location. As in the previous scenarios, such a consumer would also typically be developed using stubs. For example, Flute Bank doesn't have a contract with any supplier for office supplies. Every time an order for office supplies totaling more than a certain amount is placed, the service polls vendors from the prescreened vendor list for the lowest rate. This clearly requires standardization on the portTypes between organizations that want to form ad hoc relationships. In some vertical industries, such as finance, hotels, and travel, these types of interfaces already exist, and it seems reasonable that in the future some of them will migrate to the Web service paradigm.

Web services being developed today that use WSDL typically use static compile-time bindings and static deploy-time bindings. Organizations form business relationships with their partners and formalize the WSDL as a part of the service level agreement. The description of the service is not expected to change, and if it needs to, appropriate out-of-band measures can be taken as part of change control.

Late Binding

Another way to invoke a Web service is to download and examine the WSDL on the fly at runtime and dynamically invoke the service. This is a more robust way of invoking services that change unpredictably or that have variable characteristics. Although this method may, in general, have slower performance than an equivalent early binding implementation, changes to the consumed Web service will have less impact on the consumer, due to the loose coupling between the two.

Dynamic invocation interface (DII) and dynamic proxies actively use WSDL for this purpose, where the client needs *minimal* information about the service at compile time, and some of it is actually extracted at runtime by pointing to a URL where the WSDL is located. ▷

Similar to its early binding peers, late binding can also be described on the basis of the functional signature (portType) and network address (location) in two variations:

- **Dynamic binding.** Neither the service's functional signature (portType) nor its network address (location) is known or set at compile time. Consumers are responsible for locating a service they want to use, introspecting the portType, and subsequently invoking the service. Either dynamic invocation interface or dynamic proxies generated on the fly can be used in this case. For example, Flute Bank does not have a contract with any supplier for office supplies. Every time an order for office supplies totaling more than a certain amount is placed, the service polls vendors from the prescreened vendor list for the lowest rate. However, unlike the previous example, it needs to inspect the WSDL and then look for certain method signatures or variations of the same and their locations.

- **Dynamic binding with known location.** This is a variation of the above, where location is known but the functional signature of the service (portType) is not. In such cases consumers query the location for supported portTypes or supply the location with a portType, to check if it is supported. For example, Flute Bank always sends its quarterly report to the Securities and Exchange Commission but does not know the format, which changes every quarter.

The kinds of late binding offered by dynamic invocation interface and dynamic proxies are supported by specifications like JAX-RPC and its vendor implementations. However, the dynamic binding architectural patterns outlined are not yet practical. The mechanics of such a dynamic invocation are relatively easy to address. Considerably harder to solve are issues regarding how consumers are billed for service usage and are able to automatically select a particular service over other functionally equivalent services.

> ▷   Service consumers can be programmed using three approaches: client-side stubs, DII, or Dynamic proxies. All three modes and examples of their usage can be found in Chapter 10.

Both patterns for consuming Web services have their respective strengths and are suitable for use under different circumstances. Generally, however, because of the current maturity of vendor products and the issues yet unresolved with respect to late binding, we believe architects should first investigate early binding as the pattern of interaction.

WSDL and Server-Side Java Classes

In general, a service producer who decides to implement a Web service corresponding to a WSDL service description in Java will use the runtime vendor tools to generate the corresponding bindings for that runtime. For example, the Java WSDP reference implementation, the xrpcc, can be used to generate all necessary server-side Java ties and classes for the reference implementation. It is important to keep in mind that these classes are not portable and are specific to the vendor's runtime.

```
xrpcc  -classpath %classpath% -client -keep -d <destination directory–s
                          <source directory> <configuration file>
```

The command for using xrppc for generating server-side ties and support classes differs from the previous usage in just one flag: -server instead of -client.

Generating WSDL from Java

Java programmers who have little interest in understanding the details of a WSDL document will be encouraged to know that there are tools to generate a WSDL document, given a Java remote interface. Current tools will, however, generate only WSDL that describes an RPC style invocation for SOAP-based Web services. The xrppc utility can be used to generate a WSDL document with SOAP-HTTP binding, given a Java remote interface, using the following command:

```
xrpcc  -classpath %classpath% -server -keep -d <destination directory>
                                     <configuration xml file>
```

where the configuration file looks like the following XML document:

```
<?xml version="1.0" encoding="UTF-8"?>

<configuration xmlns="http://java.sun.com/xml/ns/jax-rpc/ri/config">
    <service name="BillPayment"
        targetNamespace="http://com.flute.webservice/billPay"
        typeNamespace="http://com.flute.webservice/types"
         packageName="com.flute.webservice">
        <interface name="com.flute.webservice.BillPay"
            servantName="com.flute.webservice.BillPayImpl"/>
    </service>
</configuration>
```

The configuration file provides the namespace to be used in the resulting WSDL document, the name of the remote interface for which the WSDL file will be generated, and the name of the generated implementation class.

> WSDL 1.2

The first working draft of WSDL 1.2 specifications has been released. The following discussion pertains to the contents of the first draft of the specification. Some of this information may not be applicable to the final 1.2 specifications. This section summarizes some of the changes between the two versions.

WSDL 1.2 is described using XML information sets. An information set (infoset) is an abstract XML data set. Its primary purpose is to provide a consistent way to describe specifications that describe information in a well-formed XML document structure. As a WSDL document is a well-formed XML document, it can be described as an *information set* (a tree) with *information items* (nodes).

The WSDL 1.2 specification introduces a clearer conceptual model for a WSDL document structure. Conceptually, a WSDL document is a container for a WSDL definitions group, which in turn is a container for *description components*, with each description component describing different parts of the Web service. For example, a message description component describes the abstract messages exchanged by the service and the portType description component describes the abstract service interface. Like WSDL 1.1, WSDL 1.2 describes Web services by defining abstract types, messages, and operations and combining operations into portTypes. However, in WSDL 1.2, a collection of portTypes is defined and called a serviceType, and a service is considered an implementation of a serviceType.

The model dictates six description components, which together provide a complete functional and location description of the service:

- Zero or one type description component
- Zero or more message description components
- Zero or more portType description components
- Zero or more serviceType description components
- Zero or more binding description components
- Zero or more service description components

WSDL 1.2 also attempts to clarify some areas of WSDL 1.1 that were not defined adequately and areas where some WSDL 1.1 service descriptions features could not be supported by all service implementation platforms. For example,

- Although WSDL 1.1 provided for solicit-response and notification type operations, there was no consensus on how these operation types were to be implemented (as callbacks? As event-based notifications?) Also, it is proposed that WSDL 1.2 define an extensible message exchange pattern (MEP), which is in line with the MEP framework defined to work with SOAP 1.2. The MEP framework for SOAP 1.2 is a means to describe a pattern of message exchanges between two SOAP nodes.

- Dropping the support for operator overloading, which was supported in WSDL 1.1 (by providing messages with the same name but different message parts) has also been proposed.

- Moving the parameter order attribute to the binding section. Because parameter order matters only to RPC style invocations, its current placement in the abstract operations description section is incorrect.

Many proposed changes to WSDL stem from the WSDL 1.2 specification's aim of supporting SOAP 1.2. Most of the proposed changes therefore deal with SOAP binding. As SOAP 1.2 specification is in draft form, the proposed changes are not discussed in this section.

To summarize, the main changes to WSDL are to describe the specification itself in a standard manner using information sets, to clarify some of the language descriptions, to remove ambiguities, and to support SOAP 1.2.

> ## Summary

This chapter described the function of WSDL for a Web-service-based architecture. WSDL provides one form of Web service description, the functional description. The functional description of Web services falls into two broad areas: the abstract service definition, containing the service interface definition, and the service implementation description, containing the protocol binding and deployment information. Vendor tools (e.g., xrpcc) may use this information to generate all the Java classes necessary for enabling a Web service client to invoke a Web service implementation.

The abstract service description is reusable across many implantations of a service, and an industry group may publish the abstract service description, so any service producer can provide a conforming implementation. A well-structured WSDL document should, therefore, separate the two and use the import element within the WSDL for service implementation to refer to the service interface WSDL.

The functional description of a Web service is essential for implementers and users of the service, but there are other forms of Web service description that WSDL does not address. Describing how Web services can be orchestrated or combined to create more complex Web services and describing the quality of service (service level agreements) promised by a Web service implementation are addressed only in the ebXML specification suite. Chapter 17 describes some emerging non-ebXML specifications that address these areas.

> ## References

Java Community Process (JCP). Java Web Services Description Language (JWSDL), Java Specification Request 110 (JSR-110), *Java API for WSDL*. *http://www.jcp.org/en/jsr/detail?id=110*.

World Wide Web Consortium (W3C). Web Services Description Language (WSDL) specification. *www.w3.org/TR/wsdl*.

Chapter {6}

UDDI

The Universal Description, Discovery and Integration (UDDI) specification defines a platform-independent framework for businesses to describe their publicly available services, discover other services, and share information about points of interaction in a global registry. UDDI is a building block that enables organizations to quickly find and conduct business transactions with other organizations, using open standards.

The UDDI specification is an attempt for organizations to accomplish the following:

- Discover the right partner to conduct business with, out of the millions that exist on the Internet today

- Create an industry–accepted, standardized approach to reach partners and customers with information on their services and convey the preferred method for integration between disparate systems

- Characterize how business transactions are used in commerce, once a preferred partner is selected through electronic means

UDDI can be the solution to many business problems. By simplifying B2B interactions, a business can discover other businesses independent of the choice of standards and protocols.

The UDDI specification is the first cross-industry initiative pushed by corporations, software vendors, and industry consortiums. It addresses many of the issues that limit the rapid adoption of commerce over the Internet. The founding fathers of UDDI were Ariba, IBM, and Microsoft. SOAP and WSDL are championed by W3C, while UDDI is an independent business undertaking.

▷ Discovering Web Services

A UDDI registry contains information about businesses and the services they offer. UDDI also contains references to industry-specific specifications a service may support, such as taxonomies and identification systems. Consumers of services can search a registry for businesses, services, or service types, either programmatically or using a Web-based interface . A UDDI business registry uses standard industry taxonomies or classification schemes, such as D-U-N-S, SIC codes, and others, to categorize businesses and the services they offer. All APIs within the UDDI specification use XML, are wrapped in a SOAP envelope, and use HTTP as the transport.

What Is a Registry?

A registry is analogous to a phone book, in that it provides the ability for service consumers to easily locate their desired business entities and the services they provide. A registry provides "white pages" that allow a consumer to look up an address, contact information, and known identifiers. This is similar to looking up either the phone number or address of a business when you know the business's name.

A registry also provides "yellow pages," which include classification information based on standard taxonomies. For example, the phone directory provides yellow pages that can be used to find an all-night pizza shop on Christmas Eve in Baltimore near the Inner Harbor. The typical implementation of yellow pages could be thought of as name-value pairs. The yellow pages metaphor allows any valid taxonomy identifier to be attached to the business white pages. The yellow pages take into account a geographical taxonomy.

Finally, a registry also provides "green pages," which describe services the business offers. Imagine looking in the phone book for the Internal Revenue Service or another government entity, trying to discover what services it offers. The "green pages" indicate the services offered and references it to a specified business process.

A registry contains four types of information:

- **Business entity.** Every business entity holds a unique identifier, the business name, simple contact information, a brief description of the business, a listing of categories that describes and classifies the business, and a URL that points to additional information about the business.

- **Business service.** Every business service entity includes a business description of the service, a listing of categories that describe and classify the service, and a URL to information about the service.

- **Specification pointers.** Each business service entity includes a list of binding templates that point to additional information about a service. A binding template may point to a URL that provides information on how a service is invoked. The specification points also contain information that associates the service with a service type.

- **Service types.** A technical model (tModel for short) defines a service type. Multiple businesses may offer the same type of service as defined by the tModel. A tModel defines the information contained for the service, such as the tModel name, the name of the organization that issued the tModel, the categories that define the service type, and pointers to specifications for the service type, including interface definitions, message protocols and formats, and security protocols. Typically, this is the WSDL document for a service. ▷

In a service-oriented architecture, we learned that this paradigm uses the find, bind, and execute approach. We learned that any service-oriented approach requires a "catalog" of services. UDDI covers the "find" aspects of a service-oriented architecture. UDDI usage is not limited to just Web services and can contain entries of other service types.

The Role of UDDI in Web Services

Figure 6.1 shows how a UDDI registry is populated with business and service information as well as how consumers use this information. Let us look at the steps involved in interacting with a registry:

1. Standards bodies and software companies define specifications specific to the vertical and register them in UDDI. These are referred to as tModels. For securities, the SEC may create tModels that define the format for a CUSIP or symbol.

2. Organizations register descriptions of their businesses and the services they provide. Each entry is assigned a Unique Universal Identifier (UUID) key. UUID keys are guaranteed to be unique across time and space and are immutable. A UUID appears as a formatted hexadecimal string, such as C1B9EF7A-322F-332A-8A3C-3214DA2E5EE1. A UUID is meaningful within the con-

▷ A *registrar* is an organization that executes registration services on behalf of other organizations. A registrar can help a business define and assemble its registry information, including the list of services the organization provides.

Figure 6.1
UDDI
interaction

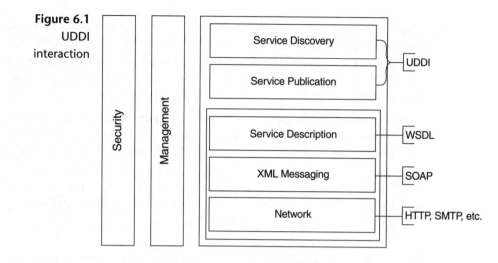

text of the registry in which it is contained. Businesses and services registered in multiple registries may be assigned different UUIDs.

3. Business applications, search engines, and intermediaries use UDDI registries to find services that satisfy the criteria they seek. They may search using any of the relevant classification schemes.

4. After a service has been found and bound, it can be executed by invoking the appropriate service interface.

Role of the UDDI Provider

UDDI is fundamental to a Web services infrastructure and provides the mechanism for organizing and managing services. The basic functions of a UDDI provider are advertising, discovery, and storage.

A UDDI provider provides a consistent way for businesses to advertise their services and make them available to others (advertising). Businesses and consumers need the ability to discover services contained in the registry (discovery). This information needs to persist the underlying XML and other resources (storage).

UDDI provides the plumbing, so each business does not have to re-create the infrastructure to support interoperability. This is where the principle of registries and repositories is formed. This common infrastructure supports metadata storage, schemas, programming interfaces, role-based authentication, and database connectivity, so a service can be located either programmatically or through human interaction, via Web pages.

UDDI is a registry that allows for registration of services, discovery of metadata, and classification of entities into predefined categories. It is not a repository, in that it does not have the ability to store XML resources such as WSDL or business process definitions that may be required to form trading agreements, nor does it present specify a security model. A repository is meant to store data, including XML documents, schemas, and other types, and supports extensive classification.

The term *registry*, when used in conjunction with Web services, means a shared resource between enterprises, accessible as a Web-based service, and the enabler of loosely coupled dynamic services. A registry can be thought of as a catalog of items, whereas a repository is the holder of items.

UDDI provides the ability to support maintenance of registry information through a set of administration pages. It is usually up to each UDDI provider to determine how to support security and registration to a UDDI registry. UDDI can be extended to support authentication using LDAP, Active Directory, or other custom credential stores.

Figures 6.2 through 6.6 are representative screen shots for registering Flute Bank in Microsoft's Test UDDI Registry.

Service Interfaces

A service interface is a published interface used to invoke a service. An interface can be implemented using any number of technologies, including WSDL, XML-RPC, COM+, CORBA (IDL), Java RMI, and others. A service interface can be described using multiple methods. A service can be described by using prose or a formal description language. In service-oriented architecture, the best approach

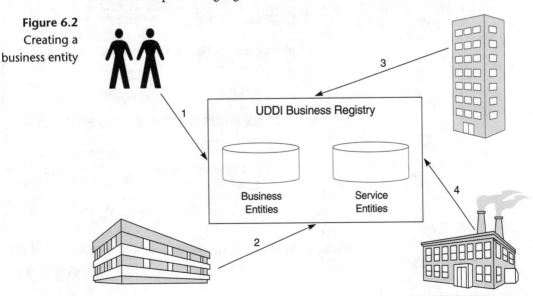

Figure 6.2
Creating a
business entity

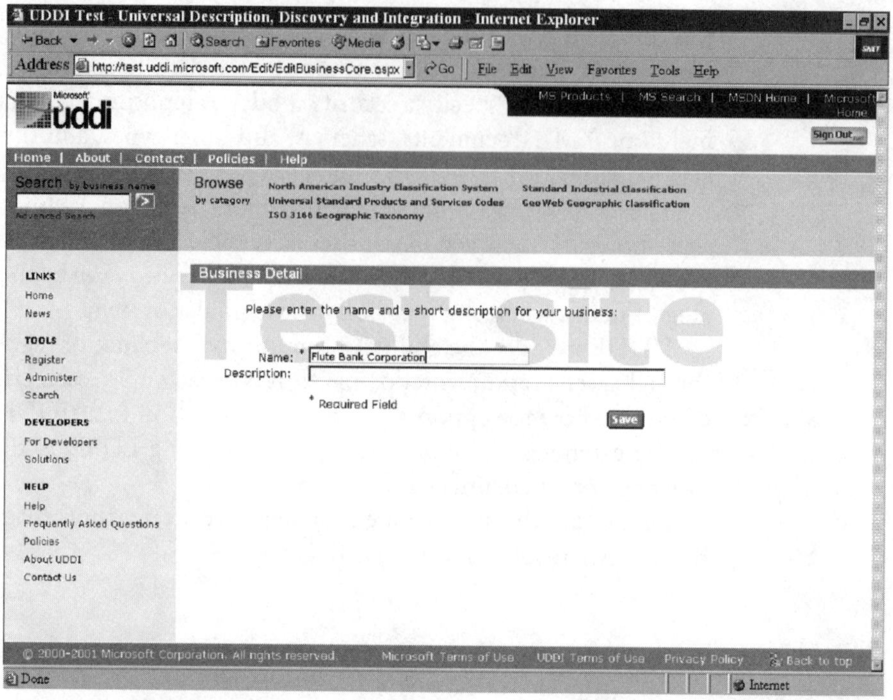

Figure 6.3
Details for the
business entity

Figure 6.4
Creating a
business service

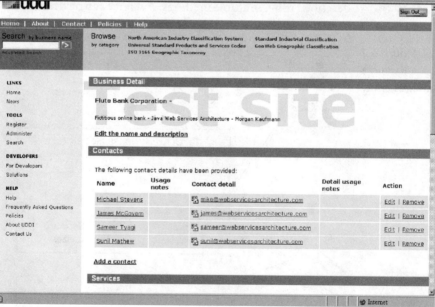

Figure 6.5
Creating a bind-
ing template

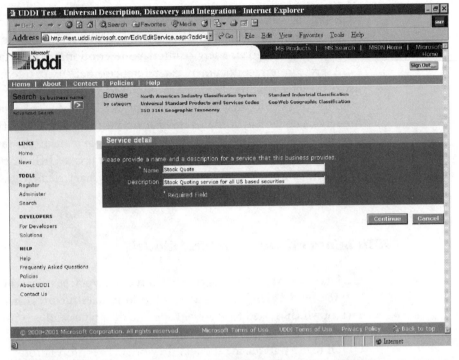

Figure 6.6
Creating a
tModel

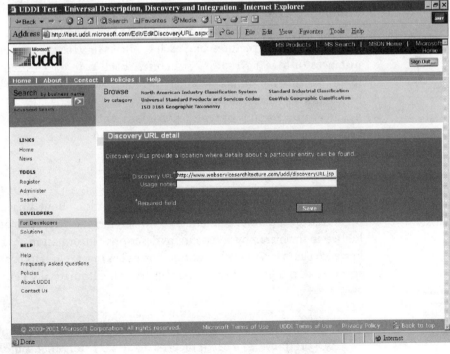

to describing services should be XML. There is merit in this approach for other forms of application development as well. In a Web services paradigm, interfaces are usually described via a service interface description language, usually WSDL.

A service interface document can reference other service interface documents using import elements. The service implementation document contains a description of a service that implements a service interface. The import element in the service document contains three attributes: namespace, location, and binding. The namespace attribute contains the URL that matches the targetNamespace in the document. The location attribute contains a URL that references the WSDL document. The binding attribute on the port element holds a reference to the binding in the document.

UDDI Informational Structural Model

UDDI contains four primary core data structure types: businessEntity, business-Service, bindingTemplate, and tModel. Additional structures can also be defined, each of which is used to represent specific data types and is organized in a relationship. For example, multiple distinct businesses can publish information in a UDDI registry about the services they offer. The information for each business and the services it offers exists as a separate instance of the core data structures within the UDDI registry.

Figure 6.7 shows that each businessEntity can contain one or more distinct businessService structures, and each businessService can contain one or more instances of bindingTemplate structures. Each core data structure is uniquely identifiable, based on uddiKeys. By default, each is publisher-assigned but can be extended so users can offer their own under challenge. Each keyed structure has an attribute that is of type Key: businessEntity has a businessKey attribute, businessService has a serviceKey attribute, and so on. ▷

businessEntity

The businessEntity structure contains information about a particular business organization and holds references to the services it offers. businessEntity is the highest in the hierarchy and contains descriptive information. As mentioned earlier, each businessEntity is identified by its businessKey. If its businessKey is not specified at publication time, the registry will automatically generate a key.

▷   UDDI provides many options for customization via extensions to cover. UDDI.org provides a best-practices document at *www.uddi.org*.

Figure 6.7
UDDI core data
structures

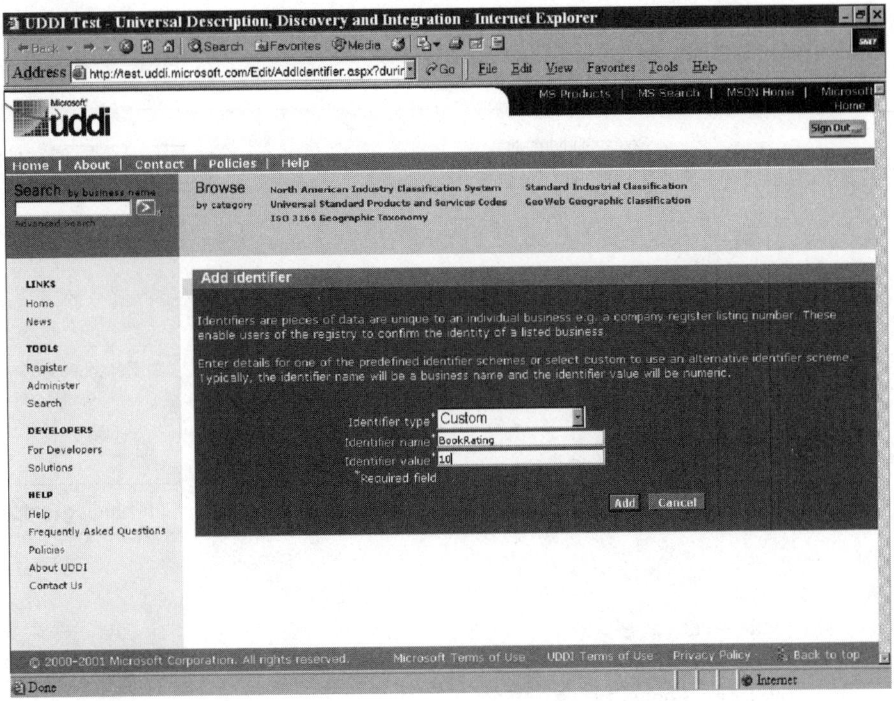

Figure 6.8 shows an example of a businessEntity and its relationship to other components of UDDI. Let us look a simple example of a businessEntity for Flute Bank:

```
<discoveryURL useType="businessEntity">
    http://www.flutebank.com?businessKey=uddi:flutebank.com:registry:support:22
</discoveryURL>
...
<contact useType="Technical support">
    <personName>Administrator</personName>
    <phone>868-555-1212</phone>
    <email>support@flutebank.com</email>
</contact>
...
<identifierBag>
    <keyedReference
        tModelKey="uddi:ubr.uddi.org:identifer:dnb.com:D-U-N-S"
        keyName="Flute Bank"
        keyValue="22-422-2232" />
</identifierBag>
...
```

Figure 6.8
`businessEntity`

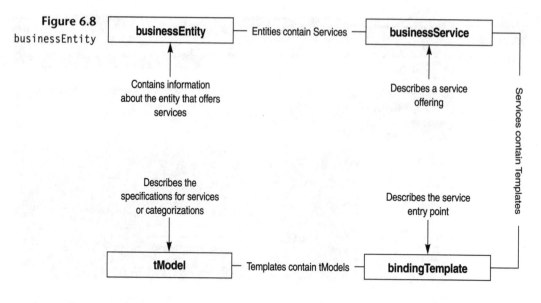

```
<categoryBag>
    <keyedReference
        tModelKey="uddi:ubr.uddi.org:categorization:geo3166-2"
        keyName="Connecticut, USA"
        keyValue="US-CT" />
</categoryBag>
```

In the above example, the businessEntity specifies basic information about Flute Bank, such as contact information, Dun & Bradstreet number, and location. We will drill deeper into each of the elements of a business entity throughout this chapter.

businessService

In UDDI, a businessService entry indicates a logical service and holds descriptive information about a Web service in business terms. A businessService is a child of a businessEntity that provides the service. Information about how a businessService can be instantiated is contained within a bindingTemplate.

Each businessService is has a unique identifier. This value is assigned by each UDDI operator and cannot be edited by the publisher. It also contains the key to its parent businessEntity. Let us look at an example:

```
<businessService businessKey="uuid:43CC32A4-4442B-2E4A-22318EAD5521"
 serviceKey="">
 <name>Flute Bank ATM Pin Service</name>
 <description>This service is used for Flute Bank customers to reset their ATM
                                                        PIN<description>
```

```
<bindingTemplates>
   ...
</bindingTemplates>
<categoryBag>
   <keyedReference
      <keyName="Flute Bank ATM Services"
       keyValue=54328910"
       tModelKey="UUID:DB44690D-9AF8-4D24-A9AD-04621E34E274"/>
 <</categoryBag>
</businessService>
```

Figures 6.9 and 6.10 show the elements of a businessEntity and business-Service. In both examples, name is required, but its description is optional. The bindingTemplate element is required and specifies technical information on various implementations of the service. We will expand on this later. The category bag is used similarly to businessService and allows for the service to be classified using multiple taxonomies.

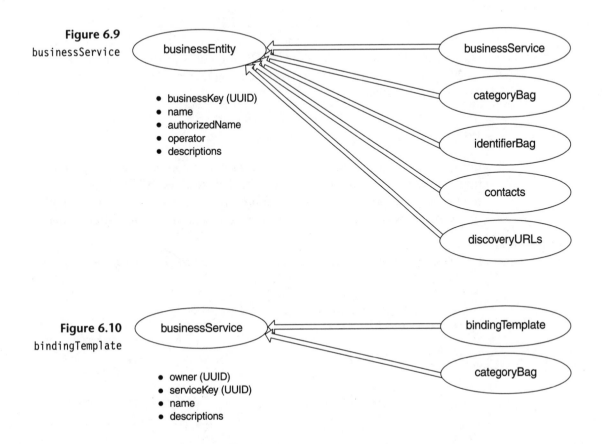

Figure 6.9
businessService

Figure 6.10
bindingTemplate

bindingTemplate

A bindingTemplate contains information necessary for a client to invoke a service. It specifies the information for a particular Web service and provides the URL of the service where it can be invoked. The bindingTemplate also contains references to tModels as well as service-specific settings. A bindingTemplate is a child of a businessService.

The key to a bindingTemplate is that it allows a service to expose what transports (e.g., bindings) it supports. A service can choose to support multiple binding protocols, including HTTP, HTTPS, SMTP, and so on. Let us look at an example of a bindingTemplate:

```
<bindingTemplates>
 <bindingTemplate bindingKey="" serviceKey=""
    <description>Flute ATM Service via HTTP</description>
    <accessPoint URLType="http">
       http://www.flutebank.com/services/accesspoint>
</bindingTemplates>
```

In the above example, the bindingTemplate specifies a URL for accessing Flute Bank's ATM service using the HTTP protocol. The accessPoint URLType specifies the actual protocol to be used. Valid values are mailto, http, https, ftp, fax, phone, and other.

tModel

Organizations require a mechanism to publish information about the specifications and their respective versions used for their services. WSDL is one of the service specifications that can use this approach. Since it is possible to have multiple revisions of a specification active at any time, a need arises to distinctly iden-

Figure 6.11
tModel

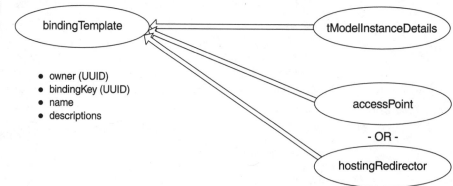

tify public specifications, and the specification in use needs to be discoverable. The information about the specification contains metadata and is called a tModel within UDDI (Figure 6.11).

tModels provide an approach that allows for reuse and standardization within a Web services framework. The concept behind tModels is useful for discovering information about services exposed for broad usage. Suppose OfficeMin purchased shopping cart/catalog software from Aspectsoft that lets customers purchase tax preparation software and cellular phones at discounted prices via the Web site. OfficeMin decides to advertise its new e-commerce site within a public UDDI registry.

Let us look at a scenario where tModels can be used. The OfficeMin Webmaster has decided to incorporate shopping cart software as part of the Web site. The software is Web service enabled and can use features of a UDDI registry. The software first contacts a UDDI registry, to determine shipping providers (UPS, FedEx, DHL, and Airborne) based on classification information. It also downloads shipping rate tables for all fifty states from each of the providers. The shopping cart also contacts the UDDI registry to determine tax information for each of the fifty states. Finally, the software uses the UDDI registry to locate several payment acceptance companies, to handle credit card acceptance.

The shopping cart was able to configure itself using tModels for:

- A list of the fifty states
- Shipping companies
- Tax tables
- Payment gateway providers
- Format information for valid credit cards

A tModel key can be thought of as a pointer to a service description. Many services will use a given domain value, such as state postal code abbreviations, zip codes, and classifications. This information is not duplicated for each individual service. Instead, a tModel key points to information about specifications via tModel entries and references. This approach has several advantages. For developers, tModels allow quick identification of compatible services, using a common point of reference. For software vendors and standards bodies, tModels provide the ability to quickly identify implementations of Web services compatible with that tModel.

tModels in Web services store the reference to WSDL in the UDDI. A tModel also contains metadata about the technical documents as well as an entity key that uniquely identifies the tModel. UDDI itself uses tModels within its own information model, to store metadata. Some of the UDDI tModels for internal usage are:

- Transport descriptions, such as HTTP, HTTPS, and SMTP (uddi-org:types)
- Postal address formats (tModels support one for each country as well as several for multilingual countries.)
- Categorization, identifiers, and namespaces (One identifier may be used to attach a tModel to an organization, such as an IRS Taxpayer Identification Number, as in the following example.)

```
<identifierBag>
    <keyedReference tModelKey="uddi:ubr.uddi.org:identifier:irs.gov.tt:TIN"
    keyName="Flute Bank"
    keyValue="868–668–921"
        </keyedReference>
</identifierBag>
```

To understand how tModels work, let us first look at the WSDL for the Flute Bank News Web service, shown in Listing 6.1.

Listing 6.1 Flute Bank News WSDL

```
<?xml version="1.0"?>
<definitions name="NewsService-interface"
  targetNamespace="http://www.flutebank.com/NewsService-interface"
  xmlns:tns="http://www.flutebank.com/NewsService-interface"
  xmlns:xsd=" http://www.w3.org/2001/XMLSchema "
  xmlns:soap="http://schemas.xmlsoap.org/wsdl/soap/"
  xmlns="http://schemas.xmlsoap.org/wsdl/">

  <message name="SymbolRequest">
  <part name="symbol" type="xsd:string"/>
  </message>

  <message name="SymbolResponse">
  <part name="news" type="xsd:string"/>
  </message>

  <portType name="NewsService">
  <operation name="getNews">
      <input message="tns:SymbolRequest"/>
      <output message="tns:SymbolResponse"/>
  </operation>
  </portType>
```

```
<binding name="SymbolBinding" type="tns:NewsService">
<soap:binding style="rpc" transport="http://schemas.xmlsoap.org/soap/http"/>
<operation name="getNews">
    <soap:operation soapAction="http://www.flutebank.com/GetNews"/>
<input>
<soap:body use="encoded" namespace="urn:symbol-news"
           encodingStyle="http://schemas.xmlsoap.org/soap/encoding/"/>
    </input>
    <output>
      <soap:body use="encoded" namespace="urn:symbol-news"
           encodingStyle="http://schemas.xmlsoap.org/soap/encoding/"/>
    </output>
   </operation>
  </binding>
</definitions>
```

When we publish the above WSDL, we will create the related UDDI tModel, shown in Listing 6.2.

Listing 6.2   UDDI tModel for Flute Bank News service

```
<?xml version="1.0"?>
<tModel tModelKey="">
  <name>http://www.flutebank.com/NewsService-interface</name>
  <description xml:lang="en">Service definition for Flute Bank News service.
                                                      </description>

  <overviewDoc>
  <description xml:lang="en">WSDL Service Interface Document</description>
  <overviewURL>http://www.flutebank.com/service/news-interface.wsdl#SymbolBinding
                                                      </overviewURL>
    </overviewDoc>
  <categoryBag>
    <keyedReference tModelKey="UUID:B1FAC26D-4569-4421-9E20-36A752A62ED4"
                 keyName="uddi-org:types" keyValue="wsdlSpec"/>
    <keyedReference tModelKey="UUID:DB44690D-9AF8-4D24-A9AD-04621E34E274"
                 keyName="Flute Bank News services"
                 keyValue="54328910"/>
  </categoryBag>
</tModel>
```

Note that the keyedReference points to the version of the WSDL specification the service uses. This allows a service to understand what type of WSDL it may receive. By using tModels, you can use UDDI to represent data and metadata about services, business entities, and other parties. The UDDI specification defines many commonly used tModels but creating your own may be worth considering for scenarios UDDI does not handle.

▷ Categorizing Services

One of the main purposes for using a registry is to maintain information about services and make it easy for clients to search for services. Having a registry without the proper taxonomic classification of data in it would not be ideal. If a client cannot quickly and efficiently discover appropriate services, UDDI becomes cumbersome to use.

Taxonomies can be used to categorize a service or other entities registered in a UDDI registry. Entities can be classified based on D-U-N-S, UN/SPC, SIC codes, or other schemes used to categorize businesses, industries, and their respective product categories. Additional classification schemes exist to specify geographic information or membership information for a specified organization. ▷

UDDI will allow a classification system to be used on every entity contained in the registry. It is generally recommended that all services be classified before being made publicly available. Whether you decide to use standard classification schemes or create your own taxonomy, it is vital that all UDDI data, such as businessEntity, businessService, bindingTemplate, and tModels, be given the appropriate classification.

UDDI inquiry APIs permit searching with different classification schemes. A query could contain criteria that use multiple classifications, such as industry codes, geographic codes, and business identification codes. This query will become an entry point to value-added search engines, such as AltaVista and Google. UDDI can also use the classification schemes optionally as validation checks. As an example, UDDI can make sure you specify a valid country code.

As part of the base specification, UDDI supports three canonical taxonomies that can be used for broad classification of businesses and the services they offer:

▷ Taxonomies are structured vocabularies that embody a relationship among terms and provide orderly classification of information. Simply, it provides a list of allowable terms or phrases.

- ISO 3166: geographic
- NAICS: industry
- UN/SPSC: products and services

UDDI registries can also provide their own additional classification schemes. Sometimes it may be necessary to define additional classification schemes for businesses and the services they offer. If you are classifying businesses for internal registries, you should create a new taxonomy that groups services by cost, quality of service, or other factors. In the Flute Bank scenario, they have decided to group all service providers into four classifications: platinum, gold, silver and regular. Flute Bank's policy is that all services offered by platinum providers must be used during market business hours. Platinum providers make their services available during business hours but also support after–business hours usage on a prioritized basis.

Many organizations have created their own internal classification schemes. This could include a preferred vendors list, preferred shipping providers, or a listing by criteria such as credit rating.

Consider the following scenario: Flute Bank decides to create a taxonomy for specifying quality of service for partners listed in its private UDDI registry. The bank determines it will use four domain values for quality of service: better, good, fair, and poor. Whenever the bank needs a particular quality of service, it will perform a taxonomy-based find operation and retrieve all business service entries that meet the requirement. To support the quality of service, Flute Bank creates a tModel and registers it in the UDDI registry. Listing 6.3 shows the XML message used to create the tModel.

Listing 6.3 Custom taxonomy

```
<save_tmodel generic="2.0" xmlns="urn:uddi-org:api_v2">
  <authInfo> ... </authInfo>
  <tModel tModelKey="">
      <name>Flute Bank Quality of Service Taxonomy</name>
      <description xml:lang="en">Flute Bank classification quality of service
                                                        </description>

      <overviewDoc>
         <overviewURL>
         http://www.flutebank.com/qos/browseQOS
         </overviewURL>
      </overviewDoc>
      <categoryBag>
          <keyReference
              keyName="Flute Bank categorization type"
```

```
                    keyValue="categorization"
                    tModelKey="UUID:B2CAF44D-2322-4333-9EF8-22D338F82AB1"/>
        </categoryBag>
    </tModel>
</save_tModel>
```

In Listing 6.3, suppliers can retrieve the tModel and use it to classify the businessServices they offer. Additionally, the registry can ensure that only specified values are used to indicate the quality of service offered. UDDI provides support for this through the validate_values API. By using a validated taxonomy, a supplier can assure that calls to the save_business, save_service, or save_tModel use only allowable values. If the validate_values API returns an error, the save_xxx API will fail.

The UDDI registry that needs to validate the quality of service values would send a validate_values message to the service registered to provide validation. The validate_values message would look similar to this:

```
<validate_values generic="2.0" xmlns="urn:uddi-org:api_v2">
    <businessService/> ... | <tModel/> ...
<validate_values>
```

Flute Bank and its validate_values service takes this message and looks for key values contained in the keyedReference element and obtains a reference to its tModelKey. It then does a lookup against all valid quality of service values to ensure validity. The Flute Bank validate_values service will ignore other information in the message.

Whenever an organization decides to create its own classification scheme, it may also decide that relationships exist between single categories. In Listing 6.3, we used categoryBags to classify quality of service. Flute Bank might want to indicate that it sells insurance products only in the United States. The categoryBags can be extended to contain keyedReferenceGroups that can contain a list of keyedReferences. Let us look at how Flute Bank can indicate its insurance products are available only in the United States:

Listing 6.4 Category grouping

```
<businessEntity businessKey="uddi:flutebank.example">
    ...
    <keyReferenceGroup
        tModelKey=
            "uddi:ubr.uddi.org:categorizationGroup:unspsc_geo3166">
```

```
    <keyedReference
        tModelKey="uddi:ubr.uddi.org:categorization:unspsc"
        keyName="UNSPSC: Insurance Products"
        keyValue="22.00.00.00.00"/>
    <keyedReference
        tModelKey="uddi:ubr.uddi.org:categorization:geo3166-2"
        keyName="GEO:United States"
        keyValue="US"/>
  </keyedReferenceGroup>
  ...
</businessEntity>
```

Listing 6.4 shows a key of "uddi:ubr.uddi.org:categorizationGroup:unspsc_ geo3166" that corresponds to category systems for UNSPSC and ISO 3166. The keyedReferenceGroup uses a tModel that describes the countries in which the product category is sold. As we can see, categorization can happen based on pre-defined classification systems or internal schemes. Classification can also be extended to support specific geographic coordinates of where the business is located and/or the services offered. Let us look at one final example of how Flute Bank can indicate where it is located, based on the World Geodetic System: ▷

Listing 6.5 businessEntity that uses categorization

```
<businessKey businessKey="uddi:flutebank.example">
    <categoryBag>
        <keyedReferenceGroup
            tModelKey="uddi:ubr.uddi.org:categorizationGroup:wgs84">
            <keyedReference
                tModelKey=
                    "uddi:ubr.uddi.org:categorization:wgs84:latitude"
                keyName="WGS 84 Latitude"
                keyValue="+41.831647"/>
            <keyedReference
                tModelKey=
                    "uddi:ubr.uddi.org:categorization:wgs84:longitude"
                keyName="WGS 84 Longitude"
                keyValue="+72.72493"/>
            <KeyedReference
                tModelKey=
```

> ▷ The world geodetic system is a classification system that specifies the longitude and latitude for a given location.

```
                    "uddi:ubr.uddi.org:categorization:geo_precision"
                keyName="Center of Street"
                keyValue="0900"/>
        </keyedReferenceGroup>
      </categoryBag>
    </businessEntity>
```

Listing 6.5 shows that Flute Bank is physically located at latitude 41.831647 and longitude 72.72493, with its position calculated based on the center of the street on which it is located.

> Identifiers

UDDI registration information has the ability to mark entities with identifiers. The primary purpose for using identifiers in the UDDI registry is to uniquely identify a business based on known schemes. Usually, identifiers are attached to either business entities and/or tModels (Table 6.1). Businesses may be registered and located based upon formal identifiers, such as their D-U-N-S number, government-issued tax number, or, if they are a public company, their stock-exchange symbol.

Private UDDI registries may also support this feature and use private identifiers. If the private UDDI registry is used in a private exchange, supplier identifiers

Table 6.1   Business Entity Identifiers

Property	Description
http.proxyHost	The hostname of the network proxy server.
http.proxyPort	The port number used by the network proxy server. This defaults to port 80.
https.proxyHost	The hostname of the network proxy server that supports SSL. This is usually the same server as HTTP.
https.proxyPort	The port number used by the network proxy server for SSL. This defaults to port 443.
socksProxy.Host	The hostname of the network proxy server that supports Socks based proxies.
socksProxy.Port	The port number used by the network proxy server.

known only to the private exchange community may be used to uniquely identify a business. Many identifiers are not immediately recognizable as such. One example might be "00–910–2001." However, once it is determined that this identifier is really a D-U-N-S number, it becomes obvious that the identifier represents a business. UDDI groups all identifiers in the registry with the identifier system, so they appear as follows: D-U-N-S Number, 00–910–2001."

UDDI allows identifiers to be attached to businessEntity and tModel structures. UDDI provides a placeholder that will allow an arbitrary number of identifiers to be attached to an entry.

Listing 6.5, the businessEntity entry for Flute Bank, specifies three identifiers in its identifierBag. Any of the three identifiers can be used in a find_business API call to locate the businessEntity in the registry. For clients who want to figure out the types of services a business offers, it is practical to search using a business identifier. Let us look at an example of Flute Bank's businessEntity, its identifierBag, and how it supports identities:

```
<businessEntity businessKey="uddi:flutebank.example">
...
  <identifierBag>
      <keyedReference
          tModelKey="uddi:ubr.uddi.org:identifier:dnb.com:D-U-N-S"
          keyName="D-U-N-S:Flute Bank Corporation"
          keyValue="00–910–2001"/>
  </identifierBag>
...
</businessEntity>
```

The identifierBag is established using three attributes of keyedReference. The tModelKey uniquely identifies the tModel that represents the identifier system. The keyName is the human-readable form of the identifier system. The keyValue is the unique identifier assigned to the business entity by the specified identifier system.

As previously mentioned, identifier systems can be discovered using the find_tModel API that looks like this:

```
<?xml version="1.0"?>
<find_tModel generic="1.0" xmlns="urn:uddi-org:api">
   <categoryBag>
      <keyedReference tModelKey="UUID:C1BBA22D-2321–2221–94D1–23B5AA42AA4"
         keyName="uddi-org:types" keyVale="wsdlSpec"/>
   </categoryBag>
</find_tModel>
```

▷ Business Entity Relationships

Large organizations need the ability to register multiple businessEntity entries yet maintain relationships amongst them. In the Flute Bank scenario, since it has a banking division regulated by the Federal Deposit Insurance Corporation (FDIC), an investment division regulated by the Securities and Exchange Commission (SEC), and an insurance division regulated by the states in which Flute Bank does business, Flute would like to register each of its subcompanies as separate business entities.

UDDI provides a find_relatedBusinesses API that allows users to view registered relationships. For relationships to be valid, each businessEntity owner must acknowledge the relationship. This prevents one business from creating misleading entries to indicate that it is related to another business when it really is not. Business entity relationships can also be useful for modeling an organization and its divisional/departmental structures.

Using the save_business API, Flute Bank can create several businessEntity entries in the UDDI registry. They would also use the add_publisherAssertion APIs, so the relationships between the bank's divisions would appear valid. Listing 6.6 shows what the add_publisherAssertions would look like.

Listing 6.6   Publisher assertions

```
<add_publisherAssertions generic="2.0" xmlns="urn:uddi-org:api_v2" >
  <authInfo> ... </authInfo>
  <publisherAssertion>
      <!--Business Key for Flute Bank Corporation.-->
      <fromKey>CBC2A349-A4C1-22D4-AE87-BC8713D2BD9</fromKey>
      <!--Business Key for Flute Bank and Trust.-->
      <toKey>CEE2A349-D4C1-23D4-AE87-BC8453D2B39</toKey>
      <keyedReference
         tModelKey="uuid:716B3D7B-FF33-470D-BCD5-B2425B529D02"
         keyValue="parent-child"/>
  </publisherAssertion>

  <publisherAssertion>
      <!--Business Key for Flute Bank Corporation.-->
      <fromKey>CBC2A349-A4C1-22D4-AE87-BC8713D2BD9</fromKey>
      <!--Business Key for Flute Bank Investments-->
      <toKey>CDE2A432-DEC1-22D4-AE87-BC8453D2E39</toKey>
```

```
    <keyedReference
        tModelKey="uuid:716B3D7B-FF33-470D-BCD5-B2425B529D02"
        keyValue="parent-child"/>
</publisherAssertion>

<publisherAssertion>
    <!--Business Key for Flute Bank Corporation.-->
    <fromKey>CBC2A349-A4C1-22D4-AE87-BC8713D2BD9</fromKey>
    <!--Business Key for Flute Bank Insurance-->
    <toKey>BEA2A319-D5C1-67D4-AE87-BC8411D2B39</toKey>
    <keyedReference
                        tModelKey="uuid:716B3D7B-FF33-470D-BCD5-B2425B529D02"
                        keyValue="parent-child"/>
</publisherAssertion>
<!--Have to also do other side of assertions-->
</add_publisherAssertions>
```

UDDI has the ability to also notify businessEntities whenever someone attempts to create an assertion through the get_assertionsStatusReport. The keyedReference in the example is a special type of tModel and can hold three possible values:

- parent-child indicates that the businessEntity indicated in the toKey is the child of the businessEntity specified in the fromKey.

- peer-peer indicates that the businessEntities in the fromKey and toKey are peers.

- identity refers to two businessEntities that are the same organization.

▶ UDDI's SOAP Interfaces

UDDI provides an API that allows for the discovery of businesses, the services they offer, and technical binding information, using a request/response approach. UDDI also supports the registration of business entities, services, bindingTemplates, and tModels. Two types of APIs are available. The first is a Publishers API, which is used for interaction between applications and the UDDI registry and provides the ability to create, modify, and delete data contained in the registry. The second is an Inquiry API, which allows applications to query the registry for information.

The Inquiry API provides three patterns that can be used to query a registry: the browse, drill-down, and invocation patterns.

Browse Pattern

The browse pattern allows users to provide general search criteria, generate a result set, then select one or more of the entries in the result set and drill down into specific entries. In UDDI, a browsing scenario may be to search for information on a particular business you know about to see if it is registered. Maybe you want to search a public UDDI registry to see what services Flute Bank has available to the public. The result set will contain overview information, such as the businessEntities that match the search criteria that were found using the find_ business API.

If you find that the Flute Bank result set returns thousands of services, you can drill deeper into the businessService information, seeking particular categories of services (e.g., investments, loans, calculators, etc.) using the find_service API call. If you happen to know the tModel signature of a product, such as news version 1.2.a1.06, and you want to see if Flute Bank has a compatible service interface, you can use the find_binding API.

Drill-Down Pattern

UDDI uses the drill-down pattern to locate entities. For example, if you wanted to locate a binding template (get_bindingDetail), you would start your search by locating the appropriate business entity (find_business). From the business entity, you would use the entity's UUID to search for services the entity provides (find_service). If you happen to know the business service's UUID, you can use the find_binding API to locate binding templates for a business service.

When searching for compatible service interfaces using the find_binding API, you could take the returned service key and pass it to get_serviceDetail to learn additional information about the service.

This pattern is typically used through the UDDI Web interface, in which you can click the "find service" action usually displayed as part of finding the appropriate business. The find service will execute in the context of a particular business entity. Likewise, the Web interface allows you to drill deeper, locating entities within the current context as you navigate the registry.

Invocation Pattern

Before Web Services, a typical software development approach for developing cross-application access was to define the interfaces in two locations. In many languages, it could also require copying stub code to various locations. In a Web services paradigm, services can be discovered dynamically and do not require stub code on the client. Instead, a client will search for particular service information and seek its bindingTemplate that contains instance-specific information for the service.

The J2EE blueprints (available at *http://java.sun.com/j2ee/blueprints*) mention the use of the Service Locator pattern. If we take the best practices and extend them to Web services, we would modify the Service Locator pattern and use an invocation pattern. Ideally, upon querying the UDDI registry for service information, the service locator could cache the bindingTemplate and bindingKey information.

Upon a failed invocation of a service, the invocation pattern could take the cached bindingKey, call the get_bindingDetails API, and get a new binding-Template. If the bindingTemplate that is returned is different, the invocation pattern can automatically retry invocation of the service and should update the cache. Using the invocation pattern in this manner allows services to become portable, survive migrations by their service provider in situations such as disaster recovery, and provide high availability. By using the invocation pattern, callers of the service automatically locate new service information without administrative intervention. Caching also helps in optimizing the service environment, by reducing unnecessary round trips to locate services and binding information in the UDDI registry.

The invocation pattern can be extended to support other situations where the basic approach will not suffice. The first scenario that breaks in a Web services paradigm using the invocation pattern is when either an application service provider or network market maker needs to control the values of the binding information.

In the Flute Bank scenario and its order execution system, Flute typically sends information about a particular order to the floor of the New York Stock Exchange. When the floor executes the trade, the exchange may decide to direct Flute to the Web service of the selling broker, to handle the clearing process. In addition, when the stock market is open, Flute always sends orders to the floor. However, when the market is closed, Flute has the desire to be directed to an electronic communication network (ECN), a facility that matches customer buy and sell orders directly through a computer, that currently has the best price to execute an after-hours trade. In scenarios where routing may be based on the time of day or identity of the caller, using retry logic and caching is not sufficient.

hostingRedirector

One of the benefits of using UDDI in service-oriented architecture is to provide a single point of reference to determine a particular service's location. When the bindingTemplate needs to be controlled by another server in scenarios of routing logic, disaster recovery, or a change of invocation address, you may need to use the accessPoint information in the bindingTemplate structure (provided you have it cached) to determine an alternative partner service.

Figure 6.12 shows the relationships of a bindingTemplate to other UDDI models. The bindingTemplate contains an element named hostingRedirector. An implementation of the invocation pattern inspects the hostingRedirector element, which points to another bindingTemplate that points to the address of a redirector service that will fulfill a get_bindingDetail message.

> UDDI and SOAP/WSDL Relationships

As you are aware, XML is a cross-platform approach to data encoding and can be used for data exchange between different applications in a self-describing manner. The SOAP specification enables one application to invoke the service interface of a service without the requirement of having both applications either written in the same language or using a distributed object infrastructure, such as COM or CORBA. SOAP is one solution to the interoperability problem, in that it uses a layered approach (Figure 6.13). SOAP is built on top of XML.

Using XML and SOAP are good first steps, but there are many gaps. When one asks the question "What do I require to have a standards–based, end-to-end

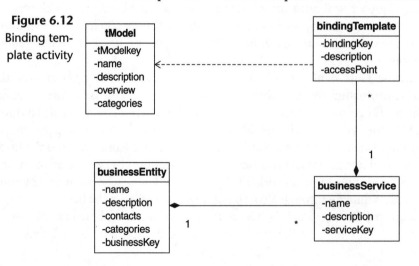

Figure 6.12
Binding template activity

Figure 6.13
UDDI inter-
operability

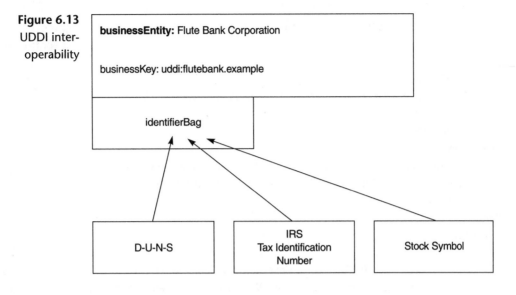

solution supported on every computing platform?" the answer becomes clear that we need additional solutions. UDDI borrows on the best practices and thoughts of XML and SOAP by defining the next layer, then enables organizations to share a mechanism to query each other's services as well as describe their own.

A UDDI business registry is accessed via SOAP. A registered service can expose any type of service interface. UDDI allows for the registration of services regardless of the type of service description means, including, but not limited to, WSDL. A service can be described via ASCII, RosettaNet, or other description approaches. Ideally, one should wherever possible use WSDL to describe the service. The primary reason for storing WSDL in UDDI is so clients can easily discover the location of the WSDL document and optionally programmatically generate a proxy to the service.

Consider the following example: Flute Bank has decided it wants to publish its news service WSDL in UDDI. It has decided to break down the news service into two separate files. The first file contains the service interface definition and exposes it at *www.flutebank.com/services/newsInterface.wsdl*. Flute will also create a tModel that references the service interface definition. The second file contains the service implementation definition and exposes it at */www.flutebank.com/services/news.wsdl*. Let us look at the SOAP message for save_service API:

```
<save_tModel generic="2.0" xmlns="urn:uddi-org:api">
  <authInfo> ... </authInfo>
  <tModel>
    <name>Flute Bank News Service Interface Definition</name>
```

```
       <description>This is the service interface definition for the news service
                                                     </description>
       <overviewDoc>
          <overviewURL>
             http://www.flutebank.com/services/newsInterface.wsdl
          </overviewURL>
       </overviewDoc>
       <categoryBag>
          <keyedReference keyName="uddi.org:types" keyValue="wsdlSpec"
             tModelKey="UUID:C1BBBA26D-9762-4344-9370-22B756E62AB4"/>
       </categoryBag>
    </tModel>
</save_tModel>
```

The tModel contains an overviewURL element that points to the location of the service interface definition (WSDL). The keyedReference element specifies its categorization as a WSDL specification document. A WSDL/UDDI-aware tool can search for this specific tModel and generate the appropriate proxy to the service.

Now that Flute Bank has generated the tModel for the news service interface, it may also want to specify that the news service businessService entity uses this tModel. The save_service API will generate the following XML:

```
<save_service generic="2.0" xmlns="urn:uddi.org:api">
   <authInfo> ... </authInfo>
   <businessService>
     <name>Flute Bank News Service</name>
     <description>This service uses the News service interface definition</description>
     <bindingTemplates><bindingTemplate>
        <description>Reference the service interface definition</description>
        <accessPoint URLType="http">www.flutebank.com/services/news</accessPoint>
        <tModelInstanceDetails>
           <tModelInstanceInfo
              tModelKey="UUID:43E24422-3E2A-11D8-222B-BAD69F5ABC12">
              <instanceDetails>
                 <overviewDoc>
                    <description>Points to service implementation WSDL</description>
                    <overviewURL>
                       www.flutebank.com/services/news.wsdl
```

```
            </overviewURL>
          </overviewDoc>
        </instanceDetails>
      </tModelInstanceInfo>
    </tModelInstanceDetails>
  </bindingTemplate></bindingTemplates>
  </businessService>
</save_service>
```

A Web service specifies the location of a service within its service implementation file (WSDL). However, our scenario specifies the URL in which the service can be invoked by using the accessPoint element. This approach provides several advantages. First, it allows for Flute Bank to move the service location without having to update the UDDI businessService entity. Second, clients receive the latest copy of the WSDL document and does not have to wait for it to replicate to all instances of a UDDI registry upon publication in a replicated environment. ▷

There are many other scenarios in which you will want to integrate WSDL into UDDI, including

- A service implementation that contains multiple service interface documents
- A service interface that references another service interface
- A service interface provider that is the same as the service provider

A service implementation may decide to implement more than one service interface definition. In this scenario, the service implementation document WSDL will contain references to all the service interface documents. For example, the Flute Bank news service will support two different service interfaces. The first supports passing in a single stock symbol to retrieve news for the company. The second allows multiple symbols to be passed in to retrieve news. The supporting interface contains a different namespace and binding.

Listing 6.7 shows the WSDL service interface for the single news service.

▷   UDDI.org publishes a best-practices document at *www.uddi.org/bestpractices .html* that should be read by anyone wanting to publish WSDL in a UDDI registry.

Listing 6.7   First WSDL document: allows a single symbol to be passed

```xml
<?xml version="1.0"?>
<definitions name="NewsService-SingleSymbol-interface"
  targetNamespace="http://www.flutebank.com/NewsService-SingleSymbol-interface"
  xmlns:tns="http://www.flutebank.com/NewsService-SingleSymbol-interface"
  xmlns:xsd=" http://www.w3.org/2001/XMLSchema "
  xmlns:soap="http://schemas.xmlsoap.org/wsdl/soap/"
  xmlns:soapenc="http://schemas.xmlsoap.org/soap/encoding/"
  xmlns="http://schemas.xmlsoap.org/wsdl/">

<documentation>
  Service interface definition for the Flute Bank News service
  Accepts a single symbol
</documentation>

<message name="SingleSymbolRequest">
  <part name="symbol" type="xsd:string"/>
</message>

<message name="SingleSymbolNewsResponse">
  <part name="news" type="xsd:string"/>
</message>

<portType name="SingleSymbolNewsService">
  <operation name="getNews">
    <input message="tns:SingleSymbolRequest"/>
    <output message="tns:SingleSymbolNewsResponse"/>
  </operation>
</portType>

<binding name="SingleSymbolBinding"
        type="tns:SingleSymbolNewsService">
  <soap:binding style="rpc"
                transport="http://schemas.xmlsoap.org/soap/http"/>
  <operation name="getNews">
    <soap:operation soapAction="http://www.flutebank.com/GetNews"/>
    <input>
      <soap:body use="encoded"
          namespace="urn:single-symbol-news"
          encodingStyle="http://schemas.xmlsoap.org/soap/encoding/"/>
    </input>
```

```
    <output>
      <soap:body use="encoded"
          namespace="urn:single-symbol-news"
          encodingStyle="http://schemas.xmlsoap.org/soap/encoding/"/>
      </output>
    </operation>
  </binding>
</definitions>
```

Listing 6.8 shows the second WSDL service interface that allows for retrieving multiple news items based on passing multiple ticker symbols.

Listing 6.8   Second WSDL document: allows multiple symbols to be passed

```
<?xml version="1.0"?>
<definitions name="NewsService-MultiSymbol-interface"
  targetNamespace="http://www.flutebank.com/NewsService-MultiSymbol-interface"
  xmlns:tns="http://www.flutebank.com/NewsService-MultiSymbol-interface"
  xmlns:xsd=" http://www.w3.org/2001/XMLSchema "
  xmlns:xsd1="http://http://www.flutebank.com/NewsService/schema"
  xmlns:soap="http://schemas.xmlsoap.org/wsdl/soap/"
  xmlns:soapenc="http://schemas.xmlsoap.org/soap/encoding/"
  xmlns="http://schemas.xmlsoap.org/wsdl/">


<documentation>
  Service interface definition for the Flute Bank News service
  Accepts multiple symbols
</documentation>


<types>
  <schema targetNamespace="http://www.flutebank.com/NewsService/schema"
    xmlns="http://www.w3.org/2001/XMLSchema"
    xmlns:wsdl="http://schemas.xmlsoap.org/wsdl/">
    <complexType name="ArrayOfString">
      <complexContent>
        <restriction base="soapenc:Array">
          <attribute ref=soapenc:arrayType
                    wsdl:arrayType="xsd:string[]"/>
        </restriction>
      </complexContent>
    </compextType>
```

```
    </schemas>
</types>

<message name="MultiSymbolRequest">
  <part name="symbols" type="xsd1:ArrayOfString"/>
</message>
<message name="MultiSymbolNewsResponse">
  <part name="news" type="xsd1:ArrayOfString"/>
</message>

<portType name="MultiSymbolNewsService">
  <operation name="getNews">
    <input message="tns:MultiSymbolRequest"/>
    <output message="tns:MultiSymbolNewsResponse"/>
  </operation>
</portType>

<binding name="MultiSymbolBinding"
         type="tns:MultiSymbolNewsService">
  <soap:binding style="rpc"
                transport="http://schemas.xmlsoap.org/soap/http"/>
  <operation name="getNews">
    <soap:operation soapAction="http://www.flutebank.com/GetNews"/>
    <input>
      <soap:body use="encoded"
          namespace="urn:multi-symbol-news"
          encodingStyle="http://schemas.xmlsoap.org/soap/encoding/"/>
    </input>
    <output>
      <soap:body use="encoded"
          namespace="urn:multi-symbol-news"
          encodingStyle="http://schemas.xmlsoap.org/soap/encoding/"/>
    </output>
  </operation>
</binding>
```

Listings 6.7 and 6.8 show two distinct WSDL documents that contain a different message, port, and binding specification for the same service. In this scenario, they will be published in a UDDI registry using distinct tModels. Note that each service interface has only a single binding. This allows the overviewURL to be generic rather than requiring it to reference a specific binding.

Listings 6.9 and 6.10 show the tModels that will be published for each WSDL document.

Listing 6.9   UDDI tModel that corresponds to a single-symbol WSDL document

```
<?xml version="1.0"?>
<tModel tModelKey="">
  <name>http://www.flutebank.com/NewsService-SingleSymbol-interface</name>
  <description xml:lang="en">
    Service interface definition for the Flute Bank News service
    Accepts a single symbol
  </description>

  <overviewDoc>
    <description xml:lang="en">
      WSDL Service Interface Document
    </description>

  <overviewURL>
    http://www.flutebank.com/services/NEWS-SingleSymbol-interface.wsdl
  </overviewURL>
</overviewDoc>

<categoryBag>
  <keyedReference tModelKey="UUID:C1ACF26D-9672-4404-9D70-39B756E62AB4"
                  keyName="uddi-org:types" keyValue="wsdlSpec"/>
  <keyedReference tModelKey="UUID:BB22457D-9AF8-4D54-AB7C-033A2A122E87"
                  keyName="flute bank News services"
                  keyValue="90210801"/>
  </categoryBag>
</tModel>
```

Listing 6.10   UDDI tModel that corresponds to a multiple-symbol WSDL document

```
<?xml version="1.0"?>
<tModel tModelKey="">
  <name>http://www.flutebank.com/NewsService-MultiSymbol-interface</name>

  <description xml:lang="en">
    Service interface definition for the Flute Bank News service
    Accepts multiple symbols
  </description>
```

```
<overviewDoc>
  <description xml:lang="en">
    WSDL Service Interface Document
  </description>
  <overviewURL>
    http://www.flutebank.com/services/NEWS-MultiSymbol-interface.wsdl
  </overviewURL>
</overviewDoc>

<categoryBag>
  <keyedReference tModelKey="UUID:C1ACF26D-9672-4404-9D70-39B756E62AB4"
                  keyName="uddi-org:types" keyValue="wsdlSpec"/>
  <keyedReference tModelKey="UUID:BB22457D-9AF8-4D54-AB7C-033A2A122E87"
                  keyName="Flute Bank News services"
                  keyValue="90210801"/>
</categoryBag>
</tModel>
```

Note that the WSDL service implementation document will contain two import elements, each of which references one of the service interface documents. Listing 6.11 shows the WSDL for the service implementation document.

Listing 6.11 WSDL service implementation

```
<definitions name="NewsService"
  targetNamespace="http://www.flutebank.com/NewsService"
  xmlns:single="http://www.flutebank.com/NewsService-SingleSymbol-interface"
  xmlns:mult="http://www.flutebank.com/NewsService-MultiSymbol-interface"
  xmlns:xsd="http://www.w3.org/2001/XMLSchema"
  xmlns:soap="http://schemas.xmlsoap.org/wsdl/soap/"
  xmlns="http://schemas.xmlsoap.org/wsdl/">

  <import
     namespace="http://www.flutebank.com/NewsService-SingleSymbol-interface"
     location="http://www.flutebank.com/wsdl/NEWS-SingleSymbol-interface.wsdl"/>

  <import
     namespace="http://www.flutebank.com/Newservice-MultiSymbol-interface"
     location="http://www.flutebank.com/wsdl/NEWS-MultSymbol-interface.wsdl"/>

  <service name="NewsService">
    <documentation>Flute Bank News Service</documentation>
```

```
    <port name="SingleSymbolService"
        binding="single:SingleSymbolBinding">
        <soap:address location="http://www.flutebank.com/newsservice"/>
    </port>

  <port name="MultiSymbolService"
      binding="mult:MultSymbolBinding">
      <soap:address location="http://www.flutebank.com/newsservice"/>
  </port>
  </service>
</definitions>
```

As you can tell, the WSDL service implementation uses the same port to support both single and multiple symbols quotes. Sometimes it is useful to have a service interface that references another service interface. This can be used by other service interface providers to specify their own bindings for the service interface. Listing 6.12 is an example.

Listing 6.12 Service interface that references another service interface

```
<?xml version="1.0"?>
<definitions name="NewsService-interface"
  targetNamespace="http://www.flutebank.com/NewsService-interface"
  xmlns:tns="http://www.flutebank.com/NewsService-interface"
  xmlns:xsd=" http://www.w3.org/2001/XMLSchema "
  xmlns:soap="http://schemas.xmlsoap.org/wsdl/soap/"
  xmlns="http://schemas.xmlsoap.org/wsdl/">

  <documentation>
    Service interface definition for the Flute Bank News service
    without bindings
  </documentation>

  <message name="SingleSymbolRequest">
    <part name="symbol" type="xsd:string"/>
  </message>

  <message name="SingleSymbolNewsResponse">
    <part name="news" type="xsd:string"/>
  </message>

  <portType name="SingleSymbolNewsService">
```

```
      <operation name="getNews">
        <input message="tns:SingleSymbolRequest"/>
        <output message="tns:SingleSymbolNewsResponse"/>
      </operation>
    </portType>
</definitions>
```

In Listing 6.12, the service interface alone contains the bindings that can be published in the registry as a tModel. The WSDL service interface document contains the types, message, and portType elements. These cannot be published in UDDI, because a UDDI tModel can point only to a WSDL service interface that contains at least one binding element.

Listing 6.13   WSDL service bindings

```
<?xml version="1.0"?>
<definitions name="NewsService-binding"
  targetNamespace="http://www.flutebank.com/NewsService-binding"
  xmlns:interface="http://www.flutebank.com/NewsService-interface"
  xmlns:xsd=" http://www.w3.org/2001/XMLSchema "
  xmlns:soap="http://schemas.xmlsoap.org/wsdl/soap/"
  xmlns="http://schemas.xmlsoap.org/wsdl/">

  <documentation>
    Service interface definition for the Flute Bank News service
  </documentation>

  <import namespace="http://www.flutebank.com/NewsService-interface/"
          location="http://www.flutebank.com/News-interface.wsdl">
  <binding name="SingleSymbolBinding"
           type="interface:SingleSymbolNewsService">
    <soap:binding style="rpc"
           transport="http://schemas.xmlsoap.org/soap/http"/>
    <operation name="getNews">
      <soap:operation soapAction="http://www.flutebank.com/GetNews"/>
      <input>
        <soap:body use="encoded"
          namespace="urn:single-symbol-news"
          encodingStyle="http://schemas.xmlsoap.org/soap/encoding/"/>
      </input>
      <output>
```

```
    <soap:body use="encoded"
        namespace="urn:single-symbol-news"
        encodingStyle="http://schemas.xmlsoap.org/soap/encoding/"/>
    </output>
  </operation>
 </binding>
</definitions>
```

The service bindings can be published as a tModel and will point to the WSDL service interface document that contains the binding definitions, as in Listing 6.13. A client will use the document to retrieve the service interface that contains the binding definitions. Tools that understand WSDL need the ability to follow an import chain. ▷

▷ Publishing WSDL Service Interfaces in UDDI

The ability to publish services in a UDDI registry requires the application used to publish the service interface definitions to understand WSDL. WSDL4J is one mechanism that allows an application to read and interpret WSDL documents and optionally create new ones programmatically.

Let us start by looking at the steps necessary to publish a WSDL service interface in UDDI. As we have previously learned, WSDL service interfaces are represented as UDDI tModels. The first step is to actually read the WSDL document. For illustrative purposes, we will demonstrate the steps using WSDL4J APIs.

```
// Read the WSDL service interface document
Definition definition = WSDLReader.readWSDL(null, wsdlURL);

// Create a new tModel to be used to map the WSDL service interface
Tmodel tModel = new tModel();
```

Next, we will specify a target namespace for the tModel as well as set the tModel description, which is optional. We will obtain the description from WSDL.

```
tModel.setName(definition.getTargetNamespace());
Element element = definition.getDocumentationElement();
```

▷   One tool that supports this capability is WSDL4J, available at www-124. ibm.com/developerworks/projects/wsdl4j/

```
String description = DOMUtils.getChildCharacterData(element);
tModel.setDefaultDescriptionString(description);
```

Now, we will create the overviewDoc. As you may remember, it contains an overviewURL that points to the location of the WSDL document:

```
OverviewDoc overviewDoc = new OverviewDoc();
OverviewURL overviewURL = new OverviewURL(wsdlURL);
tModel.setOverviewDoc(overviewDoc);
```

Remember that a tModel can point to multiple things, so in this case, we need to make sure it references a WSDL service description. We will create a categoryBag and place two keyedReferences in it. The first will contain the service description, and the second will specify the service's business description.

```
CategoryBag categoryBag  = new CategoryBag();
Vector keyedReferenceList = new Vector();

KeyedReference keyedReference = new KeyedReference("uddi-org:types", "wsdlSpec");
KeyedReference.setTModelKey("UUID:B1FAC26D-4569–4421–9E20–36A752A62ED4");
KeyedReferenceList.add(keyedReference);

KeyedReference = new KeyedReference("Flute Bank News Service", "54328910");
KeyedReference.setTModelKey("UUID:DB44690D-9AF8–4D24-A9AD-04621E34E274");
KeyedReferenceList.add(keyedReference);

CategoryBag.setKeyedReferenceVector(keyedReferenceList);
TModel.setCategoryBag(categoryBag);
```

Now that we have the WSDL and its respective tModel, it becomes necessary to publish them as bindingTemplates in the UDDI registry. We also need to create the businessService, based on the WSDL service implementation. The actual publication process will use the UDDI4J APIs, which are discussed later. In the meantime, we have only two more steps to take. The first is to create a businessService. Let us look at a code snippet that demonstrates this:

```
WsdlDefinition wsdlDefinition = new WsdlDefinition();
wsdlDefinition = WSDLReader.readWSDL(null, wsdlURL);

Service wsdlService = ((Service[]) wsdlDefinition.getServices().values().toArray(new
                                                      Service[0]))[0];
```

```
BusinessService businessService = new BusinessService();
businessService.setName(wsdlService.getQName().getLocalPar());

element = wsdlService.getDocumentationElement();
businessService.setDefaultDescriptionString(DOMUtils.getChildCharacterData(element));
```

After the WSDL document is parsed in the above example, a new businessService is created. The name of the service and its documentation is derived from its WSDL. Let us also create the corresponding bindingTemplate, using the following code:

```
BindingTemplate bindingTemplate = new BindingTemplate();

Port wsdlPort = ((Port[]) wsdlService.getPorts().values().toArray(new Port[0]))[0];
Element = wsdlPort.getDocumentationElement();
BindingTemplate.setDefaultDescriptionString(DOMUtils.getChildCharacterData(element));
```

We are using the documentation element from WSDL to create the description for the bindingTemplate. This is contained within the WSDL port element. The access point is specified in WSDL as the extensibility element, which changes depending on transport. Let us create additional code that uses the SOAP bindings:

```
Element extensibilityElement = (ExtensibilityElement)
wsdlPort.getExtensibilityElements().get(0);
AccessPoint accessPoint = new
AccessPoint((SOAPAddress)extensibilityElement).getLocationURI(), "http");
bindingTemplate.setAccessPoint(accessPoint);
```

The bindingTemplate contains a reference to the tModel associated with the WSDL service interface document and contained in the tModelInstanceInfo. Remember that the tModelInstanceInfo contains the tModelKey for the specified tModel. In addition, the bindingTemplate will contain an overviewDoc that points to the WSDL service implementation document. This is demonstrated below:

```
TModelInstanceInfo = new TmodelInstanceInfo(tModelKey);
OverviewURL overviewURL = new OverviewURL(wsdlURL);
overviewDoc.setOverviewURL(overviewURL);
instanceDetails.setOverviewDoc(overviewDoc);
```

This was the last step in parsing WSDL to create the appropriate UDDI entities. To publish this information in UDDI, you would need to use UDDI4J (discussed later in this chapter) or JAXR (discussed in its own chapter).

▷ Internationalization and Multiple Languages

Since registries need the ability to support users from all over the world, UDDI has added multiple language support in many of the entry types. The U in UDDI stands for "universal," which means the registry needs to support multiregional and international organizations and the services they offer. UDDI supports the ability to classify entities using multiple languages and/or multiple scripts of the same language. Additionally, UDDI can allow additional language-specific sort orders and provides for consistent search results in a language-independent manner.

Flute Bank also does business in Canada and Mexico and therefore needs to support English, French, and Spanish. The bank would like its name to appear in the native tongue of of service users and will provide translations in the registry. Let us look at the new businessEntity for Flute Bank:

```
<businessEntity
  businessKey="CBC2A349-A4C1-22D4-AE87-BC8713D2BD9"
  authorizedName="MattieLee"
  operator= ... >
  <name>Flute Bank</name>
  <name xml:lang="sp">banco de la flauta</name>
  <name xml:lang="fr">banque de cannelure</name>
  <name xml:lang="il">serie della scanalatura</name>
  <name xml:lang="pr">banco da flauta</name>
  <name xml:lang="gr">Flötebank</name>
...
</businessEntity>
```

UDDI registries support internationalization features through API sets and allow for multilingual business entity descriptions. UDDI registries support the following internationalization features:

- Multilingual names and descriptions
- Multiple names in the same language
- Internationalized address format
- Language-dependent collation

In the previous listing, the registration showed English, Spanish, and French, based on the Latin character set, which is the same as ASCII. Since registrations may include character sets from other languages, such as Chinese, Arabic, Hindi, and others, the xml:lang attribute can be used to specify additional language-specific information. Flute Bank can represent its name in Chinese for Chinese-speaking customers as well as in Russian for Russian-speaking customers, while also displaying its English name, using the xml:lang attribute.

```
<businessEntity>
...
  <name xml:lang="zh">长笛银行</name>
  <name xml:lang="ru">Банк флейты</name>
  <name xml:lang="en">Flute Bank</name>
  <name xml:lang="en">FB</name>
...
</businessEntity>
```

UDDI allows multiple name elements to be published. In the above listing, we have two English representations of Flute Bank—one its full name, and other its acronym. In this scenario, the first name element for each language is treated as the primary name, which would be used for all searching and sorting operations.

Each supported language within the registry is based on the Unicode 3.0 specification and ISO 10646, which support the majority of languages in use. Each language has its own unique behavior when it comes to sort-order collation, depending on whether the language's script is alphabetic, syllabic, or ideographic.

Languages that share the same alphabetic script, such as English, Spanish, and French, have different collation weights, depending on the other languages with which they're used. For languages that have both upper- and lowercase letters (bicameral), sorting depends on whether sorting is specified as case-sensitive or case-insensitive. For ideographic languages, such as Chinese and others that have large character range, collation may depend on whether stroke order or phonetic collation is specified.

The ability to support time zones is an important aspect of human communication. UDDI registries allow businesses to publish contact information, such as telephone and/or fax numbers. It is also important to have the ability to attach hours of availability. Businesses can indicate the time zone for each contact by specifying it as part of the contact's address.

UDDI also supports differing formats for postal addresses. Many parts of the world specify their postal addresses differently and may use different elements, such as lot numbers, building identification, floor numbers, subdivisions, and so on. In UDDI, the address is supported by an address element that is part of the businessEntity data structure. The address element contains a list of address-line elements.

Addresses are specified using the ubr-uddi-org:postalAddress tModel. This addresses the common subelements of an address, such as cities, states, and so on. The address element also specifies a tModelKey attribute as well as the keyName/keyValue pair for each addressLine element. Let us look at the address fragment for Flute Bank's businessEntity registration:

```
<address useType="Data Center" tModelKey="uddi:ubr.uddi.org:postalAddress">
  <addressLine keyName="Street" keyValue="60">Diana Drive</addressLine>
  <addressLine keyName="House number" keyValue="70">25</addressLine>
  <addressLine keyName="City" keyValue="40">Bloomfield</addressLine>
  ...
  <addressLine keyName="Country" keyValue="20">Trinidad</addressLine>
</address>
```

Addresses themselves may have different language representations as well. This can be accomplished by using differing addressLine elements, depending on the language. Using the keyName/keyValue pair with the codes specified in the ubr-uddi-org:postAddress tModel, you can determine proper address formatting programmatically. Let us look at one more example for Flute Bank and how this may be represented:

```
<address useType="International Office" xml:lang="en"
tModelKey="uddi:ubr.uddi.org:postalAddress">
  <addressLine keyName="House Number" keyValue="70">No. 9</addressLine>
  <addressLine keyName="Street" keyValue="60">Aberdeen Road</addressLine>
  <addressLine keyName="District" keyValue="50">Newlands Village</addressLine>
  <addressLine keyName="City" keyValue="40">Biche</addressLine>
</address>
<address useType="International Office" xml:lang="ja"
tModelKey="uddi:ubr.uddi.org:postalAddress">
  <addressLine keyName="City" keyValue="40">南路</addressLine>
  <addressLine keyName="Street" keyValue="60">本生號</addressLine>
  <addressLine keyName="District" keyValue="50">敦化</addressLine>
  <addressLine keyName="House Number" keyValue="70">台北市</addressLine>
</address>
```

As you can see, UDDI can support global usage of services in a straightforward manner. It also provides functionality that allows you to perform language-dependent collation, based on the results returned from find operations. Please see the latest UDDI specification for this support.

> Extending a UDDI Registry

UDDI registries can be extended to support additional functionality using the extended UDDI APIs and data structures. By extending a UDDI registry, additional features can easily be added to core UDDI functionality. This feature should be used with caution, as clients may over time expect all registries to support extended functionality when they do not, causing errors.

Extensions within a UDDI registry are usually associated with one or more tModels that hold reference to the extension. The tModel in this scenario indicates that it represents an extension to one or more UDDI APIs. By using tModels, clients can discover extensions to the core UDDI API. An example is shown below:

```
<keyedReference keyName="uddi-org:derivedFrom:v2_inquiry"
        keyValue="uddi:uddi.org:v2_inquiry"
        tModelKey="uddi:uddi.org:categorization:derivedFrom"/>
```

Extending the registry in this manner may require supporting two different sets of service endpoints. Additionally, each service should register additional bindingTemplates. One of the main reasons for doing this is to avoid confusion and potential collisions in API calls. For example, when a UDDI registry receives a request to get_businessDetail, the registry cannot determine whether the client can handle the extension or not. When a service supports two distinct endpoints, the UDDI registry can determine whether the client can handle the extension, based upon the endpoint the client chooses to use.

Flute Bank has decided to take advantage of the extension capabilities of UDDI to add supporting documentation as part of the UDDI publisherAssertion data structure. The bank has added a discoveryURL element to the publisherAssertion structure that will contain a URL to the business agreements and licensing terms agreed upon between Flute Bank and its partners.

Listing 6.14   Extending the publisherAssertion structure

```
<xsd:schema
  targetNamespace="http://flutebank.com/uddi_extension"
  xmlns:egExt="http://flutebank.com/uddi_extension"
  xmlns:xsd="http://www.w3.org/2001/XMLSchema"
```

```
  xmlns:uddi="urn:uddi-org:api_v3"
  elementFormDefault="qualified"
  attributeFormDefault="unqualified">


  <xsd:import namespace="urn:uddi-org:api_v3"
     schemaLocation="http://www.uddi.org/schema/uddi_v3.xsd" />
  <xsd:element name="publisherAssertionExt"

type="egExt:publisherAssertionExt"
     substitutionGroup="uddi:publisherAssertion"/>
   <xsd:complexType name=publisherAssertionExt">
     <xsd:annotation>
     <xsd:documentation>Extension of publisherAssertion</xsd:documentation>
     </xsd:annotation>
     <xsd:complexContent>
        <xsd:extension base="uddi:publisherAssertion">
           <xsd:sequence>
              <xsd:element ref="uddi:discoveryURLs" minOccurs="0" />
           </xsd:sequence>
        </xsd:extension>
     </xsd:complexContent>
  </xsd:complexType>
</xsd:schema>
```

In Listing 6.14, we are creating a UDDI extension derived from uddi:publisherAssertion. As part of extending the publisher assertion, we specify that the discovery URL is optional; hence its value of minOccurs="0". A publisher such as Flute Bank will use the assertion structure to indicate that its legal agreements are available at the discovery URL.

XML schemas support the ability to derive additional schemas from a specified base. The targetNamespace and egExt namespace take advantage of this feature. The publisherAssertion element is extended by creating a new type named publisherAssertionExt. Whenever a registry receives a request for a publisherAssertion that references the newly extended namespace but does not include the discoveryURLs element, the registry will behave in the same manner, as it would have without the extension.

There are many additional reasons that Flute Bank may want to use the UDDI extension mechanism to support its business model—including, but not limited to, supporting digital signing for all publish APIs, changing the assertion model to support custom assertion models, incorporating additional Flute Bank–specific elements on businessEntity, along with their respective services.

> UDDI4J

UDDI4J is a Java client API used to access a UDDI registry. UDDI4J objects and methods are used to build a request message in SOAP format that is sent to the registry. UDDI4J was originally developed by IBM as an open source undertaking and has the endorsement of HP, SAP, and others.

UDDI4J contains APIs that allows you to publish, find, and bind to a Web service. Because UDDI4J is open source, it comes with source code, JavaDoc, and several sample applications. It contains multiple APIs but the one most frequently used is the UDDIProxy class. Let us look at how UDDIProxy class interacts with a registry:

```
UDDIProxy proxy = new UDDIProxy();

proxy.setInquiryURL("http://www.flutebank.com/uddi/test/inquiryapi");

proxy.setPublishURL("https://www.flutebank.com/uddi/test/publishapi");
```

We start by creating an instance of the UDDIProxy class and then set the proxy to point to Flute Bank's test UDDI registry. The inquiry API is set to use HTTP protocol, because we want the inquiry to be publicly accessible. The publish URL uses HTTPS, because we want to make sure only users that are authorized can submit changes to the registry.

The publish URL can use protocols other than SSL for publication as long as it is supported by a valid Java security provider (JSSE). As you may be aware, security providers are configured in the java.security configuration file or, alternatively, can be done at runtime. The code for changing providers is simple:

```
System.setProperty("java.protocol.handler.pkgs","com.sun.net.ssl.internal.www
                                                              .protocol");
Java.security.Security.addProvider(new com.sun.net.ssl.internal.ssl.Provider());
```

The proxy class is responsible for connecting to the UDDI registry on the user's behalf and transmits the appropriate SOAP messages. The proxy class uses the underlying transport to communicate through firewalls or network bastion hosts (Network Proxy Servers). In some organizations, to communicate from inside your organization to the outside may require using an ID and password. UDDI4J supports this by supporting the system properties shown in Table 6.2.

Table 6.2   System Properties Supported by UDDI4J

Property	Description
http.proxyHost	The hostname of the network proxy server.
http.proxyPort	The port number used by the network proxy server. This defaults to port 80.
https.proxyHost	he hostname of the network proxy server that supports SSL. This is usually the same server as HTTP.
https.proxyPort	The port number used by the network proxy server for SSL. This defaults to port 443.
socksProxy.Host	The hostname of the network proxy server that supports Socks-based proxies.
socksProxy.Port	The port number used by the network proxy server.

The ultimate goal of UDDI4J is to allow discovery of businessEntities and the services they offer. UDDI4J provides several additional classes that allow you to access entity and service information from a UDDI registry. These include a BusinessInfo object that describes an individual businessEntity, a BusinessList object, which is a collection of BusinessInfo objects returned from search results, and a ServiceInfo object, which allows you to access the services offered from a particular businessEntity.

A user who wanted to find all businesses that meet a specified criterion, such as companies that start with the name "Flute," would use the find_business method of the proxy similar to this:

```
BusinessList bl = proxy.find_business("Flute", null, 0);
```

The find_business method has three parameters. The first contains the search string, the second points to an instance of a FindQualifiers object, for which we are specifying null, and the third is the number of matches to return. Zero specifies that we should return all matches. For advanced searching, you can use the FindQualifiers object to include searching on business categories, identifiers, and tModels. The BusinessList object is a collection that contains all businesses that match the search criteria.

Usually when you have a, you will want to extract information for each business. Let us look at a simple code snippet that does the job:

```
Vector biVector = bl.getBusinessInfos().getBusinessInfoVector();

for (int ii = 0; ii < biVector.size(); ii++) {

    BusinessInfo bi = (BusinessInfo)biVector.elementAt(ii);
}
```

Using UDDI4J to publish business entities to the registry is also straightforward. Publication to a UDDI registry requires authentication using SSL, so the proxy also provides a get_authToken method to handle this task. Publishing a businessEntity requires creating a new BusinessEntity object and supplying it with the various properties you want published. Let us look at a simple example that specifies the name of the business and the operator:

```
AuthToken token = proxy.get_authToken("uid","pass");

Vector entityVector = new Vector();
BusinessEntity be = new BusinessEntity("");

be.setName("Flute Bank");
be.setOperator("Administrator");

entityVector.addElement(be);
BusinessDetail bd = proxy.save_business(token.getAuthInfoString(), entityVector);
```

It is a good idea to check whether the registration was successful. You can query the registry a second time and compare BusinessDetail information. Alternatively, the majority of the proxy methods upon failure may throw UDDIException for severe errors or return an instance of a DispositionReport that indicates success or failure of an operation.

Earlier in the chapter, we mentioned that Flute Bank wanted to create multiple registrations for its insurance, banking, and investment divisions. After registering each division as a businessEntity, we will need to create a publisher assertion, which is a type of keyedReference that describes the relationship between two businessEntities. Let us look at sample code used to demonstrate how this can be accomplished programmatically:

```
// Specify which keyed reference to use
KeyedReference kr = new KeyedReference("Division", "parent-child",
                                TModel.RELATIONSHIPS_TMODEL_KEY);
```

```
// Create a new publisher assertion
PublisherAssertion pa = new PublisherAssertion(parentKey, childKey, kr);

// Link together both entities to create an assertion
DispositionReport dr = proxy.add_publisherAssertions(token.getAuthInfoString(), pa);
```

> Remember that when an assertion is added, the business entity relationship is not valid until both parties make an identical assertion that specifies they mutually agree to the relationship. The example shows only one assertion being made. Sometimes you may also want to know programmatically assertions made by other parties. In the case of Flute Bank, we want to automatically approve all assertions made against it. This can be done using this code snippet:

```
// Determine incomplete relationship where other parties have created an assertion
AssertionStatusReport asr = proxy.get_assertionStatusReport(token.getAuthInfoString(),
                                          CompletionStatus.TOKEY_INCOMPLETE);
// We need a list of partially formed relationships
Vector v = asr.getAssertionStatusItemVector();

for (int ii = 0; ii < v.size(); ii++) {
    AssertionStatusItem asi = (AssertionStatusItem)v.elementAt(ii);

    // Create a matching publisher assertion
    PublisherAssertion pa = new PublisherAssertion(asi.getFromKeyString(),
                                    asi.getToKeyString(), asi.getKeyedReference());

    // Check the disposition for errors
    DispositionReport dr = proxy.add_publisherAssertions(pa);

}
```

> In prior examples, we published information programmatically for Flute Bank. Likewise, there may be situations in which we may wish to programmatically delete information in a registry. This may require using qualifiers, as we of course want to delete specific records and do not want to use wildcard operations. An example of the qualifier we may want to use is

```
FindQualifiers findQualifiers = new FindQualifiers();
Vector qualifier = new Vector();
```

```
qualifier.add(new FindQualifier("exactNameMatch"));
findQualifiers.setFindQualifierVector(qualifier);
```

This qualifier specifies that we want to use an exact name match. Previously, we searched for all entities that start with the word "Flute." This allows us to be more specific. Flute Bank wishes to programmatically delete the businessEntity for its Biche branch and will use the code in Listing 6.15:

Listing 6.15   Creating a new business assertion

```
// Create a vector of names
Vector names = new Vector();
names.add(new Name("Flute Bank Biche")));

// Let's make search case sensitive
FindQualifiers findQualifiers = new FindQualifiers
Vector qualifier = new Vector();
qualifier.add(new FindQualifier("caseSensitiveMatch"));
findQualifiers.setFindQualifierVector(qualifier);

// Search for specified business and limit result to 10
BusinessList businessList = proxy.find_business(names, null, null, null, null,
                                                findQualifiers, 10);
Vector businessInfoVector = businessList.getBusinessInfos().getBusinessInfoVector();

// Delete any businesses returned from the search
for (int ii = 0; ii < businessInfoVector.size(); ii++) {
  BusinessInfo bi = (BusinessInfo)businessInfoVector.elementAt(ii);
  DispositionReport dr = proxy.delete_business(token.getAuthInfoString(),
                                               bi.getBusinessKey());

  if (dr.success()) {
    System.out.println("Business Deleted");
  } else
      System.out.println("Error Number: " + dr.getErrno() +
          "\n Error Code: " + dr.getErrCode() +
          "\n Error Text: " + dr.getErrInfoText());
  }
}
```

Now let us look at one more example of using UDDI4J to find a business. In the Listing 6.16, we will use UDDI4J to locate multilingual businesses. UDDI4J supports passing the preferred language identifier as a parameter.

Listing 6.16   Creating a new publisher assertion

```
Vector descriptionVector = businessInfo.getDescriptionVector();
String businessDescription = "";
String defaultDescription = "";

for (int ii = 0; ii < descriptionVector.size(); ii++) {
  Description description = (Description)descriptionVector.elementAt(ii);

  if (description.getLang().compareToIgnoreCase("en-zh") == 0) {
    businessDescription = description.getText();
    break;
  }

  // More than likely a business will have an English description.
  // Use this as default

  if (description.getLang().compareToIgnoreCase("en-us") == 0) {
    defaultDescription = description.getText();
  }

  // If none in Chinese, then use default
  if (businessDescription == "") {
    businessDescription = defaultDescription;
  }

  // Convert to appropriate character set
  businessDescription = new String(businessDescription.getBytes("ISO-8859-1"),"UTF-8");
```

UDDI4J has additional features that may prove useful. The initial version used Apache SOAP for its transport layer. Transport layers are handled via an abstract factory approach that will allow other SOAP transport providers to be used. Configuration of the transport is specified by changing a system property.

```
org.uddi4j.TransportClassName=org.uddi4j.transport.ApacheAxisTransport
```

The UDDI4J is one manner for querying a registry. The Java API for XML registries (JAXR) is another and will be covered in its own chapter.

▷ Private UDDI Registries

Many organizations may not use external Web services for years to come. Instead, they will use Web services for providing integration between legacy systems, customer relationship management applications, and other internal systems. In this scenario, it makes sense for an enterprise to consider implementing its own private UDDI registry.

A private implementation of a UDDI registry is useful for organizations that need to service-orient their systems. Once legacy systems are service-oriented, they can provide functionality to a specific group of authorized users who may be located within an intranet, extranet, or private network. Implementing a private registry has many benefits, including improving testing and quality assurance and providing a catalog of services for consumption by internal users and a mechanism for discovering services over a private network between business partners. ▷

Many large organizations and independent software vendors (ISVs) have hundreds, if not thousands, of reusable application components. By creating a private UDDI registry, an organization can register components that can be shared by internal resources. UDDI's success will most likely occur in private usage before widespread adoption of a public registry. Public registries have larger hurdles to overcome, in that they must accept registrations from multiple organizations, provide quality of service and assurance levels, and find methods to collect revenue from the registered applications. Internal registries will most likely be under the control of a single internal IT organization, which makes issues of revenue collection go away. (The authors will ignore internal chargeback models, as we are not bean counters.)

Having your own private registry brings many other benefits. Sometimes it is advisable to restrict who is allowed to view service description information, especially for sensitive services. The organization can not only control who publishes information but can also require authentication. Furthermore, auditing capabilities can be built into a private UDDI registry that allow the administrator to enumerate all clients who have executed the specified find criteria.

A public UDDI registry holds business and service information about organizations from a broad range of industry verticals. The vast majority of the businesses and the services they offer will not be of interest to most clients executing a search. Standard taxonomies used in UDDI may allow you to find a listing of businesses within a particular industry vertical but will not provide you with

> ▷   Private UDDI registry implementations are available from BEA, IONA, Microsoft, Systinet, and the Mind Electric.

useful selection criteria. One example may be to search for backup stock quote Web services providers for Flute Bank. We all know that not all providers are created equally and that a simple search based on a classification scheme will not yield the right business results.

Sometimes, for legal or process reasons, you may not want to trust the information in a registry and instead may wish to maintain your own. For business partners where contractual relationships need to be established in advance before using services, it may be a better idea to maintain the registry internally. Many organizations may want to consider using UDDI to ensure that only services from approved and verified business partners are entered in the registry. When a new partner is approved, the appropriate UDDI entries are created. Likewise, when businesses decide to no longer partner, their UDDI entries are removed.

Furthermore, a private UDDI registry, unlike its public counterpart, can be altered to change the basic behavior of many UDDI operations. One example may be a private UDDI registry that requires all `find` operations to contain a `WS_Security`, SAML (discussed in Chapter 15) or other authentication header. A private UDDI registry can be further extended to support the following business scenarios:

- Marketplace registries
- Portal registries
- Enterprise application integration registries

Marketplace Registries

Marketplace registries are hosted by industry consortiums that collaborate and compete in a particular industry vertical. Many businesses are cooperating and forming consortiums that allow them to conduct business more easily. Several examples in the market exist today where a marketplace registry would be useful. The Big Three automakers—Ford, General Motors, and Daimler/Chrysler—might want to unify their purchasing power on commodity parts. They could have their suppliers register their businesses in a marketplace registry, to promote competition. The advantage to the big three automakers in doing this is to have only qualified, prevalidated businesses appear as part of their search criteria.

Flute Bank may use a similar tactic to expose its services to previously registered external customers, such as free real-time quotes. The bank can assign each customer an authentication token. When a user visits the Web site, this token is stored as a cookie in the user's Web browser. When a user wants to invoke a Web service, the token is sent along in the SOAP header with any find operation. By taking this approach, Flute Bank can also extend the service to noncustomers. The authentication token can be used to support subscription services based on a number of factors, including, but not limited to

- Number of find operations conducted within a specified period
- Number of results returned as part of the search criteria
- Total amount of data returned in bytes of the search criteria
- Restricting the search to specific times of day

Using a registry in this manner is appropriate when you require metadata about services to be validated in advance. It is limited to a particular industry or group of users.

Portal Registries

The Internet as used today was primarily meant for humans. Only in specific instances do the Internet and its underlying protocols enable computer-to-computer interaction. Many Internet standards have been extended to support interoperability at the protocol level, which is really how bits are transmitted on the wire. However, computers today do not understand the meaning of the bits. One of the goals is to solve this dilemma by creating the *semantic web*. The semantic web provides guidance on how to facilitate integrating human and computer tasks and how to incorporate the meaning and context in which a transaction belongs. Interoperability of tasks such as searching would be more useful if computers being used understood the semantic knowledge of the data. Additional information on the semantic web is covered in Chapter 17.

Flute Bank currently maintains a presence on the World Wide Web at *www.flutebank.com*. The bank has also decided to maintain a presence on the semantic web by exposing its private UDDI registry at *www.flutebank.com/services/uddi*. It uses the portal metaphor.

The bank has exposed its UDDI registry by placing it in a DMZ segment, such that it can be queried by outside parties. In this scenario, Flute wants to allow only find operations to occur over the Internet and wants to restrict any publish operations from occurring. The bank has registered in its private UDDI registry several additional taxonomies to support the organization's procurement policies. External partners can query the bank's private UDDI registry to determine the format of purchase orders as well as the WSDL for the purchase-order service.

Flute Bank has registered itself in multiple public registries. It also populated the discoveryURL element in its businessEntity registration with the location of its private UDDI registry. A partial businessEntity registration example is shown below:

```
<businessEntity authorizedName=" ..."
  businessKey="BAB3C425-A2C3-22E1-FA23-AB2324D3BC8" ... >
  <discoveryURLs>
      <discoveryURL useType="businessEntity">
            http://www.publicuddi.com/uddiget?businessKey=BC234221 ...
      </discoveryURL>
      <discoveryURL useType="urn:uddi-inquiry-api">
            http://www.flutebank.com/services/uddi
      </discoveryURL>
    </discoveryURLs>
    <name>Flute Bank</name>
...
</businessEntity>
```

Using the portal approach to private UDDI registries allows Flute Bank to maintain control over how metadata for the services it offers is used. The bank can extend this approach by restricting who can do find operations based on who the requestor is, such as an authorized vendor specified by the procurement department. In this scenario, Flute Bank can also learn about other organizations and who has expressed an interest in rendering services for them.

Enterprise Application Integration Registries

Enterprise Application Integration registries are used in the same manner as partner registries, except that they contain services available from other departments or divisions within an organization. This form of registry is used primarily by businesses that want to restrict creation of new tModels, businessService entries, and bindingTemplates to a centralized group. This type of registry should never be exposed for external Internet access and should be restricted to internal users only.

Considerations

Here are some of the recommendations and considerations an architect of a Web services initiative should consider before implementing an in-house registry:

- The vast majority of Web services applications will not use a public registry.
- A private registry makes sense for large organizations, such as the Fortune 500, where the number of services created are used across the enterprise and/or divisional boundaries.
- A private registry makes little sense for a small IT shop, where the number of services will be small and/or used by a few applications.
- If you have either a small number of services and/or small user community, it may make better sense to publish a URL to a WSDL document instead of supporting a registry.
- When implementing a private registry, it is imperative that an organization standardize on a single vendor, hopefully in the same manner as on other corporate standards.

▷ UDDI Futures

UDDI Version 3.0 was released in July 2002. Future versions of UDDI will be built on the foundation of prior versions and incorporate many enhancement requests, including additional security functionality, advanced WSDL support, multiregistry topologies, and a new subscription API.

Digital Signatures

One of the most significant features that will be incorporated in the next version of UDDI is digital signatures for publishing UDDI entities. These will provide additional data integrity and authentication for UDDI business and service publication. Additionally, queries to a UDDI registry will now support limiting find operations to UDDI entities that have been digitally signed.

This has two advantages. First, when the registry is queried, the caller can determine whether the data was received exactly as the publisher created it upon publication. Publishers of entities can also take advantage of the digital signature to guarantee that they are not misrepresented by some malicious party who claims to own a registry. The assurance that digital signatures provide is transitive for both client and publisher, so that when an entity is copied or replicated between registries, it is guaranteed to not have changed during the process.

For a registry to become successful requires extraordinary levels of security and protection against tampering. Digital signatures, discussed in Chapter 15, are one of the most important features for UDDI.

Human-Friendly Keys

UDDI 3.0 allows for each entity within a UDDI registry to be assigned a key versus being under the registry's control. In prior versions of the specification, when a publisher wanted to copy an entry from one registry to another, the target registry would assign new keys. Preservation of the key from one registry to another was explicitly not allowed.

UDDI 3.0 introduces the concept of entity promotion, whereby a publisher is allowed to specify a a new key. It is up to the registry and its policies to determine whether this proposed key is allowed and can be inserted into the registry.

Human-friendly keys are another feature of UDDI 3.0 registries. In prior versions of UDDI, the key was based on Unique Universal Identifier (UUID) keys. Version 3.0 of UDDI removes this restriction and proposes an alternative based on DNS names. This feature allows a publisher to establish a key partition and generate keys based on that partition. For example, a version 3.0 key might look like this:

```
uddi:flutebank.com:insurance-division:67
```

This allows an organization to manage its own key space, using its own conventions.

Subscriptions

UDDI 3.0 introduces a new subscription API that allows for notification of changes to a registry. This will allow a subscriber to track registry activity in a programmatic manner. Subscribers can establish a subscription specifying either a query or set of entries in which the subscriber is interested. If the result set or underlying content of the entity changes, the subscriber is notified.

This allows for monitoring new businesses or services that are registered, monitoring of existing businesses or services, obtaining registry information from a public UDDI registry for incorporation into a private UDDI registry, and obtaining information in a marketplace or portal scenario.

> Summary

In this chapter, we looked at different UDDI considerations for implementing Web services, including

- Discovering Web services
- Categorizing services
- Business entity relationships
- Using UDDI SOAP interfaces
- UDDI and SOAP/WSDL relationships
- Publishing WSDL service interfaces in UDDI
- Extending a UDDI registry
- UDDI4J
- Private UDDI registries

Throughout this book, you may have seen dozens of differing definitions and approaches to Web services. There will be more to come. One thought is that Web services are a distributed systems architecture for enabling object-oriented applications to provide "services" to each other. Another thought is that Web services define any architecture that involves passing XML documents between disparate systems. Whatever your interpretation of a Web service, it will no doubt use SOAP, WSDL, and UDDI.

By now, you should have a crisp understanding of the fundamental concepts behind Web services: XML, SOAP, WSDL, and UDDI. The author team recommends that if there is anything so far you have not clearly understood, you take the opportunity to reread this chapter before proceeding.

Chapter {7}

ebXML

Electronic business XML (ebXML, pronounced *eee-bee-XML*) is probably the most talked about and least understood of technologies in the Web services universe. In this chapter, we present the concepts and architecture to give the reader a basic level of understanding about ebXML. We also talk about the relevance to other technologies in the WUST (WSDL-UDDI-SOAP Technologies) stack and why readers should pay close attention to the way it is transforming business-to-business communication.

To understand the relevance of ebXML, we need to revisit Electronic Data Interchange (EDI), which we briefly on touched in Chapter 4. At its fundamental level, every business is part of a supply chain that forms a link between suppliers and customers. EDI was born in the late sixties out of the need to represent this interaction electronically as structured data. In the seventies, the Transportation Data Coordinating Committee (TDCC) developed the initial transaction sets for transportation verticals (airlines, shipping corporations, etc.) and was primarily responsible for the rapid adoption of EDI interactions instead of paper exchanges. This worked well, because organizations could exchange information faster using the virtual private networks set up between participants of the supply chain. ▷

▷ **EDI Standards**

ANSI X12

In 1979, the American National Standards Institute (ANSI) created a new committee called the Accredited Standards Committee (ASC) X12, which created a set of guidelines on EDI data, outlining the structure, documents, information in each document, and so on. These were referred to as transaction sets. For example, transaction set 850 refers to purchase orders, and 810 is assigned to invoices.

Continued

Before the Internet became a household reality, e-commerce and EDI were considered the same thing. The business and technical problems with EDI and the reason for its demise were as simple as the reasons for its adoption. Though demise may seem an inappropriate term, considering that many large networks, such as airlines and customs, still use EDI, it is true—otherwise, you probably wouldn't be reading this book. These reasons are

1. Only large corporations could realize the benefits of EDI, as a result of the high costs. These were primarily due to the proprietary software that implemented handling of the EDI transaction sets, the hardware required to set up the private networks, and the cost in implementing such a technically elaborate solution.

2. The technology became fragmented, with EDI products implementing proprietary extensions.

3. EDI focused on automating information flow. For example, most EDI transaction sets landed on a printer, where EDI specialists used that information to work with the existing business process.

Standard Generalized Markup Language (SGML) originated at IBM and became an ISO standard in 1986. The advent of its subsets, XML and HTML, changed everything. Data could be represented in a self-describing and platform-independent format. The business requirements EDI proposed to solve, along with the technical capabilities of XML, gave rise to ebXML. Early in 1999, members of the United Nations Centre for Trade Facilitation and Electronic Business (UN/CEFACT) joined forces with the Organization for the Advancement of Structured Information Standards(OASIS) to produce a global XML framework

▷ **UN-EDIFACT**

To cater to the requirements of global rather than U.S. domestic trade, the United Nations developed a combination of the X12 and European standards endorsed by the International Standards Organization (ISO) that came to be known as the United Nations Electronic Data Interchange For Administration, Commerce and Transport (EDIFACT) group.

In reality, both were *guidelines* that reflected the needs of complete vertical business groups, such as transportation. Individual organizations had to create implementation guides for their own use of these guidelines, which led to fragmented EDI networks.

for e-business. Many companies participated in the initiative and, in May 2001, agreed on the first generation of ebXML specifications. ▷

Architectural Overview of ebXML

The experiences of EDI taught us that in the real world, for business-to-business (B2B) collaboration to work successfully a lot more is required than just exchanging documents. One has to deal with issues surrounding business process semantics, negotiating terms and conditions, interoperability, security, reliability, and so on. The inner circle in Figure 7.1 shows the different areas surrounding business collaboration that two partners need to address and the steps the partners must go through to realize the B2B collaboration:

1. **Process definition.** A community or consortium of trading partners defines the business processes to be used in the community according to a well-known domain model and describes them in agreed-upon formats. In ebXML, this is realized using UML and XML. Examples of such consortiums are the Open

Figure 7.1
ebXML frameworks (adapted from the ebXML Business Process Specification Schema)

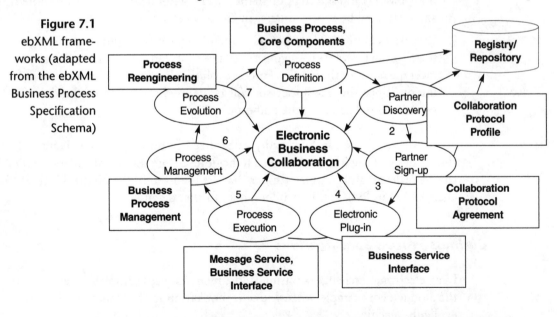

▷   OASIS (*www.oasis-open.org/about*) includes more than 150 contributing organizations and over 110 sponsors.

Travel Alliance *(www.opentravel.org)*, which includes more than one hundred key players in the travel industry; the Global Commerce Initiative *(www .globalcommerceinitiative.org)*, a group of manufacturers and retailers of consumer goods; and the Automotive Industry Action Group *(www.aiag.org)*, of key players in the automotive industry.

2. **Partner discovery.** For two partners to engage, there must be some form of discovery about each other's services and business processes. In ebXML, this is realized using a *registry-repository*.

3. **Partner sign-up.** Partners negotiate their business level and transaction level agreements. In ebXML, these are realized as a Collaboration-Protocol Profile (CPP) and Collaboration-Protocol Agreement (CPA).

4. **Electronic plug-in.** The trading partners configure their interfaces and software according to the agreed-upon business processes and details of the collaborating partner.

5. **Process execution.** Business services collaborate to do and execute the agreed-upon business processes.

6. **Process management.** The business processes defined in the process definition phase (1) and agreed upon in the partner sign-up phase (3) are monitored and facilitated by process management services.

7. **Process evolution.** The partners evaluate their existing processes, improve them through process re-engineering if necessary, and create new processes to meet the needs of the market. Process evolution brings us back to process definition, since the new processes will be defined according to the domain model and published in the community.

All of the above can be broadly categorized into two groups as Figure 7.2 shows: design time (things that need to be done before the actual collaboration can be realized) and runtime–(things that are involved in the physical B2B exchange). Let us look at this architecture in further detail.

Business Process Specifications

In an electronic exchange, a business document conveys complete intent about the product. For example, when you order books online, the request implicitly or explicitly specifies

- Who are the parties involved (the buyer and the seller).
- What commodity or product is involved.

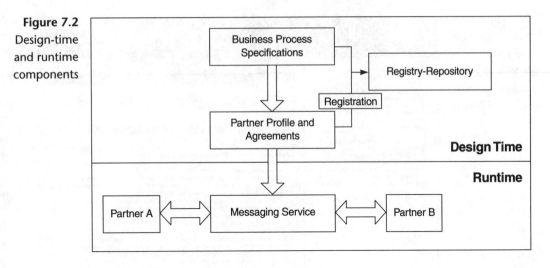

Figure 7.2
Design-time
and runtime
components

- When events occur (e.g., credit checks, inspections, shipping).
- Where the product is located.
- How it is going to be handled, shipped, packaged, and so on.

The ebXML business-process model specifies how this information can be captured in an XML format partners can use to configure their ebXML services that execute the business process. The ebXML Business Process Specification Schema (BPSS) specifies this schema that is captured through some business process modeling. To model the business process using object-oriented principles, ebXML defines a complete methodology, called UN/CEFACT modeling methodology (UMM), based on UML and XML. In the grand scheme of things, BPSS is expected to be produced as a result of business modeling using UMM, but UMM is not *required*. Any business process editor is capable of producing the standard schema, using its own modeling techniques. A few tools already support this. Figure 7.3 shows the Bind Studio product that graphically models the collaboration between Flute Bank and OfficeMin (in which Flute Bank uses OfficeMin as its vendor for office supplies—see Chapter 11) to generate the BPSS and CPP/CPA documents.

The BPSS document (schema instance) generated is an XML representation of the use cases. As Figure 7.4 shows it models a business process as a set of *collaborations* composed of discrete *transactions*. For example the document in Listing 7.1 shows how a collaboration is composed of a create order transaction between Flute Bank and OfficeMin, their roles (buyer, seller), and the states in that activity (success/failure).

Figure 7.3
Graphic process
modeling and
the Business Pro-
cess Specification
Schema

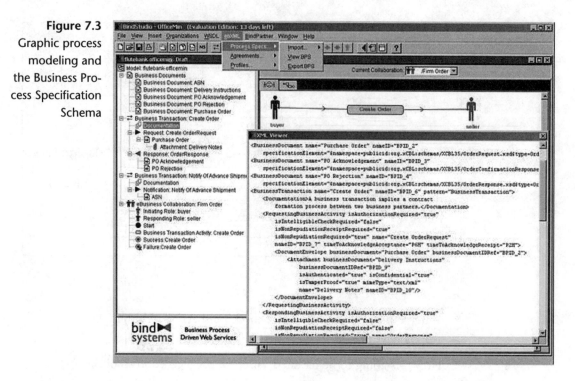

Listing 7.1 The BPSS document

```xml
<?xml version="1.0" encoding="UTF-8"?>
<ProcessSpecification name="flutebank-officemin" uuid="[1234–5678–901234]" version=
                                                                          "1.0">
    <BusinessDocument name="Purchase Order" nameID="BPID_2"specificationElement=
      "$namespace=publicid:org.xCBL:schemas/XCBL35/OrderRequest.xsd$type=OrderRequest"
      specificationLocation="http://www.flutebank.com/db/schemalibrary/xCBL/XSDL3.5/
                                                              OrderRequest.xsd"/>
    <BusinessTransaction name="Create Order" nameID="BPID_6"
                                               pattern="BusinessTransaction">
      <RequestingBusinessActivity isAuthorizationRequired="true"
          isIntelligibleCheckRequired="false" isNonRepudiationReceiptRequired="true"
          isNonRepudiationRequired="true" name="Create OrderRequest" nameID="BPID_7"
                timeToAcknowledgeAcceptance="P6H" timeToAcknowledgeReceipt="P2H">
        <DocumentEnvelope businessDocument="Purchase Order" businessDocumentIDRef=
                                                              "BPID_2">
```

```
            <Attachment businessDocument="Delivery Instructions"
                                            businessDocumentIDRef="BPID_9"
                    isAuthenticated="true" isConfidential="true" isTamperProof="true"
                    mimeType="text/xml" name="Delivery Notes" nameID="BPID_10"/>
        </DocumentEnvelope>
    </RequestingBusinessActivity>
    <RespondingBusinessActivity isAuthorizationRequired="true"
                                        isIntelligibleCheckRequired="false"
            isNonRepudiationReceiptRequired="false" isNonRepudiationRequired="true"
            name="OrderResponse" nameID="BPID_8" timeToAcknowledgeReceipt="P2H">
        <DocumentEnvelope businessDocument="PO Acknowledgement"
                                            businessDocumentIDRef="BPID_3"
                isAuthenticated="false" isConfidential="false"
                isPositiveResponse="true"   isTamperProof="false"/>
        <DocumentEnvelope businessDocument="PO Rejection" businessDocumentIDRef=
                                                            "BPID_4"
                isAuthenticated="false" isConfidential="false"
                isPositiveResponse="false" isTamperProof="false"/>
    </RespondingBusinessActivity>
  </BusinessTransaction>

<BinaryCollaboration name="Firm Order" nameID="BPID_11">
    <InitiatingRole name="buyer" nameID="BPID_12"/>
    <RespondingRole name="seller" nameID="BPID_13"/>
    <BusinessTransactionActivity businessTransaction="Create Order"
                                        businessTransactionIDRef="BPID_6"
            fromAuthorizedRole="buyer" fromAuthorizedRoleIDRef="BPID_12"
            isConcurrent="false" isLegallyBinding="false" name="Create Order"
            nameID="BPID_14" timeToPerform="P1D" toAuthorizedRole="seller"
            toAuthorizedRoleIDRef="BPID_13"/>
  <Start toBusinessState="Create Order" toBusinessStateIDRef="BPID_14"/>
   <Success conditionGuard="Success" fromBusinessState="Create Order"
                                        fromBusinessStateIDRef="BPID_14"/>
  <Failure conditionGuard="AnyFailure" fromBusinessState="Create Order"
                                        fromBusinessStateIDRef="BPID_14"/>
</BinaryCollaboration>
</ProcessSpecification>
```

Figure 7.4
Use cases map
to collaborations
grouped as dis-
crete transactions
(adapted from
the ebXML Busi-
ness Process
Specification
Schema)

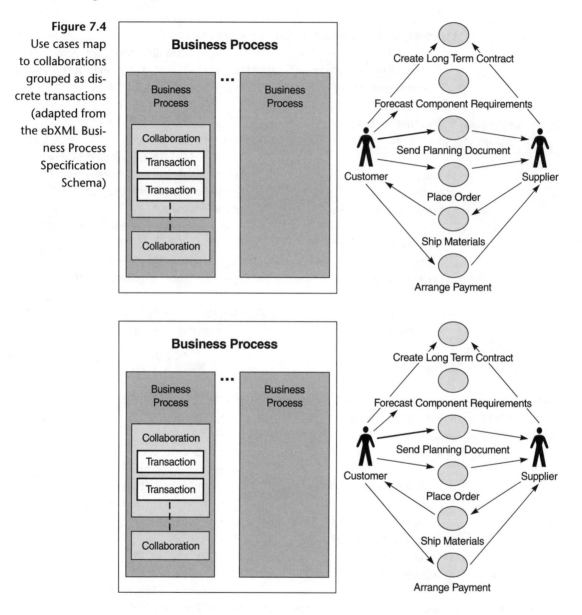

Partner Profiles and Agreements

For an organization to communicate with a business partner, it needs to know what the other end is capable of doing. We looked at how a business process can be modeled as business *collaboration*. The Collaboration-Protocol Profile describes an organization's functional and technical capabilities, such as:

- The business processes in which it can participate
- The roles played in the processes (e.g., seller, shipper)
- The transport protocols (e.g., HTTP, SMTP)
- The messaging protocols (ebXML messaging)
- The security aspects (digital signatures, etc.)

The concept of a Collaboration-*Protocol* Profile is a bit of a misnomer, since it doesn't refer to a protocol (as in networking protocol) but describes the information necessary for another partner to engage in a collaboration with it.

A CPP is an XML document that is governed by the schema defined in the ebXML collaboration protocol profile and agreement specifications. All partners register their CPP documents in an ebXML registry, so that other partners can discover them, understand the supported processes, and make choices where necessary (e.g., to HTTP or SMTP) on their side. Listing 7.2 shows a sample CPP used by OfficeMin.

Listing 7.2   The CPP document

```xml
<?xml version="1.0" encoding="UTF-8"?>
<CollaborationProtocolProfile xmlns="http://www.ebxml.org/namespaces/tradePartner"
    xmlns:xlink="http://www.w3.org/1999/xlink"
    xmlns:ds="http://www.w3.org/2000/09/xmldsig#"
xsi:schemaLocation="http://www.ebxml.org/namespaces/tradePartner
                    http://ebxml.org/project_teams/trade_partner/cpp-cpa-v1_0.xsd" >
    <PartyInfo>
        <PartyId>urn:www.officemin.com</PartyId>
        <PartyRef xlink:href="http://www.officemin.com/about.html" xlink:type="simple"/>
        <CollaborationRole id="CR1">
            <ProcessSpecification xlink:href="flutebank-officemin"
                            name="Firm Order" xlink:type="simple" version="1.0"/>
            <Role xlink:href="flutebank-officemin#seller" name="seller" xlink:type=
                                                            "simple"/>
            <ServiceBinding channelId="C1" packageId="P1">
                <Service type="uriReference">/flutebank-officemin/Firm Order/seller
                                                            </Service>
            </ServiceBinding>
        </CollaborationRole>
        <Certificate certId="CRT1">
            <ds:KeyInfo/>
        </Certificate>
```

```
<DeliveryChannel channelId="C1" docExchangeId="DE1" transportId="T0">
   <Characteristics authenticated="false" authorized="false" confidentiality=
                                                                "false"
              nonrepudiationOfOrigin="false" nonrepudiationOfReceipt="false"
              secureTransport="false" syncReplyMode="none"/>
</DeliveryChannel>
<Transport transportId="T0">
   <SendingProtocol version="1.0">HTTP</SendingProtocol>
   <ReceivingProtocol version="1.0">HTTP</ReceivingProtocol>
   <Endpoint type="allPurpose" uri="http://MACHINEB:80/bindpartner/servlet/
                                                BindMessageRouter"/>
</Transport>
<DocExchange docExchangeId="DE1">
   <ebXMLBinding version="1.0">
      <ReliableMessaging deliverySemantics="OnceAndOnlyOncet"
                                                    idempotency="false"
              messageOrderSemantics="NotGuaranteed">
        <Retries>0</Retries>
        <RetryInterval>0</RetryInterval>
        <PersistDuration>P</PersistDuration>
      </ReliableMessaging>
   </ebXMLBinding>
</DocExchange>
</PartyInfo>
<Packaging id="P1">
   <ProcessingCapabilities generate="true" parse="true"/>
   <SimplePart id="SP0" mimetype="text/xml"/>
</Packaging>
</CollaborationProtocolProfile>
```

Figure 7.5 shows the key elements of the CPP. These are:

- PartyInfo. Specifies the organization described in the CPP.

- PartyId. A unique identifier, such as a D-U-N-S code, or an industry-specific identifier, such as an airline carrier code.

- PartyRef. Describes the business partner. It can be a URL or point to an item in the repository.

- CollaborationRole. Describes the business process supported and the roles derived from the BPSS XML document (see Listing 7.1).

- Certificate. Defines the digital certificate, such as an X.509 certificate, used by the organization for nonrepudiation or authentication.

Figure 7.5
The XML elements in a Collaboration-Protocol Profile

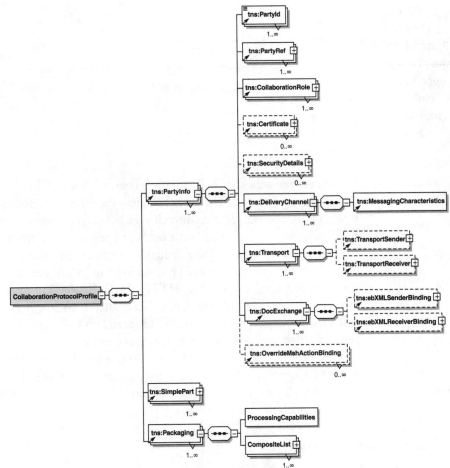

- DeliveryChannel. Defines the transport and message protocols organization supports.
- Transport. Describes the details of the messaging transport protocol, such as type, version, and endpoint.
- DocExchange. Describes the semantics of the messaging service, such as how the message is encoded, retries, deliveries, digital envelope for encryption, and namespaces. ▷

▷ A CPP is an XML document that defines the capabilities of a particular organization. An organization can be represented by multiple CPP documents.

Figure 7.6
A Collaboration-
Protocol Agree-
ment is agreed
upon based on
the Collaboration-
Protocol Profile
documents

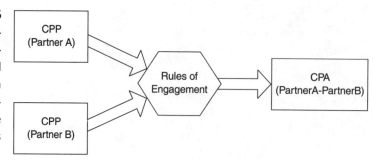

The second aspect of collaboration deals with how CPP documents for two organizations intersect. The Collaboration-Protocol Agreement defines the system level agreement for data interchange between partners, in the sense that it narrows down a subset from what both partners *can* support to what both partners *will* actually support in the exchange. A good example is the transport protocol. OfficeMin may specify HTTP and SMTP in its Collaboration-Protocol Profile, but Flute Bank can do only HTTP. The Collaboration-Protocol Agreement specifies that the ebXML exchange between the two organization will occur using the messaging service over HTTP, based on the requirements for business processes that both partners mutually agree upon.

As Figure 7.6 shows, the CPA serves, in essence, as a sort of service level agreement that, once agreed to by both parties, can be enforced by the ebXML systems on both ends of the communication. Listing 7.3 shows a sample CPA between OfficeMin and Flute Bank. ▷

Listing 7.3   The CPA document

```
<?xml version="1.0" encoding="UTF-8"?>
<!DOCTYPE CollaborationProtocolAgreement SYSTEM "http://ebxml.org/project_teams/trade_
                                          partner/cpp-cpa-v1_0.dtd">
<CollaborationProtocolAgreement cpaid="flute-officemin-cpa" xmlns="http://
                                          www.ebxml.org/namespaces/tradePartner"
    xmlns:xlink="http://www.w3.org/1999/xlink"
    xmlns:ds="http://www.w3.org/2000/09/xmldsig#">
    <Status value="proposed"/>
    <Start>2001-05-15T17:08:03.062</Start>
    <End>2032-09-27T09:16:06.124</End>
    <ConversationConstraints concurrentConversations="100" invocationLimit="10000"/>
```

> ▷   A CPA is an XML document that describes the agreement on the business conversation between two partners based on their CPP documents.

```
<PartyInfo>
   <PartyId>urn:www.officemin.com</PartyId>
   <PartyRef xlink:href="" xlink:type="simple"/>
   <CollaborationRole id="CR1">
      <ProcessSpecification xlink:href="flutebank-officemin" name="Firm Order"
                         xlink:type="simple" version="1.0"/>
      <Role xlink:href="flutebank-officemin#seller" name="seller" xlink:type=
                                                               "simple"/>
      <ServiceBinding channelId="C1" packageId="P1">
         <Service type="uriReference">/flutebank-officemin/Firm Order/seller
                                                               </Service>
      </ServiceBinding>
   </CollaborationRole>
   <Certificate certId="CRT1">
      <ds:KeyInfo/>
   </Certificate>
   <DeliveryChannel channelId="C1" docExchangeId="DE1" transportId="T1">
      <Characteristics authenticated="false" authorized="false"
                    confidentiality="false" nonrepudiationOfOrigin="false"
                    nonrepudiationOfReceipt="false"secureTransport="false"
                    syncReplyMode="none"/>
   </DeliveryChannel>
   <Transport transportId="T1">
      <SendingProtocol version="1.0">HTTP</SendingProtocol>
      <ReceivingProtocol version="1.0">HTTP</ReceivingProtocol>
      <Endpoint type="allPurpose" uri="http://machine2:80/bindpartner/servlet/
                                                      BindMessageRouter"/>
   </Transport>
   <DocExchange docExchangeId="DE1">
      <ebXMLBinding version="1.0">
         <ReliableMessaging deliverySemantics="BestEffort" idempotency="false"
                        messageOrderSemantics="NotGuaranteed">
            <Retries>0</Retries>
            <RetryInterval>0</RetryInterval>
            <PersistDuration>P</PersistDuration>
         </ReliableMessaging>
      </ebXMLBinding>
   </DocExchange>
</PartyInfo>
<PartyInfo>
   <PartyId>urn:www.flutebank.com </PartyId>
```

```
        <PartyRef xlink:href="" xlink:type="simple"/>
        <CollaborationRole id="CR2">
          <ProcessSpecification xlink:href="flutebank-officemin" name="Firm Order"
                                link:type="simple" version="1.0"/>
          <Role xlink:href="flutebank-officemin#buyer" name="buyer" xlink:type=
                                                                   "simple"/>
          <ServiceBinding channelId="C2" packageId="P1">
            <Service type="uriReference">/flutebank-officemin/Firm Order/buyer
                                                                  </Service>
          </ServiceBinding>
        </CollaborationRole>
        <Certificate certId="CRT2">
          <ds:KeyInfo/>
        </Certificate>
        <DeliveryChannel channelId="C2" docExchangeId="DE2" transportId="T2">
          <Characteristics authenticated="false" authorized="false"
                           confidentiality="false" nonrepudiationOfOrigin="false"
                           nonrepudiationOfReceipt="false" secureTransport="false"
                           syncReplyMode="none"/>
        </DeliveryChannel>
        <Transport transportId="T2">
          <SendingProtocol version="1.0">HTTP</SendingProtocol>>
          <ReceivingProtocol version="1.0">HTTP</ReceivingProtocol>
          <Endpoint type="allPurpose" uri="http://machineA:80/bindpartner/servlet/
                                                        BindMessageRouter"/>
        </Transport>
        <DocExchange docExchangeId="DE2">
          <ebXMLBinding version="1.0">
            <ReliableMessaging deliverySemantics="BestEffort" idempotency="false"
                               messageOrderSemantics="NotGuaranteed">
              <Retries>0</Retries>
              <RetryInterval>0</RetryInterval>
              <PersistDuration>P</PersistDuration>
            </ReliableMessaging>
          </ebXMLBinding>
        </DocExchange>
      </PartyInfo>
      <Packaging id="P1">
        <ProcessingCapabilities generate="true" parse="true"/>
        <SimplePart id="SP0" mimetype="text/xml"/>
      </Packaging>
</CollaborationProtocolAgreement>
```

Figure 7.7 shows the key XML elements of a Collaboration-Protocol Agreement:

- Status. One partner generates a Collaboration-Protocol Agreement and offers it to the other for approval. The status element describes the stage of agreement the CPA has reached between them. It can take only the discrete values of proposed, agreed, and signed.

- Start and End. The Start and End elements represent the beginning and end of the period during which this Collaboration-Protocol Agreement is active.

- ConversationConstraints. This optional element describes the number of *conversations* that may be held under this CPA and the number that may be held concurrently.

- PartyInfo. This is the same as the PartyInfo in the Collaboration-Protocol Profile and is used to describe the information for each partner. Note that there must be two and only two PartyInfo elements in a CPA, because a CPA is between two business partners.

- PackagingInfo. Describes the ebXML (SOAP) message headers and the attachment and its associated properties for security, MIME content, namespaces, and so on.

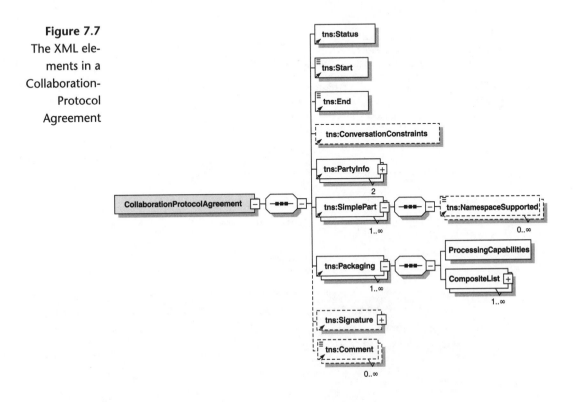

Figure 7.7
The XML elements in a Collaboration-Protocol Agreement

- Signature. Describes the digital signature as per the XML-DSIG specifications and namespace (at *www.w3.org/2000/09/xmldsig#*). ▷

Having taken a look at the BPSS and CPP-CPA, let us redraw Figure 7.2 with more detail in it to elaborate on the design-time and runtime aspects of this collaboration. This is shown in Figure 7.8. Clearly, the registry is a central interaction point between the two partners. Let us now look at this in more detail.

ebXML Registry-Repository Service

In Chapter 6, we talked about registries and their role in a business exchange. In this chapter, we will focus on the ebXML registry service and model. An ebXML registry is similar in concept to the UDDI registry but much broader in scope. In general, a registry is an important block in a business collaboration, because it serves as a central point where an organization can describe itself and its services, business semantics, and processes for other partners to retrieve.

The ebXML a registry is composed of two different concepts—*registry* and *repository.* Because of this, the ebXML registry is often referred to as the *reg-rep.* A registry is what we discussed when we were talking about UDDI, in that a registry

Figure 7.8
Design-time
and runtime
components
in detail

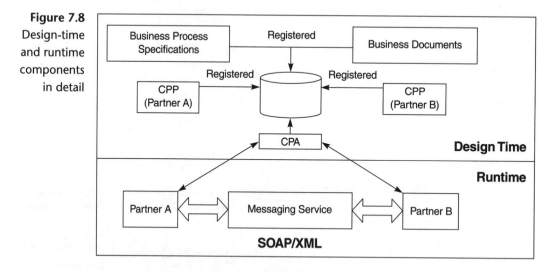

▷   JWSDL JSR-157, lead by Sybase and Cyclone Commerce, is a work in progress to provide a standard set of Java APIs for representing and manipulating CPP/CPA documents.

stores information *about* items, not the items themselves. A repository, on the other hand, is where the items are physically stored; it serves as a database that is exposed by the services of a registry. Together, they provide key functions, including discovery-storage of information and discovery-storage of information assets. This is the fundamental difference between UDDI and ebXML.

The ebXML registry service is described by two specifications that separate the static and dynamic structures of the registry into two discrete, object-oriented views:

- The *ebXML Registry Information Model* (RIM) describes the registry's static representation in terms of a model or the blueprints for the registry's logical design.
- The *ebXML Registry Services Specification* describes the registry's dynamic structure in terms of its interfaces and API. ▷

The Registry Information Model describes in terms of metadata the structures and relationships that can be stored in the registry. It is not a database schema or the registry content; it is simply an object-oriented roadmap of the data. To understand this further, recall the structures discussed about UDDI; namely, the tModels, businessEntity, businessService, and so on. That was the information model for UDDI. The ebXML information model is actually richer than the UDDI model and also more intuitive in terms of its terminology, as Figure 7.9 shows.

Figure 7.9
Relationships in the Registry Information Model

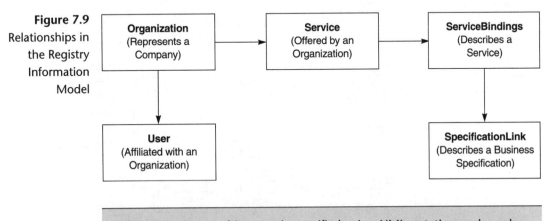

▷   ebXML registry architecture is specified using UML notation and can be implemented in any programming language. This chapter gives you an overview of what is involved in the *Registry Information Model*. We will take a closer look at RIM and registry services in Chapter 12.

Figure 7.10 shows a more detailed view of the information model. Organiza-tions have Users and Service objects that may be classified based on a ClassificationScheme. All items that represent stored metadata in the registry are subclasses of a RegistryObject. A RegistryObject can have AuditableEvents and Classifications associated with it.

The ebXML Registry Services Specification defines the registry service in ab-stract terms, using:

- A set of interfaces that must be exposed by the registry
- The set of operations that must be supported in each interface
- The parameters and responses that must be supported by each operation

These interfaces and operations are not defined in a particular programming language but are specified in abstract terms and use XML to describe the interac-tions. The ebXML registry is abstracted using the notion of a LifeCycleManager and a QueryManager interface, as Figure 7.11 shows. The LifeCycleManager is re-sponsible for exposing operations relating to the creation and management of registry objects defined in the RIM. The QueryManager interface specifies opera-tions for querying the registry and the underlying content in the repository. The client is abstracted using a RegistryClient interface that the registry can use for callbacks.

Figure 7.10
ebXML Registry
Information
Model (source:
ebXML RIM
specifications)

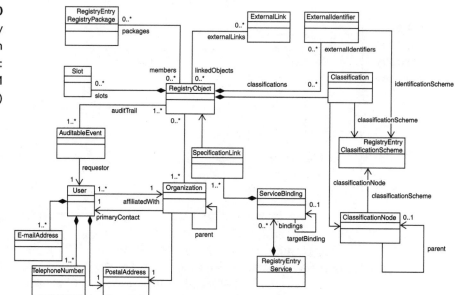

Figure 7.11
Registry
interfaces

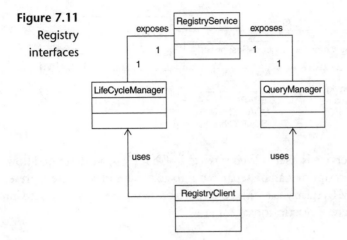

To understand how the abstractions are used, let us look at an example. The LifeCycleManager defines an operation called SubmitObjects, which clients can use to submit data to the registry, as Figure 7.11 shows. The operation takes a SubmitObjectRequest as an argument, and the registry responds by invoking the onResponse method in the RegistryClient. Each of these abstractions (Submit-ObjectsRequest, RegistryResponse etc) is defined using an XML schema. The registry service itself can be implemented in any programming language, as long as the interface supports this schema. ▷

The implementation has to expose the services of the registry using concrete protocol bindings and a wire protocol, like any other Web service. The ebXML Registry Services Specification defines two bindings. The implementation is free to use either or both:

- SOAP bindings using the HTTP protocol, shown in Figure 7.12
- ebXML Messaging Service binding

The SOAP/HTTP bindings specify the services using a document-literal binding and work similar to UDDI. The ebXML messaging service, covered in the next section, facilitates asynchronous SOAP/XML messaging between two points. When using this binding for the interaction, clients can realize the benefits of the messaging service (e.g., reliability, asynchronous invocation) but need to go though an ebXML messaging implementation on their side.

▷   The registry service interface schema is defined at *www.oasis-open.org/ committees/regrep/documents/2.0/schema/rs.xsd.*

Figure 7.12
Registry
bindings

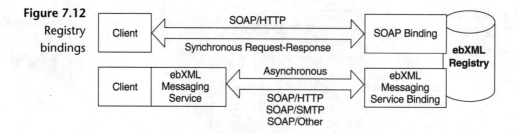

The registry service is itself a Web service. In Chapter 5, we described how a WSDL service description can be separated into abstract and concrete representations. The ebXML registry uses this concept to break up the registry service into abstract and concrete descriptions:

- The abstract representation of the ebXML registry service describes its operations and messages using the WSDL at *www.oasis-open.org/committees/regrep/documents/2.0/services/Registry.wsdl*.

- The concrete description of the registry describes the bindings to SOAP using the WSDL at *www.oasis-open.org/committees/regrep/documents/2.0/services/RegistrySOAPBinding.wsdl*.

We will break off the topic of the ebXML registry at this point, hoping to have provided sufficient information without too much detail. We revisit ebXML registries in Chapter 12, when we talk about working with registries from Java. As a final thought, we will address an often-asked question by architects on the comparison between UDDI and ebXML registries.

UDDI or ebXML

Functionally, the ebXML registry is a superset of the UDDI registry, even though UDDI may seem to have a greater momentum at present. Both specifications are now under the umbrella of the OASIS consortium and offer overlapping functionality and feature sets. A bit of confusion often surrounds the two, and in this section, we will compare and contrast them.

Information Model In Chapter 6, we looked at the UDDI information model, and in Figure 7.10, we looked at the ebXML information model. Both models came about as a result of identifying use cases for the registry, which differ in their fundamental approach. The UDDI use cases are focused more on publishing organization and service information, whereas the ebXML use cases seek to address the broader issues of B2B collaboration. This difference is reflected in the models.

The forte of the UDDI Registry Information Model is the focus on business and service *listings*. However, this model does not address some of the interactions involved in the collaboration. The ebXML RIM is described in more intuitive terms and supports the *storage* of arbitrary content, represented by a RegistryObject. This is a powerful concept, because the physical content (such as XML documents describing the WSDL, Collaboration-Protocol Profile, Collaboration-Protocol Agreement, and Business Process Specification Schema) can be stored and retrieved from the registry.

- The UDDI Registry Information Model supports a fixed set of relationships between its primary entities (the company and the service). ebXML supports the creation of arbitrary associations between any two objects, which map well to the UML associations that may be described in a business model. So, for example, two XML schemas can be stored in the ebXML registry, and an association representing a version change (i.e., supersede) can be indicated.

Taxonomies and Classifications In Chapter 6, we showed how a taxonomy is represented by a tModel in a UDDI registry. tModels are overloaded, in that they have other uses (e.g., in Chapter 12, we show how a tModel can represent the WSDL service interface). UDDI inherently supports three taxonomies (NAICS, UNSPSC, and ISO 3166), and users may submit new tModels to proxy for additional taxonomies. The issue is that since there is no way to clearly represent this taxonomy, there is no way for clients to either browse or validate the usage. ebXML, on the other hand, supports internal and external taxonomies and browsing from the client.

Registry Queries The inquiry API for both registries has been derived from the information model, which is derived from the core use cases. This is reflected in how the client can query the registry. The UDDI client API (in XML) is simple and allows for search on a business, service, or tModel. The ebXML registry, on the other hand, supports the fixed set of queries on key objects in the information model as well as declarative queries, where SQL syntax may be retrieved to search, query, and retrieve content.

Security UDDI supports a simple password-based authentication scheme over HTTP for the publishing API. HTTPS is supported in UDDI v. 2.0. The ebXML registry, on the other hand, uses digital certificates for authentication and maintains audit trails on content (e.g., who changed specific objects, and when).

Internal and external taxonomies, queries for UDDI and declarative queries on ebXML, password-based user authentication in UDDI and digital-certificate-based authentication using JAXR are all covered further in Chapter 12.

Protocol Support A registry exposes itself with an XML interface and API, which need to be accessed using some transport protocol. UDDI supports the use of these XML APIs over SOAP/HTTP and SOAP/HTTPS. The ebXML registry supports the use of these API using SOAP/HTTP directly, as UDDI does, or the ebXML messaging service. The messaging service, discussed in the next section, is layered on SOAP 1.1 with attachments and HTTP. This also allows the client to interact asynchronously with the service and the service to asynchronously respond to the client.

The options provided by the ebXML registry give business partners greater flexibility in the mechanism and infrastructure to use.

WSDL for Registry The registry itself is a Web service and is capable of being described by a WSDL. The ebXML registry clearly describes its service interface using a WSDL, as mentioned earlier. This capability of describing the UDDI registry using WSDL has been added in UDDI v. 3.0. ▷

ebXML Message Service

Successful collaboration between business partners must include a mechanism to handle the flow of requests from one end to another and take context (e.g., who is the requestor, committed service levels, privacy, prior fulfillment, and personalization) into account before determining the flow. This is the runtime component identified in Figure 7.8. The ebXML messaging service specification defines a reliable means to exchange business messages using SOAP without relying on proprietary technologies or solutions. It is a critical piece in the ebXML architecture, because it solves many of the problems inherent in the EDI messaging systems we described earlier in this chapter.

The messaging service defines two aspects of messaging:

1. How the message is packaged.
2. What different components are present in the messaging system to support the transport and processing of the message.

> ▷ An organization can expose an ebXML registry and can even register this as a Web service in UDDI—see *www.ebxml.org/specs/rrUDDI.pdf.*

In Chapter 4, we talked about the concept of vertical extensibility in SOAP, in which other specifications extend SOAP by specifying schemas for the SOAP header. This is precisely what the ebXML messaging service does, by defining a packaging scheme using the SOAP envelope, as Figure 7.13 shows.

The message package is based on SOAP with attachments and consists of a MIME-multipart structure. The package contains the SOAP envelope and the payload, which may be any business document in any format. The specifications define the ebXML specific headers extensions contained in the header element of the SOAP message and processed by the messaging server on the receiving side. The MessageHeader is added to the message with a mustUnderstand=1 attribute, so that it is processed by the other end and contains the following subelements:

Figure 7.13
The ebXML
message
(source: ebXML
Message Service
Specification)

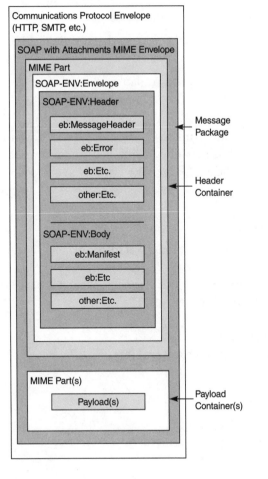

- From and To. Describe the PartyId and Role of the two parties involved in the message exchange. The PartyId and Role are based on the Collaboration-Protocol Agreement the parties have agreed upon for this exchange.

- CPAId. The Collaboration-Protocol Agreement between the two partners. It is a URI that points to the location in the reg-rep of the Collaboration-Protocol Agreement or another URL where the CPA may be mutually accessed.

- ConversationId. Collaborating business partners will typically exchange a group of messages creating a conversation. This element identifies the message as belonging to a particular conversation.

- Service. Refers to the service targeted by this message.

- Action. Refers to a particular task or action in the targeted service.

- MessageData. Contains metadata, such as the message ID, a timestamp, and time to live information about the message.

- DuplicateElimination. Tells the receiver that it should check if the message is a duplicate.

- Description. Provides a human-readable description of the message.

For example, Listing 7.4 shows the SOAP message containing the ebXML message headers from Flute Bank to OfficeMin. What is not shown is the actual message payload, the business document. The payload would be part of the MIME attachment in the SOAP message.

Listing 7.4   The ebXML SOAP message

```
<?xml version="1.0" encoding="UTF-8"?>
<soap-env:Envelope xmlns:soap-env="http://schemas.xmlsoap.org/soap/envelope/">
<soap-env:Header>
    <eb:MessageHeader xmlns:eb=http://www.ebxml.org/namespaces/messageHeader
        eb:version="1.0" soap-env:mustUnderstand="1">
        <eb:From>
            <eb:PartyId eb:type="URI">
                http://www.flutebank.com/ordersupplies
            </eb:PartyId>
        </eb:From>
        <eb:To>
            <eb:PartyId eb:type="URI">
                http://www.officemin.com/processorders
            </eb:PartyId>
        </eb:To>
        <eb:CPAId>
```

```
                http://www.flutebank.com/agreements/agreementwithofficemin.xml
    </eb:CPAId>
        <eb:ConversationId>www.flute.com/orders/829202</eb:ConversationId>
        <eb:Service eb:type="">purchaseorderservice</eb:Service>
        <eb:Action>Purchaseorder</eb:Action>
        <eb:MessageData>
            <eb:MessageId>
                    89fcfba5-fac8-4ddd-94b1-ba74339d42de
            </eb:MessageId>
            <eb:Timestamp>1031591106992</eb:Timestamp>
        </eb:MessageData>
    </eb:MessageHeader>
</soap-env:Header>
<soap-env:Body/>
</soap-env:Envelope>
```

The ebXML messaging specifications define three logical architecture levels between the business application and the network protocols that carry this SOAP message, as Figure 7.14 shows:

- The message service interface
- The message service handler
- The transport interface

The message service interface is the portion of the service that applications interact with. It forms an application interface for business applications to invoke the message handler. The message service handler (MSH) is the software system that handles the message and contains basic services, such as authentication, header parsing, encryption, and message packaging. The messaging specifications define these abstract areas of functionality, how they must act, and how the service as a whole must act. For example, the specifications define how authentication information can be included in the ebXML message headers using digital signatures and how the service must provide reliable messaging functionality.

The specifications do not define any particular implementation of these abstractions. What they define is the behavior of the messaging service and the functional areas it must support. For example, the specifications do not define an API for the message service interface. A vendor who provides the messaging software will provide the API to interact with the service. (For Java applications, this is where JAXM comes in, which we cover in Chapter 11). However, what the specifications define is the bindings with HTTP and SMTP, as Figure 7.15 shows.

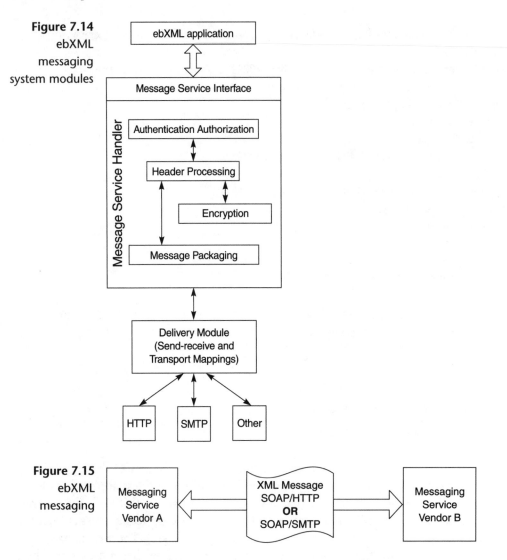

Figure 7.14
ebXML
messaging
system modules

Figure 7.15
ebXML
messaging

If two vendors conform to these bindings for the SOAP message, which is an XML document and an attachment, they will not need to bother about what technology the other is implemented in. The message package, the transport, the format on the wire, and the communication, which together form an *ebXML reliable messaging protocol,* are standardized by the specifications.

Earlier, we mentioned how the Collaboration-Protocol Agreement forms an agreement between two business partners, and the messaging service is required to enforce it at runtime. Typically, the implementation will be configured to point to the location of the CPA between the parties in an ebXML registry-repository. When the service is invoked to send the message, it will validate that the message conforms to the agreement between the two partners.

As with registries, we will again pause in our discussion on the messaging service and resume it in Chapter 11, where we talk about implementing XML messaging.

> Putting It All Together

Until now, we have talked about how a business process can be defined, how agreements set up the registry, and the messaging service. Let us see how they come together to realize the business collaboration scenario between Flute Bank and its stationery supplier, OfficeMin, which provides an online ordering service.

1. OfficeMin builds an ebXML-compliant application or buys an off-the-shelf product and implements the business process.

2. It then uploads its company profile and Collaboration-Protocol Profile to the ebXML registry. Together, they describe the business scenarios in XML and associated messages the company is able to engage in.

3. Flute Bank wants to engage in business with OfficeMin. It queries the ebXML registry-repository and retrieves OfficeMin's Collaboration-Protocol Profile.

4. Flute Bank saves its own profile and capabilities in the registry for OfficeMin or other partners to retrieve.

5. Flute Bank determines that it is able to execute a certain scenario (e.g., place a purchase order) with OfficeMin, but before engaging in that scenario, it submits a Collaboration-Protocol Agreement. This outlines the scenario it wants to use as well as certain transport- and security-related requirements.

6. OfficeMin accepts and agrees to the CPA.

7. Based on the scenarios it retrieved, Flute Bank implements its end of the system (e.g., the application to send purchase orders and process returned invoices).

8. Flute Bank and OfficeMin engage in business.

Figure 7.16 shows a simplified version of these interaction steps, without return arrows. For example, step 2 has an associated return, where the registry validates the data and sends a reply (either synchronously or asynchronously) acknowledging the data.

Figure 7.16
A business
collaboration
scenario

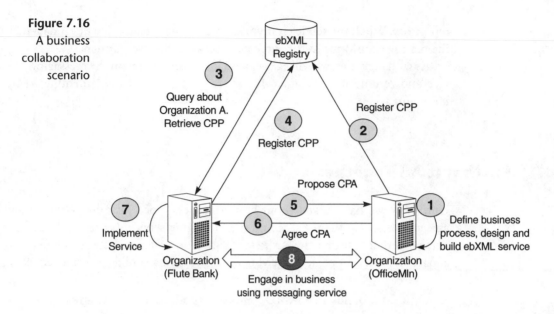

> Summary

Earlier in this book, we talked about service-oriented architecture, SOAP, UDDI, WSDL, and now, briefly, about ebXML. So, what is the value proposition of ebXML today? This will be easier to understand if we step back and take a look at the kinds of Web services that exist. These can be grouped into two broad categories:

- **Procedure-based.** A business application invokes a service and gets something back—for example, it sends a purchase order and receives a response.

- **Message-conversation-based.** A business application invokes a service that could respond asynchronously, and both sides exchange multiple messages to form a conversation—for example, it sends a purchase order and receives a response, after which the application receives an invoice and processes a payment.

Procedure-based Web services use the WSDL-UDDI-SOAP technologies (WUST) stack to realize the publish-find-bind scenarios outlined in Chapter 2. The requirements of the send category inherently impose a level of complexity on the applications. As discussed earlier in this chapter, ebXML has really come into existence to address the requirements of the collaborating businesses and seeks to solve a bigger problem.

Table 7.1   ebXML Specification Status to Date

	Version	Status
Registry	2.0	Approved standard
Messaging	2.0	Approved standard
CPP-CPA	2.0	Approved standard October 2002
BPSS	1.01	Public review v. 1.05 closed June 2002
Core components	1.85	Public review closed November 22, 2002

Even though SOAP, WSDL, and UDDI are important Web services standards in themselves, they do not address some of the issues ebXML seeks to address. For example, how do businesses describe their capabilities and processes and store them in a central place? How can the businesses engage in reliable, secure messaging?

ebXML is a community effort in which many organizations are contributors. As Table 7.1 shows, some of the specifications have evolved beyond version 2, with vendor as well as open source implementations. ▷

If ebXML is so powerful, why are few organizations actually embracing it? The issues are twofold. First is the business issue, where organizations want to wait for others to take the risk of trying out evolving technologies. The second, larger, issue is more political. For example even though Microsoft is a member of OASIS, it does not support the ebXML initiative per se, and some of its proposals overlap ebXML functionality.

ebXML has its share of issues too. Despite the success of the initiative as a consortium in defining specifications widely agreed upon, the reality is that adoption of the specification is left to vendors and implementers, which are but a handful and only in some areas (e.g., registries and messaging).

We have looked at the evolution of the ebXML effort, its high-level architecture in terms of the business process model, the agreements, the registry, and the messaging systems. Our intent has not been to position ebXML or other technologies as better (or not) but to provide the lay of the land in the ebXML world. We have not touched upon some areas of ebXML (e.g., core components and UN/CEFACT modeling methodology), because they are still evolving. We have chosen to present what is possible with ebXML today, so that architects can make an informed choice when designing applications and solutions.

▷   Open source implementations of the registry as well as the messaging service can be found at *www.freebxml.org*.

Part {Two}

The JAX APIs

In this section, we will cover all of the JAX APIs that are the foundation of Web services within Java. You will learn about both the basic usage of the APIs and several advanced techniques.

Chapter Eight *Java Web Service Developer Pack*

The Java Web Services Developer Pack is an integrated toolset that allows developers to build, test, and deploy XML applications and Web services. JWSDP provides Java standard implementations of Web services standards including SOAP, WSDL, UDDI, and ebXML.

Chapter Nine *JAXP*

The Java API for XML processing enables processing of XML documents using SAX, DOM, and XSLT. JAXP allows applications to parse and transform XML documents independent of a particular XML processing implementation.

Chapter Ten *JAX-RPC*

The Java API for XML-Based Remote Procedure Calls enables Java applications to develop SOAP-based interoperable and portable Web services.

Chapter Eleven *JAXM*

The Java API for XML Messaging enables applications to send and receive document-oriented XML messages using a pure Java API.

Chapter Twelve *JAXR*

The Java API for XML Registries provides a uniform and standard Java API for accessing XML-based registries and repositories. An XML registry is an enabling infrastructure for building, deploying, and discovering Web services.

Chapter Thirteen *JAXB*

The Java Architecture for XML Binding provides an API and tools that automate the mapping between XML documents and Java objects.

Chapter

Java Web Service Developer Pack

In the preceding chapters, we looked at the concepts surrounding service-oriented architectures and explained three fundamental technologies that make up the foundation of Web services platforms: SOAP, WSDL, and UDDI. Now that you have a grasp of the fundamental concepts and specifications, the next few chapters will introduce you to the architecture and programming of Web service applications on the Java platform. But before you can switch focus from Web service concepts to practical Web service aspects, a short tour of the development kit we have chosen for programming and running all examples in this book is in order. In this chapter, we provide an overview of the Java Web Service Developer Pack 1.0 (Java WSDP). Specific information on how to use Java WSDP for development is provided in relevant chapters.

Java WSDP is an integrated toolset, targeted at Web service developers, for building and deploying basic Web service functionality on the Java platform. To be clear, several other such kits are available for developers, such as Apache AXIS and Systinet WASP. We have chosen to develop our applications and examples on Java WSDP simply because it contains the latest (sometimes even early releases) of the standard Java APIs for XML and their runtime support libraries. Java WSDP is a free download from Sun, available at *http://java.sun.com/webservices/downloads/webservicespack.html*.

Java WSDP is a superset of the Java XML pack. The XML pack is meant for other software integrators and tool vendors and contains the Java XML APIs (the JAX pack). Java WSDP is meant for developers and adds to the JAX pack the Tomcat engine, a Web services registry server, UDDI registry browser, Ant build tool, and deployment and compile-time tools.

▷ Setting Up Java WSDP

After downloading the files, install the kit (`/bin/sh jwsdp-1_0_01-unix.sh` on UNIX or `jwsdp-1_0_01-windows-i586.exe` on Windows). The `<install_dir>/bin` should be placed in your environment `path` variable. The JAR files in the `<install_dir>/lib` should be placed in your class `path`.

▷ Java WSDP Components

The components that come with the Java WSDP download can be classified into four broad categories, shown in Figure 8.1: Java XML APIs and reference implementations, development and deployment toolsets, the runtime environment, and supporting specifications.

Java XML APIs

- **Java API for XML Processing (JAXP).** JAXP exposes standard XML parsing and validation APIs for processing and transforming XML documents in Java. JAXP 1.2_01 provides support for DOM, SAX, XSLT, and XML schemas. The download comes with the APIs and the Apache Xerces parser and XSLTC. JAXP provides a framework that allows you to use any compliant parser and transformation engine instead of the supplied implementations.

- **Java API for XML-based Remote Procedure Calls (JAX-RPC).** JAX-RPC is used to create Java Web service producers that use SOAP 1.1-based remote procedure calls. JAX-RPC also can be used to develop Java Web service consumers of these RPC services.

- **Java API for XML Messaging (JAXM).** JAXM provides an abstraction over messaging transports and enables Java applications to send and receive document-oriented XML messages. JAXM implements SOAP 1.1 and relies on the SAAJ specification for support of SOAP with attachments.

- **SOAP with Attachments API for Java (SAAJ).** SAAJ enables applications to create messages conforming to the SOAP with Attachments note. Initially a part of the JAXM API, it is now a separate API, because it is used by other JAX APIs as well.

- **Java API for XML Registries (JAXR).** JAXR provides a uniform API for accessing and modifying entries in both ebXML and UDDI registries.

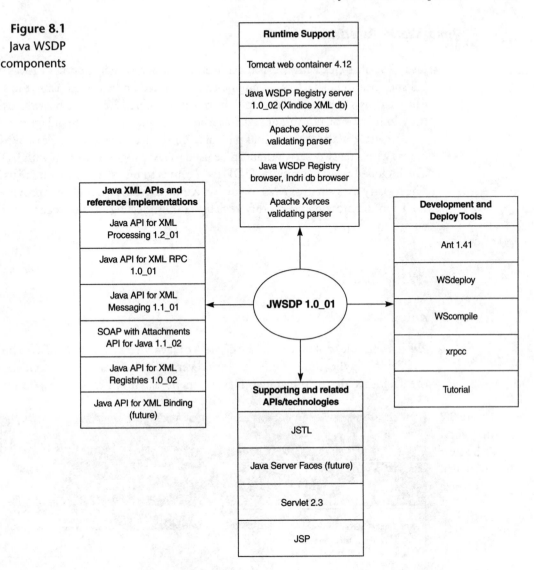

Figure 8.1
Java WSDP
components

- **Java Architecture for XML Binding (JAXB).** JAXB enables an XML schema (or DTD) to be transformed into the equivalent Java classes. The generated classes handle the details of parsing instance XML and adhering to all schema constraints. When we started work on this book, the JAXB specifications were still in draft stages and an implementation was not shipped with the Java WSDP download. The Java WSDP release now includes a JAXB 1.0 implementation.

Java WSDP Runtime

Java WSDP comes with the Tomcat Web container, which supports the Servlet 2.3 specification. The Tomcat engine can be started and stopped using the supplied scripts startup/shutdown or can be administered from the browser using the administration console at *http://localhost:8080/admin*, (shown in Figure 8.2).

A registry is also an essential part of Web services architecture. Java WSDP comes with a registry server that can be used to test programs written with JAXR. The included registry supports UDDI v. 2 and is to be used as a private registry. The registry uses a native XML database, Xindice (from Apache), and provides a GUI tool to browse and modify registry entries. Setting up the registry is discussed in Chapter 12.

Java WSDP Tools

Ant

Ant is a versatile toolkit used in the context of Java Web service and J2EE to build and deploy applications. Ant's power and versatility as a build tool is evident by the fact that many Integrated Development Environments (IDEs) provide

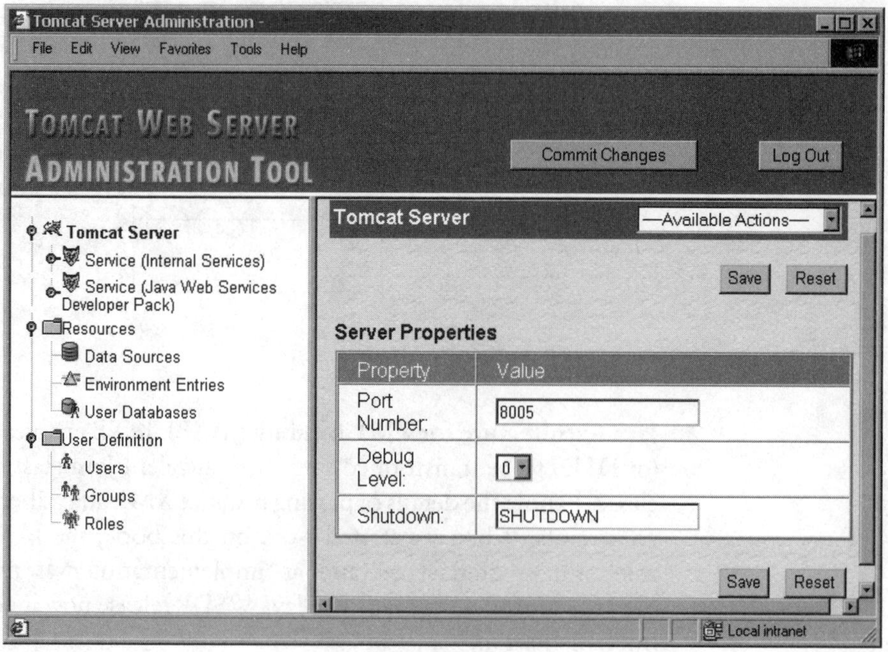

Figure 8.2
The Tomcat
Web server
administration
console

integrated Ant support. Even if you are using Ant from the command line, it is simple to deploy Web service components on a large scale. The default Ant download comes with several built-in tasks (JAR, ZIP, CAB, copy, FTP) and some product- or platform-specific tasks (for Junit testing, EJBC, etc.) in a separate optional download. Java WSDP comes with prebuilt Ant tasks for compiling stubs and skeletons and for deploying Web services to the Tomcat container.

Before using Ant to deploy Web services, you should create a build.properties file in your home directory. The file should have the username and password of the Tomcat administrator:

```
username=<user>
password=<password>
```

wsdeploy

The wsdeploy tool comes with the Java WSDP package. It is used to create a deployable WAR file that contains all the information necessary to create a JAX-RPC endpoint. The WAR file must then be deployed to Tomcat. Before looking at the syntax for invoking these tools, let's take a look at how a JAX-RPC program is deployed into the Tomcat container. This will provide a high-level introduction to these tools and to Ant. The sample Ant tasks and targets file shown in Figure 8.3 is a modified version of the scripts that come with the Java WSDP tutorial.

Note that wsdeploy is a standalone tool and can be used without using Ant. Figure 8. 4 shows the working model.

The syntax for usage is:

```
wsdeploy <options> <input war file>.
  where <options> are  :
  -classpath <path>    :   classpath (optional)
  -tmpdir <directory>  :   working directory for generated, temporary files
  -keep                :   keep temporary files generated (including WSDL
                           corresponding to the service)
  -o <output war file> :   (required) location of the generated,deployable war file
  -verbose             :   verbose output
  -version             :   print version information
```

The input WAR file contains the server-side classes and two manifest files. The first is the web.xml file, which contains the standard Web application information (see below). The second is, in this particular case, a file specific to JAX-RPC programs created using the Java WSDP and is explained in Chapter 10.

Figure 8.3
Sample tasks
for creating a
JAX-RPC server

Sample Tasks for Creating a JAX-RPC Server

```
<target name="prepare"
    description="Creates the build and dist directories" >
    <mkdir dir="${build}/client/" />
    <mkdir dir="${build}/server/" />
    <mkdir dir="${build}/shared/" />
    <mkdir dir="${build}/temp-generated" />
    <mkdir dir="${dist}" />
    <mkdir dir="${build}/WEB-INF/classes/" />
</target>
```

3. All compiled classes are moved to three different directories: client specific classes go to the /client directory, server specific classes go into the server directory and classes needed by consumers and service producers go into the /shared directory. The temp-generated directory is needed for temporary java files (ties/stubs/WSDL) that are generated by the tools.

```
<target name="compile-server" depends="prepare"
    description="Compiles the server-side source code">
    <javac
        srcdir="${proj-source}"
        destdir="${build}/shared/"
        includes="*.java"
        excludes="*Client.java"
    />
</target>
```

2. Compile-server invokes javac or another compiler and compiles source files into the build/shared directory. Build directory is a variable set in the build.xml file. This target ensures that all required directories are present by invoking the prepare target first.

```
<target name="setup-web-inf"
    description="Copies files to build/WEB-INF">
    <echo message="Setting up ${build}/WEB-INF...."/>
    <delete dir="${build}/WEB-INF" />
    <copy todir="${build}/WEB-INF/classes/">
        <fileset dir="${build}/shared/" />
        <fileset dir="${build}/server/" />
    </copy>
    <copy file="web.xml" todir="${build}/WEB-INF" />
    <copy file="jaxrpc-ri.xml" todir="${build}/WEB-INF" />
</target>
```

4. Copies compiled classes from server and shared directories into the WEB-INF/classes directory and copies manifest files for deployment into the WEB-INF directory. **web.xml** is a web-app document for providing deployment information to the Tomcat container. The **jaxrpc-ri.xml** file is specific to JAX-RPC and WSDP. It is explained in detail in the JAX-RPC chapter.

```
<target name="package"
    description="Packages the WAR file">
    <echo message="Packaging the WAR...."/>
    <delete file="${dist}/${portable-war}" />
    <jar jarfile="${dist}/${portable-war}" >
        <fileset dir="${build}" includes="WEB-INF/**" />
    </jar>
</target>
```

5. JARs the files from Step 4.

```
<target name="process-war" depends="set-ws-scripts"
    description="Runs wsdeploy to generate the ties and create a
deployable WAR file">
    <echo message="Running wsdeploy...."/>
    <delete file="${dist}/${deployable-war}" />
    <delete dir="${build}/temp/generated"/>
    <mkdir dir="${build}/temp/generated"/>
<exec executable="${wsdeploy}">
    <arg line="-tmpdir"/>
    <arg line="${build}/temp/generated"/>
    <!-- <arg line="-keep"/> -->

    <arg line="-o"/>
    <arg line="${dist}/${deployable-war}"/>
    <arg line="${dist}/${portable-war}"/>
    <arg line="-verbose"/>
</exec>
</target>
```

6. Runs the **wsdeploy** tool to generate ties, the WSDL file, and repackage the war file into a ready-to-be deployed format. This war file can then be deployed to Tomcat.

```
<target name="build-service" depends="clean,clean-wars, compile-server,
    setup-web-inf,package,process-war"
    description="Executes the targets needed to build the service.">
</target>
```

1. **"ant build-service"** command from the command line executes this target. This target executes tasks needed to compile, generate ties, and package the service producer side of the web service.
Targets clean and clean-wars are not shown here. They simply delete old directories and war files.

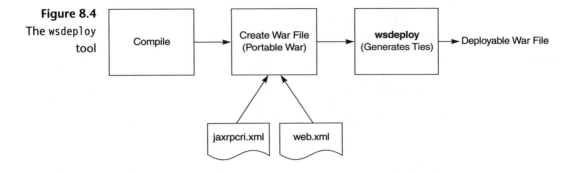

Figure 8.4
The wsdeploy tool

wscompile

The wscompile tool is used to generate the client-side stubs for RPC Web services. This tool is a newer version of the xrpcc tool. (Both provide similar functionality now, but xrpcc will presumably be replaced by wscompile in future releases). The Ant tasks shown below are a high-level illustration of how a JAX-RPC client is packaged.

The Ant tasks above provide an overview of the steps needed to create and JAR a JAX-RPC client. These are shown in Figure 8.5. The syntax for invoking wscompile to generate stubs and/or ties is

```
wscompile [options] configuration_file
where [options] include:
  -classpath <path>        classpath
  -d <directory>           destination of generated output files
  -g                       generate debugging info
  -gen                     same as -gen:client
  -gen:client              generate client artifacts (stubs, etc.)
  -gen:server              generate server artifacts (ties, etc.)
  -gen:both                generate both client and server artifacts
  -keep                    keep generated files
  -s <directory>           location for generated source files
  -verbose                 output messages about what the compiler is doing
  -version                 print version information
```

The configuration file is specific to wscompile. In this example, it provides the location of the WSDL file, so that client-side stubs can be generated from it. The listing below shows a sample configuration file used to generate client-side stubs (i.e., with the gen:client option). A more complete explanation of the configuration file is provided in Chapter 10.

Figure 8.5
Sample tasks
for creating a
JAX-RPC client

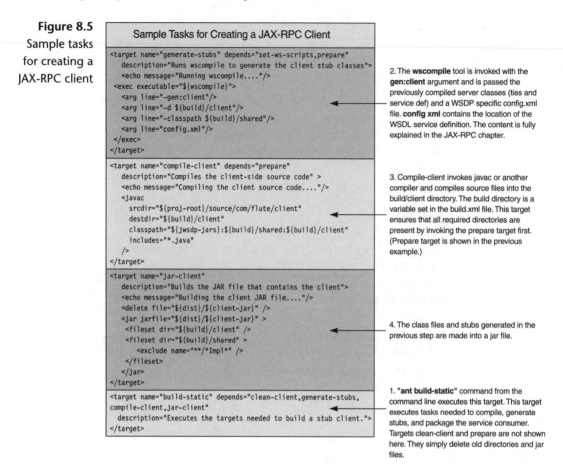

```
Sample Tasks for Creating a JAX-RPC Client

<target name="generate-stubs" depends="set-ws-scripts,prepare"
    description="Runs wscompile to generate the client stub classes">
    <echo message="Running wscompile...."/>
  <exec executable="${wscompile}">
    <arg line="-gen:client"/>
    <arg line="-d ${build}/client"/>
    <arg line="-classpath ${build}/shared"/>
    <arg line="config.xml"/>
  </exec>
</target>

<target name="compile-client" depends="prepare"
    description="Compiles the client-side source code" >
    <echo message="Compiling the client source code...."/>
    <javac
      srcdir="${proj-root}/source/com/flute/client"
      destdir="${build}/client"
      classpath="${jwsdp-jars}:${build}/shared:${build}/client"
      includes="*.java"
    />
</target>

<target name="jar-client"
    description="Builds the JAR file that contains the client">
    <echo message="Building the client JAR file...."/>
    <delete file="${dist}/${client-jar}" />
    <jar jarfile="${dist}/${client-jar}" >
      <fileset dir="${build}/client" />
      <fileset dir="${build}/shared" >
        <exclude name="**/*Impl*" />
      </fileset>
    </jar>
</target>

<target name="build-static" depends="clean-client,generate-stubs,
compile-client,jar-client"
    description="Executes the targets needed to build a stub client.">
</target>
```

2. The **wscompile** tool is invoked with the **gen:client** argument and is passed the previously compiled server classes (ties and service def) and a WSDP specific config.xml file. **config xml** contains the location of the WSDL service definition. The content is fully explained in the JAX-RPC chapter.

3. Compile-client invokes javac or another compiler and compiles source files into the build/client directory. The build directory is a variable set in the build.xml file. This target ensures that all required directories are present by invoking the prepare target first. (Prepare target is shown in the previous example.)

4. The class files and stubs generated in the previous step are made into a jar file.

1. **"ant build-static"** command from the command line executes this target. This target executes tasks needed to compile, generate stubs, and package the service consumer. Targets clean-client and prepare are not shown here. They simply delete old directories and jar files.

```
<?xml version="1.0" encoding="UTF-8"?>
<configuration
    xmlns="http://java.sun.com/xml/ns/jax-rpc/ri/config">
    <wsdl location=" WSDL location"
        packageName="generated file package name"/>
</configuration>
```

As seen from the syntax for invoking wscompile, the tool can be used to generate both client-side stubs *and* server-side ties. So far, we have used wsdeploy to generate and package server-side ties. Although not documented, wsdeploy presumably uses wscompile internally, passing it the gen:server argument to generate server-side ties.

Registry Browser

The *registry browser* is a GUI tool that can be used to search and add information to a UDDI registry. This is shown in Figure 8.6. It is implemented as a JAXR client and can be used to browse any registry, including the supplied Java WSDP registry. The code for this registry browser (JAXR) can be found in the `JAXRClient.java` class in the `<JWSDP_HOME>/samples/jaxr/jaxr-browser` directory.

Complete examples of using Ant, `wscompile`, `wsdeploy`, and the registry tool are provided in the Java WSDP tutorial, available at *http://java.sun.com/webservices/docs/1.0/tutorial/doc/JavaWSTutorialTOC.html*.

Java WSDP Supporting Specifications

Although not directly a part of the XML APIs, the Java WSDP supporting specifications form the core infrastructure of a Web services application and are shipped with the WSDP.

- **Java Server Pages Standard Tag Library (JSTL).** JSTL is a set of commonly used custom JSP tags, a framework for creating new tags, and an expression language that helps simplify page development. JSTL is explained in depth in Appendix B.

- **Java Server Faces.** Java Server Faces, a future technology, will include a standard set of JSP tags aimed at providing a single framework for creating complex HTML forms and HTML form elements within the JSP environment. Version 1.0 of Java WSDP does not include this technology.

- **Java Server Pages and Servlets.** JSP 1.2 and Servlet 2.3 are supported in this release of Java WSDP. JSP and Servlet technologies form the foundation technologies for Java Web services. As mentioned earlier, Java WSDP is shipped with the Tomcat engine, which provides support for these two specifications.

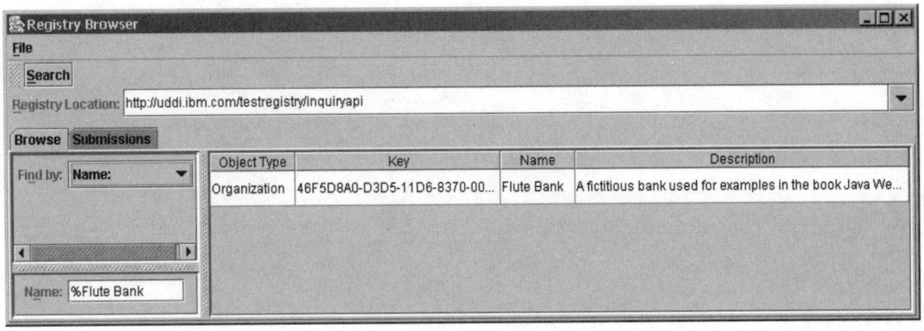

Figure 8.6
The registry
browser

▶ Summary

This short chapter provided you with an overview of Java WSDP. Each tool in the WSDP will be explained in detail in subsequent chapters where they are used. We recommend using the Ant targets as a starting point. Java WSDP does not contain any "enterprise class" features—you will have to integrate JWSDP with, say, the J2EE RI or another EJB container for writing application logic in EJBs. Java WSDP contains no reference implementation for XML security APIs (it does support basic SOAP/HTTP over SSL, however), nor does it support transaction protocols such as BTP. It is, however, a complete toolkit to model and build basic Web services that use Java APIs.

With this introduction to the Java WSDP, you are now ready to take on the next few chapters, which focus exclusively on implementing Web services on the Java platform.

Chapter

JAXP

Java API for XML Processing (JAXP) enables applications to read, write, manipulate, and transform XML data. Chapter 3 talked about XML standards and what they mean to developers. This chapter provides the reader an insight into the JAXP API and it provides a standard interface from Java applications, leveraging the same XML standards. It is assumed that the reader is sufficiently familiar with XML; this chapter is not intended to be a tutorial on XML.

From an architect's perspective, XML usage in an application can be divided into two broad categories.

- Presentation-centric: XML meant for rendering, for example, an XHTML page
- Data-centric: XML that represents data—for example, a purchase order passed between business partners

We envision that Web services will primarily use data-centric XML unless they are being used for content delivery to clients. It is interesting to note that, contrary to the general perception, the liklihood of developing Web services in Java situations where direct manipulation of XML content is required would actually be minimal. As subsequent chapters will detail, some of the other APIs, such as JAXR, JAX-RPC, JAXM, and JAXB, provide a higher level of conceptual abstraction for Java applications. Some examples of situations that would require such manipulations and direct use of JAXP would include accepting data from business partners asynchronously, validating such data against predefined schemas, transforming XML content in different rendering formats, reading configuration information in system components, and so on.

277

> JAXP Architecture

JAXP 1.0 was developed under the Java Community Process as JSR-000005 and was released in March 2000. JAXP 1.0 emerged to fill in deficiencies in the SAX 1.0 and DOM 1.0 standards. Over time, industry standards evolved (SAX 2.0, DOM 2.0), and JAXP was expanded to address those and other requirements that were identified. It was developed as JSR-63 and released as JAXP 1.1 with many new enhancements in February 2001. The specifications have subsequently undergone minor modifications in the JCP maintainence phase and have been released as JAXP 1.2, which is packaged with the JAX pack.

Beginning with J2SE 1.4 (or JDK 1.4), JAXP API is included as a part of the standard distribution and is also part of the J2EE 1.3 specifications. This means that the API will be available in all Java 1.4 runtime environments and all J2EE 1.3 containers. This is noteworthy, because prior to JAXP, there were different versions of XML parsers and transformers from different vendors that used proprietary and incompatible APIs.

JAXP is an API, but more important, it is an abstraction layer. Keep in mind that JAXP does not provide a new XML parsing mechanism or add to SAX, DOM or JDOM. As Figure 9.1a shows, it provides a standard vendor- and implementation-independendent interface for developers to use and process XML data in a meaningful way, without bothering about the details of the underlying implementation.

As Figure 9.1b shows, the abstraction in JAXP is achived from its pluggable architecture, based on the Factory pattern. JAXP defines a set of factories that return the appropriate parser or transformer. Multiple providers can be plugged under the JAXP API as long as the providers are JAXP compliant, meaning that they implement the specifications through the interfaces.

> SAX

Simple API for XML (SAX), unlike most things in the XML universe, is not a World Wide Web Consortium (W3C) specification but a public domain API that has evolved over time, through the cooperation of individuals on the xml-dev mailing list. It was originally defined as a set of Java interfaces, but working versions in other languages (e.g. C++, Perl, Python) have also evolved. ▷

> ▷ JAXP uses SAX 2.0. SAX details can be found at *www.saxproject.org* and the xml-dev mailing list at *http://xml.org/xml-dev/index.shtml.*

Figure 9.1a
Logical JAXP
architecture

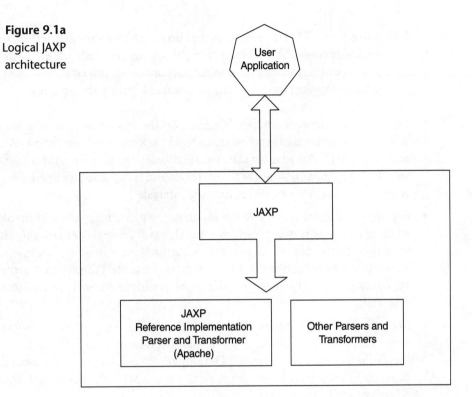

Figure 9.1b
JAXP
architecture

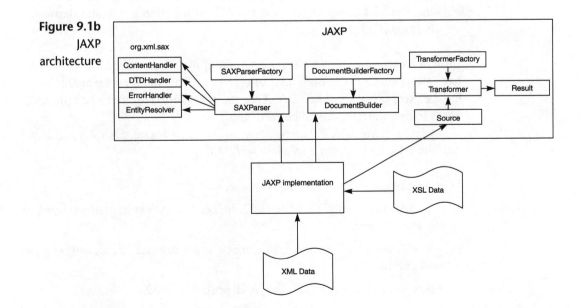

SAX parsers read XML sequentially and do event-based parsing. Effectively, the parser goes through the document serially and invokes callback methods on preconfigured handlers when major events occur during traversal.

The handlers invoked by the parser, as shown in Figure 9.1b, are as follows:

- **org.xml.sax.ContentHandler.** Methods on the implementing class are invoked when document events occur, such as startDocument(), endDocument(), or startElement(). An adaptor class DefaultHandler implements this interface with null implementations for the methods and is extended by developers to override the methods in which they are interested.

- **org.xml.sax.ErrorHandler.** Methods on the implementing class are invoked when parsing errors occur, such as error(), fatalError(), or warning(). It is usually a good idea to implement a custom error handler, because the DefaultHandler (which is also the default error handler) throws an exception for fatal errors and ignores everything else (validation errors are considered nonfatal).

- **org.xml.sax.DTDHandler.** Methods of the implementing class are invoked when a DTD is being parsed. A special handler is needed for DTDs because of their inherent non-XML syntax. Developers are unlikely to implement this interface, because Web services typically use XML schemas, which themselves are XML documents.

- **org.xml.sax.EntityResolver.** Methods of the implementing class are invoked when the SAX parser encounters an XML with a reference to an external entity (e.g., DTD or schema).

When parsing documents using SAX, the application will at a bare minimum have a ContentHandler configured to receive callbacks and an ErrorHandler to handle exceptional conditions. An ErrorHandler is also required when the XML needs to be validated, as will be seen later.

JAXP supports SAX 2.0 completely. In its current state, SAX 2.0 is divided into three packages that are overlaid with JAXP:

- org.xml.sax. Defines the SAX interfaces.
- org.xml.sax.helpers. Contains SAX helper classes that implement some of the above interfaces.
- org.xml.sax.ext. Contains SAX extensions for advanced processing (e.g., to read comments).
- javax.xml.parsers. Defines the JAXP portion of SAX.

Tables 9.1 through 9.3 describe these packages. Exceptions, deprecated classes, and classes relevant to SAX 1 are not listed.

Table 9.1 The `org.xml.sax` Package

`ContentHandler`	An interface that defines callback methods to receive notifications of XML events from the SAX parser
`DTDHandler`	An interface that defines callback methods to receive notifications of DTD parsing events
`EntityResolver`	An interface that acts as an agent of the XML reader for resolving entity references in the document
`ErrorHandler`	An interface that defines callback methods to receive notifications of error messages from the parser
`InputSource`	A class to encapsulate a single XML document for input
`Locator`	An interface for the location specification in a document
`XMLFilter`	An extension of the `XMLReader` interface to filter an `XMLReader`
`XMLReader`	An interface that defines methods to read and parse a document

Table 9.2 The `org.xml.sax.helpers` Package

`DefaultHandler`	A convenience implementation of all the core SAX handler interfaces
`LocatorImpl`	A convenience implementation of `Locator`

Table 9.3 The `org.xml.sax.ext` Package

`DeclHandler`	An interface that enables parsing of DTD declarations in an XML document
`LexicalHandler`	An interface that enables detection of normally unparsed items, such as comments and CDATA sections

JAXP and SAX

The SAX part of JAXP relevant to parsing is essentially the factory and parser class with the addition of two exception classes. This is described in Table 9.4.

Although the current implementation comes with only one SAX parser, based on a system property called `javax.xml.SAXParserFactory`, the implementation of the `SAXParserFactory` can be changed dynamically.

The following steps occur when the `SAXParserFactory` factory is instantiated to obtain a reference to a parser:

1. If the system property `javax.xml.SAXParserFactory` is set, its value is used as the class name of the parser.

2. If a `jaxp.properties` file exists in the `lib` directory of the JVM being used, it is read, and the same property is searched for.

3. If the JAR services API is available, the JAR files will be searched for the file.

4. `META-INF/services/javax.xml.parsers.SAXParserFactory`. This file contains the classname of the implementation, such as `org.apache.xerces.jaxp` `.SAXParserFactoryImpl`.

5. The default factory implementation of the reference implementation is used.

The `SAXParserFactory` can additionally be configured by using the `setFeature()` method. These properties, which are a part of SAX and not the JAXP specifications, are defined as the URI format—for example, `factory.setFeature("http://xml.org/sax/features/namespaces",true);`

Table 9.5 summarizes the relevant properties and their effects.

The factory can be informed to return a validating parser using the `setValidating(true)` method or return a parser that is namespace aware using the `setNamespaceAware(true)` method (default is false). These methods have the same effect as setting the corresponding properties above.

Let us look at a simple example of an XML file being parsed using SAX. The XML file contains administrator information for the flutebank.com server and is shown in Listing 9.1.

Table 9.4   The SAX Parsing Part of JAXP in the `javax.xml.parsers` Package

`SAXParse`	An interface that wraps an XMLReader and implementations does all the SAX parsing
`SAXParserFactory`	A factory class used to obtain a reference to the `SAXParser` and configure it if necessary, using properties

Table 9.5 Properties that Can Be Configured with the SaxPaserFactory

Property/Description	Default	Available in RI
`http://xml.org/sax/features/validation` Returns a validating parser. A parser will always check to see if the XML is well formed, but a validating parser will also validate the XML.	False	Yes
`http://xml.org/sax/features/namespaces` The parser is namespace aware and performs namespace processing.	False	Yes
`http://xml.org/sax/features/namespaces-prefixes` The parser returns the original prefixed names and attributes. If false, neither attributes nor namespace declarations are reported.	False	Yes
`http://xml.org/sax/features/string-interning` The parser internalizes `String` objects. `Strings` instantiated are pooled in the JVM during processing, using the `java.lang.String.intern()` method.	False	No. The RI uses its own string optimization.
`http://xml.org/sax/features/external-general-entities` All external text entities are included	False	True if validating parser
`http://xml.org/sax/features/external-parameter-entities` All external parameter entities and external DTD subsets are included.	False	True if validating parser

Listing 9.1 Sample XML file to be parsed with SAX

```
<?xml version="1.0"?>
<contact:flutebank xmlns:contact="http://www.flutebank.com/contacts">
    <contact:administrator type="maintenance" level="support-1">
        <contact:firstname>John</contact:firstname>
        <contact:lastname> Malkovich</contact:lastname>
        <contact:telephone>
            <contact:pager>783-393-9213</contact:pager>
            <contact:cellular>379-234-2342</contact:cellular>
            <contact:desk>322-324-2349</contact:desk>
        </contact:telephone>
```

```
            <contact:email>
                <contact:work>john.malkovich@flutebank.com</contact:work>
                <contact:personal>john.malkovich@home.com</contact:personal>
            </contact:email>
        </contact:administrator>
</contact:flutebank>
```

Listing 9.2a demonstrates the simplicity of the code needed to parse the XML with using SAX in JAXP. A factory is obtained, some properties are set, a parser is obtained from the factory, and the XML is processed using a class as the callback handler for SAX.

Listing 9.2a   SAX parsing code

```java
package com.flutebank.parsing;

import java.io.*;
import javax.xml.parsers.*;
import org.xml.sax.helpers.DefaultHandler;

public class SAXParsing {
    public static void main(String[] arg) {
        try {
        String filename = arg[0];
// Create a new factory that will create the SAX parser
        SAXParserFactory factory = SAXParserFactory.newInstance();
        factory.setNamespaceAware(true);
        SAXParser parser = factory.newSAXParser();
// Create a new handler to handle content
        DefaultHandler handler = new MySAXHandler();
// Parse the XML using the parser and the handler
        parser.parse( new File(filename), handler);
        } catch (Exception e) {
            System.out.println(e);
        }
    }
}
```

In Listing 9.2b, only some methods of the ContentHandler are overridden by the custom handler, and all three methods from the ErrorHandler are overridden to handle errors.

Listing 9.2b   SAX parsing handler

```java
package com.flutebank.parsing;
import org.xml.sax.helpers.DefaultHandler;
import org.xml.sax.*;


public class MySAXHandler extends DefaultHandler {


    /** The start of a namespace scope */
    public void startPrefixMapping(String prefix,String uri) {
        System.out.println("----Namespace scope start");
        System.out.println("      " + prefix + "=\"" + uri + "\"");
    }


    /** The end of a namespace scope */

    public void endPrefixMapping(String prefix)  {
        System.out.println("----Namespace scope end");
        System.out.println("      " + prefix);
    }



    /** The opening tag of an element.*/
    public void startElement(String namespaceURI,String localName,String
                                          qName,Attributes atts) {
        System.out.println("----Opening tag of an element");
        System.out.println("      Namespace: " + namespaceURI);
        System.out.println("     Local name: " + localName);
        System.out.println(" Qualified name: " + qName);
        for(int i=0; i<atts.getLength(); i++) {
            System.out.println("      Attribute: " + atts.getQName(i) +
                                 "=\"" + atts.getValue(i) + "\"");
        }
    }


  // Error handler methods
/** Handle warnings during parsing */
   public void warning(SAXParseException exp) throws SAXException {
        show("Warning",exp);
        throw(exp);
   }
```

```
/** Handle errors during parsing */
    public void error(SAXParseException exp) throws SAXException {
        show("Error",exp);
        throw(exp);
    }

/** Handle fatal errors during parsing */
    public void fatalError(SAXParseException exp) throws SAXException {
        show("Fatal Error",exp);
        throw(exp);
    }

/** Private method for printing details */
    private void show(String type,SAXParseException exp) {
        System.out.println(type + ": " + exp.getMessage());
        System.out.println("Line " + exp.getLineNumber() +
                            " Column " + exp.getColumnNumber());
        System.out.println("System ID: " + exp.getSystemId());
    }
}
```

The handlers can be set up in multiple ways. Either a single class extending the DefaultHandler can be passed to the instance of the parser, as in Listing 9.2b, or individual handlers can be configured using methods in the XMLReader class, as shown below.

```
    SAXParserFactory factory = SAXParserFactory.newInstance();
    SAXParser parser = factory.newSAXParser();
 // Obtain a reference to the underlying XMLReader of the Parser
    XMLReader reader = parser.getXMLReader();
 // Specify the handlers for the reader
    reader.setErrorHandler(new MyErrorHandler());
    reader.setContentHandler(new MyContentHandler());
    reader.setDTDHandler(new MyDTDHanlder());
    reader.setEntityResolver(new MyEntityResolver());
// Use the XMLReader to parse the entire file.
    InputSource input = new InputSource(filename);
// Start the SAX parsing. Relevant methods in the handlers
// will be invoked by the parser
        reader.parse(input);
```

Neither the SAXParserFactory nor the SAXParser is guaranteed to be multi-threaded, and it is a good idea to have different instances per application processing thread.

> DOM

Document Object Model (DOM) is defined by W3C as a set of recommendations. The DOM core recommendations define a set of objects, each of which represents some information relevant to the XML document. There are also well defined relationships between these objects, to represent the document's organization.

A DOM parser essentially reads the XML document and constructs a tree structure in memory that represents the original document, as Figure 9.2 shows. This tree is composed of well-defined objects. Applications can then navigate through the branches of this tree and manipulate the XML. The parser implementations, including the reference implementation, internally use a SAX parser to read the XML into memory. The XML is then analyzed for the relationships

Figure 9.2
Schema showing tree structure of DOM

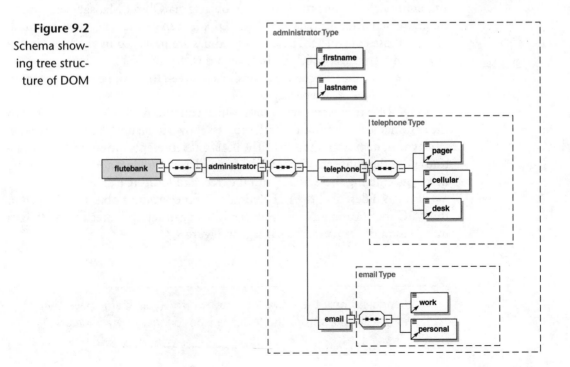

between the component parts and is organized into a tree structure that can be traversed.

DOM is organized into levels. Level 1 details the functionality and navigation of content within a document. Level 2 (also refered to as DOM 2.0) adds to Level 1 (e.g., ability to access tree members by namespace names). Level 2 is composed of a set of specifications, as shown below. Everything except the core is optional to implement for a DOM 2–compliant parser. Level 3 is a working draft.

1. DOM Level 2 Core: Defines the basic object model to represent structured data

2. DOM Level 2 Views: Allows access and update of the representation of a DOM

3. DOM Level 2 Style: Allows access and update of style sheets

4. DOM Level 2 Traversal and Range: Allows walk through, identify, modify, and delete a range of content in the DOM

Unlike SAX, DOM is specified in an implementation-independent manner and defines all its constructs for these objects via Object Management Group Interface Definition Language (OMG IDL). It then defines Java language bindings for those constructs. These Java bindings are packaged by the W3C in the org.w3c.dom package, which is also overlaid with JAXP. ▷

Figure 9.3 shows the class relationships between the major component interfaces of the org.w3c.dom package.

In DOM, a root element is a Node, which contains methods for working with the node name and attributes. Each subclass shown in Figure 9.3 represents a specific type of item from the XML. The Document represents the entire XML structure and is the conceptual root of the tree. It has methods that relate to creating nodes, assembling these nodes into the tree, and locating elements by name.

Listing 9.3 describes the IDL definition of the Document object, as defined in the W3C specification. Notice how the IDL constructs did directly map to Java interfaces in the org.w3c.dom package in Figure 9.3.

▷   JAXP endorses only the DOM 2.0 core, which is fully namespace aware. DOM specifications from the W3C can be found at *www.w3.org/DOM/ DOMTR.*

Figure 9.3 The `org.w3c.dom` package

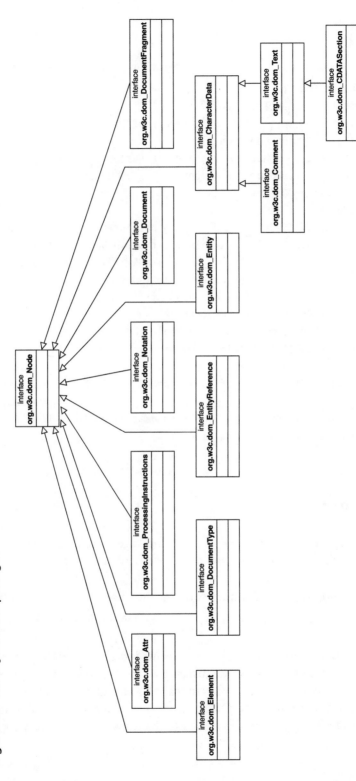

Listing 9.3   IDL description of the DOM Document objectListing

```
interface Document : Node {
  readonly attribute DocumentType  doctype;
  readonly attribute DOMImplementation  implementation;
  readonly attribute Element  documentElement;
  Element createElement(in DOMString tagName) raises(DOMException);
  DocumentFragment  createDocumentFragment();
  Text createTextNode(in DOMString data);
  Comment createComment(in DOMString data);
  CDATASection createCDATASection(in DOMString data) raises(DOMException);
  ProcessingInstruction createProcessingInstruction(in DOMString target,
                                    in DOMString data) raises(DOMException);
  Attr createAttribute(in DOMString name) raises(DOMException);
  EntityReference createEntityReference(in DOMString name) raises(DOMException);
  NodeList getElementsByTagName(in DOMString tagname);
  Node importNode(in Node importedNode, in boolean deep) raises(DOMException);
  Element createElementNS(in DOMString namespaceURI, in DOMString qualifiedName)
                                                       raises(DOMException);
  Attr createAttributeNS(in DOMString namespaceURI, in DOMString qualifiedName)
                                                       raises(DOMException);
  NodeList getElementsByTagNameNS(in DOMString namespaceURI, in DOMString localName);
  Element getElementById(in DOMString elementId);
};
```

JAXP and DOM

JAXP includes the W3C DOM package and a JAXP layer on top of it. This is similar to the SAX portion of JAXP described earlier:

- org.w3c.dom. Defines the DOM interfaces and is specified by the W3C
- javax.xml.parsers. Defines the DOM portion of JAXP, as Table 9.6 shows

The DocumentBuilderFactory is used to obtain a reference to the underlying DOM parser—that is, the instance of the DocumentBuilder interface. It can be used to select from different parsers, although the current implementation comes with only one DOM parser. The event sequence that occurs when the factory is instantiated is similar to that described previously for the SAXParser-

Table 9.6 The DOM Parsing Part of JAXP in the `javax.xml.parsers` Package

DocumentBuilder	A DOM parser capable of reading an XML document and constructing a DOM tree conforming to the DOM specification
DocumentBuilderFactory	A factory class used to obtain a reference to the DocumentBuilder and configure it if necessay using properties

Factory. First, the system property `javax.xml.parsers.DocumentBuilderFactory` is checked, then the `lib/jaxp.properties` file is checked for this property, following which the JAR files are searched for the `META-INF/services/javax.xml.parsers.DocumentBuilderFactory` file. If none of these is found, the default `DocumentBuilderFactory` of JAXP is used.

The code segment below shows the earlier `SAXParsing` example, adapted to show the basic structure used to create a DOM tree from an XML file. The flow remains the same: a `DocumentBuilderFactory` is created, a `DocumentBuilder` instance is obtained from it, and the XML is parsed using that instance.

```
package com.flutebank.parsing;

import java.io.File;
import javax.xml.parsers.*;

public class DOMParsing{
    public static void main(String[] arg) {
      try {
          String filename = arg[0];
// Create a new factory that will create the SAX parser
        DocumentBuilderFactory factory = DocumentBuilderFactory.newInstance();
        factory.setValidating(validate);
        factory.setNamespaceAware(true);
// Use the factory to create a DOM parser
          DocumentBuilder parser = factory.newDocumentBuilder();
// Create a new handler to handle content
          parser.setErrorHandler(new MyErrorHandler());
          Document xml = parser.parse(new File(filename));
```

```
// Do something useful with the XML tree represented by the Document object
        } catch (Exception e) {
            System.out.println(e);
        }
    }
}
```

Usually, the DOM representation in memory is not an exact replica of the conceptual model. The primary disparity is that the tree includes Text nodes for ignorable white spaces (white space that falls between tags—e.g., a carriage return). The parsing code has to normalize the tree and handle these node types.

▷ When to Use SAX

In general, SAX processing is faster than DOM, because it does not keep track of or build in memory trees of the document, thus consuming less memory, and does not look ahead in the document to resolve node references. Since access is sequential, it is well suited to applications interested in reading XML data and applications that do not need to manipulate the data, such as applications that read data for rendering and applications that read configuration data defined in XML. However if the primary motivation is to read the data so as to subsequently process it as Java objects, JAXB is a better choice. This is covered in Chapter 13.

Applications that need to filter XML data by adding, removing, or modifying specific elements in the data are also well suited for SAX access. The XML can be read serially and the specific element modified.

▷ When to Use DOM

The difference between SAX and DOM is the difference between sequential, read-only access and random, read-write access (an analogy is SAX parsing XML on the time axis and DOM parsing on the space axis). If, during processing, there is a need to move laterally between sibling elements or nested elements or to back up to a previous element processed, DOM is probably a better choice.

However, creating and manipulating DOMs is memory-intensive, and this makes DOM processing a bad choice if the XML is large and complicated or the JVM is memory–constrained, as in J2ME devices.

> When Not to Use Either

If the task to be performed and the XML data are simple, there usually is no need to use an XML parser; a java.io.StreamTokenizer would suffice. For example, if the task is to read a file and replace a *known* element value with another, it can be done more quickly, with fewer resources, using Strings rather than SAX and DOM.

The premise that *everything* must be XML is fundamentally flawed. A common misuse of DOM is reasoning on the following lines. "I'm developing EJBs that will be exposed as services and called by other EJBs across a tier. Therefore, the data passed between them should be XML, and a DOM Document object is best suited for this purpose." Or "My Servlet tier and EJB tier are distributed; therefore, I should use XML for communication between them." While it is true that XML is a portable data format, it is usually not the best choice to communicate with tiers of the same application that never integrate with other applications (see Chapter 2). It is also not the best choice for practical reasons, such as processing, encoding, overheads, and network bandwidth.

> JAXP and XML Schemas

An XML document can optionally be associated with the XML schema or a DTD defining its structure. While parsing the document with SAX, a DTD, as mentioned earlier, can be parsed and then validated using the DTDHandler. A special handler like a DTDHandler is needed is because DTDs are not XML documents.

With Web services, XML schemas are a preferred mechanism for defining the data. Details about DTDs, schemas, and namespaces can be found in Appendix A.

Let us now look at how JAXP works for validating XML against the schema. JAXP 1.1 did not expose any schema-related functionality at the API level. It was up to the implementation to support schema validation (the Xerces-j parsers or the reference implementation did validate schemas when validation and namespace processing were enabled).

Even though a schema may be associated with an XML document, the W3C recommendations on validating the document against schemas do not *mandate* a particular mechanism for actually locating the schemas. This makes sense, because there might be cases where the schemas are already available and known (e.g., under business agreements between business partners), or such validation may never be feasable (e.g., XML parsing on J2ME devices). ▷

To give applications flexibility and to follow the suggested W3C recommendations, JAXP 1.2 introduces two additional properties that can be passed to the SAXParser using the setProperty() method and to DocumentBuilderFactory using the setAttribute() method:

- The http://java.sun.com/xml/jaxp/properties/schemaLanguage property specifies the URI of the the schema language specification being used. For the W3C XML schema, the value is http://www.w3.org/2001/XMLSchema. This property is required for schemas to be processed.

- The http://java.sun.com/xml/jaxp/properties/schemaSource property allows the application to optionally specify the schema (or schemas) to use for validation. The source of the schema, and the value of this property, can be an InputStream, InputSource (see Table 9.1), or a File. Multiple schemas with different target namespaces can be specified by passing an array of Objects, where the values are any of these same three types.

JAXP behavior for parsing and validating schemas with these properties is in line with the W3C recommendation. Figure 9.4 summarizes the flow.

Let us look at an example of validating XML based on its schema. Listing 9.4a shows the XML from Listing 9.1 with a schema associated with it. Listing 9.4b shows the schema itself. Listing 9.4c shows the code required to validate the schema against the XML document. It differs from the previous code only in that the properties have been set and the factory told to return a namespace-aware, validating parser.

> ▷ The W3C recommendation on schemas states that the xsi:schema-Location and xsi:noNamespaceSchemaLocation attributes serve only to provide hints to the parser about the the physical location of schema documents. They do not mandate that these attributes be used to locate the schemas. However most parsers use these attributes effectively. See Appendix A for details.

Figure 9.4
XML validation
with JAXP 1.2

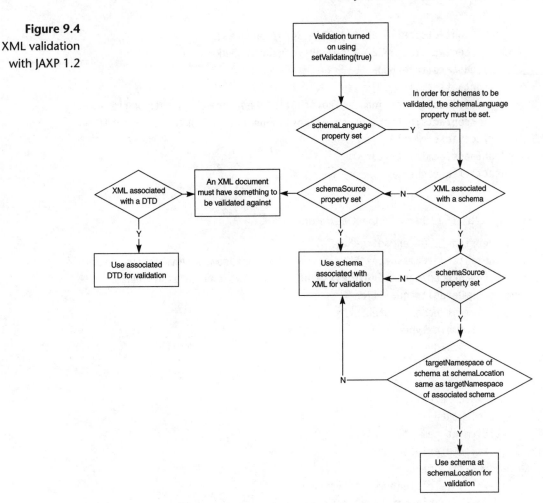

Listing 9.4a XML document with schema and namespaces

```xml
<?xml version="1.0"?>
<contacts:flutebank xmlns="http://www.flutebank.com/schema" xmlns:xsi="http://
www.w3.org/2001/XMLSchema-instance" xmlns:contacts="http://www.flutebank.com/schema"
xsi:schemaLocation="http://www.flutebank.com/schema saxexample2.xsd">
   <contacts:administrator type="maintenance" level="support-1">
      <contacts:firstname>John</contacts:firstname>
      <contacts:lastname> Malkovich</contacts:lastname>
      <contacts:telephone>
         <contacts:pager>783-393-9213</contacts:pager>
```

```
            <contacts:cellular>379-234-2342</contacts:cellular>
            <contacts:desk>322-324-2349</contacts:desk>
        </contacts:telephone>
        <contacts:email>
            <contacts:work>john.malkovich@flutebank.com</contacts:work>
            <contacts:personal>john.malkovich@home.com</contacts:personal>
        </contacts:email>
    </contacts:administrator>
</contacts:flutebank>
```

Listing 9.4b The schema for the XML document

```
<?xml version="1.0" encoding="UTF-8"?>
<xs:schema targetNamespace="http://www.flutebank.com/schema" xmlns="http://
www.flutebank.com/schema" xmlns:xs="http://www.w3.org/2001/XMLSchema"
elementFormDefault="qualified">
    <xs:element name="flutebank">
        <xs:complexType>
            <xs:sequence>
                <xs:element ref="administrator"/>
            </xs:sequence>
        </xs:complexType>
    </xs:element>
    <xs:element name="administrator">
        <xs:complexType>
            <xs:sequence>
                <xs:element ref="firstname"/>
                <xs:element ref="lastname"/>
                <xs:element ref="telephone"/>
                <xs:element ref="email"/>
            </xs:sequence>
            <xs:attribute name="type" type="xs:string" use="required"/>
            <xs:attribute name="level" type="xs:string" use="required"/>
        </xs:complexType>
    </xs:element>
    <xs:element name="firstname" type="xs:string"/>
    <xs:element name="lastname" type="xs:string"/>
    <xs:element name="telephone">
        <xs:complexType>
            <xs:sequence>
                <xs:element ref="pager"/>
                <xs:element ref="cellular"/>>
```

```
                <xs:element ref="desk"/>
            </xs:sequence>
        </xs:complexType>
    </xs:element>
    <xs:element name="pager" type="xs:string"/>
    <xs:element name="cellular" type="xs:string"/>
    <xs:element name="desk" type="xs:string"/>
    <xs:element name="email">
        <xs:complexType>
            <xs:sequence>
                <xs:element ref="work"/>
                <xs:element ref="personal"/>
            </xs:sequence>
        </xs:complexType>
    </xs:element>
    <xs:element name="work" type="xs:string"/>
    <xs:element name="personal" type="xs:string"/>
</xs:schema>
```

Listing 9.4c   The example from Listing 9.2a modified for schema validation

```
public class SAXParsingWithSchemas {
    public static void main(String[] arg) {
        try {
        // Create a new factory that will create the parser.
        SAXParserFactory factory = SAXParserFactory.newInstance();
        factory.setNamespaceAware(true);
        factory.setValidating(true);
        SAXParser parser = factory.newSAXParser();
        parser.setProperty("http://java.sun.com/xml/jaxp/properties/schemaLanguage",
                        "http://www.w3.org/2001/XMLSchema");
// If needed the schema source can be set explicitly as shown below. This example uses
// the schema associated with the XML document
//        parser.setProperty("http://java.sun.com/xml/jaxp/properties/schemaSource",
//                              , new InputSource(someuri));
        DefaultHandler handler = new MySAXHandler();
        parser.parse( new File(filename), handler);
        } catch (Exception e) {
            System.out.println(e);
        }
    }
}
```

▷ **XSLT**

XML's power lies in its ability to represent data. However, to do something useful with the XML data, especially if it is document-centric XML, it would typically need to be *translated* into another format. The technology that enables this translation is the eXtensible Stylesheet Language (XSL). XSL is a language for expressing style sheets. A style sheet is an XML document that describes how to display an XML document of a particular type. XSL is a W3C specification and is broken down into three complementary technologies:

- XSL Transformations (XSLT). Defines a language for expressing transformation rules from one class of XML document to another. XSLT specifications can be found at *www.w3.org/TR/xslt*.

- XML Path Language (XPath). An expression language used by XSLT to access or refer to parts of an XML document. XPath specifications can be found at *www.w3.org/TR/xpath*.

- XSL Formatting Objects (XSL-FO). A language for defining formatting, such as fonts and page layout. These are defined as a part of the XSL specification at *www.w3.org/TR/xsl*.

An XSLT processor, analogous to an XML parser, is an application that applies an XSL style sheet (which itself is an XML document and conforms to the XSL schema) to XML data input. Instead of modifying the original XML data, XSLT produces a result—typically HTML or XML and, in some rare cases, binary. Essentially, XSL uses XSLT to transform an XML *source tree* into an XML *result tree,* as Figure 9.5 shows.

These trees are logical structures that consists of nodes that may be produced by XML. They may be implemented as object models (e.g., DOM), a series of

Figure 9.5
XSLT transformation process

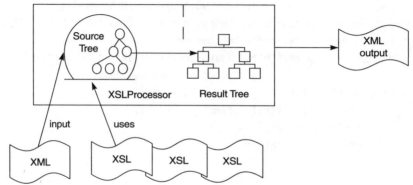

well-balanced parse events (e.g., callbacks received by the SAX ContentHandler), a series of requests (the result of which can describe a tree), or a stream of marked-up characters.

Consider the example where you want to display part of the flutebank.com administrator information from the XML in Listing 9.1. Listing 9.5 shows the XSL a processor would take. Figure 9.6 shows the resulting output from the transformation, as rendered in a browser.

Listing 9.5   The XSL style sheet used to transform the XML from Listing 9.1

```
<?xml version="1.0" encoding="UTF-8"?>
<xsl:stylesheet version="1.0" xmlns:xsl="http://www.w3.org/1999/XSL/Transform"
xmlns:n1="http://www.flutebank.com/schema" xmlns:contacts="http://www.flutebank.com/
schema" xmlns:xsi="http://www.w3.org/2001/XMLSchema-instance">
    <xsl:template match="/">
        <html>
            <body>
                <h4>Flutebank.com : Support personal contact information</h4>
                <table bgcolor="#AAB0AC" border="1" cellpadding="0" cellspacing="0"
                                                               width="50%">
                    <tr>
                        <td>
                            <h4>Name</h4>
                        </td>
                        <td>
                            <xsl:for-each select="n1:flutebank">
                                <xsl:for-each select="n1:administrator">
                                    <xsl:for-each select="n1:firstname">
                                        <xsl:apply-templates />
                                    </xsl:for-each>
                                </xsl:for-each>
                            </xsl:for-each>  <xsl:for-each select="n1:flutebank">
                                <xsl:for-each select="n1:administrator">
                                    <xsl:for-each select="n1:lastname">
                                        <xsl:apply-templates />
                                    </xsl:for-each>
                                </xsl:for-each>
                            </xsl:for-each>
                        </td>
                    </tr>
                    <tr>
                        <td>
```

```
                    <h4>Phone:</h4>
                </td>
                <td>
                    <xsl:for-each select="n1:flutebank">
                        <xsl:for-each select="n1:administrator">
                            <xsl:for-each select="n1:telephone">
                                <xsl:for-each select="n1:desk">
                                    <xsl:apply-templates />
                                </xsl:for-each>
                            </xsl:for-each>
                        </xsl:for-each>
                    </xsl:for-each>
                </td>
            </tr>
            <<tr>
                <td>
                    <h4>Email:</h4>
                </td>
                <td>
                    <xsl:for-each select="n1:flutebank">
                        <xsl:for-each select="n1:administrator">
                            <xsl:for-each select="n1:email">
                                <xsl:for-each select="n1:work">
                                    <xsl:apply-templates />
                                </xsl:for-each>
                            </xsl:for-each>
                        </xsl:for-each>
                    </xsl:for-each>
                </td>
            </tr>
        </table>
      </body>
    </html>
  </xsl:template>
  <xsl:template match="n1:administrator">
      <xsl:apply-templates />
  </xsl:template>
  <xsl:template match="n1:cellular">
      <xsl:apply-templates />
  </xsl:template>
</xsl:stylesheet>
```

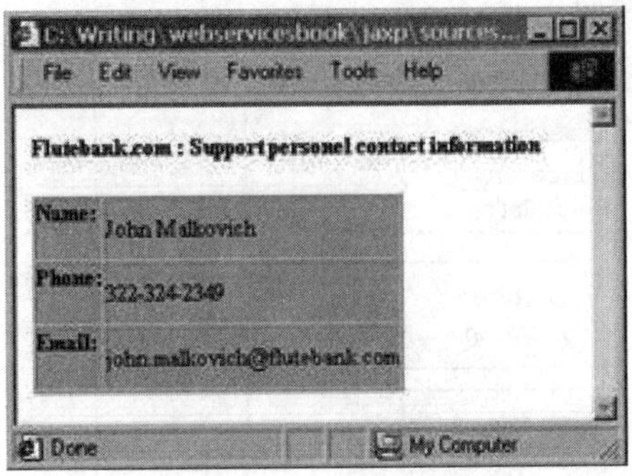

Figure 9.6
XML trans-
formed into
HTML

As with XML, this chapter is not intended to be a lesson on XSL or XPath syntax; numerous good sources are available for that. Vendor tools are also available, such as XMLSpy *(www.xmlspy.com)*, that can generate XSL code based on the input XML and desired output, with minimal knowledge of these languages on the part of the user.

So, why is XSLT important? A typical enterprise application that delivers content to users would use data from multiple EIS resources, apply some business rules and processing to the data, and serve the clients. As Figure 9.7a shows, the clients could be other applications, users, or devices, all using the same logical data. To prevent rewriting the application and the presentation tier for every interface, an XSL-based processor that transcodes same document-centric XML into different formats (XML to WML, HTML, XML, XHTML, etc.) using XSL offers a cleaner *content delivery mechanism* but the same logical data set. The logical tiering for this approach is shown in Figure 9.7b.

JAXP and XSLT

JAXP architecture accommodates XSLT by providing the same abstraction and pluggability as it does for SAX and DOM (see Figure 9.1a). ▷

As Figure 9.8 shows, JAXP is used to instantiate a `TransformerFactory`, which, in turn, is used to obtain a reference to a `Transfomer` specific to a style sheet. A `Transformer` takes a `Source` and transforms it into a `Result`. The source can be of any type: a `DOMSource`, a `SAXSource` (or the content parsed by a SAX parser), or a `StreamSource`.

▷   JAXP endorses XLST 1.0 from the W3C at *www.w3.org/TR/1999/REC-xslt-19991116.*

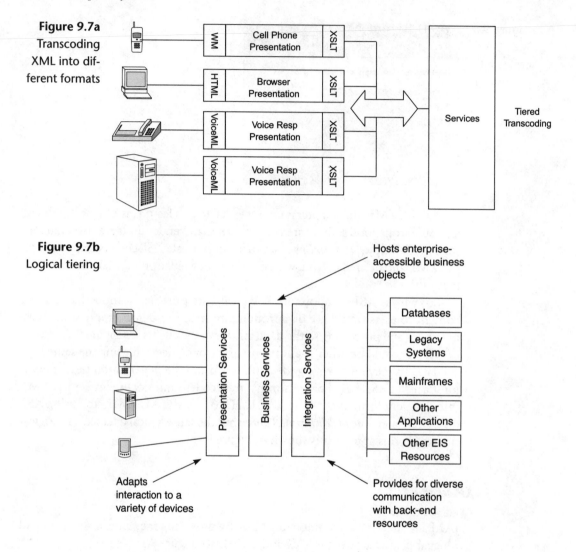

Figure 9.7a
Transcoding XML into different formats

Figure 9.7b
Logical tiering

The JAXP part that handles transformations is also known as the Transformation API for XML (TrAX) and is contained in the following packages:

- `javax.xml.transform`. Defines the core interfaces for transformation.

- `javax.xml.transform.sax`. Defines the SAX-relevant interfaces for transformation.

- `javax.xml.transform.dom`. Defines the DOM-relevant interfaces for transformation.

- `javax.xml.transform.stream`. Defines the Stream-relevant interfaces for transformation.

Figure 9.8
JAXP and XSLT

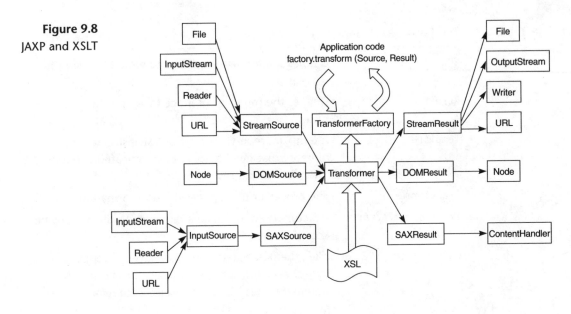

To put the earlier mention about a source tree and a result tree into perspective, it is interesting to note that if the reference implementation, Xalan, is supplied with a DOMSource, it will use this as its internal tree representation. If the input is a SAXSource or StreamSource, it uses its own internal tree representation as the source tree, called an STree. This is more efficient than a general-purpose DOM, because it contains additional sorting optimizations.

Tables 9.7 through 9.10 show the relevant interfaces in the above packages. The code to do the transformation would look something like the following:

```
        String xml = "saxexaple2.xml";
        String xsl = "fluteadmin.xsl";
// instantiate the factory
        TransformerFactory factory = TransformerFactory.newInstance();
// obtain a transformer from the factory for the XSL
        Transformer transformer = factory.newTransformer
                                    (new StreamSource(new File(xsl)));
// use the transformer to transform the source to a result
        transformer.transform(new StreamSource(new File(xml)),
                                    new StreamResult(System.out));
```

Another example would be to transform a DOM into another DOM in memory, using the XSL that is also in memory as a DOM (remember, an XSL document is also an XML document).

Table 9.7 The `javax.xml.transform` Package

Source	Defines the top level interface to wrap other specific sources.
Result	Defines the top level interface to wrap other specific results.
Templates	A template represents a set of XSL instructions in memory that need to be applied repeatedly to different XML data structures.
Transformer	The processor that applies the transformation.
TransformerFactory	A factory used to obtain a reference to the underlying Transformer.
URIResolver	Like schemas, a style sheet can have references to other style sheets, using an xsl:include or xsl:import statement. This is used to resolve such references and process them.

Table 9.8 The `javax.xml.transform.dom` Package

DOMSource	An interface to represent a DOM tree (an org.w3c.dom.Node) as the source of the XML data to be transformed
DOMResult	An interface to represent a DOM tree (an org.w3c.dom.Node) as the result of the transformation

```
            String xml = "saxexaple2.xml";
            String xsl = "fluteadmin.xsl";
// create a DOM from the XSL
            DocumentBuilderFactory domfactory = DocumentBuilderFactory.newInstance();
            domfactory.setNamespaceAware(true);
            DocumentBuilder parser = domfactory.newDocumentBuilder();
            Document xsldom = parser.parse(xsl);
// create a DOM from the source XML
            Document xmldom = parser.parse(xml);
// create the transfomer and transform the xml
            TransformerFactory factory = TransformerFactory.newInstance();
            Transformer transformer = factory.newTransformer(new DOMSource(xsldom));
            DOMResult result= new DOMResult();
            transformer.transform(new DOMSource(xmldom),result);
```

Table 9.9 The `javax.xml.transform.sax` Package

SAXSource	An interface to represent a SAX as the source of the XML data to be transformed. This wraps an `org.xml.sax.InputSource` and can futher be piped on a `java.io.InputStream`, `java.io.Reader`, or URI. (Typically, a string representing a `java.net.URL`.)
SAXResult	An interface to wrap a SAX `ContentHandler` invoked sequentially as a result of applying the transformation to the XML
TemplatesHander	A SAX `ContentHandler` that can be used to generate a `Templates` object from SAX source events
TransformerHandler	A SAX `ContentHandler` that can be used to generate a `Result` object from SAX source events
SAXTransformerFactory	A special kind of `TransformerFactory` that can be used to configure the SAX parser processing the XSL input

Table 9.10 The `javax.xml.transform.stream` Package

StreamSource	An interface to act as a pipe on different streams, as sources for the transformation (`File`, `InputStream`, `Reader`, or URL)
StreamResult	An interface to act as a pipe on different streams, as results for the transformation (`File`, `OutputStream`, `Write`, or URL)

Another example would be to use an empty transfomer not associated with a particular style sheet to transform the DOM–for example, from the code above into another form:

```
// As a convenience , print out the in memory DOM to
// the System.out using a null transform
        TransformerFactory factory = TransformerFactory.newInstance();
        Transformer nulltransformer = factory.newTransformer();
        nulltransformer.transform(new DOMSource(result.getNode()),
                        new StreamResult(System.out));
```

Another example would be to use the transformer to obtain the associated style sheet from an XML document—for example, if the XML has a processing instruction such as:

```
<?xml-stylesheet type="text/xsl" href="fluteadmin.xsl"?>:

        String xml = "pitransform.xml";
        TransformerFactory factory = TransformerFactory.newInstance();
        Source xsl = factory.getAssociatedStylesheet (
                                        new StreamSource(xml),null, null, null);
    Transformer transformer = factory.newTransformer(xsl);
    transformer.transform(new StreamSource(xml),new StreamResult(System.out));
```

A common use for transformation involves applying the same style sheet to different or dynamically generated XML data, to produce dynamic output. For example, users request a service from a flutebank.com account service, resulting in the generation of user-specific stock portfolio XML data that needs to be transformed for rendering. In such scenarios, a `Templates` object should be used instead, to obtain the `Transformer`. A `Templates` object is immutable, thread safe, and guaranteed to work across multiple threads. Also, as we shall see with XSLTc, underlying implementations may provide further optimizations to deal with repeated transformations.

```
        String xml_1 = "pitransform.xml";
        String xml_2 = "saxexample2.xml";
        String xsl = "fluteadmin.xsl";
// instantiate the factory
        TransformerFactory factory = TransformerFactory.newInstance();
// obtain a template from the factory
        Templates template = factory.newTemplates(new StreamSource(xsl));
        Transformer transformer = template.newTransformer();
// use the transformer to transform the source to a result
        transformer.transform(new StreamSource(new File(xml_1)),
                                        new StreamResult(System.out));
        transformer.transform(new StreamSource(new File(xml_2)),
                                        new StreamResult(System.out));
```

▷ **XSLTc**

XSLTc was developed by Jacek Ambroziak, at Sun Microsystems, for high performance and repeated transformations. It was released to the Apache project and is packaged with the JAXP reference implementation.

Most implementations read the style sheet sequentially using SAX, create an internal object representation from it, and use that to transform the source tree to the result tree. As Figure 9.9 shows, XSLTc takes the orginal XSL file and compiles it into Java bytecodes, called translets. The translet class, representing an optimized internal DOM (not the W3C DOM), along with the internal caching mechanism of XSLTc, increases application performance.

All the implementation details of XSLTc are hidden from the application, because of JAXP's architecture. XSLTc is treated as another implementation of the transformer underneath the API. The code to use XSLTc remains the same as earlier; only the factory implementation class, represented by the system property `javax.xml.transform.TransformerFactory`, changes from the default `org.apache`

Figure 9.9
XSLTc
architecture

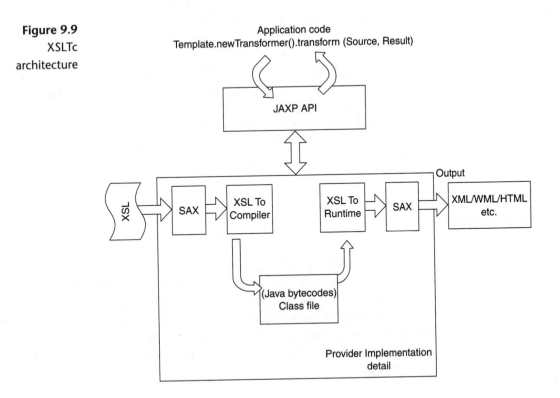

```
               .xalan.processor.TransformerFactoryImpl to org.apache.xalan.xsltc.trax
               .TransformerFactoryImpl.

       String xml_1 = "pitransform.xml";
       String xml_2 = "saxexample2.xml";
       String xsl = "fluteadmin.xsl";
       System.setProperty("javax.xml.transform.TransformerFactory",
                          "org.apache.xalan.xsltc.trax.TransformerFactoryImpl");
// instantiate the factory
       TransformerFactory factory = TransformerFactory.newInstance();
// obtain a template from the factory
// results in the stylsheet being compiled into a translet
       Templates template = factory.newTemplates(new StreamSource(xsl));
       Transformer transformer = template.newTransformer();
// use the transformer to transform the source to a result
       transformer.transform(new StreamSource(new File(xml_1)),
                                       new StreamResult(System.out));
       transformer.transform(new StreamSource(new File(xml_2)),
                                       new StreamResult(System.out));
```

When using XSLTc in a production application, the first part of the code that results in compilation would typically be handled at application startup, with only the reference to the Templates object passed around (recall that it is thread safe). XSLTc also comes with a Java API that can be used to invoke the code directly and to physically produce a class file from a style sheet. However, using that would make the code nonportable to other implementations.

> **JDOM**

Jason Hunter and Brett McLaughlin created JDOM as an open source project, but it has since been accepted as a Java Specification Request (JSR-102). At the time of writing this book, the expert group for this specification was still being formed, and only the release candidate v. 0.8 of the original code was available. This version has undergone significant changes from v. 0.7, and we believe it will evolve further as a JSR. This section gives an overview of this technology as it exists with v. 0.8. ▷

▷ The JDOM JSR can be found at *www.jcp.org/jsr/detail/102.jsp.*

JDOM came into being because Java developers really needed a straightforward model that abstracted the complexities of dealing with XML and performed well. It is similar to DOM in that it represents a tree structure, but it is not built on W3C DOM and does not use any of the DOM IDL constructs (and hence the Java bindings defined in the org.w3c.dom package). It is essentially an API used to represent an XML data tree in a format optimized for Java. From an implementation perspective, JDOM differs from DOM in the following major respects:

- It uses only concrete classes rather than interfaces.

- It makes extensive use of the Java collection classes.

- It does not require a DOM parser. It uses a SAX parser for parsing and validating an input XML document, though it can also take a previously constructed DOM as input. JDOM is not a parser; it is an XML representation model in Java.

- It includes converters to output a JDOM representation as a SAX2 event stream, a DOM model, or an XML text document.

Figure 9.10 represents the core JDOM classes in v. 0.8.

The apparent difference between DOM in Figure 9.3 and Figure 9.10 is that all the representations are classes (that implement Serializable and Cloneable) and do not inherit from a base class (such as Node in DOM). There are also no list classes, such as SAX's Attribute or DOM's NodeList and NamedNodeMap classes; the Java collections in java.util.collections (List, Map, etc.) are used instead. For example, when getAttributes() is invoked on an Element, a List is returned, as opposed to a NamedNodeMap in DOM. This simplifies a lot of things for the developer.

The good thing about having concrete classes is that they eliminate the need for factories to instantiate them. For example, a DOM can be constructed directly using the following code:

```
Element root = new Element("flutebank");
Element admin = new Element("administrator");
    admin.setText("John Malkovich");
root.addContent(admin);
    Document doc = new Document(root);
```

The output from the above would look like this:

```
<flutebank><administrator>John Malkovich</administrator></flutebank>
```

Figure 9.10
Class diagram
for JDOM.
Note the lack
of relationships
between
classes.

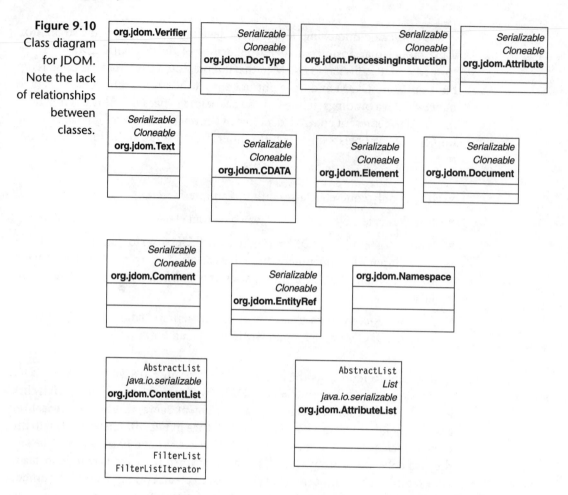

JDOM classes can also be subclassed into application-specific classes that handle specific processing tasks. For example, Element could be subclasssed into a Person, which could be subclassed into Employee and Manager by an application that held different sorting and access logic.

JDOM can also be used for transformations. It plugs into the JAXP transformation API by providing a custom JDOMSource and JDOMResult class. The code below shows how an XSL transformation can be applied with JDOM.

```
String xml = "saxexaple2.xml";
String xsl = "fluteadmin.xsl";
SAXBuilder builder = new SAXBuilder();
// Note this is a JDOM Document not a W3C DOM Document object
Document doc = builder.build(xml);
```

```
TransformerFactory factory = TransformerFactory.newInstance();
Transformer transformer= factory.newTransformer(new StreamSource(new File( xsl)));
transformer.transform(new JDOMSource(doc), new StreamResult(System.out));
```

The above code also demonstrates how JDOM relies on the *builder* classes; the two most often used are SAXBuilder and DOMBuilder, which construct a JDOM representation from set of SAX events or a DOM tree.

We envision that as the JDOM model is standardized under the Java community process, the transformation part will probably be plugged under the JAXP layer as another implementation (like XSLTc). Although JDOM holds tremendous promise, considering the early stage of the specification, it would be prudent to wait for a final version to be released as a standard Java extension API before embracing this technology completely.

▷ JAXP RI

The JAXP RI, including the JAXP bundled with J2SE 1.4 RI, uses the Apache XML project software as the implementation; namely, Xerces and Xalan. Since JAXP is now bundled with J2SE 1.4, a common question from developers is about upgrading the implementation. J2SE 1.4 provides an "Endorsed Standards Override Mechanism," which can be used to override very specific, non-core packages in the JDK itself. The new JAR files can be placed in a specific directory and passed to the JVM using a system property java.endorsed.dirs (for example, -Djava.endorsed.dirs=/usr/home/jar/). ▷

▷ Summary

In this chapter, we looked at JAXP, an API that supports processing of XML documents using DOM, SAX, and XSLT. It enables applications to parse or transform XML documents independently of a particular XML processing implementation.

> ▷ Details about the Endorsed Standards Override Mechanism can be found at *http://java.sun.com/j2se/1.4/docs/guide/standards.*

The advantage of XML is that it can be understood across programming languages and across platforms. Java has multiple ways to achieve the same end; similarly, there are many ways to manipulate and use this XML.

From an architect's perspective, the application must be analyzed, to make the appropriate decision about how to use XML. Architecturally, JAXP is just a tool that developers can use to do something useful in the business context with that XML. Its simplicity, standard API, reliance on industry-accepted XML standards, and pluggable architecture give Java developers the ability to manipulate XML for Web services independently of a particular vendor's parser implementation.

> References

Gamma E., Helm R., Johnson R., and Vlissides, J. *Design Patterns: Elements of Reusable Object-Oriented Software.* Addison-Wesley, 1994.

Chapter

JAX-RPC

Java API for XML-based RPC (JAX-RPC) is intended to be a Java API to expose remote procedure calls that use XML to business applications that occur primarily, though not exclusively, on the periphery of organizations. The need for such synchronous API increases as corporations begin to communicate with other business partners using disparate hardware and software systems.

Remote procedure call (RPC) has been around for a while, with many implementations. It essentially enables clients to work with remote procedures, or *routines*, that reside on different machines just as if the procedures were executed locally. In its simplest form, a client calls a procedure, with the name of the procedure and the arguments; the server does something useful and sends the results back to the client.

Allowing different machines or processes in different address spaces to communicate with each other isn't really a new concept. The Java RMI and CORBA models are good examples of RPC that allows objects to marshal arguments, invoke a procedure or method on an object residing on a different machine, unmarshal the results, and use them.

An almost infinite number of data formats is possible for the arguments and results. As more and more Java applications expose themselves to interoperate and move toward a Web-service-based paradigm, XML is the new choice for this data format. JAX-RPC facilitates the invocation of remote procedures, using XML as the data format and SOAP as the data protocol.

SOAP defines the XML-based protocol for exchange of information in a distributed environment, specifying the envelope structure, encoding rules, and a convention for *representing* remote procedure calls and responses. JAX-RPC provides a Java API for developers to invoke remote procedure calls, by abstracting and hiding the low-level SOAP semantics associated with RPC from applications. ▷

▷ In this chapter, *runtime* refers to a JAX-RPC–compliant implementation, such as the reference implementation packed with Java WSDP.

▷ JAX-RPC Service Model

As Figure 10.1 shows, the service model for JAX-RPC is similar to other RPC models, such as RMI-IIOP and CORBA. The model has several components.

The layers shown in Figure 10.1 correspond to the Open System Interconnection (OSI) networking model, which has these characteristics:

- The physical layer conveys the bitstream through the network.

- The data link layer encodes and decodes data packets into bits.

- The network layer provides switching, routing, packet sequencing, addressing, and forwarding between virtual circuits, to transmit data from node to node.

- The transport layer provides transparent transfer of data between hosts and is responsible for end-to-end error recovery and flow control. Clearly, the HTTP binding for SOAP lacks some of this, whereas other bindings, such as POP-SMTP, IMAP, and JMS do not.

Figure 10.1
The JAX-RPC model

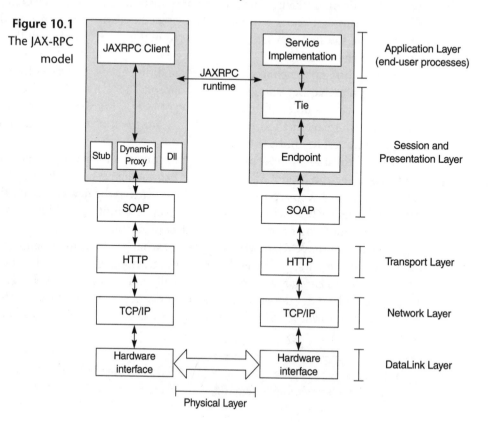

- The session layer establishes, coordinates, and terminates connections, exchanges, and dialogs between the applications.

- The presentation layer, also known as the syntax layer, provides independence from differences in data representation by translating from application to network format, and vice versa. The presentation layer works to transform data into the form the application layer can accept.

- The application layer is the actual application and end-user processes, where business functionality is addressed.

Although JAX-RPC relies on complex protocols, the API hides this complexity from the application developer. On the server side, the developer specifies the remotely accessible procedures by defining methods in a Java *service definition* interface and writing one or more Java classes that implement those methods. JAX-RPC exposes these objects as a *service endpoint* and generates the relevant ties. The client never directly communicates with the *service implementation*. The client uses a stub or other mechanisms to communicate with the endpoint (covered later in this chapter), and the endpoint uses the tie. The client then invokes the service, passing in relevant parameters, and the service returns the results to the client.

Before we dive into the internals of this model, we will take a look at the data types and see how the marshalling and unmarshalling occurs. We will then see how to use that in developing JAX-RPC services.

> Data Types and Serialization

Let us revisit some object-oriented concepts. An object at any time has state. This state, represented by its member variables at that time, is the object's snapshot. The definition of the object is the class file or compiled representation. An object with no member variables—that is, no state—is essentially just a utility that does something useful every time its methods are invoked. It may create other objects and change their states, but the *scope* of such secondary objects is limited to the method.

To do a remote procedure call, something representing *state* must be sent over the wire, and something representing *state* must be returned. Sending objects over the network is not trivial, since the network is not aware of objects; it supports only bit transmission.

The mechanism used to change the objects into a format that can be transmitted over the network is called *marshalling*, and reconstructing the objects from this format is called *unmarshalling*. Marshalling over the wire requires object state to be extracted and sent in a well-defined format. Unmarshalling requires that the format be known, for reconstruction to take place. To marshal and unmarshal successfully, both sides in the exchange must use the same protocol to *encode* and *decode* object structure and data. For example, RMI Java uses Java serialization to marshal and unmarshal objects over Java Remote Method Protocol (JRMP). CORBA uses IIOP, DCOM uses ORPC, and Gemstone uses SRP.

In summary, four things are required between communication parties in different address spaces:

1. An agreement on the data format
2. An agreement on the mechanism for transforming and reconstructing object state into this format
3. An agreement on the protocol for communication between objects
4. An agreement on the transport protocol

XML helps in achieving item 1, XML schemas and SOAP with 2 and 3, and HTTP (and others in the IP family of protocols) with 4. ▷

So how is this relevant to JAX-RPC? JAX-RPC defines

- The data type mapping of Java-XML and XML-Java for making the remote service invocation possible
- Java-WSDL and WSDL-Java for making the service description possible

This is significant, because JAX-RPC provides a *standard* for vendors to implement and makes developer code vendor-neutral, much the way any of the other Java specifications do. Just as developers write a J2EE application and expect it to behave the same across J2EE-compliant application servers from multiple vendors, JAX-RPC applications will behave the same across JAX-RPC runtimes.

This does not mean that a JAX-RPC client can call only a JAX-RPC service and a JAX-RPC service can be used only by a JAX-RPC client. An application

▷ Java (platform-independent language) + XML (platform-independent data format) + SOAP (platform-independent object communication protocol) + IP family of protocols (platform/network-independent transport) = core of what is driving Web services and their adoption today

could still use a JAX-RPC client to invoke a .NET service and a .NET client to invoke a JAX-RPC service, as we will demonstrate later. As Figure 10.2 shows, because the data format, object communication protocol, and transport protocol are platform- and vendor-implementation independent, the application can be accessed by any client on any platform, as long as it uses these standards. The data type mapping and serialization rules defined by JAX-RPC are useful when the JAX-RPC runtime is being used on the Java platform at the client or server end. ▷

From an RPC perspective, if the client and service are written in Java, the runtime needs to know the following information:

Figure 10.2
JAX-RPC client-server inter-action

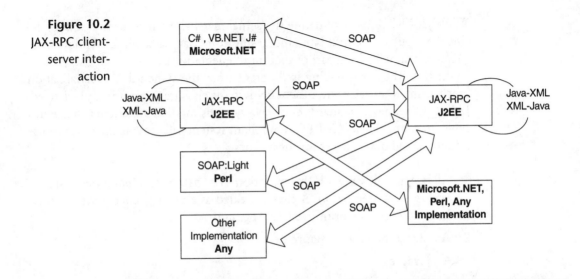

▷ RPC implementations using SOAP from different vendors:

- Apache SOAP 2.2
- Apache Axis (Alpha-1)
- HP Web Services Platform
- IBM Web Services Toolkit, WSIF
- IONA XML Bus 1.2
- Microsoft SOAP Toolkit 2.0
- Microsoft .NET
- Others: PocketSOAP, SOAP::Lite, Systinet WASP, SOAP-RMI, GLUE, Cape Clear

1. The endpoint of the service—that is, where to invoke the service

2. The method name and signature—that is, what to invoke

3. How to marshal Java data types and objects into an XML format that can be transmitted over the wire to invoke the method

4. How to unmarshal the incoming XML into Java data types and objects to process the results of that operation, if any

Java-to-XML Marshalling

While JAX-RPC does not define the actual marshalling mechanism, it does define the input and output types that result from that marshalling. Vendors write the marshalling code as part of their implementations.

In JAX-RPC, marshalling is different from the standard Java serialization mechanism, where all nontransient fields in the class are automatically serialized. JAX-RPC defines a standard set of Java types as method arguments and return types, meaning that a JAX-RPC–compliant system will provide the ready-to-use serializers and deserializers for these types:

1. All Java primitives, with the exception of a char (int, float, long, short, double, byte, Boolean). A char is treated as a String, since XML schemas have no char type primitive (see Appendix A).

2. An object that is an instance of

   • java.lang.String

   • java.util.Date

   • java.util.Calendar

   • java.math.BigInteger

   • java.math.BigDecimal

3. An object that is an instance of a class that conforms to the following restrictions:

   • It should conform to the JavaBean specification, so that its variables can be easily accessed.

   • It should not be a Remote object (i.e., should not implement java.rmi.Remote).

   • It should have a default no arguments constructor.

   These are important, because any other class is passed between the client and the server. For example, if a java.util.Map of com.flutebank.Account objects must be passed from the client to the server, a pluggable serializer and deserializer pair must be written. This is explored later in this chapter.

4. An array (with the caveat that it must contain bytes or a supported type)

5. A java.lang.Exception class ▷

The above rules differ from the standard Java serialization requirements. Table 10.1 lists the details for the same class to be used across an RMI/RMI-IIOP application as well as a JAX-RPC application. This is relevant where an existing EJB, RMI, or RMI-IIOP object must expose itself directly as a JAX-RPC service and the code must be reused across these interfaces.

Once the parameter types have been defined, rules and a standard mechanism to map these data types from Java to XML must also be defined. JAX-RPC does this, as Table 10.2 shows. ▷▷

XML-to-Java Unmarshalling

To invoke a procedure on an object with incoming XML data, an implementation must map XML data types into Java data types. This is identical to Table 10.2, with some differences explained in Tables 10.3a and 3b. XML type is declared as nillable in the schema, then it maps to its corresponding Java wrapper (primitives in Java cannot be null).

SOAP Bindings and Encoding

In Chapter 4, we looked at SOAP encoding in detail. Encoding refers to how data is serialized and sent over the wire. The parties exchanging messages have to agree on one rule to ensure that both correctly interpret the message sent from the

▷ JAX-RPC does not support a pass by reference mode for parameters and does not support passing of remote objects, because both the SOAP 1.1 and SOAP 1.2 treat objects by reference as out of scope. JAX-RPC mandates support for pass by copy semantics for parameters and return values, similar to the way nonremote objects are passed in RMI.

▷▷ JSR–31 defines the XML Data Binding Specification with JAXB, for converting an XML schema into Java classes. In the future, JAX-RPC will include the data type mapping defined by JAXB.

Table 10.1 Portability across JAX-RPC and RMI

JAX-RPC	Java serialization	A portable value object
Should not extend `Remote`.	Can extend `Remote`. It is treated as an remote object and passed by reference.	Should not implement `Remote`.
`Serializable` not required.	`Serializable` required.	Should implement `Serializable`.
`transient` fields are not serialized.	`transient` fields are not serialized.	`transient` fields are not serialized.
`static` fields are serialized.	`static` fields are not serialized.	Should not contain `static` fields.
All `public` variables are serialized.	`public transient` variables are not serialized.	Should not contain any `public` `transient` variables.
Only private, protected, package-level fields that have get/set methods are serialized.	Get/set methods are not required. Private, protected, package-level fields are still serialized.	Should have get/set methods for all private, protected, package-level fields.
Bean properties are serialized.	Bean properties are serialized.	Can have bean properties with get/set methods.

other side. They can either agree beforehand, using a predefined *encoding scheme*, or use an XML schema directly in the data to define the data types. The message with the former notation is said to be an *encoded* message; the latter is said to be a *literal* message.

SOAP encoding refers to the rules defined by the SOAP specification that the parties can follow to interpret the contents of the Body element. SOAP defines an encoding scheme, also referred to as Section 5 encoding (since it is specified in section 5 of the SOAP specifications). It outlines a schema *(http://schemas .xmlsoap.org/soap/encoding/)* containing certain basic data types that participants in the conversation can use to describe the elements in the body of the SOAP message. This encoding is not mandatory, and there is no default.

In Chapter 4, we also looked at the use of the `encodingStyle` attribute and the use of simple and compound types. To recall, the `encodingStyle` attribute in the SOAP message can be used to indicate the encoding in use. For example, the message below indicates that SOAP encodings are in use:

Table 10.2   Java-to-XML Data Type Mapping

Java type	XML type
Boolean	xsd:boolean
Byte	xsd:byte
Short	xsd:short
Int	xsd:int
Long	xsd:long
Float	xsd:float
Double	xsd:double
byte[]	xsd:base64Binary
Byte[]	xsd:base64Binary
java.lang.String	xsd:string
java.math.BigInteger	xsd:integer
java.math.BigDecimal	xsd:decimal
java.util.Calendar	xsd:dateTime
java.util.Date	xsd:dateTime
javax.xml.namespace.Qname	xsd:QName
JavaBean class whose properties are any supported Java data type or another valid JavaBean	XML schema sequence of elements
Array of any of above	SOAP array

```
<?xml version="1.0" encoding="UTF-8"?>
<env:Envelope xmlns:env="http://schemas.xmlsoap.org/soap/envelope/" xmlns:enc="http://
schemas.xmlsoap.org/soap/encoding/" xmlns:ns0="http://www.flutebank.com/xml"
env:encodingStyle="http://schemas.xmlsoap.org/soap/encoding/">
<env:Body>
<ns0:getLastPayment>
    <vendor xsi:type="enc:string">my cable tv provider</vendor>
</ns0:getLastPayment>
</env:Body>
</env:Envelope>
```

Table 10.3a   XML-to-Java Data Type Mapping for Basic Types

XML type	Java type	When declared as nillable
xsd:boolean	Boolean	java.lang.Boolean
xsd:byte	Byte	java.lang.Byte
xsd:short	Short	java.lang.Short
xsd:int	Int	java.lang.Integer
xsd:long	Long	java.lang.Long
xsd:float	Float	java.lang.Float
xsd:double	double	java.lang.Double
xsd:base64Binary	byte[]	
xsd:hexBinary	byte[]	
xsd:string	java.lang.String	
xsd:integer	java.math.BigInteger	
xsd:decimal	java.math.BigDecimal	
xsd:dateTime	java.util.Calendar	
xsd:Qname	javax.xml.namespace.Qname	

The message shows that the vendor element is of type enc:string defined in the encoding schema, represented by the encodingStyle attribute. The receiver of this message, processing the vendor element, knows it is a SOAP-encoded string, which it can then translate into the language in which the service is implemented.

The SOAP specification does not define any language bindings for the data types described by its encoding schema. Instead, the types are generic enough to model some of the typical data types found in Java and most other programming languages. JAX-RPC defines how the simple types in the SOAP encoding are mapped to Java, as per Table 10.4.

Note that the data types in Table 10.4 are the same as the nillable types in Table 10.3a, because they map to the same underlying basic XML schema types. Of particular interest is the Array type, which maps to Java arrays. In the previous

Table 10.3b   XML-to-Java Data Type Mapping

XML construct	Java construct
ComplexType	JavaBeans class with the same name.
	Its properties are mapped from the element's name and type.
	Complex types derived by extension are mapped into classes with similar hierarchies.

Example

```
<complexType name="PaymentConfirmation">
    <sequence>
        <element name="confirmationNum" type="int"/>
        <element name="payee" type="string"/>
        <element name="amt" type="double"/>
    </sequence>
</complexType>

public class PaymentConfirmation {
    private int confirmationNum;
    private String payee;
    private double amt;
    public PaymentConfirmation() {
    }

    public PaymentConfirmation(int confirmationNum,
                            java.lang.String payee, double amt) {
        this.confirmationNum = confirmationNum;
        this.payee = payee;
        this.amt = amt;
    }

// getXXX/setXXX methods for each member property
}
```

(continued)

Table 10.3b XML-to-Java Data Type Mapping (Cont'd)

XML construct	Java construct
Enumerations	A Java class with the same name as the enumeration. The class must contain 1. The enumerated values as members of the enumeration type 2. A getValue method that returns the current value 3. Two static methods for each label

Example

```
<simpleType name="PaymentDetail" >
    <restriction base="xsd:string" >
        <enumeration value="checking" />
        <enumeration value="saving" />
        <enumeration value="brokerage" />
    </restriction>
</simpleType>


public class PaymentDetail implements Serializable {
    private String value;
    public static final String _checkingString = "checking";
    public static final String _savingString = "saving";
    public static final String _brokerageString = "brokerage";

    public static final String _checking = new String
                                    (_checkingString);
    public static final String _saving = new String(_savingString);
    public static final String _brokerage = new String
                                    (_brokerageString);

    public static final PaymentDetail checking =
                                    new PaymentDetail(_checking);
    public static final PaymentDetail saving = new PaymentDetail
                                    (_saving);
    public static final PaymentDetail brokerage =
                                    new PaymentDetail(_brokerage);
```

Table 10.3b   XML-to-Java Data Type Mapping (Cont'd)

```java
    protected PaymentDetail(String value) {
        this.value = value;
    }

    public String getValue() {
        return value;
    }

    public static PaymentDetail fromValue(String value)
        throws IllegalStateException {
        if (checking.value.equals(value)) {
            return checking;
        } else if (saving.value.equals(value)) {
            return saving;
        } else if (brokerage.value.equals(value)) {
            return brokerage;
        }
        throw new IllegalArgumentException();
    }

    public static PaymentDetail fromString(String value)
        throws IllegalStateException {
        if (value.equals(_checkingString)) {
            return checking;
        } else if (value.equals(_savingString)) {
            return saving;
        } else if (value.equals(_brokerageString)) {
            return brokerage;
        }
        throw new IllegalArgumentException();
        }
    }
// other methods not shown
    }
```

Table 10.4 Mapping of SOAP Simple Types to Java

SOAP-encoded simple type	Java type
String	java.lang.String
Boolean	java.lang.Boolean
Float	java.lang.Float
Double	java.lang.Double
Decimal	java.math.BigDecimal
Int	java.lang.Integer
Short	java.lang.Short
Byte	java.lang.Byte
Base64	byte[]
Array	Java array

extract, if the SOAP body contained something like the following, it would be mapped to an array of String[] objects in the Java side by JAX-RPC, and vice versa:

```
<ns0:getLastPayment>
<vendor enc:arrayType="xsd:string[4]" xsi:type="enc:Array">
   <item xsi:type="xsd:string">AT&T</item>
   <item xsi:type="xsd:string">Sprint PCS</item>
   <item xsi:type="xsd:string">Flute Electric Co</item>
</vendor>
</ns0:getLastPayment>
```

While mapping arrays, the type of the array is determined from the schema type. The size is determined at runtime rather than at declaration time. JAX-RPC also supports multidimensional arrays, where the types are supported JAX-RPC types. Listing 10.1 shows how a multidimensional array of application-defined PaymentDetail objects may be mapped on the wire using SOAP encoding:

Listing 10.1 A multidimensional array of application-defined PaymentDetail objects mapped on the wire using SOAP encoding

```
<env:Envelope xmlns:env="http://schemas.xmlsoap.org/soap/envelope/"
xmlns:enc="http://schemas.xmlsoap.org/soap/encoding/"
```

```
xmlns:ns0="http://www.flutebank.com/xml"
// other namespaces >
<env:Body>
// other XML
<ns0:ArrayOfArrayOfPaymentDetail id="ID1" xsi:type="enc:Array"
enc:arrayType="ns0:PaymentDetail[2,2]">
          <item href="#ID2"/>
          <item href="#ID3"/>
          <item href="#ID4"/>
          <item href="#ID5"/>
</ns0:ArrayOfArrayOfPaymentDetail>
     <ns0:PaymentDetail id="ID2" xsi:type="ns0:PaymentDetail">
          <date xsi:type="xsd:dateTime">2002-08-26T21:17:37.678Z</date>
          <account xsi:type="xsd:string">Credit</account>
          <payeeName xsi:type="xsd:string">Digital Credit Union</payeeName>
          <amt xsi:type="xsd:double">2000.0</amt>
     </ns0:PaymentDetail>

     <ns0:PaymentDetail id="ID3" xsi:type="ns0:PaymentDetail">
          <date xsi:type="xsd:dateTime">2002-08-26T21:17:37.678Z</date>
          <account xsi:type="xsd:string">Credit</account>
          <payeeName xsi:type="xsd:string">Auto Loan Company</payeeName>
          <amt xsi:type="xsd:double">299.0</amt>
     </ns0:PaymentDetail>

     <ns0:PaymentDetail id="ID4" xsi:type="ns0:PaymentDetail">
          <date xsi:type="xsd:dateTime">2002-08-26T21:17:37.678Z</date>
          <account xsi:type="xsd:string">Credit</account>
          <payeeName xsi:type="xsd:string">AT&amp;T Wireless</payeeName>
          <amt xsi:type="xsd:double">20.0</amt>
     </ns0:PaymentDetail>

     <ns0:PaymentDetail id="ID5" xsi:type="ns0:PaymentDetail">
          <date xsi:type="xsd:dateTime">2002-08-26T21:17:37.678Z</date>
          <account xsi:type="xsd:string">Credit</account>
          <payeeName xsi:type="xsd:string">AT&amp;T Long distance</payeeName>
          <amt xsi:type="xsd:double">12.0</amt>
     </ns0:PaymentDetail>
</env:Body>
</env:Envelope>
```

In Chapter 4, we introduced the concept of RPC/document *style*. Recall that a SOAP message on the wire can be represented in either in *RPC* style or *document* style, which affects the body of the message. In RPC style, the client invokes a method on the server, by sending in the body of the SOAP message all information necessary for that method's execution. It receives a response in the same fashion. All SOAP messages shown till now in this chapter have been in RPC style.

In document style, the client and server communicate using XML documents. The client sends an XML document such as a purchase order; the server does something with it and returns an XML document such as an invoice as a result (Figure 10.3).

Thus, based on the style (RPC or document) and use (encoded or literal), four combinations result:

- RPC/encoded
- RPC/literal
- Document/encoded
- Document/literal

In Chapter 5, we looked at how WSDL could represent these combinations using the style and use attributes of the binding element. Let us elaborate on that with a detailed example. The WSDL extract below shows a sample schema and message extracts. The schema has two elements, Amount and details, and a custom type, PaymentDetail. The message element shown has four parts: part1, which is of type PaymentDetail; part2, which is of type int; part3, which is a sim-

Figure 10.3
(a) RPC style.
(b) Document style.

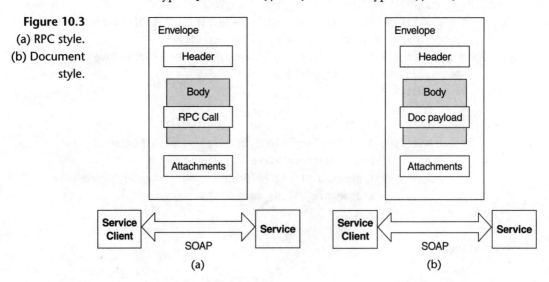

ple element Amount; and part4, which is an element of complex type Payment-Detail. Table 10.5 compares the combinations. ▷

```
<definitions
  targetNamespace="(namespace for service WSDL)"
  xml:typens="(namespace for service schema)">

<types>
<schema targetNamespace="(namespace for the schema)">
  <element name="Amount" type="xsd:int"/>
  <element name="details" type="typens:PaymentDetail"/>
<!--user defined data type-->
  <complexType name="PaymentDetail">
    <sequence>
        <element name="balance" type="xsd:int"/>
        <element name="payeeName" type="xsd:string"/>
    </sequence>
  </complexType>
</schema>
</types>

<message...>
  <part name='part1' type="typens: PaymentDetail"/>
  <part name='part2' type="xsd:int"/>
  <part name='part3' element="typens:Amount"/>
  <part name='part4' element="typens:details"/>
</message>
...
</definitions>
```

> In document/literal style, the contents between <SOAP-ENC:Body> and </SOAP-ENC:Body> are sent as an XML string to the application, which is responsible for parsing the XML.
>
> JAX-RPC requires RPC/encoded and document/literal support. These are optional for the other two combinations.
>
> For more about the style use combinations of RPC/literal, document/literal, PRC/encoded, and document/encoded, see Chapter 5.

Table 10.5 Examples of RPC/Encoded, RPC/Literal, Document/Literal, and Document/ Encoded Combinations

Style

RPC/encoded

WSDL

```
<operation name="schedulePayment" style="rpc" ... >
<input>
<soap:body parts="part1 part2"
        use="encoded"
        encoding= "http://schemas.xmlsoap.org/soap/encoding/"
 namespace="(namespace for message)"/>
</input>
</operation>
```

The WSDL extract shows an RPC operation named schedulePayment being invoked in RPC/encoded format, with SOAP encodings and two input parameters.

SOAP message

```
<soapenv:body xmlns:mns="(namespace for message)">
<mns:schedulePayment>
    <part1 HREF="#1" TARGET="_self"/>
    <part2>5688</part2>
</mns:schedulePayment>

<mns:PaymentDetails id="#1">
    <balance>8933</balance>
    <payeeName>johnmalkovich</payeeName>
</mns:PaymentDetails>
</soapenv:body>
```

Style

RPC/literal

```
<operation name="schedulePayment"
        style="rpc" ... >
  <input>
    <soap:body use="literal"
        parts="part1 part2 part3 part4"
```

Table 10.5   Examples of RPC/Encoded, RPC/Literal, Document/Literal, and Document/Encoded Combinations (Cont'd)

```
namespace="(namespace for message)"/>
  </input>
// ...
</operation>
```

The WSDL extract shows an RPC operation named schedulePayment being invoked in RPC/literal format, with four input parameters. It shows how data types can be passed and how a schema element is sent across the wire directly, without any encoding.

SOAP message

```
<soapenv:body xmlns:mns="(namespace for message)"
        xmlns:typens="(namespace for service schema)".. >
<mns:schedulePayment>


<mns:part1>


<typens:balance>8933</typens:balance>
    <typens:payeeName>johnmalkovich
                </typens:payeeName>
</mns:part1>


<mns:part2>5688</mns:part2>


<mns:part3>


<typens:Amount>5688</typens:Amount>
</mns:part3>


<mns:part4>
      <typens:PaymentDetail>
      <typens:balance>8933</typens:balance>
      <typens:payeeName>johnmalkovich
                  </typens:payeeName>
</typens:PaymentDetail>
</mns:part4>


</mns:schedulePayment>
</soapenv:body>
```

(Continued)

Table 10.5 Examples of RPC/Encoded, RPC/Literal, Document/Literal, and Document/ Encoded Combinations (Cont'd)

Style

Document/literal

```
<operation name="schedulePayment"
                style="document" ... >
<input>
<soap:body parts="part1 part3 part4"
            use="literal">
</input>
</operation>
```

The WSDL extract shows a document-style message being sent in literal format with four input parameters. It shows how data types can be passed and how a schema element is sent across the wire directly, without any encoding.

SOAP message

```
<soapenv:body
                xmlns:typens="(namespace for service schema)" ... >


<typens:balance>8933</typens:balance>
<typens:payeeName>johnmalkovich
                </typens:payeeName>


<typens:Amount>5688</typens:Amount>


<typens:details>
    <typens:balance>5688</typens:balance>
    <typens:payeeName>johnmalkovich


</typens:payeeName>
</typens:details>
</soapenv:body>
```

Table 10.5   Examples of RPC/Encoded, RPC/Literal, Document/Literal, and Document/Encoded Combinations (Cont'd)

Style

Document/encoded

```
<operation name="schedulePayment"
            style="document" ... >
<input>
<soap:body parts="part1 part2"
            use="encoded"
            encoding=
"http://schemas.xmlsoap.org/soap/encoding/"
    namespace="(namespace for message)"/>
</input>
</operation>
```

The WSDL extract shows a document style message being sent with SOAP encoding and four input parameters. It shows how data types can be passed and how a schema element is sent across the wire directly.

SOAP message

```
<soapenv:body ...
            xmlns:mns="(namespace for message)">
<mns:PaymentDetails>
    <balance>8933</balance>
    <payeeName>johnmalkovich</payeeName>
</mns:PaymentDetails>

<soapenc:int>5688</soapenc:int>
</soapenv:body>
```

When to Use RPC/Encoded and Document/Literal

To best choose a particular style, an architect would need to understand the implementation or desired use. In general, however, the effort and complexity involved in document style service is greater than for RPC style—for example, in negotiating the schema design with the business partners and validating the document against the schema. When architecting applications, these are some of the decision points for deciding between RPC or document style:

1. **State maintenance.** If multiple service invocations are involved in a single business transaction, with state maintained between the service invocations, the service must maintain state. Maintaining state is nontrivial and is usually not as simple as exposing a stateful EJB as a Web service over multiple RPC invocations. One alternative is to use document style, pass the contents of an entire transaction in the document, and allow the service implementation to ensure the sequence and state maintenance in the transaction. Information about that state can be returned in a token or in the resulting document to the client if needed.

   If the service consumer is only requesting information or persisting information in a specific format (e.g., industry-standard XML schema), a document style message makes more sense, because it is not constrained by the RPC-oriented encoding.

2. **Integration with external parties and decoupled interfaces.** Service consumers outside the enterprise typically have little control over the use and consequences of changes to the service interface. RPC interfaces are expected not to change, because any change would break the contract between the service and its consumers. In scenarios where a large number of applications have produced stub code from the service's WSDL document (we will see how to do this later in this chapter), changing the WSDL would cause all the applications that rely on a specific method signature to break. If you anticipate frequent changes, you can use a document/literal style, because the impact on the WSDL can be minimized. This is useful for the *late binding pattern* discussed in Chapter 5.

3. **Validate business documents.** A Web service can use the capabilities of a validating parser and schemas to describe and validate high-level business documents. This is opposed to RPC, where the XML describes the method and parameters encoded for that method call, which cannot be used to enforce high-level business rules.

   To enforce these rules for the document with RPC, a message must include an XML document as a string parameter or attachment and must hide the validation in the implementation of the method being called. If an attachment is not used, the service will have to deal with custom marshalling and unmarshalling code for a possibly complex XML structure. This often leads to valid calls with invalid parameters that are not detected till the entire structure has been processed. In short, if the service is accepting or returning a complex XML structure, a document style is better suited. The XML can be validated against the schema prior to calling the service, and no custom marshalling code is required.

4. **Performance and memory limitations.** Marshalling and unmarsalling parameters to XML in memory can be an intensive process. The SOAP model inherently requires DOM-based processing of the envelope, which can lead to large DOM trees in memory if the XML representation is complex. However, document style services can choose SAX handling of the including XML document, to perform quicker and less memory intensive parsing. This is critical for services that handle many simultaneous requests.

5. **For fine-grained communication.** With RPC calls, only a limited amount of data can be passed around in a single invocation, and it is not possible to include multiple RPC calls in a single SOAP envelope. If the application requires a significant amount of data to be passed around, RPC style with an attachment (e.g.. an XML document) is better suited.

6. **Request-response processing.** SOAP messages are, by nature, one-way transmissions from a sender to a receiver, but they are usually combined to implement a request/response model. SOAP piggybacking on top of a request-response–oriented transport, such as HTTP and JAX-RPC, is well suited to applications that require synchronous request-response processing. Such applications typically involve retrieval of results based on some remote procedure execution, for which RPC/encoded messages are well suited.

7. **Encoding scheme.** The default encoding scheme specified by SOAP is usually sufficient. If you determine a need to use custom encoding (e.g., the SOAP encoding doesn't meet your needs because you have complex types not addressed by JAX-RPC and SOAP), we recommend that you investigate the document style route instead, since schemas are by far a richer metalanguage than SOAP encoding. This allows for a more complex arrangement of information.

Document style combined with literal encoding allows validation. Changing that to *RPC/literal* takes that benefit away, because the surrounding RPC element does not appear in the schemas. A possible example where *RPC/literal* can be used instead of *document/literal* is when multiple RPC operations return XML documents using the same schema. *Document/encoded* takes away the benefits of *RPC/encoded* but does not add anything in return.

> JAX-RPC Development

We have just covered how data can be transferred over the wire, along with the rules and associated mechanics governing that. In this section, we will look at how services can be developed and realized using JAX-RPC and the steps involved in doing so.

Developing and consuming a JAX-RPC service can be categorized into five steps:

1. Service definition
2. Service implementation
3. Service deployment
4. Service description
5. Service consumption

In walking through these steps we will develop the service example introduced in Chapter 5. The example illustrates a bill payment service developed by Flute Bank as part of its online operations.

1. Service Definition

The term *service definition* is used to refer to the abstraction that defines the publicly surfaced view of the service. The service definition is represented as a Java interface that exposes the service's operations. The service definition is also called a remote interface, because it must extend the java.rmi.Remote interface, and because all methods in it must throw a java.rmi.RemoteException. The code below shows the BillPay Web service:

```
package com.flutebank.billpayservice;

import java.util.Date;
import java.rmi.Remote;
import java.rmi.RemoteException;

public interface BillPay extends Remote {
    public PaymentConfirmation schedulePayment(Date date, String nickName, double
                        amount) throws ScheduleFailedException, RemoteException;
```

```
    public PaymentDetail[] listScheduledPayments() throws RemoteException;
    public double getLastPayment(String nickname) throws RemoteException;
}
```

The methods in the interface must have valid JAX-RPC data types (disussed earlier) as arguments and return types. If they are not a supported data type (e.g. java.util.Map), then appropriate *serializers* and *deserializers* must be available, so that these types can be marshaled and unmarshalled to and from their corresponding XML representations. The data type can also be a *holder* class. Holders and pluggable serializers are covered later in this chapter.

An implemenatation will usually verify this type information at compile time and warn the developer if it is not correct. A request sent with incorrect type information at runtime will generate a SOAP fault, because it will not be able to unmarshall the XML.

2. Service Implementation

The *service implementation,* also known as a *servant,* is the concrete representation of the abstract service definition; it is a class that provides the implementation or the service definition. The Java class must have a default constructor and must implement the remote interface that defines the service. Listing 10.2 shows the implementation for the BillPay service.

Listing 10.2   Implementation for Flute Bank's BillPay service

```
package com.flutebank.billpayservice;

import java.util.Date;

public class BillPayImpl implements BillPay {

public BillPayImpl(){}

public PaymentConfirmation schedulePayment(Date date, String nickName, double
                                    amount) throws ScheduleFailedException {
    // invoke business logic like EJBs here
        return new PaymentConfirmation(81263767,"Sprint PCS", amount);
    }
```

```
public PaymentDetail[] listScheduledPayments() {
     // lookup the detail objects and other business logic from EJBs here
     PaymentDetail details[]=new PaymentDetail[1];
     PaymentDetail dummy= new PaymentDetail("Digital Credit
                                             Union","Credit",2000, new Date());
     details[0]=dummy;
     return details;
  }


public double getLastPayment(String nickname) {
   // lookup the detail objects and other business logic from EJBs for this
   // nickname based on the callers user id
           if(nickname.equalsIgnoreCase("my cable tv provider"))
                 return 829;
           else
                 return 272;
  }
}
```

Services are deployed in a JAX-RPC *runtime,* which is a container that implements the JAX-RPC specifications. By default, the runtime will just invoke the methods corresponding to the RPC request in the Java implemenatation. The service implementation can choose to provide hooks to allow the runtime to manage the service's lifecyle and allow the container to invoke callbacks on the service when major lifecycle events occur. The "hook" is defined as a javax.xml .rpc.server.ServiceLifeCycle interface that the service can implement. The container will then invoke methods on this service appropriately, via this interface. The interface defines an init(Object context) and a destroy() method:

```
public interface ServiceLifecycle{
      public void init(Object obj) throws ServiceException;
      public void destroy();
  }
```

The behavior of these methods is similar to the init() and destroy() methods in a servlet. When the implementation is first instantiated, the init() method is invoked, and a context object passed to it, the destroy() method is called before the implementation needs to be removed (e.g., at shutdown or during a resource crunch). These methods are good places to initialize and release expensive resources, such as database connections and remote references. The con-

Figure 10.4
Service
deployment

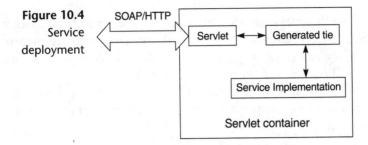

text is defined as an `Object`, to allow for different endpoint types to be used, as we will see later (e.g., the context will be different for an HTTP endpoint and a JMS endpoint).

As with a servlet, an implementation should not hold a client-specific state in instance variables, because the runtime can invoke methods from multiple threads. Architects should also avoid synchronizing the methods themselves. There are other ways to maintain client state, as discussed in the next section.

3. Service Deployment

We mentioned earlier that a service is deployed in a JAX-RPC runtime. A *service endpoint* is the perimeter where the SOAP message is received and the response dispatched. It is the physical entity exposed to service consumers that essentially services client requests. An endpoint is provided by the runtime and is not written by developers. An endpoint is bound to the transport protocol. Because a runtime is required to support an HTTP transport, JAX-RPC also defines the behavior of an endpoint for this protocol as a Java servlet, as Figure 10.4 shows. ▷

The servlet receives the SOAP message as the HTTP request, determines the servant to use for servicing that request, and delegates to it or its proxy representation (the tie). Once the service has done its work, the servlet is responsible for packaging the SOAP message and sending it back over HTTP.

The exact implementation of the servlet endpoint is left up to the runtime. The reference implementation contains a single servlet (`com.sun.xml.rpc.server` `.http.JAXRPCServlet`) that delegates to a tie, based on the xrpcc-generated prop-

> ▷ Even though a JAX-RPC runtime must support HTTP, it can use other transports as well. The JAX-RPC architecture is designed to be transport–independent, even though it describes the way HTTP is used if it is chosen as transport.

erties file (we will see this later in the chapter). Because the endpoint is a servlet, it requires a Servlet 2.2–compliant container. Also, the packaging and deployment to the endpoint of the service has to be the standard J2EE WAR file, with its defined structure (WEB-INF/classes and the web.xml file, etc.)

If a service implementation implements the `ServiceLifeCycle` interface, the context object passed in the `init()` is of type `javax.xml.rpc.server.Servlet-EndpointContext`:

```
public interface ServletEndpointContext{
        public MessageContext getMessageContext();
        public Principal getUserPrincipal();
        public HttpSession getHttpSession();
        public ServletContext getServletContext();
}
```

This context provides methods to access the `MessageContext`, `Principal`, `HttpSession` and `ServletContext` objects associated with the user. The listing below shows an example of how this can be used. These objects are good places for maintaining different kinds of state information:

- The `HttpSession` is a good place to maintain *client*-specific state, using the `getAttribute()` and `setAttribute()` methods.

- The `ServletContext` is a good place to access *application*-specific state, such as configuration parameters, Java Naming and Directory Interface (JNDI) names, and JNDI contexts, using the `getAttribute()` and `setAttribute()` methods.

- The `MessageContext` is a good place to obtain state set by message handlers during preprocessing of the message. Handlers are covered in detail later in the chapter.

```
public class BillPayImpl implements BillPay, ServiceLifecycle {
    private ServletEndpointContext ctx;
 public void init(java.lang.Object context){
      ctx=(ServletEndpointContext)context;
    }
public PaymentDetail[] listScheduledPayments() {
     SOAPMessageContext msgctx= (SOAPMessageContext) (ctx.getMessageContext());
     HttpSession session = ctx.getHttpSession();
       ServletContext servletctx= ctx.getServletContext()
```

```
    // other code
    }
}
```

The usage of the ServletEndpointContext is analogous to the SessionContext and EntityContext in EJBs.

4. Service Description

Once the service is defined, implemented, and ready for deployment as an end-point, it also must be *described* clearly for service consumers. This is where WDSL comes in. Based on the service definition, the WSDL document describes the service, its operations, arguments, return types, and the schema for the data types used in them.

xrpcc *Internals*

The JAX-RPC reference implementation comes with the xrpcc (XML-based RPC Compiler) tool, which reads a tool-specific XML configuration file and generates the client- or server-side bindings shown in Figure 10.5. A developer can start with

- A remote interface and use xrpcc to generate the stubs, ties, and WSDL
- A WSDL document and generate the stubs to consume the service
- A WSDL document and generate the stubs, ties, and remote interface and implement the service

Listing 10.3 shows the format for the XML configuration file xrpcc reads.

Figure 10.5
xrpcc artifacts

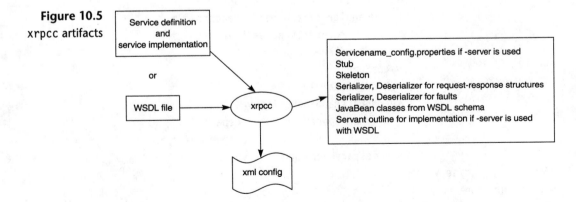

Listing 10.3 xrpcc configuration in the reference implementation

```xml
<?xml version="1.0" encoding="UTF-8"?>
<configuration xmlns="http://java.sun.com/xml/ns/jax-rpc/ri/config">
<service name="" packageName="" targetNamespace="" typeNamespace="">
  <interface name="" servantName="" soapAction="" soapActionBase="">
      <handlerChains>
        <chain runAt=" " roles="">
                    <handler className="" headers="">
                     <property name="" value=""/>
                    </handler>
                </chain>
              </handlerChains>
</interface>
      <typeMappingRegistry>
              <import>
                  <schema namespace="" location=""/>
              </import>
              <typeMapping encodingStyle="">
                  <entry schemaType=""
                          javaType=""
                          serializerFactory=""
                          deserializerFactory=""/>
              </typeMapping>
              <additionalTypes>
                  <class name=""/>
              </additionalTypes>
            </typeMappingRegistry>
              <handlerChains>
                  <chain runAt="client" roles="">
                      <handler className="" headers="">
                          <property name="" value=""/>
                      </handler>
                  </chain>
                  </handlerChains>
                  <namespaceMappingRegistry>
                      <namespaceMapping namespace=""
                                        packageName=""/>
                  </namespaceMappingRegistry>
            </service>
</configuration>
```

Key XML elements of the configuration are discussed below. Some refer to concepts covered later in the chapter (e.g., `handlers` and `typemappings`).

Service Element. This describes the overall service. Only one service can be defined in the XML descriptor, to prevent potential name clashes in the generated code for the different services and the types they use.

- `name`. The name of the service. This is also used as the value for the `service` element in the generated WSDL.

- `package`. The package name for the generated service classes. `xrpcc` generates the stubs with the same package name as the service interface.

- `targetnamespace`. The target namespace for the generated WSDL document.

- `typenamespace`. The namespace for the schema portion of the generated WSDL document.

Interface element. This defines details about the interface the service supports. A service can have multiple interfaces.

- `name`. Fully qualified name of an interface, such as `com.flutebank.billpay` `.Billpay`.

- `servant`. Fully qualified name of the service interface implementation.

- `soapAction`. Value to be used as the `SOAPAction` for all operations in the corresponding port (optional).

- `soapaActionBase`. Value used as a prefix for the `SOAPAction` strings for the operations in the corresponding port (optional).

Handlerchain element. Defines information about handlers for this service. The `handler` element can be defined inside a service. If so, it is available to all interfaces inside the `interface` element, in which case it is specific only to that interface.

- `runAt`. Defines where the handler is to be executed. Possible values are `client` or `server`.

- `roles`. Lists or defines the roles that the handler will run as. This is the whitespace-separated `List (xsd:anyURI)` value returned by `HandlerChain` `.getRoles()`.

- `className`. Fully qualified name of the handler class.

- headers. The header blocks processed by the handler. This is the whitespace-separated List(xsd:QName)-qualified name of a header block's outermost element.

- property. Multiple and arbitrary name-value pairs the handler can use internally, such as configuration and initialization parameters. These properties are passed as input to Handler.init(HandlerInfo config) through the "config" argument. The HandlerInfo.getHandlerConfig() method returns a Map containing all property name-value pairs specified in the <property/> elements.

Typemapping registry element.

- import. Specifies a list of schema documents to import and is used to generate the corresponding <wsdl:import/> and <schema:import/> elements.

- typeMapping. Contains one or more entry elements.

- entry. Specifies the encodingStyle, schemaType, Java class, and class for the serializer and deserializer factories.

- additionalTypes. Specifies a list of Java classes that do not appear in the remote interface but are still passed to JAX-RPC. For example, if in a method with a signature

```
public java.util.List getPaymentDetails() throws RemoteException;
```

contains PaymentDetail objects, and the PaymentDetail class is not referenced by any other method in the remote interface, then for xrpcc to generate and register a serializer for the PaymentDetail type, this element must be specified:

```
<additionalTypes>
    <class name="com.flutebank.PaymentDetail "/>
</additionalType>
```

Namespace mapping registry.

- namespaceMapping

The –both option of the xrpcc tool can be used to generate stubs and ties together. Alternatively, the server and client code can be generated separately, using the –server and –client options. Note that the –keep option must be used to retain the WSDL file.

One of the artifacts xrpcc generates when it reads the XML descriptor is an *additional* configuration file. So, what is this new configuration file? Remember,

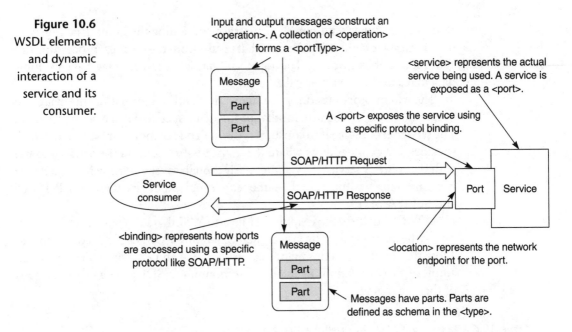

Figure 10.6
WSDL elements and dynamic interaction of a service and its consumer.

the service is being deployed in a servlet container, where the runtime-provided endpoint exists (the reference implementation defined the endpoint as a com.sun.xml.rpc.server.http.JAX-RPCServlet). This configuration file is used to hook the endpoint with the service implementation. It is just an implementation detail that, like xrpcc itself, is specific to the reference implementation and is not a part of the specifications. Other vendors may use a completely different tool with its own mechanism. ▷

Java-WSDL Mappings

In Chapter 4, we discussed the WSDL structure, the role of vendor tools, and the significance of a standard specification to map WSDL elements to Java (and vice versa). To understand this mapping, let us revisit the role of WSDL elements from that chapter (Figure 10.6).

A Web service exposes groups of business operations for service consumers to use. Operations are grouped together to form portTypes. To invoke an opera-

---

▷ The final version of the Hava WSDP and JAX pack include a tool called wscompile. Currently there is no difference in the behavior of wscompile and xrpcc; however in future versions wscompile is likely to evolve, whereas xrpcc may not.

tion, the consumer sends an input message containing the input data. It gets an output message containing the data that results from the business processing, or a fault if a problem occurs. The input and output messages may have multiple data items in them; each is called a part.

The wire protocol used for the invocation and the format of the input and output messages on the wire for that protocol are specified in a binding element. The service exposes itself to consumers through one or more ports, each of which specifies a network address where the service is located and the binding to use with that port. A service may render itself though several ports, where each port has a different binding (e.g., the same service may expose itself via SOAP/HTTP and SOAP/SMTP).

JAX-RPC defines the mapping of Java to WSDL data types, and vice versa. This is the mapping used by xrpcc when generating a WSDL file or consuming it. Table 10.6 summarizes this mapping. Listings 10.4 and 10.5 show a complete example of a service definition and its corresponding WSDL generated on the basis of these mappings.

Table 10.6   Data Type Mapping between Java and WSDL

Java type	WSDL mapping
Package	WSDL document

Sample extract code

The namespace definition in a WSDL is mapped to a Java package name.

Java type	WSDL mapping
Interface	wsdl:portType

Sample extract code

```
public interface BillPay extends java.rmi.Remote {
// methods here
}
```

```
<portType name="BillPay">
   // operations here
</portType>
```

Text continued on p. 355

Table 10.6   Data Type Mapping between Java and WSDL (Cont'd)

Java type	WSDL mapping
Method	`wsdl:operation` 1. The WSDL operation name is the same as the method name. 2. Overloaded methods can map to multiple operations with the same name or unique names that are implementation-specific.

Sample extract code

```
public interface BillPay extends java.rmi.Remote {
    public PaymentDetail[] listScheduledPayments()
        throws RemoteException;
    public PaymentConfirmation schedulePayment(
        Date date, String payee, double amt)
      throws ScheduleFailedException, RemoteException;

public double getLastPayment(String nickname) throws
                                RemoteException;
}
```

```
<portType name="BillPay">
    <operation name="listScheduledPayments">
     // input output messages for this operation
</operation>
    <operation name="schedulePayment">
     // input output messages for this operation
    </operation>
<operation name="getLastPayment">
     // input output messages for this operation
</portType>
```

Java type	WSDL mapping
Extended interface	`wsdl:portType` with a complete set of inherited operations.

(Continued)

Table 10.6   Data Type Mapping between Java and WSDL (Cont'd)

Sample extract code

```
Public interface LinkedBillPay extends BillPay {
public String getStatus() throws
java.rmi.RemoteException, StatusUnavilableException;
}
<portType name="LinkedBillPay">
   <operation name="listScheduledPayments">
    // input output messages for this operation
</operation>
   <operation name="schedulePayment">
    // input output messages for this operation
  </operation>
   <operation name="getStatus">
    // input output messages for this operation
   </operation>
   </operation>
</portType>
```

Java type	WSDL mapping

Method arguments   wsdl:input and corresponding wsdl:message elements.

Sample extract code

```
public interface BillPay extends java.rmi.Remote {
   public PaymentDetail[] listScheduledPayments()
      throws RemoteException;
public PaymentConfirmation schedulePayment(Date
date, String payee, double amt)
   throws ScheduleFailedException, RemoteException;
public double getLastPayment(String nickname) throws
RemoteException;
}

  <portType name="BillPay">
    <operation name="getLastPayment"">
      <input message="tns:BillPay_getLastPayment"/>
      // output message
```

Table 10.6   Data Type Mapping between Java and WSDL (Cont'd)

```
</operation>
    <operation name="listScheduledPayments">
      <input message="tns:BillPay_listScheduledPayments"/>
      // output message
</operation>
  <operation name="schedulePayment" >
    <input message="tns:BillPay_schedulePayment"/>
    // output message
</operation>
</portType>

<message name="BillPay_getLastPayment">
    <part name="String_1" type="xsd:string"/></message>
  <message name="BillPay_listScheduledPayments"/>
  <message name="BillPay_schedulePayment">
    <part name="Date_1" type="xsd:dateTime"/>
    <part name="String_2" type="xsd:string"/>
    <part name="double_3" type="xsd:double"/></message>
```

Java type	WSDL mapping
Method returns	`wsdl:output` and corresponding `wsdl:message` elements.

Sample extract code

```
public interface BillPay extends java.rmi.Remote {
    public PaymentDetail[] listScheduledPayments()
        throws RemoteException;
public PaymentConfirmation schedulePayment(Date date, String payee,
                                                    double amt)

    throws ScheduleFailedException, RemoteException;
public double getLastPayment(String nickname) throws
RemoteException;
```

```
<message name="BillPay_getLastPaymentResponse">
  <part name="result" type="xsd:double"/></message>
<message name="BillPay_listScheduledPaymentsResponse">
  <part name="result" type="tns:ArrayOfPaymentDetail"/></message>
```

(Continued)

Table 10.6   Data Type Mapping between Java and WSDL (Cont'd)

```
<message name="BillPay_schedulePaymentResponse">
   <part name="result" type="tns:PaymentConfirmation"/></message>
<portType name="BillPay">
   <operation name="getLastPayment" parameterOrder="String_1">
       // input message here
   <output message="tns:BillPay_getLastPaymentResponse"/>
                                                       </operation>
   <operation name="listScheduledPayments" parameterOrder="">
       // input message here
     <output message="tns:BillPay_listScheduledPaymentsResponse"/>
                                                       </operation>
   <operation name="schedulePayment" parameterOrder="Date_1
                                          String_2 double_3">
     <output message="tns:BillPay_schedulePaymentResponse"/>
</operation></portType>
```

Java type	WSDL mapping
Checked exceptions	wsdl:fault

1. wsdl:message name is the same as the exception name.

2. RemoteExceptions are mapped to standard SOAP faults.

3. The exception and its hierarchies get mapped to XML types in the schema, using the standard complexType extension mechanism.

Sample extract code

```
public interface BillPay extends java.rmi.Remote {
   // other code
public PaymentConfirmation schedulePayment(Date
date, String payee, double amt)
    throws ScheduleFailedException, RemoteException;
 }
```

Table 10.6   Data Type Mapping between Java and WSDL (Cont'd)

```
<operation name="schedulePayment">
    // input  and output elements
  <fault name="ScheduleFailedException">
      <soap:fault encodingStyle="http://schemas.xmlsoap.org/soap/
encoding/" use="encoded" namespace="http://www.flutebank.com/xml"/>
                                                    </fault>

      <soap:operation soapAction=""/>
</operation>
<message name="ScheduleFailedException">
   <part name="ScheduleFailedException" type=
                        "tns:ScheduleFailedException"/></message>
```

Java type	WSDL mapping
Java identifiers	XML name.

Sample extract code

Java identifiers are already legal XML names.

```
public class PaymentDetail {
  private String payeeName;
  private String account;
  private double amt;
  private Date date;
  // other code
```

```
<types>
// other code
<complexType name="PaymentDetail">
      <sequence>
        <element name="date" type="dateTime"/>
        <element name="account" type="string"/>
        <element name="payeeName" type="string"/>
        <element name="amt" type="double"/></sequence>
                                            </complexType>
   </types>
```

Listing 10.4 Source file for BillPay.java

```java
package com.flutebank.billpayservice;

import java.util.*;
import java.rmi.Remote;
import java.rmi.RemoteException;

public interface BillPay extends Remote {

public PaymentConfirmation schedulePayment(Date date, String nickName, double amount)
throws ScheduleFailedException, RemoteException;

public PaymentDetail[] listScheduledPayments() throws RemoteException;

public double getLastPayment(String nickname) throws RemoteException;
}
```

Listing 10.5 WSDL billservice.java corresponding to Listing 10.4

```xml
<?xml version="1.0" encoding="UTF-8"?>
<definitions name="billpayservice" targetNamespace="http://www.flutebank.com/xml"
xmlns:tns="http://www.flutebank.com/xml" xmlns="http://schemas.xmlsoap.org/wsdl/"
xmlns:xsd="http://www.w3.org/2001/XMLSchema" xmlns:soap="http://schemas.xmlsoap.org/
wsdl/soap/">
    <types>
        <schema targetNamespace="http://www.flutebank.com/xml" xmlns:wsdl="http://
schemas.xmlsoap.org/wsdl/" xmlns:tns="http://www.flutebank.com/xml" xmlns:xsi="http://
www.w3.org/2001/XMLSchema-instance" xmlns:soap-enc="http://schemas.xmlsoap.org/soap/
encoding/" xmlns="http://www.w3.org/2001/XMLSchema">
            <import namespace="http://schemas.xmlsoap.org/soap/encoding/"/>
            <complexType name="ArrayOfPaymentDetail">
                <complexContent>
                    <restriction base="soap-enc:Array">
                        <attribute ref="soap-enc:arrayType" wsdl:arrayType=
                                                    "tns:PaymentDetail[]"/>
                    </restriction>
                </complexContent>
            </complexType>
            <complexType name="PaymentDetail">
                <sequence>
                    <element name="date" type="dateTime"/>
```

```
            <element name="account" type="string"/>
            <element name="payeeName" type="string"/>
            <element name="amt" type="double"/>
            </sequence>
        </complexType>
        <complexType name="PaymentConfirmation">
            <sequence>
                <element name="confirmationNum" type="int"/>
                <element name="payee" type="string"/>
                <element name="amt" type="double"/>
                </sequence>
        </complexType>
        <complexType name="ScheduleFailedException">
            <sequence>
                <element name="message" type="string"/>
                <element name="localizedMessage" type="string"/>
            </sequence>
        </complexType>
    </schema>
</types>
<message name="BillPay_getLastPayment">
    <part name="String_1" type="xsd:string"/>
</message>
<message name="BillPay_getLastPaymentResponse">
    <part name="result" type="xsd:double"/>
</message>
<message name="BillPay_listScheduledPayments"/>
<message name="BillPay_listScheduledPaymentsResponse">
    <part name="result" type="tns:ArrayOfPaymentDetail"/>
</message>
<message name="BillPay_schedulePayment">
    <part name="Date_1" type="xsd:dateTime"/>
    <part name="String_2" type="xsd:string"/>
    <part name="double_3" type="xsd:double"/>
</message>
<message name="BillPay_schedulePaymentResponse">
    <part name="result" type="tns:PaymentConfirmation"/>
</message>
<message name="ScheduleFailedException">
    <part name="ScheduleFailedException" type="tns:ScheduleFailedException"/>
</message>
```

```
<portType name="BillPay">
   <operation name="getLastPayment" parameterOrder="String_1">
      <input message="tns:BillPay_getLastPayment"/>
      <output message="tns:BillPay_getLastPaymentResponse"/>
   </operation>
   <operation name="listScheduledPayments" parameterOrder="">
      <input message="tns:BillPay_listScheduledPayments"/>
      <output message="tns:BillPay_listScheduledPaymentsResponse"/>
   </operation>
   <operation name="schedulePayment" parameterOrder="Date_1 String_2
                                                  double_3">
      <input message="tns:BillPay_schedulePayment"/>
      <output message="tns:BillPay_schedulePaymentResponse"/>
      <fault name="ScheduleFailedException" message=
                                  "tns:ScheduleFailedException"/>
   </operation>
   </portType>
<binding name="BillPayBinding" type="tns:BillPay">
   <operation name="getLastPayment">
      <input>
         <soap:body encodingStyle="http://schemas.xmlsoap.org/soap/encoding/"
                    use="encoded" namespace="http://www.flutebank.com/xml"/>
      </input>
      <output>
         <soap:body encodingStyle="http://schemas.xmlsoap.org/soap/encoding/"
                    use="encoded" namespace="http://www.flutebank.com/xml"/>
      </output>
      <soap:operation soapAction=""/>
</operation>
<operation name="listScheduledPayments">
   <input>
      <soap:body encodingStyle="http://schemas.xmlsoap.org/soap/encoding/"
                 use="encoded" namespace="http://www.flutebank.com/xml"/>
   </input>
   <output>
      <soap:body encodingStyle="http://schemas.xmlsoap.org/soap/encoding/"
                 use="encoded" namespace="http://www.flutebank.com/xml"/>
   </output>
   <soap:operation soapAction=""/>
</operation>
```

```
    <operation name="schedulePayment">
      <input>
        <soap:body encodingStyle="http://schemas.xmlsoap.org/soap/encoding/"
                      use="encoded" namespace="http://www.flutebank.com/xml"/>
      </input>
      <output>
        <soap:body encodingStyle="http://schemas.xmlsoap.org/soap/encoding/"
                      use="encoded" namespace="http://www.flutebank.com/xml"/>
      </output>
      <fault name="ScheduleFailedException">
        <soap:fault encodingStyle="http://schemas.xmlsoap.org/soap/encoding/"
                      use="encoded" namespace="http://www.flutebank.com/xml"/>
      </fault>
      <soap:operation soapAction=""/>
    </operation>
    <soap:binding transport="http://schemas.xmlsoap.org/soap/http" style="rpc"/>
  </binding>
  <service name="Billpayservice">
    <port name="BillPayPort" binding="tns:BillPayBinding">
      <soap:address location="http://127.0.0.1:9090/billpayservice/jaxrpc/BillPay"/>
    </port>
  </service>
</definitions>
```

5. Service Consumption

Until now, we have seen how to define, implement, and deploy a JAX-RPC service. Let us now look at how such a service can be consumed. A *service consumer* represents the abstraction of the entity invoking the facilities of an existing service. Invocation modes for doing so fall into three broad categories:

- **Synchronous request-response.** The client invokes a remote procedure and blocks until a response or an exception is received from the service. The client cannot do any other work while awaiting the response. This is analogous to making a phone call. Either someone responds by picking up the handset on the other end, or a busy tone is received.

- **One-way RPC.** The client invokes a remote procedure but does not block or wait to receive a return and is free to do other work. In fact the client does not receive any return parameters. This is analogous to sending a fax (fire and forget!). When a fax is sent, a person does not need to pick up the phone on the receiving end for the fax to go through.

- **Nonblocking RPC invocation.** The client invokes a remote procedure and continues processing without waiting for a return. The client may process the return later by polling some service or by using some other notification mechanism. This is analogous to making a phone call and getting an answering machine. The caller leaves a message and continues. The person on the other end gets the message and returns the call by dialing the number left on the machine or a number he or she already knows.

The significant difference between one-way and nonblocking invocation is that in the former, the client will not receive a return value.

As a bare minimum, JAX-RPC implementations must support the first two modes for client invocation and HTTP 1.1 as the transport binding for SOAP. The sematics of nonblocking RPC are quite complicated. For example, the client must inform the service of an endpoint to which the service can repond, and both parties must deal with issues of reliability and availability. If your application requires asynchronous communication, messaging is probably more appropriate. See Chapter 11 for details.

Let us now look at the mechanisms an RPC client can use to consume the service in these invocation modes. The client can be written to invoke the service using one of the following three mechanisms:

- Stub
- Dynamic invocation interface
- Dynamic proxies

In Chapter 5, we described WSDL use cases and early/late binding patterns associated with them. The reader is encouraged to revisit that section before continuing. Recall the usage patterns:

- Static compile-time binding
- Static deploy-time binding
- Static runtime binding

- Dynamic binding
- Dynamic binding with known location

The examples of clients in the following sections show how some of these patterns can be realized.

Clients Using Stubs

Figure 10.1 introduced the concept of stubs. Clients locate the service endpoint by specifying a URI, then simply invoke the methods on a local object, a stub that represents the remote service. JAX-RPC stubs, or *proxies,* as they are sometime referred to, are very different from RMI-IIOP stubs. Keep the following in mind:

- A stub is never required to be downloaded or distributed to clients.
- A client is not a required artifact on the client side. The end result of the invocation is that the required SOAP envelope must be sent on the transport protocol. The client can be written in a completely different programming language, as shown later in the JAX_RPC Interoperability section.
- The stub is implemented in Java and is relevant only for a JAX-RPC client runtime.
- A stub can be dynamically generated by the client side at runtime.
- A stub is specific to the client runtime.
- A stub is specific to a protocol and transport.
- A stub must implement the `javax.xml.rpc.Stub` interface.

The tie represents the server-side skeleton for the implementation. It is used by the endpoint to communicate with the implementation and is generated using tools (such as `xrpcc`) when the implementation is deployed.

Using stubs is also sometime referred to as *static* invocation, because the stub must know the remote interface about the service at *compile* time. It must have the class file representing the remote interface and the implementation available for stub generation to proceed. The client does not need the WSDL file describing the service at runtime. Stubs are specific to a particular runtime and are not portable across vendor implementations.

The code in Listing 10.6 shows the fragment for invoking the `Billpayservice` developed previously.

Listing 10.6 Client using stubs

```java
// import generated xrpcc classes + interface class + Helper classes for interface
  import com.flutebank.billpayservice.*;
  import java.util.Date;

public class StubClient {
    public static void main(String[] args) throws Exception {

  String endpoint="http://127.0.0.1:8080/billpayservice/jaxrpc/BillPay";
  String namespace = "http://www.flutebank.com/xml";
  String wsldport = "BillPayPort";
  Billpayservice_Impl serviceproxy= new Billpayservice_Impl();
  BillPay_Stub stub=(BillPay_Stub)(serviceproxy.getBillPayPort());
  stub._setProperty(javax.xml.rpc.Stub.ENDPOINT_ADDRESS_PROPERTY,endpoint);
  PaymentConfirmation conf= stub.schedulePayment(new Date(),
                                                 "my account at sprint", 190);
    System.out.println("Payment was scheduled " + conf.getConfirmationNum());
    PaymentDetail detail[]=stub.listScheduledPayments();
  for(int i=0;i<detail.length;i++) {
        System.out.println("Payee name "+ detail[i].getPayeeName());
        System.out.println("Account "+ detail[i].getAccount());
        System.out.println("Amount "+ detail[i].getAmt());
        System.out.println("Will be paid on " + detail[i].getDate());
        }
    double lastpaid= stub.getLastPayment("my cable tv provider");
    System.out.println("Last payment was " + lastpaid);
  }
}
```

Before using a stub, a client must first obtain a reference to it. The exact mechanism is specific to the implementation. The reference implementation for the stub is obtained by instantiating the service implementation class. The code below shows the mechanism another vendor might use:

```java
InitialContext ctx = new InitialContext();
Billpayservice service =
        (Billpayservice) ctx.lookup("myserver:soap:Billpayservice");
BillPay bill = service. getBillPayPort ();
Stub stub= ((Stub) bill;
```

The stub can be configured by passing it name-value pairs of properties. The `javax.xml.rpc.Stub` interface defines four standard properties to configure the stub, using the `stub._setProperty(java.lang.String name, java.lang.Object value)` method:

- `javax.xml.rpc.security.auth.username`. Username for authentication.
- `javax.xml.rpc.security.auth.username.password`. Password for authentication.
- `javax.xml.rpc.service.endpoint.address`. Optional string for the endpoint service.
- `javax.xml.rpc.session.maintain`. Use `java.lang.Boolean` to indicate that the server needs to maintain session for the client.

Clients Using DII

The second way a consumer can access a service involves the use of dynamic invocation interface (DII) instead of *static* stubs. DII is a concept that, like most other things in JAX-RPC, should be familiar to CORBA developers. Unlike static invocation, which requires that the client application include a client stub, DII enables a client application to invoke a service whose data types were unknown at the time the client was compiled. This allows a client to discover interfaces dynamically—in other words, at runtime rather than compile time—and invoke methods on objects that implement those interfaces.

JAX-RPC supports DII with the `javax.xml.rpc.Call` interface. A `Call` object can be created on a `javax.xml.rpc.Service` using the `port name` and `service name`. Then, during runtime, the following details are set:

- Operation to invoke
- Port type for the service
- Address of the endpoint
- Name, type, and mode (`in`, `out`, `inout`) of the arguments
- Return type

This information is derived by looking at the WSDL file for the service. For example, the service name is the `service name="Billpayservice">` element, the portname is the `port name="BillPayPort"` element, and so on. Listing 10.7 shows a DII client where a `Call` object is configured for the `getLastPayment` method.

The client code wraps the DII request in a Call object. DII can be used directly, by passing these values (port, operation, location, and part information) to the Call, or indirectly, by passing the WSDL to the Call. Listing 10.7 shows how a DII client can be written using the former. (QName is a common class used to represent a qualified name in different XML APIs. The qualified name of an XML element consists of its namespace declaration and its local name in the namespace.)

Listing 10.7 Client using DII directly, where all parameters are known (WSDL is not passed)

```
import javax.xml.namespace.QName;
import javax.xml.rpc.Call;
import javax.xml.rpc.Service;
import javax.xml.rpc.ParameterMode;
import javax.xml.rpc.ServiceFactory;

public class DIIClient_NoWSDL{
  public static void main(String[] args) throws Exception {

    String endpoint="http://127.0.0.1:9090/billpayservice/jaxrpc/BillPay";
    String namespace = "http://www.flutebank.com/xml";
    String schemanamespace = "http://www.w3.org/2001/XMLSchema";
    String serviceName = "Billpayservice";

    ServiceFactory factory = ServiceFactory.newInstance();
    // the Billpayservice service does not exist
    // (no stub, skeleton, or Service was generated by xrpcc)
    // but createService will return a Service object
    // that can be used to create the dynamic call

    Service service = (Service) factory.createService
                                      (new QName(namespace,serviceName));

    QName portName =      new QName(namespace,"BillPayPort");
    QName operationName = new QName(namespace,"getLastPayment");
    Call call = service.createCall(portName, operationName);
    call.setTargetEndpointAddress(endpoint);
    call.setProperty(Call.ENCODINGSTYLE_URI_PROPERTY,
              "http://schemas.xmlsoap.org/soap/encoding/");

    QName paramtype = new QName(schemanamespace, "string");
```

```
    QName returntype = new QName(schemanamespace, "double");

    call.addParameter("String_1", paramtype, ParameterMode.IN);
    call.setReturnType(returntype);

    Object[] params = {"my cable tv provider"};
    Object lastpaid= (Double)call.invoke(params);
    System.out.println("Last payment was " + lastpaid);
    }
}
```

What is relevant in Listing 10.7 is that there is no coupling between the service interface and the client (e.g., see import statements).

In indirect DII, only the port and operation names are knowm at compile time. The runtime will determine the type information about the part and location, based on the WSDL. In this case, the parameters and return types do *not* need to be configured using the addParameter or setReturnType method. Listing 10.8 shows a sample DII client using the WSDL.

Listing 10.8   Client using DII indirectly, where all parameters are not known (WSDL is dynamically inspected)

```
public class DIIClient_WSDL{

    public static void main(String[] args) throws Exception {

  String wsdllocation= http://127.0.0.1:9090/billpayservice/billpayservice.wsdl";

    String namespace = "http://www.flutebank.com/xml";
    String serviceName = "Billpayservice";

    ServiceFactory factory = ServiceFactory.newInstance();
    Service service = (Service) factory.createService
                    (new URL(wsdllocation),new QName(namespace,serviceName));

    QName portName = new QName(namespace,"BillPayPort");
    QName operationName = new QName(namespace,"getLastPayment");
    Call call = service.createCall(portName, operationName);
```

```
    Object[] params = {"my cable tv provider"};
    Object lastpaid= (Double)call.invoke(params);
    System.out.println("Last payment was " + lastpaid);
  }
}
```

Note that neither use of DII generates stubs.

WSDL with DII. When deciding whether to use WSDL or not in the client, keep in mind that though it may be more convenient to use, it requires an extra network call and processing overhead for the runtime to fetch and process the WSDL and perhaps even validate the call against the WSDL.

One of the major differences between static invocation and dynamic invocation is that, while both support synchronous communication, only DII supports one-way communication. From an API perspective, instead of using the invoke() method, DII can be used to invoke the invokeOneWay(java.lang.Object[] inputParams) method. Attempting to invoke a call.getOutputParams() in a one-way invocation will result in a JAX-RPCException.

Clients Using Dynamic Proxies

The JAX-RPC specification also specifies a third way for clients to access services: using the concept of dynamic proxy classes available in the standard J2SE Reflection API (the java.lang.reflect.Proxy class and the java.lang.reflect.InvocationHandler interface). A dynamic proxy class implements a list of interfaces specified at runtime. The client can use this proxy or façade as though it actually implemented these interfaces, although it actually delegates the invocation to the implementation.

Classes allowing any method on any of these interfaces can be called directly on the proxy (after casting it). Thus, a dynamic proxy class is used to create a type-safe proxy object for an interface list without requiring pregeneration of the proxy class, as you would with compile-time tools. Listing 10.9 shows how a client can use dynamic proxies.

Listing 10.9   Client using dynamic proxies

```
// jaxrpc classes
import javax.xml.namespace.QName;
import javax.xml.rpc.Service;
import javax.xml.rpc.ServiceFactory;
```

```java
// java classes
import java.util.Date;
import java.net.URL;
// Interface class
import com.flutebank.billpayservice.BillPay;

public class DynamicProxyClient {
  public static void main(String[] args) throws Exception{
      String namespace = "http://www.flutebank.com/xml";
      String wsldport = "BillPayPort";
      String wsdlservice = "Billpayservice";
      String wsdllocation =
                       "http://127.0.0.1:8080/billpayservice/billpayservice.wsdl";
      URL wsldurl = new URL(wsdllocation);
      ServiceFactory factory = ServiceFactory.newInstance();
      Service service = factory.createService(wsldurl,
                                        new QName(namespace, wsdlservice));
// make the call to get the stub corresponding to this service and interface
      BillPay stub = (BillPay) service.getPort(new QName(namespace,wsldport),
                                                    BillPay.class);
// invoke methods on the service
      double lastpaid= stub.getLastPayment("my cable tv provider");
      System.out.println("Last payment was " + lastpaid);
  }
}
```

In Listing 10.9, there is no compile-time stub generation. The getPort() method will return the proxy, which is also required to implement the Stub interface at runtime—that is, the stub is generated internally at runtime. Again, CORBA developers will see the similarity in the above code with its counterpart:

```java
BillPay stub = (BillPay)PortableRemoteObject.narrow(initial.lookup("Billpayservice"),
                                                    BillPay.class);
```

Clients Using WSDL

Until now, we have seen how to start with a Java service definition and implement it as an XML-RPC Web service. One could also do the reverse:

- *Start* with a WSDL file for an existing service and generate the stubs, to consume the service.

- *Start* with a WSDL file and generate the ties (and stubs if needed) and remote interfaces, and fill in appropriate business logic to implement the service.

Let us look at how to consume the Billpayservice Web service using the service's WSDL and the WSDL 1.1–compliant xrpcc tool. The client-side bindings are generated from the WSDL using xrpcc, with only a configuration file change:

```
<?xml version="1.0" encoding="UTF-8"?>
    <configuration xmlns="http://java.sun.com/xml/ns/jax-rpc/ri/config">
        <wsdl location=http://127.0.0.1:9090/billpayservice/billpayservice.wsdl
                packageName="generated">
            </wsdl>
    </configuration>
```

The client-side code is identical to the StubClient shown previously, except that

- The client no longer depends on the server interfaces but is coupled to the tool-*generated* classes—which, from the above configuration, reside in a generated package (see import statement).

- The Date parameter has been changed to Calendar, as per the date type mappings from XML to Java specified in Tables 10.3a and 10.3b.

- The endpoint does not need to be configured (unless you want to) and is picked from the soap:address element in the WSDL by the tool.

```
import generated.*; // generated classes by xrpcc from WSDL file
import java.util.Calendar;

public class WSDLClient {
    public static void main(String[] args) throws Exception {
        String namespace = "http://www.flutebank.com/xml";
        String wsldport = "BillPayPort";
        Billpayservice_Impl serviceproxy= new Billpayservice_Impl();
        BillPay_Stub stub=(BillPay_Stub)(serviceproxy.getBillPayPort());
        PaymentConfirmation conf=stub.schedulePayment(Calendar.getInstance(),
                                        "my account at sprint", 190);
        System.out.println("Payment was scheduled " +
                                            conf.getConfirmationNum());
```

```
      PaymentDetail detail[]=stub.listScheduledPayments();
      for(int i=0;i<detail.length;i++) {
        System.out.println("Payee name "+ detail[i].getPayeeName());
        System.out.println("Account "+ detail[i].getAccount());
        System.out.println("Amount "+ detail[i].getAmt());
        System.out.println("Will be paid on " +
                                        detail[i].getDate().getTime());
      }
      double lastpaid= stub.getLastPayment("my cable tv provider");
      System.out.println("Last payment was " + lastpaid);
  }
}
```

What Client Is Right for Me?

Choosing either option shown above to implement the client affects only client-side development. When a server method is invoked, that server has no knowledge of whether a method was invoked via the conventional static stub mechanism, through DII, through proxies, or even by a non-Java client. From the server's perspective, it receives a SOAP request and generates a SOAP response; these are identical for all client types. For example, Listings 10.10a and 10.10b show SOAP request and response messages for the getLastPayment() method, which is identical for stubs, DII (with or without WSDL), dynamic proxies, or WSDL.

Listing 10.10a   SOAP request

```
POST /billpayservice/jaxrpc/BillPay HTTP/1.1
Content-Type: text/xml; charset="utf-8"
Content-Length: 506
SOAPAction: ""
User-Agent: Java1.3.1_01
Host: 127.0.0.1:9090
Accept: text/html, image/gif, image/jpeg, *; q=.2, */*; q=.2
Connection: keep-alive

<?xml version="1.0" encoding="UTF-8"?>
<env:Envelope xmlns:env="http://schemas.xmlsoap.org/soap/envelope/" xmlns:xsd=
"http://www.w3.org/2001/XMLSchema" xmlns:xsi="http://www.w3.org/2001/XMLSchema-
instance" xmlns:enc="http://schemas.xmlsoap.org/soap/encoding/" xmlns:ns0="http://
www.flutebank.com/xml" env:encodingStyle="http://schemas.xmlsoap.org/soap/encoding/">
```

```
<env:Body>
<ns0:getLastPayment>
    <String_1 xsi:type="xsd:string">my cable tv provider</String_1>
</ns0:getLastPayment>
</env:Body>
</env:Envelope>
```

Listing 10.10b SOAP response

```
HTTP/1.1 200 OK
Content-Type: text/xml; charset="utf-8"
SOAPAction: ""
Transfer-Encoding: chunked
Date: Mon, 29 Jul 2002 19:28:50 GMT
Server: Apache Coyote HTTP/1.1 Connector [1.0]

<?xml version="1.0" encoding="UTF-8"?>
<env:Envelope xmlns:env="http://schemas.xmlsoap.org/soap/envelope/" xmlns:xsd=
"http://www.w3.org/2001/XMLSchema" xmlns:xsi="http://www.w3.org/2001/XMLSchema-
instance" xmlns:enc="http://schemas.xmlsoap.org/soap/encoding/" xmlns:ns0="http://
www.flutebank.com/xml" env:encodingStyle="http://schemas.xmlsoap.org/soap/encoding/">
    <env:Body>
        <ns0:getLastPaymentResponse>
            <result xsi:type="xsd:double">829.0</result>
        </ns0:getLastPaymentResponse>
    </env:Body>
</env:Envelope>
```

In most practical situations, an enterprise will develop a service and publish its WSDL. Service consumers will use the WSDL and a vendor-provided tool (such as xrpcc) to generate client-side bindings and invoke the service. This has several advantages. There is no distribution of client code (e.g., remote interfaces), and in most cases, the tool will generate the serializers and deserializers, using the encoding scheme. For example, xrpcc generates the serializers and deserializers using the SOAP encoding scheme for PaymentDetail[] and PaymentDetail and maps the supported XML Schema types to Java.

Using stubs directly has the disadvantage of having to share the Java interface (and interface-dependent classes) with the service consumer. However, in scenarios where services will be developed within the boundaries of the enterprise, static stubs are the preferred client model, along the same lines as above. The performance with stubs is also expected to be better, since all type casting information is built in. All that occurs at runtime is service invocation.

DII is quite attractive, because it allows dynamic creation and invocation of object requests. In most cases, the architect of an application knows the kind of objects the application will need to access, and if not, WSDL should suffice. In some cases, such as object browsers and object brokers, DII is useful, but we don't envision these as frequent.

In practical situations and architecturally, DII is also not completely dynamic. Let us explain this further. Enterprise-level Web services will be coarse-grained and will frequently deal with passing data objects, such as the JavaBean's (e.g., `PaymentDetail` or `PaymentConfirmation`, as in the `StubClient.java` example). Simple data types will not suffice. For a DII client to be able to invoke these services, it *will* need the classes at compile time for the objects being passed around. (For example, if the DII code above invoked the `schedulePayment` method, the result would be a `PaymentConfirmation` object). The question is, where do these classes come from? The alternatives include using the same classes as the service, producing a coupling, or producing the classes from WSDL, using a tool (xrpcc). Further, if the data type that needs to be passed around is a custom type and not a JavaBean (e.g., a vector), a serializer and deserializer would need to be written for it. All this offsets the benefits DII offers of being a "dynamic invocation" at runtime.

> Advanced JAX-RPC

Attachments in JAX-RPC

A SOAP message may also contain one or more attachments using the MIME encoding, as Listing 10.11 shows. This is often refered to as a *compound* message. The attachments are referenced in the SOAP message with an HREF, analogous to how HTML anchor tags are used to create links on the same Web page. The special characters in Listing 10.11 are the binary content of the attachment printed as text.

Listing 10.11 A compound message with a MIME attachment

```xml
<?xml version="1.0" encoding="UTF-8"?>
<env:Envelope... >
<env:Body>
<storeDocumentService>
        <!--Some XML Here-->
        <something xsi:type="ns1:something" href="cid:ID1"/>
```

```
</storeDocumentService>
</env:Body>
</env:Envelope>

--3317565.1028340932732.JavaMail.Administrator.BYTECODE
Content-Type: application/octet-stream
Content-Id: ID1
```

ÐÏ_âì±_á

Sending information in an attachment rather than in the SOAP message body is more efficient, because smaller SOAP message bodies are processed faster. The message contains only a reference to the data and not the data itself, which reduces the translation time in mapping the data to Java objects. JAX-RPC uses the JavaBeans activation framework for dealing with SOAP attachments. When unmarshalling this message to Java, the JAX-RPC runtime can use either of two mapping techniques:

- It can map well-known MIME types to Java objects, as per Table 10.7, and vice versa, using built-in DataHandlers and DataContentHandlers in the runtime.
- It can map the attachment to a javax.activation.DataHandler using the JavaBeans Activation framework, and vice versa.

What this essentially means is that if a method in a service implementation is exposed in a Web service and has a return type that contains either a Java type, as per the mappings shown in Table 10.2, or a DataHandler, the runtime will marshal that as an attachment to the outgoing SOAP message. If the argument is of the type in Table 10.7 or is a DataHandler, it will be passed the corresponding attachment from the incoming SOAP message. The content of the attachment can then be extracted using a getContent() on the DataHandler. If the installed DataContentHandler does not understand the content, it will return a java.io .InputStream object with the raw bytes. ▷

▷ The JavaBeans Activation framework is a standard extension API originally designed for bean components. It adds support for typing arbitrary blocks of data and handling the content accordingly.

Table 10.7   MIME-to-Java Data Type Mapping

MIME	Type
image/gif	java.awt.Image
image/jpeg	java.awt.Image
text/plain	java.lang.String
multipart/*	javax.mail.internet.MimeMultipart
text/xml or application/xml	javax.xml.transform.Source

Let us now look at an example of a Flute Bank Web service that stores and archives any incoming documents it receives from partners. The remote interface defines a single method, as shown in the following code.

```
public interface AttachmentService extends Remote{
    public String storeDocumentService(DataHandler dh,String filename)
                                                throws RemoteException;
}
```

The service implementation (Listing 10.12a) is also straightforward; it just extracts the content from the DataHandler and stores it to a file. It returns a date/timestamp to the caller.

Listing 10.12a   Service implementation for processing attachments

```
public class AttachmentServiceImpl implements AttachmentService {
    /**
     * This method implements a web service that stores any attachment it receives.
     */
    public String storeDocumentService(DataHandler dh, String filename) {
        try{
                BufferedOutputStream out = new BufferedOutputStream(new
                                        FileOutputStream (filename));
                BufferedInputStream in = new BufferedInputStream (dh.getInputStream());

                byte[] buffer = new byte[256];
                while (true) {
            int bytesRead = in.read(buffer);
                    if (bytesRead == -1)
                            break;
```

```
                    out.write(buffer, 0, bytesRead);
                      }
                    in.close();
                    out.close();
                    }catch(Exception e){
                                System.out.println(e);
                                return e.toString();

                    }
                    return ("File processes succesfully " + filename + " " + new Date());
        }
}
```

Listing 10.12b shows the xrpcc configuration used to generate stubs and ties.

Listing 10.12b xrpcc configuration for stub and tie generation

```
<?xml version="1.0" encoding="UTF-8"?>
<configuration
  xmlns="http://java.sun.com/xml/ns/jax-rpc/ri/config">
  <service name="attachservice"
      targetNamespace="http://www.flutebank.com/xml"
      typeNamespace="http://www.flutebank.com/xml"
      packageName="com.flutebank.attachmentservice">
      <interface name="com.flutebank.attachmentservice.AttachmentService"
          servantName="com.flutebank.attachmentservice.AttachmentServiceImpl"/>
      </service>
</configuration>
```

The relevant extract from the client code is shown below, where the stub is instantiated and the service invoked:

```
  Attachservice_Impl() service =new Attachservice_Impl();
AttachmentService_Stub stub=(AttachmentService_Stub)
                          (service.getAttachmentServicePort());
stub._setProperty(javax.xml.rpc.Stub.ENDPOINT_ADDRESS_PROPERTY,url);
  DataHandler dh = new DataHandler(new FileDataSource(filename));
  String response = stub.storeDocumentService(dh,filename);
  System.out.println("Response from server " + response);
```

The SOAP request to the server includes an attachment, as shown below. The MIME segments are highlighted:

```
POST /attachmentservice/jaxrpc/AttachmentService HTTP/1.1
Content-Type: multipart/related; type="text/xml"; boundary=
3317565.1028340932732.JavaMail.Administrator.BYTECODE
Content-Length: 26994
SOAPAction: ""
User-Agent: Java1.3.1_01
Host: 127.0.0.1:9090
Accept: text/html, image/gif, image/jpeg, *; q=.2, */*; q=.2
Connection: keep-alive

--3317565.1028340932732.JavaMail.Administrator.BYTECODE
Content-Type: text/xml

<?xml version="1.0" encoding="UTF-8"?>
<env:Envelope xmlns:env="http://schemas.xmlsoap.org/soap/envelope/" xmlns:xsd=
"http://www.w3.org/2001/XMLSchema" xmlns:xsi="http://www.w3.org/2001/XMLSchema-
instance" xmlns:enc="http://schemas.xmlsoap.org/soap/encoding/" xmlns:ns0=
"http://www.flutebank.com/xml" xmlns:ns1="http://java.sun.com/jax-rpc-ri/internal"
env:encodingStyle="http://schemas.xmlsoap.org/soap/encoding/"><env:Body>
<ns0:storeDocumentService><DataHandler_1 xsi:type="ns1:datahandler" href="cid:ID1"/>
<String_2 xsi:type="xsd:string">Uploadme.doc</String_2></ns0:storeDocumentService>
</env:Body></env:Envelope>

--3317565.1028340932732.JavaMail.Administrator.BYTECODE
Content-Type: application/octet-stream
Content-Id: ID1

ÐÏ_àì±_â
```

xrpcc contains an option—Xdatahandleronly—that forces attachments to always map to the **DataHandler**, instead of to the mappings shown in Table 10.7.

MessageHandlers *and* HandlerChains

A SOAP message handler is a Java class that provides a filtering mechanism for preprocessing and postprocessing the SOAP message, by intercepting it and acting on the SOAP request and response. As Figure 10.7 shows, a handler can be used on the client side, server side, or both. Handlers can be used to add features to a service call and are a good means to layer additional functionality over the core message. They are useful because they provide the ability to introduce

Figure 10.7
Handler
architecture

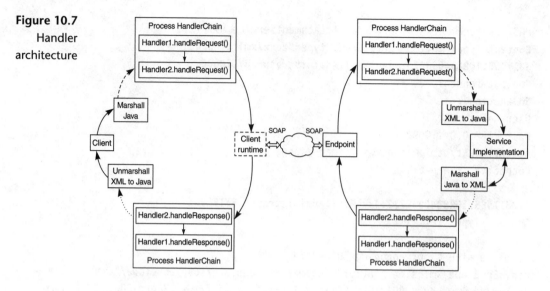

security services, business processing, and error handling. They also permit managing the selection of content creation strategies in both service consumers and service implementations without changing client or server code.

All handler implementations must implement the javax.xml.rpc.handler.Handler interface shown below:

```
public interface Handler{
    public abstract void init(HandlerInfo handlerinfo);
    public abstract boolean handleRequest(MessageContext messagecontext);
    public abstract boolean handleResponse(MessageContext messagecontext);
    public abstract boolean handleFault(MessageContext messagecontext);
    public abstract void destroy();
    public abstract QName[] getHeaders();
}
```

The handler is passed an instance of a MessageContext, which can be used to access the underlying Soap with Attachments API for Java (SAAJ) javax.xml.soap.SOAPMessage that represents the actual message. It can also be used to pass objects between handlers in the chain, to share state information specific to a request. Note that a handler is always stateless itself and should not hold any message-specific state in an instance variable. The lifecycle of a handler instance is quite similar to that of a servlet:

1. The runtime initializes the handler by calling the `init()` method and passing configuration information to the instance via the `HandlerInfo` object. This is a useful place to obtain references to reusable resources.

2. Depending on the stage of request processing, the `handleRequest()`, `handle-Response()`, or `handleFault()` method is invoked.

3. The runtime can call these methods multiple times from different threads that handle different requests and can even pool handler instances for optimization.

4. When the runtime is done or is under resource constraints, it will invoke the `destroy()` method, which is a good place to release the resources obtained in the `init()` method.

Multiple handlers can be combined together an ordered group called a *handler chain*. Chained handlers are invoked in the order in which they are configured. When a handler completes its processing, it passes the result to the next handler in the chain. Chaining and managing communication between handlers in a chain is done by the runtime. Developers write handlers as individual units that do not need to be aware of other handlers and are thus highly reusable.

The order in which handlers are deployed is important. For example, if a client sends an encrypted request in a compressed format, the handlers on the server must first decompress and then decrypt the input. Like individual handlers, chains can be defined on the client, the server, or both. The steps below describe how execution occurs in a chain (see Figure 10.7):

1. The `handleRequest()` methods of the handlers in the chain on the client are all executed, in the order specified. Any of these `handleRequest()` methods might change the SOAP message request.

2. When the `handleRequest()` method of the last handler in the chain has been executed on the client side, the runtime dispatches the request to the server.

3. When the endpoint receives the request, it invokes the `handleRequest()` methods of the handlers in the chain on the server, in the order specified in the chain.

4 When all the handlers are done processing the request, the endpoint delegates the invocation to the service implementation via the tie.

5. When the service has completed its work, the runtime invokes the `handle-Response()` methods of the handlers in the chain on the server, in reverse

order. The last handler to process the request will be the first to process the response. Any of these `handleResponse()` methods might change the SOAP message response.

6. When the client receives the response from the server, the `handleResponse()` methods of the chain on the client are executed in the same reverse manner. Any handler can change the SOAP message.

7. The response is then returned to the client application that invoked the Web service.

In a chain, if any of the `handle` methods in the handler return `true`, the next handler in the chain is invoked.

Request processing can be terminated by returning `false`. As Figure 10.8 shows, developers can throw a `SOAPFaultException` to indicate a SOAP fault or a `JAX-RPCException` and trigger the `handleFault` callbacks in the handler. Table 10.8 describes the main classes and interfaces relevant to handlers.

Handler Advantages

Handlers and handler chains offer a valuable tool to architects. We list below some best practices and usage scenarios for handlers:

* **Introducing security.** A handler can be used to encrypt and decrypt the header or body data, using symmetric or asymmetric ciphering techniques. Clients use a handler to encrypt data before sending the SOAP request. A handler on the server decrypts the data before invoking business components, such as EJBs, and encrypts the outgoing response after business processing occurs.

Figure 10.8
Fault handling
in handlers

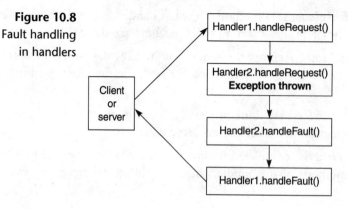

Table 10.8   Handler-Specific API in JAX-RPC

`javax.xml.rpc.handler.Handler`	Must be implemented by a handler class.
`javax.xml.rpc.handler.HandlerInfo`	Contains information about the handler—in particular, the initialization parameters.
`javax.xml.rpc.handler.MessageContext`	Abstracts the message processed by the handler and contains `getProperty(String)` and `setProperty(String,Object)` methods that can be used to share state between handlers in a handler chain. This is analogous to the `pageContext` in JSPs or a `ServletContext` in servlets.
`javax.xml.rpc.handler.soap.SOAPMessageContext`	Extends the `MessageContext` and provides access to the actual SOAP message. It also contains the `getRoles()` method, which returns the SOAP actor roles associated with the `HandlerChain`.
`javax.xml.soap.SOAPMessage`	Object that contains the actual request or response SOAP message, including its header, body, and attachment.
`javax.xml.rpc.handler.HandlerChain`	Implemented by the JAX-RPC implementation to represent a chain. A `HandlerChain` can have SOAP actor roles associated with it.

- **Processing metadata.** A handler can be used to access and manipulate the SOAP header containing metadata or context information about the service invocation or service consumer.

- **Validating data.** Intercepting the request before any processing occurs on the data and validating the request or attachment in the request against a schema, especially for a handling compound messages with XML attachments is best done using handlers.

- **Handling data content.** Handlers can be used to process SOAP attachments—for example, plain text, XML, JPEG images, and octet streams.

- **Optimizing and improving performance.** Handlers can be used to introduce optimizations in service processing by introducing features such as

  o Data caching or result caching for frequently accessed results

  o Prefetching of additional data that may be required during request processing

○ Initializing, preparing, and caching resources that may otherwise introduce latencies

• **Implementing intermediaries.** Chapter 4 introduced the concepts of actors, intermediaries, and roles. To recall, a SOAP message may pass though *intermediaries* capable of processing and forwarding the request. The SOAP message may contain *header* information intended only for an intermediary's consumption. The targeted intermediary will process that particular header and ensure that it is not passed along. The SOAP actor attribute is a URI that indicates whom the header intended for. The actor next corresponds to a URI of http://schemas.xmlsoap.org/soap/actor/next and indicates that the header element is intended for the first SOAP application that processes the message.

Handlers offer a good mechanism to implement SOAP intermediaries and process headers. When the handler chain executes, the runtime will identify the SOAP *actor roles* for which the chain is configured and ensure that the handlers are passed the header blocks they need. If the processing was unsuccessful or any of the mandatory headers is not present, a corresponding SOAP fault (e.g., a SOAP MustUnderstand fault) is generated and propagated back to the client.

Configuring Handlers

Message handlers can be configured in two ways: programmatically, using JAX-RPC API, or declaratively, using a JAX-RPC runtime-provided tool or deployment descriptor. Client-side handlers can be configured either way, but server-side handlers can be be configured only declaratively. The fragment below shows the relevant extract for xrpcc in the reference implementation given in Listing 10.3. The runAt property can be client or server, indicating where the handler is to be deployed, and the property fields indicate arbitrary properties (e.g., configuration information) required by the handlers. Multiple handlers can be registered per interface or per service.

```
<handlerChains>
    <chain runAt="client|serverw" roles="">
        <handler className="" headers="">
                <property name="" value=""/>
        </handler>
    </chain>
</handlerChains>
```

Programmatic registration of handlers on the client can be done in code such as the following:

```
ServiceFactory factory = ServiceFactory.newInstance();
Service service = factory.createService (...);
HandlerRegistry registry = service.getHandlerRegistry();
// pass the namespace and portname to get the handler chain object
List chain = registry.getHandlerChain(new QName(...));
Map config =... //configuration poperties
Qname headers[]=... //headers
HandlerInfo info = new HandlerInfo(MyHandler.class, config,headers);
chain.add(info);
```

Let us now look at an example of using handlers. Flute Bank has exposed a service that allows third-party vendors to send sensitive information about customers as a part of a larger business transaction. The code below shows how a handler can be implemented on both the client and server sides to first compress that information and then encrypt it, using password-based symmetric ciphering (PBEWithMD5AndDES).

As Figure 10.9 shows, the client-side handler intercepts the request, compresses the outgoing data, and encrypts it, using a symmetric cipher. (Listing 10.13 uses JCE, the Java Cryptography Extension API bundled with JDK 1.4.) Once this is done, it places the data back in the SOAP message and sends the request on its way to the service.

Listing 10.13   Client-side handler

```
public class SecureZipClientHandler implements Handler {
    private static final byte salt[] = new byte[8];
    private static final int iterations =1;
    private final static String algorithm = "PBEWithMD5AndDES";
    private static SecretKeyFactory skf;
    private static PBEParameterSpec aps;
    private final static char[] password = "1eallysecurepassword".toCharArray();

    public void init(HandlerInfo hi) {
        try {
            // Initialize JCE and the key factory
            Security.addProvider(new com.sun.crypto.provider.SunJCE());
```

```
            skf = SecretKeyFactory.getInstance(algorithm);
            aps = new PBEParameterSpec(salt,iterations);
        } catch (Exception e) {
            System.out.println(e);
        }
    }
/**
The handlerequest method that intercepts the outgoing request from the client
*/
    public boolean handleRequest(MessageContext context) {
        try {
            SOAPMessageContext smc = (SOAPMessageContext)context;
            SOAPMessage msg = smc.getMessage();
            SOAPPart sp = msg.getSOAPPart();
            SOAPEnvelope se = sp.getEnvelope();
    // next step based on the processing model for this handler
            SOAPBody body = se.getBody();
            Iterator it = body.getChildElements();
            SOAPElement opElem = (SOAPElement)it.next();
            it = opElem.getChildElements();
            SOAPElement pin = (SOAPElement)it.next();
            it = pin.getChildElements();
            Text textNode = (Text)it.next();
            textNode.detachNode();
            String encContent = textNode.getValue();

    // Use a utility class to decode the Base64 encoded binary SOAP data
            byte[] contentBytes = Base64.decode(encContent);
            // zip the content
            ByteArrayOutputStream baos = new ByteArrayOutputStream();
            GZIPOutputStream zos = new GZIPOutputStream(baos);
            zos.write(contentBytes);
            zos.flush();
            zos.finish();
            zos.close();

    // Encrypt the content
            byte[] zippedbytes = encrypt(baos.toByteArray());

    // Use a utility class to encode the bytes back to the binary SOAP data
```

```
          String zippedContent = Base64.encode(zippedbytes);
          System.out.println("Client handler done with encryption and compression");

  // Add the content to the outgoing message
          pin.addTextNode(zippedContent);
          return true;
    }
    catch (Exception e) {
          System.out.println(e);
          return false;
    }
}


    private static byte[] encrypt(byte[] clear) throws Exception {
        byte[] ciphertext = null;
        PBEKeySpec ks = new PBEKeySpec(password);
        SecretKey key = skf.generateSecret(ks);
        Cipher desCipher = Cipher.getInstance(algorithm);
        desCipher.init(Cipher.ENCRYPT_MODE, key,aps);
        ciphertext = desCipher.doFinal(clear);
        return ciphertext;
    }
/* The handleResponse method does nothing on the response returned from the
 * server. Only outgoing data needs to be encrypted and compressed.
 */
    public boolean handleResponse(MessageContext context) {
        return true;
    }

// Other Handler methods with empty implementations not shown
}
```

The handler on the server side intercepts the request from the endpoint, decrypts the data using the same password as the client, and decompresses the data. It then places the data back on the SOAP request and sends it on the way to the service implementation or tie, as Listing 10.14 shows.

Figure 10.9
Handler
example

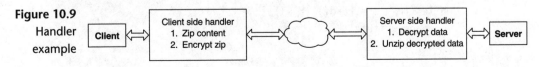

Listing 10.14 Server-side handler

```java
public class SecureZipServerHandler implements Handler {
// member variables are identical to client handler shown previously

    public void init(HandlerInfo hi) {
// Initialize JCE here identically to the client handler shown previously
    }

    public boolean handleRequest(MessageContext context) {
        try {
            SOAPMessageContext smc = (SOAPMessageContext)context;
            SOAPMessage msg = smc.getMessage();
            SOAPPart sp = msg.getSOAPPart();
            SOAPEnvelope se = sp.getEnvelope();

// next step based on the processing model for this handler
            SOAPBody body = se.getBody();
            Iterator it = body.getChildElements();
            SOAPElement op = (SOAPElement)it.next();
            SOAPElement param = (SOAPElement)op.getChildElements().next();
            Text textNode = (Text)param.getChildElements().next();
            String zippedenccontent = textNode.getValue();
            System.out.println(zippedenccontent);
            textNode.detachNode();

// Use a utility class to decode the Base64 encoded binary SOAP data
            byte[] rawbytes = Base64.decode(zippedenccontent);

// First decrypt the data using ciphers
            rawbytes = decrypt(rawbytes);

// unzip the data
            ByteArrayInputStream bais = new ByteArrayInputStream(rawbytes);
            GZIPInputStream zis = new GZIPInputStream(bais);
            ByteArrayOutputStream baos = new ByteArrayOutputStream();
            int c = -1;
            while ((c = zis.read())!= -1) {
                baos.write(c);
            }
```

```
                baos.flush();
                byte[] contentBytes = baos.toByteArray();
                System.out.println("Server handler done with decryption and
                                                        decompression");
// Use a utility class to encode bytes to Base64 binary SOAP data
                String encContent = Base64.encode(contentBytes);
                param.addTextNode(encContent);
                return true;
            }
            catch (Exception e) {
                System.out.println(e);
                return false;
            }
        }


// method to decrypt bytes
        private static byte[] decrypt(byte[] input) throws Exception {
            byte[] cleartext1 = null;
            PBEKeySpec ks = new PBEKeySpec(password);
            SecretKey key = skf.generateSecret(ks);
            Cipher desCipher = Cipher.getInstance(algorithm);
            desCipher.init(Cipher.DECRYPT_MODE, key,aps);
            cleartext1 = desCipher.doFinal(input);
            return cleartext1;
        }

// The server does not need to process the outgoing response to the client

    public boolean handleResponse(MessageContext context) {
            return true;
        }

// Other Handler methods with empty implementations not shown
}
```

The service implementation in Listing 10.15 is no different from any of the previous examples and requires no additional code. Note that in this case, the service implementation is not aware of any of the changes (compression, encryption, decryption, and decompression) applied to the SOAP message between the time the client initiated the request and the time it was processed.

Listing 10.15 Service implementation

```
public interface Fileservice extends Remote{
    public String acceptContent(byte[] parameter_in) throws RemoteException;
}

public class FileserviceImpl implements Fileservice {

    public String acceptContent(byte[] input) throws RemoteException {
                try {
        BufferedOutputStream fos= new BufferedOutputStream
                                            (new FileOutputStream("Myfile.doc"));
                fos.write(input,0,input.length);
                fos.flush();
                fos.close();
                }catch(Exception e){
                        System.out.println(e);
                }
    return "Data sucessfully processed and timestamped as:"+ new Date();
    }
```

The client code also does not require any modification and remains the same as any of the previous examples:

```
// instantiate the service.
Contentservice_Impl service = new Contentservice_Impl();
Fileservice_Stub stub =(Fileservice_Stub) service.getFileservicePort();
stub._setProperty(javax.xml.rpc.Stub.ENDPOINT_ADDRESS_PROPERTY,args[0]);

// get the content of file to be sent
byte[] rawbytes = readFile(args[1]);
// send the content
String timestamp= stub.acceptContent(rawbytes);
```

What is different from the previous examples is the configuration file shown in Listing 10.16 for xrpcc, where the handlers are declaratively specified.

Listing 10.16 xrpcc configuration for handlers

```
<?xml version="1.0" encoding="UTF-8"?>
<configuration xmlns="http://java.sun.com/xml/ns/jax-rpc/ri/config">
  <service name="Contentservice" targetNamespace="http://www.flutebank.com/xml"
            typeNamespace=http://www.flutebank.com/xml
```

```
            packageName="com.flutebank.encryptedposervice">
<interface name="com.flutebank.encryptedposervice.Fileservice"
  servantName="com.flutebank.encryptedposervice.FileserviceImpl"/>
<handlerChains>
  <chain runAt="client">
        <handler className="com.flutebank.encryptedposervice.SecureZipClientHandler">
      </handler>
    </chain>
  <chain runAt="server">
        <handler className="com.flutebank.encryptedposervice.SecureZipServerHandler">
        </handler>
  </chain>
</handlerChains>
  </service>
</configuration>
```

Handler Disadvantages

Though handlers offer a nice way of pre- and postprocessing the SOAP message, certain issues must be kept in mind:

- If the handler code introduces propietary modifications in the outgoing SOAP message, the service may no longer be interoperable with other platforms. For example, just based on WSDL, the caller of the above service will never be able to deduce that the server endpoint expects the data in a particular compressed and encrypted format.

- Introducing handlers that alter the response message at an endpoint may break existing clients written for the service interface.

- Introducing another layer of pre- and postprocessing of the SOAP message may degrade performance by increasing reponse times.

Asynchronous Invocation with Attachments and Handlers

Earlier in this chapter, we mentioned the use of attachements for creating compound messages. Let us look at a possible realization, shown in Figure 10.10.

A business document, such as a purchase order or invoice in XML format, is sent as an attachment to the SOAP message in the request. The service definition exposes a method similar to

```
public String submitInvoice(Source invoice) throws RemoteException;
```

Figure 10.10
Using XML
attachments
with JAX-RPC
for asynchron-
ous invocation

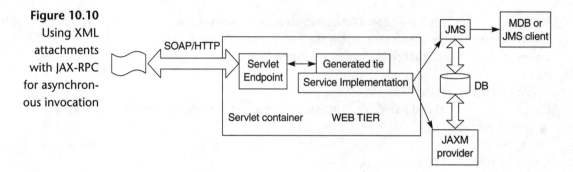

which receives the message and in turn maps the attachment as per the mapping
in Table 10.7. An XML attachment (text/xml MIME type) automatically maps to
the javax.xml.transform.Source. The service could then process that XML representation in many ways. For example, it could parsed and transformed it, place
it on a JMS queue, or even pass it to a JAXM provider, as Figure 10.10 shows.
Additionally, handlers could intercept the message and perform a hard validation against a schema for the document, if necessary.

The difference between this asynchronous model and the one-way RPC is essentially that the client receives a response from the endpoint, because of its
asynchronous persistence framework using JMS. If, as a result of HTTP issues,
the client could not receive that response, it is the client's prerogative to retry the
invocation or query the service. The latter would require introspection into the integration tier (e.g., JMS queue). The service has no way to communicate back to
the HTTP client with a callback unless the client realizes a similar service on its side.
This realization, though useful in most scenarios, is *pseudo-asynchronous*. Look at
asynchronous messaging with JAXM and messaging profiles in Chapter 11.

Holder Classes

CORBA developers would already be familiar with the concept of in, out, and
inout parameters and Holder classes. Like IDL, operations in WSDL may take
out or inout parameters as well as in parameters. To understand the in, out, and
inout concepts, consider the following signature:

```
public Something myMethod(Somearg somearg) {
// code
}
```

In Java, the somearg is the argument the method receives, and the Something is what the method returns after doing its work. However if clients pass the somearg as an object and expect the method to change that value, it is an inout parameter. For example, consider the following code:

```
Somearg param= Somearg(...).;
Something val= myMethod(param);
if (param.xxx){
    //
}
```

The above coding practice is discouraged in Java but is used in other languages, such as C and C++. Java passes parameters only by value and has no concept of out or inout parameters; therefore, in JAX-RPC these are mapped Holder classes. In place of the out parameter, a Java method will take an instance of the Holder class of the corresponding type. The result assigned to the out or inout parameter is assigned to the value field of the Holder class. ▷

A service operation signature written in Java will typically return a single value: a primitive or a JavaBean. If there is a need for the service operation to return multiple values, the data type of the return value can be a complex type, such as an object with multiple parts (e.g. a Portfolio object with many Position objects) or an array. The third alternative is to specify that one or more of the parameters of the Web service operation be out or inout parameters.

For example, assume a Web service operation contains one out parameter, and the operation is implemented with a Java method. The method sets the value of the out parameter and sends this value back the client application that invoked it. The client application can then access the value of this out parameter as if it were a return value. The code below illustrates this with a method whose second parameter is an inout parameter:

▷   In WSDL, if a part name appears

- In both the input and output message, it is an inout parameter

- In only the input message, it is an in parameter

- In only the output message, it is an out parameter

out parameters are undefined when the operation is invoked but defined when the operation completes; inout parameters are defined when invoked and when completed.

```
public float payBalance(String userid,javax.xml.rpc.holders.IntHolder balance) {
        System.out.println ("The input value is: " + balance.value);
        // do some work here
        balance.value = 90; // the new value of the out parameter
    }
```

When the client invokes the above method with two parameters, a String and an integer, it will be returned two values: a float and an integer. If at invocation the balance parameter value was 1000 when the method completed, the value of the second parameter is now 90 and will also be returned to the client.

```
IntHolder inoutbalance = new IntHolder(1000);
System.out.println("Holder value is " + inoutbalance.value);
float interest= service.payBalance("johnmalkovich",inoutbalance);
System.out.println("Interest charged on credit card is " + interest);
System.out.println("Remaining balance,holder value is " + inoutbalance.value);
```

The above client code invoking the above service implementation will produce the following output:

```
Holder value is 1000
Interest charged on credit card is 9.0
Remaining balance, holder value is 90
```

Holder classes for out and inout parameters must implement the javax.xml .rpc.holders.Holder interface. In the service implementation, use the value field to first access the input value of an inout parameter and then set the value of out and inout parameters.

If the out or inout parameter is a standard data type, JAX-RPC provides a set of holder classes in the javax.xml.rpc.holders package, listed in Table 10.9.

If the data type of the parameter is not provided, developers must create their own implementation of the javax.xml.rpc.holders.Holder interface to handle out and inout parameters, based on the following guidelines:

- Name the implementation class XXXHolder, where XXX is the name of the complex type. For example, if the complex type is called Portfolio, the implementation class is called PortfolioHolder.

- Create a public field called value, whose data type is the same as that of the parameter.

Table 10.9   JAX-RPC–Defined Holder Classes

Built-in holder class	Java data type it holds
javax.xml.rpc.holders.BooleanHolder	boolean
javax.xml.rpc.holders.ByteHolder	Byte
javax.xml.rpc.holders.ShortHolder	short
javax.xml.rpc.holders.IntHolder	Int
javax.xml.rpc.holders.LongHolder	Long
javax.xml.rpc.holders.FloatHolder	float
javax.xml.rpc.holders.DoubleHolder	double
javax.xml.rpc.holders.BigDecimalHolder	Java.math.BigDecimal
javax.xml.rpc.holders.BigIntegerHolder	Java.math.BigInteger
javax.xml.rpc.holders.ByteArrayHolder	Byte[]
javax.xml.rpc.holders.CalendarHolder	Java.util.Calendar
javax.xml.rpc.holders.QnameHolder	javax.xml.namespace.QName
javax.xml.rpc.holders.StringHolder	Java.lang.String

- Create a default constructor that initializes the value field to a default.
- Create a constructor that sets the value field to the passed parameter.

The following example shows the outline of a custom PortfolioHolder implementation class:

```
package com.flutebank.brokerage;
public final class PortfolioHolder implements javax.xml.rpc.holders.Holder {
     public Portfolio value;
     public PortfolioHolder() {
     }
         // set the value variable to a default value
     }
     public PortfolioHolder(Portfolio value) {
         // set the value variable to the passed in value
     }
}
```

Using Custom Data Types

Besides the data types supported by JAX-RPC discussed earlier, it may be necessary to pass data types that do not satisfy the requirements. For example, BillPay.java demonstrated earlier could define the listScheduledPayments() to return a java.util.Vector of PaymentDetail objects, instead of the PaymentDetail[]it did return. Note that a Vector is not a supported data type, as per the mappings in Table 10.2.

JAX-RPC supports the concept of pluggable serializers and deserializers for such custom data types. A serializer marshals a Java object to an XML representation, and a deserializer unmarshals an XML representation to a Java object. As Figure 10.11 shows, serialization and deserialization are symmetrical functions and both use *type mapping* to map the Java and XML data types.

Developers can specify the serializer and deserializer to use for a service on the server using the deployment tool. xrpcc has the typemapping element for this purpose. This allows the endpoint to unmarshal the XML to the corresponding Java type, and vice versa. For example, a com.fluebank.Vector may be serialized as

```
<avector xmlns:tns="http://www.flutebank.com" xsi:type=" tns:Vector">
<item xsi:type="xsd:string">some value here</item>
<item xsi:type="xsd:anyType" xsi:null="true"/>
</avector >
```

If the server know that this namespace and type correspond to a com.flutebank.Vector, it can invoke the corresponding deserializer and create and pass the

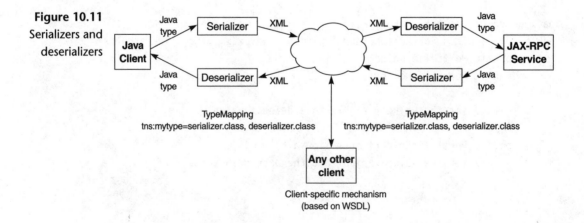

Figure 10.11
Serializers and
deserializers

corresponding com.flutebank.Vector object to the service implementation. When the service client is written, the developers will need to write a similar serializer and deserializer on the client-side runtime or take a shortcut and use the same classes from the server, if the same vendor runtime is used. If it is not used, the runtime will not know what to do when it comes across this custom data type and will throw a serialization exception.

JAX-RPC Pluggability Mechanism

The JAX-RPC part of the API, the type system relevant to development of pluggable serializers and deserializers, is simple and is shown in Figure 10.12 and Table 10.10.

The base serializer and deserializer interfaces are implemented by a runtime-specific class or extended by a runtime-specific interface. Developers use this to write their serializers and deserializers for that particular runtime. However, a larger issue is at hand. A closer look at the Serializer, DeSerializer, SerializationContext, and DeSerializationContext interfaces reveals no methods relate to serialization or deserialization and that these are just marker interfaces. What

Figure 10.12
The type mapping system

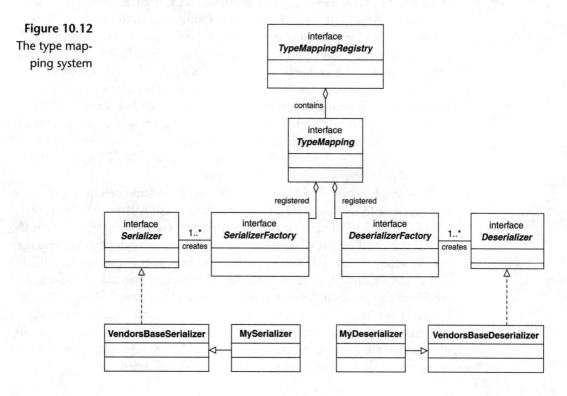

Table 10.10 The Type Mapping System API

TypeMappingRegistry	Defines an internal registry that holds a mapping of encoding styles and the corresponding TypeMapping.
TypeMapping	Maintains a set of tuples of the type {Java type, SerializerFactory, DeserializerFactory, XML type}.
Serializer	The base interface for serializers to implement.
DeSerializer	The base interface for deserializers to implement.
SerializationContext	Passed to the serializer as context information.
DeSerializationContext	Passed to the deserializer as context information.

this means is that serializers and deserializers are not guaranteed to be *portable* across implementations, because there is no contract with the runtime. They are specific to and pluggable only in a particular implementation. For example, if a developer writes a serializer and deserializer for the JAX-RPC RI, these classes are not guaranteed to be usable in another vendor's JAX-RPC implementation.

The API is structured like this for a very good reason. Different runtimes may (and do) use different XML parsing techniques (e.g., DOM parser, SAX parser, streaming pull). Porting a serializer written for SAX parsing (i.e., one that expects a SAX stream) into a runtime that uses a different parsing mechanism cannot be done completely transparently. The next version of the JAX-RPC specification is supposed to address transparent pluggability further.

Most vendors will provide several built-in serializers and deserializers, to help developers as utility classes for their runtimes. The code will never be aware of the need for a serializer/deserializer for that particular custom data type, as long the code is deployed in that vendor's runtime. (If you move it to another, you may need to write the serializer and deserializer yourself.) For example, JAX-RPC 1.0 RI supports a subset of Java collection classes and provides corresponding serializers and deserializers as utilities for developers (Table 10.11).

So if the listScheduledPayments() method returned a java.util.ArrayList, even though it is not a data type for which a standard Java-XML mapping exists, the runtime will generate the corresponding SOAP message and response, based on internal type mapping and custom serializers and deserializers.

Table 10.11   Deserializers and Serializers Provided
as Utilities by the Reference Implementation

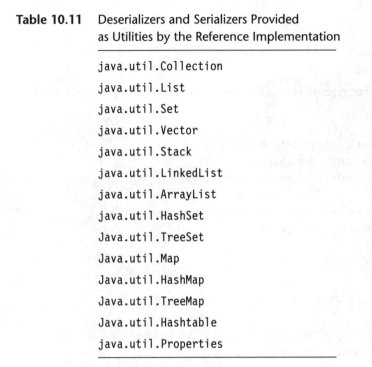

```
java.util.Collection
java.util.List
java.util.Set
java.util.Vector
java.util.Stack
java.util.LinkedList
java.util.ArrayList
java.util.HashSet
Java.util.TreeSet
Java.util.Map
Java.util.HashMap
Java.util.TreeMap
Java.util.Hashtable
java.util.Properties
```

Configuring Custom Serializers and Deserializers

Like message handlers, pluggable serializers and deserializers can be configured in two ways: programmatically, using JAX-RPC API, or declaratively, using a JAX-RPC runtime-provided tool or deployment descriptor. Client-side serializers and deserializers can be configured in either way, but server-side handlers can be be configured only declaratively. The fragment below shows the relevant extract for xrpcc in the reference implementation given in Listing 10.3.

```
<typeMappingRegistry>
    <import>
        <schema namespace="" location=""/>
    </import>
    <typeMapping encodingStyle="">
    <entry schemaType="" javaType="" serializerFactory="" deserializerFactory=""/>
    </typeMapping>
    <additionalTypes>
```

```
      <class name=""/>
    </additionalTypes>
</typeMappingRegistry>
```

Programmatic registration on the client can be done in code similar to the following:

```
ServiceFactory factory = ServiceFactory.newInstance();
Service service = factory.createService (...);
TypeMappingRegistry registry = service. getTypeMappingRegistry();

TypeMappingRegistry maprping = registry.createTypeMapping()
// or registry.getDefaultTypeMapping();

  SerializerFactory sfactory= // some runtime specific code

  DeserializerFactory dfactory= // some runtime specific code

// register the custom handlers passing the Java class, the namespace, the serializer
// factory to use and the deserializer factory to use

  mapping.register(myclass, qname, sfactory, dfactory)
  registry.register(encodingStyleURI,mapping)
```

JAX-RPC and Security

Security has multiple aspects; Chapter 15 covers them in detail. From a JAX-RPC perspective, there are two major points:

- **Securing the transport layer.** JAX-RPC does not explicitly require runtimes to support Hypertext Transfer Protocol Secure (HTTPS). However most servlet containers where the HTTP endpoints are deployed potentially support HTTPS (e.g., Tomcat). Just switching on HTTPS on the server will be enough for the service deployment. To enable SSL support on the client side, however, JSSE must be used to change the default HTTP handlers.

- **Securing users.** JAX-RPC requires support for basic HTTP authentication. The username and password on the client side can be passed via the javax .xml.rpc.security.auth.username and javax.xml.rpc.security.auth.user-name.password properties discussed in the Clients Using Stubs section earlier in this chapter. If at runtime the username or password is not found or is incorrect, the server code will send the client an HTTP code 401 along with the basic HTTP authentication header (WWW-Authenticate). In the service implementation, the service can access the java.security.Principal via the getUserPrincipal() in the ServletEndpointContext, as shown earlier.

> JAX-RPC Interoperability

In the context of Web services, interoperability can be summarized as meaning that the functional characteristics of the service should remain immutable across differing application platforms, programming languages, hardware, operating systems, and application data models. By definition, Web services should be interoperable, and the service consumer should not be tied to the service implementation.

However there are bound to be issues when applications use disparate SOAP libraries that generate and manipulate the underlying SOAP message, disparate programming languages, and disparate hardware-software stacks. The following are common causes for interoperability problems between these libraries or toolkits:

- Implementations conform only to a subset of the full SOAP or other XML specifications.

- Implementations depend on optional aspects of the SOAP specifications. For example:
  - Sending type information for encoded parameters is optional; however, if an implementation assumes this will be present in messages it receives, it may not interoperate with others that do not send this information.
  - There is no differentiation between SOAPAction values of "" and null in the specifications, but some implementations support both, whereas others do not quote this value at all for non-null SOAPActions.

- Implementations interpret ambiguous definitions of the SOAP specification differently. For example:
  - It is not clear how a service should represent an RPC response with a void return and no out parameters. It could be an empty SOAP envelope, an empty SOAP response element, or even an HTTP 204 ("No Response") code.

○ A null value can be represented either by not including that XML element or by an element with the xsi:nil="true". ▷

In general, architects should keep the following in mind while designing Web services:

1. **Avoid propeietary extensions.** Avoid building dependencies into the application that use any vendor-specific extension to the specifications JAX-RPC depends on (SOAP, WSDL, XML schemas, and HTTP).

2. **Test interoperability.** Never assume things will work as they should. It is essential to test interoperability of the service implementation across multiple consumers, especially if the consumers are outside the boundaries of the organization. Public interoperability tests are also available from the Web Services Interoperability organization *(www.ws-i.org)* and White Mesa *(www .whitemesa.com)*. ▷▷

3. **Analyze disparate data models.** When a service is used to integrate applications that have disparate data models, the models may need to be resolved by creating an intermediate model. For example, flutebank.com integrates with brokerage.com to provide customers the ability to view their accounts simultaneously online when in any of the portals. The data model for an account as represented in flutebank.com may be quite different from an account in

---

▷ The only real mechanism for ensuring interoperability is to verify compliance with standards:

- HTTP 1.1 for the transport protocol
- XML Schema to describe your data
- WSDL 1.1 to describe your Web service
- SOAP 1.1 for the message format

The JAX-RPC API and SAAJ provide a standard interface for Java developers leveraging these same standards.

▷▷ Testing! To promote SOAP-level interoperability and address issues between implementations, the SOAPBuilders community—with members as diverse as IBM, Microsoft, Sun Microsystems, Apache, and even individuals—has come together to develop an interoperability test suite specification and regularly conduct testing of their endpoints against this specification. See *http://soapinterop.java.sun.com/soapbuilders/index.shtml* and *www.xmethods.net/ilab*.

brokerage.com. In this scenario, the architects will need to reconcile the models by creating an XML schema acceptable to both parties.

4. **Analyze disparate data types.** Data types passed as arguments and return types from the service invocation can impact interoperability.

   - **JAX-RPC–defined data types.** The data types and mappings defined in the specifications are available in all JAX-RPC runtimes. Because they are subsets of the XML schema specifications and map directly to the data types in the SOAP encoding, they are completely interoperable.

   - **Custom data types.** If the data type is custom defined (e.g., a `java.util.HashMap` of `com.flutebank.accounts.Account` objects), an XML schema must be created to describe the representation of the data and the custom serializer and deserializer for that data on the server. Such a schema may not be completely interoperable. In addition, the JAX-RPC client would need to write serializers and deserializers to invoke the service. We looked at handling custom data types earlier in this chapter. In summary, custom data types may not be completely interoperable across all service consumers.

5. **Avoid custom data types.** Custom data types that force the use of custom serializers and deserializers can potentially cause interoperability issues with other implementations. For example, a `List` may be represented differently by implementations from vendors A and B. If vendor A's client runtime is used to invoke a service deployed in vendor B's runtime, serialization errors may occur, because each implementation uses its own XML mapping of that data type. If the mapping is not available, the corresponding serailizers and deserializers will need to be written.

   For collection classes in particular, the SOAPBuilders community plans to pursue interoperability testing across vendor runtime implementations.

6. **Customize data, protocols, and encoding schemes.** Architects should be wary of any code that customizes the messages. A good example is the Compress-Secure handlers example in Listing 10.13. The endpoint of that service cannot be invoked by clients that are not aware of the compression and security algorithm used and understood by the service. From a service perspective, there is no standard way to communicate this information (e.g., it cannot be specified in WSDL).

7. **Promote portability of client code between JAX-RPC implementations.** J2EE developers would be familiar with the concept of writing an EJB and deploying it transparently in a J2EE server. The EJB *client* can be written with complete transparency and used in any J2SE environment by simply altering configuration properties. This portability of client code does not translate

identically in the JAX-RPC environment, especially when using custom data types. A JAX-RPC client is not guaranteed to be portable if it uses anything beyond the simple data types. This is tied to the way the serializers and deserializers are written, as discussed earlier. In other words, if architects choose vendor A's implementation of JAX-RPC and write client code that uses serializers and deserializers to invoke the service, they should not expect to simply take the *client* code and use it in vendor B's runtime. Applications should be designed to abstract away the specificity, minimizing the changes needed.

Let us now look at an example of interoperability in action. We will write a Microsoft C#.NET client to demonstrate how a JAX-RPC Web service can be consumed from a Microsoft.NET environment. We will use the BillPay service developed and deployed previously in this chapter. As in most practical service consumer scenarios, we will invoke a service based on the WSDL describing it.

During service deployment, xrpcc was used to generate the WSDL. This WSDL file can now be passed to the Microsoft.NET wsdl compiler, to generate the client-side stubs:

```
wsdl /l:CS /protocol:SOAP http://127.0.0.1:9090/billpayservice/billpayservice.wsdl
```

The above generates the C# source file Billpayservice.cs, which contains the structures and serialization rules based on the schema and bindings defined in WSDL.

Next, we build a Windows DLL out of the generated proxy code using the C# compiler, passing it the referenced dlls from the .NET framework:

```
csc /t:library /r:System.Web.Services.dll /r:System.Xml.dll Billpayservice.cs
```

The next step is to write a client and invoke the three methods exposed by the JAX-RPC Web service. Listing 10.17 shows the C# client code for this purpose.

Listing 10.17 C# client for JAX-RPC

```
BillPay service
using System;
namespace BillpayClient{
    /// <summary>
    /// This is a simple C# client to invoke the flutebank.com Web service.
```

```
/// @Author Sameer Tyagi
/// </summary>
class JAX-RPCClient{
       /// <summary>
       /// The main entry point for the application.
       /// </summary>
       [STAThread]
       static void Main(string[] args) {

// Instantiate the stub/proxy
            Billpayservice serv = new Billpayservice();
// Set the endpoint URL
         if(args.Length ==1)
              serv.Url=args[0];
         else
              serv.Url= "http://127.0.0.1:9090/billpayservice/jaxrpc/BillPay";

// Invoke the schedule payment method
         PaymentConfirmation conf = serv.schedulePayment(DateTime.Today,"my
                                                account at sprint",190);
         Console.WriteLine("Payment was scheduled "+ conf.confirmationNum);

// Invoke the listSchedulePayment method
         PaymentDetail[] detail= serv.listScheduledPayments();
             for(int i=0;i< detail.Length;i++){
                 Console.WriteLine("Payee name "+ detail[i].payeeName);
                 Console.WriteLine("Payee name "+ detail[i].account);
                 Console.WriteLine("Payee name "+ detail[i].amt);
                 Console.WriteLine("Payee name "+ detail[i].date);
             }
// Invoke the getLastPayment method
         Double lastpaid= serv.getLastPayment("my cable tv provider");
         Console.WriteLine("Last payment was "+ lastpaid);
         }
     }
}
```

The C# client code is remarkably similar to the JAX-RPC stub client written earlier, because of the syntactic and semantic similarities between the two programming languages. The client code can now be compiled and executed. The output will be similar to the following:

```
C:\Dotnetclient>billpayClient
Payment was scheduled 81263767
Payee name Digital Credit Union
Payee name Credit
Payee name 2000
Payee name 8/1/2002 11:27:33 PM
Last payment was 829 ▷
```

We have just developed a Web service in Java, deployed it in a JAX-RPC runtime, and exposed the service with only a WSDL interface. WSDL was used to develop a client in a completely different language and platform, C# and .NET, yet produced identical behavior.

▷ JAX-RPC and J2EE

Three specifications tightly integrate JAX-RPC with J2EE:

- J2EE 1.4 specifications (JSR-151)
- EJB 2.1 specifications (JSR-153)
- Web services for J2EE (JSR-109)

J2EE 1.4 includes JAX-RPC as a required API, which means that all J2EE 1.4 application servers will support JAX-RPC. The EJB 2.1 specifications–part of J2EE 1.4–also define how an EJB can be exposed as a Web service and how EJBs can consume a Web service. The *Implementing Enterprise Web Services* specification will lay out the deployment and service requirements for portability of client and server code across containers.

> ▷ The complete C# project and Microsoft .NET runtime distributable can be found on the CD. Java developers can think of the runtime distributable as the JRE. It allows developers to execute the compiled code. To build the source, however, Microsoft .NET Visual Studio is needed.

JAX-RPC and JSR 153

EJB 2.1 allows a *stateless* session bean to be exposed as a Web service, by defining a new interface type in addition to the home, local, and remote interfaces. It is called an *endpoint interface* and is essentially the JAX-RPC service definition. EJB developers provide the service definition and the EJB class. As Figure 10.13 shows, the container generates the implementation of the endpoint interface. much as it generates the implementation of the EJBObject during deployment.

The container exposes the EJB through its service endpoint interface and a WSDL document that clients can use. Once it is deployed, clients use it like any other JAX-RPC service—that is, they access this stateless session bean using the JAX-RPC client APIs over an HTTP transport, just like clients covered earlier in the chapter.

EJBs can look up other Web services with Java Naming and Directory Interface (JNDI), using a logical name called a *service reference*. It maps to a service-ref element in the deployment descriptor, obtains a stub instance for a Web service endpoint, and invokes a method on that endpoint. The J2EE client or EJB can do this, as Figure 10.14 and Listing 10.18 show.

Listing 10.18   EJB client and deployment descriptor code extract

```
InitialContext ctx = new InitialContext();
BillPayService service = (BillPayService)ctx.lookup
                              ("java:comp/env/service/billpayservice");
BillPay stub=(BillPay)(serviceproxy.getBillPayPort());
PaymentConfirmation conf= stub.schedulePayment(new Date(),
                                        "my account at sprint",190);


<enterprise-beans>
<session>
      <service-endpoint> com.flutebank.billpayservice.BillPay</service-endpoint>
      <ejb-class> com.flutebank.billpayservice.BillPayEJB </ejb-class>
    <service-ref>
          <service-ref-name> service/billpayservice</service-ref-name>
          <service-ref-type>com.flutebank.BillPayImpl</service-ref-type>
      </service-ref>
</session>
</enterprise-beans>
```

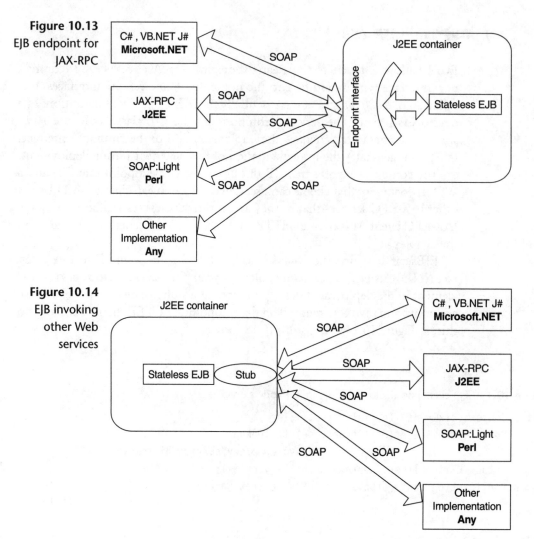

Figure 10.13
EJB endpoint for
JAX-RPC

Figure 10.14
EJB invoking
other Web
services

What Implementation Is Right for Me?

Implementing a JAX-RPC service as an EJB in a J2EE container has four significant advantages:

- Integrated support for transactions
- A comprehensive security model
- Integration with existing business logic
- Scalability through the application server (e.g., clustering and failover)

If the service was implemented as a class and *not* deployed in a J2EE container, it forgoes the advantage of the ACID (atomic, consistent, isolated, and durable) characteristics of the Java Transaction API (JTA) transaction. A non-EJB class in a J2EE container could still leverage a JTA transaction by directly using the `javax.transaction.UserTransaction` object though a JNDI lookup. The stateless EJB with its service endpoint interface, like other EJBs, can propagate and demarcate transactions in a J2EE container and also use bean-managed transactions. It can also leverage the role-based security features the J2EE container provides. (Note, however, that transaction context *propagation* is not required by the current JAX-RPC specifications.)

Using just a servlet endpoint and a Java class(s) (without an EJB) implementation has the following advantages:

- Generally better performance
- Simplicity in deployment
- No need for a full-blown J2EE application server; any Servlet 2.3–compliant Web server or container can be used

JAX-RPC and JSR-109

Implementing Enterprise Web Services (JSR-109) defines a complete mechanism for deploying Web services in a container, using a `webservices.xml` file for a module and a `webservicesclient.xml` file for the clients. The key elements of the former are shown below.

```
<webservices>
   <description>A sample file </description>
   <webservice-description>
      <wsdl-file>billpayservice.wsdl</wsdl-file>
      <port-component>
         <port-component-name>BillPayerComponent</port-component-name>
         <port-qname-namespace>http://www.flutebank.com/xml</port-qname-namespace>
         <port-qname-localname>BillPayService</port-qname-localname>
         <service-def-interface>com.flutebank.billpayservice.BillPayt
                         </service-def-interface>
         <service-impl-bean>
      <!--If the service implementation is an EJB →
           <ejb-link >com.flutebank.billpayservice.BillPayEJB </ejb-link>
```

```
<!--If the service implementation is a Servlet →
    <servlet-link>com.sun.xml.rpc.server.http.JAXRPCServlet</servlet-link>
  </service-impl-bean>
 </port-component>
 </webservice-description>
</webservices>
```

At the time of writing, all three of these specifications were still in draft form. They may possibly undergo changes as a part of the Java community process.

> Summary

So, why do you need JAX-RPC? And more important, what value do these APIs add to architects? Should developers stop writing RMI, RMI-IIOP, and Java-IDL/CORBA applications and discard code that consumed significant time and money, just because newer technology is available?

The answer is an obvious no. Those APIs are as integral a part of J2EE specifications as JAX-RPC is in J2EE 1.4.

JAX-RPC adds value only if you are sure you want to use SOAP, because it allows developers to write distributed and loosely coupled applications using this technology: distributed because the objects may not be colocated, and loosely coupled because the model inherently enforces a level of independence between the implementation and the calling code. As with all software, architects have to understand the tradeoffs in integration with existing and new applications, performance, bandwidth, and accessibility. However, there are possibly two major use cases where JAX-RPC API can be exploited.

The RMI Analogy

Just as in RMI developers write a remote interface, the implementation, and use the rmic compiler to generate the stubs and ties, you could write a service definition, the service implementation, and use a JAX-RPC tool (e.g., xrpcc) to generate the relevant JAX-RPC stubs, ties, and the WSDL file. The client could then use the WDSL file and stubs to invoke the service. This is something architects can do to expose existing business logic contained in RMI objects or EJBs as Web services.

The CORBA Analogy

J2SE has the idlj compiler that reads an IDL file and generates the Java bindings. Developers can do something similar with the JAX-RPC tools (e.g., xrpcc) and consume a WSDL file to generate the client, server, or both sides of the code, to serve as relevant adaptors for the servant code they write. This is something architects can do to implement a service that conforms to a given interface or consume an existing Web service on the JAX-RPC or on a completely different platform, such as Microsoft.NET.

This chapter was meant to give you an insight into JAX-RPC, an API that provides an invaluable *standard* for developers and architects who want to build XML-RPC based Web services.

Chapter **{11}**

JAXM

In this chapter, we will look at Java API for XML Messaging (JAXM). JAXM provides a standard extension API for applications to send and receive document-oriented XML messages synchronously and asynchronously, using SOAP. JAXM is a part of the JAX family of Java APIs and was started under the Java Community Process (JCP) in November 2001 as JSR-67. It is now a part of the JAX pack and the Java WSDP.

JAXM has been designed to help architects create business applications that use XML messaging with SOAP and protocols built on SOAP. Developers can use JAXM to build, send, receive, and decompose SOAP messages for their applications instead of programming low-level XML routines that deal with "angle brackets" and messaging infrastructure.

Before we discuss JAXM in detail, we will discuss the role of message-oriented middleware (MOM), a concept central to messaging. We will then discuss *provider*-based messaging options in Java and how they can be used for SOAP messaging. We recommend reading Chapter 10 before this, because this chapter contains frequent comparisons and references to content therein.

▷ Messaging and MOM

Even though computing technologies have evolved from dumb-terminal-based computing systems with small green screens to complex distributed enterprise systems, the most elementary purpose of these applications remains the same—to enable the exchange of data between different pieces of computing software. Message-oriented middleware (MOM) is typically a piece of software that sits between communicating parties and provides the infrastructure responsible for handling disparate dependencies between them, such as operating systems, hardware, and communication protocols. It enables participants involved in the data exchange to focus on the application domain rather than on the mechanics of how the communication takes place.

A MOM exposes its facilities using an API that defines how distributed applications should use the underlying MOM to communicate with each other. MOM can be thought of as the postal service of messaging technology. People write a letter (the message), include the from/to address details on the envelope (the headers), and drop it in the mailbox, which acts as the standard interface for the post office (the API). The postal service (MOM) takes care of picking up the message, sorting the address details, and transporting it to the mailbox of the addressee (the receiver). The mail (message) is passed between parties (applications) via the postal service (MOM) in a manner that does not block the sender of that message from doing other work—that is, the sender can allow the postal service (MOM) to ensure that the message arrives without waiting for a response from the receiver (Figure 11.1).

In general, messaging refers to the act of sending metadata or information about the message and the message content itself, using one or more MOMs, between applications typically located on the periphery of the enterprise. These MOM-based messaging solutions can be architected in three broad topologies:

- **Centralized MOM topology.** A MOM may be deployed in a centralized hub-and-spoke topology, shown in Figure 11.2, where the MOM acts as a message bus between application components. The bus component was introduced in Chapter 2. In this approach, the components communicate with a central MOM (typically a vendor's MOM server) that behaves like a hub and is responsible for routing messages to the recipients. It also provides other features, such as persistence to ensure reliability and clustering for availability.

  The advantages of such a topology are numerous and allow messaging parties to be added and removed on the fly, without breaking other communication paths or affecting other parties. The disadvantages include increased network overhead, the single point of failure, performance of the hub (it has to do extra work in acting like the post office to sort mail), and possibly increased latency.

- **Decentralized MOM topology.** The decentralized topology shown in Figure 11.3 breaks up the hub-spoke layout to an application-centric approach. Each communicating party typically has its local MOM that acts as a sort of messaging proxy, receiving messages as though it were the intended recipient and then dispatching them to the respective applications.

Figure 11.1
MOM

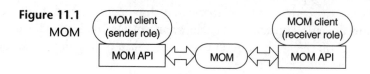

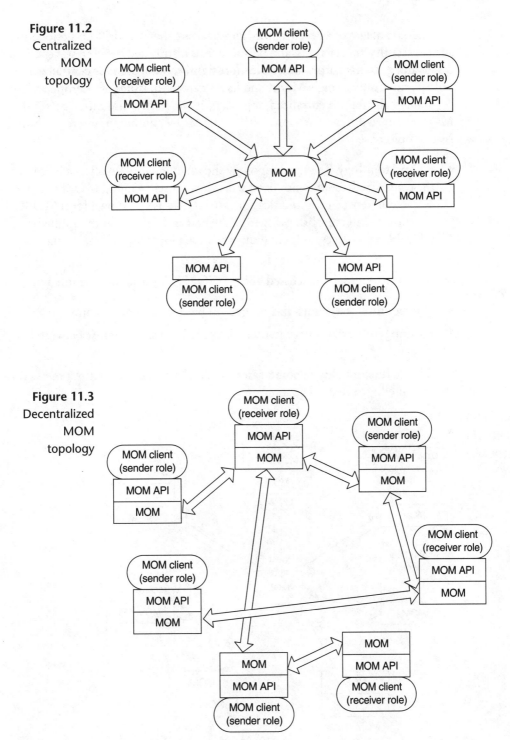

Figure 11.2
Centralized
MOM
topology

Figure 11.3
Decentralized
MOM
topology

The advantages of a decentralized approach are that the MOM functionality, such as security, transactions, and persistence, is distributed between servers. The disadvantage is that parties are a little more tightly coupled. In the centralized topology, since only a single MOM and its API are used, issues of interoperability are limited. In the decentralized approach, if the parties use different vendor MOMs or even different versions of the same MOM, numerous interoperability issues could arise.

- **Hybrid topology.** The third topology shown in Figure 11.4 offers a hybrid of the centralized and decentralized scenarios. It uses a central MOM that acts as a router between communication parties that use their own local MOMs. A hybrid architecture brings together the best and worst of both topologies. It is flexible yet most complex in terms of use, deployment, and maintenance.

In all the topologies discussed above, MOMs play a significant role by

- Not requiring the sender and receiver to be simultaneously connected
- Ensuring strong delivery guarantees on the request and response between participants
- Adding functionality in some cases by translating and formatting messages en route between participants

Figure 11.4
Hybrid MOM
topology

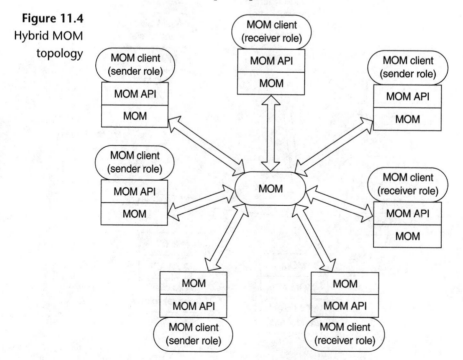

MOM-based messaging solutions are typically a good fit for five broad application categories:

- **Applications requiring asynchronous communication.** Synchronous or connection-based applications typically send requests at a known instance of a receiver and block until that request is processed. This results in directly shared state information between the two applications for the duration of the call—that is, the receiver uses the input data for processing, and the message sender must know the outcome of that processing to continue its own processing. This approach is not always practical. For example, applications that require guaranteed delivery cannot wait for the receiver to be online, or the recipient may not always be known in advance (especially with multiple recipients). MOMs, with their inherent proxying capabilities, offer a good solution for applications that require asynchronous behavior.

- **Store-and-forward applications.** In these applications, one or more of the eventual message receivers is not expected to be available. For example, some data processing applications run only after normal business hours, because of their intense consumption of computing resources, but they must receive the data they process from applications that run only during business hours. MOM-based messaging facilities ensure that messages will be delivered as soon as connectivity is restored or applications become available to begin their processing.

- **Applications that require a higher level of reliability.** Often termed *guarded communication applications,* these are also a good candidate. In this variation of store-and-forward applications, the messaging participants do not rely on the availability of connectivity to participating applications and are precognizant of the *intermittent* network. Because MOM acts as a proxy for the eventual receiver, it ensures that messages are protected against communication losses by delivering them reliably.

- **Application with multiple recipients.** Applications requiring delivery of the same initial message to multiple recipients are best implemented using a MOM-based solution. This is often known as the publish-subscribe messaging design. MOM takes the responsibility of asynchronously delivering messages to multiple receivers and also offers the capability of receiving their responses on behalf of the message initiator.

- **Applications requiring message trails.** Most MOM implementations offer the ability to maintain detailed message trails. Applications that require the ability to create records of all communications activity for logging, auditing, error recovery, and other quality of service measures can use these services.

> **Messaging and Web Services**

From a Web service use case perspective, XML messaging in the form of SOAP requests, between applications can be either synchronous or asynchronous. Figure 11.5 shows an example of a synchronous message exchange. Flute Bank places an order for office supplies with OfficeMin and sends a purchase order (an XML document). The purchase order maps specifically to the service's logical interface (e.g., an RPC call). OfficeMin's service checks the inventory and verifies all items in the purchase order are in stock. It acknowledges the purchase order by generating an invoice (an XML document) indicating that the order will be shipped. This entire interaction happens in a request-response manner.

An alternative approach, shown in Figure 11.6, also begins with Flute Bank sending a purchase order to OfficeMin. OfficeMin acknowledges it, using a confirmation mechanism (e.g., replying with an email or even a response to the re-

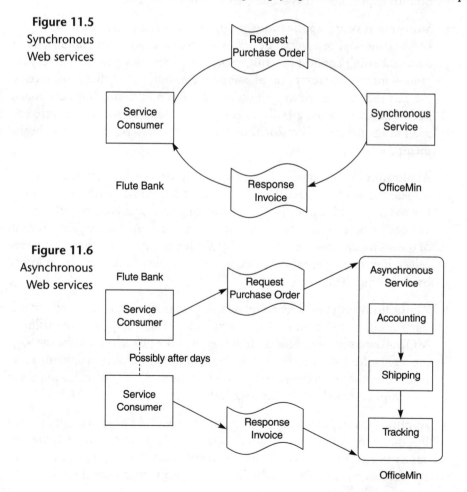

Figure 11.5
Synchronous
Web services

Figure 11.6
Asynchronous
Web services

quest) indicating that the purchase order was received and is being processed. The purchase order goes though OfficeMin's processing system, where it is processed, flutebank.com charged, and the order shipped. OfficeMin then generates an XML document describing the invoice and sends it to flutebank.com.

In subsequent sections of this chapter we will talk about how these use cases can be implemented.

> Messaging in Java

JMS

We have just discussed MOMs and the kinds of applications that may require their use. Java Message Service (JMS) provides Java applications with a standard and consistent interface to the messaging services of a MOM provider or a messaging server. This benefits architects, because they no longer need to use the messaging vendor's proprietary Java interface, if one exists at all.

JMS-based communication is a potential solution in any distributed computing scenario that needs to pass data, not references, either synchronously or asynchronously between application components. It offers a good solution for business integration in heterogeneous environments and for connecting to legacy systems. For example, an enterprise computing strategy can use JMS-based distributed software components as a middleware solution that functions as a bridge among legacy applications.

Architecturally, the JMS stack revolves around the concept of providers. This provides the underlying queuing and guaranteed delivery, ensuring that "offline" applications get the messages later, when they are capable of receiving them. Figure 11.7 shows how message delivery and acknowledgment works for a *durable* message consumer and how the provider acts as a proxy that actually receives messages on behalf of the eventual recipients.

Figure 11.7
Conceptual
model for JMS

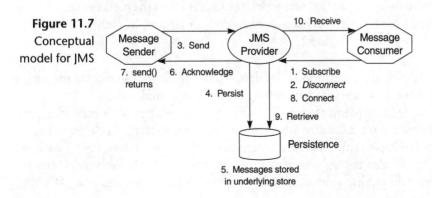

Figure 11.8a
Point-to-point
messaging

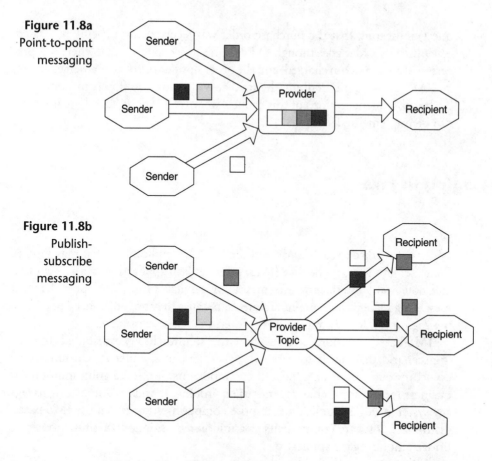

Figure 11.8b
Publish-
subscribe
messaging

From a messaging perspective, JMS supports two messaging models:

- **Point-to-point.** In this model, the sender sends the message, which is put on a *queue*, and a single consumer reads the message off the queue. There is exactly one recipient (Figure 11.8a).

- **Publish-subscribe.** In this model, the sender sends the message, which is put on a *topic*. Multiple recipients can subscribe to the topic; each receives a copy of the message (Figure 11.8b).

Without going into too much detail about JMS, we will discuss messaging with it and how XML/SOAP messages can be delivered with it.

The JMS implementations of point-to-point and publish-subscribe paradigms use the same fundamental concepts but have specialized classes to handle them. In simple terms, there is a common set of base interfaces. Each base interface has at least two sub-interfaces: one for the point-to-point model, and the other for the publish-subscribe model. Figure 11.9 shows the core of the JMS API.

Figure 11.9 The JMS API

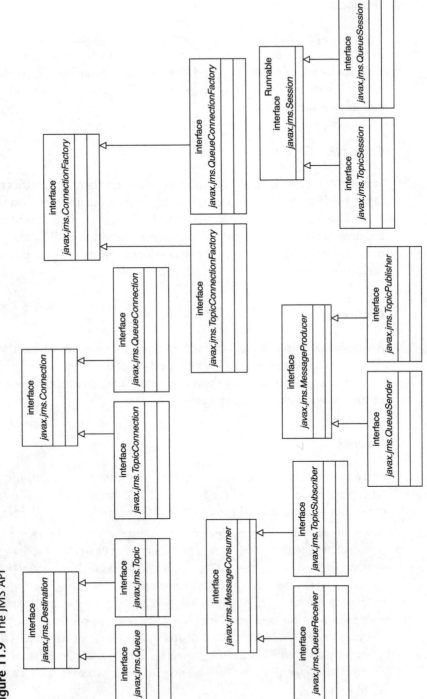

Destination

Destination represents an abstraction of a message delivery or endpoint. The provider uses this interface to define the location where messages are delivered The provider is, of course, free to choose any underlying implementation mechanism. Clients use the sub-interfaces javax.jms.Queue and javax.jms.Topic, depending on the message style.

Connection Factory

ConnectionFactory is an abstraction used to encapsulate the specifics of connecting to a JMS provider from an application. The task of a connection factory is to create a provider-specific *connection* to the JMS provider. This is similar to the way the driver manager (java.sql.DriverManager) works in JDBC. The application programmer needs only to get the database-specific driver, which returns a connection to the database. ▷

Connection

An application uses ConnectionFactory to create a connection to the JMS provider. The connection is a network connection of some type (a socket, RMI reference, etc., depending on how the provider implements it) and represents a single communication channel to the provider.

Sessions

Once a Connection is obtained to a provider, a Session is started, and all activity takes place in the context of the Session. A Session represents a conversation or collection of transactional interactions with the underlying provider.

> ▷   In JMS, the term *administered object* refers to an object the application program retrieves from the JNDI context and works with as though it were a local object. The application administrator configure these objects in the application setup. The closest analogy is configuring the long-distance carrier on a telephone line. The phone company can configure the administered "carrier" object as MCI or AT&T. To the client, the calls work the same, without the need to buy a new telephone every time the calling plan or carrier changes. **Destination** and **ConnectionFactory** are administered objects.

Message Producers

To send a message to a Destination, a client must ask the Session to create a MessageProducer. For point-to-point messaging, a javax.jms.QueueSender is created, and for publish-subscribe messaging, a javax.jms.TopicPublisher is created.

Message Consumers

Message consumers are created by the Session for clients that want to receive messages. Message consumers are attached to a Destination and, depending on the messaging style, the javax.jms.QueueReciever or javax.jms.TopicSubscriber is used. The client can attach javax.jms.MessageListener with the consumer, with which the callback method onMessage() is invoked asynchronously when a message arrives.

We have taken a high-level view of the different parts of the JMS API. The basic steps, as summarized in Figure 11.10, are:

Figure 11.10
JMS messaging

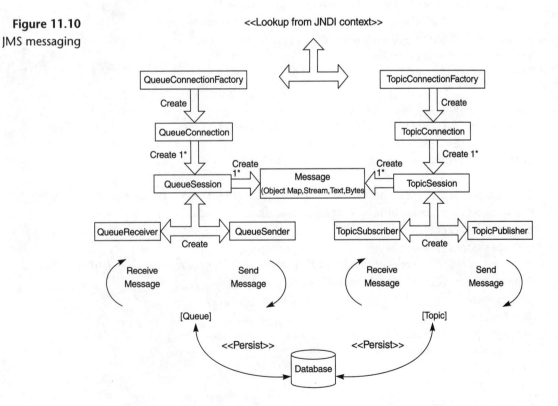

1. Obtain the ConnectionFactory from JNDI.

2. Obtain the Destination from JNDI.

3. Use the connection factory to create a Connection.

4. Use the connection to start a Session.

5. Use the Session and Destination to create MessageConsumers and MessageProducers as necessary and attach a MessageListeners.

6. Send messages with the producer and receive messages with the consumer.

For application A to send messages to Application B with JMS, using point-to-point messaging (Figure 11.11), the code would look like Listings 11.1 and 11.2.

Listing 11.1 Application A: Sending the message

```
String message="Some message here ";
// JMS factories and queues are administered objects.
String JNDIFACTORY="weblogic.jndi.WLInitialContextFactory";
String JMSFACTORY ="myQueueFactory";
String QNAME="mymessagequeue";
String endpoint= "t3://192.168.0.1:9090";

Hashtable env = new Hashtable();
env.put(Context.INITIALCONTEXTFACTORY, JNDIFACTORY);
env.put(Context.PROVIDERURL, endpoint);
InitialContext ctx = new InitialContext(env);

QueueConnectionFactory factory = (QueueConnectionFactory) ctx.lookup(JMSFACTORY);
QueueConnection connection = factory.createQueueConnection ();
connection.start();
QueueSession session =
                connection.createQueueSession(false,QueueSession.AUTOACKNOWLEDGE );
Queue queue = (Queue) ctx.lookup(QNAME);
QueueSender queuesender =session.createSender(queue);
TextMessage message = session.createTextMessage();
message.setText( MESSAGE );
queuesender.send(message);
ctx.close();
session.close();
connection.close();
```

Listing 11.2   Application B: Receiving the message

```
String JNDIFACTORY="weblogic.jndi.WLInitialContextFactory";
// JMS factories and queues are adminsitered objects.
String JMSFACTORY="myQueueFactory";
String QNAME="mymessagequeue";
String endpoint= "t3://192.168.0.1:9090";

Hashtable env = new Hashtable();
env.put(Context.INITIALCONTEXTFACTORY, JNDIFACTORY);
env.put(Context.PROVIDERURL,endpoint);
InitialContext ctx = new InitialContext(env);
QueueConnectionFactory factory = (QueueConnectionFactory) ctx.lookup(JMSFACTORY);
QueueConnection connection = factory.createQueueConnection ();
connection.start();
QueueSession session =
                connection.createQueueSession(false,QueueSession.AUTOACKNOWLEDGE );
Queue queue = (Queue) ctx.lookup(QNAME);
QueueReceiver receiver = session.createReceiver(queue);
receiver.setMessageListener (new MyListener(){
    public void onMessage(Message msg) {
            String msgText;
            if (msg instanceof TextMessage) {
                msgText = ((TextMessage)msg).getText();
            } else{
                    msgText = msg.toString();
                    }
            System.out.println("Message Received: "+ msgText );
            }
        });
ctx.close();
session.close();
connection.close();
```

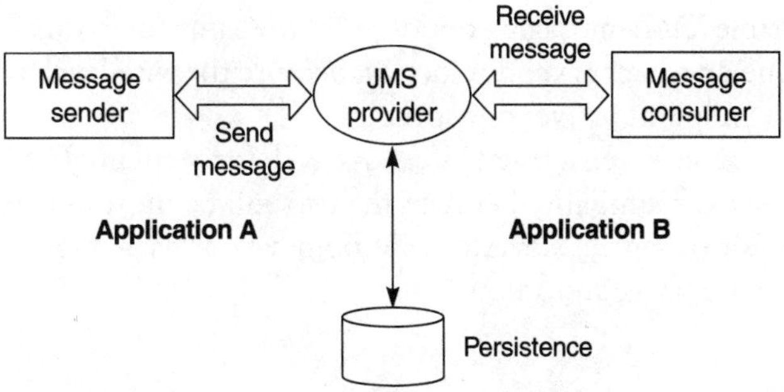

Figure 11.11
Sending
messages with
point-to-point
messaging

The model shown in Listings 11.1 and 11.2 is quite robust and works well for enterprise-level messaging. It supports a variety of message types (e.g., `Bytes-Message`, `MapMessage`, `ObjectMessage`, `StreamMessage`, and `TextMessage`), of which the above code fragment demonstrates the latter. JMS can also easily be adapted for XML messaging. The text message shown above could be replaced with an XML document and sent from application A to application B. However, JMS is just a specification. It does not define the wire-level protocol or encodings the provider uses to implement the messaging.

For example, in Listings 11.1 and 11.2, `provider_url` points to "t3:// 192.168.0.1:9090", showing that the underlying implementation uses a t3 protocol or BEA's implementation of RMI to connect to the provider. In this case, if the client were anything other than BEA, to receive the messages it would need BEA's API or client files, containing the factories and implementation classes, to connect to BEA's provider.

JMS vendors often provide the ability to extend themselves across firewall boundaries, using some form of HTTP tunneling. However as described above, it still requires a slice of the JMS vendor's software to be installed at *every remote location*. Applications within the enterprise boundaries usually control every remote node involved in the communication, which is a perfectly viable solution. Unfortunately, this is not usually the case for interenterprise communications.

Many vendors have enhanced their JMS provider implementations to support SOAP messaging over HTTP. They use HTTP as the transport under the JMS API and pass SOAP messages as the JMS `TextMessage` (this is often referred to as SOAP over JMS). The message format used to transport data over HTTP is vendor–proprietary, usually some form of multipart MIME. This is quite a robust messaging approach, but the problem remains that JMS was not really intended for this purpose. For example, there is no way to create and manipulate a SOAP message envelope with an attachment in JMS. Developers would have to use complicated, error-prone `String` operations or the provider's proprietary API.

Some JMS vendors have taken this approach one step further, by using SOAP with Attachments API for Java (SAAJ) to create and manipulate messages, HTTP transport, and a SOAP message (instead of an HTTP multipart message). This is also a viable XML messaging option, with the same functionality as a JAXM provider. The drawback is vendor lock-in, because the wire-level SOAP message format and endpoint are vendor-specific.

Our reason for covering JMS above is that essentially JAXM has its roots in JMS. The close similarity between the two will be more apparent further in the chapter. For example, JMS and JAXM both have a `ConnectionFactory`, a `Message-Listener` interface, and so on.

JavaMail

JMS is the preferred technology for integration and messaging between loosely coupled Java applications. While JMS is a specification that creates an abstraction at the application level, as opposed to the wire protocol, JavaMail can be thought of as an object-oriented wrapper around the standard messaging protocols—SMTP, POP3, and IMAP. SMTP is used to send email, and POP3 and IMAP are used to retrieve email. In this section, we will look at an alternative messaging mechanism—JavaMail—and, more important, how SOAP can be used with JavaMail for asynchronous XML messaging between applications. ▷

Email applications can be divided into two broad categories: Mail User Agent (MUA) and Mail Transfer Agent (MTA) applications. MUA applications, such as Eudora, Netscape Messenger, and Microsoft Outlook, allow messages to be composed, accessed, and sent. MTA applications, such as iPlanet Messaging server and Microsoft Exchange, handle the actual physical delivery. JavaMail, shown in Figure 11.12, is a standard extension API focused on building MUA functionality into Java applications. Like JMS, it is designed with provider-based architecture, for wire protocol independence. Several MTAs are freely available, including "JAMES" from Apache, which uses POP3/SMTP protocols. It can be found

Figure 11.12
Conceptual
JavaMail model

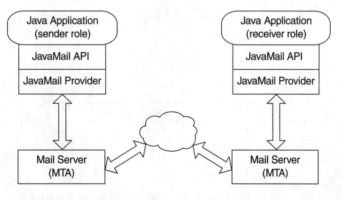

▷ The Simple Mail Transfer Protocol (SMTP) specified in RFC 821 *(www.ietf .org/rfc/rfc821.txt)* defines the mechanism for delivery of email to a SMTP server. The server relays the message to the recipients' SMTP server, from which users download the mail using POP (Post Office Protocol) or IMAP (Internet Message Access Protocol). POP and IMAP are defined by RFC 1939 *(www.ietf.org/rfc/rfc1939.txt)* and RFC 2060 *(www.ietf.org/rfc/rfc2060 .txt)*, respectively.

at *http://jakarta.apache.org/james/index.html* and is included in the CD for this book.

The JavaMail API, shown in Figure 11.13, consist of three packages that contain both the client API and the API that serves as a contract for providers to implement. These packages also contain the classes and interfaces to model events, notifications, and searching. We will not discuss all these features in detail but will limit our discussion to sending and receiving messages.

Figure 11.14 illustrates the concept behind sending mail messages using the JavaMail API. A Session is created to a server, using an underlying Provider. Message objects are created and sent using the Transport for that provider session. The semantics of how a provider establishes a session and the physical connection are completely abstracted from the application code.

Figure 11.13
The JavaMail
API

Figure 11.14
Sending mail
using JavaMail

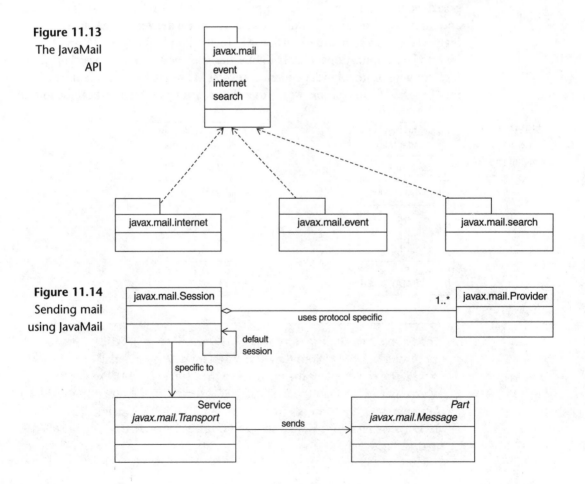

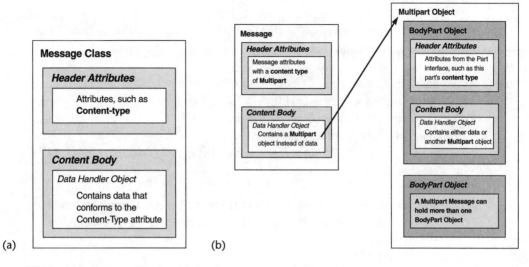

Figure 11.15   Message structure for *(a)* simple messages and *(b)* multipart messages

The Message is logically composed of different sections, as Figures 11.15a and 11.15b illustrate. It has some Header attributes (To, From, Subject, etc.) and the content data. Email messages that contain attachments are modeled as Multipart messages. In a Multipart message, the body consists of many BodyPart objects.

Let us now look at an example of asynchronous messaging, in which Flute Bank sends a purchase order to OfficeMin, using SOAP. To send a SOAP message, we will follow the steps outlined in Figure 11.14. We will replace the body of the mail message with the SOAP envelope structure and attach the XML file that represents the purchase order. Listing 11.3 shows the code for sending this mail from purchaseorders@flutebank.com to invoices@officemin.com. The JavaMail API comes with providers from Sun for POP3, SMTP, and IMAP, so no vendor products (such as MOM implementations) are needed to run this example.

Listing 11.3   The SoapMailSender application

```
package com.flutebank.javamail

import java.util.*;
import java.io.*;
import javax.mail.*;
import javax.mail.internet.*;
import javax.activation.*;
```

```
/**
 * SoapMailSender creates a message with the SOAP envelope as the body and the
 * business document exchanged between companies as the attachment.
 */
public class SoapMailSender {
    private static String messageText1 =
        "<?xml version=\"1.0\" encoding=\"UTF-8\"?>" +
        "<soap-env:Envelope xmlns:soap-env=
                        \"http://schemas.xmlsoap.org/soap/envelope/\">" +
      "<soap-env:Header/>" +
        "<soap-env:Body>" +
            "<po:PurchaseOrder xmlns:po=\"http://www.flutebank.com/schema\">"+
              "<senderid>myuserid@Mon Aug 19 23:55:28 EDT 2002</senderid>"+
            "</po:PurchaseOrder>"+
        "</soap-env:Body>"+
      "</soap-env:Envelope>";

    public static void main(String[] args) {
    try {
        String to = args[0];
        String from = args[1];
        String host = args[2];
        boolean debug = Boolean.valueOf(args[3]).booleanValue();

// create some properties and get the default Session
        Properties props = new Properties();
        props.put("mail.smtp.host", host);

        Session session = Session.getDefaultInstance(props, null);

// create a message
        MimeMessage message = new MimeMessage(session);
// create the from
        message.setFrom(new InternetAddress(from));
// create the recipient headers
        InternetAddress[] address = {new InternetAddress(to)};
        message.setRecipients(Message.RecipientType.TO, address);
// create the subject and date header
```

```
      message.setSubject("PurchaseOrder");
      message.setSentDate(new Date());

// create and fill the first message part
      MimeBodyPart mbp1 = new MimeBodyPart();
      mbp1.setText(messageText1);

// create and fill the second message part
      MimeBodyPart attachment = new MimeBodyPart();

// attach the purchaseorder.xml file to the message
      FileDataSource fds= new FileDataSource("purchaseorder.xml");
      attachment.setDataHandler(new DataHandler(fds));
      attachment.setFileName("purchaseorder.xml");
// create the Multipart and its parts
      Multipart mp = new MimeMultipart();
      mp.addBodyPart(mbp1);
      mp.addBodyPart(attachment);

// add the Multipart to the message
       message.setContent(mp);

// send the message
      Transport.send(message);
    } catch (Exception mex) {
        mex.printStackTrace();
      }
    }
}
```

The mail message can be retrieved at officemin.com. Figure 11.16 shows the minimum steps required to retrieve mail using an underlying provider. A Session object is used to obtain a Store created for the POP3 protocol. The Store is connected to a server by a username and password, and the user's Folder is opened. Messages in the Folder are then accessed and downloaded.

Listing 11.4 shows the code on OfficeMin's side to access the POP3 server and download all messages with JavaMail. The code dumps the message headers, content, and attachments to the console.

Figure 11.16
Retrieving mail
using JavaMail

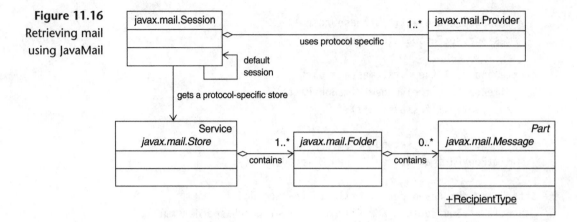

Listing 11.4 The SoapMailReceiver application

```
package com.officemin.purchaseorderservice;

import javax.mail.*;
import javax.mail.internet.*;
import java.util.*;
import java.io.*;
/**
  * A Receives a mail message and prints out the contents
  */
  public class SoapMailReceiver{

    public static void main(String args[]) throws Exception {
        String server=args[0];
        String username=args[1];
        String password=args[2];

// get the default session
        Properties props = System.getProperties();
        Session session = Session.getDefaultInstance(props);
// get the POP3 message store and connect to it
        Store store = session.getStore("pop3");
        store.connect(server, username, password);

// get the default folder in the store
        Folder folder = store.getDefaultFolder();
// get the INBOX folder in the default folder
        folder = folder.getFolder("INBOX");
```

```
// download the message or leave it on the server.
// we leave it on the server by using read-only
        folder.open(Folder.READ_ONLY);

// Get the messages
        Message[] msgs = folder.getMessages();

// process the messages
        for (int msgNum = 0; msgNum < msgs.length; msgNum++){
        // insert business logic here to process the message
        // for now we just print it out
            processMessage(msgs[msgNum]);
        }
// close everything
        folder.close(false);
        store.close();
    }


/**
 * Dump the message contents to the console
 */
public static void processMessage(Message message){
  try{
// get the header information
    String from=((InternetAddress)message.getFrom()[0]).getPersonal();
    if (from==null)
        from=((InternetAddress)message.getFrom()[0]).getAddress();
    System.out.println("FROM: "+from);
    String subject=message.getSubject();
    System.out.println("SUBJECT: "+subject);

// get the message part (i.e., the message itself)
    Part messagePart=message;
    Object content=messagePart.getContent();

    for(int i=0;i < ((Multipart)content).getCount(); i++){
        messagePart=((Multipart)content).getBodyPart(i);

        InputStream is = messagePart.getInputStream();
        BufferedReader reader  =new BufferedReader(new InputStreamReader(is));
        String thisLine=reader.readLine();
```

```
      while (thisLine!=null) {
        System.out.println(thisLine);
        thisLine=reader.readLine();
      }
  }
}catch (Exception ex){
    ex.printStackTrace();
    }
  }
}
```

The simple JavaMail API can be used to build complex messaging applications. Consider the business use case of flutebank.com and officemin.com discussed earlier. Flute Bank places a regular order for its main branch with OfficeMin, by sending a purchase order. OfficeMin processes the purchase order and ships the supplies. OfficeMin then sends an invoice to Flute Bank that Flute's accounting processes. Flute then sends an electronic payment to OfficeMin. Figure 11.17 shows how this can be realized:

1. The client application initiates the business exchange by sending a SOAP message with the purchase order as an XML attachment, using SMTP. The sender and recipient are indicated by the from and to email headers. Flute's local mail server acts as a sort of messaging provider and stores the message, which is reliably delivered (possibly with a delivery receipt) to officemin.com. We looked at this code in Listing 11.3.

Figure 11.17
Asynchronous
B2B messaging
using JavaMail

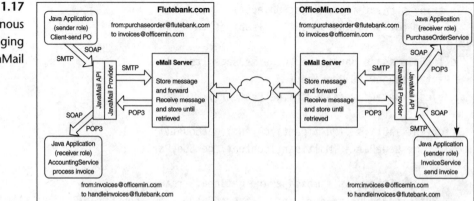

2. The `PurchaseOrderService` at OfficeMin either picks up the mail or is notified when it arrives. It downloads the mail and processes the headers and the body, which contains a SOAP message. It also extracts the attachment, which contains the order, and processes it. We looked at this code in Listing 11.4.

3. The `SendInvoice` application is invoked, which now acts like a client and sends the invoice to Flute Bank, as in step 1.

4. Flute's `AccountingService` picks up the message containing the invoice, as in step 2, and processes the payment to OfficeMin.

The above scenario shows how an asynchronous message-exchange scenario can be built using JavaMail and XML technologies. It is not necessary that Java be used on both sides. For example, OfficeMin could use Visual Basic or C++ to download email from its servers.

Messaging with JavaMail—and in particular, SOAP messaging with JavaMail—offers several advantages:

- **Eliminates messaging MOMs.** The sender and receiver do not need any JMS infrastructure or vendor software. This is especially significant for non-Java environments.

- **Supports security.** Two broad concerns affect most email applications: authentication and encryption. Basic authentication is built into email, and a majority of enterprise email servers provide secure mail, using techniques such as PGP and S/MIME. In short, the work required to build security into the application layer is reduced.

- **Leverages existing infrastructure.** Email is the first enterprise solution any company implements. Most organizations have sophisticated hardware and software infrastructures, to assure a high quality of service for this corporate lifeline. Messaging with JavaMail and XML can leverage this existing infrastructure to build interoperable asynchronous messaging solutions.

- **Provides message sorting facilities.** Messages in the server can be searched, sorted, and filtered from applications using headers (subject, to, from, etc.) and even message content, if needed.

- **Supports notifications.** Mailbox monitoring features allow monitoring of message servers for new messages rather than using a latent polling approach.

- **Supports delivery to multiple recipients.** The same message can be delivered to multiple recipients. Audit trail services can also be built, using the "bcc" feature.

- **Reduces implementation cost.** Messaging solutions using JavaMail are generally less expensive, because most of the infrastructure already exists, and no MOM products are required. ▷

Using JavaMail for enterprise messaging and integration does have some limitations:

- **No transaction support.** Although mail-based messaging solutions use tried-and-tested technology, they do no support transactions across enterprise boundaries. Most architects interpret this as an absolute design constraint for any adoption. Without a stringent requirement on transactions across enterprise boundaries, architectures such as those outlined in Figure 11.5 can be a good fit. If is this is not the case, see Chapter 14 for details on transactions in Web services.

- **Repeated delivery of the same message.** Just as receiving an email in your mailbox twice is a common occurrence, the same message may be delivered to applications multiple times. In short, a mail based solution offers no guaranteed one-time delivery support . The application layer must incorporate the logic of filtering this out if such an event would affect the business process. For example, receiving the same purchase order twice can trigger two shipments, but receiving the same free stock quote twice may not be so critical an issue.

▷ JAXM Architecture

We have looked at some messaging options in Java, such as JMS and JavaMail, and how they can be leveraged to send SOAP messages. Let us now look at JAXM, its architecture, and how it can be used for XML messaging.

> ▷ While an email is an asynchronous one-way message exchange, SMTP offers a delivery notification mechanism called Delivery Status Notification (DSN) and a Message Disposition Notification (MDN), in which a receipt email message is sent back.

Providers

Conceptually, JAXM is based around the notion of *providers,* which is analogous to MOM. As Figure 11.18 shows, a provider is a simplified message broker that sits in the middle of the two messaging points. A provider supplies the services necessary for persisting and forwarding messages, reliability, routing, and additional infrastructure-related features to improve quality of service, such as scalability, availability, and security. The chief requirement for a JAXM provider is that it must support HTTP and SOAP with Attachments.

The concept of the provider has its roots in JMS. Like JMS, JAXM sits on top of a provider implementation. Figure 11.19 shows the architectural stack for JAXM and the provider's relative position in it. The provider plays a proxying role, in the sense that when the application uses a provider, all messages go *via* the provider. When a JAXM application sends a message, it actually sends it to the provider, which then handles transmission to the final destination(s). Similarly, when a JAXM consumer receives a message, the underlying provider has actually received the message and then forwarded it to the application code. A provider will typically use the services of a J2EE container, because the container requires

- An interface to interact with the outside world. This is provided by servlets or message-driven EJBs.

- A mechanism to be administered by the environment. This involves setting up administered objects in JNDI, factories, and so on (just like the JMS-administered objects).

Conceptually, a JAXM provider sits somewhere between an email server and a MOM broker. However all of the discussion about MOMs in this chapter so far is valid for JAXM providers (e.g., topologies) as well.

Figure 11.18
Conceptual
model for
JAXM

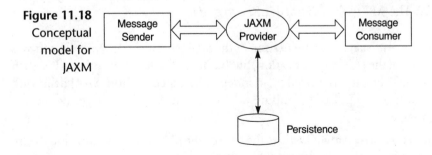

Figure 11.19
Architectural
stack for JAXM

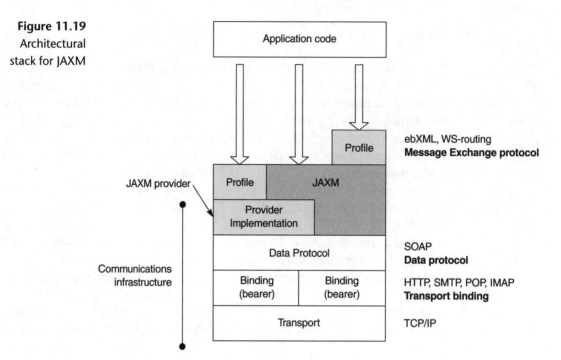

JAXM API

Earlier in the chapter, we talked about MOMs and how the JMS API provides a standard Java-based interface to the messaging services of a MOM or a messaging broker. The JAXM API takes on the task of providing a standard Java interface for applications to use the services of a provider capable of XML messaging with SOAP. The API itself is divided into two parts:

1. **javax.xml.soap**. Implementation of the SAAJ specification. Initially, this was a part of the JAXM specification, but because of reuse across other APIs, such as JAX-RPC, it was moved to an independent specification. SAAJ deals with creating, manipulating, sending, and receiving SOAP messages (without a provider).

2. **javax.xml.messaging**: Defines the core of the JAXM specification and the interactions with the messaging provider.

Subsequent sections of this chapter cover the API in further detail.

Profiles

Like JMS, JAXM API provides only the lightweight mechanism for connecting and communicating with a provider and requires nothing of the message content except that it must meet the SOAP standard. Real-world business applications, however, often need to control and agree on what *kind* of information and in what *structure* it is being passed. The SOAP 1.1 and SOAP with Attachments standards provide a basic packaging model. All they require is that a message sent from point A to point B be composed of an outer envelope that can contain a header and a body. This falls short on many fronts. For example, to successfully implement XML messaging, parties to the communication must be capable of performing tasks such as the following:

- **Addressing.** Parties must agree on a standard addressing scheme and provide a mechanism to correlate a request to a response—that is, the "from-to correlation."

- **Content processing.** Parties must know what the message is in the context of their business. For example, a purchase order must conform to particular set of rules, and both parties must understand the schema for the document.

- **Header processing.** Both parties must be able of examining the SOAP header fields of incoming messages to process some metacontent and metadata about the message.

- **Security checks and encryption/decryption.** Parties should be able to examine the message to determine that the message is from an authenticated sender who is authorized to perform the task and that the data in the message is securely encrypted.

- **Error and exception handling.** Parties must be able to ensure that senders receive appropriate faults when the incoming messages does not contain sufficient or accurate information.

- **Routing.** Parties must be able to route the message, meaning they must be capable of handling the branching logic that determines the intended recipients of the message and deliver the message in the order it was intended to be delivered to those recipients. ▷

▷ JAXM requires support for SOAP 1.1 with Attachments. The attachments are important, because *choreographed* messaging with compound messages (i.e., SOAP messages with a body and one more attachments that contain the message content) dictates slightly different semantics than traditional request-response-based SOAP communication.

JAXM does not describe the semantics that address the above requirements and govern the SOAP/XML message exchange protocol. They are described by the common XML protocol defined by a *profile* and XML schemas associated with that profile.

The profile layer in Figure 11.20 refers to the implementation of a specific message-exchange protocol based on SOAP 1.1 with Attachments. A profile is really an industry standard, such as the ebXML Message Handling Service defined by OASIS or the W3C's XMLP. The latter defines well-established rules for message processing and represents a higher level of abstraction on top of SOAP that governs how business partners can leverage XML messaging. By layering a profile on JAXM, the application uses the profile-specific API and not JAXM directly. So, for example, an ebXML profile from a vendor may use a specialized subclass `com.myprovider.EbxmlMessage` object instead of the `javax.xmk.soap` `.SOAPMessage` object.

A profile may not even be built on top of JAXM and may be supplied by a vendor directly. In either case, the output on the wire is the same SOAP message, conforming to the ebXML Message Service Specification.

Profiles are closely tied to SOAP headers. In fact, a profile can be thought of as a specific *usage* of a SOAP header, because the headers contain most of the pro-

Figure 11.20
SOAP message
structure with
a profile

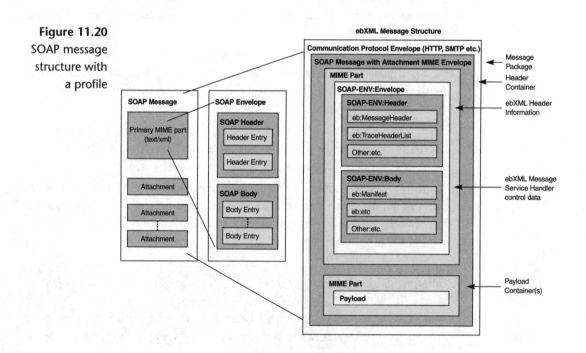

file-specific information. The payload or business content of the message would remain the same, no matter what message exchange protocol was used.

In short, the profile and the schemas associated with that profile describe the set of rules and procedures all parties must understand and agree upon for effective XML messaging. ▷

▷ ### ebXML

The ebXML initiative by UN/CEFACT (United Nations Centre for Trade Facilitation and Electronic Business) and OASIS (Organization for the Advancement of Structured Information Standards) is a set of specifications for message formatting, business processes, and registry services, among others. ebXML concepts were covered in Chapter 7.

ebXML Messaging

In ebXML, an entire message is called a *message package.* A message package has one *header container* and zero or more *payload containers.* Most of the messaging-specific XML elements reside in the header container and describe the messaging routing, operations performed, the unique identifier for the message, and so on. The payload containers hold the message content, which can be anything from XML documents, such as purchase orders and invoices, to scanned x-ray images.

Some ebXML SOAP Headers

- To and From. URIs that identify the sender and receiver.

- CPAId. Based on the Collaboration Protocol Profile and Collaboration Protocol Agreement specifications, the messaging parties agree on the interaction semantics. This results in an XML document describing the business process and messaging interaction. The **CPAId** header refers to an ID defined according to this agreement.

- ConversationId. Uniquely identifies a set of related message exchanges that constitute a conversation between messaging parties.

- Service. Denotes the service that processes the message at the destination (the To element).

- Action. Specifies the action the receiving service should take on the message.

- MessageId. Uniquely identifies the message.

- Timestamp. Specifies the time the message was created.

▶ Designing with JAXM

Architecturally, JAXM-based messaging applications fall into two broad categories, which determine the messaging capabilities the application can support: applications that do not use a JAXM provider (synchronous messaging) and those that use a JAXM provider (asynchronous messaging). We will now look at these in further detail and the type of business use cases each category can address.

Synchronous Messaging

Without a provider, messaging requires simultaneous engagement of both end-points of the exchange. This is called synchronous request-response (or point-to-point) messaging (Figure 11.21) and was described in Chapter 10. The client sends a message and blocks until a reply or fault is received from the service. It cannot do any other work while awaiting the response. This is analogous to making a phone call. Either someone responds by picking up the handset on the other end, or a busy tone is received.

At a lower level, synchronous communication between a message sender and receiver falls into two categories:

- **Synchronous with response.** The sender is blocked till the response to the message is received (Figure 11.22). This usually implements use cases corresponding to a read-only messaging pattern called *synchronous-inquiry,* in which data on the receiver's side is not changed as a result of the invocation. For example, the request contains a purchase order. The service processes that order and returns an invoice and shipping details.

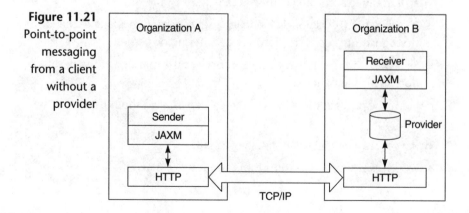

Figure 11.21
Point-to-point messaging from a client without a provider

- **Synchronous with acknowledgment.** The receiver does not send a response but sends more of a "got it" acknowledgment (Figure 11.23). The client remains blocked until it receives the acknowledgment, which may not even relate to the original message (but usually does). Its purpose is to notify the client that the message was received and to unblock the calling thread. This is often used to implement use cases corresponding to a *synchronous-update* messaging pattern. This involves changing business data that may potentially be used by other services or consumers on the receiver's side. For example,

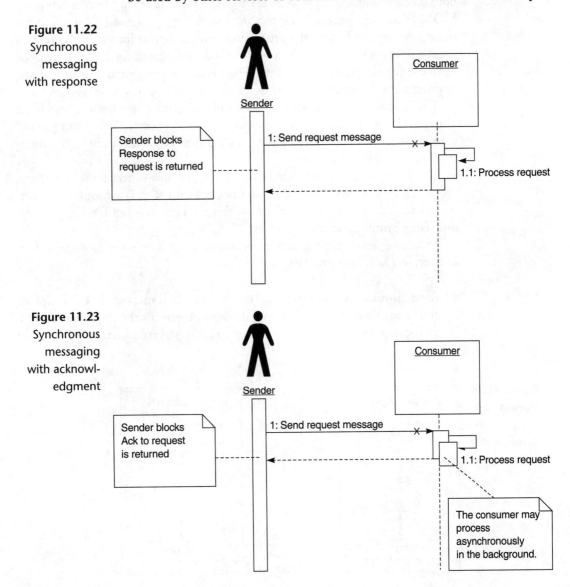

Figure 11.22 Synchronous messaging with response

Figure 11.23 Synchronous messaging with acknowledgment

the request contains a change of address form, and the service responds by acknowledging that it was received.

Asynchronous Messaging

An application that use an underlying JAXM provider can provide support for both synchronous and asynchronous messaging, because the provider acts like a MOM or message broker. In asynchronous messaging (Figure 11.24), the client sends a message and continues processing without waiting for a return. Based on some a priori agreement (such as a predefined and agreed-upon endpoint), the service sends a response to the client. There is no requirement on the time frame or other physical aspects (such as using the same transport or connection).

This is analogous to making a phone call and getting an answering machine. The caller leaves a message and continues. The person on the other end gets the message and returns the call by dialing the number left on the machine or a number he or she already knows.

This gives rise to the problem of co-relation, or how to relate a response to a previously sent request. This problem does not exist with synchronous messaging per se. JAXM does not specify how this co-relation is built, relying on the messaging profile layer for it.

At a lower level, asynchronous communication between a message sender and receiver falls into two categories:

- **Asynchronous with response.** The client sends a message to the recipient and expects a response. However, it does not wait for the response to arrive and continues doing other work (Figure 11.25). The recipient asynchronously

Figure 11.24
Provider roles in asynchronous messaging

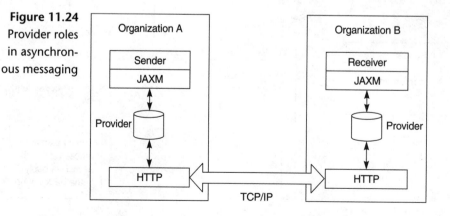

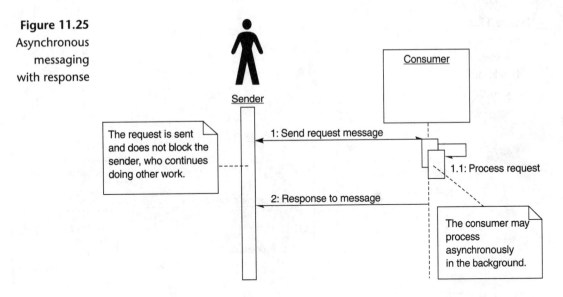

Figure 11.25
Asynchronous messaging with response

sends a reply to the sender when it has done the work on its side, with no time limitation on its doing so. This often implements use cases corresponding to an *asynchronous inquiry* messaging pattern. This is a read-only operation; data on the receivers side is unchanged.

- **Asynchronous with acknowledgment.** This is similar to asynchronous with response, with the difference that the message consumer sends a confirmation or acknowledgment to the sender (Figure 11.26) correlated to a request previously sent. The semantics of the correlation are not specified by JAXM and are typically at the profile level. This usually implements use cases corresponding to an *asynchronous-update* messaging pattern, where business data that may potentially be used by other consumers undergoes some mutation on the receiver's side.

- **One-way messaging.** The client sends a message and does not block or wait to receive a reply (Figure 11.27). It is free to do other work. This is analogous to sending a fax (fire and forget!) A number is dialed and a fax sent. You do not need a person to answer the other phone (just a fax machine). This also implements use cases corresponding to an *asynchronous-update* pattern, in which data on the receiver's side is updated with new values.

In the asynchronous application models, an analogy can be drawn between the messaging provider and an email server that we looked at with JavaMail earlier. A mail is sent, and one may or may not receive a response or acknowledgment, depending on the details of the message and how the system is configured.

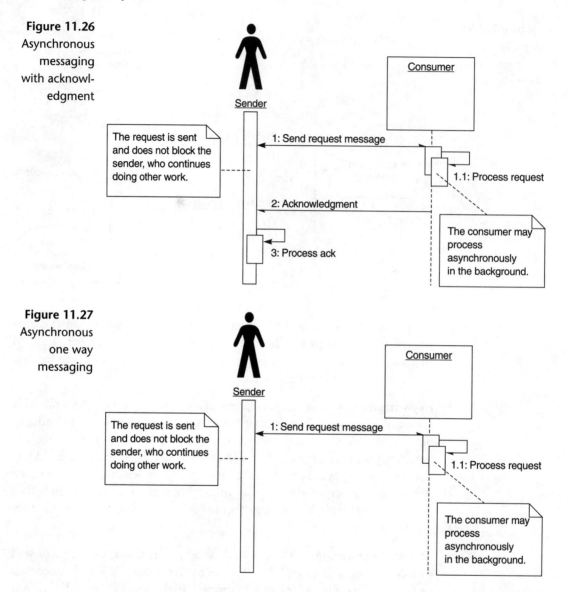

Figure 11.26
Asynchronous
messaging
with acknowl-
edgment

Figure 11.27
Asynchronous
one way
messaging

A message sender and consumer (or client and server) are more logical views than physical entities in an architecture. An application using a JAXM provider can function in a client as well as service role, meaning it is capable of switching between a message sender and message consumer. An application that does not use a JAXM provider can support only a client role and can send messages only synchronously (such applications are also referred to as *standalone* JAXM clients).

We have looked at five design approaches (two synchronous and three asynchronous). The decision on where and when to use a provider depends on which of the five use cases models the business requirement accurately. Most asynchronous messaging environments can also operate in synchronously if necessary, which explains the popularity of message-oriented middleware as the underlying mechanism. Most businesses work both asynchronously and synchronously, and it is useful to have a single medium that supports both.

For example, a car rental company offering online reservations may choose to process credit cards asynchronously in batches for frequent customers with gold memberships, because bulk authorizations are cheaper. and these customers have established their creditworthiness. It may also choose to authorize cards synchronously for new customers before completing a reservation. It is useful to have a single underlying design that can support both these business requirements, which provider-based architecture offers. It also simplifies application development for architects, because they no longer need to account for different transports based on the business's requirements at a particular time.

> Developing with JAXM

Synchronous Messaging

The SOAP specification does not provide a programming model or even an API for the construction of SOAP messages; it simply defines the XML schema to be used in packaging a SOAP message. The SAAJ specifications and the java.xml .soap package defines objects to construct and deconstruct a SOAP message and send them without the support of a provider. The SAAJ API introduced in Chapter 4 essentially provides a DOM-like tree representation of a SOAP message to developers. Figure 11.28 shows the relationships between the core objects in the javax.xml.soap package and how they model the physical SOAP message.

Let us look at the steps involved on the message sender's side for point-to-point or synchronous XML messaging with JAXM. The steps involved (also shown in Figure 11.29) are remarkably similar to the steps outlined for JMS earlier:

1. Create a `MessageFactory` for creating message objects.

2 Create a `Message` from the message factory.

3. Populate the message with the relevant information and content (such as attachments).

4. Create a `SOAPConnectionFactory`.

5. Create the `SOAPConnection` from the factory.

Figure 11.28
SAAJ model in
the `javax.xml`
`.soap` package

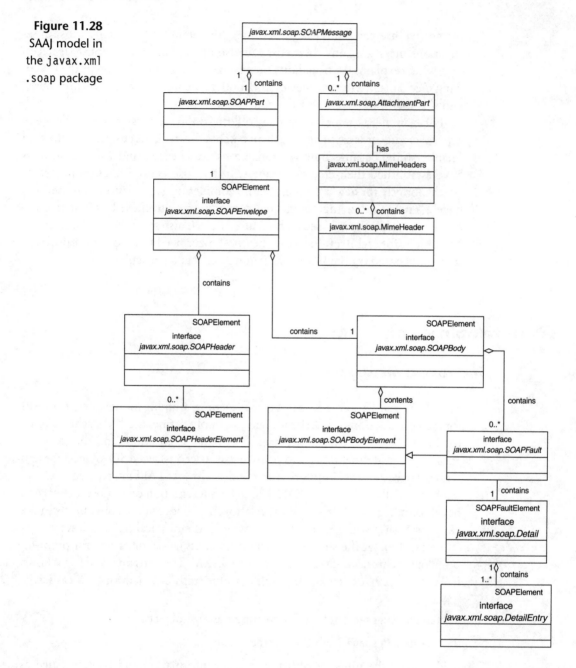

Figure 11.29
Synchronous
messaging

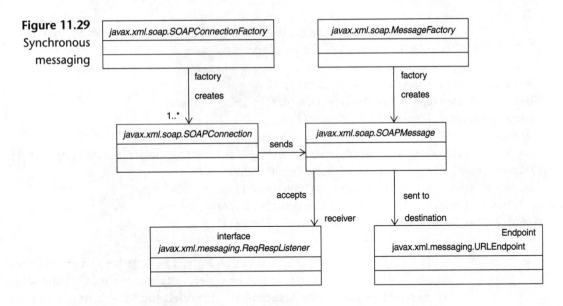

6. Create the Endpoint for the connection.

7. Send the message to the endpoint using the connection and receive the SOAPMessage as the response.

A MessageFactory is a factory to instantiate and create messages. Without a provider, the client uses the default method:

```
MessageFactory mfactory = MessageFactory.newInstance();
SOAPMessage message = mfactory.createMessage();
```

The message object created from the factory contains the logical SAAJ DOM representation of the SOAP message. The SOAPMessage message object above contains

- A SOAPPart object that contains
  - A SOAPEnvelope object that contains
    An empty SOAPHeader object
- An empty SOAPBody object

Once the SOAPMessage has been created, the client can add content to it by accessing the subparts of the envelope:

```
SOAPPart soapPart = message.getSOAPPart();
SOAPEnvelope envelope = soapPart.getEnvelope();
SOAPHeader header = envelope.getHeader();
SOAPBody body = envelope.getBody();
Name name=envelope.createName("PurchaseOrder",  "po","http://www.flutebank.com/xml");
SOAPBodyElement element = body.addBodyElement(name);
Name sendername = envelope.createName("senderid");
SOAPElement symbol = element.addChildElement(sendername);
symbol.addTextNode("myuserid@"+new Date().toString()) ;
```

The payload(s) can be attached as necessary. The code below demonstrates how an XML file representing a purchase order is attached to the SOAP message. As Figure 11.29 shows, the AttachmentPart models the MIME attachments in the physical SOAP message.

```
AttachmentPart ap1 = message.createAttachmentPart();
ap1.setContent(new StreamSource("sample.xml"), "text/xml");
message.addAttachmentPart(ap1);
```

Once the message is ready and available to be processed, it must be sent. To create a connection factory, the SAAJ API's javax.xml.soap.SOAPConnectionFactory class is used, which has a default implementation:

```
SOAPConnectionFactory factory = SOAPConnectionFactory.newInstance();
```

Alternatively, because factories are administered objects (as in JMS), they can be obtained from the JNDI context in the client's runtime, if the vendor supports it. In that case, the code would look something like the following:

```
Hashtable env = new Hashtable();
//set environment properties in
InitialContext ctx = new InitialContext(env);
SOAPConnectionFactory factory = (SOAPConnectionFactory) ctx.lookup(SOAPFACTORY);
```

Once the factory is available, it is used to create the underlying connection. A SOAPConnection represents a point-to-point connection between a sender and a receiver. Note that creating a connection does not imply that a socket has been opened or any underlying network connections have been established, because the destination or *endpoint* has not been configured until now.

```
SOAPConnection con = factory.createConnection();
```

Now that we have created our message, we want to send it, using the connection we made earlier:

```
SOAPConnection connection = factory.createConnection();
URLEndpoint endpoint = new URLEndpoint (url);
SOAPMessage response = connection.call(message, endpoint);
```

The SOAPMessage returned from the above call can either be traversed using the SAAJ methods or just dumped to a stream for debugging response.writeTo(System.out);

Listing 11.5 shows the SOAP message created and sent by JAXM.

Listing 11.5 The SOAP request sent synchronously.

```
POST /flutejaxmsync/syncjaxm HTTP/1.1
Content-Type: multipart/related; type="text/xml";
    boundary="-----=_Part_0_3237557.1029815730110"
Content-Length: 1229
SOAPAction: ""
User-Agent: Java1.3.1_04
Host: 127.0.0.1:9090
Accept: text/html, image/gif, image/jpeg, *; q=.2, */*; q=.2
Connection: keep-alive


------=_Part_0_3237557.1029815730110
Content-Type: text/xml

<?xml version="1.0" encoding="UTF-8"?>
<soap-env:Envelope xmlns:soap-env="http://schemas.xmlsoap.org/soap/envelope/">
<soap-env:Header/>
<soap-env:Body>
        <po:PurchaseOrder xmlns:po="http://www.flutebank.com/schema">
        <senderid>myuserid@Mon Aug 19 23:55:28 EDT 2002</senderid>
        </po:PurchaseOrder>
</soap-env:Body>
</soap-env:Envelope>
```

```
------=_Part_0_3237557.1029815730110
Content-Type: text/xml

<?xml version="1.0" encoding="UTF-8"?>
<purchaseorder xmlns="http://www.flutebank.com/schema" xmlns:xsi=
"http://www.w3.org/2001/XMLSchema-instance" xmlns:po="http://www.flutebank.com/schema"
xsi:schemaLocation="http://www.flutebank.com/schema purchaseorder.xsd">
    <identifier>87 6784365876JHITRYUE</identifier>
    <date>29 October 2002</date>
    <billingaddress>
        <name>John Malkovich</name>
        <street>256 Eight Bit Lane</street>
        <city>Burlington</city>
        <state>MA</state>
        <zip>01803-6326</zip>
    </billingaddress>
    <items>
        <item>
            <quantity>3</quantity>
            <productnumber>229AXH</productnumber>
            <description>High speed photocopier machine with automatic sensors
                                                        </description>
            <unitcost>1939.99</unitcost>
        </item>
        <item>
            <quantity>1</quantity>
            <productnumber>1632</productnumber>
            <description>One box of color toner cartridges</description>
            <unitcost>43.95</unitcost>
        </item>
    </items>
</purchaseorder>
------=_Part_0_3237557.1029815730110--
```

Just as the SOAPMessage was created and populated using the SAAJ API, the response SOAPMessage returned by the service can be parsed and extracted:

```
SOAPPart sp = response.getSOAPPart();
SOAPEnvelope se = sp.getEnvelope();
SOAPBody sb = se.getBody();
Iterator it = sb.getChildElements();
```

```
while (it.hasNext()) {
  SOAPBodyElement bodyElement = (SOAPBodyElement) it.next();
System.out.println(bodyElement.getElementName().getQualifiedName() + "
                      namepace uri=" +bodyElement.getElementName().getURI());
Iterator it2 = bodyElement.getChildElements();
while (it2.hasNext()) {
  SOAPElement element2 = (SOAPElement) it2.next();
  System.out.print(element2.getElementName().getQualifiedName() +" = ");
  System.out.println(element2.getValue());
  }
}
```

The attachments in the messages returned from the server can also be processed, as shown below. Since the attachment is of text/xml type, it maps to a javax.xml.Source type. Table 11.1 shows the three mappings between MIME types and Java objects defined by the SAAJ specifications, which all implementations must support. Though the mappings are a subset of those defined in the JAX-RPC specifications, they follow the same guidelines and use the JavaBeans Activation framework.

```
Iterator attachments = response.getAttachments();
while(attachments.hasNext()){
AttachmentPart part= (AttachmentPart)attachments.next();
System.out.println("Message returned has attachment of type :" +
                                         part.getContentType());
System.out.println("Message returned has attachment content : \n" );
// use a null transformer. See Chapter 9 for details
Transformer nulltransformer =TransformerFactory.newInstance().newTransformer();
nulltransformer.transform((StreamSource)part.getContent(),
                                   new StreamResult(System.out));

}
```

Table 11.1   The MIME Mappings that Must Be Supported by Every SAAJ Implementation

MIME type	Java type
text/plain	java.lang.String
multipart/*	javax.mail.internet.MimeMultipart
text/xml or application/xml	javax.xml.transform.Source

Once the client has been compiled, it can be executed. Note that unlike with JAX-RPC, there is no concept of stubs, DII, or dynamic proxies in messaging. Conceptually, messaging is all about *senders* and *receivers*. Listing 11.6 shows the output from the client.

Listing 11.6   Client-side output

```
C:\webservices>java SyncClient
cid:CorrelationID namepace uri=http://www.flutebank.com/schema
messageid = 9812398ABHCOIUU
timestamp = Tue Aug 20 01:46:47 EDT 2002
Message returned has attachment of type :text/xml
Message returned has attachment content :

<?xml version="1.0" encoding="UTF-8"?>
<invoice xmlns="http://www.officemin.com/schema" xmlns:xsi=
"http://www.w3.org/2001/XMLSchema-instance" xmlns:po="http://www.officemin.com/schema"
xsi:schemaLocation="http://www.officemin.com/schema invoice.xsd">
    <purchaseorder>
        <identifier>87 6784365876JHITRYUE</identifier>
        <date>29 October 2002</date>
    </purchaseorder>
    <items>
        <item>
            <quantity>3</quantity>
            <productnumber>229AXH</productnumber>
            <description>High speed photocopier machine
                        with automatic sensors</description>
            <unitcost>1939.99</unitcost>
        </item>
        <item>
            <quantity>1</quantity>
            <productnumber>1632</productnumber>
            <description>One box of color toner cartridges</description>
            <unitcost>43.95</unitcost>
        </item>
    </items>
    <paymentdetails>
        <invoicenumber>8912737821ATYWER </invoicenumber>
        <currency>USD</currency>
        <total>5864</total>
```

```
        <payableto>officemin.com</payableto>
        <mailingaddress> 64 Bit True Unix Street,
                    Windsor, CT, USA</mailingaddress>
    </paymentdetails>
</invoice>
```

We have looked at how to develop a synchronous client that sends a message to a service. Let us now look at how the message receiver can be implemented.

A developer-written service that exhibits synchronous or request-response behavior must implement the javax.xml.messaging.ReqRespListener interface. The service itself can be deployed as a servlet endpoint or EJB endpoint. We will look at EJBs later in the chapter. For the service to be deployed as a servlet endpoint requires the servlet to implement the javax.xml.messaging.ReqResp-Listener interface, which has one method:

```
public SOAPMessage onMessage(SOAPMessage message);
```

The logic to process the request must be plugged into the implementation of this method, because the implementation receives the incoming SOAP message and returns the response to that message. Developers must still write the code that extracts the SOAPMessage from the incoming HTTP request and invoke this method in their servlet implementations. To save time, the JAXM reference implementation comes with a utility in the form of the javax.xml.messaging .JAXMServlet, which contains this logic and can be extended by developers (giving the appearance that onMessage() is invoked automatically). Note that this is not a part of the JAXM specifications. Vendors are not required to provide this utility, and developers are not required to use it. ▷

Figure 11.30 shows the implementation scheme for a synchronous service. It implements the ReqRespListener and optionally extends JAXMServlet. Listing 11.7 shows the code for the service. Ideally, the XML representing the purchase order would be extracted from the SOAPMessage, and business logic applied to it. This example just returns an invoice document without looking at the contents of the request.

▷   The JAXM reference implementation has been released under the Sun source code community license. Developers can download complete source code from *www.sun.com* and see how the JAXMServlet has been implemented.

Figure 11.30
Implementing
a synchronous
service

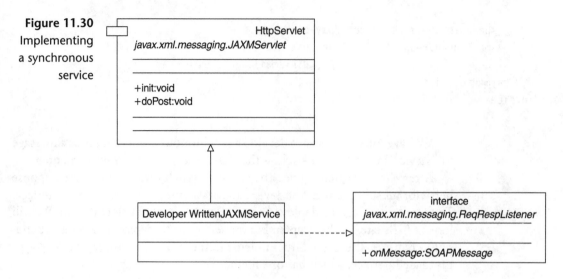

In point-to-point messaging if the client does not receive a response because of a communication error, the server or client cannot recover automatically. The logic for retrying the communication must be built into the client. Request-response services must take this into account, and architects must design a correlation-retry mechanism. This may include schemes such as message initiators sending every request with a unique ID and servers keeping track of the request IDs processed. The PurchaseOrderService example in Listing 11.7 includes some dummy timestamp and ID information in the response it sends back.

Because the service is exposed with a servlet endpoint, it can be deployed in the standard WAR archive format. Listing 11.8 shows the response returned by the service.

Listing 11.7 The synchronous PurchaseOrderService

```
package com.flutebank.jaxmservice;
// imports not shown for brevity
public class PurchaseOrderService extends JAXMServlet implements
                                                ReqRespListener {
    private ServletContext context ;

// Servlet init method
    public void init(ServletConfig servletConfig) throws ServletException {
      super.init(servletConfig);
        context=servletConfig.getServletContext();
    }
    /**
    * SOAP Message containing the purchase order is received, and a SOAP
```

```
     * message containing an invoice is returned
     *
   */
  public SOAPMessage onMessage (SOAPMessage soapMessage) {
        // insert some logic here to process the incoming  message
        // with the purchase order here
        // Then return the invoice
        try{
// create a message to return
        MessageFactory mfactory = MessageFactory.newInstance();
        SOAPMessage message = mfactory.createMessage();
// get the body of the message created
        SOAPPart soap = message.getSOAPPart();
        SOAPEnvelope envelope = soap.getEnvelope();
        SOAPHeader header = envelope.getHeader();
        SOAPBody body = envelope.getBody();
// add some elements to the body
        Name name=envelope.createName("CorrelationID",
                          "cid","http://www.flutebank.com/schema");
        SOAPBodyElement element = body.addBodyElement(name);
        Name messageid = envelope.createName("messageid");
        SOAPElement msg = element.addChildElement(messageid);
        msg.addTextNode("9812398ABHCOIUU") ;
        Name timestamp = envelope.createName("timestamp");
        SOAPElement date = element.addChildElement(timestamp);
        date.addTextNode(new Date().toString()) ;
// add the invoice as an attachment to the message
        AttachmentPart attach = message.createAttachmentPart(
                          new DataHandler(context.getResource
                                    ("/WEB-INF/invoice.xml")));

        attach.setContentType("text/xml");
        message.addAttachmentPart(attach);
        message.saveChanges();
// return the newly create SOAP message with the attachment
        return message;
    }catch(Exception e){
        System.out.println("Exception occured in onMessage() "+e);
        // return the original message in case of a problem.
        return soapMessage;
        }
    }
}
```

Listing 11.8 The response returned by the synchronous PurchaseOrderService

```
HTTP/1.1 200 OK
Content-Type: multipart/related; type="text/xml";
    boundary="----=_Part_1_2588785.1031512962862"
Content-Length: 1636
SOAPAction: ""
Date: Sun, 08 Sep 2002 19:22:42 GMT
Server: Apache Coyote HTTP/1.1 Connector [1.0]


------=_Part_1_2588785.1031512962862
Content-Type: text/xml


<?xml version="1.0" encoding="UTF-8"?>
<soap-env:Envelope xmlns:soap-env="http://schemas.xmlsoap.org/soap/envelope/">
<soap-env:Header/>
 <soap-env:Body>
     <cid:CorrelationID xmlns:cid="http://www.flutebank.com/schema">
             <messageid>9812398ABHCOIUU</messageid>
             <timestamp>Sun Sep 08 15:22:42 EDT 2002</timestamp>
     </cid:CorrelationID>
 </soap-env:Body>
</soap-env:Envelope>
------=_Part_1_2588785.1031512962862
Content-Type: text/xml


<?xml version="1.0" encoding="UTF-8"?>
<!--edited by Sameer Tyagi (none)-->
<invoice xmlns="http://www.officemin.com/schema" xmlns:xsi=
"http://www.w3.org/2001/XMLSchema-instance" xmlns:po="http://www.officemin.com/schema"
xsi:schemaLocation="http://www.officemin.com/schema invoice.xsd">
    <purchaseorder>
        <identifier>87 6784365876JHITRYUE</identifier>
        <date>29 October 2002</date>
    </purchaseorder>
    <items>
        <item>
            <quantity>3</quantity>
            <productnumber>229AXH</productnumber>
            <description>High speed photocopier machine with
                        automatic sensors</description>
```

```
            <unitcost>1939.99</unitcost>
        </item>
        <item>
            <quantity>1</quantity>
            <productnumber>1632</productnumber>
            <description>One box of color toner cartridges</description>
            <unitcost>43.95</unitcost>
        </item>
    </items>
    <paymentdetails>
        <invoicenumber>8912737821ATYWER </invoicenumber>
        <currency>USD</currency>
        <total>5864</total>
        <payableto>officemin.com</payableto>
        <mailingaddress> 64 Bit True Unix Street,
                         Windsor, CT, USA</mailingaddress>
    </paymentdetails>
</invoice>

------=_Part_1_2588785.1031512962862--
```

Asynchronous Messaging

Earlier in the chapter, we discussed the concept of providers. The client-side provider plays a proxying role and accepts the message on behalf of the intended recipients, providing an asynchronous façade to the client application. To send a message asynchronously, a service client must meet two requirements: it *must* use a JAXM provider, and it *must* use a messaging profile with the provider.

If a client does not use a provider to deliver its messages, it is essentially behaving like a synchronous client. As discussed in the MOM topologies, it is not necessary that a provider and its client coexist in the same address space (e.g., process). However, if the provider does not expose itself remotely (e.g., the client API for connecting to the provider is not implemented with the ability to connect to the provider over the network), the client and provider must coexist. This is the case with the reference implementation. The way an application communicates with its provider is vendor-implementation-specific and is not imposed by JAXM.

The core of the JAXM API that relates to asynchronous messaging resides in the javax.xml.messaging package and is shown in Table 11.2.

Table 11.2   Core Interfaces in the `javax.xml.messaging` Package

OnewayListener	An interface for services intended to be consumers of asynchronous messages
ProviderConnection	Represents a connection to a provider
ProviderConnectionFactory	Factory for creating ProviderConnection objects
ProviderMetaData	Provides information about the provider
ReqRespListener	An interface for components intended to be consumers of synchronous messages

Figure 11.31
Asynchronous
messaging

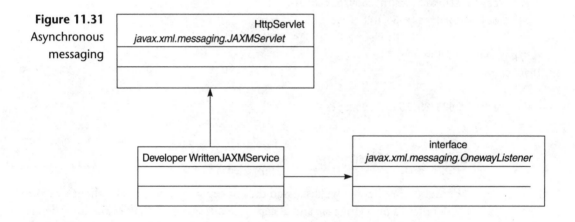

The class diagram in Figure 11.31 shows how a JAXM client can send a message asynchronously using a provider, and the steps involved:

1. Create a connection to the provider.

2. Use the connection to the provider to create messages.

3. Populate the message with the relevant information and content (such as attachments).

4. Send the message to the endpoint, using the connection to the provider.

A connection to the provider is represented by `ProviderConnection` and is obtained using a `ProviderConnectionFactory`. Clients can use the default `Provider-`

ConnectionFactory instantiation mechanism, which will pick up the default configuration. Alternatively, they can use JNDI for the lookup, using a logical name. For JNDI lookups, the `ProviderConnection` factory is configured at deployment time with the relevant information to connect to a particular provider and bound to the JNDI tree in the J2EE container with a logical name. Applications look up the tree using the logical name as a key and get back the instance. (JNDI lookups are a standard technique in J2EE but will work only for J2EE containers that support JNDI, which Tomcat and the Java WSDP do not.) This is analogous to JMS-administered objects and the manner in which `QueueConnectionFactory` and `TopicConnectionFactory` are located.

```
ProviderConnectionFactory providerFactory =
                              ProviderConnectionFactory.newInstance();
// alternate technique
HashMap properties = new HashMap();
properties.put("some property", "some value");
// set other properties.
InitialContext ctx = new InitialContext(properties);
ProviderConnectionFactory providerFactory =(ProviderConnectionFactory)
                    ctx.lookup("java:comp/env/jaxm/providerfactory");
```

The `ProviderConnectionFactory` is used to create the `ProviderConnection`, which represents an active connection to the provider.

```
ProviderConnection  fluteprovider = providerFactory.createConnection();
```

The `ProviderConnection` is a heavyweight reference, because its instantiation might lead to possible network communications and authentication calls with the provider (depending on the topology used). Therefore, keeping the reference longer than necessary will keep those resources blocked (this is analogous to how a JDBC `Connection` is set up). Because of this, the connection should be closed as soon it is not needed. Vendors are free to implement pooling and other optimization techniques for this connection.

Once a `ProviderConnection` has been obtained, it can be used to instantiate one or more `MessageFactory` objects, which in turn can be used to create `SOAPMessage` objects.

```
Messagefactory messageFactory = fluteprovider.createMessageFactory("ebxml");
```

Earlier in the chapter, we talked about the need for messaging profiles. A messaging profile is required for asynchronous delivery by a provider to some eventual destination, because the provider has to know the messaging semantics to actually deliver the message. These are not inherently defined by SOAP. (Note that a MessageFactory can be instantiated only for a particular profile.) If a profile name is not specified, the provider must default to some internal profile that may be vendor–specific. In such cases, the application may not interoperate with other applications that rely on standard profile information.

Once the factory is available, it can be used to generate empty SOAPMessage objects, which are then populated with the message data.

```
SOAPMessage message = messageFactory.createMessage();
```

Typically, the messages created by the factory will either use vendor utility API or be profile-specific vendor-implementation subclasses of SOAPMessage that expose methods to wrap the profile-specific information (such as messaging headers). For example, the reference implementation contains minimal profiles for ebXML messaging ("ebxml") and Web Services Routing Protocol ("soaprp"). The message class corresponding to these profiles are com.sun.xml.messaging .jaxm.ebxml.EbXMLMessageImpl and com.sun.xml.messaging.jaxm.soaprp.SOAP-RPMessageImpl respectively.

```
EbXMLMessageImpl message = (EbXMLMessageImpl)messageFactory.createMessage();
```

This can now be populated with the ebXML-specific headers, using convenient methods to construct relevant XML tags:

```
// set send and receive provider
message.setSender(new Party(from));
message.setReceiver(new Party(to));
message.setCPAId(
           "http://www.flutebank.com/agreements/agreementwithofficemin.xml");
message.setConversationId("www.flute.com/orders/829202");
message.setService(new Service("purchaseorderservice"));
message.setAction("Purchaseorder");
```

Once the message has been created, it can be sent using the connection to the provider that was created earlier.

```
fluteprovider.send(message);
```

Note that this invocation does not return anything; the provider simply accepts the message and delivers it later. The significant difference between sending messages using a provider and using the SOAPConnection discussed earlier is that no endpoint information is passed in the former. The model of "self-addressed messages" that carry the "from-to" information in a standard format as a part of the message is central to the concept of asynchronous messaging. Only self-addressed messages can be routed independently of the infrastructure. For example, the "from-to" address is contained on letters, which does not tie the postal service to a particular train or airplane route.

Let us now look at a detailed messaging example involving asynchronous communication between two organizations. We will continue to use the business use case of flutebank.com and officemin.com already covered with JavaMail and synchronous messaging. Using its JAXM provider, the Flute Bank application sends a purchase order as an ebXML message to OfficeMin asynchronously. The Flute Bank provider takes on the responsibility of delivering the message to the eventual recipient registered with it—in this case, OfficeMin's JAXM provider—which accepts the message on behalf of OfficeMin's Web service. The service processes the message and sends an ebXML message back to Flute Bank later, along with the invoice.

This provider-to-provider communication, where both sides have a role to initiate and are also in a responder mode, is typical of XML messaging across enterprise boundaries. Figure 11.32 shows how such an application can be implemented. Multiple components are involved, and to understand the workings, let us look at each in detail:

- AsynClient. The Flute Bank application that sends a purchase order asynchronously
- PurchaseOrderService. The OfficeMin service that handles the order and sends an invoice to Flute Bank
- CallbackProcessor. The Flute Bank service that asynchronously handles invoices returned by OfficeMin

AsynClient

AsyncClient, shown in Listing 11.9, is the message initiator and is implemented using the guidelines discussed previously for constructing an asynchronous client (Figure 11.33 shows how the mapping is realized). AsyncClient connects to a provider, constructs an ebXML message, and sends it. Not that it does not use any physical destination (URL) anywhere in the code. The mapping of the destination to the physical endpoint is configured in the JAXM provider, using administrative tools such as the console shown in Figure 11.34.

Figure 11.32
Sequence diagram of provider-to-provider communication

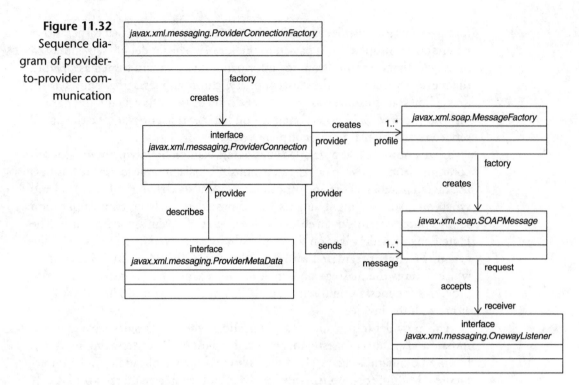

Listing 11.9   An asynchronous message sender

```
package com.flutebank.jaxmservice;

import java.io.*;
import javax.servlet.http.*;
import javax.servlet.*;
import javax.xml.messaging.*;
import javax.xml.soap.*;
import javax.activation.DataHandler;
// ebXML package
import com.sun.xml.messaging.jaxm.ebxml.*;

public class AsyncClient extends HttpServlet {
    private ProviderConnection fluteprovider;
    private MessageFactory messageFactory;
    // source and destination endpoints for messages
    private String from = "http://www.flutebank.com/ordersupplies";
```

```
    private String to = "http://www.officemin.com/processorders";
    private ServletContext context;

    public void init(ServletConfig servletConfig) throws ServletException {
        try {
            super.init(servletConfig);
            context = servletConfig.getServletContext();
            ProviderConnectionFactory providerFactory =
                            ProviderConnectionFactory.newInstance();
            fluteprovider = providerFactory.createConnection();
            ProviderMetaData metaData = fluteprovider.getMetaData();
            messageFactory = fluteprovider.createMessageFactory("ebxml");
        } catch (JAXMException e) {
            // handle exception in connecting to provider
            System.out.println("Exception >> " + e);
        }
    }


/**
  * Invoked from browser when client makes a request. The method constructs
  * an ebXML message containing a purchaseorder.xml as the attachment. It
  * then sends the message to its JAXM provider, which sends the message to
  * officemin.com's JAXM provider, based on a URI to URL mapping.
  * The flutebank.com JAXM provider has an endpoint mapping that maps the URI
  * http://www.officemin.com/processorders  to the URL
  * http://machineB:8081/jaxm-provider/receiver/ebxml
  */
public void service(HttpServletRequest request,
                    HttpServletResponse response) throws ServletException {
    // create ebXML message for fluteprovider
    try {
        // create ebXML message
EbXMLMessageImpl message = (EbXMLMessageImpl)messageFactory.createMessage();
        // set send and receive provider
message.setSender(new Party(from));
message.setReceiver(new Party(to));
message.setCPAId(
        "http://www.flutebank.com/agreements/agreementwithofficemin.xml");
message.setConversationId("www.flute.com/orders/829202");
```

```
  message.setService(new Service("purchaseorderservice"));
  message.setAction("Purchaseorder");
// create and add an attachment to the message
  AttachmentPart attachment = message.createAttachmentPart(
        new DataHandler(context.getResource("/WEB-INF/purchaseorder.xml")));
  attachment.setContentType("text/xml");
  message.addAttachmentPart(attachment);
  message.saveChanges();
// send message from fluteprovider to Web service
  fluteprovider.send(message);
// display HTML confirmation message to client
  ServletOutputStream out = response.getOutputStream();
  out.println("<html>");
  out.println("<body> <b>Order placed</b> <hr> <pre>");
  message.writeTo(out);
  out.println("</pre></body></html>");
  out.flush();
  } catch (Exception e) {
        // handle exception in using message provider
      System.out.println("Exception in service " + e);
    }
  }


/**
  * Servlets destroy method. Typically used to release any resources
  */
    public void destroy(){
        try{
            fluteprovider.close();
        }catch (JAXMException e) {
            System.out.println("Exception in service " + e);
        }
    }
}
```

PurchaseOrderService

The JAXM service to receive messages, PurchaseOrderService, is similar to the synchronous version developed earlier. The significant difference is that the servlet realizing the asynchronous service does not return a message. It also implements the javax.xml.messaging.OnewayListener interface, which contains a

Figure 11.33 Sequence diagram of provider-to-provider communication

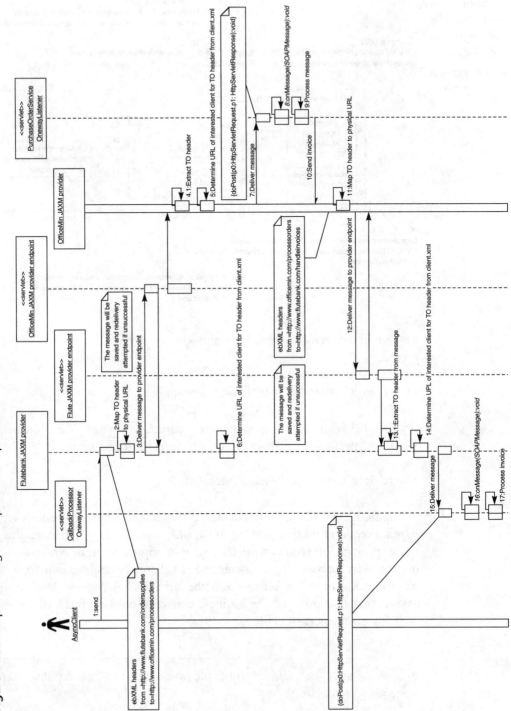

Figure 11.34
JAXM Provider
Administration in
the reference
implementation

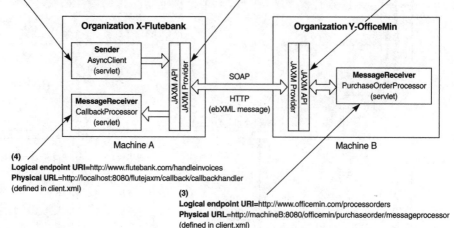

(1) Logical URIs
from=http://www.flutebank.com/ordersupplies
to=http://www.officemin.com/processorders

(2) Provider mapping
Endpoint URI=http://www.officemin.com/processorders
Physical URL=http://machineY:8081/jaxm-provider/receiver/ebxml

(4) Provider mapping
Endpoint URI=http://www.flutebank.com/handleinvoices
Physical URL=http://machineX:8081/jaxm-provider/receiver/ebxml

(4)
Logical endpoint URI=http://www.flutebank.com/handleinvoices
Physical URL=http://localhost:8080/flutejaxm/callback/callbackhandler
(defined in client.xml)

(3)
Logical endpoint URI=http://www.officemin.com/processorders
Physical URL=http://machineB:8080/officemin/purchaseorder/messageprocessor
(defined in client.xml)

single method invoked when the message is delivered to the service by the provider:

```
public void onMessage(SOAPMessage message);
```

The behavior and signature are identical to its JMS counterpart, `javax.jms.MessageListener` interface, which has a similar method:

```
public void onMessage(Message message);
```

Figure 11.35 shows an implementation scheme for an asynchronous service. Again, keep in mind that `JAXMServlet` is only a utility class, and extending it is not a specification requirement. The sample implementation *acts in dual roles,* both as a server processing messages and as a client, by sending an invoice using its own JAXM provider. When doing the latter, its behavior is identical to the `AsyncClient` that initiated the business conversation. Listing 11.10 shows the code for `PurchaseOrderService`. ▷

▷   A JAXM service is required to handle one-way or request-response messages but not both.

Figure 11.35
Realizing an
asynchronous
JAXM service

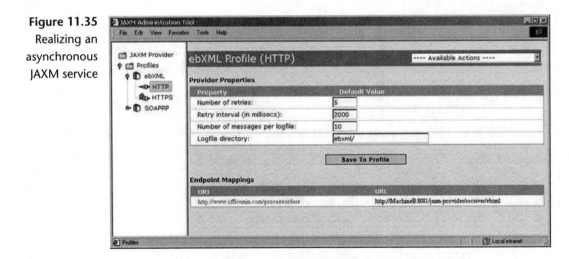

Listing 11.10   The PurchaseOrderService handles asynchronous messages and also acts as a client.

```
package com.supplier.messageprocessor;

import java.io.*;
import javax.servlet.http.*;
import javax.servlet.*;
import javax.xml.messaging.*;
import javax.xml.soap.*;
// ebXML packages
import com.sun.xml.messaging.jaxm.ebxml.*;
import java.io.PrintWriter;
import javax.xml.transform.stream.StreamSource;
import javax.activation.*;

/**
 * This JAXM service on officemin.com receives an ebXML message containing a purchase
 *                                        order from the sender, flutebank.com.
 * It responds to the sender asynchronously with an invoice.
 * It sends the message to a   URI http://www.flutebank.com/handleinvoices that is
 *                                        registered in officemin.com's provider
 *  * and maps to a URL http://machineA:8080/
 */
public class PurchaseOrderService extends JAXMServlet implements OnewayListener {
    private ProviderConnection officeminprovider;
    private MessageFactory messageFactory;
```

```java
    // source and destination endpoints for messages
    private String from = "http://www.officemin.com/processorders";
    private String to = "http://www.flutebank.com/handleinvoices";
    // setup connection to message provider
    private ServletContext context;

    public void init(ServletConfig servletConfig) throws ServletException {
        try {
            super.init(servletConfig);
            context = servletConfig.getServletContext();
            // establish connection to provider
            ProviderConnectionFactory providerFactory =
                            ProviderConnectionFactory.newInstance();
            officeminprovider = providerFactory.createConnection();
        } catch (JAXMException e) {
            // handle exception in connecting to provider
            System.out.println("Exception >> " + e);
        }
    } // end method init

/**
 * This is the method called by officemin.com's JAXM provider when
 * it receives an ebXML message marked with a destination that
 * matches this client's URI - http://www.officemin.com/processorders
 * The client specifies its URI in the client.xml file. This method receives
 * the message and prints the attachment (which
 * is the purchaseorder.xml sent by flutebank) to the console. It then sends
 * a message to flutebank.com (through
 * the mapping defined in officemin.com's provider to flutebank.com's provider)
 * containing an invoice.xml as the attachment. The officeMin.com JAXM provider
 * contains a URI to URL mapping that maps the URI
 * http://www.flutebank.com/handleinvoices to the URL
 * http://machineA:8081/jaxm-provider/receiver/ebxml
 * which corresponds to the URL for the JAXM provider on flutebank.com
 */
public void onMessage(SOAPMessage soapMessage) {
 try {
 // insert some business logic to process the message
 // for now we just dump it to the console and a file
    soapMessage.writeTo(System.out);
    soapMessage.writeTo(new FileOutputStream("/temp/receivedonofficemax.txt"));
```

```
   // send an ebXML. In this case this service is now acting in a client role
      sendMessageBack();
   } catch (Exception e) {
           System.out.println("Exception in PoService " + e);
      }
    }

/** Private method for constructing and sending an ebXML message
 * to flutebank.com's provider
 */
private void sendMessageBack() {
  try {
      // create ebXML message for officeminprovider
   messageFactory = officeminprovider.createMessageFactory("ebxml");
   // create ebXML message
   EbXMLMessageImpl message = (EbXMLMessageImpl)messageFactory.createMessage();
   // set send and receive provider
   message.setSender(new Party(from));
   message.setReceiver(new Party(to));
// set other ebXML message headers
message.setCPAId("http://www.officemin.com/agreements/agreementwithflute.xml");
    message.setConversationId("www.flute.com/orders/829202");
    message.setService(new Service("invoiceservice"));
    message.setAction("Invoice");

// Add the attachment with an invoice
   AttachmentPart attach = message.createAttachmentPart(
               (new DataHandler(context.getResource("/WEB-INF/invoice.xml"))));
   attach.setContentType("text/xml");
   message.addAttachmentPart(attach);
   message.saveChanges();
//send message from officeminprovider to Web service
  officeminprovider.send(message);
  } catch (Exception e) {
       System.out.println("Exception in PoService " + e);
     }
  }// end sendMessage

/** Servlets destroy method
 */
public void destroy(){
```

```
    try{
        officeminprovider.close();
        }catch (JAXMException e) {
            System.out.println("Exception in service " + e);
        }
    }
}
}
```

CallbackProcessor

The third component is the CallbackProcessor service, which is deployed along with AsyncClient on Flute Bank's servers. AsyncClient simply sends the message without expecting any reply. From a business exchange perspective, however, the recipient may need to send a message back with the response—that is, the "Asynchronous messaging with response" or "Asynchronous messaging with acknowledgment" pattern discussed earlier in Figures 11.25 and 11.26. Listing 11.11 shows the code for CallbackProcessor that implements the OneWayListener and simply displays the attachments (i.e., the invoice) for now.

Listing 11.11   The CallbackProcessor service on flutebank.com

```
package com.flutebank.jaxmservice;

import java.io.*;
import javax.servlet.http.*;
import javax.servlet.*;
import javax.xml.messaging.*;
import javax.xml.soap.*;

import javax.xml.transform.stream.*;
import javax.xml.transform.*;
import java.util.Iterator;

/**Class to handle the asynchronous returns from officemin.com's JAXM provider
 * installed on a different machine on the network. officemin.com received the
 * purchaseorder.xml sent by flutebank.com and responds asynchronously
 * with an invoice.xml to the sender (flutebank.com). This client is registered
 * with flutebank.com's JAXM provider to handle these messages.
 */
public class CallbackProcessor extends JAXMServlet implements OnewayListener {
```

```java
    public void init(ServletConfig servletConfig) throws ServletException {
        try {
            super.init(servletConfig);
            ProviderConnectionFactory providerFactory =
                                ProviderConnectionFactory.newInstance();
            ProviderConnection fluteprovider =
                                providerFactory.createConnection();
            ProviderMetaData metaData = fluteprovider.getMetaData();
        } catch (JAXMException e) {
            // handle exception in connecting to provider
            System.out.println("Exception >> " + e);
        }
    }


/**
 * Method  from OneWayListener interface. Implemented by this class for
 * receiving callbacks. Notice the void return. Called by superclass during
 * its service method. It dumps the entire message to
 * /temp/callbackreceived received.txt file and also shows the attachment in
 * the message (invoice.xml) on the console
 * @param message, the SOAPMessage object received
 */
public void onMessage(SOAPMessage message) {
  try {
    message.writeTo(new FileOutputStream("/temp/callbackreceivedonflute.txt"));
    Iterator attachments = message.getAttachments();
    while(attachments.hasNext()){
        AttachmentPart part= (AttachmentPart)attachments.next();
    // use a null transformer for dumping attachment to console.
    // See Chapter 9 for details
    Transformer nulltransformer =
                        TransformerFactory.newInstance().newTransformer();
     nulltransformer.transform((StreamSource)part.getContent(),
                                        new StreamResult(System.out));
    }
  } catch (Exception e) {
        System.out.println("Exception occurred in onMessage" + e);
    }
  }
}
```

We have not covered an important deployment detail. An asynchronous JAXM client application consists of one or more Web components deployed in the servlet container. Java WSDP uses an XML descriptor that accompanies each service and resides in WEB-INF/classes. This descriptor contains a mapping of a logical endpoint (URI) and a physical endpoint (URL) that describe any services that act as *clients to the provider* and receive messages. For example, the descriptor for Flute Bank looks like this:

```
<?xml version="1.0" encoding="ISO-8859-1"?>
<!DOCTYPE ClientConfig
    PUBLIC "-//Sun Microsystems, Inc.//DTD JAXM Client//EN"
    "http://java.sun.com/xml/dtds/jaxm_client_1_0.dtd">
<ClientConfig>
    <Endpoint> http://www.flutebank.com/handleinvoices  </Endpoint>
    <CallbackURL>
              http://MachineA:8080/flutejaxm/callback/callbackhandler
    </CallbackURL>

    <Provider>
      <URI>http://java.sun.com/xml/jaxm/provider</URI>
      <URL>http://127.0.0.1:8081/jaxm-provider/sender</URL>
    </Provider>
</ClientConfig>
```

A similar descriptor must be deployed on the OfficeMin server. These mappings correspond to items 3 and 4 in Figure 11.33. To help the reader visualize the message exchange, Listings 11.12 and 11.13 show the underlying ebXML messages transmitted on the wire.

Listing 11.12   The ebXML message sent from Flute Bank to OfficeMin

```
------=_Part_3_3866500.1031591037579
             Content-Type: text/xml

<?xml version="1.0" encoding="UTF-8"?>
<soap-env:Envelope xmlns:soap-env="http://schemas.xmlsoap.org/soap/envelope/">
<soap-env:Header>
    <eb:MessageHeader xmlns:eb=http://www.ebxml.org/namespaces/messageHeader
        eb:version="1.0" soap-env:mustUnderstand="1">
        <eb:From>
            <eb:PartyId eb:type="URI">
                http://www.flutebank.com/ordersupplies
```

```
            </eb:PartyId>
        </eb:From>
        <eb:To>
            <eb:PartyId eb:type="URI">
                http://www.officemin.com/processorders
            </eb:PartyId>
        </eb:To>
    <eb:CPAId>
                http://www.flutebank.com/agreements/agreementwithofficemin.xml
    </eb:CPAId>
        <eb:ConversationId>www.flute.com/orders/829202</eb:ConversationId>
        <eb:Service eb:type="">purchaseorderservice</eb:Service>
        <eb:Action>Purchaseorder</eb:Action>
        <eb:MessageData>
            <eb:MessageId>
                    89fcfba5-fac8-4ddd-94b1-ba74339d42de
                </eb:MessageId>
                <eb:Timestamp>1031591106992</eb:Timestamp>
        </eb:MessageData>
    </eb:MessageHeader>
</soap-env:Header>
<soap-env:Body/>
</soap-env:Envelope>
-------=_Part_3_3866500.1031591037579
Content-Type: text/xml

<?xml version="1.0" encoding="UTF-8"?>
<purchaseorder xmlns="http://www.flutebank.com/schema" xmlns:xsi=
"http://www.w3.org/2001/XMLSchema-instance" xmlns:po="http://www.flutebank.com/schema"
            xsi:schemaLocation="http://www.flutebank.com/schema purchaseorder.xsd">
    <identifier>87 6784365876JHITRYUE</identifier>
    <date>29 October 2002</date>
    <billingaddress>
        <name>FluteBank Inc</name>
        <street>256 Eight Bit Lane</street>
        <city>Burlington</city>
        <state>MA</state>
        <zip>01803-6326</zip>
    </billingaddress>
    <items>
        <item>
```

```
            <quantity>3</quantity>
            <productnumber>229AXH</productnumber>
            <description>High speed photocopier machine with automatic sensors
                                                      </description>
            <unitcost>1939.99</unitcost>
        </item>
        <item>
            <quantity>1</quantity>
            <productnumber>1632</productnumber>
            <description>One box of color toner cartridges</description>
            <unitcost>43.95</unitcost>
        </item>
    </items>
</purchaseorder>
------=_Part_3_3866500.1031591037579--
```

Listing 11.13   The ebXML message sent from OfficeMin to Flute Bank

```
------=_Part_8_176822.1031591108715
Content-Type: text/xml


<?xml version="1.0" encoding="UTF-8"?>
    <soap-env:Envelope xmlns:soap-env="http://schemas.xmlsoap.org/soap/envelope/">
    <soap-env:Header>
    <eb:MessageHeader xmlns:eb="http://www.ebxml.org/namespaces/messageHeader"
                                       eb:version="1.0" soap-env:mustUnderstand="1">
    <eb:From>
        <eb:PartyId eb:type="URI">http://www.officemin.com/processorders</eb:PartyId>
    </eb:From>
    <eb:To>
        <eb:PartyId eb:type="URI">http://www.flutebank.com/handleinvoices</eb:PartyId>
    </eb:To>
    <eb:CPAId>http://www.officemin.com/agreements/agreementwithflute.xml</eb:CPAId>
    <eb:ConversationId>www.flute.com/orders/829202</eb:ConversationId>
    <eb:Service eb:type="">invoiceservice</eb:Service>
    <eb:Action>Invoice</eb:Action>
    <eb:MessageData>
        <eb:MessageId>687f2de1-586a-4391-94f9-c9795a6dd0b4</eb:MessageId>
        <eb:Timestamp>1031591037579</eb:Timestamp></eb:MessageData>
    </eb:MessageHeader>
</soap-env:Header>
```

```
<soap-env:Body/>
</soap-env:Envelope>
------=_Part_8_176822.1031591108715
Content-Type: text/xml

<?xml version="1.0" encoding="UTF-8"?>
<!--edited by Sameer Tyagi (none)-- >
<invoice xmlns="http://www.officemin.com/schema" xmlns:xsi=
"http://www.w3.org/2001/XMLSchema-instance" xmlns:po="http://www.officemin.com/schema"
xsi:schemaLocation="http://www.officemin.com/schema invoice.xsd">
    <purchaseorder>
        <identifier>87 6784365876JHITRYUE</identifier>
        <date>29 October 2002</date>
    </purchaseorder>
    <items>
        <item>
            <quantity>3</quantity>
            <productnumber>229AXH</productnumber>
            <description>High speed photocopier machine with automatic sensors
                                            </description>
            <unitcost>1939.99</unitcost>
        </item>
        <item>
            <quantity>1</quantity>
            <productnumber>1632</productnumber>
            <description>One box of color toner cartridges</description>
            <unitcost>43.95</unitcost>
        </item>
    </items>
    <paymentdetails>
        <invoicenumber>8912737821ATYWER </invoicenumber>
        <currency>USD</currency>
        <total>5864</total>
        <payabletoo>officemin.com</payabletoo>
        <mailingaddress> 64 Bit True Unix Street, Windsor, CT,
                        USA</mailingaddress>
    </paymentdetails>
</invoice>

 ------=_Part_8_176822.1031591108715--
```

JAXM and EJB 2.1

The EJB 2.1 specifications developed under the JCP as JSR-153 are a required part of the J2EE 1.4 platform and define how a message-driven EJB can realize a JAXM service. A message-driven bean (MDB) was initially intended to be a consumer of JMS messages from queues and topics sent from JMS clients. A message-driven bean is completely decoupled from any clients, in the sense that a client cannot access a message-driven bean through its EJB interfaces. Message-driven beans do not have a home, local home, or remote or local interface. They are intended to receive messages and serve as an abstraction layer for asynchronous processing in J2EE. Message-driven beans are completely stateless, in the sense that they hold no conversational state. Therefore, multiple instances of the bean can process multiple messages concurrently.

Based on the same lines as its servlet counterpart, the message-driven bean can implement the `javax.xml.messaging.ReqRespListener` or the `javax.xml.messaging.OnewayListener` interface, which specifies synchronous or asynchronous behavior for the EJB respectively. The advantage of using an EJB as the listener is that it leverage the transactional services of the EJB container upon receipt of the message. ▷

▷   BizTalk is a Microsoft messaging and orchestration product for Windows 2000 that enables B2B messaging using SOAP/XML, flat files, and EDI.

- The BizTalk Orchestration Designer is a graphic orchestration tool based on Visio, for designing and defining the business processes and messages exchanged using XLANG schedules. Developers do not need to write code to bind the business processes together or the implementation that holds them together, only the individual components that handle the specialized business logic.

- The BizTalk editor helps create XML schema definitions for the messages exchanged in the business process.

- The BizTalk Mapper can then be used to configure the BizTalk Messaging Services for these documents.

The code below shows the Flute Bank purchase order request as a BizTalk message. The SOAP headers contain descriptions about the sender and destination (to-from), document identifiers (`sentAt`, `expiresAt`, `topic`), business process identifiers, delivery services, and so on. The significant difference between this message structure and the ebXML messages shown earlier is that the business document is sent in the body rather than as an attachment.

At the time of writing, EJB 2.1 specifications were in proposed final draft state.

```
<SOAP-ENV:Envelope
        xmlns:SOAP-ENV=http://schemas.xmlsoap.org/soap/envelope/
        xmlns:xsi="http://www.w3.org/1999/XMLSchema-instance">
<SOAP-ENV:Header>
 <eps:endpoints SOAP-ENV:mustUnderstand="1"
            xmlns:eps="http://schemas.biztalk.org/btf-2-0/endpoints"
            xmlns:agr="http://www.trading-agreements.org/types/">
  <eps:to>
    <eps:address xsi:type="agr:department">Accounting </eps:address>
  </eps:to>
  <eps:from>
    <eps:address xsi:type="agr:organization">Flute Bank</eps:address>
  </eps:from>
 </eps:endpoints>
 <prop:properties SOAP-ENV:mustUnderstand="1"
            xmlns:prop="http://schemas.biztalk.org/btf-2-0/properties">
      <prop:identity>
            uuid:74b9f5d0-33fb-4a81-b02b-5b760641c1d6
      </prop:identity>
      <prop:sentAt>2002-09-14T03:00:00+08:00</prop:sentAt>
      <prop:expiresAt>2003-12-30T04:00:00+08:00</prop:expiresAt>
      <prop:topic>
            http://www.flutebank.com/schema purchaseorder.xsd
      </prop:topic>
 </prop:properties>
</SOAP-ENV:Header>

<SOAP-ENV:Body>
  <purchaseorder xmlns="http://www.flutebank.com/schema"
            xmlns:xsi="http://www.w3.org/2001/XMLSchema-instance"
            xmlns:po="http://www.flutebank.com/schema"
            xsi:schemaLocation="http://www.flutebank.com/schema
                                               purchaseorder.xsd">
<!--Other elements and data from the purchase
   order, as in previous examples-->
  </purchaseorder>
</SOAP-ENV:Body>
</SOAP-ENV:Envelope>
```

Interoperability

Two parties exchanging business messages using disparate hardware and software platforms who wish to interoperate must agree on the following:

- A means to specify, package, publish, and exchange both structured and unstructured information across application or enterprise boundaries
- Application-level communication protocols for communicating this information
- Mechanisms for securing messages for integrity, privacy, and nonrepudiation.

Because the messages are structured in XML, passed in a standard format based on the SOAP specification, and use a standard protocol such as HTTP, message senders and consumers are *somewhat* interoperable with each other. A JAXM service must be able to consume SOAP 1.1 with attachment messages. The service is unaware of the source of the messages and could be generated by an application using any technology.

However, the larger picture remains. Both parties have to agree upon and understand the structure of the information in a business context as well as the semantics of *how* the exchange takes place. This can be achived only by agreeing on the messaging profile layered on top of messaging providers. As long as the client and the service agree on the profile, they do not necessarily need to use the same SOAP provider or even be written in the same language. Only the packaging of the message (i.e., the SOAP envelope) must be standardized. Figure 11.37 shows a possible interoperability scenario. For a JAXM client or service to interoperate with a service or client using a different provider, the parties must use the same transport bindings (the same transport protocol, such as HTTP) and the same profile in constructing the SOAP message being sent.

▷ What Is Right for Me—JAXM or JAX-RPC?

A question commonly asked by architects while developing distributed applications is centered around the guidelines for using synchronous/asynchronous communication or JAX-RPC/JAXM. Typically, this mutates into the traditional and unproductive RPC-versus-MOM argument. In reality, neither messaging nor RPC is better. Each plays a different but significant role and is relevant to Web services architecture. ▷

Figure 11.36
JAXM,
JAX-RPC, and
relationship
to SAAJ

Figure 11.37
JAXM
interoperability
scenarios

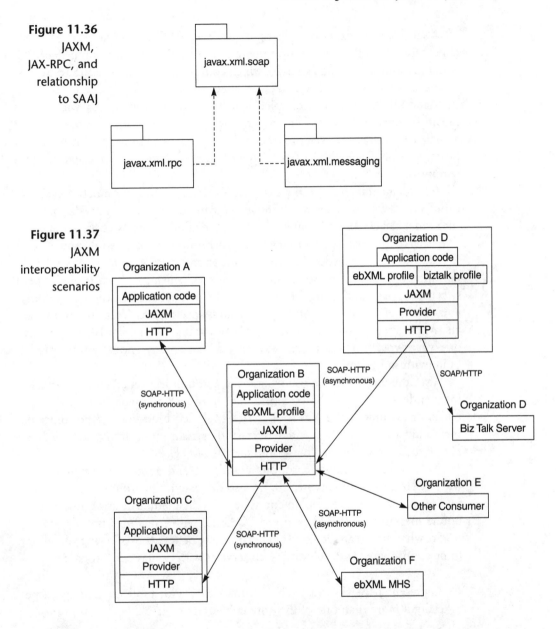

▷ Both JAXM and JAX-RPC use the **javax.xml.soap** package or SAAJ and use SOAP 1.1 with Attachments. JAXM supports asynchronous, document–oriented, reliable messaging, with support for messaging profiles. JAX-RPC supports synchronous procedure invocations.

A successful realization of the tightly coupled RPC-driven model is *n*-tier architecture, where the presentation tier (e.g., a servlet) communicates using RPC with the business tier (e.g., an EJB), which communicates with the EIS resources on the backend. Microsoft's DNA is architecturally similar to ASPs and COM+. In essence, RPC systems are coupled, synchronous, and usually deal with multiple fine-grained operations (remember, a single SOAP message can contain only a single RPC call). However, this does not mean that everything synchronous can be implemented *only* with JAX-RPC. Recall how point-to-point messaging is synchronous.

A fundamental concept in messaging is that communication between applications is *asynchronous* and via some *middleware*. Once a message is dispatched, the sender can continue about its business; the middlware takes care of delivery. The reply to that message, if any, arrives asynchronously and possibly much later.

Another aspect needed for successful communication is reliability though guaranteed delivery. The store-and-forward mechanism, where a provider persists the message until it has been successfully delivered, offers high availability and quality of service capabilities for business applications. This does not mean all asynchronous applications *have* to use messaging. In Chapter 10, we saw how one-way invocations can be dispatched and how asynchronous systems can be built (with some work).

Also, the underlying transport and the communication styles are mutually independent. JAX-RPC–based blocking or nonblocking invocations (either encoded or document style) as well as JAX-M–based blocking and nonblocking messaging can be implemented over both synchronous transports, such as HTTP, and asynchronous transports, such as SMTP.

We have discussed synchronous messaging and asynchronous messaging with JAXM earlier. In Chapter 10, we also discussed synchronous and one-way invocation and how to implement asynchronous communication using compound messages. Both APIs support SOAP 1.1 with Attachments.

So, what should architects use? In general, we believe the following guidelines to be appropriate for developing Web services with the Java API today:

1. At present, JAX-RPC should be a primary choice for application design, especially if more than one of the criteria below is met:

    • The application design is based around synchronous behavior.
    • The application design can support a blocking call.
    • File-and-forget *invocation* can suffice.
    • The service must be exposed and published in registries. JAXM now and by itself offers no support in this area.
    • Multiple recipients for a single invocation are not required.

- Document-centric communication is required. Given the current state of various choreography and orchestration specifications, vendor support, and the assumption that most service consumers will reside in J2EE-capable containers that are themselves capable of hosting JAX-RPC endpoints, we believe applications-based compound message exchanges can be architected with JAX-RPC using attachments. There is no doubt that doing so involves a greater degree of complexity and design.

2. Use JAXM with a messaging profile such as ebXML when

   - Asynchronous messaging is required and the message exchange in a business context is closely associated with reliability and guaranteed delivery, possibly to multiple recipients. Applications can be architected with JAX-RPC for asynchronous behavior using compound messages, but the *store-and-forward* services offered by a messaging profile-provider combination must be developed by architects. In Chapter 10, we briefly discussed a server-side architecture that used such an approach.

   - The application design is centered around callbacks, long-lived business transactions (e.g., spanning days), or a conversational message exchange model.

3. Using JAXM without a provider.

   - We do not believe this is a viable deployment for applications (on the client or server role), because it dictates synchronous behavior for which JAX-RPC is better suited.

4. Using JAXM as an interface to JMS.

   - One approach to achieving reliable, asynchronous messaging is to provide a reliable messaging protocol at the SOAP level, such as ebXML. (See Figure 11.38.) Another approach is to use a higher level of abstraction, such as JMS, for its guaranteed delivery semantics. We discussed SOAP over JMS earlier in the chapter. In fact, the first generation of JAXM implementations are from JMS vendors such as Sun ONE MQ, BEA, and Sonic MQ, who have chosen the logical route of exposing their existing JMS messaging bus and infrastructure, using one of the following techniques from a high level:

     - Using SAAJ and enhancing the transport layer to support HTTP. This combination gives service consumers asynchronous capabilities. It also provides JMS benefits, such as guaranteed delivery, reliability, and scalability of the MOM transport, and works around the firewall issue.

     - Exposing JMS destinations as SOAP services and using the JAX-RPC Call API to invoke them asynchronously from the clients.

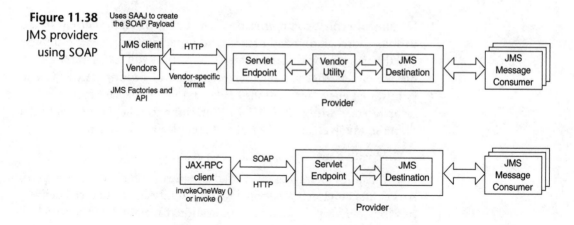

Figure 11.38 JMS providers using SOAP

In the former approach, the wire-level message format and service implementation are specific to the vendor implementation. The latter is closer to the JAXM model, in that even though the server role is tied to a particular vendor implementation, the clients are not, and the service can be described as a traditional JAX-RPC service using WSDL.

> Summary

Pieces in the JAXM puzzle are still missing. For example, JAXM does not place any requirements on message security. En route encryption of message content is considered a provider implementation detail (e.g., HTTPs, PGP, or S/MIME). JAXM also has no requirements for authentication of clients to the JAXM providers.

Nor does JAXM specify the means to describe a JAXM service. WSDL does not suffice for messaging, because it cannot conveniently describe messaging conversations (as, for example, the ebXML CPP/CPA can). Nor does JAXM define any data types or relation to the data types defined by JAX-RPC.

JAXM is the Java community's first kick at the can for XML messaging. Like any new specification, it will evolve and must gain vendor acceptance. There is a belief in the community that JMS should have been extended to handle XML/SOAP payloads for asynchronous messaging instead of developing a new API such as JAXM *(www.jcp.org/jsr/results/67-15-1.jsp)*.

However, with the move to service-oriented architecture, architects are striving to reach the outer edges of their enterprise boundaries. Simple interfaces such as JAXM provide a convenient mechanism for exchanging information with business partners. We believe JAXM is not just another event service and that in combination with messaging profiles such as ebXML, it gives a viable, provider-centric abstraction—where developers must work with and worry about the client and service and allow the vendor's provider software to do the legwork. We believe JAXM is a solution that businesses and architects can rely on for building XML/SOAP-based asynchronous messaging applications.

Chapter {12}

JAXR

In Chapter 2, we looked at the role of registries in service-oriented architectures. The Java API for XML Registries (JAXR) allows Java applications to communicate and interact with service registries and repositories for Web services. As corporations begin to develop an increasing number of services for consumption by business partners, or even internally within their organizations, they need a standard API to undertake this task of interacting with the registries. Using a vendor-, protocol-, or implementation-specific API for this purpose couples the Web service to the vendor implementation.

JAXR is a standard extension API which, like the other XML APIs, has been developed by the collaborative effort of the community as part of the Java Community Process under JSR-93, which became a final specification in April 2002. The JAXR reference implementation is included in the JAX pack and is also packaged with JWSDP.

> Registries and Repositories

Before we look at JAXR, let us revisit some of the concepts regarding registries introduced in Chapter 6. A naming service is a critical building block in an enterprise network. It allows names to be associated with objects and objects to be located by name. For example, a Domain Name Service (DNS) holds a mapping between a domain name and an IP address. When queried for *www.webservicesarchitecture.com,* it returns the IP address 66.45.57.100. A phone book is an example of a naming service where listings are a little more organized by name and, in the yellow pages, by category (lawyers, movers, restaurants, etc.)

A registry is a special form of naming service. It not only allows such a lookup but also allows entities, objects, and so on to be *registered* with it. The first registry and lookup API any Java developer comes across are the RMI registry and JNDI API.

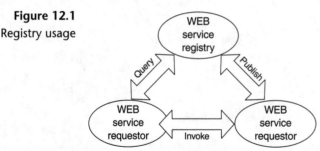

Figure 12.1
Registry usage

Let's examine what happens within an RMI registry. Developers create a remote object and publish it in the registry, by associating it with a name. Other applications use the JNDI API to query that registry for the name and get a remote reference (or stub) back for the object.

A registry in the context of Web services serves essentially the same purpose. It gives applications and businesses a central point to store information about their Web services. It also facilitates consumption of these Web services by giving clients the ability to query and retrieve details about the business, the services offered, and details about the services, such as how and where to invoke them (Figure 12.1).

Every registry has an *information model* or domain object model that business applications develop. An information model is a detailed schema that lays out the blueprint for the registry. It provides information about the type of data that can be stored and how that data is organized in the registry. It is important to understand that the information model does not represent the actual content stored in the registry but the logical metadata for that content. The content itself (e.g., the WSDL describing the service) is stored in a repository, which serves as an implementation detail under the registry.

A registry for Web services also defines a standard set of services it provides. These services are themselves exposed as Web services. For example, well-defined SOAP requests define the interactions involved in querying and publishing to the registry.

JAXR Architecture

At present, two dominant industry standards for Web service registries are the registry as defined by the UDDI specifications and the registry and repository as defined by the ebXML specifications. Each of these standards defines its information model and a set of registry services; however, Java developers need a standard API to access these heterogeneous registries from applications and services developed in Java. This is where JAXR plays a significant role. It provides a layer of abstraction and gives architects the ability to design applications with a simple and standard API in Java that can interact with a varied set of business registries (such as UDDI and ebXML). However, this should not be construed to mean that JAXR is a new registry specification or a lowest common denominator API. ▷

Providers

JAXR architecture is based around the concept of pluggable providers, as Figure 12.2 shows. Developers write applications using a standard JAXR client API and a standard information model (or domain object model) defined by JAXR. JAXR provides a pluggable mechanism for registry-specific providers, to be used by the client. The provider layer under the standard API supplies the API implementation and maps the JAXR information model as well as client invocations to the underlying registry's capabilities. In other words, the registry-specific provider knows how to interact with the specific registry type it supports. It maps the method invocations into the corresponding SOAP message invocations based on the registry's API specification and interacts with the registry over the wire, using a protocol such as HTTP.

Although the concept of pluggable providers is similar to the way JAXP, JAXM, and other APIs enable provider pluggability there is a subtle difference between the JAXR provider and the JAXM providers discussed in Chapter 11, which is that the JAXR provider is accessed locally. The only network communication point in the JAXR architecture is between the provider and the registry server. Everything else is colocated in the same virtual machine.

Capability Profiles

Earlier, we used the term registry *capability*, which has a specific meaning in JAXR terminology. JAXR's object model provides a superset of existing registry models; not all registry implementations support every JAXR feature. To logically group these features, each individual method in the JAXR API is assigned a *capability* level; providers declare what capability level they support.

> ▷ JAXR is a simple, rich, and standard Java extension API for accessing diverse business registries. It should not be confused with a new registry specification or as a lowest common denominator API.

Figure 12.2
JAXR
Architecture

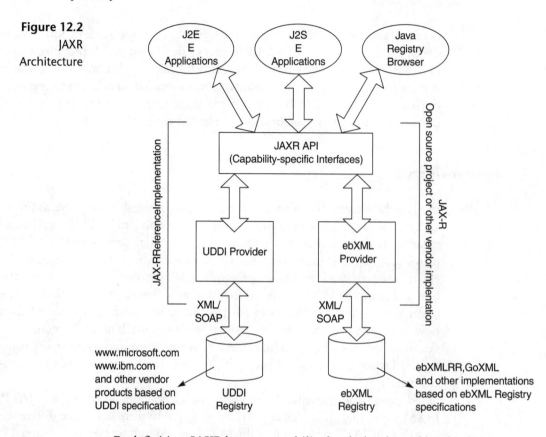

By definition, JAXR has two capability levels: level 0 and level 1. When a provider declares support for level 0, it means the provider supports all methods in the API marked as level 0. A level 1 provider supports level 0 and level 1 API calls (support for a higher level by a provider also implies support for a lower level). Coincidentally, UDDI providers map to level 0 profile, and ebXML registry providers map to level 1 profile. ▷

All JAXR providers are required to support level 0 (and hence UDDI); support for level 1 is optional. In short, a JAXR client for a standard registry specification (e.g., UDDI) is guaranteed to be portable across JAXR providers from any vendor for that capability, and similarly for any vendor's registry implementation that is compliant to the specifications. ▷▷

▷   JAXR is also a part of J2EE 1.4 and application servers will be required to provide a level 0 JAXR registry implementation. In practical terms what this means is that J2EE 4 servers will come with a UDDI registry.

▷ The JAXR Information Model

Application developers using JAXR interact *only* with JAXR's domain object model; the provider translates that into the model of the specific registry standards.

The JAXR information model is contained in the `javax.xml.registry` `.infomodel` package and is quite straightforward. The model consists of two logical groups of classes:

- Interfaces that model metadata that can be submitted to the registry (e.g., business and service information)

- Interfaces that describe how to get the metadata and content out of the registry-repository

Let us look at the object that models business entity relationships in the information model shown in Figure 12.3:

- A business, such as a corporation whose data is contained in the registry, is represented by an `Organization` instance. An `Organization` can have multiple `Organizations` under it or can refer to another organization as a parent (for example, a business may have multiple divisions or may be a subsidiary of another).

- People are represented as `User` objects. There is an obvious relationship between `Organizations` and `Users`. An `Organization` has a primary contact person represented by a `User`, it can have multiple `Users` who make up the `Organization`, or individual `Users` can be affiliated with an organization. A `User` will also have one or more `EmailAddress` objects where he or she receives email, a `PersonName`, and, optionally, a URL, such as a home page location (Figure 12.3 does not show the `java.net.URL`).

- A physical address is represented as a `PostalAddress` object. An `Organization` will have a primary address (e.g., a corporate headquarters), and a `User` will have a `PostalAddress` as a part of the contact information. Similarly, an `Organization` and a `User` will have telephone numbers associated with them, represented as `TelephoneNumber` objects.

▷▷ The JAXR reference implementation comes with a level 0–compliant provider to support UDDI 2.0. The ebXML provider for JAXR and the ebXML registry itself are available in an open source effort for the reference implementation of the OASIS ebXML registry at *http://ebxmlrr.sourceforge.net.*

Figure 12.3
The core JAXR
information
model

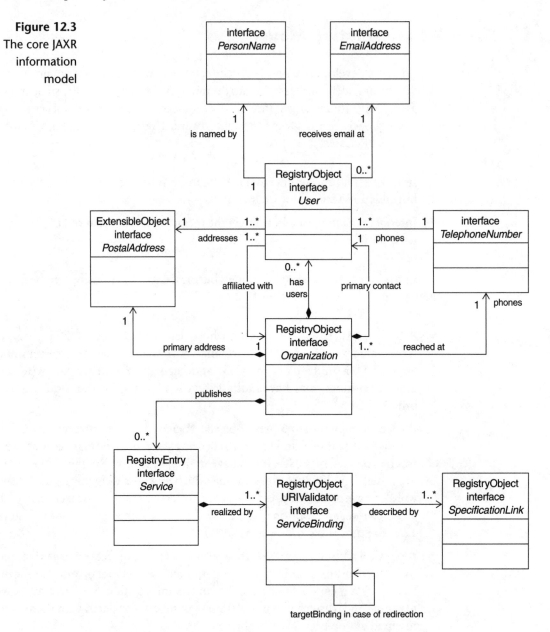

- An Organization can offer one or more services, represented by Service objects. Each Service can have multiple ServiceBindings that specify the details about the protocol binding information for that service. (Recall that in Chapter 5 we looked at how the same abstract definition can have multiple binding elements.)

- A ServiceBinding has attributes that describe the location where the service can be accessed and, optionally, another ServiceBinding, in case the service is redirected.

- A ServiceBinding is associated with one or more SpecificationLink objects that point to the technical specifications defining the service (e.g., a WSDL file for the Web service).

Keep in mind that this information model refers to the logical relationships in the JAXR level. It is not the content itself but logical metadata about the content that is stored in the underlying repository. Storing an Organization does *not* mean an Organization object is serialized and stored in the registry. It means that application clients can describe a business as an Organization. When the appropriate JAXR API is called to publish the Organization, this Organization will be translated into the model of the underlying registry by the JAXR provider (e.g., an Organization maps to a businessEntity in UDDI), and the appropriate API for the registry will be invoked (e.g., save_business) with the required SOAP message. We will look at this mapping in further detail later in this chapter. ▷

The JAXR information model has been developed with an object-oriented approach and is therefore easy to understand. It uses inheritance between different interfaces to abstract out the common behavior. At the core of the information model is a javax.xml.registry.infomodel.RegistryObject.

Figure 12.4 shows the physical generalization relationship. All the objects discussed till now, as well as some others discussed in subsequent sections that conceptually must be represented or sent to the registry, implement this interface. In short, from an abstract perspective, everything *in* the registry is a RegistryObject.

Classification of Registry Data

In Chapter 6, we discussed taxonomies and classification in the UDDI registry. Arranging and grouping the logical relationships in the information model is one of the code features of any registry. A good example of arranging information is a Web-based search engine, such as Yahoo.com. For example, a person looking for a bank near home in Connecticut could drill down through the following categories:

▷   All elements of this model are described as interfaces. The actual implementations are provided by the JAXR vendor implementation.

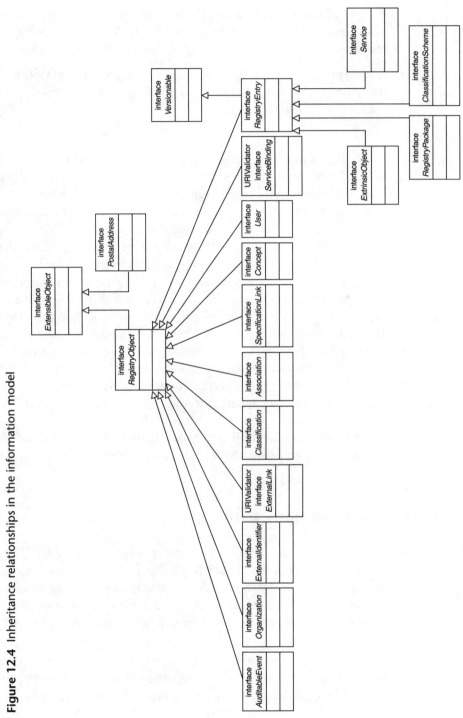

Figure 12.4 Inheritance relationships in the information model

Home > Business and Economy > Shopping and Services > Financial Services > Banking > Banks > By Region > U.S. States > Connecticut and arrive at a listing for Flute Bank (our fictitious bank). There are other ways to reach the same listing, including

U.S. States > Connecticut > Cities > Manchester > Business and Shopping > Business to Business >

This arrangement or categorization based on names is referred to as a *taxonomy*— a generally accepted standard of grouping. Taxonomy is important because it allows RegistryObjects to be discovered quickly and published in a logical manner. In JAXR, a RegistryObject is classified using the Classification interface, analogous to the catgegoryBag in UDDI. A RegistryObject can have multiple Classifications. For example, in a registry, Flute Bank, which is an Organization, can be classified by geographical location, accounts offered, banking type (Internet or branch-based), and so on. Each Classification may belong to one ClassificationScheme or taxonomy (Figure 12.5).

For example, the first lesson in junior high chemistry begins by grouping matter as in Figure 12.6. This "matter" scheme is valid for matter but not for, say, library books. For these, another scheme, the Dewey Decimal system, uses a combination of letters and numbers to coordinate materials on the same and related subjects, to make them easier to find on library shelves. Similarly, business organizations use two common classification schemes: D-U-N-S and NAICS. ▷

Figure 12.5
Classification of
registry objects

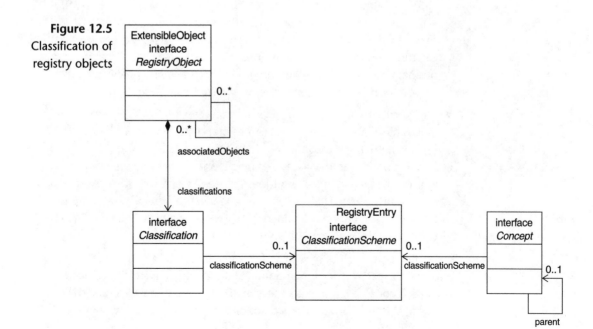

Figure 12.6
The basic
subdivisions
of matter

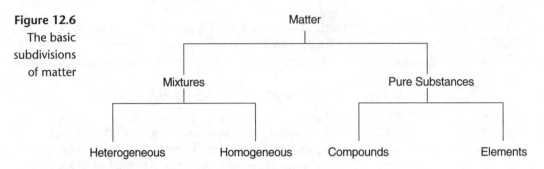

Figure 12.6 The basic subdivisions of matter

The taxonomy itself can be internal or external to the provider, meaning that its structure is resident inside the provider or is represented somewhere outside. NAICS is an example of an internal taxonomy, because the scheme and all the codes are available inside the JAXR provider (even though NAICS is maintained and specified by an external organization). In Chapter 11, we used the example of Flute Bank and its business partner, OfficeMin. Figure 12.7 shows how NAICS assigns codes to organizations such as OfficeMin. ▷▷

Figure 12.8 shows the realization of the OfficeMin NAICS classification and is called an internal classification in JAXR, because it uses an internal taxonomy. Because internal taxonomies are directly available in the JAXR provider layer, the

▷
- The Dun & Bradstreet (D&B) Data Universal Numbering System (D-U-N-S) is a unique nine-digit identification sequence that provides identifiers for single business entities while linking corporate family structures together. It is now the standard for all United States federal government electronic commerce transactions. A company that plans to engage in business with the U.S. government will need a D&B D-U-N-S number. More information is available at *www.dnb.com/duns_update.*

- The North American Industry Classification System (NAICS, pronounced *nakes*) has replaced the United States Standard Industrial Classification (SIC) system. It is a taxonomy for e-business devised by the U.S. Census Bureau and is used to classify businesses and services by the industry to which they belong and the business processes they follow. It was developed jointly by the U.S., Canada, and Mexico to provide new comparability in statistics about business activity across North America. Details can be found at *www.census.gov/epcd/www/naics.html.*

▷▷ For UDDI registries, the JAXR specifications require that NAICS, ISO 3166, and the United Nations Standard Product and Services Classification (UNSPSC) code be internal taxonomies. This is one of the value-added features of JAXR for UDDI. Internal taxonomies are supported only by level 1 JAXR providers.

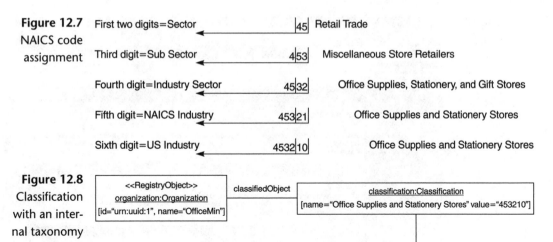

Figure 12.7
NAICS code
assignment

First two digits=Sector	|45|	Retail Trade
Third digit=Sub Sector	4|53|	Miscellaneous Store Retailers
Fourth digit=Industry Sector	45|32|	Office Supplies, Stationery, and Gift Stores
Fifth digit=NAICS Industry	453|21|	Office Supplies and Stationery Stores
Sixth digit=US Industry	4532|10|	Office Supplies and Stationery Stores

Figure 12.8
Classification
with an inter-
nal taxonomy

client can browse the taxonomy structure and the provider can enforce validation rules for registry objects classified against such a scheme.

An example of an external taxonomy is the microsoft-com:geoweb:2000 scheme (based on the ISO 3166 standard) in the Microsoft registry shown in Figure 12.9, which allows classification by geographical location.

The taxonomy is represented by ClassificationScheme interface instances. Its taxonomy values and structure are represented by Concept interface instances. Figure 12.10 shows how the microsoft-com:geoweb:2000 taxonomy can be represented with the topmost element of the tree as a ClassificationScheme and subsequent levels as Concepts. ▷

Association of Registry Data

Just as the UML model allows a relationship between two classes to be stereotyped as an association class, JAXR defines an Association interface, which can be used to set up a relationship between a source RegistryObject and a target RegistryObject instance.

A User can associate two objects owned or created by that user. For example, an administrator may create a parent-subsidiary association between two Organizations. Associations can be created between objects owned by separate users and may require confirmation by one or more of those users.

▷ Internal taxonomies are supported by level 1 JAXR providers.

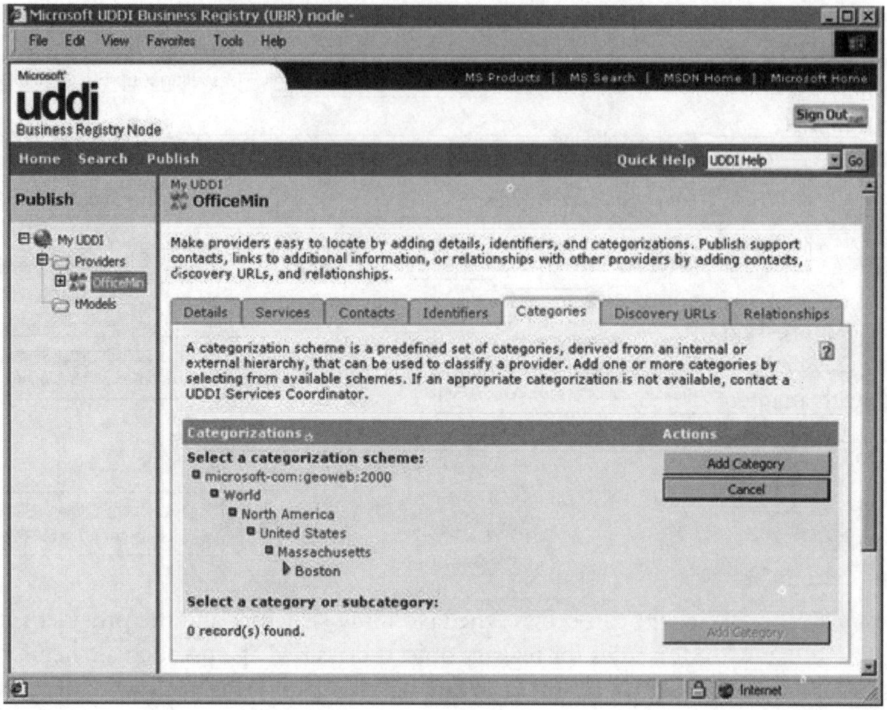

Figure 12.9
An example of
an external
taxonomy

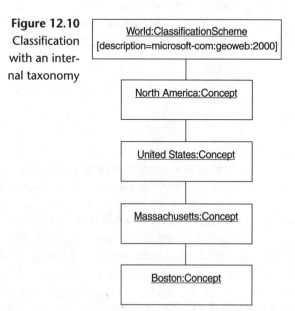

Figure 12.10
Classification
with an inter-
nal taxonomy

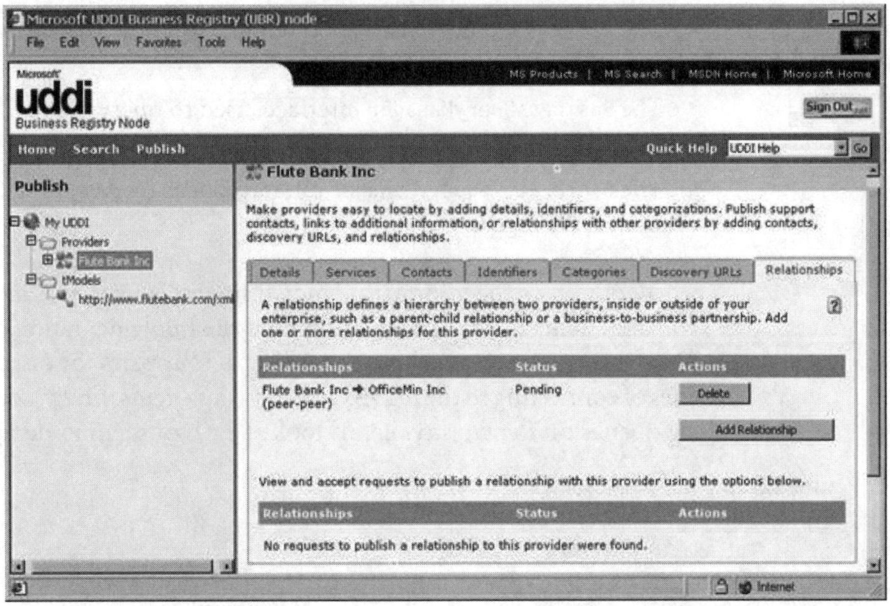

Figure 12.11
An extramural
association
between two
organizations

In Figure 12.11, a UDDI user creates a peer-peer relationship between Flute Bank and OfficeMin. The contact person for OfficeMin has to confirm and accept this relationship. JAXR provides APIs to create, update, and confirm these associations programmatically, as we will see later. ▷

▷ The JAXR API

So far, we have discussed at a conceptual level the object model defined by JAXR. Let us now look at the API that client applications use to interact with the registry and work with this model.

RegistryService is the main interface implemented by the JAXR pluggable provider layer. It allows the client to query the implementation for the capability level it supports and also obtain references to the three main interfaces from the underlying registry-specific providers. These are:

> ▷   An association is called *intramural* if the objects are owned by the same user
> and *extramural* if the owners are different.

- The `BusinessLifeCyleManager` interface, used for creating objects based on the information model
- The `BusinessQueryManager` interface, used to query the registry using objects from the information model
- The `DeclarativeQueryManager` interface, used to execute statement type queries on the registry

All objects in the information model are implemented as interfaces in JAXR. The underlying registry provider supplies the implementation classes. As Figure 12.12 shows, we will break up the API into four parts for discussion, along the lines of connecting to the registry, creating data items, finding data, and performing queries on the registry. Let us look at each of them in detail.

Figure 12.12
JAXR API

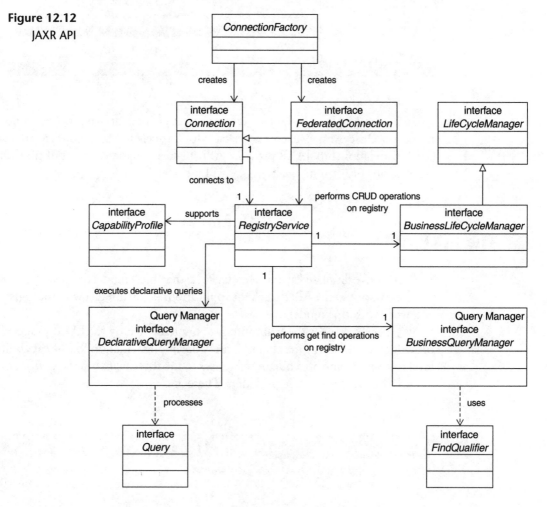

JAXR and Connections

The first few step in any JAXR application is to establish a connection to the underlying registry, which is abstracted with a RegistryService interface. In general, all JAXR applications have the following sequence:

1. Create a ConnectionFactory.
2. Create a Connection object from that factory to the registry.
3. Pass the Connection the appropriate user credentials (e.g., username and password) required by the registry operator.
4. Obtain the reference to the RegistryService from the connection.
5. Do some work with the RegistryService.

JAXR uses the Factory pattern and a ConnectionFactory that can be configured with properties for initializing the underlying Connection object. Just like the JAXM factories discussed in Chapter 11, the JAXR factory can be obtained from the J2EE container's JNDI context, as shown below:

```
HashMap properties = new HashMap();
properties.put("some property", "some value");
// set other properties.
InitialContext ctx = new InitialContext(properties);

ConnectionFactory connfactory =
     (ConnectionFactory)ctx.lookup("java:comp/env/jaxr/connectionfactory");
```

Note that the JNDI mechanism can be used only if the container supports it. Tomcat and the reference implementation servlet container do not have this feature. EJB containers such as the J2EE reference implementation do have this feature. ▷

Table 12.1 shows the properties specified by JAXR. The only required setting is the javax.xml.registry.queryManagerURL property; others are optional. The factory can also be instantiated by the default mechanism using the newInstance() method, as shown below:

▷   Tomcat 4.1 and above can be enabled to use JNDI with some effort; see details at *http://jakarta.apache.org/tomcat/tomcat-4.1-doc/index.html.*

```
// Set the properties for the factory
        Properties environment = new Properties();
        environment.setProperty("javax.xml.registry.queryManagerURL", QUERY_URL);
        environment.setProperty("javax.xml.registry.lifeCycleManagerURL",
                                                        PUBLISH_URL);
 // Instantiate the factory and create a connection from it
        ConnectionFactory connfactory = ConnectionFactory.newInstance();
        connfactory.setProperties(environment);
        Connection connection = connfactory.createConnection();
// Authenticate the username and password with the registry
      PasswordAuthentication passwdAuth = new PasswordAuthentication(uddiusername,
                                                uddipassword.toCharArray());
            Set credentials = new HashSet();
            credentials.add(passwdAuth);
            connection conn.setCredentials(credentials);
// Obtain a reference to the registry service
        RegistryService registryservice = connection.getRegistryService();
```

JAXR and Create-Replace-Update-Delete (CRUD) Operations

The second part of the JAXR API deals with how applications can work with and manipulate objects in the information model with operations that can be used to create, update, delete, and save data in the underlying registry. The JAXR provider is responsible for translating these operations into the underlying registry's API calls.

The `LifeCycleManager` and the `BusinessLifeCycleManager` in the `javax.xml`.`registry` package shown in Figure 12.12 primarily abstracts all these operations, which are shown in Figure 12.13. The two lifecycle managers contain overloaded methods for:

- Creating metadata entries such as `Associations`, `Classification`, `Classlifi-cationScheme`, and `Concept`
- Creating data entries such as `Organization`, `User`, `PostalAddress`, `Telephone-number`, `Service`, and `ServiceBinding`
- Saving and deleting the `Organization`, `Service`, `Concepts`, `Associations`, and so on

Earlier in the chapter, we mentioned how everything in the information model is represented by an interface and that the implementation classes are vendor-

Table 12.1   The JAXR Connection Properties

Connection property	Description
`javax.xml.registry` `.queryManagerURL`	A required string that specifies the URL to the query manager service for the provider.
`javax.xml.registry` `.lifeCycleManagerURL`	An optional string that specifies the URL to the lifecycle manager service for the provider.
`javax.xml.registry` `.semanticEquivalences`	An optional set of tuples that specifies how two Concepts in two different ClassificationSchemes for the internal taxonomy may be considered equivalent (for example, microsoft-com:geoweb:2000:United States, microsoft-com:geoweb:2000:USA | microsoft-com:geoweb:2000:Netherland, microsoft-com:geoweb:2000:Holland)
`javax.xml.registry.security` `.authenticationMethod`	An optional string that may be used to tell the provider about the authentication method to use
`javax.xml.registry.uddi` `.maxRows`	An optional integer that tells UDDI registries the maximum number of rows that should be returned for find operations
`javax.xml.registry` `.postalAddressScheme`	The PostalAddress object in the information model has well-defined attributes (e.g., street, city, postal code), whereas some registries, such as the UDDI registry, may represent address attributes simply as a set of lines. This optional string property can be used to specify a ClassificationScheme (i.e., a postal address scheme) the provider uses to map the structured information in JAXR and unstructured information in the underlying registry.

provided. The BusinessLifeCyleManager is used as a factory for instantiating these objects in application classes. For example, empty User and Telephone-Number objects can be created as shown below and subsequently populated with relevant attributes:

```
User contact = lifecyclemgr.createUser();
    TelephoneNumber telnum = lifecyclemgr.createTelephoneNumber();
```

Figure 12.13
The Life-
CycleManager
and the
BusinessLife-
CycleManager

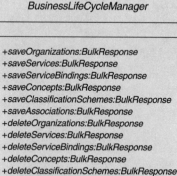

Figure 12.13 The LifeCycleManager and the BusinessLifeCycleManager

JAXR and Get-Find Operations

The third part of the API relates to searching the registry using get-find type operations. These operations relating to retrieving data from the underlying registry are abstracted by the `QueryManager` and the `BusinessQueryManager` interfaces in the `javax.xml.registry` package, as Figure 12.14 shows. Both these query managers contain overloaded methods that relate to different mechanisms for searching and retrieving information on existing data in the registry. The data could relate to `Associations`, `Organizations`, `Concepts`, or other objects from the information model. The JAXR provider takes care of translating these operations into the underlying registry's API and generating the corresponding SOAP messages.

A registry can be queried for different fields (e.g., `Organization`, `Concepts`, `ServiceBindings`, `Service`, `Associations`) using the `BusinessQueryManager` interface. Each argument to the methods in this interface is of type `java.util.Collection`, which represents the following:

- `findQualifiers`. Constants specified in the `javax.xml.registry.FindQualifier` interface that specify the `find` criteria (e.g., sorting, searching, etc.) For example, to search in a case-sensitive manner and have the results arranged in descending order, the qualifier parameter would look like this:

```
Collection findqualifier= new ArrayList();
findqualifier.add(FindQualifier. CASE_SENSITIVE_MATCH);
findqualifier.add(FindQualifier. SORT_BY_NAME_DESC);
```

- `namePatterns`. The wildcard pattern based on the syntax of the SQL LIKE clause to search on (e.g., `%Flute%`, `%Flute,Flute,Flute%`, etc.)

Figure 12.14
The Query-
Manager and
the Business-
QueryManager

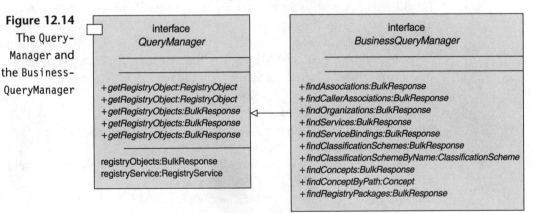

- For example, to search for an organization whose name contains starts with "Flute" in a case-sensitive manner and have the results arranged in descending order, the code would look like this:

```
Collection findqualifier= new ArrayList();
findqualifier.add(FindQualifier. CASE_SENSITIVE_MATCH);
findqualifier.add(FindQualifier. SORT_BY_NAME_DESC);
Collection searchpattern = new ArrayList();
searchpattern.add("%Flute");
BulkResponse response = querymgr.findOrganizations(findqualifier,searchpattern,
                null, null, null, null);
```

- `classifications`. The `Classification` objects to use during the `find` operation.
- `specifications`. The `javax.xml.registry.infomodel.Concept` or `javax.xml.registry.infomodel.ExtrinsicObject` objects to use during the `find` operation.
- `externalIdentifiers`. The `javax.xml.registry.infomodel.ExternalIdentifiers` objects to use during the `find` operation.
- `externalLinks`. The `javax.xml.registry.infomodel.ExternalLink` objects to use during the `find` operation.

Typical use cases covered later in this chapter will show more detailed code using these parameters in the corresponding `find` operations.

JAXR and Declarative Queries

Level 1 registries, such as the ebXML registry, expose clients with the ability to execute declarative queries against the registry (Figure 12.15). JAXR abstracts this using the `Query` and `DelarativeQuery` interfaces. JAXR at present supports only SQL-92 and the OASIS ebXML registry filter queries. An example of a simple query that returns all the organizations in the registry is shown below:

```
// obtain a connection here
RegistryService registryservice = conn.getRegistryService();
DeclarativeQueryManager decquerymgr
                    = registryservice. getDeclarativeQueryManager;
String querystr = "SELECT * FROM Organization"
Query query = decquerymgr.createQuery(Query.QUERY_TYPE_SQL, querystr);
BulkResponse response = dqm.executeQuery(query); ▷
```

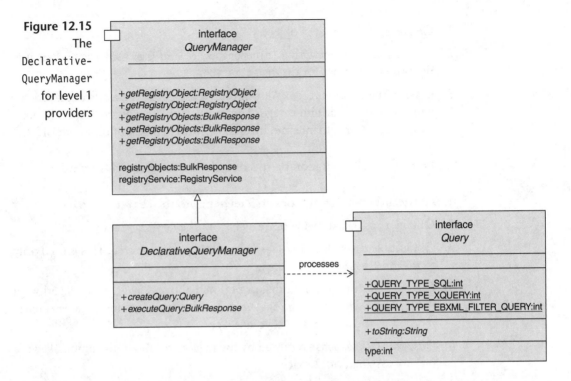

Figure 12.15
The
`Declarative-`
`QueryManager`
for level 1
providers

Publishing Company Information to a UDDI Registry

The JAXR API provides a higher level of abstraction. There are essentially two ways to register the business and the services it provides with a UDDI registry. UDDI specifications require that a UDDI provider expose the registry though a Web-based HTML interface, such as that shown in earlier figures. In this section, we will show how the JAXR API can be used to register details about Flute Bank and its bill payment Web service in the UDDI registry. ▷

From an information model perspective, here are the steps that need to be followed to create the conceptual representation:

▷ The relational schema definition for SQL queries required by the ebXML Registry Service can be found at *www.oasis-open.org/committees/regrep/ documents/2.0/sql/database.sql*. The stored procedures that must be supported by the SQL query feature are defined at *www.oasis-open.org/committees/regrep/documents/2.0/sql/storedProcedures.sql*.

1. Create an Organization object.

2. Create a User object with a TelephoneNumber and EmailAddress and set it as the primary contact for the Organization.

3. Classify the Organization. We will follow the NAICS classification scheme and assign the code and category description that fits Flute Bank: the high-level category of "Finance and Insurance," with a corresponding code of 52.

From an implementation perspective, the steps are straightforward:

1. Create a Connection and obtain a reference to the RegistryService.

2. Obtain a BusinessLifeCycleManager from the RegistryService.

3. Obtain a BusinessQueryManager from the RegistryService. This is used only to set the ClassificationScheme.

4. Create the information model, as outlined above. Save the organization in the registry by invoking the saveOrganizations(Collection organizations) method in the BusinessLifeCycleManager.

5. Parse the BulkResponse returned by the registry to obtain the unique key the registry assigned our service.

6. Close the connection to the registry.

Listing 12.1 shows the complete code for these steps. Upon successful registration, the registry assigns a unique key and discovery URL to Flute Bank, which are printed in the output of the example. The successful registration can be verified using the Web interface of the registry, shown in Figure 12.16.

Listing 12.1   Publishing organization information

```
import javax.xml.registry.infomodel.*;
import javax.xml.registry.*;
import java.util.*;
import java.net.PasswordAuthentication;

public class UDDIPublishOrg {
        private static final String QUERY_URL=
            "http://www-3.ibm.com:80/services/uddi/v2beta/inquiryapi";
    private static final String PUBLISH_URL =
        "https://www-3.ibm.com:443/services/uddi/v2beta/protect/publishapi";
        private static String uddiusername;
        private static String uddipassword;
```

```
    public static void main(String[] args) {
        if(args.length!=2){
            System.out.println("Usage java UDDIPublish username uddipassword");
            return;
        }
        uddiusername = args[0];
    uddipassword = args[1];
try{

// Set the properties for the ConnectionFactory
Properties environment = new Properties();
environment.setProperty("javax.xml.registry.queryManagerURL", QUERY_URL);
environment.setProperty("javax.xml.registry.lifeCycleManagerURL",PUBLISH_URL);

 // Instantiate the factory and create a connection from it
    ConnectionFactory connfactory = ConnectionFactory.newInstance();
    connfactory.setProperties(environment);
    Connection conn = connfactory.createConnection();

  // Authenticate the username and password with the registry
    PasswordAuthentication passwdAuth = new PasswordAuthentication
                                (uddiusername, uddipassword.toCharArray());
    Set credentials = new HashSet();
    credentials.add(passwdAuth);
    conn.setCredentials(credentials);

 // Obtain a reference to the RegistryService, the BusinessLifeCycleManager, and
 //   the BusinessQueryManager
    RegistryService registryservice = conn.getRegistryService();
    BusinessLifeCycleManager lifecyclemgr
                        =registryservice.getBusinessLifeCycleManager();
    BusinessQueryManager querymgr = registryservice.getBusinessQueryManager();

// Create an organization object
    Organization company =   lifecyclemgr.createOrganization("Flute Bank");
    InternationalString description = lifecyclemgr.createInternationalString("A
        fictitious bank used for examples in the book Java Web Services Architecture,
            "+                "published by Morgan Kaufman, ISBN 1-55860-900-8." +
"The authors can be reached at   webservicesbook@yahoogroups.com OR" +
    "www.javawebservicesarchitecture.com. ");
    company.setDescription(description);
```

```
// Create a user object
    User contact = lifecyclemgr.createUser();
    PersonName name = lifecyclemgr.createPersonName("John Malkovich");
    contact.setPersonName(name);


// Create and set the user's telephone number
    TelephoneNumber telnum = lifecyclemgr.createTelephoneNumber();
    telnum.setNumber("1-800-FLUTE-US");
    Collection phonenumbers = new ArrayList();
    phonenumbers.add(telnum);
    contact.setTelephoneNumbers(phonenumbers);


// Create and set the user's email address
    EmailAddress email = lifecyclemgr.createEmailAddress
                                        ("uddiadmin@flutebank.com");
            Collection emaillist = new ArrayList();
            emaillist.add(email);
            contact.setEmailAddresses(emaillist);


// Set the user as the primary contact for the organization
            company.setPrimaryContact(contact);
    ClassificationScheme scheme =
            querymgr.findClassificationSchemeByName(null,"ntis-gov:naics");


// Create the classification using the above scheme and pass the relevant category
                                                    code and description
            Classification classification =
(Classification)lifecyclemgr.createClassification(scheme, "Finance and Insurance",
                                                            "52");
            Collection classificationlist = new ArrayList();
            classificationlist.add(classification);
            company.addClassifications(classificationlist);


// Set the organization in the list of organizations
// An organization list is a list of organizations, because a user could choose to
                                        publish multiple organizations
            Collection organizationlist = new ArrayList();
            organizationlist.add(company);
```

```
// make the final call to the registry and get a response
          BulkResponse response = lifecyclemgr.saveOrganizations(organizationlist);
          Collection exceptions = response.getExceptions();

// If there are no exceptions, the publish action was successful
          if (exceptions == null) {
             Collection keys = response.getCollection();
             Iterator iterator = keys.iterator();
             Key key = (Key) iterator.next();
             String uid = key.getId();
             System.out.println("The unique ID returned by the UDDI registry for
                                        the Organization is " + uid);

             company.setKey(key);
             }
// This means exceptions occurred during the publish action
          else {
             Iterator iterator = exceptions.iterator();
             while (iterator.hasNext()) {
                Exception exception = (Exception) iterator.next();
                System.out.println("Exception occurred while saving to the
                                        registry: " + exception);

             }
          }
// Finally, close the connection
          conn.close();
       } catch (Exception exception) {
          System.out.println("General exception occurred: " + exception);
       }
    }
} ▷
```

Let us examine what happens under the hood when the example class UDDIPublish is executed. Publication calls to UDDI happen only as a set of authenticated operations where the authentication is token-based. The JAXR pro-

> ▷ Remember that although we are publishing to a UDDI registry, developers using JAXR never have to do anything UDDI-specific. JAXR providers take care of all the wiring under the hood.

Figure 12.16
Flute Bank as
registered
in the IBM
UDDI registry

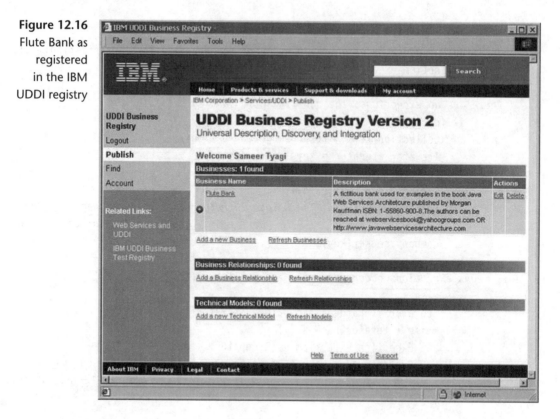

vider connects to the registry using SSL and verifies the username and password
by making the get_authToken call. The registry returns the XML response with
the authToken element. The request sent looks like this:

```
<?xml version="1.0" encoding="UTF-8"?>
<soap-env:Envelope xmlns:soap-env="http://schemas.xmlsoap.org/soap/envelope/">
  <soap-env:Body>
      <get_authToken generic="2.0" userID="fluteuddi" cred="fluteuddi"
             xmlns="urn:uddi-org:api_v2"/>
  </soap-env:Body>
</soap-env:Envelope>
```

The response from the registry looks like this:

```
<?xml version="1.0" encoding="UTF-8"?>
    <authToken generic="2.0" xmlns="urn:uddi-org:api_v2"
                      operator="www.ibm.com/services/uddi">
<authInfo>xyzi2892somesecuretoken</authInfo>
  </authToken>
```

The provider then sends another SOAP request, which includes the token and XML structure, based on the save_business UDDI operation:

```
<soap-env:Envelope xmlns:soap-env="http://schemas.xmlsoap.org/soap/envelope/">
<soap-env:Body>
<save_business generic="2.0" xmlns="urn:uddi-org:api_v2">
  <authInfo>xyzi2892somesecuretoken</authInfo>
  <businessEntity businessKey="">
    <name xml:lang="en">Flute Bank</name>
    <description xml:lang="en">A fictitious bank used for examples in the book
            Java Web Services Architecture, published by Morgan Kaufman, ISBN
        1-55860-900-8. The authors can be reached at webservicesbook@yahoogroups.com OR
http://www.javawebservicesarchitecture.com.
      </description>
    <contacts>
    <contact>
        <description xml:lang="en">
                The primary contact person for Flute web services
            </description>
        <personName>John Malkovich</personName>
        <phone useType="">1-800-FLUTE-US</phone>
        <email>uddiadmin@flutebank.com</email>
    </contact>
    </contacts>
    <businessServices>
      <businessService serviceKey="">
       <name xml:lang="en">Billpayservice</name>
       <description xml:lang="en">A web service allowing online account holders to
                                        pay bills online</description>
    <bindingTemplates>
       <bindingTemplate bindingKey="">
                <description>Flute Bank, beyond providing simple account-related
                services, also has the infrastructure to support online bill payments.
    The online bill payment system is offered to customers as a value-added service.
            </description>
                <accessPoint URLType="http">
                    http://127.0.0.1:8080/billpayservice/jaxrpc/BillPay
                </accessPoint>
                <tModelInstanceDetails/>
            </bindingTemplate>
    </bindingTemplates>
    </businessService>
```

```
  </businessServices>
  <categoryBag>
    <keyedReference tModelKey="uuid:C0B9FE13-179F-413D-8A5B-5004DB8E5BB2"
                            keyName="Finance and Insurance" keyValue="52"/>
  </categoryBag>
</businessEntity>
</save_business>
</soap-env:Body>
</soap-env:Envelope>
```

In response to this request, the registry returns the businessDetail structure, which is the top-level element in the UDDI information model. It is used to represent information about an entity or business, as shown below:

```
<?xml version="1.0" encoding="UTF-8"?>
<businessDetail generic="2.0" xmlns="urn:uddi-org:api_v2" operator="www.ibm.com/
services/uddi">
    <businessEntity businessKey="25BF1920-D020-11D6-9314-000629DC0A7B"
                    operator="www.ibm.com/services/uddi" authorizedName="100000CTU6">
    <discoveryURLs>
        <discoveryURL useType="businessEntity">
            http://uddi.ibm.com/testregistry/uddiget?businessKey=25BF1920-D020-11D6-
                                                  9314-000629DC0A7B
        </discoveryURL>
    </discoveryURLs>
    <name xml:lang="en">Flute Bank</name>
    <description xml:lang="en">A fictitious bank used for examples in the book
        Java Web Services Architecture, published by Morgan Kaufman, ISBN 1-55860-900-8.
                     The authors can be reached at webservicesbook@yahoogroups.com OR
                                 http://www.javawebservicesarchitecture.com.
    </description>
    <contacts>
        <contact>
        <description xml:lang="en">The primary contact person for Flute Web services
                                                  </description>
        <personName>John Malkovich</personName>
        <phone useType="">1-800-FLUTE-US</phone>
        <email>uddiadmin@flutebank.com</email>
        </contact>
    </contacts>
    <businessServices>
```

```
<businessService serviceKey="25E12010-D020-11D6-9314-000629DC0A7B"
                 businessKey="25BF1920- D020-11D6-9314-000629DC0A7B">
<name xml:lang="en">Billpayservice</name>
<description xml:lang="en">A Web service allowing account holders to pay bills
                                                    online</description>
<bindingTemplates>
    <bindingTemplate bindingKey="2606F790-D020-11D6-9314-000629DC0A7B"
                     serviceKey="25E12010-D020-11D6-9314-000629DC0A7B">
        <description xml:lang="en">Flute Bank, beyond providing simple
            account-related services, also has the infrastructure to support
            online bill payments. The online bill payment system is offered
                                    to customers as a value-added service.
        </description>
        <accessPoint
    URLType="http">http://127.0.0.1:8080/billpayservice/jaxrpc/BillPay
                </accessPoint>
        <tModelInstanceDetails/>
    </bindingTemplate>
</bindingTemplates>
</businessService>
</businessServices>
<categoryBag>
<keyedReference tModelKey="UUID:C0B9FE13-179F-413D-8A5B-5004DB8E5BB2"
                keyName="Finance and Insurance" keyValue="52"/>
</categoryBag>
</businessEntity>
</businessDetail>
```

Notice that in the businessDetail structure of the response, the registry has assigned the unique identifier to the entity and filled out the businessKey, operator, and authorizedName attributes. It has also assigned a unique discovery URL, where the XML describing the UDDI businessEntity structure for Flute Bank can be accessed.

All this communication and these SOAP messages are transparent to the Java application. The application deals only with the JAXR API and the information model objects contained therein; the provider takes care of the details. ▷

▷   Because publication to UDDI happens over SSL, the SOAP messages cannot be captured on the wire using HTTP tools. JAXR debugging can be enabled by using the options

`-Dorg.apache.commons.logging.log=org.apache.commons.logging.impl.SimpleLog` and
`-Dorg.apache.commons.logging.simplelog.defaultlog=debug`.

Additionally, using `-DuseSOAP=true` enables JAXR to switch Soap4J instead of JAXM internally. This can be helpful when using JDK 1.4.

Publishing Service Information to a UDDI Registry

WSDL, with its abstract and concrete sections, was covered in Chapter 5; in Chapter 6, UDDI and how the WSDL elements map to UDDI elements was discussed. Let us now look at how JAXR can be used to publish service descriptions contained in the WSDL programmatically to a registry. ▷

Let us look at the earlier example of the bill payment service. Suppose all the banks in the Good Banking Consortium got together and agreed to have a common bill payment service interface, so that customers of one bank could use the bill payment service of another bank to address a wider merchant account base. They could describe the `billpayserviceinterface.wsdl` shown in Listing 12.2a. (This is the same WSDL we covered in previous chapters.) Flute Bank could then implement this standard service and expose it as an endpoint. The WSDL is shown in Listing 12.2c. Notice that the schema definitions in `billpayservice` `.wsdl` have also been separated into their own XSD file, so that they can be reused across multiple service interfaces. Listing 12.2b shows the schema.

> ▷   The service interface consists of the abstract description (`types`, `messages`, `operations`, and `portTypes`, and `elements`) and a protocol binding (`binding` `element`), which describe the Web service interface. The service implementation consists of the `imported` service interface and the WSDL `service` element, which describe `port` implementation details, such as `location`. Typically, the service interface and the service implementation can and should be defined in different WSDL documents. The rationale behind this from the UDDI consortium is that different industry verticals will define a set of service interfaces that will be made publicly available. Organizations will then build services that conform to these industry-standard specifications (i.e., the abstract definition and the protocol binding for the service), implement them, and expose the endpoints. These recommendations from the UDDI consortium can be found at *www.uddi.org/bestpractices* *.html*.

Listing 12.2a   Service interface separated into `billpayinterface.wsdl`

```
<?xml version="1.0" encoding="UTF-8"?>
<definitions name="billpayservice-abstractinterface" targetNamespace="http://
www.flutebank.com/xml" xmlns:tns="http://www.flutebank.com/xml" xmlns="http://
schemas.xmlsoap.org/wsdl/" xmlns:xsd="http://www.w3.org/2001/XMLSchema" xmlns:soap=
"http://schemas.xmlsoap.org/wsdl/soap/">
    <types>
        <schema targetNamespace="billpaydatatypes.xsd" xmlns:wsdl="http://
schemas.xmlsoap.org/wsdl/" xmlns:soap-enc="http://schemas.xmlsoap.org/soap/encoding/"
xmlns="http://www.w3.org/2001/XMLSchema"/>
    </types>
    <message name="BillPay_getLastPayment">
        <part name="String_1" type="xsd:string"/>
    </message>
    <message name="BillPay_getLastPaymentResponse">
        <part name="result" type="xsd:double"/>
    </message>
    <message name="BillPay_listScheduledPayments"/>
    <message name="BillPay_listScheduledPaymentsResponse">
        <part name="result" type="tns:ArrayOfPaymentDetail"/>
    </message>
    <message name="BillPay_schedulePayment">
        <part name="Date_1" type="xsd:dateTime"/>
        <part name="String_2" type="xsd:string"/>
        <part name="double_3" type="xsd:double"/>
    </message>
    <message name="BillPay_schedulePaymentResponse">
        <part name="result" type="tns:PaymentConfirmation"/>
    </message>
    <message name="ScheduleFailedException">
        <part name="ScheduleFailedException"
                    type="tns:ScheduleFailedException"/>
    </message>
    <portType name="BillPay">
        <operation name="getLastPayment" parameterOrder="String_1">
            <input message="tns:BillPay_getLastPayment"/>
            <output message="tns:BillPay_getLastPaymentResponse"/>
        </operation>
```

```
<operation name="listScheduledPayments" parameterOrder="">
    <input message="tns:BillPay_listScheduledPayments"/>
    <output message="tns:BillPay_listScheduledPaymentsResponse"/>
</operation>
<operation name="schedulePayment"
                        parameterOrder="Date_1 String_2 double_3">
    <input message="tns:BillPay_schedulePayment"/>
    <output message="tns:BillPay_schedulePaymentResponse"/>
    <fault name="ScheduleFailedException"
            message="tns:ScheduleFailedException"/>
</operation>
</portType>
<binding name="BillPayBinding" type="tns:BillPay">
    <operation name="getLastPayment">
        <input>
            <soap:body
                encodingStyle="http://schemas.xmlsoap.org/soap/encoding/"
                use="encoded" namespace="http://www.flutebank.com/xml"/>
        </input>
        <output>
            <soap:body
                encodingStyle="http://schemas.xmlsoap.org/soap/encoding/"
                use="encoded" namespace="http://www.flutebank.com/xml"/>
        </output>
        <soap:operation soapAction=""/>
    </operation>
    <operation name="listScheduledPayments">
        <input>
            <soap:body
                encodingStyle="http://schemas.xmlsoap.org/soap/encoding/"
                use="encoded" namespace="http://www.flutebank.com/xml"/>
        </input>
        <output>
            <soap:body
                encodingStyle="http://schemas.xmlsoap.org/soap/encoding/"
                use="encoded" namespace="http://www.flutebank.com/xml"/>
        </output>
        <soap:operation soapAction=""/>
    </operation>
    <operation name="schedulePayment">
        <input>
```

```
                    <soap:body encodingStyle="http://schemas.xmlsoap.org/soap/encoding/"
                             use="encoded" namespace="http://www.flutebank.com/xml"/>
                </input>
                <output>
                    <soap:body encodingStyle="http://schemas.xmlsoap.org/soap/encoding/"
                             use="encoded" namespace="http://www.flutebank.com/xml"/>
                </output>
                <fault name="ScheduleFailedException">
                    <soap:fault encodingStyle="http://schemas.xmlsoap.org/soap/encoding/"
                             use="encoded" namespace="http://www.flutebank.com/xml"/>
                </fault>
                <soap:operation soapAction=""/>
            </operation>
            <soap:binding transport="http://schemas.xmlsoap.org/soap/http" style="rpc"/>
        </binding>
</definitions>
```

Listing 12.2b   The schema definition referenced by `billpayservice.wsdl`

```
<?xml version="1.0" encoding="UTF-8"?>
<schema targetNamespace="http://www.flutebank.com/xml" xmlns="http://www.w3.org/2001/
XMLSchema" xmlns:soap-enc="http://schemas.xmlsoap.org/soap/encoding/" xmlns:xsi=
"http://www.w3.org/2001/XMLSchema-instance" xmlns:tns="http://www.flutebank.com/xml"
xmlns:wsdl="http://schemas.xmlsoap.org/wsdl/">
    <import namespace="http://schemas.xmlsoap.org/soap/encoding/"/>
    <complexType name="ArrayOfPaymentDetail">
        <complexContent>
            <restriction base="soap-enc:Array">
                <attribute ref="soap-enc:arrayType" wsdl:arrayType=
"tns:PaymentDetail[]"/>
            </restriction>
        </complexContent>
    </complexType>
    <complexType name="PaymentDetail">
        <sequence>
            <element name="date" type="dateTime"/>
            <element name="account" type="string"/>
            <element name="payeeName" type="string"/>
            <element name="amt" type="double"/>
        </sequence>
    </complexType>
```

```
    <complexType name="PaymentConfirmation">
        <sequence>
            <element name="confirmationNum" type="int"/>
            <element name="payee" type="string"/>
            <element name="amt" type="double"/>
        </sequence>
    </complexType>
    <complexType name="ScheduleFailedException">
        <sequence>
            <element name="message" type="string"/>
            <element name="localizedMessage" type="string"/>
        </sequence>
    </complexType>
</schema>
```

Listing 12.2c   The `billpayservice.wsdl` implemented by Flute Bank

```
<?xml version="1.0" encoding="UTF-8"?>

<definitions name="billpayservice" targetNamespace="http://www.flutebank.com/
billpayservice" xmlns:tns="http://www.flutebank.com/xml" xmlns="http://
schemas.xmlsoap.org/wsdl/" xmlns:xsd="http://www.w3.org/2001/XMLSchema" xmlns:soap=
"http://schemas.xmlsoap.org/wsdl/soap/">

<import namespace="http://www.flutebank.com/xml"
        location="baillpayinterface.wsdl"/>

  <service name="Billpayservice">
    <port name="BillPayPort" binding="tns:BillPayBinding">
      <soap:address
            location="http://127.0.0.1:8080/billpayservice/jaxrpc/BillPay"/>
    </port>
  </service>
</definitions>
```

In Chapter 5, we mentioned best practices relating to how the WSDL elements should be stored in the registry. The WSDL service interface should be represented as a tModel, so that it can be reused across service implementations. The service and port elements in the service implementation descriptions map to the businessService and bindingTemplate in the UDDI registry. Figure 12.17

Figure 12.17
WSDL representation in UDDI

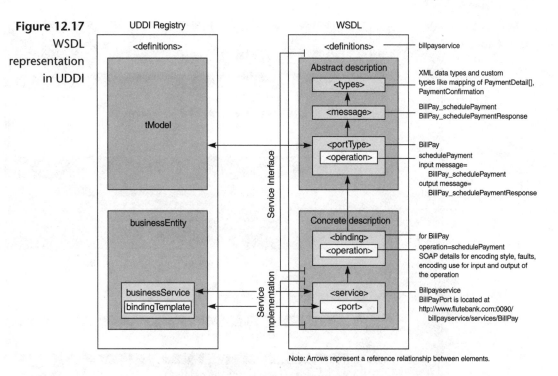

Note: Arrows represent a reference relationship between elements.

shows the mapping of the WSDL elements to the UDDI structures for the BillPay Web service. Figure 12.18 shows the WSDL information as it would appear in the UDDI registry browser.

All the above mappings can be realized quite easily using JAXR. Let us look at how the WSDL can be published to a UDDI registry and examine the JAXR code for doing so. The JAXR client should:

1. Connect to the registry and authenticate with the username and password.

2. Locate the organization in the registry using the BusinessQueryManager. The organization should have been published previously, using either JAXR (previous example) or the provider's Web interface.

3. Publish the WSDL service interface of the Web service (i.e., the billpayserviceinterface.wsdl) as a tModel. In JAXR terms, this is a Concept with the namespace, description, and a link to the binding element specified in the service interface.

4. Classify the service interface as a WSDL specification in the UDDI registry. UDDI has defined the type wsdlSpec for this purpose.

5. Save the Concept and get a key for it. This will correspond to a key for the tModel in UDDI.

Figure 12.18
WSDL information published in UDDI

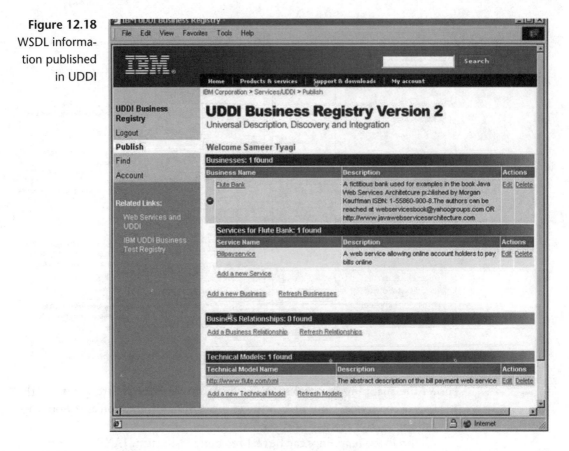

6. Publish the WSDL describing the service implementation (i.e., the `bill-payservice.wsdl`) and reference the `tModel` used by the service. In JAXR terms, this means creating and saving a `Service`, the `ServiceBinding`, and a `SpecificationLink` object that links the bindings to the `Concept` in the above step.

7. Save the `Service` using the `LifeCycleManager`.

Note that in the ideal situation, steps 1 to 6 would be performed by the industry consortium (such as the Good Banking Consortium). Flute Bank would perform only step 6 and publish it under the service implementation within its own organization. In most cases today, however, the service interface and description would be published by the same business entity. The code in Listing 12.3 shows details about doing so with JAXR.

Listing 12.3 JAXR application to publish the WSDL

```java
// imports not shown
public class WSDLPublisher {
    private static final String QUERY_URL =
        "http://www-3.ibm.com:80/services/uddi/v2beta/inquiryapi";
    private static final String PUBLISH_URL =
        "https://www-3.ibm.com:443/services/uddi/v2beta/protect/publishapi";
    private static String uddiusername;
    private static String uddipassword;

/**
 * Main method to publish the WSDL to the UDDI registry
 */
    public static void main(String[] args) {
        if(args.length!=2){
            System.out.println("Usage java UDDIPublish username uddipassword");
            return;
        }
        uddiusername = args[0];
        uddipassword = args[1];
    try{

// Set the properties for the ConnectionFactory
        Properties environment = new Properties();
        environment.setProperty("javax.xml.registry.queryManagerURL",
                                                    QUERY_URL);
        environment.setProperty("javax.xml.registry.lifeCycleManagerURL",
                                                    PUBLISH_URL);

    // Instantiate the factory and create a connection from it
        ConnectionFactory connfactory = ConnectionFactory.newInstance();
        connfactory.setProperties(environment);
        Connection conn = connfactory.createConnection();

        // Authenticate the username and password with the registry
        PasswordAuthentication passwdAuth =
            new PasswordAuthentication(uddiusername, uddipassword.toCharArray());
        Set credentials = new HashSet();
        credentials.add(passwdAuth);
        conn.setCredentials(credentials);
```

```
// Obtain a reference to the RegistryService, the BusinessLifeCycleManager,
// and the BusinessQueryManager
    RegistryService registryservice = conn.getRegistryService();
    BusinessLifeCycleManager lifecyclemgr =
                        registryservice.getBusinessLifeCycleManager();
    BusinessQueryManager querymgr =
                        registryservice.getBusinessQueryManager();


// First find the organization (this would already be registered from the
// previous examples)
    Collection searchpattern = new ArrayList();
    searchpattern.add("Flute Bank");
    Collection findqualifier= new ArrayList();
    findqualifier.add(FindQualifier.EXACT_NAME_MATCH);
    BulkResponse orgresponse =  querymgr.findOrganizations(findqualifier,
                            searchpattern, null, null, null, null);
    Collection orgs = orgresponse.getCollection();
    Iterator orgiter= orgs.iterator();
// We don't need to iterate, because we know there is only one organization in the
                                                        registry
// called Flute Bank
    Organization fluteorg = (Organization) orgiter.next();


// Create a concept for the service interface of the WSDL
    Concept concept=
            lifecyclemgr.createConcept(null,"http://www.flutebank.com/xml",null);
    InternationalString conceptdescription =
            lifecyclemgr.createInternationalString("The service interface of the
                                        bill payment Web service");
    concept.setDescription(conceptdescription);
// Note that the WSDL at this URL must be physically accessible. JAXR will access
//the URL and ensure that the WSDL is valid
    ExternalLink link=lifecyclemgr.createExternalLink(
        "http://127.0.0.1:8080/billpayservice/
billpayserviceinterface.wsdl#BillPayBinding",
        "Wsdl service interface document");
    concept.addExternalLink (link);


// Classify the service interface as the WSDL
    Collection classification=new ArrayList();
```

```
    ClassificationScheme uddiOrgTypes =
     querymgr.findClassificationSchemeByName(null, "uddi-org:types");
    Classification wsdlclassification =
        lifecyclemgr.createClassification(uddiOrgTypes, "wsdlSpec", "wsdlSpec");
    classification.add(wsdlclassification);
    concept.setClassifications(classification);

// Save the concept (the UDDI registry will save this as a tModel and return a
// Key to it)
    Collection concepts = new ArrayList();
    concepts.add(concept);
    BulkResponse savedConcepts =lifecyclemgr.saveConcepts(concepts);
    Iterator conceptIterator =savedConcepts.getCollection().iterator();
    if (conceptIterator.hasNext()){
        javax.xml.registry.infomodel.Key key
                    =(javax.xml.registry.infomodel.Key) conceptIterator.next();
        concept.setKey(key);
        System.out.println("tModel key: " + key.getId());
            }

// the service interface has been saved and the tModel created in the UDDI
// registry
// Create the concrete service (this maps to the businessService)
    Service service = lifecyclemgr.createService("Billpayservice");
    InternationalString servicedescription =
                        lifecyclemgr.createInternationalString("A Web service
allowing account holders to pay bills online");
    service.setDescription(servicedescription);

// Create the service bindings for the Web service
    Collection serviceBindings = new ArrayList();
    ServiceBinding binding = lifecyclemgr.createServiceBinding();
    InternationalString bindingdescription =
                    lifecyclemgr.createInternationalString("HTTP bindings for
                                        the Billpayservice Web service");
    binding.setDescription(bindingdescription);
// replace with the actual URL where the service is deployed
    binding.setAccessURI("http://127.0.0.1:8080/billpayservice/jaxrpc/BillPay");
// Create the specification link for the Web service
    SpecificationLink specLink=lifecyclemgr.createSpecificationLink();
```

```
// the concept now has the key created for the tModel
    specLink.setSpecificationObject(concept);
    binding.addSpecificationLink(specLink);
    serviceBindings.add(binding);

// Add the service bindings to service
    service.addServiceBindings(serviceBindings);
// Link the service to the provider
    service.setProvidingOrganization(fluteorg);

// Add the Web service to the list of services, then add the list of services to
// the organization
    Collection servicelist = new ArrayList();
    servicelist.add(service);

// Make the final call to the registry to save the services and get a response
    BulkResponse response = lifecyclemgr.saveServices(servicelist);
    System.out.println("services saved");
    Collection exceptions = response.getExceptions();

// If there are no exceptions, the publish action was successful
    if (exceptions == null) {
        Collection keys = response.getCollection();
        Iterator iterator = keys.iterator();
        Key key = (Key) iterator.next();
        String uid = key.getId();
        System.out.println("The unique ID returned by the UDDI registry for the
                                        Organization is " + uid);
        }
// This means exceptions occurred during the publish action
    else {
        Iterator iterator = exceptions.iterator();
        while (iterator.hasNext()) {
            Exception exception = (Exception) iterator.next();
            System.out.println("Exception occurred while saving to the registry: "
                                        + exception);
            exception.printStackTrace();
            }
        }
```

```
// Finally, close the connection
          conn.close();
      } catch (Exception exception) {
        System.out.println("General exception occurred: " + exception);
      }
   }
} ▷
```

Although five usage combinations can be derived and are outlined below based on the concept of separating the service interface and service implementation, we believe that usage is currently typically centered around two use cases (items two and three).

1. Publishing the service interface only. This can be realized as the first part of Listing 12.3.

2. Publishing the service interface with one service implementation. This is Listing 12.3.

3. Publishing a complete WSDL document that contains both a service interface and service implementation interface. The realization for this would be identical to Listing 12.3.

4. Publishing a service implementation definition that uses multiple service interfaces. This would be the case if, for example, Flute Bank decided to implement two services, as shown below:

```
<import namespace="http://www.goodbankconsortium.com/xml"
     location=" http://www.goodbankconsortium.com/creditcardinterface.wsdl"/>
<import namespace="http://www.betterbankconsortium.com/xml"
     location=" http://www.betterbankconsortium bankacountdebit.wsdl"/>

<service name="Billpayservice">
  <port name="CreditCardBillPayPort" binding="good:BillPayBinding">
    <soap:address
        location="http://www.flutebank.com:8080/billpayservice/CardBillPay"/>
    </port>
```

> ▷ By default, JAXR will download and verify that the WSDL is available at the URLs when publishing. The validation can be bypassed by using the `setValidateURI(false)` method.

```
<port name="AccountBillPayPort" binding="better:BillPayBinding">
  <soap:address
   location="http://www.flutebankx.com:8080/billpayservice/AccountBillPay"/>
  </port>
</service>
```

The only difference between the realization for this and Listing 12.3 would be multiple `ServiceBinding` objects associated with the `Service`.

5. Publishing an abstract description that references another abstract description. In this case, instead of a `Service`, another `Concept` that refers would be created and published.

Querying UDDI Registry with JAXR

We have already covered the case of *finding* entities in the registry in the previous two examples, where we searched for an organization called Flute Bank and also for classifications.

Steps 1 through 8 remain the same as in the section Publishing Company Information to a UDDI Registry and in Listing 12.1, with one exception. Per the UDDI specifications, no authentication or SSL is needed to query the registry. Let us look at the subsequent steps:

1. Use the reference to the `BusinessQueryManager` and one of the `find` methods (see Figure 12.14) to query the registry. Listing 12.4 queries the registry for an organization whose name must exactly match "Flute Bank." This should return one or more organizations, one of which would be the organization we published in Listing 12.1.

2. Create a pattern to query on. For the above criteria, this would be `FluteBank`.

3. Create the qualifiers for the `find` operation.

4. Invoke the `findOrganizations` method on the `BusinessQueryManager`.

5. Parse the `BulkResponse` object returned from the `find` method and obtain the collection of `Organization` objects.

6. Query each `Organization` object to obtain details about the primary contact and services registered.

7. Close the `Connection` to the registry

Listing 12.4a shows the code; Listing 12.4b shows the corresponding output.

Listing 12.4a Querying organization information from UDDI

```java
import javax.xml.registry.infomodel.*;
import javax.xml.registry.*;
import java.util.*;

public class UDDIQueryOrg {

public static void main(String[] args) {
// Set the properties for the ConnectionFactory
Properties environment = new Properties();
environment.setProperty("javax.xml.registry.queryManagerURL", QUERY_URL);
environment.setProperty("javax.xml.registry.lifeCycleManagerURL", PUBLISH_URL);

 // Instantiate the factory and create a connection from it
ConnectionFactory connfactory = ConnectionFactory.newInstance();
connfactory.setProperties(environment);
Connection conn = connfactory.createConnection();

Collection searchpattern = new ArrayList();
searchpattern.add("Flute Bank");

Collection findqualifier= new ArrayList();
findqualifier.add(FindQualifier.EXACT_NAME_MATCH);

// Find using the name
BulkResponse response =  querymgr.findOrganizations(findqualifier,
                         searchpattern, null, null, null, null);

// Display information about the organizations found
Collection orgs = response.getCollection();
Iterator orgiterator = orgs.iterator();

while (orgiterator.hasNext()) {
    Organization org =  (Organization) orgiterator.next();
    System.out.println("\t Organization name: " + org.getName().getValue());
    System.out.println("\t Organization description: " +
org.getDescription().getValue());
    System.out.println("\t Organization uid: " + org.getKey().getId());
```

```
// Display information about the discovery URLs found
    Collection links = org.getExternalLinks();
    Iterator linkiterator = links.iterator();
    while(linkiterator.hasNext()){
        ExternalLink link = (ExternalLink)linkiterator.next();
        System.out.println("\t\t Link URI = " +link.getExternalURI());
    }

// Display information about the discovery URLs found
    Collection classify = org.getClassifications();
    Iterator classifyiterator = classify.iterator();
    while(linkiterator.hasNext()){
        Classification clasf = (Classification)linkiterator.next();
        System.out.println("\t\t Classification value = " +clasf.getValue());
    }

// Display primary contact information
    User pc = org.getPrimaryContact();
    if (pc != null) {
        PersonName pcName = pc.getPersonName();
        System.out.println("\t\t Primary contact name: " +
                                        pcName.getFullName());
        Collection phNums =  pc.getTelephoneNumbers(pc.getType());
        Iterator phIter = phNums.iterator();
        while (phIter.hasNext()) {
        TelephoneNumber num = (TelephoneNumber) phIter.next();
        System.out.println("\t\t Phone number: " +  num.getNumber());
        }
        Collection eAddrs = pc.getEmailAddresses();
        Iterator eaIter = eAddrs.iterator();
        while (phIter.hasNext()) {
        System.out.println("\t\tEmail Address: " +
                                    (EmailAddress) eaIter.next());
        }
    }
  }
 }
}
```

Listing 12.4b   Output of `UDDIQuery`

```
C:\jaxr\jwsa>java UDDIQueryOrg fluteadmin flutepassword
Organization name: Flute Bank
Organization description: A fictitious bank used for examples in the book Java Web
    Services Architecture, published by Morgan Kaufman, ISBN 1-55860-900-8. The authors
                                                                    can be reached at

        webservicesbook@yahoogroups.com OR
        www.javawebservicesarchitecture.com.
Organization uid: 38920050-D028-11D6-9314-000629DC0A7B
    Link URI = http://uddi.ibm.com/testregistry/uddiget?
                businessKey=38920050-D028-11D6-9314-000629DC0A7B
    Primary contact name: John Malkovich
    Phone number: 1-800-FLUTE-US
```

Finding Services Information in UDDI

We have looked at how service information can be published. Let us now look at how it can be retrieved from the registry by JAXR client applications. There are two broad use cases for retrieving the WSDL definition:

- The client knows the organization and wants to retrieve one or more interfaces published by it.
- The client knows the namespace corresponding to the service.

In the first case, the client must query the registry for a particular organization. It can retrieve this information based on name, classification, external identifiers, and other criteria. The organization can then be queried for the services published under it. Listing 12.5a shows how the WSDL published earlier can be retrieved using the Flute Bank organization name. Listing 12.5b shows its corresponding output.

Listing 12.5a   Querying the registry for service information

```
import javax.xml.registry.infomodel.*;
import javax.xml.registry.*;
import java.util.*;
```

```java
public class UDDIQueryServices {
    private static final String QUERY_URL =
                    "http://www-3.ibm.com:80/services/uddi/v2beta/inquiryapi";

/* Main method */
    public static void main(String[] args) {
    try{

// Set the properties for the ConnectionFactory
        Properties environment = new Properties();
        environment.setProperty("javax.xml.registry.queryManagerURL", QUERY_URL);

// Instantiate the factory and create a connection from it
        ConnectionFactory connfactory = ConnectionFactory.newInstance();
        connfactory.setProperties(environment);
        Connection conn = connfactory.createConnection();

// Obtain a reference to the RegistryService,the BusinessLifeCycleManager,
 //  and the BusinessQueryManager
        RegistryService registryservice = conn.getRegistryService();
        BusinessLifeCycleManager lifecyclemgr =
                            registryservice.getBusinessLifeCycleManager();
        BusinessQueryManager querymgr = registryservice.getBusinessQueryManager();

// prepare the arguments for the find operation
        Collection searchpattern = new ArrayList();
        searchpattern.add("Flute Bank");
        Collection findqualifier= new ArrayList();
         findqualifier.add(FindQualifier.EXACT_NAME_MATCH);

// Find using the name
        BulkResponse response =  querymgr.findOrganizations(findqualifier,
                                        searchpattern, null, null, null, null);

// Display information about the organizations found
// In our case, only one should be returned
        Collection orgs = response.getCollection();
        Iterator orgiterator = orgs.iterator();
        while (orgiterator.hasNext()) {
            Organization org =  (Organization) orgiterator.next();
            System.out.println("Organization name: "+org.getName().getValue());
```

```
        System.out.println("Organization uid: " + org.getKey().getId());

//Display service and binding information
        Collection services = org.getServices();
        Iterator svcIter = services.iterator();
        while (svcIter.hasNext()) {
            Service svc = (Service) svcIter.next();
            System.out.println("\t\t Service name: " +
                                            svc.getName().getValue());
            System.out.println("\t\t Service description: " +
                                            svc.getDescription().getValue());
            Collection serviceBindings =  svc.getServiceBindings();
            Iterator sbIter = serviceBindings.iterator();
            while (sbIter.hasNext()) {
                ServiceBinding sb =(ServiceBinding) sbIter.next();
                System.out.println("\t\t\t  Binding " +
                            "Description: " +sb.getDescription().getValue());
                System.out.println("\t\t\t  Access URI: " +
                                                sb.getAccessURI());
                Collection servicespecs= sb.getSpecificationLinks();
                Iterator servicespecit=servicespecs.iterator();
                while(servicespecit.hasNext()){
                SpecificationLink spec=
                                (SpecificationLink)servicespecit.next();
            Concept tModel= (Concept)spec.getSpecificationObject();
// get the tModel
                System.out.println("\t\t\t\t Service Interface :"
                            +tModel.getDescription().getValue());
                Iterator extlinks=tModel.getExternalLinks().iterator();
                while(extlinks.hasNext()){
                    ExternalLink extlink=(ExternalLink)extlinks.next();
                    System.out.println("\t\t\t\t Service Interface
                                location : "+extlink.getExternalURI());
                    System.out.println("\t\t\t\t Location
                                    description:"
                                +extlink.getDescription().getValue());
                    }
                }
            }
        }
    }
```

```
// Finally, close the connection
    conn.close();
  } catch (Exception exception) {
    System.out.println("General exception occurred: " + exception);
        }
      }
    }
```

Listing 12.5b   Client side output of a service query

```
C:\jaxr\jwsa>java UDDIQueryServices flutebank fluteadmin
Organization name: Flute Bank
Organization uid: 46F5D8A0-D3D5-11D6-8370-000629DC0A7B
    Service name: Billpayservice
    Service description: A Web service allowing account holders to pay bills online
          Binding Description: HTTP bindings for the
                          Billpayservice Web service
        Access URI: http://127.0.0.1:8080/billpayservice/jaxrpc/BillPay
            Service Interface: The service interface of the bill payment Web
                                                                      service
          Service Interface location:
http://127.0.0.1:8080/billpayservice/billpayserviceinterface.wsdl#BillPayBinding
              Location description: Wsdl service interface document
```

In the second case, the client can query the registry based on the namespace declaration from the WSDL defining the service interface. The namespace corresponds to the name of the concept (i.e., the tModel name) classified with the wsdlSpec in UDDI, as shown earlier. This may be helpful in two cases:

- The parties can agree upon the namespace as part of the service level agreement between them.

- The client may want to query the registry to find service implementation based on service interfaces defined by industry verticals. For example, we mentioned earlier how the Good Banking Consortium may define the BillPay service implemented by Flute. The namespace of this service interface will be that as defined by the consortium.

Listing 12.6a shows how the service can be queried on namespace. Listing 12.6b shows the corresponding output.

Listing 12.6a   Service discovery based on namespace

```
import javax.xml.registry.*;
import javax.xml.registry.infomodel.*;
import java.util.*;

public class UDDIQueryServicesByNamespace {
private static final String QUERY_URL="http://uddi.microsoft.com:80/inquire";

/* Main method of the class*/
    public static void main(String[] args) {
    try{
// Set the properties for the ConnectionFactory
    Properties environment = new Properties();
    environment.setProperty("javax.xml.registry.queryManagerURL", QUERY_URL);
// Instantiate the factory and create a connection from it
    ConnectionFactory connfactory = ConnectionFactory.newInstance();
    connfactory.setProperties(environment);
    Connection conn = connfactory.createConnection();
// Obtain a reference to the RegistryService,the BusinessLifeCycleManager
//  and the BusinessQueryManager
    RegistryService registryservice = conn.getRegistryService();
    BusinessLifeCycleManager lifecyclemgr =
                                registryservice.getBusinessLifeCycleManager();
    BusinessQueryManager querymgr =
                                registryservice.getBusinessQueryManager();

// prepare the parameters for the find operation
    Collection findqualifier= new ArrayList();
    findqualifier.add(FindQualifier.EXACT_NAME_MATCH);

// WSDL tModels must be classified under the wsdlSpec classification in UDDI
    Collection  classifications = new ArrayList();
    ClassificationScheme uddiOrgTypes =
                querymgr.findClassificationSchemeByName(null, "uddi-org:types");
    Classification wsdlSpecClassification =
        lifecyclemgr.createClassification(uddiOrgTypes, "wsdlSpec", "wsdlSpec");
    classifications.add(wsdlSpecClassification);
```

```
// WSDLs corresponding to this namespace
    Collection searchpattern = new ArrayList();
    searchpattern.add("%http://www.flutebank.com/xml%");

// find the Concepts (i.e., the tModels)
    BulkResponse response = querymgr.findConcepts(null, searchpattern,
                                             classifications, null, null);
    Collection specConcepts = response.getCollection();
    Iterator iter = specConcepts.iterator();
    while (iter.hasNext()) {
    try {
        Concept concept = (Concept)iter.next();
        String name = concept.getName().getValue();
        Collection extlinks = concept.getExternalLinks();
        System.out.println("WSDL :\n\t Namespace: " + name +
            "\n\t Key: " + concept.getKey().getId() +
        "\n\t Description: " + concept.getDescription().getValue());
        Iterator linkiter=extlinks.iterator();
        while(linkiter.hasNext()) {
        ExternalLink link = (ExternalLink)linkiter.next();
        System.out.println("\t WSDL location : " + link.getExternalURI());
        }
    // Find all the organizations using this WSDL definition
        Collection tmodels = new ArrayList();
        tmodels.add(concept);
        response = querymgr.findOrganizations(null, null, null, tmodels, null, null);
        Collection orgs = response.getCollection();
        Iterator orgIter = orgs.iterator();
        if (orgIter.hasNext())
            System.out.println("Organizations using the " + name + " WSDL
                                                        namespace:");
        else
            System.out.println("No Organizations using the WSDL " + name);
                                                    while (orgIter.hasNext()) {
            Organization org = (Organization)orgIter.next();
            System.out.println("\t Name: " + org.getName().getValue() +
                "\n\t Key: " + org.getKey().getId() +
                "\n\t Description: " + org.getDescription().getValue());
                }
```

```
    }catch (JAXRException e) {
        e.printStackTrace();
        }
    }
    } catch (JAXRException e) {
        e.printStackTrace();
        }
    }
}
```

Listing 12.6b   The client side output

```
C:\jaxr\jwsa>java UDDIQueryServicesByNamespace
WSDL :
    Namespace: http://www.flutebank.com/xml
    Key: UUID:67191F10-D3D6-11D6-8370-000629DC0A7B
    Description: The service interface of the bill payment Web service
WSDL location:
http://127.0.0.1:8080/billpayservice/billpayserviceinterface.wsdl#BillPayBinding
Organizations with service implementations for namespace www.flutebank.com/xml
    Name: Flute Bank
    Key: 46F5D8A0-D3D5-11D6-8370-000629DC0A7B
    Description: A fictitious bank used for examples in the book Java Web Services
Architecture, published by Morgan Kaufman, ISBN 1-55860-900-8. The authors can be
    reached at webservicesbook@yahoogroups.com OR
    http://www.javawebservicesarchitecture.com.
```

Runtime Service Discovery from UDDI

We have just looked at how the service information can be published and retrieved from the UDDI registry. In Chapter 2, we talked about the register-find-bind scenario for Web services. In most cases, service consumers will locate the WSDL and generate the client-side code in Java or other languages for consuming that service.

In Chapter 9, we looked at how to do this for both Java and C#. This is a typical use of the *static compile-time binding* pattern discussed in Chapter 5. In most cases, clients will not look up the UDDI registry at runtime for this information, because the WSDL published in the registry will be part of some service level or business agreement and will not be expected to change often.

We also discussed the second *static deploy-time binding* pattern, where the portType is known but the location is retrieved at runtime. Let us look at a strategy for implementing this pattern:

1. Design-time tools can discover the service in the UDDI registry and retrieve its service interface and the service implementation. Though we looked at how to do this programmatically with JAXR, we envision that vendor-provided tools will perform this task at design time, using APIs such as those provided by JSR-110 (Java API for WSDL) in combination with JAXR.

2. Either way, the client application will have complete service information described by the JAXR Service and ServiceBinding (containing the key), Concept, and ExternalLink. It can then store the ServiceBinding key, which corresponds to the UDDI bindingKey in some configuration variable.

3. When the client is executed, it can use this stored ServiceBinding key to retrieve the ServiceBinding information from the BusinessQueryManager. For example:

```
BulkResponse response=querymgr.findServiceBindings(serviceKey,null,null,null);
```

We have already discussed this static deploy-time pattern earlier but clearly this can be useful if:

- The service location changes.
- The client is created and distributed by the service provider to different service consumers.
- The service invocation fails, at which time the client can query the registry for a mirror location for the same service defined by the service provider.

Deployment-Time Publication to UDDI

Though we have discussed how information can be published progammatically to the registry, it is quite common for an enterprise to follow an administrator-driven approach during application deployment into production environments Here, for example, a designated person is responsible for publishing information in the UDDI registry using the browser-based interface. This also makes sense, because information such as company address, contact information, and service location is expected to remain static and is included as part of the service level agreements forged with business partners.

> ## JAXR to UDDI Mapping

In the previous sections, we looked at how different operations can be performed on the UDDI registry using JAXR. While developers never interact directly with the registry in any form, it is worth noting how JAXR defines the mapping between its information model and UDDI. Table 12.2 shows the high-level mapping between the information models. Table 12.3 shows the UDDI SOAP-publishing-related API mapped by JAXR, and Table 12.4 shows the Inquiry API. We encourage you to refer to the specifications for detailed attribute-level mapping.

We would like to mention three important details about all that has been covered in this chapter relating to UDDI:

- Though we have talked about publishing WSDL, it should be noted that the WSDL file itself is not being stored in UDDI, only the information or metadata about the service contained therein. The WSDL must still be located on a Web server. UDDI is not a repository.

- Use of the Microsoft and IBM public registries in the examples above should not imply that JAXR is only for publishing to public registries. From a developer's perspective, it does not matter if the registry is public, private, or from

Table 12.2   Information Model Mapping

JAXR interface	UDDI data structure
Organization	businessEntity
Service	businessService
ServiceBinding	bindingTemplate
Concept	tModel (fingerprint)
ClassificationScheme	tModel (namespace)
ExternalLink	discoveryURL
User	contact
Collection of ExternalIdentifier instances	identifierBag
Collection of Classification instances	categoryBag
PostalAddress	address
ExternalLink	overviewDoc
Classification	keyedReference (in categoryBag)
ExternalIdentifier	keyedReference (in identifierBag)

Table 12.3 Mapping of UDDI Publisher API to JAXR

JAXR BusinessLifeCycleManager	UDDI method
saveAssociations	add_publisherAssertions
deleteServiceBindings	delete_binding
deleteOrganizations	delete_business
deleteAssociations	delete_publisherAssertions
deleteServices	delete_service
deleteClassificationsSchemes and deleteConcepts	delete_tModel
findAssociations	get_assertionStatusReport
QueryManager.getRegistryObjects	get_publisherAssertions
QueryManager.getRegistryObjects	get_registeredInfo
saveServiceBindings	save_binding
saveOrganizations	save_business
saveServices	save_service
saveClassificationsSchemes and saveConcepts	save_tModel
saveAssociations	set_publisherAssertions

Table 12.4 Mapping of UDDI Inquiry API to JAXR

JAXR BusinessQueryManager	UDDI method
findServiceBindings	Find_binding
findOrganizations	find_business
findAssociatedObjects	find_related_business
findServices	find_service
findConcepts and findClassificationSchemes	find_tModel

any particular vendor. The code remains the same; only the URLs pointing to the registry change.

- Though we have covered UDDI, the code to realize any of the use cases will not change for other registry *types;* only the underlying provider will. For example, if a JAXR provider was available for a foo-bar registry that supported the capability levels used, simply switching the underlying providers would be enough, because the provider would take care of how the JAXR model maps to that registry. In short, JAXR code is portable across registry providers for the same or higher capability levels.

> JAXR and ebXML Registry

In practical terms, the JAXR information model is based on the ebXML information model. This makes sense from two perspectives: the ebXML v. 2.0 Registry Information Model (RIM) is functionally larger than the UDDI v. 2.0 information model, and developing such detailed models based on community consensus takes time.

As mentioned previously, all the previous discussion about using JAXR and UDDI remains unchanged with an ebXML registry, because of the API's abstraction. In this section, we will discuss how client applications can leverage some of JAXR's level 1 capability features. ▷

Publishing Organizations in ebXML Registries

One of the significant differences between UDDI and ebXML registries is how client applications are authenticated. While UDDI requires only password-based authentication, the ebXML Registry Service allows for digital certificates to be used in the SOAP headers. The SOAP message in Listing 12.7 shows how the X.509 certificate is included using XML D-Sig specifications.

Listing 12.7   SOAP request to the registry with the X.509 certificate

```
<soap-env:Envelope xmlns:soap-env="http://schemas.xmlsoap.org/soap/envelope/">
<soap-env:Header>
    <ds:Signature xmlns:ds="http://www.w3.org/2000/09/xmldsig#">
    <ds:SignedInfo>
    <ds:CanonicalizationMethod
            Algorithm="http://www.w3.org/TR/2001/REC-xml-c14n-20010315">
        </ds:CanonicalizationMethod>
    <ds:SignatureMethod
            Algorithm="http://www.w3.org/2000/09/xmldsig#dsa-sha1">
        </ds:SignatureMethod>
```

> ▷   The ebXML Registry Service and Registry Information Model specifications can be found at *www.oasis-open.org/committees/regrep.*

```
<ds:Reference URI="">
<ds:Transforms>
<ds:Transform
        Algorithm="http://www.w3.org/2000/09/xmldsig#enveloped-signature">
    </ds:Transform>
<ds:Transform
    Algorithm="http://www.w3.org/TR/2001/REC-xml-c14n-20010315#WithComments">
        </ds:Transform>
</ds:Transforms>
<ds:DigestMethod Algorithm="http://www.w3.org/2000/09/xmldsig#sha1">
    </ds:DigestMethod>
<ds:DigestValue>bT5BLPViSpaLoRE3fjnHORpQ6Jw=</ds:DigestValue>
</ds:Reference>
</ds:SignedInfo>

<ds:SignatureValue>YJZAHweU7komyE1p9yOiutWrwZR46/L2GByohkd/b16iVurDQ3ik1g==
        </ds:SignatureValue>
<ds:KeyInfo>
<ds:X509Data>
<ds:X509Certificate>
MIIC2DCCApYCBD2WJLAwCwYHKoZIzjgEAwUAMFIxDDAKBgNVBAYTA1VTQTEVMBMGA1UEChMMU
cmN1IEZvcmd1MRAwDgYDVQQLEwd1YnhtbHJyMRkwFwYDVQQDExBSZWdpc3RyeU9wZXJhdG9yM
DTAyMDkyODIxNTI0OFoXDTAyMTIyNzIxNTI0OFowUjEMMAoGA1UEBhMDVVNBMRUwEwYDVQQKE
b3VyY2UgRm9yZ2UxEDAOBgNVBAsTB2VieG1scnIxGTAXBgNVBAMTEFJ1Z21zdHJ5T3B1cmF0b
ggG3MIIBLAYHKoZIzjgEATCCAR8CgYEA/X9TgR11Ei1S3OqcLuzk5/YRt1I870QAwx4/gLZRJ
XUAiUftZPY1Y+r/F9bow9subVWzXgTuAHTRv8mZgt2uZUKWkn5/oBHsQIsJPu6nX/rfGG/g7V
qKYVDwT7g/bTxR7DAjVUE1oWkTL2dfOuK2HXKu/yIgMZndFIAccCFQCXYFCPFSMLzLKSuYKi6
8Fgc9QKBgQD34aCF1ps93su8q1w2uFe5eZSvu/o66oL5VOwLPQeCZ1FZV4661F1P5nEHEIGAt
cSPoTCgWE7fPCTKMyKbhPBZ6i1R8jSjgo64eK7OmdZFuo38L+iE1YvH7YnoBJDvMpPG+qFGQi
3+Fa5Z8GkotmXoB7VSVkAUw7/s9JKgOBhAACgYB19I45gtWIm14LIQXNNZS/u43ams5pjzjD9
drOvoIUc/cWm/odiLnoNj4YNaRKncI8f5o91QYX4y4QGusbVLVVUd7u4Xby5OseuOnvAxh9//
BHaQgHA/JTvatcmZwjXqqpZyBYrEYfXpHAFTY6fLJFKpp31Ai045gcXGIzALBgcqhkjOOAQDB
LwAwLAIUYODY/SLIho4PA11VC4ZnCavE57cCFCtmGUi+oFftL8m29PdZqkW4XMK1
</ds:X509Certificate>
</ds:X509Data>
<ds:KeyValue>
<ds:DSAKeyValue>
<ds:P>
/X9TgR11Ei1S3OqcLuzk5/YRt1I870QAwx4/gLZRJm1FXUAiUftZPY1Y+r/F9bow9subVWzXg
HTRv8mZgt2uZUKWkn5/oBHsQIsJPu6nX/rfGG/g7V+fGqKYVDwT7g/bTxR7DAjVUE1oWkTL2d
K2HXKu/yIgMZndFIAcc=
</ds:P>
```

```
        <ds:Q>12BQjxUjC8yykrmCouuEC/BYHPU=</ds:Q>
        <ds:G>
        9+GghdabPd7LvKtcNrhXuXmUr7v6OuqC+VdMCzOHgmdRWVeOutRZT+ZxBxCBgLRJFnEj6EwoF
        zwkyjMim4TwWeotUfIOo4KOuHiuzpnWRbqN/C/ohNWLx+2J6ASQ7zKTxvqhRkImog9/hWuWfB
        Z16Ae1U1ZAFMO/7PSSo=
        </ds:G>
        <ds:Y>
        dfSOOYLViJpeCyEFzTWUv7uN2prOaY84w/Q1THa9L6CFHP3Fpv6HYi56DY+GDWkSp3CPH+aPZ
        +MuEBrrG1S1VVHe7uF28udLHrtJ7wMYff/w9KgR2kIBwPyU72rXJmcI16qqWcgWKxGH16RwBU
        yyRSqad9QItOOYHFxiM=
        </ds:Y>
        </ds:DSAKeyValue>
        </ds:KeyValue>
        </ds:KeyInfo>
        </ds:Signature>
</soap-env:Header>
<soap-env:Body>
    <SubmitObjectsRequest
            xmlns="urn:oasis:names:tc:ebxml-regrep:registry:xsd:2.1">
    <LeafRegistryObjectList>
        <RegistryPackage id="urn:uuid:bfef9997-508d-4131-a826-edebc7a47836" objectType=
                                                            "RegistryPackage">

    <Name>
            <LocalizedString charset="UTF-8" lang="en-us"
            value="Flute Bank Agreements">
             </LocalizedString>
    </Name>
    <Description>
            <LocalizedString charset="UTF-8" lang="en-us" value="">
     </LocalizedString>
    </Description>
    </RegistryPackage>
    </LeafRegistryObjectList>
    </SubmitObjectsRequest>
</soap-env:Body>
</soap-env:Envelope>
```

Let us look at how a client can publish Organization information in the ebXML registry using JAXR. Listing 12.8 shows how the JAXR provider for ebXML (available under open source) can be used. The example is identical to Listing 12.1, which published the information to a UDDI registry. The only difference is the manner in which the connection is passed the user's credentials for authentication. Instead of a username and password, the user sends the X.509 certificate.

Listing 12.8 Using the open source JAXR provider to include the X.509 certificate

```
import java.security.*;
import java.security.cert.X509Certificate;
// other imports

public class ebXMLPublishOrg {

public static void main (String args[]){
// keystore location and alias

// Start JAXR provider imsplementation specific code
    String alias = "mykey";
    String location="c:/temp/rr/jaxr/keystore.jks";
    String storepass="ebxmlrr";
    String keypass="password";
HashSet creds = new HashSet();
// get the keystore
KeyStore keyStore = KeyStore.getInstance("JKS");
keyStore.load(new FileInputStream(location), storepass.toCharArray());
X509Certificate cert =(X509Certificate)keyStore.getCertificate(alias);
PrivateKey privateKey=
(PrivateKey)keyStore.getKey(alias,keypass.toCharArray());
    X500PrivateCredential credential=
                              new X500PrivateCredential(cert,privateKey,alias);
// End  JAXR provider implementation specific code
    creds.add(credential);

// Create the connection factory, which can be set by the system property
//-Djavax.xml.registry.ConnectionFactoryClass=
//                   com.sun.xml.registry.ebxml.ConnectionFactoryImpl
 ConnectionFactory factory = ConnectionFactory.newInstance();
 Connection connection = connFactory.createConnection();
 connection.setCredentials(creds);
// create organization and other objects with BusinessLifeCyleManager and
// use the BusinessLifeCyleManager.saveOrganizations(orgs) method
    }
} ▷
```

Publishing Content to ebXML Registry

One of the advantages of using an ebXML registry is that it can store arbitrary content, such as business process descriptions (BPML documents), and business agreements, such as the CPP and CPA agreements used in ebXML messaging systems. This is different from storing WSDL in UDDI, in the sense that the *actual* business document is stored in the repository, which the registry service exposes. For example, the code in Listing 12.3 publishes a URL only to the WSDL document, whereas in an ebXML registry, the actual WSDL document may be published to the registry. In this sense, the ebXML registry plays a sort of content management role.

In JAXR, the `ExtrinsicObject` is used to model the metadata representing such content. Let us look at some code extracts that show how this can be used. Flute Bank can choose to store its CPP/CPA with OfficeMin as the following code shows.

▷ **X.509**

Digital certificates are based on public-key crytography, in which an individual is issued a private and a public key. X.509 is a widely used industry standard maintained by the International Telecommunications Union (ITU). It is used in various code-signing schemes, (e.g., signed JAR files and Microsoft Authenticode) and protocols such as secure email (PEM and S/MIME) and SSL. The certificate contains information about the issuer, the validity period, the subject's distinguished name (e.g., CN=John Malkovich, OU=Billing Department, O=Flute Bank, C=US) and the subject's public key.

Typically, authentication is performed by the user's sending the X.509 certificate containing the public key. The server sends a challenge back to the user that contains a randomly generated sequence of characters. The user then encrypts it with the private key and returns the encrypted string to the server. If the encrypted string can be successfully decrypted using the public key supplied in the certificate, the server can be sure the user is in possession of the private key and is the person to whom the certificate was issued.

Working with X.509 Certificates

The JDK comes with a the tool called `keytool` that can be used to create public-private key pairs; display, import, and export X.509 v. 1, v. 2, and v. 3 certificates stored as files; and generate new self-signed v. 1 certificates. `keytool` also manages the keystore, which is a protected database that holds keys and certificates. The API for using these certificates in Java is included in the core package, `ava.security.cert`.

```
// Create a connection and authenticate with the registry
// Obtain the BusinessLifeCyleManager instance from the connection
// Now get the XML file
URL url = getClass().getResource("/agreements/officemin.xml");
DataHandler handler = new DataHandler(url);
// Create an ExtrinsicObject
ExtrinsicObject obj = lifecyclemgr.createExtrinsicObject(handler);
obj.setRepositoryItem(handler);
// Save the arbitrary content
Collection data = new ArrayList();
data.add(obj);
BulkResponse response = lifecyclemgr.saveObjects(data);
if(response.getStatus()==BulkResponse.STATUS_SUCCESS){
    System.out.println("CPP successfully saved");
     System.out.println("ID is :+obj.getKey().getId()");
        }
```

Note that in the above example, the resource can be any arbitrary content, such as graphic files, XML schemas, or Word documents.

In practical terms, content will be grouped into RegistryPackage objects that can be associated with any RegistryObject. RegistryPackages are a powerful level 1 feature. Any registry object can have multiple RegistryPackages associated with it and can also be associated with multiple packages. Therefore, business documents such as privacy policies, grouped under a package named "Policies" and associated with an Organization, can be retrieved as shown below:

```
// Locate the Organization
    BulkResponse response = querymgr.findOrganizations(findqualifier,
                                    searchpattern, null, null, null,
// Iterate and get to the individual Organization
    Organization org =  (Organization) orgiterator.next();
     Collection packages =org.getRegistryPackages();
 // Iterate and get to the package we are interested in
     if(package.getName().getValue().equals("Policies"){
        Collection extobjects=package.getRegistryObjects();
 //  Iterate and get individual ExtrinsicObject elements
         ExtrinsicObject obj=eoiter.next();
// get underlying content
         DataHandler handler= obj.getRepositoryItem();
```

Documents such as the CPP and CPA, which relate to the Service, can also be queried and stored in a similar manner under the associated Service object (which is also an instance of a RegistryObject).

As a general programming note, while interacting with the ebXML registry, client applications will rely more on the generic methods defined in the LifeCycleManager rather than the subclass BusinessLifeCycleManager to create and save objects. Similarly, they will rely more on the declarative queries and the DeclarativeQueryManager looked at earlier to find data in the registry, as opposed to the BusinessQueryManager looked at for UDDI.

A Complete ebXML Example

Let us look at a complete example of publishing information to an ebXML registry, using the open source JAXR provider and ebXML registry implementation. We have slightly modified the UDDI example from Listing 12.1, for two reasons: the ebXML registry has tighter validation rules than UDDI (e.g., a contact person for an Organization is required), and we wanted to show the use of some level 1 capabilities.

Listing 12.9 publishes Flute Bank's information, its BillPay service information, some associated documents (we will use Flute's BPSS and CPA XML documents used in Chapter 7), and creates a package object in the registry and an association. For the sake of brevity, we have not included the SOAP messages exchanged between the client and the registry. Upon successful execution, the results can be viewed using the graphical registry browser, as Figure 12.19 shows.

Figure 12.19
ebXML registry
browser

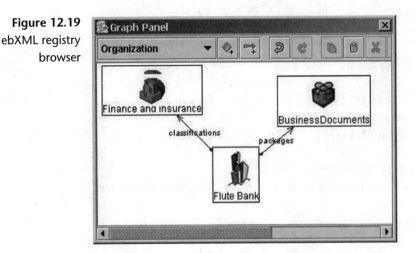

Listing 12.9   Publishing with the JAXR provider

```
import javax.xml.registry.infomodel.*;
import javax.xml.registry.*;
import java.util.*;
import java.net.URL;
import javax.activation.*;
import java.security.*;
import java.io.FileInputStream;
import java.security.cert.X509Certificate;
import javax.security.auth.x500.X500PrivateCredential;


public class ebXMLPublishOrg{
  private static final String QUERY_URL= "http://localhost:9090/ebxmlrr/registry";
  private static final String PUBLISH_URL="http://localhost:9090/ebxmlrr/registry";
  public static void main(String[] args) throws Exception {
// Set the properties for the ConnectionFactory
Properties environment = new Properties();
environment.setProperty("javax.xml.registry.queryManagerURL", QUERY_URL);
environment.setProperty("javax.xml.registry.lifeCycleManagerURL", PUBLISH_URL);

// Instantiate the factory and create a connection from it
    ConnectionFactory connfactory = ConnectionFactory.newInstance();
    connfactory.setProperties(environment);
    Connection conn = connfactory.createConnection();
// Authenticate the username and password with the registry

//////////////// Start JAXR provider implementation-specific code
    String alias = "mykey";
    String location="c:/temp/rr/jaxr/keystore.jks";
    String storepass="ebxmlrr";
    String keypass="password";
    HashSet creds = new HashSet();
// get the keystore
  KeyStore  keyStore = KeyStore.getInstance("JKS");
    keyStore.load(new FileInputStream(location), storepass.toCharArray());

  X509Certificate cert =(X509Certificate)keyStore.getCertificate(alias);
  PrivateKey privateKey =
                (PrivateKey)keyStore.getKey(alias,keypass.toCharArray());
```

```
  X500PrivateCredential credential=
                           new X500PrivateCredential(cert,privateKey,alias);
    creds.add(credential);
/////////////// END JAXR provider implementation-specific code
    conn.setCredentials(creds);

// Obtain a reference to the RegistryService, the BusinessLifeCycleManager, and
// the BusinessQueryManager
RegistryService registryservice = conn.getRegistryService();
BusinessLifeCycleManager lifecyclemgr =
                           registryservice.getBusinessLifeCycleManager();
BusinessQueryManager querymgr = registryservice.getBusinessQueryManager();

// Create a user object
User contact = lifecyclemgr.createUser();
PersonName name = lifecyclemgr.createPersonName("John Malkovich");
contact.setPersonName(name);
InternationalString contactdescription = lifecyclemgr.createInternationalString
                          ("The primary contact person for Flute Web services");
contact.setDescription(contactdescription);

// Create and set the user's telephone number
TelephoneNumber telnum = lifecyclemgr.createTelephoneNumber();
telnum.setNumber("1-800-FLUTE-US");
Collection phonenumbers = new ArrayList();
phonenumbers.add(telnum);
contact.setTelephoneNumbers(phonenumbers);

// Create and set the user's email address
EmailAddress email =  lifecyclemgr.createEmailAddress(
                                        "ebxml-admin@flutebank.com");
Collection emaillist = new ArrayList();
emaillist.add(email);
contact.setEmailAddresses(emaillist);

PostalAddress addr = lifecyclemgr.createPostalAddress("64","Bit
                     Street","Windsor","CT","USA","03060","Office Address");
ArrayList addresses = new ArrayList();
addresses.add(addr);
contact.setPostalAddresses(addresses);
```

```
// Create an organization object
Organization company =   lifecyclemgr.createOrganization("Flute Bank");
InternationalString description = lifecyclemgr.createInternationalString
                    "A fictitious bank used for examples in the book Java Web
Services Architecture, published by Morgan Kaufman, ISBN 1-55860-900-8. The authors
can be reached at webservicesbook@yahoogroups.com OR
www.javawebservicesarchitecture.com. ");
company.setDescription(description);

// Set the user as the primary contact for the organization. User's address and
// company address are same
company.setPrimaryContact(contact);
company.setPostalAddress(addr);
company.setTelephoneNumbers(phonenumbers);

ExternalLink website = lifecyclemgr.createExternalLink("http://www.flutebank.com",
"Flute Bank Inc");
website.setValidateURI(false);
company.addExternalLink(website);

// We now have the objects representing our information model
// To publish it, we must classify it. We decide to use the
//   NAICS scheme
ClassificationScheme scheme =
            querymgr.findClassificationSchemeByName(null,"ntis-gov:naics");

// Create the classification using the above scheme and pass the relevant
// category code and description

Classification classification =
(Classification)lifecyclemgr.createClassification(scheme,"Finance and Insurance", "52");
Collection classificationlist = new ArrayList();
classificationlist.add(classification);
company.addClassifications(classificationlist);

// Create the concrete service (this maps to the businessService)
Service service = lifecyclemgr.createService("Billpayservice");
company.addService(service);
InternationalString servicedescription =
```

```
                              lifecyclemgr.createInternationalString("A Web
                         service allowing account holders to pay bills online");
service.setDescription(servicedescription);

ExternalLink link1 = lifecyclemgr.createExternalLink
 ("http://127.0.0.1:8080/billpayservice/billpayservice.wsdl", "Service WSDL");
link1.setValidateURI(false);
service.addExternalLink(link1);

// Create the service bindings for the Web service
ServiceBinding binding = lifecyclemgr.createServiceBinding();
binding.setValidateURI(false);
InternationalString bindingdescription =
    lifecyclemgr.createInternationalString("HTTP bindings for the Billpayservice Web
                                                                       service");
binding.setDescription(bindingdescription);
// replace with the actual URL where the service is deployed
binding.setAccessURI("http://127.0.0.1:8080/billpayservice/jaxrpc/BillPay");
service.addServiceBinding(binding);

DataHandler upload1 = new DataHandler( new FileDataSource("C:/rr/jaxr/build/test/
classes/bpss.xml" ));
DataHandler upload2 = new DataHandler( new FileDataSource("C:/rr/jaxr/build/test/
classes/cpa.xml" ));

// Create an ExtrinsicObject
ExtrinsicObject obj1 = lifecyclemgr.createExtrinsicObject(upload1);
ExtrinsicObject obj2 = lifecyclemgr.createExtrinsicObject(upload2);

RegistryPackage docs =lifecyclemgr.createRegistryPackage("BusinessDocuments");
docs.addRegistryObject(obj1);
docs.addRegistryObject(obj2);

Concept assType = querymgr.findConceptByPath("/AssociationType/packages");
Association ass = lifecyclemgr.createAssociation(docs, assType);
company.addAssociation(ass);
// make the final call to the registry and get a response
// This could have been used instead
//BulkResponse response = lifecyclemgr.saveOrganizations(organizationlist);
```

```
// We show the more general method below

ArrayList objs = new ArrayList();
objs.add(company);
objs.add(service);
objs.add(binding);
objs.add(contact);
objs.add(docs);
objs.add(website);

BulkResponse response = lifecyclemgr.saveObjects(objs);
if (response.getStatus()==JAXRResponse.STATUS_SUCCESS)
        System.out.println("The request was processed successfully");
// Finally, close the connection
conn.close();
    }
}
```

Mapping of ebXML Registry Information Model to JAXR

No mapping is required from the JAXR model to the ebXML Registry Information Model, because they are identical (e.g., Organization interface in JAXR maps to an Organization object in RIM, etc.) Also, JAXR supports all features and functionality defined by OASIS for the ebXML registry.

> Summary

In this chapter, we looked at JAXR and its functionality. So, why is this API important, and why should developers use it? For businesses to communicate with their partners and forge relationships, not only do they need to expose their functions as Web services, they also need to publish them in a manner accessible by different partners. Using open standards such as XML, UDDI/ebXML registry, and SOAP eliminates the dependence between disparate hardware and software stacks and facilitates a loosely coupled architecture. JAXR removes the dependence between applications and nonstandard toolkits by giving developers a rich, simple, standard extension API to communicate with registry providers using these very same open standards. It allows applications accessing XML registries to remain vendor-neutral and portable across disparate registry implementations.

Chapter  {13}

JAXB

Java API for XML Binding (JAXB) is the much-anticipated Java API designed to provide a programmatic association between XML and Java. Like much of the other JAX APIs, JAXB is designed to provide an abstraction layer at the Java code level, insulating developers from dealing with building, reading, and processing the underlying XML constructs. In general, binding provides developers with a programming-language-centric view of the underlying XML. Though binding developers deal only with objects and classes in their Java code, these objects and classes correspond to underlying XML constructs. ▷

▷ The Need for Binding and JAXB

In Chapter 9, we introduced the concept of parsing XML using SAX and DOM. However, we also mentioned that this would not be necessary, because developers will work with JAXB. Let us now expand on this.

The traditional design approach when dealing with XML in application code has centered around retrieval and parsing of XML, using XML parsers and API (such as JAXP and SAX/DOM) and manipulating the result of that parsing exercise. For example, with SAX, developers run though an XML file in a serial manner, access data, and use its programmatic representation—their own Java objects. Alternatively, developers parse the XML using a tree-based approach and create object tree representations in memory, using a model defined by some other party (e.g., the W3C DOM) or JDOM. In either case, there is a disconnect between the XML data definitions.

▷ At the time of writing this book, the JAXB specifications were public draft version 0.75 and Reference Implementation 1.0. We do not anticipate significant changes between these and the FCS.

545

For example, the purchase order used in Listing 11.5 is represented by an XML schema shown in Listing 13.1. The schema was not listed earlier for brevity but is included with the example code.

Listing 13.1   The `purchaseorder.xsd` schema from Chapter 9

```
<?xml version="1.0" encoding="UTF-8"?>
<xsd:schema targetNamespace="http://www.flutebank.com/schema" xmlns:xsd="http://
www.w3.org/2001/XMLSchema" xmlns="http://www.flutebank.com/schema" elementFormDefault=
"qualified">
    <xsd:element name="billingaddress">
        <xsd:complexType>
            <xsd:sequence>
                <xsd:element ref="name"/>
                <xsd:element ref="street"/>
                <xsd:element ref="city"/>
                <xsd:element ref="state"/>
                <xsd:element ref="zip"/>
            </xsd:sequence>
        </xsd:complexType>
    </xsd:element>
    <xsd:element name="city" type="xsd:string"/>
    <xsd:element name="date" type="xsd:string"/>
    <xsd:element name="description" type="xsd:string"/>
    <xsd:element name="identifier" type="xsd:string"/>
    <xsd:element name="item">
        <xsd:complexType>
            <xsd:sequence>
                <xsd:element ref="quantity"/>
                <xsd:element ref="productnumber"/>
                <xsd:element ref="description"/>
                <xsd:element ref="unitcost"/>
            </xsd:sequence>
        </xsd:complexType>
    </xsd:element>
    <xsd:element name="items">
        <xsd:complexType>
            <xsd:sequence>
                <xsd:element ref="item" maxOccurs="unbounded"/>
```

```
            </xsd:sequence>
        </xsd:complexType>
    </xsd:element>
    <xsd:element name="name" type="xsd:string"/>
    <xsd:element name="productnumber" type="xsd:string"/>
    <xsd:element name="purchaseorder">
        <xsd:complexType>
            <xsd:sequence>
                <xsd:element ref="identifier"/>
                <xsd:element ref="date"/>
                <xsd:element ref="billingaddress"/>
                <xsd:element ref="items"/>
            </xsd:sequence>
        </xsd:complexType>
    </xsd:element>
    <xsd:element name="quantity" type="xsd:int"/>
    <xsd:element name="state" type="xsd:string"/>
    <xsd:element name="street" type="xsd:string"/>
    <xsd:element name="unitcost" type="xsd:decimal"/>
    <xsd:element name="zip" type="xsd:string"/>
</xsd:schema> ▷
```

To pass this logical collection of data around in their code, developers often define a Java class that wraps the data into a JavaBean-type construct, with get/set methods or the attributes. However, the class is developer-designed and -defined and is therefore based on the developer's interpretation of the XML schema. For example, based on the schema in Listing 13.1, a developer may create an Item bean as follows:

```
package com.jwsa.mybeans;
public class Item {
    private String Quantity;
    private String Productnumber;
    private String Description;
    private String Unitcost;
```

> ▷   SML schemas are explained briefly in Appendix A for those readers who are unfamiliar with them.

```
        public String getQuantity() {
            return Quantity;
        }
        public void setQuantity(String quantity) {
            Quantity = quantity;
        }
        public String getProductnumber() {
            return Productnumber;
        }
        public void setProductnumber(String productnumber) {
            Productnumber = productnumber;
        }
        public String getDescription() {
            return Description;
        }
        public void setDescription(String description) {
            Description = description;
        }
        public String getUnitcost() {
            return Unitcost;
        }
        public void setUnitcost(String unitcost) {
            Unitcost = unitcost;
        }
    }
```

Another developer may create another class with a completely different representation or even a different hierarchy. Both would parse the corresponding XML, validate it against the schema, populate their Item bean (or whatever other representation they define), and use it in the code. This approach has issues.

- It requires manual effort and extra coding.
- Any change in the schema requires changes to Java code, reducing the inherent flexibility of using XML in an application.
- It produces code that may vary from developer to developer.
- The programmatic representation may be inaccurate.
- The code is not portable, because of developer interpretation. Two applications using the same XML schema may end up using completely different PurchaseOrder objects that are mutually incompatible.

- To generate the XML representation back from the object representation, developers have to write extra code. For example, developers frequently include a `toString()` method in their objects (e.g., `PurchaseOrder`) that creates an XML string conformant to the schema based on the object properties.

JAXB aims at resolving these issues by giving developers a standard API to program to and automating the Java-XML marshalling and XML-Java unmarshalling with round-trip support between XML and Java. ▷

▷ **When to Use JAXB**

In Chapter 9, we hypothesized that developers would rarely deal with XML constructs directly in their application code when developing Web services, as a result of *other* JAX APIs. In Chapters 10 , 11, and 12, we looked how different APIs (such as JAX-RPC, JAXM, and JAXR, respectively) provide some of this abstraction. JAXB is intended to be used in cases where XML must be handled directly in application code. Some of the scenarios where JAXB would be appropriate typically involve applications that:

- Read, write, or process XML-based configuration information.
- Must pass XML data between applications independently of the SOAP-XML–based messaging and RPC protocol.
- Persist data in XML format or read XML data from a persistent storage, such as an XML database. In such cases, JAXB can be used to marshall and unmarshall the XML directly into Java objects.
- Access XML data and must update or modify that data at runtime. Rather than using SAX/DOM parsing, JAXB can be used to unmarshall the data to Java, change it as necessary, and marshall it back to the XML representation.
- Must marshall value objects into XML and pass them between tiers.

The preceding is meant to be only an illustration of scenarios where JAXB may be appropriate and is not an exhaustive list.

▷   Recall from Chapter 10 that marshalling is the process of creating the XML representation from Java objects—that is, Java-XML—and the reverse process is called unmarshalling.

> JAXB Architecture

JAXB architecture uses a design similar to the other JAX APIs . Developers use standard interfaces and classes provided by the specifications, and vendors provide the implementation. Figure 13.1 shows the overall architecture. Developers write application code and business logic that uses Java classes and interfaces representing XML constructs. These classes are generated from XML schemas using JAXB-provided tools.

When the code must unmarshall XML supplied by some external entity, such as a Web service, the JAXB API is invoked to unmarshall the XML, and the data represented therein is populated in its corresponding Java classes.

To change the Java classes to the corresponding XML representation, developers invoke the JAXB API, and the Java classes are marshalled into the schema-compliant XML format.

Figure 13.1
JAXB
architecture

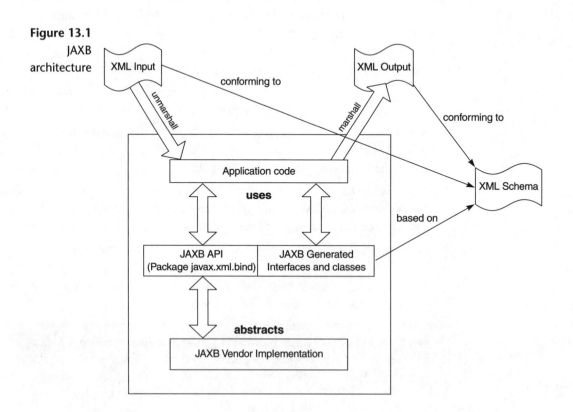

▶ Developing with JAXB

JAXB's workings and the associated development process are best understood through an example. We will quickly walk though an example and then look at different aspects of JAXB from that example in detail.

OfficeMin can receive purchase orders in many ways. In Chapter 11, we saw how a customer such as Flute Bank can use JAXM to send XML messages. Another customer, Piggy Bank, uses a proprietary financial package but is capable of generating and saving purchase order details in XML format. OfficeMin's Web service can process these XML orders.

Generate Java Classes

The first step for OfficeMin to consume the XML is to generate the Java representation of the agreed-upon schema. We will use the schema covered in Chapter 11 and shown in Listing 13.1.

The JAXB specifications require that all JAXB implementations provide a tool called a *schema compiler* or *binding compiler* (Figure 13.2), which should be able to generate the Java code according to the rules and guidelines defined in the JAXB specification. In the reference implementation provided by Sun, the tool is called the XML-to-Java compiler (xjc). ▷

Figure 13.2
The binding
compiler

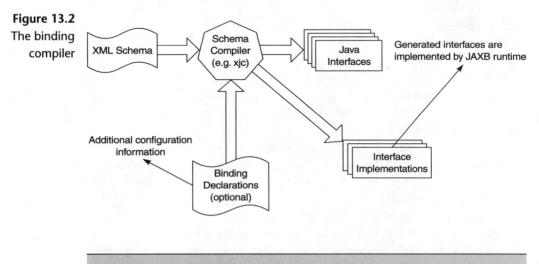

▷   xjc can be found in the JAXB_HOME/bin directory of the reference implementation.

Execute the schema compiler on the purchase order interface:

```
xjc-d output generated purchaseorder.xsd
```

This will generate two sets of files:

- Interfaces that correspond to the XML elements according to the mapping rules defined in JAXB (e.g., PurchaseOrder.java, Billingaddress.java, State.java, Street.java) in a com.flutebank.schema. package. We will discuss this in the next section.
- Implementation classes for the interfaces that are specific to the JAXB runtime. (e.g., PurchaseOrderImpl.java, BillingaddressImpl.java, StateImpl.java) in a com.flutebank.schema.impl package.

Write Application Code

The application in the example *reads in* an XML file and does something useful (for now, it just changes some information around) and writes out an XML file. The file we will read in, purchaseorder.xml, was used in Chapter 9.

Listing 13.2   Simple JAXB code to read an XML document

```java
import java.io.*;
import java.util.*;
// import JAXB API
import javax.xml.bind.*;
// import java content classes generated by binding compiler
import com.flutebank.schema.*;

public class ReadWritePO {
    public static void main( String[] args ) throws Exception {
// create a JAXBContext capable of handling classes in the generated package
    JAXBContext context = JAXBContext.newInstance( "com.flutebank.schema" );
// create an Unmarshaller
    Unmarshaller unmars = context.createUnmarshaller();
// unmarshall an XML document into its Java representation
    Purchaseorder po = (Purchaseorder)unmars.unmarshall( new FileInputStream(
"purchaseorder.xml" ) );
// display the shipping address
```

```
    Billingaddress address = po.getBillingaddress();
    Name name= address.getName();
    Street street= address.getStreet();
    City city= address.getCity();
    State state = address.getState();
    Zip zip= address.getZip();
    System.out.println( "Billing address in the XML is : " );
    System.out.println("Name :" + name.getValue());
    System.out.println("Street :" + street.getValue());
    System.out.println("City :" + city.getValue());
    System.out.println("State :" + state.getValue());
    System.out.println("Zip :" + zip.getValue());
    Items order=po.getItems();
    Iterator it=order.getItem().iterator();
    while(it.hasNext()){
        Item item=      (Item)it.next();
        System.out.println("Order contains" );
        System.out.println("     Description: " + item.getDescription().getValue());
        System.out.println("     Product number: " +
                                    item.getProductnumber().getValue());
        System.out.println("     Quantity: " + item.getQuantity().getValue());
        System.out.println("     Unit cost: " + item.getUnitcost().getValue());
    }
// Change some information
    name.setValue("Sameer Tyagi");
    zip.setValue("90210");
// Marshall Java to XML
    Marshaller mars = context.createMarshaller();
    mars.setProperty( Marshaller.JAXB_FORMATTED_OUTPUT, Boolean.TRUE );
    mars.setProperty (Marshaller.JAXB_SCHEMA_LOCATION,"http://www.flutebank.com/schema
                                    purchaseorder.xsd");
    mars.marshall( po, new FileOutputStream("modifiedpurchaseorder.xml"));
    }
}
```

It should be apparent that the code in Listing 13.1 does not involve any parsing logic whatsoever. The application code uses the JAXB API (e.g., Unmarshaller and JAXBContext) when dealing with the marshalling and unmarshalling and uses the generated interfaces when dealing with the object representation. Listing 13.3 shows the output saved in modifiedpurchaseorder.xml.

Listing 13.3 The XML marshalled out by application code in Listing 13.2

```
<?xml version="1.0" encoding="UTF-8" standalone="yes"?>
<ns1:purchaseorder xsi:schemaLocation="http://www.flutebank.com/schema
purchaseorder.xsd" xmlns:ns1="http://www.flutebank.com/schema" xmlns:xsi="http://
www.w3.org/2001/XMLSchema-instance">
    <ns1:identifier>87 6784365876JHITRYUE</ns1:identifier>
    <ns1:date>29 October 2002</ns1:date>
    <ns1:billingaddress>
        <ns1:name>Sameer Tyagi</ns1:name>
        <ns1:street>256 Eight Bit Lane</ns1:street>
        <ns1:city>Burlington</ns1:city>
        <ns1:state>MA</ns1:state>
        <ns1:zip>90210</ns1:zip>
    </ns1:billingaddress>
    <ns1:items>
        <ns1:item>
            <ns1:quantity>3</ns1:quantity>
            <ns1:productnumber>229AXH</ns1:productnumber>
            <ns1:description>High speed photocopier machine with automatic sensors
                                                        </ns1:description>
            <ns1:unitcost>1939.99</ns1:unitcost>
        </ns1:item>
        <ns1:item>
            <ns1:quantity>1</ns1:quantity>
            <ns1:productnumber>1632</ns1:productnumber>
            <ns1:description>One box of color toner cartridges</ns1:description>
            <ns1:unitcost>43.95</ns1:unitcost>
        </ns1:item>
    </ns1:items>
</ns1:purchaseorder>
```

The preceding example should have helped clarify how JAXB works and the simplified approach it provides to developers. No more parsing! Looking at Listing 13.1, it should also be apparent that it has two parts:

- Code generated using the binding compiler that binds XML schemas to Java types
- Code that uses API defined in the JAXB specifications and deals with Java-XML marshalling and unmarshalling

Let us now look at the underpinnings of JAXB in these two areas.

▷ XML-to-Java Mapping

JAXB defines the basic mapping rules between XML and Java that all JAXB implementations must support. These are referred to as default bindings, and the schema compiler uses them by default. In addition, JAXB is flexible enough to allow custom bindings, though by passing in the "configuration" in the form of *binding declarations* to the binding compiler.

In Chapter 10, we discussed how JAX-RPC maps and marshalls XML to Java. The default binding defined by JAXB is identical to the mapping specified in JAX-RPC. In this section, we will discuss some commonly used additional details and mappings . We encourage you to refer to the JAXB specifications for syntactical details regarding XML-Java mappings. ▷

Primitives and Simple Types

In addition to the types defined by JAX-RPC (Chapter 10, Table 10.3a), JAXB addresses mapping for the types shown in Table 13.1.

Enumerations

XML enumerations map to Java classes where the name of the class is the name of the enumeration and the package corresponds to the target namespace. This

Table 13.1 Additional Mappings Defined in JAXB

XML type	Java type
xsd:unsignedInt	long
xsd:unsignedShort	int
xsd:unsignedByte	Short
xsd:time	java.util.Calendar
xsd:date	java.util.Calendar
xsd:anySimpleType	java.lang.String

▷   For the sake of brevity, concepts pertaining to XML-Java mapping covered in Chapter 10 are not repeated here. We suggest reading that chapter, particularly the section "XML to Java Unmarshalling," before this section.

was discussed in Chapter 10 (see Table 10.3b). JAXB generates similar mappings, and the generated interface has a getValue and setValue method to access the underlying value. Listings 13.4a and 13.4b show a sample XML schema and its corresponding Java interface.

Listing 13.4a   A schema with enumerations

```
<xsd:schema xmlns:xsd="http://www.w3.org/2001/XMLSchema">
    <xsd:element name="Day">
     <xsd:simpleType >
       <xsd:restriction base="xsd:string">
       <xsd:enumeration value="Saturday"></xsd:enumeration>
           <xsd:enumeration value="Sunday"></xsd:enumeration>
          <xsd:enumeration value="Monday"></xsd:enumeration>
           <xsd:enumeration value="Tuesday"></xsd:enumeration>
          <xsd:enumeration value="Wednesday"></xsd:enumeration>
           <xsd:enumeration value="Thursday"></xsd:enumeration>
           <xsd:enumeration value="Friday"></xsd:enumeration>
        </xsd:restriction>
      </xsd:simpleType>
    </xsd:element>
</xsd:schema>
```

Listing 13.4b   The generated interface for an enumeration in Listing 13.4a

```
public interface Days extends javax.xml.bind.Element{
  String getValue();
    void setValue(String value);
```

typesafe *Enumerations*

typesafe enumeration is an important concept. Because Java was designed to avoid using the C/C++ type enumerations (*enum*), developers often define simple sets of primitive values:

```
public class Days{
    public static final int MONDAY= "Monday";
    public static final int TUESDAY= "Tuesday";
    public static final int WEDNESDAY= "Wednesday";
// And so on
} ▷
```

The problem with using Strings is that it causes numerous string comparisons and embeds the values in the code. The typesafe enum pattern takes the approach of using `static final` primitives one step further and essentially replaces the primitive constants with a set of `static final` object references encapsulated in a class:

```
public final class Days {
    public static final Days MONDAY = new Days();
    public static final Days TUESDAY = new Days();
    public static final Days WEDNESDAY = new Days();
// And so on
    private Daya() {}
}
```

The static fields will be initialized when the class is loaded. Because the only way to construct the objects is internal to the class, there can be no other instance of these Days objects. Because the fields are final, the identity comparison (`==`) can be easily used instead of the `equals()` method—for example, `if(someday== Days.TUESDAY) {}`. This is analogous to comparing pointers in C/C++. ▷▷

JAXB allows developers to specify that code generated for the enumerations in the schema use this `typesafe` enumeration pattern. By default, only XML enumerations derived by restriction from the base type `"xsd:NCName"` are mapped to typesafe enumeration classes. ▷▷▷

Lists

XML lists map to `java.util.List` instances. The data types contained in the collection are either the Java mappings of the basic data types or objects based on the enumeration mapping. For example, consider this schema fragment:

▷ The above approach using primitive `int`s was originally proposed by James Gosling and Henry McGilton in *The Java Language Environment* whitepaper (see section 2.2.3, "No Enums") at *http://java.sun.com/docs/white/langenv /Simple.doc2.html.*

▷▷ Details on `typesafe` enumerations and their complexities can be found in Joshua Bloch's *Effective Java Programming Language Guide* (Addison-Wesley, 2001). Some discussion is available at *http://developer.java.sun.com/devel-oper/Books/shiftintojava/page1.html.*

▷▷▷ If the Java object is being serialized, then the enum class must implement the read Resolve() method, because the private constructor state is lost during serialization.

```
<xsd:schema xmlns:xsd="http://www.w3.org/2001/XMLSchema">
<xsd:element name="Catalog">
        <xsd:simpleType>
                <xsd:list itemType="xsd:string"/>
        </xsd:simpleType>
  </xsd:element>
</xsd:schema>
```

The element would map to a `Catalog` class object, and the `getValue()` would return a `List` of `String` objects:

```
public interface Catalog extends javax.xml.bind.Element{
        java.util.List getValue();
}
```

If the `itemType` in the schema were an enumeration or a complex type, the `List` would contain the corresponding Java classes—for example, a `List` of `Billingaddress` objects. ▷

Complex Types

As in JAX-RPC, XML complex types are mapped to Java interfaces. For example, Listings 13.5a and 13.5b show how the `billingaddress` element is mapped to Java.

Listing 13.5a   A complex element

```
<xsd:element name="billingaddress">
     <xsd:complexType>
         <xsd:sequence>
             <xsd:element ref="name"/>
             <xsd:element ref="street"/>
             <xsd:element ref="city"/>
             <xsd:element ref="state"/>
             <xsd:element ref="zip"/>
         </xsd:sequence>
     </xsd:complexType>
  </xsd:element>
```

> ▷   Recall that in JAX-RPC the Java mapping for the list and union type are optional.

Listing 13.5b   Generated binding interface for a complex element

```
package com.flutebank.schema;
public interface Billingaddress
    extends javax.xml.bind.Element, com.flutebank.schema.BillingaddressType{
}


package com.flutebank.schema;
public interface BillingaddressType {
    com.flutebank.schema.Name getName();
    void setName(com.flutebank.schema.Name value);
    com.flutebank.schema.Zip getZip();
    void setZip(com.flutebank.schema.Zip value);
    com.flutebank.schema.State getState();
    void setState(com.flutebank.schema.State value);
    com.flutebank.schema.City getCity();
    void setCity(com.flutebank.schema.City value);
    com.flutebank.schema.Street getStreet();
    void setStreet(com.flutebank.schema.Street value);
}
```

Mappings in JAXB and JAX-RPC

Although the JAXB and JAX-RPC API were developed independently, and JAXB was released after JAX-RPC, both specify XML-to-Java and Java-to-XML mappings. We looked at the JAX-RPC mappings in Chapter 10. JAXB concentrates on the binding issue and therefore seeks to solve the larger problem of how XML and Java can work seamlessly through the use of compile-time bindings. Therefore, the treatment in JAXB is much more detailed and thorough. This should not be construed to mean that there are two sets of bindings. The bindings defined by JAX-RPC and discussed in Chapter 10 can be considered a subset of details addressed in JAXB. JAXB also allows for customization using the binding declaration mechanism.

> The JAXB API

The JAXB specifications defines three basic packages, shown in Table 13.2. Let us look at the javax.xml.bind package in detail.

Table 13.2   JAXB Packages

`javax.xml.bind`	Defines the interfaces and classes to be used by developers. Deals with marshalling, unmarshalling, and validation.
`javax.xml.bind.util`	Contains useful utility classes for use by developers.
`javax.xml.bind.helper`	Not intended to be used by developers. The package provides default implementations of some interfaces in the `javax.xml.bind` package, for providers to use.

JAXBContext

The entry point for any developer code into JAXB will be a `JAXBContext` object using the `newInstance()` method:

```
JAXBContext context = JAXBContext.newInstance( "com.flutebank.schema" );
```

The JAXB context initializes the underlying JAXB runtime with the appropriate factory information. The file named `jaxb.properties` is searched for in the classpath and the class indicated by the `javax.xml.bind.context.factory` property and is used to create the context. The context is passed the package name, which contains the binding information (multiple package names can be specified using the colon separator, ":"; this allows JAXB to manage the multiple schemas at one time).

The packages specified must contain binding information generated by a single vendor (who provides the JAXB implementation). With multiple packages, the same context can be used to marshall and unmarshall multiple XML documents from different schemas in a single invocation. The JAXB implementation will ensure that each package on the context path has a `jaxb.properties` file containing a value for the `javax.xml.bind.context.factory` property and that all these values resolve to the same provider—in short, that the context is specific to a JAXB implementation.

As mentioned earlier, the binding compiler generates the interfaces corresponding to schema constructs as well as the implementation for such interfaces. This raises the question of how multiple implementations can be used in a single application—for example, where an application component must be packaged and distributed and may potentially be used with other application components using another vendor's JAXB implementation. To facilitate such situations, different JAXB contexts would need to be created for different packages and possibly with different class loaders, using the alternate newInstance() method:

```
JAXBContext context = JAXBContext.newInstance( "com.flutebank.schema", myclassloader );
```

Unmarshaller

The javax.xml.bind.Unmarshaller is responsible for unmarshalling XML documents (which are based on the schema) into Java object representations. An Unmarshaller is created from a JAXBContext, using the createUnmarshaller() method:

```
JAXBContext context = JAXBContext.newInstance( "com.flutebank.schema" );
// create an Unmarshaller
Unmarshaller unmars = context.createUnmarshaller(); ▷
```

Once created, the Unmarshaller can be applied to many different XML sources using convenient methods, as Table 13.3 shows.

The Unmarshaller has two other important functions:

- Performing validation during unmarshalling, to verify that the XML conforms to the schema. Upon invoking the setValidating(true), the Marshaller instance will be marked as a validating unmarshaller, and the JAXB provider performs XML validation against the schema used to generate the binding information:

```
JAXBContext context = JAXBContext.newInstance( "com.flutebank.schema" );
// create an Unmarshaller
Unmarshaller unmars = context.createUnmarshaller();
unmars.setValidating(true);
// Any XML instance unmarshalled will now be validated against the schema used by the
// binding compiler
```

> ▷ The Java object representations that the XML is Unmarshalled into and Marshalled from are collectively called *content trees*. The tree represents a collection of object references defined by JAXB binding-compiler-generated interfaces.

Table 13.3 Unmarshalling from Different Sources

Unmarshalling method	Unmarshall from
`public void Object umarshall(java.io.File f)`	XML data from a file
`public void Object unmarshall` `(org.xml.sax.InputSource source)`	From the specified SAX InputSource (See Chapter 9)
`public void Object unmarshall` `(java.io.InputStream is)`	From any InputStream
`public Object unmarshall` `(org.w3c.dom.Node node)`	From a W3C DOM tree (See Chapter 9)
`public void Object unmarshall` `(javax.xml.transform.Source source)`	From the XML Source object. (See Chapter 9)
`public void Object` `unmarshall(java.net.URL url)`	From a network URL

- Registering application-defined event handlers that are notified of validation events. Developers write the event handlers by implementing the `javax.xml.bind.ValidationEventHandler` method and registering this handler with the Unmarshaller, using the `setEventHandler` method:

```
JAXBContext context = JAXBContext.newInstance( "com.flutebank.schema" );
  // create an Unmarshaller
    Unmarshaller unmars = context.createUnmarshaller();
    MyValidator validr=new MyValidator():
    unmars.setEventHandler(validr);
```

The default validation handler in JAXB will terminate processing upon encountering the first fatal error. So if your application must recover gracefully or conditionally process the XML, consider overriding the default handler. This is analogous to the SAX handlers in Chapter 9.

Marshaller

The `javax.xml.bind.Marshaller` can be used to marshall object representations into XML format. The XML is based on the schema passed to the binding compiler and used to generate the initial Java bindings.

The marshaller is also created from the context:

```
JAXBContext context = JAXBContext.newInstance( "com.flutebank.schema" );
    // Other code here
    Marshaller mars = context.createMarshaller();
    mars.setProperty( Marshaller.JAXB_FORMATTED_OUTPUT, Boolean.TRUE );
    mars.setProperty (Marshaller.JAXB_SCHEMA_LOCATION,
                    "http://www.flutebank.com/schema purchaseorder.xsd");
mars.marshall( po, new FileOutputStream("modifiedpurchaseorder.xml"));
```

Much like the Unmarshaller, the Marshaller can marshal the Java object and its referenced objects (the content tree) into different destinations–files, DOM trees, and so on–summarized in Table 13.4.

JAXB does not require that the Java content tree be valid or validated against the schema during the marshalling process to give the JAXB implementation the ability to support use cases where partial XML is generated. The provider may choose to disallow marshalling of invalid content and throw a MarshallException.

As with the Unmarshaller, event handlers can be registered with the Marshaller using the setEventHandler(ValidationEventHandler handler) method. Even though there is no way to programmatically enable validation during the marshall operation, it is possible for validation events to be received by the handler. The default handler will stop the marshalling when the first fatal error is encountered.

Table 13.4   Marshalling Object Trees into Different Destinations

Marshalling method	Marshall the object and referenced objects therein into
public void marshall(Object obj, org.xml.sax.ContentHandler handler)	SAX2 events
public void marshall(Object obj, org.w3c.dom.Node node)	A DOM tree
public void marshall(Object obj, java.io.OutputStream os)	An output stream
public void marshall(Object obj, javax.xml.transform.Result result)	A javax.xml.transform.Result
Public void marshall(Object obj, java.io.Writer writer)	A Writer stream.

Configuring the Marshaller

The Marshaller can be configured using four standard properties, described in Table 13.5, that affect the XML formatting and output. The properties are passed as name-value pairs using the setProperty method, as shown below.

```
Marshaller mars = context.createMarshaller();
Mars.setProperty( Marshaller.JAXB_FORMATTED_OUTPUT, Boolean.TRUE );
 mars.setProperty (Marshaller.JAXB_SCHEMA_LOCATION,
               "http://www.flutebank.com/schema purchaseorder.xsd");
```

The Element *Interface*

JAXB defines the javax.xml.bind.Element interface used by the runtime as a marker for identifying the JAXB-generated binding interfaces. It has no methods. In some situations, application developers would need to write code implementing this interface. JAXB users always work with the generated Java binding interface and its methods, which encapsulate the name and value of the corresponding XML element. For example, the billingaddress element is mapped to the

Table 13.5 Marshaller Properties

Property	Description
jaxb.encoding	The Marshaller will use "UTF-8" by default. If needed the encoding can be changed using this property.
jaxb.formatted.output	By default the Marshaller will not format the output with line breaks and indentations. If this property is set to true the XML generated will be formatted for human readability.
jaxb.schemaLocation	Used to set the xsi:schemaLocation attribute in the generated XML. (See Chapter 9 for details on this property.)
jaxb.noNamespaceSchemaLocation	Used to set the xsi:noNamespaceSchemaLocation property in the generated XML. (See Chapter 9 for details on this property.)

Billingaddress interface, which has methods to get/set the relevant types, which themselves are generated bindings. This was shown in Listing 13.2.

In XML schemas, the xsd:any element can be used to refer to elements not specified in the schema. For example, in the following fragment, the occupation element can be extended to include other content with the any element:

```
<?xml version="1.0" encoding="UTF-8"?>
<xsd:schema xmlns:xsd="http://www.w3.org/2001/XMLSchema" elementFormDefault=
                                                            "qualified">

    <xsd:element name="occupation">
        <xsd:complexType>
            <xsd:sequence>
                <xsd:element name="Engineer" type="xsd:string"/>
                <xsd:element name="SeniorEngineer" type="xsd:string"/>
                <xsd:element name="TechnicalWriter" type="xsd:string"/>

<xsd:any minOccurs="0"/>
            </xsd:sequence>
        </xsd:complexType>
    </xsd:element>
</xsd:schema>
```

This schema results in the generated binding shown below, which must cater to the potential of arbitrary XML elements being specified whose name or value is not known at compile time.

```
public interface OccupationType {
    String getEngineer();
    void setEngineer(String value);
    javax.xml.bind.Element getAny();
    void setAny(javax.xml.bind.Element value);
    String getTechnicalWriter();
    void setTechnicalWriter(String value);
    String getSeniorEngineer();
    void setSeniorEngineer(String value);
}
```

When using this interface in application code, the code is responsible for passing an instance that implements the javax.bind.xml.Element interface, as opposed to the procedure with other Java data types.

▷ **Validation with JAXB**

One aspect of validation–unmarshall-time validation–has already been discussed in preceding sections. In this section, we will discuss another aspect of validation: on-demand validation. At times, developers may need to validate partial (or even complete) content trees. For example, it may be useful to validate only the Billingaddress object when user input is accepted, or, alternatively, the entire Purchaseorder and all the referenced objects against the XML schema when needed.

JAXB defines the javax.xml.bind.Validator interface for this purpose. Once the reference to this is obtained, an event handler can be set if needed and the relevant object passed for validation:

```
    JAXBContext context = JAXBContext.newInstance( "com.flutebank.schema" );
// create an Unmarshaller
    Unmarshaller unmars = context.createUnmarshaller();
// unmarshall an XML document into its Java representation
    Purchaseorder po = (Purchaseorder)unmars.unmarshall( new FileInputStream(
                        "purchaseorder.xml" ) );
    Billingaddress address = po.getBillingaddress();
// do some work here changing the attributes of Purchaseorder
//
// create a Validator
        Validator v = context.createValidator();
// validate the entire content tree
        boolean isvalid = v.validateRoot( po );
        System.out.println(isvalid);
// validate partial content tree
        isvalid = v.validate(address);
        System.out.println(isvalid);
```

Developers can write a class that implements the ValidationEventHandler and register the implementation with the Validator instance to receive callbacks when appropriate ValiationEvents occur. This is analogous to the way SAX handlers are registered to receive events during parsing, discussed in Chapter 9.

```
JAXBContext context = JAXBContext.newInstance( "com.flutebank.schema" );
        Validator v = context.createValidator();
// MyValidator is developer written and implements
javax.xml.bind.ValidationEventHandler
```

```
MyValidator validr=new MyValidator():
v.setEventHandler(validr);
```

In initial versions of the specifications, the logic and infrastructure to facilitate validation, marshalling, and unmarshalling were required to be included in the generated classes themselves. This not only opened the door for potential redundancy but also meant existing classes could not be used and increased the coupling between the generated code and the implementation. The current approach of logically separating the validation from the generated code is a lot cleaner.

> Customizing JAXB

Figure 13.2 showed the use of custom binding declarations with the binding compiler, to override the default binding behavior. The binding declarations are XML elements themselves. JAXB specifies two techniques to pass them to the binding compiler:

- They can be passed as separate XML input, as Figure 13.2 shows.
- They can be inlined with the source XML schema itself. This is the mechanism supported by the JAXB reference implementation.

When inlined, the declarations are included, using the xsd:annotation and xsd:appinfo tags.

In XML schemas, the annotation element is a top-level element that specifies comments treated as inline documentation by schema parsers. The annotation may have any number of documentation or appInfo elements as child elements. appinfo specifies information specific to the application. A sample schema fragment is shown below:

```
<xsd:schema xmlns:xsd="http://www.w3.org/2001/XMLSchema">
<xsd:annotation>
  <xsd:appInfo>W3Schools Note</xsd:appInfo>
  <xsd:documentation xml:lang="en">
     Some application documentation here
  </xsd:documentation>
</xsd:annotation>
<!--other elements here with possibly any number of annotations-->
</xsd:schema>
```

When inlining declarations with the source schema, JAXB uses these annotation and appInfo elements to insert the JAXB specific information, using the following syntax:

```
<xsd:annotation>
      <xsd:appinfo>
            <binding declaration>
      </xsd:appinfo>
</xsd:annotation>
```

If an external file is used to specify the declarations, the file follows this format:

```
<jaxb:bindings schemaLocation = "location of schema here">
    <jaxb:bindings node = "XPath String referencing node here">
        <binding declaration>
    <jaxb:bindings>
</jaxb:bindings>
```

For example, an external binding declaration referencing the billingaddress node in the purchaseorder.xsd schema may look like this:

```
<jaxb:bindingsxmlns:jaxb="http://java.sun.com/xml/jaxb"
             xmlns:xsd="http://www.w3.org/2001/XMLSchema"
             xmlns:ens="http://www.flutebank.com/schema" version="1.0">
      <jaxb:bindings schemaLocation="purchaseorder.xsd">
        <jaxb:binding node="./xs:attribute[@name='billingaddress']">
        <jaxb:property name="country"/>
        </jaxb:binding>
      </jaxb:binding>
</jaxb:bindings>
```

A binding declaration has scope that specifies the schema elements to which it applies. There are four levels of scope, described below and shown in Figure 13.3, ranging from the generic to the specific. The more specific scope (e.g., component) overrides the higher-level (e.g., global) scope.

- **Global scope** applies to all schema elements in the source schema and all schemas included or imported.

- **Schema scope** applies to all schema elements in a schema's target namespace.

Figure 13.3
Declaration
scope

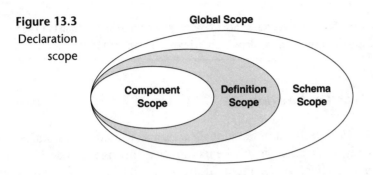

- **Definition scope** applies to all schema elements that reference the type definition or the global declaration.

- **Component scope** applies only to the schema element annotated with the binding declaration.

Our treatment of the declarations in the subsequent paragraphs has purposely been kept light. We recommend the JAXB specifications for detailed syntax use, for two reasons:

- Most developers are likely to use the default mechanism.

- We anticipate vendor tools and a wizard to be provided that would minimize hand insertions. The tools will use the standard declarations and, because these declarations are specified in a standard manner by JAXB, would be portable across implementations.

JAXB defines seven distinct custom declarations that can be annotated to XML schemas. Let us look at an example of how custom bindings can be used with the purchaseorder.xsd schema in Listing 13.1. We will walk down the different steps and also the specifics of the syntax for the declarations used.

Including the JAXB Namespace

When using inlined annotations to specify the custom bindings, the XML schema must include the namespace and version number defined in JAXB. The modified declaration for the purchase order is shown below, with modifications highlighted in bold:

```
<?xml version="1.0" encoding="UTF-8"?>
<xsd:schema targetNamespace="http://www.flutebank.com/schema"
        xmlns:xsd="http://www.w3.org/2001/XMLSchema"
```

```
xmlns="http://www.flutebank.com/schema" elementFormDefault="qualified"
xmlns:jaxb="http://java.sun.com/xml/ns/jaxb" jaxb:version="1.0">
```

The globalBindings *Declaration*

The globalBindings declaration has global scope and is used to customize the bindings globally for all schemas. A schema can have only one such declaration, and the declaration affects all the imported and included schemas. The syntax for this declaration is shown below:

```
<globalBindings>
[ collectionType = "collectionType" ]
[ fixedAttributeAsConstantProperty= "true" | "false" | "1" | "0"]
[ generateIsSetMethod= "true" | "false" | "1" | "0" ]
[ enableFailFastCheck = "true" | "false" | "1" | "0" ]
[ choiceContentProperty = "true" | "false" | "1" | "0" ]
[ underscoreBinding = "asWordSeparator" | "asCharInWord" ]
[ typesafeEnumBase = "typesafeEnumBase" ]
[ typesafeEnumMemberName = "generateName" | "generateError" ]
[ enableJavaNamingConventions = "true" | "false" | "1" | "0" ]
[ modelGroupAsClass = "true" | "false" | "1" | "0" ]
[ <javaType> . . . </javaType> ]*
</globalBindings>
```

Previously we looked at how some elements, such as the Catalog, mapped to a java.util.List. A globally scoped globalBinding declaration can be used to specify the exact implementation the generated code may use:

```
<xsd:annotation>
      <xsd:appinfo>
           <jaxb:globalBindings collectionType="java.util.Vector"/>
      </xsd:appinfo>
</xsd:annotation>
```

The schemaBindings *Declaration*

The schemaBindings declaration has schema scope and is used to customize the bindings for the specific schema. The syntax for this declaration is shown below:

```
<schemaBindings>
    <package [ name = "packageName" ]
        [ <javadoc> . . . </javadoc> ]
    </package>
    <nameXmlTransform>
        [ <typeName [ suffix="suffix" ]
        [ prefix="prefix" ] /> ]
        [ <elementName [ suffix="suffix" ]
        [ prefix="prefix" ] />]
        [ <modelGroupName [ suffix="suffix" ]
        [ prefix="prefix" ] />]
        [ <anonymousTypeName [ suffix="suffix" ]
        [ prefix="prefix" ] />]
    </nameXmlTransform>
</schemaBindings>
```

The nameXmlTransform element in this declaration is specifically intended for use with UDDI 2.0, which contains many declarations that may cause duplicate names (or collisions) during generation of the Java bindings. For example, the following element in a UDDI schema will cause a fatal error:

```
<element name="bindingTemplate" type="uddi:bindingTemplate"/>
```

The nameXmlTransform element can be used to apply a suffix and prefix to such elements and avoid collisions.

In the original purchaseorder.xsd example, the Java code was generated by default in the com.flutebank.schema package corresponding to the target namespace http://www.flutebank.com/schema of the schema. This can be changed to com.flutebank.custompackage by using a schema scoped schemaBinding declaration:

```
<xsd:annotation>
    <xsd:appinfo>
        <jaxb:globalBindings collectionType="java.util.Vector"/>
        <jaxb:schemaBindings>
            <jaxb:package name="com.flutebank.custompackage"/>
        </jaxb:schemaBindings>
    </xsd:appinfo>
</xsd:annotation>
<!--The rest of the original schema from Listing 13.1-->
```

The `javadoc` *Declaration*

This general-purpose declaration can be used to insert text that will appear as Javadoc comments in the generated Java code. It can be used only for component scope declaration. The syntax is:

```
<javadoc> Contents in Javadoc format </javadoc>
```

The sample usage of this declaration is shown below, along with the `class` declaration.

The `class` *Declaration*

This declaration can be used to specify the name of the Java interface or the implementation class to use for a specific element. This will be useful for tool vendors and providers in specifying their own implementation classes rather than the default JAXB implementation code.

```
<class [ name = "className"]>
    [ implClass= "implClass" ]
    [ <javadoc> . . . </javadoc> ]
</class>
```

In the original `purchaseorder.xsd` example, the `billingaddress` element was mapped to a Java interface named `Billingaddress` by default. This can be customized to the name `PrimaryBillingAddress`:

```
<xsd:element name="billingaddress">
    <xsd:complexType>
        <xsd:annotation>
         <xsd:appinfo>
           <jaxb:class name="PrimaryBillingAddress">
            <jaxb:javadoc>
              The custom Java interface corresponding to the billingaddress element
                                                       in the schema
            </jaxb:javadoc>
           </jaxb:class>
         </xsd:appinfo>
        </xsd:annotation>
<!--The rest of the orignal schema from Listing 13.1-->
```

Listing 13.6 shows the effect of these annotations on the generated code. The interface is named `PrimaryBillingAddress`, it is now in the package `com.flute-bank.custompackage`, and the specified Javadoc comments precede the standard comments.

Listing 13.6   Bindings affected by `class` and `javadoc` declarations

```
package com.flutebank.custompackage;
/**
 *
 *The custom Java interface corresponding to the billingaddress element in the schema
 * Java content class for anonymous complex type.
 *   <p>The following schema fragment specifies the expected content contained within this
 * java content object.
 * <p>
 * <pre>
 * &lt;complexType>
 *   &lt;complexContent>
 *     &lt;restriction base="{http://www.w3.org/2001/XMLSchema}anyType">
 *       &lt;sequence>
 *         &lt;element ref="{http://www.flutebank.com/schema}name"/>
 *         &lt;element ref="{http://www.flutebank.com/schema}street"/>
 *         &lt;element ref="{http://www.flutebank.com/schema}city"/>
 *         &lt;element ref="{http://www.flutebank.com/schema}state"/>
 *         &lt;element ref="{http://www.flutebank.com/schema}zip"/>
 *       &lt;/sequence>
 *     &lt;/restriction>
 *   &lt;/complexContent>
 * &lt;/complexType>
 * </pre>
 *
 */
public interface PrimaryBillingAddress {
    com.flutebank.custompackage.Name getName();
    void setName(com.flutebank.custompackage.Name value);
    com.flutebank.custompackage.Zip getZip();
    void setZip(com.flutebank.custompackage.Zip value);
    com.flutebank.custompackage.State getState();
    void setState(com.flutebank.custompackage.State value);
    com.flutebank.custompackage.City getCity();
```

```
    void setCity(com.flutebank.custompackage.City value);
    com.flutebank.custompackage.Street getStreet();
    void setStreet(com.flutebank.custompackage.Street value);
}
```

The property Declaration

This declaration is used to customize the binding of an XML schema element to the Java representation as a property. The syntax for the property declaration is shown below:

```
<property
[ name = "propertyName"]
[ baseType = "propertyBaseType"]
[ collectionType = "propertyCollectionType" ]
[ fixedAttributeAsConstantProperty= "true" | "false" | "1" | "0"]
[ generateIsSetMethod= "true" | "false" | "1" | "0" ]
[ enableFailFastCheck="true" | "false" | "1" | "0" ]
[ choiceContentProperty = "true" | "false" | "1" | "0" ]
[ <javadoc> . . . </javadoc> ]
</property>
```

The generateIsSetMethod customization is important because it causes two additional property methods, isSetXXX() and unsetXXX(), to be included in the generated code (where XXX is the property name). The application code can use these methods to distinguish between schema default values and values occurring explicitly within an instance document.

For example, the city and date elements are annotated in the original schema as shown below. This causes the name of the property in the Java code to be changed from city to billingcity and date to dateorderplaced. Had the original property been named Date, it might have caused a collision with the class java.util.Date during code generation, requiring a custom declaration.

```
<xsd:element name="city" type="xsd:string">
     <xsd:annotation>
       <xsd:appinfo>
          <jaxb:property name="billingcity" generateIsSetMethod="true"/>
       </xsd:appinfo>
     </xsd:annotation>
   </xsd:element>
```

```
<xsd:element name="date" type="xsd:string">
      <xsd:annotation>
        <xsd:appinfo>
            <jaxb:property name="dateorderplaced"/>
        </xsd:appinfo>
      </xsd:annotation>
    </xsd:element>
```

The effect of these declarations can be seen in the code generated for the interface PrimaryBillingAddress, which now contains the following methods:

```
package com.flutebank.custompackage;
public interface PrimaryBillingAddress {
// Other Java code here not shown
        com.flutebank.custompackage.City getBillingcity();
        void setBillingcity(com.flutebank.custompackage.City value);
        boolean isSetBillingcity();
        void unsetBillingcity();
    }
```

The javaType *Declaration*

This declaration is used to customize the bindings of an XML schema data type to the corresponding Java data type. The Java data type can be a Java built-in data type or a custom-defined type (e.g., an application-defined class).

This declaration can be applied as an annotation to a specific element or included in the globalBinding declaration. The syntax for the javaType declaration is shown below:

```
<javaType name="javaType"
[ xmlType="xmlType" ]
[ parseMethod="parseMethod" ]
[ printMethod="printMethod" ]>
```

In the original purchaseorder.xsd, the identifier element was defined as a string and therefore automatically mapped to a Java interface called Identifier, with getValue and setValue methods that treated the underlying property as a String. If it is known that this value will always be an integer, the default mapping can be overridden with the javaType declaration, as shown below:

```
<xsd:element name="identifier" type="xsd:string">
    <xsd:annotation>
        <xsd:appinfo>
            <jaxb:javaType name="int"/>
        </xsd:appinfo>
    </xsd:annotation>
</xsd:element>
```

The Java interface generated as a result of this annotation is:

```
package com.flutebank.custompackage;
 public interface Identifier extends javax.xml.bind.Element{
    int getValue();
    void setValue(int value);
}
```

The typesafeEnum *Declaration*

Earlier, we mentioned how an enumeration of base type "xs:NCName" maps to typesafe class. This binding declaration can be used to customize the generated bindings for simple type definitions with enumeration facets. The syntax is shown below:

```
<typesafeEnumClass name = "enumClassName">
    <typesafeEnumMember name = "enumMemberName">
        [ value = "enumMemberValue" ]
        [ <javadoc> enumMemberJavadoc </javadoc> ]
    </typesafeEnumMember>
    [ <javadoc> enumClassJavadoc </javadoc> ]
</typesafeEnumClass>
```

Using typesafeEnums enables schema enumeration values to be mapped to Java constants. This optimizes performance by making it possible for constants to be compared, instead of string comparisons. To understand the difference, let us look at the sample schema discussed earlier in the "Enumerations" section:

```
<?xml version="1.0" encoding="UTF-8"?>
<xsd:schema xmlns:xsd="http://www.w3.org/2001/XMLSchema"
         elementFormDefault="qualified" >

    <xsd:element name="Day">
```

```
            <xsd:simpleType>
                <xsd:restriction base="xsd:string">
                    <xsd:enumeration value="Saturday"/>
                    <xsd:enumeration value="Sunday"/>
                    <xsd:enumeration value="Monday"/>
                    <xsd:enumeration value="Tuesday"/>
                    <xsd:enumeration value="Wednesday"/>
                    <xsd:enumeration value="Thursday"/>
                    <xsd:enumeration value="Friday"/>
                </xsd:restriction>
            </xsd:simpleType>
        </xsd:element>
    </xsd:schema>
```

When compiled, this generates the Day interface, corresponding to the enumeration:

```
public interface Day extends javax.xml.bind.Element{
    String getValue();
    void setValue(String value);
}
```

This same schema can be customized with the typesafeEnum declaration, as shown below:

```
<?xml version="1.0" encoding="UTF-8"?>
<xsd:schema xmlns:xsd="http://www.w3.org/2001/XMLSchema"
            elementFormDefault="qualified"
            xmlns:jaxb="http://java.sun.com/xml/ns/jaxb" jaxb:version="1.0">
    <xsd:element name="Day">
        <xsd:simpleType>
            <xsd:annotation>
                <xsd:appinfo>
                    <jaxb:typesafeEnumClass name="WeekDays"/>
                </xsd:appinfo>
            </xsd:annotation>
            <xsd:restriction base="xsd:string">
                <xsd:enumeration value="Saturday"/>
                <xsd:enumeration value="Sunday"/>
                <xsd:enumeration value="Monday"/>
                <xsd:enumeration value="Tuesday"/>
                <xsd:enumeration value="Wednesday"/>
```

```
            <xsd:enumeration value="Thursday"/>
            <xsd:enumeration value="Friday"/>
        </xsd:restriction>
      </xsd:simpleType>
    </xsd:element>
</xsd:schema>
```

When compiled, the Day interface now uses a type-safe class instead of strings:

```
public interface Day extends javax.xml.bind.Element{
    generated.WeekDays getValue();
    void setValue(generated.WeekDays value);
}
```

Listing 13.7 also shows the generated class Weekdays. Notice the private constructor and the parse method.

Listing 13.7 A typesafe-enumeration-generated binding

```
public class WeekDays {
    public final static WeekDays SATURDAY = new WeekDays("Saturday");
    private final static Object $$$_SATURDAY = "Saturday";
    public final static WeekDays SUNDAY = new WeekDays("Sunday");
    private final static Object $$$_SUNDAY = "Sunday";
    public final static WeekDays MONDAY = new WeekDays("Monday");
    private final static Object $$$_MONDAY = "Monday";
    public final static WeekDays TUESDAY = new WeekDays("Tuesday");
    private final static Object $$$_TUESDAY = "Tuesday";
    public final static WeekDays WEDNESDAY = new WeekDays("Wednesday");
    private final static Object $$$_WEDNESDAY = "Wednesday";
    public final static WeekDays THURSDAY = new WeekDays("Thursday");
    private final static Object $$$_THURSDAY = "Thursday";
    public final static WeekDays FRIDAY = new WeekDays("Friday");
    private final static Object $$$_FRIDAY = "Friday";
    private final String value;
    private WeekDays(String v) {
        value = v;
    }
    public String toString() {
        return value;
    }
```

```java
    public final int hashCode() {
        return super.hashCode();
    }
    public final boolean equals(Object o) {
        return super.equals(o);
    }
    public static WeekDays parse(String str) {
        if ($$$_SATURDAY.equals(str)) {
            return SATURDAY;
        }
        if ($$$_SUNDAY.equals(str)) {
            return SUNDAY;
        }
        if ($$$_MONDAY.equals(str)) {
            return MONDAY;
        }
        if ($$$_TUESDAY.equals(str)) {
            return TUESDAY;
        }
        if ($$$_WEDNESDAY.equals(str)) {
            return WEDNESDAY;
        }
        if ($$$_THURSDAY.equals(str)) {
            return THURSDAY;
        }
        if ($$$_FRIDAY.equals(str)) {
            return FRIDAY;
        }
        return null;
    }
}
```

> ## When to Use Custom Declarations

In certain situations, developers find it appropriate to override the default bindings by using the custom declarations. Some examples of such use cases are:

- Automatically creating Javadoc style documentation in the generated code. By using the `javadoc` annotation in the schema, developers can include descriptive information in the Java code emitted by the binding compiler.

- Providing application-specific Java identifiers. For example:
  - Developers may sometimes need to specify a particular package name for the generated code rather than using the default package name, which maps to the namespace.
  - XML schemas may sometime contain elements that conflict with Java language keywords or identifiers, causing "collisions." The binding compiler will detect such collisions, throw a fatal error, and exit. Custom bindings can be used to rectify such errors.
- Override the default bindings used by the schema compiler for application-specific behavior or optimization. For example, it may be useful to map constants in the schema to a `public` static final String rather than a `String`.

> Summary

In this chapter we discussed how JAXB can be used to generate Java bindings for XML schemas. The functionality JAXB offers will be important to developers, because it alleviates the need to manually parse and validate XML structures to and from their representations in code.

We looked not only at how JAXB can be used as is, but also how it can be customized with binding declarations to tailor specific application requirements. From a design perspective, JAXB is a robust and standard API that provides a layer of abstraction over the handling of XML data types and constructs in Java code. There has long been a need for such a specification, and JAXB serves to fill that need quite aptly.

Part {Three} Advanced Topics

In this section, we investigate advanced topics that are not only applicable to developing a Web service using Java but are also applicable to non-Java applications. This section finishes with checklists, tips, and additional sources of information required for successful architecture.

Chapter Fourteen *Transaction Management*

To conduct electronic commerce using Web services, a service will need to support ACID like transaction models.

Chapter Fifteen *Security*

The ability to provide security to SOAP messages is vital in a Web services architecture. This chapter covers the specifications that allow one to ensure message integrity, confidentiality, and single message authentication.

Chapter Sixteen *Practical Considerations*

Designing highly available robust Web services can be difficult. Many issues could arise from implementing applications that incorporate Web services. This chapter looks at various design considerations involved with architecting high-performance Web services architectures.

Chapter Seventeen *Future Standards*

The future for Web services will be tools that allow for fully automatic software generation, use of leased services, the semantic web, and other standards. This chapter explores the arising issues that must be considered in future development.

Chapter **{14}**

Transaction Management

The notion of a transaction is fundamental to business systems architectures. A transaction, simply put, ensures that only agreed-upon, consistent, and acceptable state changes are made to a system—regardless of system failure or concurrent access to the system's resources.

With the advent of Web service architectures, distributed applications (macroservices) are being built by assembling existing, smaller services (microservices). The microservices are usually built with no a priori knowledge of how they may be combined. The resulting complex architectures introduce new challenges to existing transaction models. Several new standards are being proposed that specify how application servers and transaction managers implement new transaction models that accommodate the introduced complexities.

The first sections of this chapter introduce the fundamental concepts behind transactions and explain how transactions are managed within the current Java/J2EE platforms. Later sections discuss the challenges of using existing transaction models for Web services, explain newly proposed models and standards for Web service transactions, and finally, detail proposed implementations of these new models on the Java platform.

> Concepts

A transaction may be thought of as an interaction with the system, resulting in a change to the system state. While the interaction is in the process of changing system state, any number of events can interrupt the interaction, leaving the state change incomplete and the system state in an inconsistent, undesirable form. Any change to system state within a transaction boundary, therefore, has to ensure that the change leaves the system in a stable and consistent state.

A transactional unit of work is one in which the following four fundamental transactional properties are satisfied: atomicity, consistency, isolation, and durability (ACID). We will examine each property in detail.

Atomicity

It is common to refer to a transaction as a "unit of work." In describing a transaction as a unit of work, we are describing one fundamental property of a transaction: that the activities within it must be considered indivisible—that is, *atomic*.

A Flute Bank customer may interact with Flute's ATM and transfer money from a checking account to a savings account. Within the Flute Bank software system, a transfer transaction involves two actions: debit of the checking account and credit to the savings account. For the transfer transaction to be successful, both actions must complete successfully. If either one fails, the transaction fails. The atomic property of transactions dictates that all individual actions that constitute a transaction must succeed for the transaction to succeed, and, conversely, that if any individual action fails, the transaction as a whole must fail.

Consistency

A database or other persistent store usually defines referential and entity integrity rules to ensure that data in the store is *consistent*. A transaction that changes the data must ensure that the data remains in a consistent state—that data integrity rules are not violated, regardless of whether the transaction succeeded or failed. The data in the store may not be consistent during the duration of the transaction, but the inconsistency is invisible to other transactions, and consistency must be restored when the transaction completes.

Isolation

When multiple transactions are in progress, one transaction may want to read the same data another transaction has changed but not committed. Until the transaction commits, the changes it has made should be treated as transient state, because the transaction could roll back the change. If other transactions read intermediate or transient states caused by a transaction in progress, additional application logic must be executed to handle the effects of some transactions having read potentially erroneous data. The *isolation* property of transactions dictates how concurrent transactions that act on the same subset of data behave. That is, the isolation property determines the degree to which effects of multiple transactions, acting on the same subset of application state, are isolated from each other.

At the lowest level of isolation, a transaction may read data that is in the process of being changed by another transaction but that has not yet been committed. If the first transaction is rolled back, the transaction that read the data would have read a value that was not committed. This level of isolation—*read uncommitted*, or "dirty read"—can cause erroneous results but ensures the highest concurrency.

An isolation of *read committed* ensures that a transaction can read only data that has been committed. This level of isolation is more restrictive (and consequently provides less concurrency) than a read uncommitted isolation level and helps avoid the problem associated with the latter level of isolation.

An isolation level of *repeatable read* signifies that a transaction that read a piece of data is guaranteed that the data will not be changed by another transaction until the transaction completes. The name "repeatable read" for this level of isolation comes from the fact that a transaction with this isolation level can read the same data repeatedly and be guaranteed to see the same value.

The most restrictive form of isolation is *serializable*. This level of isolation combines the properties of repeatable-read and read-committed isolation levels, effectively ensuring that transactions that act on the same piece of data are serialized and will not execute concurrently.

Durability

The *durability* property of transactions refers to the fact that the effect of a transaction must endure beyond the life of a transaction and application. That is, state changes made within a transactional boundary must be persisted onto permanent storage media, such as disks, databases, or file systems. If the application fails after the transaction has committed, the system should guarantee that the effects of the transaction will be visible when the application restarts. Transactional resources are also recoverable: should the persisted data be destroyed, recovery procedures can be executed to recover the data to a point in time (provided the necessary administrative tasks were properly executed). Any change committed by one transaction must be durable until another valid transaction changes the data. ▷

Transaction Manager

In a simple Java application that interacts with a database management system (DBMS), the application can demarcate transaction boundaries using explicit SQL commits and rollbacks. A more sophisticated application environment, with multiple transactional resources distributed across a network, requires a dedicated component to manage the complexity of coordinating transactions to completion.

A *transaction manager* works with applications and application servers to provide services to control the scope and duration of transactions. A transaction manager also helps coordinate the completion of global transactions across multiple transactional resource managers (e.g., database management systems), pro-

> ## Isolation Levels and Locking
>
> Traditionally, transaction isolation levels are achieved by taking locks on the data that they access until the transaction completes. There are two primary modes for taking locks: optimistic and pessimistic. These two modes are necessitated by the fact that when a transaction accesses data, its intention to change (or not change) the data may not be readily apparent.
>
> Some systems take a *pessimistic* approach and lock the data so that other transactions may read but not update the data accessed by the first transaction until the first transaction completes. Pessimistic locking guarantees that the first transaction can always apply a change to the data it first accessed.
>
> In an *optimistic* locking mode, the first transaction accesses data but does not take a lock on it. A second transaction may change the data while the first transaction is in progress. If the first transaction later decides to change the data it accessed, it has to detect the fact that the data is now changed and inform the initiator of the fact. In optimistic locking, therefore, the fact that a transaction accessed data first does not guarantee that it can, at a later stage, update it.
>
> At the most fundamental level, locks can be classified into (in increasingly restrictive order) shared, update, and exclusive locks. A *shared* lock signifies that another transaction can take an update or another shared lock on the same piece of data. Shared locks are used when data is read (usually in pessimistic locking mode).
>
> An *update* lock ensures that another transaction can take only a shared lock on the same data. Update locks are held by transactions that intend to change data (not just read it).
>
> If a transaction locks a piece of data with an *exclusive* lock, no other transaction may take a lock on the data. For example, a transaction with an isolation level of read uncommitted does not result in any locks on the data read by the transaction, and a transaction with repeatable read isolation can take only a share lock on data it has read.
>
> Locking to achieve transaction isolation may not be practical for all transactional environments; however, it remains the most common mechanism to achieve transaction isolation.

vides support for transaction synchronization and recovery, and may provide the ability to communicate with other transaction manager instances.

A transaction context contains information about a transaction. Conceptually, a transaction context is a data structure that contains a unique transaction identifier, a timeout value, and the reference to the transaction manager that controls the transaction scope. In Java applications, a transaction manager associates a transaction context with the currently executing thread. Multiple threads may be associated with the same transaction context—dividing a transaction's work into parallel tasks, if possible. The context also has to be passed from one transaction manager to another if a transaction spans multiple transaction managers (see Figure 14.4).

Two separate but interconnected Java specifications pertain to the operation and implementation of Java transaction managers. These are detailed in the next sections. ▷

Two-Phase Commit and Global Transactions

Global transactions span multiple resource managers. To coordinate global transactions, the coordinating transaction manager and all participating resource managers should implement a multiphased completion protocol, such as the *two-phasecommit (2PC) protocol* (Figure 14.1). Although there are several proprietary implementations of the this protocol, X/Open XA is the industry standard. Two distinct phases ensure that either all the participants commit or all of them roll back changes.

During the first, or *prepare phase,* the global coordinator inquires if all participants are prepared to commit changes. If the participants respond in the affirmative (if they feel that the work can be committed), the transaction progresses to the second, or *commit phase,* in which all participants are asked to commit changes.

▷   **Transaction Manager versus TP Monitor**

Transaction processing (TP) monitors, such as CICS and IMS/DC, enhance the underlying operating system's scalability and its ability to manage large transaction volumes, by taking on some of the roles of the underlying operating system. For example, a TP monitor, in addition to managing transactions, also performs connection pooling and task/thread pooling and scheduling. Transaction management is only one function of a TP monitor. In today's J2EE environment, application servers perform a similar function and may be thought of as modern equivalents of TP monitors.

Figure 14.1 **Two phase commit and Global transactions**

The two-phase
commit
protocol

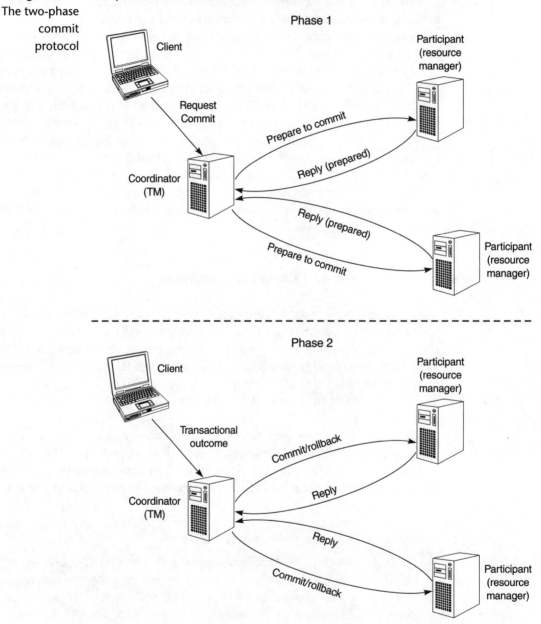

The two-phase commit protocol ensures that either all participants commit changes or none of them does. A simplified explanation follows of how this happens in a typical transaction manager. To keep the discussion brief, we examine only a few failure scenarios. Once a transaction starts, it is said to be *in-flight*. If a machine or communication failure occurs when the transaction is in-flight, the transaction will be rolled back eventually.

In the prepare phase, participants log their responses (preparedness to commit) to the coordinator, and the state of the transaction for each participant is marked *in-doubt*. At the end of the prepare phase, the transaction is in-doubt. If a participant cannot communicate with the global coordinator after it is in the in-doubt state, it will wait for resynchronization with the coordinator. If resynchronization cannot take place within a predefined time, the participant may make a heuristic decision either to roll back or commit that unit of work. (Heuristic or arbitrary decisions taken by the participant are a rare occurrence. We emphasize this because it is a conceptual difference between current transaction models and those such as BTP, discussed later in the chapter).

During the second phase, the coordinator asks all participants to commit changes. The participants log the request and begin commit processing. If a failure occurs during commit processing at one of the participants, the commit is retried when the participant restarts.

Transaction Models

Transactions managers can provide transactional support for applications using different implementation models. The most common is the flat transaction model. A transaction manager that follows the flat transaction model does not allow transactions to be nested within other transactions. The flat transaction model can be illustrated by examining the transaction model employed in J2EE application servers today.

As an example, Flute Bank provides a bill payment service. The service is implemented by an EJB that interacts with two other EJBs the account management EJB (to update account balance) and the check writing EJB (to write out a check to the payee).

Table 14.1a illustrates the scope of transactions in the scenario where all three EJBs are deployed with declarative transaction attribute of Required.

Table 14.1b illustrates the scope of transactions where the bill payment service EJB and account management EJB are deployed with transaction attribute Required but the check writing EJB is deployed with a transaction policy of RequiresNew. In this scenario, when the check writing EJB method is executed, the container suspends T1 and starts a new transaction, T2. Check writing occurs within the scope of the second transaction. When control returns to the bill payment EJB, T2 is committed, and the previous transaction is activated. So, in a flat transaction model, two transactions are executed in different scopes—T2's scope is not within T1's scope.

Table 14.1a   All EJBs Deployed with Transaction Attribute `Required`

Component	BillPayment EJB	AccountMgmt EJB	CheckWrite EJB	BillPayment EJB
Transaction	T1	T1	T1	T1 (terminates)

Table 14.1b   Account Management EJB with Transaction Attribute `RequiresNew`

Component	BillPayment EJB	AccountMgmt EJB	CheckWrite EJB	BillPayment EJB
Transaction	T1	T1	T2 (started, then terminated)	(T1 resumed, then terminated)

In effect, one business activity (bill payment) is executed under the scope of two separate transactions. In a flat transaction model, the only way to correctly control the scope of transactions that span multiple services is to reach an agreement beforehand on how these services will be combined for a business activity and to apply appropriate transaction policies for the services by agreement.

What if the check writing service were created and hosted by a different company? What if the check writing company did not want its deployment attributes to be dictated by Flute Bank? What if other customers (Flute Bank's competitor) of the check writing company wanted a contradictory transaction policy? Would it not be in Flute Bank's interest to have its bill payment transaction control the outcome of the business activity, regardless of whether the check writing company decided to start a new transaction or not?

A *nested transaction model,* shown in Figure 14.2, is one solution to the above problem. It allows transactions to consist of other transactions: a top-level transaction may contain subtransactions. In a *nested transaction model,* with respect to the above example, the bill payment service would start a top-level transaction (*t*). Both the account management service and the check writing service are free to start new transactions (*ts1* and *ts2*). But both these subtransactions are within the scope of the top-level transaction (*t*). Transactions in a nested transaction model also adhere to the ACID properties of transactions—that is, *t* completes successfully only if *ts1* and *ts2* both complete successfully. If either subtransaction fails, the top-level transaction would fail, thereby guaranteeing atomicity.

A nested transaction model allows services to be built independently and later combined into applications. Each service can determine the scope of its transaction boundaries. The application or service that orchestrates the combination of services controls the scope of the top-level transaction.

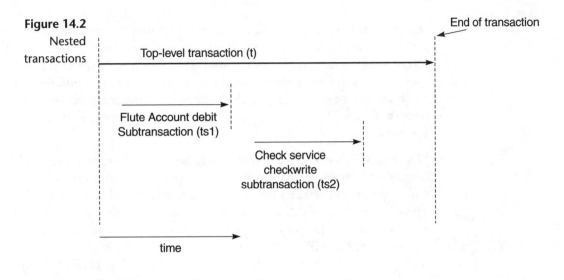

Figure 14.2
Nested transactions

Java Transaction API (JTA)

In a J2EE environment, the transaction manager has to communicate with the application server, the application program, and the resource managers, using a well-defined and standard API. The Java Transaction API (JTA) is defined precisely for this purpose. It does not specify how the transaction manager itself has to be implemented but how components external to the transaction manager communicate with it. The JTA defines a set of high-level interfaces that describe the contract between the transaction manager and three application components that interact with it: the application program, resource manager, and application server. These are described below. The next section describes the Java Transaction Service (JTS) specification—a related specification that deals with the implementation details of transaction managers.

- **JTA contract between transaction managers and application programs.** In J2EE applications, a client application or server EJB component whose transaction policy is managed in the bean code (TX_BEAN_MANAGED) can explicitly demarcate (i.e., start and stop) transactions. For this purpose, the application gets a reference to a user transaction object that implements the javax.transaction.UserTransaction interface. This interface defines methods, among others, that allow the application to commit, roll back, or suspend a transaction. The transaction that is started or stopped is associated with the calling user thread.

- In a Java client application, the UserTransaction object is obtained by looking up the application server's JNDI-based registry. There is no standard JNDI name for storing the UserTransaction reference, so the client application must know beforehand (usually by reading a configuration file) how to obtain the UserTransaction object from the application server's JNDI registry. In an EJB, the UserTransaction object is exposed through the EJBContext.

- **JTA contract between transaction managers and application servers.** J2EE containers are required to support container-managed transactions. The container demarcates transactions and manages thread and resource pooling. This requires the application server to work closely with the transaction manager. For example, in an EJB where the container has to manage transaction demarcation, the EJB container has to communicate with the transaction manager to start, commit, and suspend transactions. The J2EE application server and transaction manager communicate via the javax.transaction .TransactionManager interface.

- **JTA contract between transaction managers and transactional resource managers.** Resource managers provide an application access to resources, which can be databases, JMS queues, or any other transactional resource. An example of a global transaction is the one that changes a Flute Bank employee's address: it involves updating the employee master database (Oracle) and posting a message to a JMS queue (MQSeries) for the external payroll company (because payroll taxes can change based on employee address). For the transaction manager to coordinate and synchronize the transaction with different resource managers (in this example, Oracle and MQSeries), it must use a standards-based, well-known transaction protocol that both resource managers understand (such as X/Open XA).

- JTA defines the javax.transaction.xa.XAResource interface, which allows a transactional resource manager, such as a DBMS or JMS implementation, to participate in a global transaction. The XAResource interface is a Java mapping of the industry-standard X/Open XA. J2EE applications communicate to the resource managers via a resource adapter (e.g., JDBC connection), and JDBC 2.0 extensions support distributed transactions. JDBC 2.0 provides two interfaces that support JTA-compliant resources: the javax.sql.XAConnection and javax.sql.XADataSource.

- Similarly, JMS providers implement the javax.jms.XAConnection and the javax.jms.XASession interfaces in supporting JTA transaction managers.

Java Transaction Service

The JTA specification's main purpose is to define how a client application, the application server, and the resource managers communicate with the transaction manager. Because JTA provides interfaces that map to X/Open standards, a JTA-compliant transaction manager can control and coordinate a transaction that spans multiple resource managers (*distributed* transactions). JTA does not specify how a transaction manager is to be implemented, nor does it address how multiple transaction managers communicate with each other to participate in the same transaction. That is, it does not specify how a transaction context can be propagated from one transaction manager to another. The Java Transaction Service (JTS) specification addresses these concepts.

JTS specifies the implementation contracts for Java transaction managers. It is the Java mapping of the CORBA Object Transaction Service (OTS) 1.1 specification. The OTS specification defines a standard mechanism for generating and propagating a transaction context between transaction managers, using the IIOP protocol. JTS uses the OTS interfaces (primarily `org.omg.CosTransactions` and `org.omg.CosTSPortability`) for interoperability and portability. Because JTS is based on OTS, it is not unusual to find implementations that support transactions propagating from non-Java CORBA clients as well.

Within a JTS-compliant transaction manager implementation, a communication resource manager component handles incoming and outgoing transaction requests. Details of the interaction between the application server and a JTS transaction manager can be found in the JTS specification document.

In addition to being a Java mapping of OTS, the JTS specification also mandates that a JTS-compliant transaction manager implement all JTA interfaces—that is, a JTS-based transaction manager interfaces with an application program, the application server, and resource managers, using the JTA. Figure 14.3 shows the relationship between the application components involved in a transaction.

▷ A Transaction Model for Web Services

So far, we have examined the properties, transactions, and specifications for transaction managers in the current Java/J2EE environment. Most, if not all, of today's Java transaction managers implement the flat transaction model, in compliance with JTA and/or JTS. Also, most transactions today are executed within

Figure 14.3
JTS transaction
manager
components

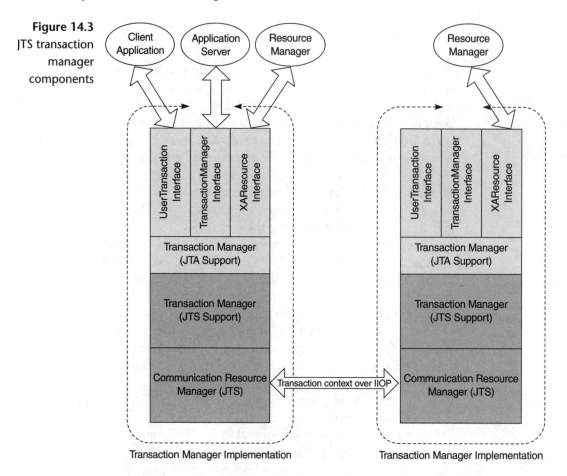

Transaction Manager Implementation   Transaction Manager Implementation

the scope of one enterprise, within one trust domain, and with all resources under the control of one transaction manager. A *business transaction* may be defined as a consistent state change in the business relationship among *two or more parties,* with each party maintaining an independent application system (or Web service) that maintains the state of each application. Business transactions form a good number of transaction types in Web services.

While the flat transaction model is well suited for traditional business computing environments, a Web services environment can create new, interesting challenges for flat transactions:

- **Loose coupling among services.** A Web service application is a loose coupling of constituent Web services and is often constructed by combining Web services from multiple organizations. In this scenario, each service may implement a standalone business process and therefore demarcate transaction boundaries within the service. Because transactions are started and committed within each service, it is not possible to use a simple flat transaction model within the combined application.

For example, in Flute Bank's bill payment service, Flute works with an external check writing service to mail payment checks on behalf of its customers. That is, when a Flute customer transacts with Flute's bill payment service, the service has to accomplish two separate functions as a part of one atomic transaction: it has to debit the customer's checking account, and it has to transact with the external check-writing service and send details of the payee (payee address, payment amount, etc.) If the external check-writing service demarcates its own transaction, a flat transaction model may be inadequate to guarantee atomicity to the Flute consumer's action. (The consumer's interaction is internally implemented as two distinct transactions).

It should be said that a nested transaction model will accommodate this situation, but it is not the only model that can do so. A flat transaction model that supports interposition also can accommodate this situation; we look at interposition in the later sections that explain the Business Transaction Protocol (BTP).

- **Long-running transactions.** Many business transactions are long-running—some may run for hours or days. As transaction isolation is achieved by holding locks on resources, long-running transactions may reduce transaction concurrency to unacceptable levels. Moreover, in a business transaction, the actions of one party affect how long another's resources are locked, opening the door for denial-of-service attacks. It is clear that the isolation property (which controls locking) must be relaxed in such transactions.

  Because a business transaction can take a long time to complete, businesses often impose a time limit on certain types of transactions. For example, an airline may hold a tentative reservation for a travel agency for two days. When the time limit is reached, the airline may decide to either cancel or confirm the reservation automatically. The time period for timeout and the result (confirm or cancel) should be a business agreement between the two parties. The transaction protocol should anticipate such events and allow for negotiation between the participants.

- **Optional subtransactions.** In some business transactions, a subset of activities may be optional. An example of a fictitious travel agency will better illustrate such a situation.

  Assume that the travel service will search with multiple airline services to find flights, based on a consumer's request. Further assume that the airlines all take a pessimistic approach to their commitment: when the travel agent service requests seats on a particular flight, if enough seats are available, the airlines lock the seats for the travel agent and marks the seats unavailable to other requests. Figure 14.4 depicts the participants in this example.

In such a scenario, a transaction initiated by a consumer request will result in the agency requesting seats from one or more airline systems (in the example airlines A, B, and C), a rental car agency, and a hotel. Some airline systems may decline to participate in the transaction (perhaps because no seats are available, as is the case with airline C), and more than one may lock seats for the request (airlines A and B both have seats and confirm them).

Airline C's failure to commit seats cannot be considered a failure of the reservation transaction as a whole, because the application can determine the *atomic subset* of participants, based on business logic. As a result, the atomic property of the transaction need not be satisfied. Moreover, should multiple airlines lock seats (Airlines A and B), a compensating transaction that releases previously booked seats will have to be generated for Airline B, so that only one airline eventually reserves the required seats. This, in effect, conceptually relaxes the durability property of the reservation transaction initiated by the travel service. For this solution to work, application logic has to be written to

Figure 14.4
Atomicity relaxed, travel agency example

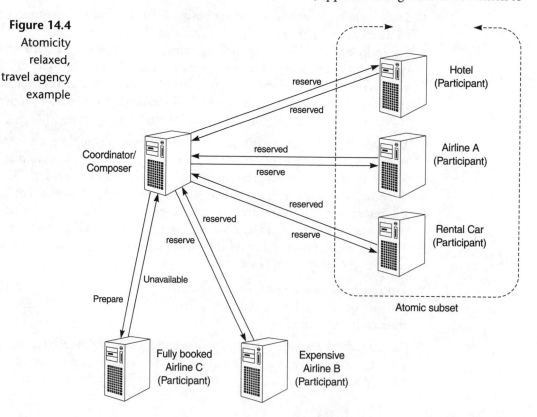

select the subset of activities that must be considered atomic and also to generate compensation transactions.

- **Transaction context propagation.** A Web service application that combines Web services from different organizations will have transactions that span the services. The constituent services may be implemented using different technologies on different platforms (e.g., UNIX, Windows) and may store state in heterogeneous databases. When a transaction spans these disparate services, the transaction context must be passed from service to service. In a JTS environment, JTS specifies how a compliant transaction manager propagates the context from one transaction manager to another over IIOP. A Web service transaction manager must accommodate XML-based transaction contexts propagated over Web service protocols.

This section has illustrated the need for a new model for transactions and transaction management. In the new model, a transaction is viewed as a series of business activities with the context of the transaction made available to each activity. The execution of activities is coordinated, but individual activities may decide to commit the effects of the transaction and make the effects visible before the larger transaction is completed. However, the flat transaction model is adequate for a large number of Web service applications—those that feature short transactions and those in which individual services persist data into a central database or databases within the same enterprise. The new model therefore has to support both the properties of ACID transactions and the relaxed ACID properties demanded by loosely coupled, long-running business transactions. ▷

Table 14.2 summarizes the differences between traditional transaction models and the new model.

▷ New Transaction Specifications

In this section, we discuss three important proposed standards that implement new transaction models: Business Transaction Protocol (BTP) from OASIS, WS-Transaction from IBM and Microsoft, and Activity Service from OMG. Their purpose is to coordinate Web services into applications that provide reliable out-

▷ Strictly speaking, adoption of this new model is not dictated primarily by Web service architectures but by the fundamental long-running nature of business transactions. Web service architecture has simply accentuated the need for it.

Table 14.2 Properties of Traditional and Business Transaction Models

Property	Traditional transactions	Business transactions
Atomicity	Required; all or nothing.	Depends; sometimes desirable, sometimes may be applicable only to a subset of functions.
Consistency	Required.	Required; temporary inconsistencies rectified.
Isolation	Required; state change is not visible until transaction completes.	Relaxed; each service controls degree of visibility.
Durability	Required; effects persist.	Required, but based on atomicity property; some parts may be volatile.
Context propagation	Relaxed; may not be required.	Required.

comes. Of the three, BTP is the most mature and sophisticated. We examine it first and in the most detail.

Business Transaction Protocol (BTP)

In May 2002, the OASIS Business Transaction Technical Committee (BTTC) published a specification, BTP 1.0, for coordinating transactions between applications controlled by multiple autonomous parties. BTP 1.0 is the work of several companies (BEA, IBM, Sun, HP, Choreology, ORACLE, and others) that addresses the challenges posed by business transactions to traditional transaction models.

Examining BTP messages and interactions in detail is beyond the scope of this book. Our intention is to describe the concepts and motivations behind BTP. The full BTP specification can be found at *www.oasis-open.org/committees/business-transactions*.

BTP recognizes that in a business transaction, no single party controls all resources needed. In such an environment, parties manage their own resources but coordinate in a defined manner to accomplish the work scoped by a transaction. Individual service providers either agree to join a transaction or not. If they agree, they are required to provide a mechanism to confirm or cancel their commitments to the transaction. They may, however, autonomously decide when to un-lock resources they hold and/or whether to use compensating transactions to roll back transient states that were persisted.

The BTP specification did not arise out of the need created by Web services architecture but was formed to address the needs of interorganizational transactions and of workflow systems. However, the authors realized early on the limitations of similar coordination protocols tied to communication protocols.

BTP defines an abstract message set and a binding to communication protocols. Its ability to coordinate transactions across multiple autonomous services and its use of XML messages makes it particularly suited for adoption in Web service architectures. BTP is designed such that the protocol may be bound to any carrier protocol, and BTP implementations bound to the same carrier protocols should be interoperable. The current specification describes a SOAP 1.1/HTTP binding.

Transaction and security aspects of an application system are often related, but the BTP specification consciously does not address how a BTP transaction will integrate with a security system, because Web services security standards are still evolving (independently of the transaction specifications).

Application and BTP Elements

BTP is a *protocol*—a set of well-defined messages exchanged between the application systems involved in a business transaction. Each system that participates in a business transaction can be thought of as having two elements—an *application element* and a *BTP element* (Figure 14.5).

Figure 14.5
Application
and BTP
elements
overview

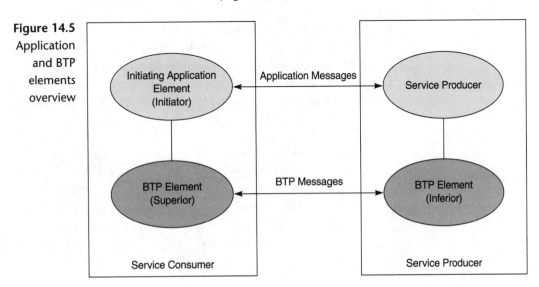

The application elements exchange messages to accomplish the business function. When Flute Bank's bill payment service sends a message to the check writing service with details of the payee's name, address, and payment amount, the application elements of the two services are exchanging a message.

The BTP elements of the two services also exchange messages that help compose, control, and coordinate a reliable outcome for the message sent between the application elements.

The application element pertains to the service consumer and service producer components the application programmer deploys—that is, application/business logic. The BTP elements are supplied by the BTP vendor. The separation of system components into BTP and application elements is a logical one. These elements may or may not coexist in a single address space.

With respect to a BTP transaction, application elements play the role of *initiator* (the Web service that starts the transaction) and *terminator* (the Web service that decides to commit or end the transaction). The initiator and terminator of a transaction are usually played by the same application element.

BTP elements play either a *superior* or *inferior* role. The BTP element associated with the application element that starts a business transaction is usually assigned the *superior* role. The superior informs the inferior when to prepare to terminate the transaction and waits for the inferior to report back on the result of its request. The following sections detail roles played by BTP elements and the nature and content of BTP messages.

Types of BTP Transactions

Table 14.2 summarized the transactional properties business transactions must satisfy. In all types of business transactions, the isolation property is relaxed. Some business transactions require the entire transaction to be treated as an atomic operation, while another class of business transactions requires that the atomic property also be relaxed. BTP accommodates both types of transaction needs. BTP Atomic Business Transactions, or *atoms*, are like traditional transactions, with a relaxed isolation property. ▷

▷ In traditional transactions, a transaction manger will cancel (roll back) a transaction if any resource manager participating in the transaction cannot commit or cannot prepare. In BTP, this is not *always* the case; the set of participants that must confirm before a transaction can be committed is called a *confirm-set*. The confirm-set may be the set of all participants or a subset of participants.

BTP Cohesive Business Transactions, or *cohesions,* are transactions where both isolation and atomicity properties are relaxed.

Atoms *Atoms* are business transactions where all participants have to agree before a transaction can be committed that is, all participants in an atom are guaranteed to see the same ending to the transaction. If any participant cannot confirm, the entire transaction is canceled. Because BTP transactions do not require strict isolation, it is up to each participating service to determine how to implement transaction isolation.

Figure 14.6 depicts a Web service consumer invoking two business methods on two different services, within the scope of a transaction. If the overall transaction is an atom, the BTP element (superior) at the service consumer end is called an *atom coordinator* or simply a *coordinator.* The BTP element plays the coordinator role and coordinates a BTP atomic transaction. It does this by exchanging BTP messages with the BTP elements associated with the two service producers when the application asks it to complete the transaction.

As Figure 14.6 also shows, inferior BTP elements are called *participants.* The participant is in charge of persisting the state change made by the associated application element (service producer), which it does by following instructions (via BTP messages) from the superior (coordinator). If either participant informs the superior that it cannot confirm the transaction, the transaction is rolled back—that is, the confirm-set in this example is "participant a" and "participant b." ▷

Cohesions *Cohesions* are transactions where not all involved parties must agree to commit their changes before a transaction is committed. Only some subset of the parties may need to agree. The subset of parties that need to agree before a transaction can be completed is determined using business logic and is called the confirm-set.

In the example illustrated by Figure 14.4, airline C refuses to reserve seats on the requested flight, because it is fully booked. This refusal to participate in the transaction does not mean that the transaction should be rolled back, because the application logic is able to determine that two other airlines have reserved seats on their flights. Furthermore, because two airlines have reserved seats, the application element must instruct the BTP superior to cancel the more expensive reservation. The BTP superior that composes the transaction based on instructions from the initiating application element is called a *cohesion composer.* The

▷   An atom is a BTP transaction whose confirm-set is the set of *all* inferiors—that is, in an atom, any inferior has power to veto the transaction.

Figure 14.6
Application
and BTP ele-
ments in an
atom/cohesion

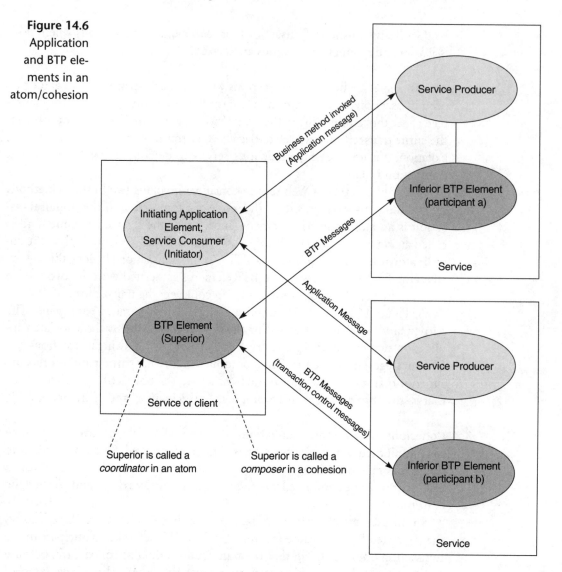

confirm-set in the example is the BTP elements associated with the Web services of Airline A, the rental car agency, and the hotel.

Referring to Figure 14.6, in a *cohesion* scenario, the BTP element (superior) at the service consumer end is called a *cohesion composer* or simply a *composer*. The BTP element associated with the service producer is called a *participant*. In a cohesion scenario, the business logic in application element (initiating element) can determine whether the transaction can be completed—that is, whether "participant a" only need confirm, "participant b" only need confirm, or both must confirm. If only one participant must confirm but both eventually confirm, the composer will ask the unwanted participant to cancel.

In BTP, the actions of transaction coordinator or composer can be influenced by application elements (i.e., business logic). In a cohesion, the initiating application element determines which subset of activities is to be included in the overall transaction by providing that information to the superior. Application elements can also influence the control and coordination of the transaction by providing the superior with additional context information (via *qualifiers;* see next section), such as transaction time limits and other application-specific values. ▷

BTP Transactions and Locking

For both atoms and cohesions, the isolation level for cohesions is left up to each service. Isolation can be achieved by:

- Making changes but applying locks, as in traditional transactions
- Deferring changes until a transaction commits (perhaps by writing a log of changes that will be applied later)
- Making changes and making the interim results visible to others

If the third option is chosen, the effect of making interim changes visible is called the *provisional effect.* If a service makes visible provisional changes and the transaction is ultimately rolled back, new transactions (compensations) may have to be generated to undo the changes made (This is known as the *counter effect*).

BTP Actors, Roles, and Messages

As mentioned earlier, the BTP element associated with the initiator plays the superior role. The initiator is also usually the *terminator* of the initiated transaction. Depending on the type of business transaction, superiors are either coordinators or composers of the business transaction—an atom is coordinated by an *atom coordinator (coordinator),* and a cohesion is composed by a *cohesive composer (composer).* All other BTP elements are inferiors to this superior. In the simplest case, with only one superior and one inferior (i.e., only two parties are involved in the business transaction), the inferior is called a participant.

> ▷ A cohesion is a transaction whose confirm-set is a subset of all inferiors participating in the transaction—that is, only inferiors in the confirm-set have the power to veto the transaction. This subset is determined by application logic, and the application element passes the confirm-set to the composer before asking the composer to complete the transaction.

Figure 14.7 shows a more detailed version of Figure 14.5. The application *(initiator)* first asks a BTP element called the *factory* to create the coordinator/composer. The *factory* creates the superior and returns the transaction *context*. The *initiator* then invokes the business method on the service consumer and passes the context to the service.

How the context is passed depends on the protocol binding. It is, for example, stuffed as a header block in a SOAP message. At the other end, the invoked service asks a BTP element called *enroller* to enroll in the transaction, passing the received context. The enroller creates the inferior (*participant*) and enrolls in the transaction with the *superior.* Finally, the service provides the response to the business method and passes along the *context reply.* The message sequence diagram in Figure 14.8 details the exchange of messages between the different elements.

BTP messages must be bound to a protocol such as SOAP. Because we have not yet described the BTP binding to SOAP, the following section shows only abstract forms of BTP messages.

All BTP messages have an associated schema. The CONTEXT message shown below is an example of a BTP message.

```
<btp:context id>
<btp:superior-address> address</btp:superior-address>
<btp:superior-identifier> URI </btp:superior-identifier>
```

Figure 14.7
BTP and
application
elements

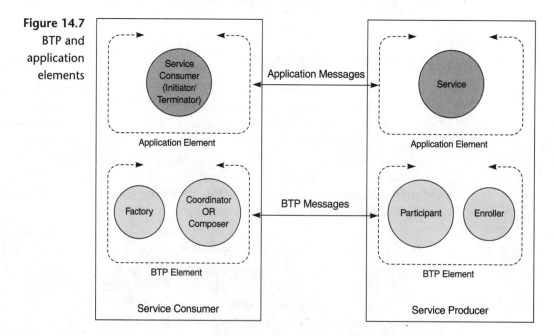

```
<btp:superior-type>atom</btp:superior-type>
<btp:qualifiers> qualifiers </btp:qualifiers>
<btp:reply-address> address </btp:reply-address>
</btp:context>
```

The superior-address element contains the address to which ENROLL and other messages from an inferior are to be sent. Every BTP address element (superior-address, reply-address, etc.) has the following XML format:

```
<btp:superior-address>
    <btp:binding-name> </btp:binding-name>
    <btp:binding-address></btp:binding-address>
    <btp:additional-information>information ... </btp:additional-
    information>
</btp:superior-address>
```

Figure 14.8
BTP actors and
messages over-
view

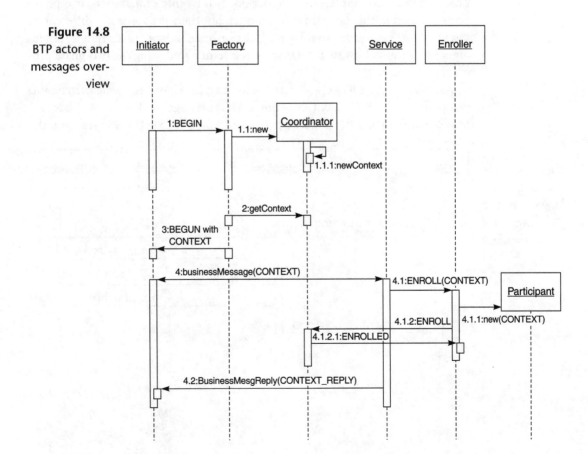

superior-identifier contains a unique identifier (URI) for the superior. superior-type indicates whether the context is for a transaction that is an atom or a cohesion. The qualifiers element provides a means for application elements to have some control over transaction management. Qualifiers are data structures whose contents can influence how the transaction coordinator/composer controls the transaction. BTP defines a few standard qualifiers (such as transaction time limit), but BTP vendors can define more such parameters.

The reply-address element contains the address to which a CONTEXT_REPLY message is to be sent (this is required only if the BTP message is not sent over a request-response transport).

BTP Two-Phase Protocol

Once the initiating application decides to terminate the transaction, it asks the BTP superior to confirm the transaction. The BTP elements then follow a two-phase protocol to complete the transaction. This is quite similar to the two-phase protocol used in the flat transaction model, but there are some key differences, discussed later in this section. Figure 14.8 illustrated how a transaction is started. Figure 14.9 shows how such a transaction is terminated using the two-phase protocol.

On receiving a PREPARE message, an inferior (in Figure 14.9, the participant) can reply with a PREPARED, CANCEL, or RESIGN message. In Figure 14.9, because only one inferior exists, the participant must reply with a PREPARED message if the

Figure 14.9
A simple atom example illustrating the BTP two-phase protocol

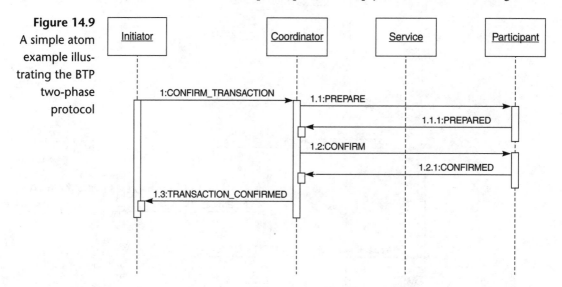

transaction is to be confirmed and progress to phase 2 (CONFIRM). An example of the BTP message for PREPARE is shown below:

```
<btp:prepare id>
    <btp:inferior-identifier> URI </btp:inferior-identifier>
    <btp:qualifiers>qualifiers</btp:qualifiers>
    <btp:target-additional-information>
        additional address information
    </btp:target-additional-information>
    <btp:sender-address>address</btp:sender-address>
</btp:prepare>
```

As explained previously, the qualifiers element contains a set of standard or application-specific qualifiers. The timeout for inferiors is one of the qualifiers that should be sent for a PREPARE message. target-address points to the address of the inferior that was ENROLLed. The PREPARE message will be sent to that address. The sender-address points to address of the superior.

The effect on the outcome of a final transaction of having multiple inferiors depends on whether the transaction is a cohesion or is an atom. The set of inferiors that must eventually return CONFIRMED to a CONFIRM message for the transaction to be committed is called a *confirm-set*. For an atomic transaction, the set consist of *all* of a superior's inferiors. For a cohesion, the confirm-set is a subset of all its inferiors. The subset is decided by the application element associated with the superior (this implies that business logic is involved).

Figure 14.10 illustrates how a composer with multiple participants confirms a cohesion with the two-phase protocol. The application element (the *initiator* and the *terminator* of the transaction) decides that only participants 1 and 2 should confirm—that the *confirm-set* consists of participants 1 and 2. To accomplish this,

1. The terminator sends a CONFIRM_TRANSACTION with the IDs of the participants in the *confirm-set*.

2. The *decider* (composer) sends PREPARE messages to participants 1 and 2 and a CANCEL message to participant 3.

3. As soon as PREPARED messages return from participants in the confirm-set, the decider sends out CONFIRM (phase 2) messages.

4. When the confirm-set replies with CONFIRMED messages, the transaction is confirmed.

Figure 14.10
Cohesion
completion

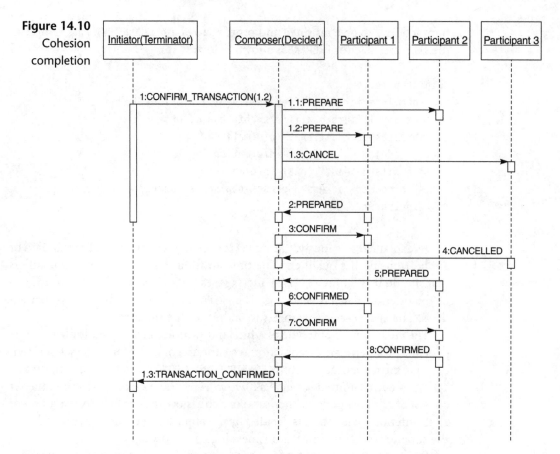

How the confirm subset is passed to the decider is better understood by examining the CONFIRM_TRANSACTION message structure:

```
<btp:confirm-transaction id>
    <btp:transaction-identifier> ... URI ... </btp:transaction-identifier>
    <btp:inferiors-list>
        <btp:inferior-identifier> inferior URI</btp:inferior-identifier>
        <btp:inferior-identifier> inferior URI</btp:inferior-identifier
    </btp:inferiors-list>
    <btp:report-hazard>true</btp:report-hazard>
    <btp:qualifiers>qualifiers</btp:qualifiers>
    <btp:target-additional-information>
        info
    </btp:target-additional-information>
    <btp:reply-address> decider address</btp:reply-address>
</btp: confirm_transaction>
```

Note that `inferiors-list` contains only the confirm-set of inferiors. If this element is absent, *all* inferiors are part of the confirm-set. For an atom, because all participants are in the confirm set, this element must not be present.

The `report-hazard` element defines when the decider informs the application that the transaction is conformed (`TRANSACTION_CONFIRMED` message):

- If `report-hazard` is `true`, the decider waits to hear from all inferiors, not just the confirm-set, before informing the terminator.

- If `report-hazard` is `false`, the decider must wait for all elements (even elements that receive a `CANCEL` message) to reply before communicating the outcome of the transaction to the terminator.

`report-hazard` is useful when the application element wants to know if there was a hazard (problem) with any inferior. ▷

Differences between the BTP and Current Two-Phase Commit Protocols

As discussed in the "Isolation Levels and Locking" sidebar earlier, BTP does not require a participant waiting for a confirm message to hold locks for maintaining application state. A prepared participant can choose to apply application state changes to the database and make this interim "provisional effect" visible. In doing so, it has to hold a compensating transaction ready to be applied (the counter effect), in case of the need to cancel.

Because Web service transactions can span networks prone to communication failure or congestion, a participant and its superior may not be able to communicate readily. BTP recognizes this and accommodates possible communication failures. A participant can limit the promise made in sending `PREPARED` back to its superior. by retaining the right to autonomously confirm or cancel application state changes it controls. This autonomous decision is very much like the heuristic decision made by in-doubt resources in a normal two-phase commit protocol. The difference is that whereas other transaction models consider heuristic decisions rare occurrences, BTP anticipates such problems and allows participants to indicate how long they are willing to be in a prepared state.

▷ If a coordinator or composer has only one inferior, it may decide to use a single-phase confirm operation and skip the two-phase protocol. Instead of a `PREPARE + CONFIRM` message exchange, it may send a `CONFIRM_ONE_PHASE` message to the inferior.

The two-phase protocol used in BTP ensures that either the entire transaction is canceled or that a consistent set of participants is confirmed.

What happens when a participant, having informed its superior that it is prepared to confirm, makes an autonomous decision to cancel, because it has not received the phase-two CONFIRM message within the allotted time? What if, after the autonomous decision is made to cancel, the superior sends out a CONFIRM message? In such cases, the superior will eventually recognize and log a contradiction, inform management/monitoring systems, and send a CONTRADICTION message to the participant. By sending a contradiction message, the superior acknowledges the contradiction and informs the inferior that it knows and has tried to cope with it.

The differences between BTP 2PC and current 2PC can be summed up as follows:

- In BTP, the application determines the confirm-set.

- BTP provides a means for applications to "tune" the two-phase protocol, by passing qualifiers to the coordinator. These qualifiers include standard BTP qualifiers, such as how long a participant is to wait before making an autonomous decision. Qualifiers can also be BTP vendor- or application-specific.

- BTP does not require two-phase locking. This can lead to contradictions if participants make autonomous decisions. Unlike other models, however, which treat heuristic decisions as rare occurrences, BTP anticipates such problems and tries to accommodate them.

Complex BTP Element Relationships

So far, we have examined the BTP elements, roles, and message in a rather simple scenario. A business transaction can span multiple organizations and multiple services, and BTP accommodates such complex scenarios by describing a tree structure for relationships between BTP elements. Figure 14.11 illustrates such a complex relationship. The BTP elements associated with services B and C are both superiors to other inferiors but are inferiors to the superior (composer A, also known as the *decider*). BTP element B is a composer of the transaction cohesion Tc1. As B is an inferior to A, B is called a *sub-composer*. Similarly, BTP element C coordinates the atom Ta1 and is a superior to F and G but an inferior to A , so C is a *sub-coordinator.*

A sub-composer or sub-coordinator is not a participant; it controls other participants and reports to its superior. On receiving PREPARE and CONFIRM messages from its superior, the sub-composer or sub-coordinator asks its confirm-set to

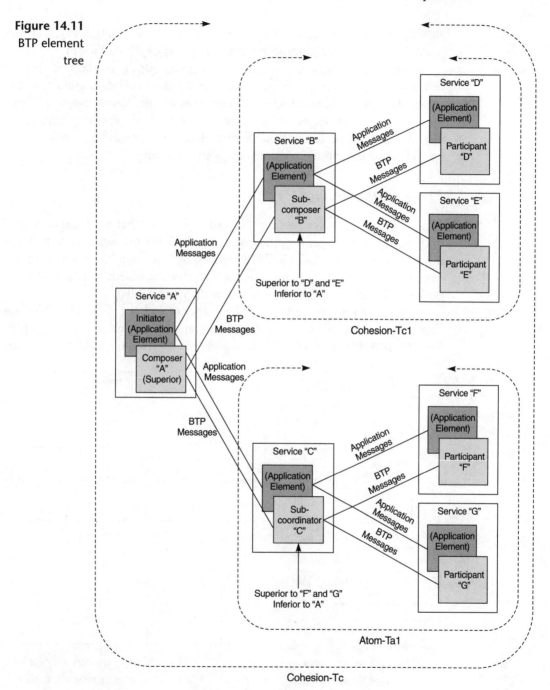

Figure 14.11
BTP element
tree

PREPARE and CONFIRM and reports the result to its superior. In this way, BTP supports the creation of relationship trees of arbitrary depth and width. ▷

To summarize, if an *inferior* is a *superior* to other nodes, it may be a *sub-composer* or a *sub-coordinator*. A *sub-coordinator* treats its inferior's actions as atomic, while a *sub-composer* treats only a subset of its inferiors as atomic. A *participant* is a BTP inferior element that has no children; it is responsible for applying application state changes to a persistent store. Figure 14.12 shows the different roles played by BTP elements and the relationships between them.

BTP and SOAP Binding

BTP defines an abstract message set and a protocol that are independent of underlying communication protocols over which the messages are to be transmitted. For BTP to be viable for Web services, BTP messages must be transmitted over the de facto messaging standard for Web services: SOAP. BTP specifications define a binding for SOAP (and SOAP with Attachments).

As discussed above, most BTP messages are exchanged between BTP elements and are not mixed with any application-element business messages (e.g., PREPARE, CONFIRM). All such BTP messages are sent within the SOAP body under

Figure 14.12
Roles played by
superiors and
inferiors

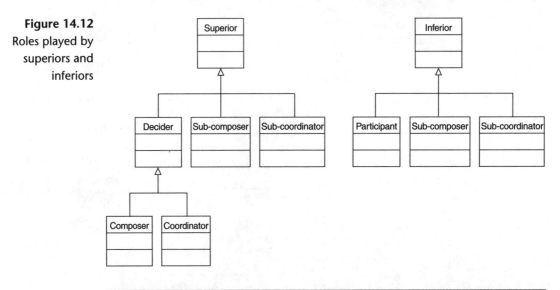

> ▷   Sub-composers and sub-coordinators are *interposed* (as in *injected* or *inserted*) into the transaction. By default, BTP supports an interposed transaction model, not a nested transaction model.

the `btp:messages` element. A few BTP messages are sent along with application messages.

One example of this type of message is CONTEXT. The BTP CONTEXT is propagated from a BTP superior to a BTP inferior when the initiating application element invokes a business method on a service. The BTP CONTEXT message, therefore, must be sent along with the application business message. For such messages, the BTP message is sent in the SOAP header under a single `btp:messages` element, and the application message is sent within the SOAP body. All BTP messages are sent without any encoding (application messages may be encoded).

The following example of a SOAP message starts a BTP atomic transaction in Flute Bank's bill payment service. The business method invoked is `getLast-Payment`. As a new transaction is started, the BTP CONTEXT message is passed, along with the application message. The CONTEXT message is passed as a part of the SOAP header. The header is not encoded, but the body, which carries the application message, is RPC/encoded.

```
<?xml version="1.0" encoding="UTF-8"?>
<env:Envelope xmlns:env="http://schemas.xmlsoap.org/soap/envelope/"
    xmlns:xsd="http://www.w3.org/2001/XMLSchema"
    xmlns:xsi="http://www.w3.org/2001/XMLSchema-instance"
    xmlns:enc="http://schemas.xmlsoap.org/soap/encoding/"
    env:encodingStyle="">

    <env:Header>

        <btp:messages
            xmlns:btp="urn:oasis:names:tc:BTP:1.0:core">
            <btp:context>
                <btp:superior-address>
                    <btp:binding>soap-http-1</btp:binding>
                    <btp:binding-address>
                            http://www.flute.com/btpengine
                    </btp:binding-address>
                </btp:superior-address>

                <btp:superior-identifier>
                    http://www.flute.com/btp01
                </btp:superior-identifier>
```

```
            <btp:qualifiers>
                <btpq:transaction-timelimit>
        xmlns:btpq="urn:oasis:names:tc:BTP:1.0:qualifiers">
                <btpq:timelimit>500</btpq:timelimit>
                </btpq:transaction-timelimit>
            </btp:qualifiers>
        </btp:context>
    </btp:messages>
  </env:Header>

  <env:Body>
    <ans1:getLastPayment
        xmlns:ans1="http://com.flute.webservice/billPay/wsdl/billPay">
        env:encodingStyle=" http://schemas.xmlsoap.org/soap/encoding/"

        <String_1 xsi:type="xsd:string">horizon_wireless </String_1>
    </ans1:getLastPayment>
  </env:Body>

</env:Envelope>
```

Although application architects and developers rarely concern themselves with messages exchanged between BTP elements, let us look at more examples, to help visualize the transaction coordination. The listing below shows the BEGIN BTP message over SOAP from the initiating application element to the associated BTP factory (Figure 14.13). This BEGIN message starts a cohesion.

```
<?xml version="1.0" encoding="UTF-8"?>
<soap-env:Envelope xmlns:soap-env="http://schemas.xmlsoap.org/soap/envelope/"
        encodingStyle="http://schemas.xmlsoap.org/soap/encoding/">
<soap-env:Body>
    <btp:begin transaction-type="cohesion"
                        xmlns:btp="urn:oasis:names:tc:BTP:xml"/>
  </soap-env:Body>
</soap-env:Envelope>
```

The following listing shows a SOAP message with a CANCEL request from a transaction coordinator to a participant.

Figure 14.13
BTP SOAP
message shown
pictorially

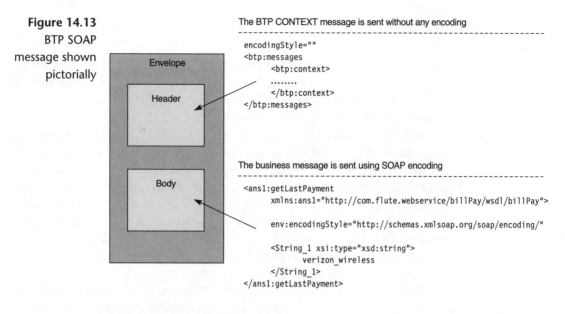

```
<?xml version="1.0" encoding="UTF-8"?>
<soap-env:Envelope xmlns:soap-env="http://schemas.xmlsoap.org/soap/envelope/"
        encodingStyle="http://schemas.xmlsoap.org/soap/encoding/">
<soap-env:Body>
    <btp:cancel xmlns:btp="urn:oasis:names:tc:BTP:xml">
    <btp:inferior-identifier>
    http://www.flute.com/btp01/Fluteparticipant/-74c4a3c4:8dd-6ce8fec8:1
    </btp:inferior-identifier>
    <btp:superior-identifier>
    http://www.flute.com/btp01/TransactionManager/-77e2b3e4:8aa-3ce8fec8:9
    </btp:superior-identifier>
    </btp:cancel>
</soap-env:Body>
</soap-env:Envelope> ▷
```

> **HP Web Services Transactions (HP-WST)**
>
> HP's Web Services Transactions (WST) is the first implementation of a transaction manager based on the BTP specifications. The implementation, available at *www.hpmiddleware.com,* supports both cohesive and atomic transactions. HP-WST includes an HP-WST coordinator component, Java libraries for transaction participants, and libraries for Java clients.

WS-Transaction

WS-Transaction (WS-TX) and the related WS-Coordination specifications are relatively new (released in August 2002). They describe mechanisms to coordinate the executions of individual Web services into reliable applications. The two specifications, created jointly by Microsoft, IBM, and BEA, rely on or are built on existing Web services specifications of WSDL, SOAP, and WS-Security.

The execution of a Web service application is seen as a series of activities, each of which may be executed in a different Web service. WS-Coordination describes a general mechanism to create, register, and coordinate those activities across multiple Web services. When a participant Web service creates and registers the activity, it also identifies the coordination protocol—that is, the way collaboration occurs between activities. The specification does not describe protocols for coordination,. which can be achieved in many ways. Some coordination protocols may be transactional; some may not.

WS-Coordination provides a generalized framework that allows Web services to specify the coordination protocol. WS-Transaction describes protocols for two common transactional coordination patterns that may be used with the WS-Coordination framework: the atomic transaction coordination pattern and the business activity transaction pattern. Figure 14.14 shows the relationship between WS-Coordination and WS-Transaction.

Before describing the WS-Transaction coordination protocols, a brief explanation of the coordination framework described in WS-Coordination is necessary. The latter describes a standard coordination framework, consisting of an

Figure 14.14 Relationship between WS-Coordination and WS-Transaction

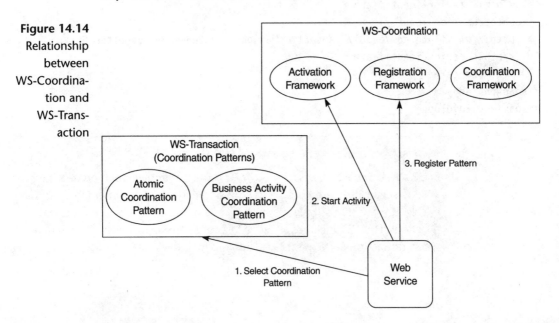

activation service, which helps create a new activity; a *registration service,* to register an activity's participants; and a *coordination service,* to process an activity's completion.

An application contacts the activation service to create an activity, which is identified by a coordination context. The context is a container (defined by an XML schema) with elements for an ID, a context expiration time, the coordination type (the coordination protocols to be used), and other extensible elements. Web services that participate in the same activity receive application messages with the context attached. Web services then use the context to identify the registration service and register as participants to the original activity. The coordination service controls the completion of the activity, based on the selected coordination protocol.

A WS-TX atomic transaction coordination pattern preserves the ACID properties of transactions. The application requests that a new activity be created by the activity service. The activity service creates a coordination context that has the coordinationType element set to the URI http://schemas.xmlsoap.org/ws/ 2002/08/wstx. The coordination context allows for coordination-protocol-specific elements to be added to the context, using the extensibility mechanism (e.g., a context for an atomic transaction may also carry the isolation level value).

The Web service that created the transaction also registers with the registration service the coordination or completion pattern service for the completion protocol. The coordination service controls the completion of the activity, based on the registered completion protocol.

The BTP and WS-Transaction/WS-Coordination specifications provide for similar transactional needs. One important difference between them is that although BTP provides bindings for SOAP 1.1, it is independent of current de facto Web service standards, although WS-Transaction is built on or relies on SOAP, WSDL, and WS-Security.

Activity Service

Activity Service framework is a submission to OMG in response to OMG's call for additional structuring mechanisms for Object Transaction Service (OTS). OTS, you will recall, is the specification for the CORBA transaction manager. The Activity Service specification submission, like the BTP specification, addresses the transactional needs of complex, long-running transactions. The submission can be found at *http://cgi.omg.org/cgi-bin/doc?orbos/2000–06–19.*

This specification, unlike BTP, is directly tied to and based on the OMG Object Request Broker (ORB) and OTS specifications. The lack of support for XML-based messages and Activity Service's tie to OTS may mean that Web services implemented in compliance to it may not transact transparently with services written on, say, the .NET platform. However, because most current Java transaction managers implement JTS (which is a Java mapping of OTS), Activity Service is likely to have a high impact on how Java transaction managers are implemented.

▷ JSRs for Web Service Transaction Support

As described earlier, JTA- and JTS-based transaction managers are limited, in that they are meant to manage and coordinate distributed, ACID transactions. A new specification is needed to address the complex distributed transactions prevalent in Web service and workflow applications.

JSR-95, *J2EE Activity Service for Extended Transactions,* proposes a low-level API for J2EE containers and transaction managers. JSR-95 borrows from the OMG Activity Service submission and leverages concepts defined by JTA and EJB specifications.

JSR-156, *XML Transactions for Java (JAXTX),* also proposes support for extended transaction support in J2EE systems. Unlike JSR–95, JSR-156 proposes a closer relationship to the BTP specification, using XML messaging for transaction management and coordination. This proposed Java API also has a loftier long-term goal: to isolate application programmers and application servers from the underlying transaction manager implementation (BTP, WS-Transaction, and Activity Service). ▷

> ▷ The acronym "JAXTX," in an attempt at consistency with other JAX* APIs, is, in our opinion, misleading. The other JAX* APIs (e.g., JAXM) are meant to be used primarily by application programmers. The J2EE specifications have tried to minimize programmatic transaction demarcation, making the **UserTransaction** interface the only JTA interface exposed to the application.
>
> We recognize that coordinated, non-atomic transactions (e.g., cohesive BTP transactions and business transactions in the WS-Transaction specification) will require application logic to generate compensation transactions. We also recognize that in determining the subset of activities treated as atomic, the interface exposed to application programmers must be expanded beyond the current JTA **UserTransaction** interface. But the vast majority of transaction coordination messages are meant to be exchanged by components below the application layer. Therefore, we feel that "JAXTX" is misleading.

> Summary

J2EE servers are required only to implement the flat transaction model. This model is sufficient in situations where the transactional resources are centralized and under the control of one party. The ACID properties of such transactions can be maintained without compromise. This transactional model is adequate for Web service applications with short-running transactions and those in which transactions do not span organizational boundaries.

The flat transaction mode is inadequate to address the transactional needs of some business transactions in Web services, which frequently involve the assembly of disparate services. These disparate services may have been written with their own, autonomous transaction boundaries and may control their own resources. Web services for business-to-business integration can also be long-running, causing inefficiency as a result of the locking mechanism used for achieving isolation in traditional transaction models.

Relaxing the isolation property of transactions and allowing subtransactions to make visible state-change effects before the larger transaction completes solves the problem of inefficient resource locking in long-running transactions. Allowing a transaction to complete even if only a subset of subtransactions completes (i.e., relaxing the atomic property) allows a business transaction to be composed based on application needs.

The BTP, WS-TX, and Activity Service specifications address the needs of coordinating long-running business transactions that span autonomous, loosely coupled services while accommodating the needs of short-running, centralized transactions. BTP specifies the working of atomic and cohesive transactions, and WS-TX describes the atomic and business activity patterns for coordination. The Activity Service submission to OMG also provides a specification for business transactions but does not reference XML-based messages specifically. (Because Activity Service is based on OMG OTS, it does provide IDL specifications.)

Two JSRs, JSR-95 and JSR-156 propose an extended transaction model for the J2EE platform. As of now, no implementations of BTP or Activity Service transaction managers work seamlessly with J2EE servers. It will be some time before the relevant JSRs are fleshed out and we see servers with embedded, standards-based transaction support for extended transaction models. Until then, our current JTA- and JTS-based flat transaction managers will have to suffice.

Chapter

Security

The coupling of Web services has an inherent security risk, in that a chain of Web services is as strong as its weakest link. The Web service that has the weakest link may not even belong to your organization, but its vulnerabilities will have significant consequences. A breach of the weakest link can compromise the Web service in several ways:

- Allowing interception of data that flows between services, to provide information about servers, usernames, passwords, or personal, financial, medical or other sensitive information

- Allowing alteration of data that flows between services, to return incorrect results or redirect the flow to other services.

- Simply shutting down the service itself, so that other dependent services can no longer function, disrupting multiple users from multiple access points. ▷

▶ Security Considerations for Web Services

Design Time

In earlier chapters, we learned that SOAP is a basic message format that has two parts, the header and body. The header contains metadata associated with the request, and the body is used for holding basic data associated with the message. The simple fact of sending metadata with the message should scare most security-conscious people. Identifying the person sending the message is important to

▷ A honey pot is a computer system used to attract and "trap" people who attempt to penetrate computer systems.

621

any security approach. Security for financial, medical, and other secure transactions usually requires a certificate, Kerberos ticket, or similar mechanisms.

One approach is to create a credentials header that contains an unlimited number of credentials. Inclusion of multiple credentials can be used for more than just authentication. As an example, you could include the certificate that holds the public key used to encrypt a session key. Other certificates can be included that specify the certificate authority chain for another included certificate. Later in this chapter, we drill down into WS_Security—one specification that allows for creating SOAP security headers.

Deployment Time

Whether you decide to use a UDDI- or ebXML-based registry, you will most likely have many of the following security concerns:

- Is the information in the registry up to date?
- How can you ensure that data in the registry was placed there by a valid publisher?
- How can you ensure that only legitimate publishers can add information to the registry?
- How does a registry publisher restrict access to specific registry readers?
- How does a registry provide selective access to partners that need usage data?
- How are credentials (authentication and authorization) transferred to federated registries?
- How can you bind the registry's security mechanism to the security infrastructure of a particular organization?

If the service you want to expose requires security, and access is limited to selected parties, the first step should be to consider avoiding altogether putting it in the registry. Other alternatives may include running the UDDI/ebXML service on a nondefault TCP/IP port. If you know in advance which computers need to access your Web service, you can take advantage of firewall security or Internet Protocol Security (IPSec) to further restrict access. IPSec allows you to establish secure communication between two servers and is a feature provided at the network layer by many operating systems. This approach works well for private networks but may be harder to implement if your Web service will be exposed to the Internet.

Run-time

A Web server and application server in a Web services infrastructure are typically distributed for additional security. A well-thought-out security plan will use the security authentication features built into the Web server tier. The three popular Web server platforms (Apache, IIS, and Sun ONE Web Server) all support several authentication mechanisms for HTTP. Table 15.1 shows five standards-based mechanisms that can be used at the Web server tier to secure your service.

Secure Sockets Layer (SSL) (Figure 15.1) will be the method that secures most Web services. It has become the de facto standard to encrypt data transmitted between HTTP requesters (usually Web browsers) and HTTP servers (Web servers).

Table 15.1 Authentication Methods

Authentication method	Description	Limitation
Basic	Allows for the basic identification of a Web services client based on an ID and password	The ID and password are sent in plain text that could allow credential stealing.
Basic over SSL	Same as basic, but ID and password are sent over the network using Secure Sockets Layer (SSL) encryption instead of plain text.	SSL is a good choice for Internet-based Web services but requires more CPU usage than simple basic authentication. This can be offset in large infrastructures by hardware-based devices for SSL processing.
Kerberos	A Web services client is issued a ticket for access to each Web service it is authorized to use.	This is the most secure approach but can be used only with intranets. Kerberos cannot be used with clients accessing a Web service through a proxy server or a firewall that does Network Address Translation.
Client certificates	Digital certificates can be used to validate the identity of a client and for signing and nonrepudiation.	Each client is required to obtain a certificate, which has a significant cost. Although server certificates have been used for a long time, client certificates are not widely used.
Digest	Uses hashing algorithms to transmit client credentials securely.	Relatively new standard, so it may require upgrading to the latest versions of Web server software.

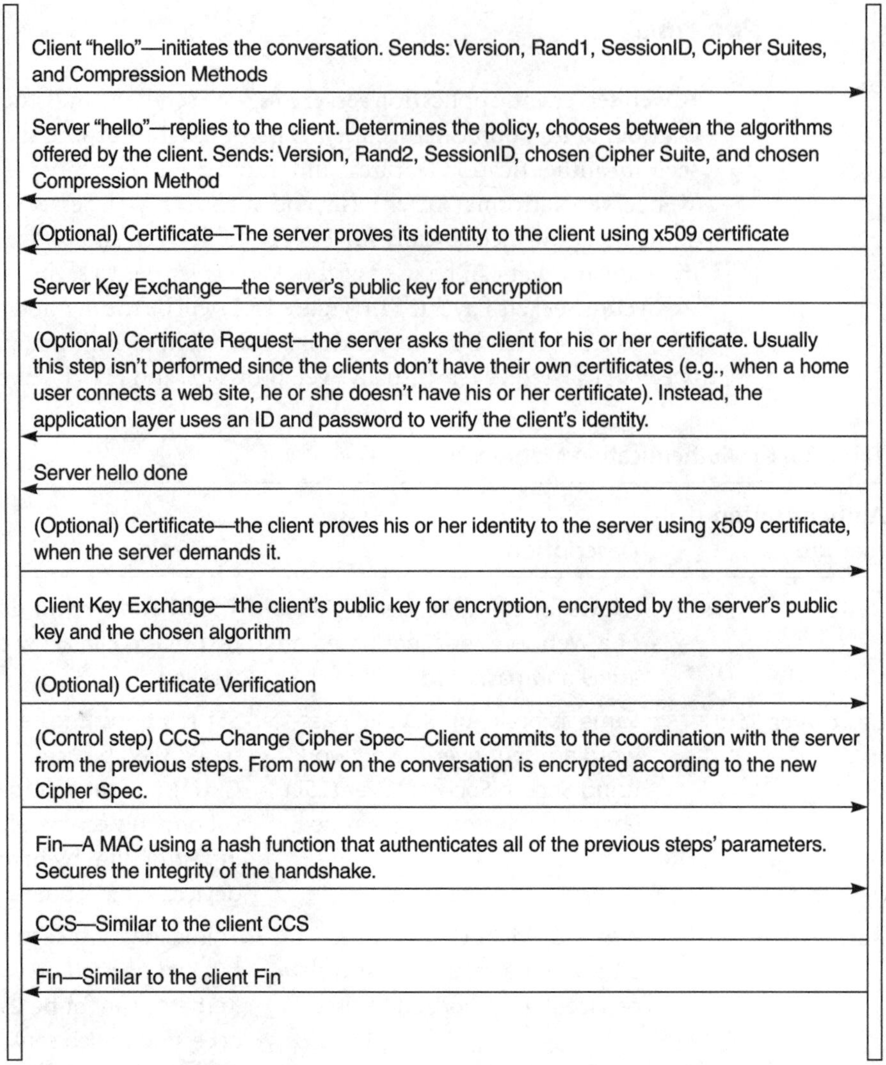

Figure 15.1

Secure Sockets

Layer

Client "hello"—initiates the conversation. Sends: Version, Rand1, SessionID, Cipher Suites, and Compression Methods

Server "hello"—replies to the client. Determines the policy, chooses between the algorithms offered by the client. Sends: Version, Rand2, SessionID, chosen Cipher Suite, and chosen Compression Method

(Optional) Certificate—The server proves its identity to the client using x509 certificate

Server Key Exchange—the server's public key for encryption

(Optional) Certificate Request—the server asks the client for his or her certificate. Usually this step isn't performed since the clients don't have their own certificates (e.g., when a home user connects a web site, he or she doesn't have his or her certificate). Instead, the application layer uses an ID and password to verify the client's identity.

Server hello done

(Optional) Certificate—the client proves his or her identity to the server using x509 certificate, when the server demands it.

Client Key Exchange—the client's public key for encryption, encrypted by the server's public key and the chosen algorithm

(Optional) Certificate Verification

(Control step) CCS—Change Cipher Spec—Client commits to the coordination with the server from the previous steps. From now on the conversation is encrypted according to the new Cipher Spec.

Fin—A MAC using a hash function that authenticates all of the previous steps' parameters. Secures the integrity of the handshake.

CCS—Similar to the client CCS

Fin—Similar to the client Fin

Secure Sockets Layer operates at the session layer of the OSI stack and provides point-to-point confidentiality and either one-way or two-way authentication. Establishing a secure session involves the following steps:

1. The server is registered with a certificate authority (e.g., VeriSign, Thawte) and is assigned a unique certificate.

2. The server transmits its public key to the client.

3. The requestor takes the public key and uses it to encrypt a random number generated by the client (known as a premaster secret). The server will decrypt the premaster secret using its private key.

4. The server creates a new session key based on the premaster secret. The key can be decrypted and used only by the requestor that generated the premaster secret.

The actions taken by the server and requestor to create a session where all traffic between the two is encrypted allows the service to handle authentication, confidentiality, and integrity. SSL in its de facto implementation does not always provide a suitable method for authentication. Most SSL deployment uses server-side certificates, in which the client obtains a copy of the server's certificate, allowing it to authenticate the server and create an encrypted channel. This is the typical model in an e-commerce Web site, because of its ease of implementation and low risk. The main risk in this situation is that a third party may acquire credit-card or other personal information. ▷

SSL will be used for initial Web services security until the proper security schemes are fully developed. In a Web service, SOAP can expose functionality that goes beyond simple low-risk transactions. Therefore, it may be important to also authenticate the requestors in addition to the servers, unlike the typical B2C scenario. SSL also does not protect a Web service against traditional forms of attack, such as buffer overviews. A hacker could create a buffer overview attack by sending parameters that are longer than the Web service expects. A hack could also create a replay attack by playing back a message twice to impersonate the sender.

Transports that use SSL or similar mechanisms help ensure the confidentiality of a message in flight but cannot provide secure end-to-end communication, because they can secure communication only to the next hop. A message may sometimes travel through untrusted links or use communication that cannot be secure. The only way to truly have end-to-end security is by incorporating it at the application level.

Incorporating security into an application is difficult for all but the best architects who have a detailed understanding of cryptographic technologies. Incorporating algorithms into an application itself may actually increase an organization's security exposure if used incorrectly. The most attractive architecture would use an approach where security was close to the application but not incorporated into it. Adding security to the message level is the best solution for Web services.

Skilled Java developers can develop custom authentication mechanisms, so there may be merit in exploring the development of your own. To do so, define

> ▷ The big players in the digital certificate arena are Entrust, Thawte, Valicert, and Verisign.

your Web service so that client credentials are passed in the SOAP header. Alternatively, credentials can be passed as elements in the message body. The Web service would retrieve the credentials from the message and pass it to a custom authentication handler. The logic could compare the credentials to an LDAP server, relational database, or other data stores.

In the Chapter 10, we learned how to expose services with and without Secure Sockets Layer (SSL). Using what we have learned so far, we could define a custom login authentication operation for our Web services that could return a session key. This, of course, is best done over SSL, to prevent hijacking. The communication between the Web services client and server could occur normally over HTTP. The client would include the session identifier in the SOAP header.

This approach would allow for efficient use of server resources and provide a moderate level of security. It does run the risk that the session key could be hijacked but limits exposure that would allow the client's password to be stolen. Alternatively, you could use both SSL and the session key approach for maximum security.

Trust integration is the most difficult of all security principles to implement in Web services architecture. A trust service is typically implemented as a Web service that other Web services call to enable trust for their own transactions. Trust services provide the security functions (e.g., encryption, signing, timestamping, administrative) to other Web services that require a guarantee of their transactions. This approach allows for developers and architects to avoid having to learn the complexity of public-key initiatives and requires only that they invoke the appropriate trust service at the right time.

Trust services as part of your Web services architecture will also allow you to outsource many of your security functions. If you needed to calculate the digital signature for an XML service response, the calculation could be outsourced to a digital signature trust service. One standard that will be included in many trust services is the XML Key Management Specification (XKMS). It is not responsible for encryption or signing and handles only key registration and validation functionality.

> Web Services Security Initiatives

SOAP is simplistic: it allows for basic communication between services through structured data exchange, independent of language or platform. It depends upon underlying transport protocols (e.g., HTTPS and others) for its security. The initial SOAP specification focused primarily on extensibility and made security a second-class citizen.

One principle of Web services is to build on and extend what already exists and implement by merging existing technologies. SOAP is the foundation of the Web services infrastructure and is the focus of emerging security efforts. To create enterprise Web services, security considerations must extend past the SOAP specifications and go deeper into the underlying messaging approach. Many business transactions, such as establishing trust relationships and exchanging confidential information, require building additional security into SOAP.

Some of the XML specifications covered in this chapter are encryption, digital signatures, and key management services. Other standards-based organizations, such as OASIS and WS-I, are working on additional specifications related to SOAP security, including Extensible Access Control Markup Language (XACML) and Security Assertion Markup Language (SAML). The above standards provide the security foundation for SOAP and other XML-based messaging paradigms. This will become crucial for XML messages that pass through intermediaries.

Message Layer Security

Compared to transport-based security schemes such as SSL, incorporating security into the SOAP message provides several important advantages in Web services architecture. First, the interoperable nature of SOAP allows it to use a variety of transport protocols, including HTTP, SMTP, and others. In these scenarios, the message is transported from the originator through one-to-many intermediaries to the ultimate destination. When an intermediary receives a SOAP message, it processes entries contained in the header intended for itself and removes them before sending the message to the next destination.

Design

Privacy for Web services and the sensitivity of the messages over the public Internet could mandate the use of encryption in your architecture. *Encryption* is the act of taking data (usually referred to as clear text) and a short string (the key) and producing data (cipher text). The resulting cipher text is meaningless to a third party who does not know the key. Decryption is the inverse of encryption: taking cipher text and key and producing clear text.

Password encryption derives an encryption key from a user-supplied password. To make the task of discovering the key from the password more time-consuming, many implementations mix in a random variable, known as a *salt,* to create the key.

Several industry-standard algorithms can be chosen for a custom encryption mechanism. One of the elements to consider is whether the encrypted data needs to be decrypted once encrypted. Some algorithms are appropriate for one-way encryption, typically used in login and authentication scenarios. *One-way encryption* prevents the data from being reversed, which is important for credentials. *Two-way encryption* allows for reversible encryption.

A *key agreement* is a protocol in which two or more parties establish the same cryptographic keys without exchanging any secret information. Message authentication codes are a way for two parties to check the integrity of information stored in or transmitted over an unreliable medium and are based on a secret key. Typically, both parties have the same key, referred to as a *shared secret*.

Using Secure Sockets Layer to access your Web service will prevent "man-in-the-middle" attacks and stop data from being read or modified in transit. As previously mentioned, SSL does require additional processing overhead if done in software. This can be alleviated by using SSL accelerator network-interface cards.

XML Digital Signatures

XML Digital Signatures is a standard that allows for specifying the syntax and processing rules for attaching digital signatures to XML documents. An XML digital signature takes data objects, calculates a *digest* (fixed-length representation of a variable-length stream), and places the result into the signature element.

The standard allows XML to functionally sign itself over an insecure network. XML signatures can be attached to any form of digital content, including XML (data objects). An XML signature can sign more than one type of resource, such as HTML, binary-encoded data (GIFs and JPEGs), or an XML-encoded section of an XML file.

Security Assertions Markup Language

Security Assertions Markup Language (SAML) is an XML-based framework used to exchange security information between business partners over the Internet. The driving force behind the creation of SAML is to enable interoperability between different security service providers. Prior to Web services, security was implemented primarily within a single organization. Now that organizations need to collaborate with business partners electronically, the ability to authenticate a user or service across organizations becomes imperative.

A Web services transaction started by one Web service can be completed at a different Web service and may require security information to be shared across all services involved in the transaction. SAML allows services to exchange authentication, authorization, and attribute information without organizations and their partners having to modify their current security solutions. SAML is designed to work with multiple industry-standard protocols such as HTTP and SMTP and integrates document-exchange protocols such as SOAP, BizTalk, and EbXML.

Extensible Access Control Markup Language

Extensible Access Control Markup Language (XACML) defines standardized security access control using XML to state authorization rules over a public connection. XACML also allows validation and revocation, based on defined authorization rules.

Key Management Specification

XML Key Management Specification (XKMS) is a standard that detail protocols for registration and distribution of public keys, so that the keys can be used in combination with XML digital signatures and encryption. XKMS was created to simplify the integration of digital certificates and public key infrastructure (PKI) with a multitude of applications. Applications that use this specification can easily integrate authentication, digital signature, and encryption services. XKMS includes support for certificate processing and revocation status checking.

Encryption Algorithm Selection

Algorithms can be generically categorized as either *symmetric* or *asymmetric*. A *symmetric-key algorithm,* better known as a shared secret, uses a single key for encryption and decryption. This is suitable when two parties have established a relationship in advance. Table 15.2 shows some of the algorithms that can be used in a symmetric scenario.

Asymmetric algorithms are better known as *public/private-key.* This encryption is best used between two parties who have no prior knowledge of each other but want to exchange data securely. Unlike symmetric algorithms, asymmetric algorithms use two different cryptographic keys to encrypt and decrypt plain text. The two keys have a mathematical relationship. A message encrypted by the algorithm using one key can be decrypted by the same algorithm using the other key. Some asymmetric algorithms have the property that one key is deducible from

Table 15.2   Symmetric Algorithms

Algorithm	Length of key	Block size
AES	256	128
Blowfish	576	64
CAST-256	256	128
GOST	256	64
IDEA	128	64
RC-6	2040	128
Serpent	256	128
Twofish	256	128

the other. These algorithms are typically incorporated into public/private-key algorithms commonly used by certificate providers.

Encryption mechanisms typically use various algorithms for their routines. Listed below are some of the algorithms that can be used to develop your own encryption mechanism, along with their relative strengths and weaknesses. Many other encryption algorithms can be part of your toolkit but are not in widespread usage. If you want to go down this path, we recommend *Applied Cryptography,* by Bruce Schneier (Wiley, 1996).

Blowfish

Blowfish is a 64-bit block cipher algorithm. This essentially means that data is encrypted in 64-bit chunks. The Blowfish algorithm allows for varying key lengths, from 32 to 448 bits, and uses sixteen iterations of the main algorithm. The number of iterations is exponentially proportional to the time required to find a key using a brute-force attack. As the number of iterations increases, so does the algorithm's security.

SkipJack

SkipJack is 64-bit algorithm that transforms a 64-bit input block into a 64-bit output block. The transformation is parameterized by an 80-bit key and involves performing 32 iterations of a nonlinear complex function. In a key-based algorithm, the number of possible keys is directly related to the length of the key. Since SkipJack uses 80-bit keys, it means that there are 280, or more than one trillion trillion, possible keys.

Twofish

Twofish is a 128-bit block cipher algorithm. This essentially means that data is encrypted in 128-bit chunks. The Twofish algorithm allows for varying key lengths. It also uses sixteen iterations of its main algorithm, to ensure maximum security. This algorithm has been compromised with five iterations but never with sixteen. More than sixteen iterations can be used, but the tradeoff in slower speed is not worth the higher security.

Triple DES

The DES algorithm was invented by IBM around 1970 and was initially designed with a key size of 128 bits. This algorithm has been successfully cracked by a group of Internet users (DESCHALL) using spare computer cycles. Based on current computer technology, this algorithm can be cracked in anywhere from six hours to as little as three minutes. Triple DES uses the DES algorithm but encrypts data with DES three times, using three different keys. It is useful for securing low-security data, such as grade books or diaries.

MD5 and SHA1

A *digest,* such as MD5 or SHA1, takes an arbitrary-sized byte array and generates a fixed-size output, commonly referred to as a digest or hash. The fundamental requirements of a digest are that it should never reveal anything about the input used to generate it. While two different messages could potentially generate the same hash value, it should be computationally infeasible to do so. These algorithms are typically used for "fingerprinting" or digital signatures.

S/MIME

S/MIME is an emerging standard that uses a 40-bit symmetrical encryption for all messages. The message contains a digital signature the receiving party must receive before decrypting the message.

Ralph Merkle's Puzzle Protocol

A puzzle is a string that takes precisely a known amount of time to decrypt. For example, one way to create a puzzle is to encrypt a message with a symmetric cipher and a very short key of 20 bits. Let us say that no better way exists for attacking the cipher than brute force. Therefore, anyone attempting to crack the puzzle will have to try every possible 20-bit key. Searching the entire key space will take

220 operations. The odds are good that the key will be discovered halfway through, so it is expected to take 219 operations.

Diffie-Hellman

The Diffie-Hellman key agreement protocol, developed in 1996, allows two users to exchange a secret key over an insecure medium without any prior secrets. This protocol depends on a discrete logarithmic problem for its security. It makes the assumption that it is computationally unfeasible to calculate a shared secret key, given two public values that are sufficiently large. This protocol has limitations, in that it does not validate either party.

DSA

The National Institute for Standards and Technology (NIST) published the Digital Signature Algorithm (DSA) as part of the government's Capstone project, which seeks to develop a standard for publicly available cryptography. The Capstone project used 80-bit symmetric keys.

DSA signature generation is significantly faster than signature verification and is therefore not an optimal algorithm compared to RSA. Typically, a message may be signed once but read many times. Therefore, it is advantageous to have faster signature verification.

RSA

The first known asymmetric algorithm was invented by Clifford Cocks but was not public. It was therefore reinvented by Ronald Rivest, Adi Shamir, and Leonard Adelman, (RSA) at MIT during the 1970s. RSA is a public-key cryptographic approach that allows for both encryption and digital signatures. The RSA algorithm relies for its security on factoring very large integers. Encryption and authentication occur without sharing private keys. Each party uses the other's public key or its own private key for operations. Any party can send an encrypted message and/or verify a signed message, but only the party that possesses the correct private key can decrypt or sign a message. RSA has certain weaknesses and is vulnerable to attack by factoring the modulus part of the public key.

Elliptic Curves

Elliptic-curve algorithms, created by Victor Miller and Neal Koblitz in the mid-1980s, are analogs of existing public-key approaches in which elliptic curves replace modular arithmetic operations. An elliptic curve is a mathematical construction from number theory and algebraic geometry and can be defined over any field.

Example: Asymmetric Puzzles

Let us look at the procedure for using Merkle's Puzzle to encrypt legal documents sent between Flute Bank's Loan Officer (Rodney) and a customer (Alicia):

1. Alicia creates a puzzle using the signed contract received from Rodney. Alicia encrypts her signed contract with a very long, randomly chosen key, using a symmetric algorithm such as Blowfish. Since the key is large, Alicia will not wait for Rodney to read the contract, because it will take a long time to be decrypted.

2. Alicia sends the puzzle to Rodney and asks for a return receipt.

3. Alicia receives the return receipt, whereby Rodney asks for a "hint" for the puzzle. Rodney will use this hint to solve the puzzle instead of computing it himself. The hint does not reveal the contract (message).

4. Alicia in turn sends Rodney the first few bits of the key and asks for a return receipt for the hint.

5. When Alicia receives no additional requests for hints, this means that either the mathematical combinations have been reduced to a point where they are easy to calculate or the puzzle has been solved.

When Rodney sends Alicia a return receipt for the puzzle, she knows he possesses enough information to reconstruct the message. Every time she receives a request for a hint from him, she knows how much time is left until he can read the message. Also, because she does not give out hints until Rodney requests them by sending a return receipt, she knows how much of a hint he has.

You may have noticed that asymmetric algorithms are slower than comparably secure symmetric algorithms—sometimes on the order of magnitude of one hundred times slower. Many cryptographic systems use a combination of both approaches, where a receiver's public key encrypts a symmetric-key algorithm used to encrypt a message. This uses the best of both worlds when properly done.

Organizations that operate outside the United States and Canada must be aware of national laws and export regulations. Many of the encryption algorithms that use large keys cannot be exported to certain foreign countries: Afghanistan, Cuba, Iran, Iraq, Libya, North Korea, Serbia, Sudan, Syria, and others. France also has its own unique laws in this regard. For further information on export rules, visit *www.bxa.doc.gov*.

Many open source activities, such as *www.openjce.org,* provide additional algorithms that are secure and do not have export restrictions. It is up to you to determine which of the listed algorithms fits your business needs and falls within legal guidelines.

> Canonical XML

Many standards mentioned in this chapter, such as XML signatures and XML encryption, require a common way to represent XML documents. XML documents can have the same logical meaning but different physical implementations, based on character encoding, attribute ordering, or even structure. Let us look at a simple example:

```
<img src="burney.gif" width="100" height="50"/>
<img src="burney.gif" height="50" width="100"/>
```

A string comparison of the two elements above will not equate, yet they are equivalent. The XML 1.0 specification states that order of attributes is not noteworthy. Two equivalent XML documents may differ based on physical structure or character encoding. Nor are the amount of whitespace between attributes and whether default values are included. The ability to check XML documents for equivalence is important, especially in conjunction with checksums, digital signatures, and version control. W3C has defined a canonical form for XML documents that provides a solution to these problems.

The Canonical XML specification establishes the concept of equivalence between XML documents and provides the ability to test at the syntactic level. It allows you to determine whether logically equivalent documents are byte-for-byte identical. Canonical XML does not use Unicode for its processing; it relies on UTF-8. This is done primarily because the Unicode standard allows multiple representations of certain characters. Two XML documents with equivalent content may contain differing character sequences. For example:

```
<?xml version="1.0" encoding="ISO-8859-1"?>
<lang>Español</lang>
```

Here, the character "ñ" is represented as #xF1 in Unicode, based on the specified ISO-8859–1 encoding ("ISO Latin-1"). UTF-8 represents all characters as two bytes and will therefore represent "ñ" as #xC3 and #xB1. Many other XML constructs have similar representations.

A canonicalized XML document depends on its standalone document declaration. A document must be self-contained and cannot contain external references that affect its canonical form. Suppose an XML document named government.xml contains the sentence "The government is responsible!" and the document is also stored in the same directory:

```
<!DOCTYPE d [
 <!ENTITY lsb '['>
 <!ENTITY rsb ']'>
 <!ENTITY government SYSTEM "government.xml">
]>
<d>&lsb;&bum;&rsb;</d>
```

The canonical form of this document would become:

```
<d>[The government is responsible!]</d>
```

Using the canonical form of an XML document is vital for digital signatures and encryption. Otherwise, a recipient may improperly determine that a document has been altered, when in fact it is still intact. This is important for signing and nonrepudiation in Web services architecture.

Because the Canonical XML specification is evolving, we recommend that you visit *www.w3.org* for the latest draft of the CharModel, Namespaces, and XML specifications.

> XML Digital Signatures

Consider a scenario where you are developing a healthcare Web service for a hospital that exposes medical records and other patient information. An insurance company or HMO would need to see the details of a lab test and the interactions between the doctor and patient. A doctor would need to see details not only of a patient's current stay at the hospital but also any past visits. The doctor should not need to know whether the patient has insurance deductibles. A nurse may need to see information related only to the current visit. A medical researcher may need to see medical history but not personal details. Many other combinations of information could, of course, be contained in an XML message.

The W3C and the Internet Engineering Task Force (IETF) have put together a joint proposal for using XML-based digital signatures. Java Community Process *(www.jcp.org)* is also working to define a specification for XML Digital Signatures (JSR-105) within Java. Digitally signing the entire XML document is simplistic. What if a document such as a medical record requires digital signatures on different portions by different medical personnel? Furthermore, signature in this scenario implies order. The admissions department should ideally sign its section before the discharge department does.

The primary use for digital signatures is for nonrepudiation. For example, Flute Bank can receive a signed document and know exactly who sent it, because the signature contains a message digest signed by using the sender's private key. XML signatures define a `signature` element that contains the information to process a digital signature. Each digital signature refers to one of three things:

- An XML element in the signature element

- An external XML document referenced by a URI in the document

- An external non-XML resource referenced by a URI in the XML document

Consider the following XML document for placing a check order:

```
<flutebank:checkOrder xmlns:flutebank="http://flutebank.com/CheckOrders">
    <flutebank:checkType>flutebank:Dilbert</flutebank:checkType>
    <flutebank:quantity>1,000</flutebank:quantity>
    <flutebank:account>ABC123</flutebank:account>
    <flutebank:startnum>2000</flutebank:startnum>
</flutebank:checkOrder>
```

If a customer of Flutebank.com sent this order to our Web service, the service will need to validate that the order truly came from the account holder, regardless of the specified account number. One approach would be for the customer to digitally sign the above XML document, as in Listing 15.1.

Listing 15.1   Signed check order

```
<flutebank:signedCheckOrder xmlns:flutebank="http://flutebank.com/CheckOrders">
  <Signature xmlns="http://www.w3.org/2000/09/xmldsig#">
    <SignedInfo>
```

```
<CanonicalizationMethod Algorithm="http://www.w3.org/TR/2001/REC-xml-c14n-
                                                             20010315"/>
<SignatureMethod Algorithm="http://www.w3.org/2000/09/xmldsig#rsa-sha1"/>
<Reference URI=""/>
  <Transforms>
    <Transform Algorithm="http://www.w3.org/2000/09/xmldsig#enveloped-
                                                         signature"/>
  </Transforms>
  <DigestMethod Algorithm="http://www.w3.org/2000/09/xmldsig#sha1"/>
  <DigestValue>j6lbgp5EPmSfTb3atsSuNbeVu8nk=</DigestValue>
</Reference>
</SignedInfo>
<SignatureValue>aiYECAxGoPiLOv3sSamm3rXup5zJa ... </SignatureValue>
<KeyInfo>
  <X509Data>
    <X509Certificate>MIIDa1sY+mAyIBA ... </X509Certificate>
  </X509Data>
</KeyInfo>
</Signature>
<flutebank:checkOrder>
  <flutebank:OrderID>64B4A0D1-814E-4FF6-918A-DD7E7E1AECEA</flutebank:OrderID>
  <flutebank:checkType>flutebank:Dilbert</flutebank:checkType>
  <flutebank:quantity>1,000</flutebank:quantity>
  <flutebank:account>ABC123</flutebank:account>
  <flutebank:startnum>2000</flutebank:startnum>
</flutebank:checkOrder>
</flutebank:signedCheckOrder>
```

Here, the original checkOrder now becomes a child element of the root signedCheckOrders and adds an additional child, the signature element, which contains the digital signature information. Included it are elements that identify the algorithms used to canonicalize the data, the digest algorithm, and the signature algorithm.

The reference element points to the data we are interested in validating. In Listing 15.1, the element contains a null URI, which means that the entire XML document containing the signature element should be signed. This attribute could also include an XPointer reference, to state a specific portion of the document used to compute the signature.

The transforms element performs an XPath transform that removes the signature element. This is required in this scenario, because we are signing the entire document that envelops the signature. The DigestValue, calculated as part of the signing process, will obviously change if you include the digest itself. The trans- forms element removes the entire signature element from the data that must be digested and signed. This approach prevents recursion issues. ▷

The keyinfo element holds key information required for validation of the sig- nature. In our scenario, it contains an X.509 certificate, which holds the public key for the account holder. This is how Flute Bank can validate that the check or- der originated from a specific account holder.

The final feature that is critical in this example is the OrderID element. It con- tains a unique identifier that could be based on a timestamp or other calculated value. We have provided an additional level of protection by tagging each order with a unique identifier, preventing the success of a replay attack. Without the unique identifier, an attacker could simply replay the signed message, causing hundreds of duplicate orders to be created. This could be used to drain the bank account. The Flute Bank Check Order Web service checks to see if it has already processed an order with this unique identifier and ignores any duplicates.

In the above example, the check order was sent directly from the client to Flute Bank. If the check order were routed through other intermediaries, chang- ing the order identifier would cause the signature validation check to fail. Re- member that a digest is calculated based on the contents of the message. Rear- ranging the order within the document will also cause the message digest value to change. Likewise, replaying the same order would be flagged and ignored. Detec- tion of replay attacks can be part of the message or header and can use one or more of the following approaches: timestamps, sequence numbers, expiration message, and correlation.

The XML digital signature specification also incorporates the XML canoni- cal specification for generating the physical document, for scenarios where two XML documents may differ in their exact textual representation but are logically equivalent. Otherwise, documents may become suspect without valid cause. Both digital signature generation and validation are typically done using message digests. For a signature, the digest is calculated on the XML's canonical form. If the digests between two canonical forms of XML match, you can be sure the docu- ment has not been tampered with, even though the textual forms may vary. ▷▷

▷ XPath is a language that describes a method to locate and process items within XML documents. The method uses an addressing syntax on a path through the document's logical structure or hierarchy.

▷▷ A message digest takes an input message of arbitrary length and produces a fixed-length output.

If you decide to use digital signatures as part of your Web service, you must become aware of the security implications involved. Digital signatures require public and private key pairs, and the validity of the public key has to be provided by other technologies. A certificate trust model is required—either peer-to-peer or hierarchical. A method to generate and maintain trusted key pairs and certificates is also necessary. Finally, it must be possible to validate that the certificate has not been revoked. ▷

Many implementations of XML digital signatures are available, including:

- IAIK XML Signature Library: *http://jcewww.iaik.tu-graz.ac.at/products/ixsil/index.php*

- IBM's XML Security Suite: *www.alphaworks.ibm.com/tech/xmlsecuritysuite*

- InfoMosaic SecureXML: *www.infomosiac.net*

- NEC XML Digital Signature Software Library: *www.sw.nec.co/jp/soft/xml_s/appform_e.html*

- Phaos XML: *www.phaos.com/e_security/dl_xml.html*

- RSA BSAFE: *www.rsasecurity.com/products/bsafe/certj.html*

- Verisign XML Signature SDK: *www.xmltrustcenter.org/xmlsig/developer/verisign/index.htm*

Providing digital signatures as part of a Web services architecture increases the ability to support nonrepudiation and signer authentication aspects of your services.

▷ Apache XML Security

Now that you have a thorough understand of how XML signatures work, let us look at one implementation of an API provided by Apache that allows a user to sign and verify digital signatures in a document. The source code is available at *http://xml.apache.org/security/index.html*. We will first sign a document named axisSignature.xml. Listing 15.2 demonstrates XML signatures for this document.

▷   For additional information on XML digital signatures, please visit *www .w3.org/TR/2002/REC-xmldsig-core-20020212.*

Listing 15.2 Apache Axis signer

```java
/* <http://www.apache.org/>.
 */
package org.apache.xml.security.samples;

import java.io.*;
import java.security.*;
import java.security.cert.*;
import java.util.*;
import org.apache.xpath.XPathAPI;
import org.w3c.dom.*;
import org.apache.xml.security.algorithms.MessageDigestAlgorithm;
import org.apache.xml.security.c14n.*;
import org.apache.xml.security.exceptions.XMLSecurityException;
import org.apache.xml.security.signature.*;
import org.apache.xml.security.keys.*;
import org.apache.xml.security.keys.content.*;
import org.apache.xml.security.keys.content.x509.*;
import org.apache.xml.security.keys.keyresolver.*;
import org.apache.xml.security.keys.storage.*;
import org.apache.xml.security.keys.storage.implementations.*;
import org.apache.xml.security.utils.*;
import org.apache.xml.security.transforms.*;
import org.apache.xml.security.Init;
import org.apache.xml.security.samples.utils.resolver.OfflineResolver;
import org.apache.xml.serialize.*;

/**
 *
 * @author $Author: geuerp $
 */
public class AxisSigner {

   /** Field AXIS_SIGNATURE_FILENAME           */
    public static final String AXIS_SIGNATURE_FILENAME = "axisSignature.xml";

   /**
    * Method main
    *
    * @param unused
```

```
 * @throws Exception
 */
public static void main(String unused[]) throws Exception {

    org.apache.xml.security.Init.init();

    //J-
    String keystoreType = "JKS";
    String keystoreFile = "data/org/apache/xml/security/samples/input/
                                                      keystore.jks";
    String keystorePass = "xmlsecurity";
    String privateKeyAlias = "test";
    String privateKeyPass = "xmlsecurity";
    String certificateAlias = "test";
    File signatureFile = new File(AXIS_SIGNATURE_FILENAME);
    //J+
    KeyStore ks = KeyStore.getInstance(keystoreType);
    FileInputStream fis = new FileInputStream(keystoreFile);

    ks.load(fis, keystorePass.toCharArray());

    PrivateKey privateKey = (PrivateKey) ks.getKey(privateKeyAlias,
                            privateKeyPass.toCharArray());
    javax.xml.parsers.DocumentBuilderFactory dbf =
        javax.xml.parsers.DocumentBuilderFactory.newInstance();

    dbf.setNamespaceAware(true);

    javax.xml.parsers.DocumentBuilder db = dbf.newDocumentBuilder();
    org.w3c.dom.Document doc = db.newDocument();

    /*
     * Start SOAP infrastructure code. This is to be made compatible with Axis.
     *
     */
    String soapNS = "http://www.w3.org/2001/12/soap-envelope";
    String env = "env";
    String envPrefix = env + ":";
    Element envelopeElement = doc.createElementNS(soapNS,
                            envPrefix + "Envelope");
```

```
envelopeElement.setAttribute("xmlns:" + env, soapNS);
doc.appendChild(envelopeElement);

Element headerElem = doc.createElementNS(soapNS, envPrefix + "Header");
Element bodyElem = doc.createElementNS(soapNS, envPrefix + "Body");

envelopeElement.appendChild(doc.createTextNode("\n"));
envelopeElement.appendChild(headerElem);
envelopeElement.appendChild(doc.createTextNode("\n"));
envelopeElement.appendChild(bodyElem);
envelopeElement.appendChild(doc.createTextNode("\n"));
bodyElem
    .appendChild(doc
        .createTextNode("This is signed together with its Body ancestor"));
String SOAPSECNS = "http://schemas.xmlsoap.org/soap/security/2000-12";
String SOAPSECprefix = "SOAP-SEC";

bodyElem.setAttributeNS(SOAPSECNS, SOAPSECprefix + ":" + "id", "Body");

Element soapSignatureElem = doc.createElementNS(SOAPSECNS,
                               SOAPSECprefix + ":" + "Signature");

envelopeElement.setAttribute("xmlns:" + SOAPSECprefix, SOAPSECNS);
envelopeElement.setAttribute(env + ":" + "actor", "some-uri");
envelopeElement.setAttribute(env + ":" + "mustUnderstand", "1");
envelopeElement.appendChild(doc.createTextNode("\n"));
headerElem.appendChild(soapSignatureElem);

/*
 *
 * End SOAP infrastructure code. This is to be made compatible with Axis.
 */
String BaseURI = signatureFile.toURL().toString();
XMLSignature sig = new XMLSignature(doc, BaseURI,
                                 XMLSignature.ALGO_ID_SIGNATURE_DSA);

soapSignatureElem.appendChild(sig.getElement());
{
    // sig.addDocument("#Body");
    Transforms transforms = new Transforms(doc);
    transforms.addTransform(Transforms.TRANSFORM_ENVELOPED_SIGNATURE);
```

```
      sig.addDocument("", transforms);
   }
   {
      X509Certificate cert =
         (X509Certificate) ks.getCertificate(certificateAlias);
      sig.addKeyInfo(cert);
      sig.addKeyInfo(cert.getPublicKey());
      sig.sign(privateKey);
   }

   FileOutputStream f = new FileOutputStream(signatureFile);
   XMLUtils.outputDOMc14nWithComments(doc, f);
   f.close();
   System.out.println("Wrote signature to " + BaseURI);

   for (int i = 0; i < sig.getSignedInfo().getSignedContentLength(); i++) {
      System.out.println("-- Signed Content follows--");
      System.out
         .println(new String(sig.getSignedInfo().getSignedContentItem(i)));
   }
  }
 }
}
```

In the above example, we specify the keystore type as Java Keystore (JKS), with its location and password. Additionally, we specify the private-key password and alias used for the keystore. We then retrieve the private key from the keystore:

```
PrivateKey privateKey = (PrivateKey) ks.getKey(privateKeyAlias,
                        privateKeyPass.toCharArray());
```

Once we have the private key, we create a new XML document:

```
javax.xml.parsers.DocumentBuilderFactory dbf =
   javax.xml.parsers.DocumentBuilderFactory.newInstance();

dbf.setNamespaceAware(true);

javax.xml.parsers.DocumentBuilder db = dbf.newDocumentBuilder();
org.w3c.dom.Document doc = db.newDocument();
```

Because we are signing a SOAP message, we need additional elements in the SOAP header and body for our signature:

```
Element envelopeElement = doc.createElementNS(soapNS,
                              envPrefix + "Envelope");

envelopeElement.setAttribute("xmlns:" + env, soapNS);
doc.appendChild(envelopeElement);

Element headerElem = doc.createElementNS(soapNS, envPrefix + "Header");
Element bodyElem = doc.createElementNS(soapNS, envPrefix + "Body");

envelopeElement.appendChild(doc.createTextNode("\n"));
envelopeElement.appendChild(headerElem);
envelopeElement.appendChild(doc.createTextNode("\n"));
envelopeElement.appendChild(bodyElem);
envelopeElement.appendChild(doc.createTextNode("\n"));
bodyElem
    .appendChild(doc
        .createTextNode("This is signed together with its Body ancestor"));

String SOAPSECNS = "http://schemas.xmlsoap.org/soap/security/2000-12";
String SOAPSECprefix = "SOAP-SEC";

bodyElem.setAttributeNS(SOAPSECNS, SOAPSECprefix + ":" + "id", "Body");

Element soapSignatureElem = doc.createElementNS(SOAPSECNS,
                              SOAPSECprefix + ":" + "Signature");

envelopeElement.setAttribute("xmlns:" + SOAPSECprefix, SOAPSECNS);
envelopeElement.setAttribute(env + ":" + "actor", "some-uri");
envelopeElement.setAttribute(env + ":" + "mustUnderstand", "1");
envelopeElement.appendChild(doc.createTextNode("\n"));
headerElem.appendChild(soapSignatureElem);
```

We then create a new XML signature using DSA (two-way asymmetric) and SHA1 (one-way hash) as our algorithm:

```
String BaseURI = signatureFile.toURL().toString();
XMLSignature sig = new XMLSignature(doc, BaseURI,
                        XMLSignature.ALGO_ID_SIGNATURE_DSA);
```

By incorporating a signature, we are changing the contents of the document, which will require performing transformations on it. The input to the first transform results in dereferencing the URI attribute of the reference element. The output from the last transform is the input for the DigestMethod algorithm:

```
Transforms transforms = new Transforms(doc);
transforms.addTransform(Transforms.TRANSFORM_ENVELOPED_SIGNATURE);
sig.addDocument("", transforms);
```

Next, we retrieve the X.509 certificate from our keystore and add the certificate's public key to the signature:

```
X509Certificate cert =
    (X509Certificate) ks.getCertificate(certificateAlias);

sig.addKeyInfo(cert);
sig.addKeyInfo(cert.getPublicKey());
```

Finally, we sign the document using the certificate's private key and write its output to the file:

```
sig.sign(privateKey);
FileOutputStream f = new FileOutputStream(signatureFile);
XMLUtils.outputDOMc14nWithComments(doc, f);
f.close();
```

As you can see, signing an XML document is straightforward. In our example, the newly generated signature is stored separately from the original document in the local directory.

Now let us look at validating a digital signature using the Apache Axis verifier in Listing 15.3.

Listing 15.3   Apache Axis verifier

```
/* For more information on the Apache Software Foundation, please see
 * <http://www.apache.org/>.
 */
package org.apache.xml.security.samples;

import java.io.*;
import java.security.*;
```

```
import java.security.cert.*;
import java.util.*;
import org.apache.xpath.CachedXPathAPI;
import org.w3c.dom.*;
import org.apache.xml.security.algorithms.MessageDigestAlgorithm;
import org.apache.xml.security.c14n.*;
import org.apache.xml.security.exceptions.XMLSecurityException;
import org.apache.xml.security.signature.*;
import org.apache.xml.security.keys.*;
import org.apache.xml.security.keys.content.*;
import org.apache.xml.security.keys.content.x509.*;
import org.apache.xml.security.keys.keyresolver.*;
import org.apache.xml.security.keys.storage.*;
import org.apache.xml.security.keys.storage.implementations.*;
import org.apache.xml.security.utils.*;
import org.apache.xml.security.transforms.*;
import org.apache.xml.security.Init;
import org.apache.xml.security.samples.utils.resolver.OfflineResolver;
import org.apache.xml.serialize.*;

/**
 *
 * @author $Author: geuerp $
 */
public class AxisVerifier {

    /**
     * Method main
     *
     * @param unused
     * @throws Exception
     */
    public static void main(String unused[]) throws Exception {

        org.apache.xml.security.Init.init();

        File signatureFile = new File(AxisSigner.AXIS_SIGNATURE_FILENAME);
        javax.xml.parsers.DocumentBuilderFactory dbf =
            javax.xml.parsers.DocumentBuilderFactory.newInstance();

        dbf.setNamespaceAware(true);
```

```
        javax.xml.parsers.DocumentBuilder db = dbf.newDocumentBuilder();
        org.w3c.dom.Document doc = db.parse(new FileInputStream(signatureFile));
        String BaseURI = signatureFile.toURL().toString();
        CachedXPathAPI xpathAPI = new CachedXPathAPI();
        Element nsctx = doc.createElement("nsctx");

        nsctx.setAttribute("xmlns:ds", Constants.SignatureSpecNS);

        Element signatureElem = (Element) xpathAPI.selectSingleNode(doc,
                                "//ds:Signature", nsctx);
        XMLSignature sig = new XMLSignature(signatureElem, BaseURI);
        boolean verify = sig.checkSignatureValue(sig.getKeyInfo().getPublicKey());
        System.out.println("The signature is" + (verify
                                ? " "
                                : " not ") + "valid");


        for (int i = 0; i < sig.getSignedInfo().getSignedContentLength(); i++) {
            boolean thisOneWasSigned = sig.getSignedInfo().getVerificationResult(i);
            if (thisOneWasSigned) {
                System.out.println("-- Signed Content follows--");
                System.out.println(new
String(sig.getSignedInfo().getSignedContentItem(i)));
            }
        }
        System.out.println("");
        System.out.println("Prior transforms");
        System.out.println(new
String(sig.getSignedInfo().getReferencedContentBeforeTransformsItem(0).getBytes()));


    }
}
```

In the above example, the first several lines of code locate the signature within the XML document. Once the signature element is located, we will create an instance of the XMLSignature class and call its checkSignatureValue method:

```
XMLSignature sig = new XMLSignature(signatureElem, BaseURI);
boolean verify = sig.checkSignatureValue(sig.getKeyInfo().getPublicKey());
```

The checkSignatureValue method takes as an argument an X.509 certificate, which was used to sign the document. Within this method, the public key that signed the document is retrieved and validates the signature in the element. If the signature cannot be validated using the retrieved public key, the document is assumed to be invalid. The document's signature is considered invalid if it was not signed by the corresponding private key and/or the contents have been tampered with.

Digital signatures provide strong signer authentication, which helps realize the goal of nonrepudiation when implementing a Web service architecture. When tied with other technologies, such as encryption, the notion of trust can be incorporated into a Web service.

▷ XML Encryption

The W3C and IETF are working on an XML encryption specification. Java Community Process *(www.jcp.org)* is working to define a standard *Java API for XML Encryption* (JSR-106). In our discussion above, we outlined how to use SSL for encryption of messages over the transport. SSL addresses the needs to secure the document over the transport but does not handle the security requirements of a document once it is persisted. It also does not address when different parts of a document require different levels of protection.

The core element in XML encryption is the EncryptedData element, used with the EncryptedKey element to transport encryption keys from the originator to a known recipient. It derives from the EncryptedType abstract type. When an element is encrypted, the EncryptedData element replaces the element in the encrypted version of the XML document. The easiest way to demonstrate XML encryption is by showing unencrypted and encrypted XML documents, as in Listings 15.4 and 15.5.

Listing 15.4 Unencrypted XML document

```
<?xml version='1.0'?>
<InsuranceInfo xmlns='http://insurance.org/HMOv2'>
    <Name>Sylvester James</Name>
    <Employer>Planet Fruit</Employer>
    <IDCard Deductible='5,000' Currency='TT'>
        <Number>XJABAC 34534</Number>
        <Issuer>Dispute Insurance</Issuer>
        <Expiration>04/02</Expiration>
    </IDCard>
    <Insured>Soogia Rattan</Insured>
</InsuranceInfo>
```

Listing 15.5   Encrypted XML document

```
<?xml version='1.0'?>
<InsuranceInfo xmlns='http://insurance.org/HMOv2'>
    <Name>Sylvester James</Name>
    <Employer>Planet Fruit</Employer>
    <EncryptedData Type='http://www.w3.org/2001/04/xmlenc#Element'
    xmlns='http://www.w3.org/2001/04/xmlenc#'>
        <CipherData><CipherValue>A1B2C3D4E5F</CipherValue></CipherData>
    </EncryptedData>
    <Insured>Soogia Rattan</Insured>
</InsuranceInfo>
```

In the above example, we have hidden the currency amounts. Sometimes it is necessary to encrypt the entire document (Listing 15.6).

Listing 15.6   Completely encrypted XML document

```
<?xml version='1.0'?>
    <EncryptedData xmlns='http://www.w3.org/2001/04/xmlenc#'
    Type='http://www.isi.edu/in-notes/iana/assignments/media-types/text/xml'>
    <CipherData><CipherValue>B1CH3TR1N1</CipherValue><</CipherData>
</EncryptedData>
```

Business messages must ensure authenticity (Who was the sender?), data privacy (Was it modified in transit?) and nonrepudiation (Can the sender deny sending it?) So far, we have discussed using Web server authentication for knowing the sender. We have considered use of SSL to secure the transport. We have thought about using either custom or XML encryption to make sure documents cannot be modified by intermediate parties.

In our solution, we have not considered whether we need to support nonrepudiation. Flute bank needs to ensure that transactions sent to Flute Bank services come from authorized customers who cannot deny having sent transactions. This can be handled using multiple techniques.

Public key infrastructure (PKI) describes the processes, policies, and standards that govern the issuance and revocation of the certificates and public and private keys that encryption and signing operations use. Public-key cryptography allows Web services to exchange data across an insecure network such as the Internet with the assurance that messages will neither be modified nor inappropriately accessed.

The basis premise is that data is transformed according to an algorithm parameterized by a pair of keys (public and private). Each participant in the exchange has such a pair of keys. Users make their public key freely available to anyone wishing to establish a dialog with their services and keep the other key private and appropriately secured. Information encoded using one key can be decoded using the other. If someone else intercepts a message, it would remain unusable, because the private key is needed decrypt the message.

The advantages of using public-key infrastructure over other approaches based on shared secrets are not only scalability, in not having to distribute the secret to unknown parties in advance, but also the ability to validate the sender, because everyone has a unique private key.

To digitally sign a message, an algorithm that accepts the sender's private key transforms the data in the message. The detransformation can occur in reverse only if it uses the sender's public key, This assures the recipient of the message's true origin. If the data can be confirmed using the sender's public key, it must have been signed using the corresponding private key, to which only the sender has access. A certificate authority provides an assertion of a public key's validity and asserts that it actually does belong to the sender. Otherwise, an impostor could arbitrarily create or steal others' certificates, presenting himself as the owner.

Typically, public-key approaches do not encode an entire message. Instead, they create a small, unique thumbprint of the document, typically referred to as a digest or hash. Hashing algorithms are aware of changes to a source message and therefore provide a way for the recipient to validate that the message has not been altered. The digest is transformed using the sender's private key, creating a digital signature. This also allows the recipient to verify that the sender performed the transformation.

Listed below are some of the implementations of XML encryption:

- Phaos XML: *www.phaos.com/e_security/prod_xml.html*
- Trust Services Integration Kit: *www.xmltrustcenter.org/developer/verisign/tsik/indes.htm*
- XML Security Library: *www.aleksey.com/xmlsec*
- XML Security Suite: *www.alphaworks.ibm.com/tech/xmlsecuritysuite*

> **Security Assertions Markup Language**

The SAML specification is part of the Oasis Security Services Technical Committee, but the original ideas for SAML originated from Netegrity. The specification will address interoperability between security providers for multiple areas of security that do not exist today. The main area of concentration is in authentication and authorization across multiple Web sites, to gain single sign-on (SSO) functionality (Figure 15.2).

SAML is based on the principle of *assertions*. An assertion is a statement regarding the properties of a given user that one party exchanges with another party. In the security context, an assertion becomes the exchange of security properties among security providers. Because each security provider may implement security differently (username/password, certificates, etc.), the assertion states that the user was authenticated at a specific time using a certain type of authentication.

SAML defines a protocol and format for distributing SAML data among trusted third parties in a business relationship. It supports pushing of data assertions from an authoritative source to a receiver and can also support pulling of data assertions from an authoritative source to a receiver. This allows SAML to exchange event notifications between trusted partners in a relationship. SAML also handles different assertion types for decisions and attribute assertions.

The SAML specification provides specifications in the following four categories:

- Assertions and protocols. Defines the semantics and syntax for XML-based SAML assertions, protocol requests, and responses.

- Bindings and profiles. Defines the frameworks for encapsulating and transporting SAML assertion requests and responses.

Figure 15.2
SAML

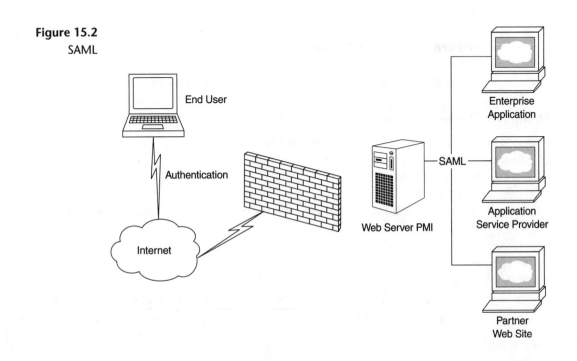

- Security and privacy. Defines, for implementers of SAML, guidelines to mitigate security risks for threats against a SAML-based implementation. All implementers should read this document.

- Conformance. Defines a mechanism to ensure compatibility and interoperability among the various SAML implementations.

SAML Architecture

All SAML assertions contain the following common elements: assertion ID, issuer and issuance timestamp, subject, advice, and conditions. In SAML, a subject specifies the name and security domain for which an assertion is requested/issued. The subject can optionally contain additional information for authenticating the subject. The advice element consists of optional additional information the issuing authority wishes to provide to the relying party regarding how the assertion was made and can support proof of assertion claims.

The conditions element specifies that the assertion is valid only when an evaluation of conditions is provided. This can include specifying a validity period, restrictions on whom the assertion is valid for (audience), and target restrictions, including target parties who have received authority to use this assertion. Target restrictions state that if a party decides to consume an assertion for which it is not the intended target, it must throw the assertion away.

Authentication Assertion

Listing 15.7 shows a request that would be sent to an issuing authority.

Listing 15.7   Authentication assertion

```
<saml:Request MajorVersion="1" MinorVersion="0"
    RequestID="987.65.432.10.12345678">
    <samlp:AuthenticationQuery>
        <saml:Subject>
            <saml:NameIdentifier SecurityDomain="flutebank.com" Name="rlimbaugh"/>
        </saml:Subject>
    </saml:AuthenticationQuery>
</saml:Request>
```

In the above example, a party authorized to issue assertion requests creates a request for a subject whose name is "rlimbaugh" in the security domain "flutebank.com". A SAML response will be generated based on this request. Listing 15.8 shows the response.

Listing 15.8 Authentication assertion response

```
<saml:Response MajorVersion=1" MinorVersion="0"
    InResponseTo="987.65.432.10.12345678"
    StatusCode="Success">
    <saml:Assertion MajorVersion="1" MinorVersion="0"
        AssertionID="987.65.432.10.12345678"
        Issuer="flutebank.com"
        IssueInstant="2001-09-11T09:48:00Z">
        <saml:Conditions
            NotBefore="2001-09-11T09:48:00Z"
            NotAfter="2001-09-11T11:26:00Z"/>
        <saml:AuthenticationStatement
            AuthenticationMethod="Password"
            AuthenticationInstant="2001-09-11T09:48:00Z">
            <saml:Subject>
                <saml:NameIdentifier
                    SecurityDomain="flutebank.com" Name="rlimbaugh"/>
            </saml:Subject>
        </saml:AuthenticationStatement>
    </saml:Assertion>
</saml:Response>
```

Here, the assertion is valid for only the specified time period, according to the saml:Conditions element. saml:AuthenticationStatement states the authentication method used. In our example, subject "rlimbaugh" is a member of the security domain "flutebank.com" and was authenticated using password authentication. ▷

Attribute Assertion

An *attribute assertion* verifies the result of an evaluation of an access control policy, such as whether an end user is authorized to perform a specific transaction at

▷ SAML is responsible for making assertions about authentication and authorization but does not provide the mechanism to perform these actions.

a specified time. The key point to remember is that it is an assertion, not a fact. Listing 15.9 shows an attribute assertion request.

Listing 15.9   Attribute assertion request

```
<saml:Request MajorVersion="1" MinorVersion="0"
   RequestID="123.45.000.11.12345678">
   <samlp:AttributeQuery>
      <saml:Subject>
         <saml:NameIdentifier
            SecurityDomain="flutebank.com"
            Name="rlimbaugh"/>
      </saml:Subject>
      ...
      <saml:AttributeDesignator
         AttributeName="Employee_ID"
         AttributeNamespace="flutebank.com"/>
   </saml:AttributeQuery>
<saml:Request>
```

In this example, a request for attribute assertion is sent to the issuing authority (in this case flutebank.com), to assert the value of certain attributes.

Authorization Assertion

An *authorization assertion* does not state that a user is allowed to perform a certain type of transaction but indicates only that the user is permitted to perform a particular instance of that type of transaction at a given time.

An authorization assertion communicates information about the attributes of a particular subject. One example may be an airline site that wants to determine whether the user is a Gold, Chairman's, or Medallion frequent flyer, to allow a user access to special services. Other examples may be whether the user's account balance is up to date or on the verge of being reported to a credit agency. Listing 15.10 shows an authorization assertion that will check whether a current Flute Bank customer can access an external service.

Listing 15.10   Authorization assertion

```
<saml:Request MajorVersion="1" MinorVersion="0"
   RequestID="123.45.000.11.12345678">
   <samlp:AuthorizationQuery
      Resource="http://www.loans.co.tt/members/accountAccess">
```

```
        ...
        <saml:Subject>
          <saml:NameIdentifer
              SecurityDomain="flutebank.com"
              Name="rlimbaugh"/>
        </saml:Subject>
        <saml:Actions Namespace="flutebank.com">
          <saml:Action>Read</saml:Action>
          <saml:Action>Change</saml:Action>
        </saml:Actions>
        <saml:Evidence>
          <saml:Assertion>
              ... Assertion Information ...
          </saml:Assertion>
        </saml:Evidence>
    </saml:AuthorizationQuery>
</saml:Request>
```

In this example, a SAML request for authorization assert is sent to the issuing authority (Flute Bank) to assert whether the subject is allowed to access the specified resource given the specific evidence. Evidence is an assertion on which an issuing party can make authorization decisions. The example demonstrates the request being sent to an issuing authority to assert whether subject "rlimbaugh" can be allowed read and change access to the specified resource. Listing 15.11 shows the response.

Listing 15.11 Authorization assertion response

```
<saml:Response ... >
   <saml:Assertion ... >
      <saml:Conditions ... />
      ...
      <saml:AuthorizationStatement
          Decision="Permit"
          Resource="http://www.loans.co.tt/members/accountAccess">

          <saml:Subject>
            <saml:NameIdentifier
                SecurityDomain="flutebank.com"
                Name="rlimbaugh"/>
          </saml:Subject>
```

```
      <saml:AuthorizationStatement>
   </saml:Assertion>
<saml:Response>
```

Here, the returned authorization assertion contains `saml:Authorization-Statement`, which permits the subject "rlimbaugh" access to the specified resource.

Let us look at a scenario in which SAML may be used in a Web service transaction between two organizations. In this example, we will need to pass several types of information securely manner for a SAML-enabled provider to make a decision, as Figure 15.3 shows.

A user is logged into the luxurycarscheap.com Web site and has decided to pay for his dream Porsche Boxster by applying for a loan. He would also like to purchase insurance for his vehicle at the same time. Luxurycarscheap.com has a partnership with a lender named flutebank.com for auto loans. Luxurycarscheap .com also has a partnership with a company called reallycheapinsurance.com, which provides the insurance that luxurycarscheap.com sells via a Web service. Both flutebank.com and reallycheapinsurance.com need information on who is requesting a loan and insurance and some attributes about them. We would also like to interact with our state's motor vehicle division and automatically register the purchased vehicle. Figure 15.4 shows the flow of information that could occur in this scenario. ▷

Figure 15.3
SAML assertion

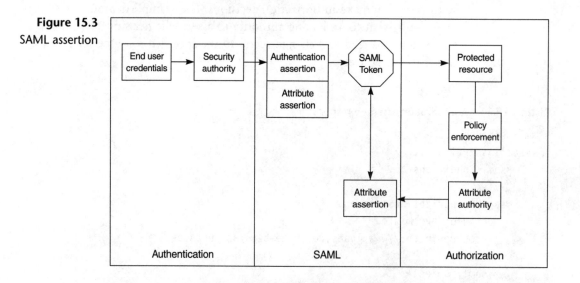

▷ Applications that use SAML can also define their own custom assertions.

Figure 15.4
SAML assertion
response

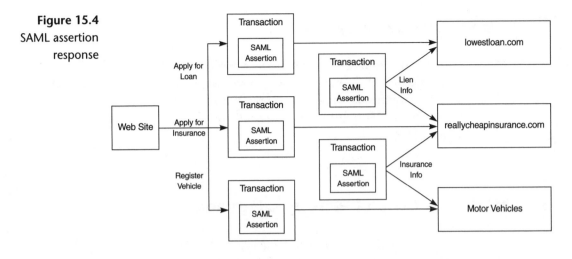

As you can see from the figures, SAML uses a common XML schema for basic information that includes the assertion ID, date and time of issuance, and the time interval for which the assertion is valid. Assertions may depend on additional information from an asserting party or on other valid assertions.

SAML Bindings and Profiles

SAML can be used over a variety of network/application protocols. A SAML binding specifies how SAML is transported over particular protocols and how request-response messages should be handled. For example, the SAML SOAP binding describes how SAML request-response messages are mapped into SOAP messages. The HTTP binding for SAML specifies how request-response messages are mapped into HTTP messages. To date, the SAML specification has defined only how a SAML request-response is handled using SOAP over HTTP. ▷

Some of the products and vendors that have implemented support for SAML include Baltimore SelectAccess, Entegrity, Netegrity Siteminder, Securant, Sun ONE Identity Server, Systinet WASP, and Verisign Trust Services Integration Kit.

> ▷   Applications can define their own custom protocol for exchanging SAML assertions. A SAML profile describes how an originating party embeds SAML assertions in other object types for transport. For example, the SAML profile for SOAP specifies how SAML assertions are added to SOAP messages as well as how the SOAP headers are affected by SAML assertions.

▷ Web Services Security Assertions

SAML is the leading standard for security assertions. Java Specification Request 155 (JSR-155), *Web Services Security Assertions,* provides a standard set of APIs to exchange assertions using request-response and synchronous and asynchronous mechanisms. More information about JSR-155 is available at *www.jcp.org/jsr/detail/155.jsp.*

▷ XML Access Control Markup Language

XML Access Control Markup Language (XACML) provides XML documents with support for access control lists on the document and elements. Access control can be as fine-grained as a single element in an XML document. Access control supports four types of actions: create, read, write, and delete. It is organized around triplets of object, subject, and action.

An XACML object represents a single element or a set of elements in a XML document. The elements are specified through an XPATH expression. Let us look at a typical bank transaction document:

```
<?xml version="1.0"?>
<transaction>
    <name>Sherry Ann Rattan</name>
    <zipcode>06002</zipcode>>
    <action>debit</action>
    <merchant>Porsche</merchant>
    <description>2003 Boxster</description>
    <creditcardnumber>2222 111 232 23222</creditcardnumber>
    <expiration>19770216</expiration>
    <amount>98222.22</amount>
</transaction>
```

Let's say that the Web service has the ability to read the amount but does not have the ability to write to it. We would simply define the appropriate access control:

```
<?xml version="1.0"?>
<policy>
   <xacl>
   <object href="amount"/>
      <rule>
```

```
        <acl>
        <subject>
           <uid>WebServiceOne</uid>
        </subject>
        <action name="read" permission="grant"/>
        <action name="write" permission="deny"/>
        </acl>
      </rule>
   </xacl>
</policy>
```

This specification is controlled by the OASIS Technical Committee and may undergo several changes before it becomes a standard. The ability to apply field-level access-control lists coupled with encryption and other security options will make security integration between disparate Web services a lot easier. XACML will allow this to happen in a standards-based, open manner.

> XML Key Management Specification

The XML Key Management Specification (XKMS) provides a standard, XML-based messaging protocol that allows application developers to outsource the processing of key management (registration, verification, and so on) to trust services accessed through the Internet.

Using XKMS moves the public key infrastructure complexity and processing burden to a different server. This approach allows PKI code to be tightly integrated on remote servers accessed through self-describing XML interfaces. The example below shows an XKMS message indicating that a supplied key should be revoked:

```
<?xml version="1.0"?>
<Request>
    <Prototype>
    <AssertionStatus>Invalid</AssertionStatus>
    <KeyID>unique_key_identifier</KeyID>
    <ds:KeyInfo> ... </ds:KeyInfo>
    </Prototype>
    <AuthInfo><AuthUserInfo>
    <ProofOfPossession>[RSA-Sign]</ProofOfPossession>
    </AuthUserInfo></AuthInfo>
    <Respond>
```

```
        <string>KeyName</string>
      </Respond>
</Request>
```

AssertionStatus indicates that the revocation request should include making the ID specified in the KeyID tag invalid. To prevent misuse, the ProofOfPossession tag provides a level of assurance that the request comes from a source authorized to make such a request.

▶ WS-I Specifications

IBM and Microsoft have developed an initial set of Web services security specifications (Table 15.3 and Figure 15.5) that will initially be built into the .NET architecture but have been turned over to the OASIS working group. These sets of specifications will include a message security model (WS-Security) that will be the foundation for other WS-I specifications.

Table 15.3   WS-I Specifications

Specification	Description
WS-Security	Describes how to attach security tokens (certificates and Kerberos tickets), signatures, and encryption headers to SOAP messages.
WS-Policy	Describes the features and limitations of the security policies on intermediaries and endpoints.
WS-Trust	Describes a framework for secure interoperation of trust models between Web services.
WS-Privacy	Describes how both Web services and their requestors specify subject privacy preferences and organizational privacy practice statements.
WS-SecureConversation	Describes how to authenticate and manage message exchange between parties.
WS-Federation	Describes how to manage and broker the trust relationships in a heterogeneous federated environment.
WS-Authorization	Describes how to manage authorization data and policies.

Figure 15.5
WS-I
specifications

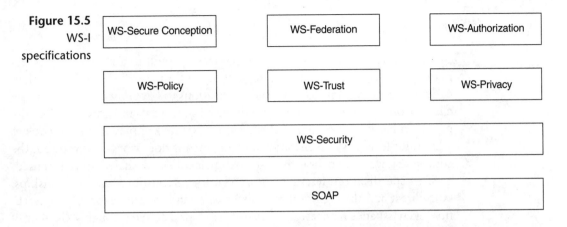

These specifications are evolving and continue to change over time. As each comes closer to its public final release date, the security aspects of your Web service may require some changes.

WS-Security

This specification provides a general-purpose means for joining messages with security tokens. WS-Security supports multiple security-token formats and can be used independently or in conjunction to accommodate an assortment of security models and encryption technologies. This could be useful in situations where a requestor may require proof of identity and assurance that the party has a particular business certification.

WS-Security leverages the XML encryption specification along with security tokens to keep portions of SOAP messages confidential. The encryption features can also support encryption technologies, processes, and operations by multiple parties.

WS-Policy

WS-Policy specifies how senders and receivers can state their requirements and capabilities regarding policies they require to conduct business in an electronic format. This specification is highly extensible and will support identification of service attributes, including encoding formats, privacy attributes, security token requirements, and supported algorithms.

WS-Policy defines a generic SOAP policy format that supports more than simply security policies. With this feature, you can also define service policies and attach them to SOAP messages.

WS-Trust

In a connected world, many users of services are built in a manner that is not hardware-independent and require identity information embedded in their code. It is unreasonable to expect all applications to have equal capability to secure personal information and maintain message and data integrity. The Web site paradigm has been a failure in this regard. Several examples are use of cookies and multiple Web site registrations. Even when it does work as advertised, the consumer is ignorant of how the information is collected, shared, stored, or used.

This specification describes the model for establishing trust relationships, both direct and through brokers (third parties and intermediaries), using security-token issuance services. Security tokens are transferred through WS-Security to ensure their confidentiality and integrity. The specification also describes how one to many existing trust mechanisms can be used in conjunction with this trust model. The model can be further extended to support delegation and impersonation by principals. Delegation is an extension of impersonation but with the ability to include additional levels of traceability.

WS-Privacy

Personal information becomes public in many ways, including, but not limited to, sharing of customer data through disclosure agreements and partnerships, unsecured personal information stored on the Internet, and lack of dynamic engagement protocols. WS-Privacy allows organizations to state their privacy policies and require that incoming requests make claims about the initiator's adherence to these policies. Organizations can state and indicate conformance to privacy polices by using a combination of WS-Security, WS-Policy, and WS-Trust.

WS-Privacy also describes how WS-Trust mechanisms can be used to evaluate privacy claims for organizational practice as well as user preferences. This specification will become extremely important in the not-too-distant future, as many governments pass laws to protect sharing of personal information without the owner's knowledge or permission.

WS-SecureConversation

This specification describes how services can exchange assertions about security attributes. WS-SecureConversation extends the concepts of security token mechanisms defined by WS-Security and WS-Trust. It also describes how to establish session keys and per-message keys. A service implementing this specification could implement support for creating security tokens that use either symmetric (shared-secret) key algorithm or asymmetric (public/private) algorithms.

Unlike SSL, which secures the transport, secure conversations operate at the SOAP messaging layer. Messages can travel over an assortment of transports and through various intermediaries. WS-SecureConversation can be used in conjunction with other messaging frameworks and may be combined with transport-level security and WS-Security implementations.

WS-Federation

Federations are based on defining and managing trust relationships between service providers. A trust policy is usually introduced to specify and identify the type of trust being brokered. Trust relationships in a Web services scenario will use WS-Security, WS-Policy, WS-Trust, and WS-SecureConversation specifications.

Federations are important in a Web services business-transaction scenario. In a nonelectronic business transaction, the first event is the establishment of a relationship. When one establishes a relationship with another party in real life, the first thing built up is trust. After trust is established, then usually comes some form of convenience in not having to prove oneself each time. Finally, a history of prior positive interactions is formed. Because one service cannot go out on a blind date with another service, an electronic equivalent is required.

WS-Authorization

This specification describes how Web service access policies are managed. It covers the description of how assertions can be made within security tokens as well as how they will be interpreted by each endpoint. This is important because each security provider may have a different authorization format and language.

As an example, a PKI implementation behaves differently from a Kerberos-based implementation. PKI depends on certificates based on public asymmetric keys. The certificate authorities use assertions to validate properties such as identity. This model is different from Kerberos, in that it does not validate key ownership. The WS-Authorization specification may be incorporated into future firewalls (Checkpoint, Cisco) and proxy devices (Alteon, Cisco, F5, Radware) to provide greater flexibility in rules and inspection of messages. This model will also support delegation models for services.

Let us look at a scenario that demonstrates delegation models (see also Figure 15.6):

Figure 15.6
Married couple
interaction

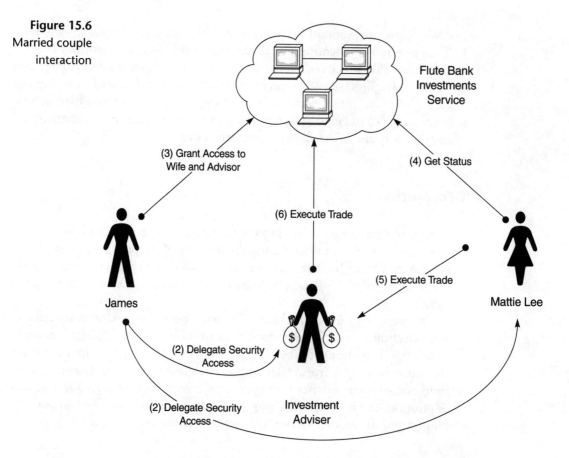

1. James and his wife, Mattie, do all their financial services transactions through Flute Bank. They also take advantage of the Flute Bank Investments Web service that allows them to perform portfolio management activities as well as interact with their investment adviser. Currently, James is the only account that can access this service.

2. James would like to give both his wife and investment adviser access to his portfolio and creates a delegation token for each of them

3. James later decides he would like to update the authorization list at Flute Bank to contain both his wife and investment adviser, so he does not have to delegate access each time.

4. Now Mattie has access to the portfolio, she looks at the various securities in the portfolio and discusses her options with her adviser.

5. Mattie decides she wants to dump all stock for companies located on Easter Island and purchase Microsoft stock. She believes that the Windows platform will outpace its competitors over the next several years.

6. The investment adviser agrees with Mattie's assertion and contacts the Flute Bank Investment service to execute the trade.

The above example demonstrates how the delegation model works. Listing 15.12 is an example of using WS-Authorization to permit access to the Flute Bank quoting service.

Listing 15.12 WS-Security example

```
<?xml version="1.0" encoding="utf-8"?>
    <env:Envelope xmlns:env="http://www.w3.org/2001/12/soap-envelope"
        xmlns:ds="http://www.w3.org/2000/09/xmldsig#">
    <env:Header>
    <m:path xmlns:m="http://schemas.xmlsoap.org/rp/">
        <m:action>http://flutebank.com/getQuote</m:action>
        <m:to>http://flutebank.com/stocks</m:to>
        <m:id>uuid:84b9f5d0-33fb-4a81-b02b-5b760641c1d6</m:id>
    </m:path>
    <wsse:Security
    xmlns:wsse="http://schemas.xmlsoap.org/ws/2002/04/secext">
    wsse:UsernameToken Id="MyID">
    <wsse:Username>Pinto</wsse:Username>
    </wsse:UsernameToken>
    <ds:Signature>
    <ds:SignedInfo>
        <ds:CanonicalizationMethod Algorithm= "http://www.w3.org/2001/10/xml-exc-
                                                                        c14n#"/>
        <ds:SignatureMethod Algorithm= "http://www.w3.org/2000/09/xmldsig#hmac-sha1"/>
        <ds:Reference URI="#MsgBody">
        <ds:DigestMethod Algorithm= "http://www.w3.org/2000/09/xmldsig#sha1"/>
        <ds:DigestValue>Ll1tT13mAnPU ... </ds:DigestValue>
        </ds:Reference>
        </ds:SignedInfo>
    <ds:SignatureValue>D34adm5gK ... </ds:SignatureValue>
    <ds:KeyInfo>
        <wsse:SecurityTokenReference>
        <wsse:Reference URI="#MyID"/>
        </wsse:SecurityTokenReference>
    </ds:KeyInfo>
    </ds:Signature>
    </wsse:Security>
    </env:Header>
```

```
<env:Body Id="MsgBody">
    <tru:StockSymbol xmlns:tru="http://flutebank.com/payloads">
    http://www.flutebank.com/service/ws-secure
    HIG
    </tru:StockSymbol>
</env:Body>
</env:Envelope>
```

The first two lines are the start of the SOAP envelope. The m:path tag specifies how this message should be routed according to the WS-Routing specification. The Security tag defines the security information for the intended receiver. The UsernameToken tag specifies a security token associated with the message. In this scenario, it defines the username of the client. The ds:CanonicalizationMethod tag specifies the canonicalization method used as part of the XML signature specification. The ds:Reference URI=#MsbBody element indicates that only the message body is signed. The wsse:SecurityTokenReference tag provides the hint on the location of the security token associated with the digital signature.

The Security header provides the ability to attach security-related information targeted toward the end recipient or an intermediary. A SOAP message may have multiple security headers, and an intermediary may create new headers as necessary. The intermediary may read SOAP security headers but should not remove them until they reach their final destination.

Where validation of a security token, encryption, or a signature fail, the service can choose to respond with supported formats or not to respond, because the failure may be a cryptographic, replay, or denial-of-service attack. A service that decides to return a message to the sender should use one of the security fault codes shown in Table 15.4.

WS-Coordination

The WS-Coordination specification addresses the concerns for coordinating distributed application. Coordination is used to support a number of applications where each must reach a consistent agreement on the outcome of distributed transactions. An application using this specification creates a context to other services that register themselves for coordination events. It provides an abstraction layer for services that require transaction processing, workflow, and coordination in distributed heterogeneous environments.

A coordination service consists of three components: activation, registration, and coordination. An *activation* service is responsible for creating a coordination context and is called by the initiating Web service. The context holds the re-

Table 15.4   WS-Security Faults

Error	Fault
An unsupported algorithm was used.	**wsse:UnsupportedAlgorithm**
An unsupported token was used.	**wsse:UnsupportedSecurityToken**
The security token could not be authenticated.	**wsse:FailedAuthentication**
The signature was invalid.	**Wsse:FailedCheck**
Error discovered while processing the \<Security> header.	**Wsse:InvalidSecurity**
An invalid security token was used.	**wsse:InvalidSecurityToken**

quired information to register into an activity and specifies the behavior the calling service should use. The *registration* service allows a service to register for coordination protocols. The *coor*dination context may use the registration service of either the original Web service or an intermediary trusted coordinator. This allows for an arbitrary collection of services to coordinate their operations seamlessly. A coordination context travels within SOAP messages between participating parties. Listing 15.13 shows a simple coordination context that supports a transaction service.

Listing 15.13   Coordination context

```
<?xml version="1.0" encoding="utf-8"?>
<S:Envelope xmlns:s="http://www.w3.org/2001/12/soap-envelope"
   <S:Header>
   ...
      <wscoor:CoordinationContext
         xmlns:wsu="http://schemas.xmlsoap.org/ws/2002/07/utility"
         xmlns:wscoor="http://schemas.xmlsoap.org/ws/2002/08/wscoor"
         xmlns:myApp="http://www.flutebank.com/myApp">
         <wsu:Expires>2002-08-24T12:02:00.000-06:00</wsu:Expires>
         <wsu:Identifier>http://www.flutebank.com/coor/abcd</wsu:Identifier>
         <wscoor:CoordinationType>
            http://schemas.xmlsoap.org/ws/2002/08/wstx
         </wscoor:CoordinationType>
         <wscoor:RegistrationService>
            <wsu:Address>
               http://www.chiltown.com/coordinationservice/registration
```

```
          </wsu:Address>
          <myApp:BetaMark> ... </myApp:BetaMark>
          <myApp:EBDCode> ... </myApp:EBDCode>
      </wscoor:RegistrationService>
      <myApp:IsolationLevel>RepeatableRead</myApp:IsolationLevel>
    </wscoor:CoordinationContext>
  ...
</S:Header>
```

Coordination messages are typically used in conjunction with WS-Security messages to ensure that messages are neither modified nor forged between destinations. The coordination message also contains an expiration timestamp. By using the WS-Security, you could ensure that the coordination message is not reused or replayed. Digital signatures should also be used to make sure the security header cannot be separated from coordination messages.

Web services must function over a variety of topologies, through intermediaries such as firewalls (e.g., Checkpoint, Cisco), messaging gateways (e.g., Actional, MQSeries, Sonic, Tibco), and load-balancing appliances (e.g., F5 Big IP, CSS 11000, CoyotePoint). These intermediaries provide additional layers of security for a Web services infrastructure but do not address all possible security breaches. The need for additional security specifications is evident. It is important that any new specification extend existing security assets within an organization. The WS-I specifications are the first step in defining an all-inclusive security strategy.

▷ SOAP and Firewalls

SOAP is a messaging format that can ride on top of other transport protocols, such as SMTP, but is primarily used with HTTP. One of the design goals for SOAP was that it should easily pass through firewalls (this is good and bad). This creates a problem, because many firewalls cannot adequately filter a SOAP message, which uses the same approach as a standard HTTP POST method. The early version of SOAP had a SOAPAction header that any firewall could inspect, but this is now deprecated.

For a firewall to adequately secure SOAP traffic, it must also perform XML parsing. The real problem comes in trying to figure out what to look for. Throughout this book we have seen SOAP with and without headers, at times using RPC encoding and method names, and sometimes not. This makes determining the security of a SOAP message difficult at best from the perspective of your firewall administrator.

The typical firewall administrator's reaction to coming under attack is to shut down specific firewall ports. Because SOAP may travel over port 80 (HTTP) or 443 (HTTPS), the administrator will shut down not only SOAP traffic but all Web-related traffic. Many organizations have used URL filtering approaching to enhance security. HTTP-based services typically support GET, PUT, POST, and DELETE. Security administrators can automatically look for PUT and DELETE requests and not allow them to traverse the network. The problem with SOAP is that it does not use these directives.

Our recommendation in this regard is to make sure that your security and firewall personnel spend the time to understand Web services security and that this is not left in the hands of developers alone. All players within a Web services architecture including developers, security administrators, project managers, and architects should purchase books on Web services that provide additional information on topics presented in this chapter.

> Security and J2EE

J2EE provides a rich set of security-related functions for authentication, authorization, attribution, and access control through the Java Naming and Directory Interface (JNDI) and Java Authentication and Authorization Service (JAAS).

JAAS

The Java security model provides policy-based access controls for Java applications. This security model provides protection based on the physical origin of the classes in use as well as identity services supported by their digital signature. The Java Authentication and Authorization Service APIs further extend the Java security model by allowing an application at runtime to take into account a user's identity. These APIs make a powerful combination for custom authentication and authorization in your Web service.

The Java Authentication and Authorization Service allows pluggable authentication (Figure 15.7) into an application, using several techniques. First, the authentication interfaces hide the complexity of the actual authentication mechanisms. Applications using this approach will not need to know nor care about what authentication protocol is in use. Second, JAAS allows authentication protocols to be stacked. In your Web service, you may require multiple authentication mechanisms be used before identity is established. As an example, accessing a payroll Web service may require a Kerberos login and a SQL server login. JAAS

Figure 15.7
JAAS pluggable
authentication

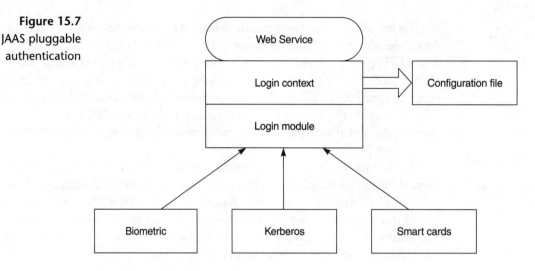

comes with sample authentication modules for Java Naming and Directory Interface (JNDI), Unix (NIS), Windows NT (Domains), Kerberos, and Keystore.

Using Java Authentication and Authorization Service within a Web service is simple to implement but subtly different from normal Java security. Unlike Java security, authentication is not associated with the instantiation of a class or invocation of an instance method. When using JAAS, an application wishing to authenticate a user constructs a `javax.security.auth.LoginContext` and calls its `login()` method. When the application no longer requires the authenticated identity, it calls the `LoginContext`'s `logout()` method.

You may have noted that neither `login()` nor `logout()` takes any arguments. This was done for ease of use. The `LoginContext` constructor does require parameters, however. The first parameter is the JAAS configuration file name. The configuration file contains the appropriate JAAS `LoginModule(s)`, to authenticate the current user.

Let us look at simple configuration file:

```
// JAAS Security Policy record

grant Codebase "www.flutebank.com", Signedby "peanut" {
    Principal com.flutebank.Principal "pamela" {
    FilePermission "/web/service/-", "read";
}
```

```
// Login module configuration record

InternalLogin {
    internal.TrustedLoginModule required debug=true;
}

ExternalLogin {
    internal.TrustedLoginModule required;
    com.sun.security.auth.module.NTLoginModule sufficient;
    com.chiltown.Kerberos optional debug=true;
};
```

The above configuration file indicates that an attempt by InternalLogin to authenticate a subject will be successful only if the TrustedLoginModule succeeds. Likewise, if the ExternalLogin tries to validate a subject, it can use other authentication providers. A Web services provider may implement code similar to the following:

```
import java.security.*;
import javax.security.auth.*;

// Create a new login context
LoginContext ctx = new LoginContext("ContextName", CallbackHandler);

// Authenticate the subject
ctx.login();

// Get the subject
Subject sub = ctx.getSubject();

// Enforce Access Controls
Subject.doAs(sub, action);
```

JAAS APIs supports a wide variety of pluggable authentication modules (PAM). In some authentication scenarios, authentication could consist of specifying a username and password. In other scenarios, the service may require name and a fingerprint, retinal scan and distinguished name, digital certificates and voice recognition, or some authentication mechanism that hasn't yet been invented.

The login() takes no methods. The approach used to get credentials to an authentication provider is to call the initialize() method of each LoginModule and pass in zero to *n* of javax.security.auth.callback.CallbackHandler. As an example, if you wanted to authenticate a user based on username and password, the LoginModule would examine the Callback array and look for instances of javax.security.auth.callback.NameCallback and javax.security.auth.callback.PasswordCallback. The LoginModule can then authenticate the user appropriately.

The common classes shared by both JAAS authentication and authorization are located in javax.security.auth.Subject, which contains information for an entity such as principals and public and private credentials. The interface java.security.Principal represents a principal. A Web service may need to authorize access to a particular resource but must first authenticate the source of the request. The term subject represents the source of the request. Once authenticated, the subject is populated with associated identities.

A person named Daisy who uses your service may have a name principal ("Daisy Burney") and an SSN principal ("987–00–123") that distinguishes her from other subjects. Subjects may own security-related attributes, known as credentials. Sensitive credentials that require special protection are stored with a private credential set. These types of credentials are usually private cryptographic keys. Credentials such as digital certificates are stored in a public credential set. ▷

▷ Java Cryptography Extensions

Java Cryptography Extensions (JCE) provide a framework and implementation for encryption, key generation, and authentication algorithms. Encryption support includes asymmetric, symmetric, block, and stream ciphers. These extensions also support secure streams and sealed objects. JCE is part of the Java 2 SDK version 1.4 and was an optional package in earlier JDKs. It is contained in the javax.crypto package.

The principle behind the Java Cryptography Extensions is to provide an API that allows pluggable algorithms and implementations, using provider architecture. The framework can use providers signed by a trusted entity. This also allows algorithms that have not yet been created to be inserted in the future.

> ▷ More information on JAAS is available at *http://java.sun.com/products/jaas*.

The base JDK comes with the SunJCE provider and provides support for the following services:

- DES and Triple DES
- Blowfish
- Cipher Block Chaining (CBC) and Propagating Cipher Block Chaining (PCBC)
- Cipher Feedback (CFB) and Output Feedback (OFB)
- MD5 and SHA1 hashes
- MD5 with DES Cipher Block Chaining password-based encryption as defined in PKCS #5
- A Diffie-Hellman key pair generator used to generate a pair of public and private values
- A key store implementation for the proprietary key store type named "JCEKS" ▷

Let's look at a simplistic example of using the Java Cryptography Extensions to generate a one-way hash using the MD5 algorithm:

```
import java.security.*;

// Use the MD5 Algorithm
MessageDigest md = MessageDigest.getInstance("MD5");

// Take message and convert to bytes
byte buf[] = Message.getBytes();

// Populate the buffer with the message
md.update(buf);

// Create the digest
byte digestBuf[] = md.digest();
```

▷ Remember when using a one-way hash, the output cannot be used to determine the input. Hashing in this instance produces a unique digest.

In this scenario, if the message varies, so will the digest, as Table 15.5 shows.

JCE also generates reversible encryption. Lets look at an example that uses the Blowfish algorithm:

```
import java.security.*;
import javax.crypto.*;

// Get a cryptography provider
Provider sunJce = new com.sun.crypto.provider.SunJCE();

// Obtain an instance of the Blowfish cipher
Cipher c = Cipher.getInstance("Blowfish");

// Obtain an instance of a key generator
KeyGenerator kg = KeyGenerator.getInstance("Blowfish");

// Generate the key specification
SecretKey sk = kg.generateKey();
byte[] raw = sk.getEncoded();
SecretKeySpec ks = new SecretKeySpec(raw, "Blowfish");

// Initialize the cipher using the key specification
cipher.init(Cipher.ENCRYPT_MODE, ks);

// Update the buffers
while (msg[ii] != null)
    enc = cipher.update(msg[ii].getBytes());

// Finish processing
enc = cipher.doFinal();
```

Table 15.5   MD5 Example

Message	MD5 Digest
I need a raise of $10,000.	9i5nud5r2a9idskjs2tbuop2ildax
I need a raise of $100,000.	8m4ikijuelaidsfg8asyfnasdfgl1
I need a raise of $1,000,000.	4M9i2t8c7h436l712t1h4e1d1otg7

You should notice that the first thing we did was obtain a reference to a cryptographic provider. This mechanism allows you to plug in at will other third-party providers approved by Sun. Additionally, the providers themselves cannot be used as standalones and will work only in the context of the JCE framework.

Export restrictions on the use of certain encryption algorithms is controlled by jurisdiction policy files of JCE. These policy files are typically stored under the `java-home` directory in lib/security. A supplemental version of JCE is available that allows for "unlimited strength" algorithms for those living in eligible countries. The download URL is available at *http://java.sun.com/products/jce/index-14.html*.

Core Classes

The implementation of JCE as of JDK 1.4 is feature rich and provides many methods to make your application secure. Let us look at a small subset of some of the classes that are part of the package:

- **Cipher.** Provides a cryptographic cipher for use in encryption and decryption.

- **CipherStream.** Combines an InputStream or OutputStream with a cipher object. Secure streams are provided by CipherInputStream and CipherOutputStream classes.

- **CipherInputStream.** Represents a secure input stream into which a cipher object has been interposed. It is derived from `java.io.FilterInputStream`.

- **CipherOutputStream.** Represents a secure output stream into which a cipher object has been interposed. It is derived from `java.io.FilterOutputStream`.

- **KeyGenerator.** Used to generate secret keys for symmetric algorithms.

- **SecretKeyFactory.** Represents a factory for creating secret keys.

- **SealedObject.** Enables a developer to create an object and protect its confidentiality with a cryptographic algorithm. This is useful when you want to encapsulate a serializable object using an algorithm such as DES, to protect its confidentiality. The encrypted content can be decrypted and deserialized to produce the original object.

- **KeyAgreement.** Provides the functionality of a key agreement protocol. Using one of the key generators (KeyPairGenerator or KeyGenerator), the resulting keys are used to establish a shared secret.

- **MAC.** Responsible for creating a Message Authentication Code object.

- **Provider.** Contains the interface to the concrete implementation of the Java 2 SDK security API features.

- **Security.** Manages installed providers and security-wide properties. This class is never instantiated and contains only static methods. Only Trusted programs can execute it.

- **MessageDigest.** Provides secure message digests, such as SHA1 or MD5.

- **Signature.** Provides a digital signature implementation, such as DSA or RSA with MD5. It takes an arbitrary-sized input and a private key and generates a relatively short string of bytes, known as the signature. Given the public key corresponding to the private key used to generate the signature, you can validate the authenticity and integrity of the input.

Keystore

The default keystore in JDK 1.4 is the Sun provider. JCE provides its own implementation of `java.security.KeyStore` and is referred to as "SunJCE." The SunJCE keystore uses a password-based encryption along with Triple DES for protection of private keys. To use the special implementation of the JCE keystore, you can specify "JCEKS" as the keystore type. ▷

▷ Implementation Scenarios

Many of the security specifications discussed in this chapter can be applied to your security needs. Let us briefly discuss some scenarios that use in a business context some of the specifications covered.

Many organizations have specific business policies that must be enforced. A Web service may mandate that consumers have a certain rating with a specific auditing company. Policies that Web services use can be validated in a standardized manner, which has the advantage of simplifying the Web services process.

For example, the Flute Bank wire transfer Web service takes the approach shown in Figure 15.8. This scenario defines security token use. The bank's Web

> ▷   A keystore is a container or common repository that holds cryptographic keys and certificates.

Figure 15.8
Bank wire
transfer
process

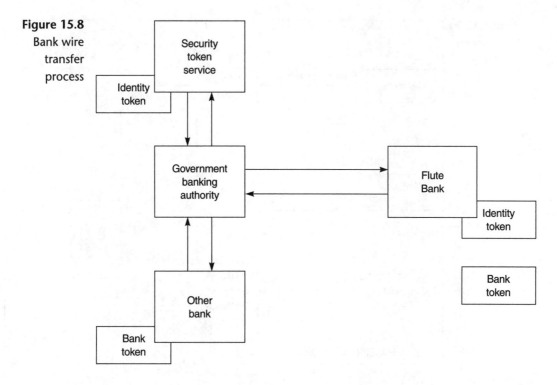

service interacts with other banks to transfer money on behalf of its customers. The service must validate that the receiving bank is certified by the government banking authority. This authority could go to the other bank, present its identity security token gathered from the Security Token Service, and request a security token from the other bank confirming that it is a government-certified bank. The government banking authority could then contact Flute Bank and provide both security tokens.

Flute Bank could codify its business policy into a service policy and shift proof of policy conformance from a backend process to a front-loaded process handled by the government banking authority. The service policy could also identify restrictions on what information each bank could store, to ensure compliance with the bank's privacy policy.

Flute Bank also allows wire transfer requests to be initiated through cellular phones and other forms of wireless communication. Mobile devices typically have limitations on the types of cryptography they implement. This is primarily a result of limited memory, storage, and computational capabilities. Many wireless service providers provide gateways that act on behalf of the wireless device (Figure 15.9).

Wireless network operators and their gateways may use SOAP to provide the intermediary functionality for their wireless devices to communicate with Web

Figure 15.9
Mobile access
through
gateways

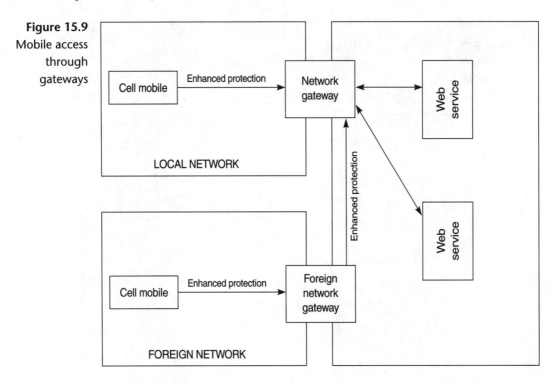

services. The wireless devices themselves may include unique encryption algorithms. The wireless gateway can alter and/or supplement the security tokens and the message protection. This security model is also valid when the wireless device is roaming on a foreign network.

Many Web services will also use a federation model. Let us say that Annika, a customer of Flute Bank, wants to use a currency Web service at the First & Last Bank of Tunapuna (a company with which Flute maintains a relationship). The currency Web service allows only requests with a security token issued by Flute Bank. Annika's security token can be used only with identity claims. In this situation, Annika can access only the currency Web service, if the First & Last Bank of Tunapuna is willing to permit security federation with Flute Bank.

As Figure 15.10 shows, Annika presents her Flute Bank security token to the First & Last Bank of Tunapuna's security token service and receives a security token. Annika then presents the new token to the currency service. The federated model may use public-key security tokens to facilitate security federations. Each service could additionally specify for its policy that it may accept Kerberos security tokens from its Key Distribution Center (KDC).

Web service security may also support delegated operations. Another Flute Bank customer, Kelon, uses the investments Web service to manage his portfolio. He wants to allow his investment adviser, Demesha, and his wife, Victoria, to access his holdings. Demesha does not do portfolio analysis and management directly and instead uses an application service provider. Whenever Demesha observes market activity with a particular stock, she places buy/sell recommendations that are broadcast to each of her clients.

Kelon provides both Victoria and Demesha with a security token that allows both of them to access his portfolio (Figure 15.11). The security token contains claims that limit Demesha's ability to analyze the parts of his portfolio that do not contain stocks. This security token also allows Demesha to create successive security tokens, as long as the portfolio analysis service can prove it has a privacy certification from the third-party trust service.

The trust service provider may audit each of the services on a periodic basis, so that any security token issued by the service asserts the privacy certification. When the portfolio analysis service accesses Kelon's portfolio, it can confirm proof of possession of its privacy certification and its assertion to access and schedule a trade, based on the security tokens from Kelon through Demesha to itself.

Figure 15.10
Security
federations

Figure 15.11
Delegation
of trust

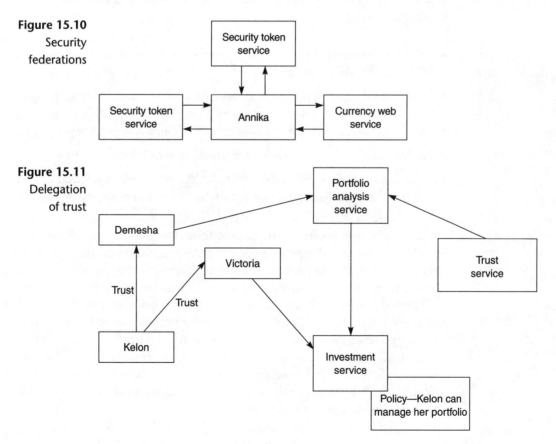

Hopefully, you have learned how to apply many of the standards we have discussed so far to design and/or implement a secure Web services infrastructure. Let us step into the final discussion point, on identity management.

> Identity Management

The concept of identity management in the physical world is strongly linked to context and relationships. When computers and the services they support seek to interoperate, the incorporation of identities becomes important. In the future, most applications will take advantage of identity information for security, billing, and recognition of friends, family, and consumers as well as for conducting activities in our daily lives that extend past commerce and touch political and social interactions. The architects of the world will struggle to unify and make consistent the accuracy of identity information. This is primarily a result of several opposing factors:

- The pervasiveness of information systems that have stored their own identities in a proprietary manner.

- The sheer sloppiness of data in an organization and the lack of anything that remotely resembles a data architecture. In many Fortune 500 companies, customer information can be found in at least 20 databases, none of which agree.

- Individuals' desire to make any information about them private.

- The ability of criminal-minded individuals to either misrepresent themselves and/or use identity information to gain advantage or escape accountability.

Part of the problems in creating a ubiquitous identity-management approach is tied to governmental regulations and friendly neighborhood ambulance chasers (e.g. lawyers). Today, no legal precedent states who is responsible for errors, omissions, quality control and assurance, redundancies, and dispute resolution.

Many systems have been created (some are still being created this way) that introduced their own notions of a user, password, and authorization scheme. Other applications within an organization, such as a payroll system, maintained detailed, accurate information about users, was just records. One of the evolutions in information technology encouraged architects to think about process and not data. While this provided some benefit, today we are left with databases that applications simply manipulate.

Storing information in a database is simple. The industry understands rules of normalization (not always practiced), but bridging authenticated identity realtime is not yet fully realized. The ideal situation would be, in real time, to authorize or deny access to a user, to treat a referred customer as a welcome guest instead of a stranger, or even to globally revoke all access immediately to fired employees (Sun has mastered this). These are some of the potential issues an identity management architecture can solve.

Identity management permits creating flexible definitions for people and things, such as classes or groups, that permit attaching policies or drawing conclusions. Many of us have moved physically from one place to another and taken items with us. Likewise, in a digital sense, electronic users will want to take information with them.

Components of Identity Management

The infrastructure components that constitute identity management include a data store (usually a directory or relational database) and processes that read and update the data, such as authentication and authorization that provide access control to a resource. A directory such as LDAP is a significant component in identity management but is not the last stop. The directory can provide a central place to store credentials but still allow authentication and authorization policies to be embedded in an application. The ideal scenario is to externalize these rules so that they can be executed anywhere, including in an application or by a centralized security service.

An identity management solution allows an architect to simply plug in a separate authentication layer without having to reinvent the wheel. This allows each application to have its own authentication rules without having to create its own authentication mechanisms. Identity management allows authentication systems to interact in a federated manner. This approach also becomes the first step in enabling single sign-on. The ability to be authenticated once and have a different authorization service for each resource ensures that personal information is not being passed. This process also allows the ability to specify explicitly what data can be passed from one resource to another, adding another level of security.

The Next Minute

Web services will enable many people and systems to be discoverable and knowable. These entities' visibility will increase; they will not simply disappear into cyberspace, as they do today. The actions and interactions of people and systems will persist, and architects will be called on to categorize, visualize, and filter knowledge, not simply store it. Individuals will control their identities in the same manner as they control their finances, most likely using third parties in the same manner a bank holds money. This relationship will extend to their software.

> Liberty Alliance

The Liberty Alliance is an industry consortium comprised of more than 70 companies, whose goal is to make it easier for businesses and consumers to conduct commerce while providing protection mechanisms for privacy and identity information. The Liberty Alliance has established a specification for an open standard of federated network identity that integrates with a variety of products and services.

A federated identity model will allow business and consumers alike to conduct business dynamically, without having to form relationships in advance. A federated identity in a consumer scenario may be used to provide a unified view of a consumer's information across providers. Consumers can unify their personal information, such as name, address, phone numbers, credit records, payment information, and other sensitive personal data. A federated identity provides important capabilities, such as allowing credentials from different originating organizations to be linked. This will provide single sign-on as well as allow business partners to interact with each other in a secure, trusted manner, without adding overhead by duplicating credentials across organizational boundaries.

Extending the federated identity approach over a network will allow consumers and business to manage diverse sets of identity information. An account federation allows for the association and binding of a consumer's multiple credentials within an affiliated group among commercial organizations that have some legal agreement. The account federation allows a user to sign on with one member of an affiliate group and subsequently use other access points within the group without having to reauthenticate.

The main objectives of Project Liberty are:

- To allow consumers to secure their network identity and enable privacy for it
- To enable businesses to manage their customer relationships without third-party participation or intervention
- To provide an open standard for single sign-on that uses a decentralized authentication and authorization model with the ability to incorporate multiple security providers

- To allow federated identity infrastructure components to work across all current and emerging network access devices

- To allow for the creation of new revenue opportunities that leverage existing relationships with consumers and partners cost-effectively

- To provide a framework in which businesses can give consumers the choice, convenience, and control of their information when using any device connected to the Internet

Internet users today have multiple login IDs, passwords, and other aspects that make up an identity. This information is spread throughout the Internet, buried in multiple sites. The thought of having a cohesive network identity is not realizable today. The Liberty Alliance allows the goal of a network identity to be realized, enabling two essential elements: circles of trust and local identities.

Circles of trust (Figure 15.12) are defined between business affiliates that use Liberty-enabled technology and that have established mutual operational agreements defining trust relationships between each party. *Local identities* allow each business to have its own set of credentials but provide a way to federate these credentials across organizations. A circle of trust is a federation of identity and ser-

Figure 15.12
Federated network identity

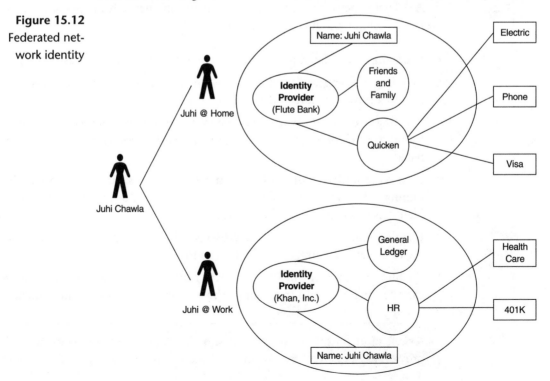

vice providers who have formed technical and legal relationships that allow users to transact business securely and seamlessly. ▷

Let's look at a scenario in which Flute Bank would use the Liberty Alliance. The Bank wants to ensure that all its consumers can access services created by Flute Bank and those provided by third parties. Flute Bank respects the privacy of its consumers and wants to delegate to them responsibility for protecting their information. The bank has a relationship with a travel company that allows bank customers to purchase airline tickets to international destinations economically. The airline ticket site has a relationship with an online bookseller that allows customers of the airline site to purchase travel-related books economically. The airline ticket site also has a relationship with a restaurant reservation service that can automatically arrange for reservations at top-tier restaurants at the selected destinations.

Flute Bank will use the circle of trust not only to avoid the need for customers to establish new identities or reauthenticate themselves to each provider but also to tie together payment information that will furnish the Flute Bank credit card number securely to each vendor. This example realizes the goal of the Liberty Alliance, in that identity becomes united but stays decentralized, so that information (credit card number) is available only at the time of engagement, in conjunction with a business transaction.

A federated network identity provides many strategic advantages to an organization, including, but not limited to:

- Reducing costs related to identity and access management infrastructure

- Enabling self-help (self-service) for customers, employees, and business partners in a private, secure and trusted manner

- Creating an opportunity to collaborate with business partners without fear of losing your customers, because the need to reveal customer identities is eliminated

- Improving understanding of customer needs across business partners, by mining information and sharing preferences without revealing customer identities or intruding on their privacy

- Enabling consumers to access advertised services anonymously, without having to undergo a barrage of solicitations for services.

- Enabling deployment of business-critical functions more quickly, because they no longer have to incorporate the overhead of identity management

▷   A circle of trust exists when the user and service providers rely on identity providers as trusted sources for authenticated user information.

Network identity is the first step in creating a viable trust model on the Internet, whereby personal information is secure and the information-sharing policy is clear and authorized by consumers. Network identity also has the ability to reduce online transaction fraud and the costs of integration and support for providers. We believe that network identity is inevitable and that no organization should simply be in standby mode, postponing decisions about it.

Network identity will also help organizations stay within legal compliance for many governmental actions, such as the Healthcare Information Portability Act (HIPA). It is imperative for architects to embrace network identity as part of the technology infrastructure and for business architects to incorporate it into all business processes. It is in your organization's best interest to respect consumers' privacy, earn their trust, and make services easy to use (eliminating multiple credentials).

The Liberty Alliance specification will incorporate and ratify many of the specifications discussed in this chapter.

▷ SourceID

SourceID is an open source project that will incorporate ideas, protocols, and software to support open identity as well as the creation of an open-source identity management system. Several of the projects under this initiative include development of a federated identity exchange to enable seamless single sign-on that will be 100% interoperable with the Liberty Alliance project. Development of an identity server, to provide identity in an open peer-to-peer manner for use by enterprises and service providers, is also underway. The SourceID project is the sole identity solution that puts control of identity into the hands of the identity owner. Other initiatives, such as Passport and the Liberty Alliance, are driven by corporations and software vendors. SourceID will allow users to host identity on their own computers if they desire. ▷

SourceID's goal is important because developers currently do not have any tools or libraries to develop solutions to interact with single sign-on protocols, such as Liberty Alliance. SourceID provides value to developers at large corporations who do not have time to learn SAML, Liberty, or other APIs that will be developed as part of the Java Community Process.

SourceID tools provide well-documented plug-in points that allow developers to insert bridge code into the SourceID SSO kernel. These plug points

▷ Additional information on SourceID is available at *www.pingid.org.*

support identity storage, retrieval, authentication, and authorization. The first release of the API is targeted toward developers who write Java servlets and JavaServer Pages. Future releases of SourceID will also support Microsoft's ASP.NET.

To understand SourceID a little better requires understanding the strengths and limitations of competing and complementary technologies, such as SAML and The Liberty Alliance. Let's compare SourceID to SAML first. SAML is a complete specification but also offers more than SSO requires. It does provide benefits, such as specifying a timestamp and network location of the identity host, which help prevent forgery, but it is also verbose in its layers. SourceID will use SAML for authentication but will defer to other protocols for identity management.

The Liberty Alliance specification addresses federated authentication among identity and service providers and works based on circles of trust. Liberty Alliance was originally started by Sun Microsystems under the guise of open standards. The Liberty Alliance specifications specify how to join identities from various sources, such as the companies that make up the alliance. Each pair of companies that participates has many user accounts between them, but no relationship information is available. Liberty Alliance allows these identities to be joined, making it convenient when consumers visit their sites. By joining identity across sites, the organizations that adopt this standard can reduce the cost of business, which can result in reduced cost to consumers.

SourceID has a different focus. It provides the ability to host identities from a centralized location, which could be the user's personal computer, rather than spreading this information across multiple identity providers. Given the choice, consumers would rather have identity stored 100% in their control but would defer where appropriate to federated identity providers.

An open identity-management solution must provide the following features:

- Metadirectory
- Self-service and workflow provisioning
- Delegated administration
- Unified developer kit and tools
- Security providers for Web and Web services
- Federated identity exchange functionality

Metadirectories provide the ability to abstract differences between disparate storage mediums that hold identity information, such as relational databases, LDAP, NIS, Active Directory, and others. This layer provides the capability to have a unified management and access facility for single sign-on applications. Provisioning of identity, especially in a self-service manner, will be vital for use on the Internet, where consumers may not be known to the businesses with which they intend to conduct commerce.

The ability to support provisioning and self-service allows an organization to enjoy significant cost savings. For example, employees of Flute Bank can self-provision an identity for using services offered. Consumers of Flute Bank can also self-provision an identity, which can be submitted for approval before access is granted. Incorporation of workflow is important, especially if it requires governmental licensing, security clearances, or other nontrivial validation procedures.

Delegated administration is an important feature that can help reduce calls to a central help desk. For example, a husband can have delegated authority to reset his wife's password. Software development kits are required for developers to programmatically access identity information and build functionality into their Web sites and backend infrastructure. Ideally, they will use an open standard, such as SOAP.

Authentication, authorization, and the ability to protect resources should be supported so that they can be configured to work with Web servers, such as Apache and Microsoft's IIS. These proxies support the ability to intercept requests for resources (URLs) and validate that the end user is authorized to access the resource. Proxies should also support the ability to inspect SOAP messages and optionally be inserted into application servers, such as BEA's WebLogic and IBM's WebSphere, as a custom authentication realm.

Many identity provider solutions will be available, from custom-built to products such as Netegrity's Siteminder to implementations that conform to the Liberty Alliance specification. Interoperability between SourceID supports these implementations and will seek to address scenarios not currently covered by the Liberty Alliance, such as peer-to-peer exchanges, auto forms population, and global lost and found.

Peer-to-peer exchanges are inherently ad hoc and counter the notion of circles of trust. Yet in a peer-to-peer exchange, the notion of identity exchange occurs. One example is when using a wireless phone or Bluetooth-enabled device. You can keep a copy of your contacts in Microsoft Outlook on your Bluetooth-enabled Compaq iPaq. Whenever someone walks into range, the iPaq can notify you that his or her contact information is out of date and automatically update it, based on automatic credential exchanges that could be built into each wireless device.

The constant task of updating data with each visit to a Web site or Web service can be frustrating. One would be to simply provide a SourceID network address that points to your identity. The Web site or service could automatically query and retrieve all basic information you have permitted, without user intervention.

The site could do this on a periodic basis, to keep basic information up to date within its own systems. This could be further extended to automatically populate forms in Web sites or even fat clients.

The notion of a global lost and found could be extended to wireless devices, which could have universally unique identifiers assigned to them. This would allow these devices to be accessed and managed through a Web service interface from anywhere in the world. The devices and their owners could also be registered with a service that monitors usage. If a registered device is lost or stolen, the owner could report it and render it useless by removing its identity. This could be extended to cars, televisions, airplanes, and other valuables.

Implementing identity management will be difficult for organizations. Tradeoffs exist in whether you want a single software company (e.g., Microsoft) to provide the solution (Passport), a consortium of large organizations who pay significant membership fees to participate in a consortium (Liberty Alliance). or identity presented via grassroots efforts (SourceID) without any form of vendor support. The discussion of this topic is highly religious and subject to debate even among the author team. What is important is that when constructing your architecture, you do homework on all the options presented. The best solution over time will always win.

> Summary

This chapter covers the processes, tools, and standards necessary to develop the right solution for your organization. Many of the topics build on other technologies and industry specifications. Implementing any one specification does not mean a Web service cannot be compromised. Even implementing multiple specifications will not guarantee security but will make a breach harder.

We have seen how security can impact the overall design of a Web service, what standards are involved, and how Java can be applied. It is good practice to always assume the worst–case, because eventually you will be proven correct. Careful attention to the specifications mentioned in this chapter will provide benefits now and in the future.

Chapter

Practical Considerations

Web services are being implemented by many enterprises at an intense pace, with little regard for infrastructure concerns such as systems management, high availability, or even interoperability. Many organizations will believe the hype and think they can become application service providers by simply publishing their service in a public registry. While we believe that success in this regard requires more than just technology (a good business plan is what is really needed), we can only provide you with sound, industry-proven technology recommendations.

We have striven to provide you with a complete, 360-degree view of Web services in a manner that will help you architect the right solution for your problem. In prior chapters, the focus was primarily on technology. This chapter will jump into topics, namely systems management, interoperability, payment models, XMLPay specification, service level agreements, testing Web services, performance, availability, scalability, clustering, fault tolerance, and grid computing, that did not fit neatly into other chapters. Its primary focus will be to provide you with best practices and additional considerations for making your architecture become scalable, available, reliable, and on budget.

> Systems Management

Many aspects of a comprehensive Web services solution will have components that reside outside the control of IT. Many services, such as credit card authorization, external caching, and public key infrastructure (which is used for authentication and authorization), are vital to the Web services nervous system. The typical Web service infrastructure is composed of a mix of both hardware and software technologies, along with a variety of complex processes to maintain the system's health.

A good systems management strategy allows a centralized, automated approach, to minimize operation errors and ensure compliance with infrastructure policies. This requires both proactive and reactive actions. Proactive monitoring takes into account trends, potential capacity problems, and opportunities for optimization. Reactive actions usually involve monitoring the components in the Web service infrastructure for faults.

Systems management is one solution that can address three business problems: availability, productivity, and efficiency. Availability of a Web service can be defined as the time the service is fully available to internal and external users. Increasing availability may have several benefits, including the ability for internal users to work additional hours and less revenue lost to downtime.

Efficiency of the systems management function can decrease time and travel of support services. This also has the side effect of increasing the user-to-service management ratio. In many organizations today, IT personnel costs and their growth have far outstripped the rate of revenue growth. The time saved in not having to perform user administration, operation functions, and support will free up both management and the technical staff for more proactive tasks.

Systems management requires sound management policies and procedures. Incorporating tight change control to reduce the chance of unexpected results is crucial. A well-thought-out authorization policy, restricting IT permissions to what is needed for personnel to accomplish tasks for which they are responsible, is also a good idea.

Components of a Systems Management Strategy

A complete systems management strategy requires multiple components. Table 16.1 lists management components we feel are required for a Web services environment. Many systems management vendors, such as BMC, CA Unicenter, and Tivoli, may offer additional functionality.

> Interoperability

One of the driving goals of the original SOAP was for interoperability. As with any first draft, it left many things up for interpretation. A group of industry participants referred to as Soap Builders are working on interoperability among the various SOAP implementations. Interoperability issues are constantly changing; refer to *http://groups.yahoo.com/group/soapbuilders* for the latest status.

Table 16.1 Components of a Systems Management Strategy

Component	Description
Systems	Enables monitoring of operating systems, disk drives, CPU, and network appliances within a business context.
Performance	Enables monitoring end-to-end performance of a Web service, including bandwidth, network response times, and service performance from the perspective of the end user.
Network	Enables monitoring of network components, such as TCP/IP, routers, switches, hubs, intrusion detection, firewalls, and appliances.
Service level	Enables monitoring of the effectiveness of service delivery and objectives in a manner understandable by the business community.
Scheduling	Enables centralized, event-driven scheduling and error recovery across an organization.
Console	Enables remote control and access from a central location to the components of a Web service infrastructure and eliminates the need to have local staff for routine systems maintenance.
Delivery	Enables the ability to install, configure, remove, and manage software on target servers from a central server. This can include servers, PDAs, laptops, and so on.
Service	Enables the collection and recording of system problems and their resolutions in a centralized database.
Capacity	Enables an organization to make sure that the Web services infrastructure is running at acceptable levels and allows what-if scenarios to help plan for the future.
Backup and recovery	Enables the ability to centrally back up and recover both local and remote servers.

Many implementations of SOAP do not agree on how SOAP headers should be handled. One example is that the SOAPAction header is permitted to be null (no value specified), an empty string (no intent specified), or an arbitrary quoted string. The SOAPAction header indicates the intent of the message for its target. Some SOAP implementations (e.g., Apache SOAP) do not support dispatching using the SOAPAction header. Instead, they route based on the namespace URI of the first child element contained in the SOAP:Body element. SOAP also allows for un-namespaced body entries, which cause their own issues.

Some aspects of SOAP have not been implemented by all parties. One example is character set encoding. For a SOAP message to be understood, both the originator and the recipient must use the same encoding of the character set. SOAP does not force a particular encoding standard. For interoperability, SOAP also requires all message interchanges to use the same protocol bindings, such as HTTP. Although HTTP is pervasive, the ability to use other bindings may interfere with interoperability.

Many SOAP toolkits are used to generate WSDL files. Depending on the particular toolkit in use and when the service was first generated, you could run into schema incompatibilities. The early IBM Web service toolkits could generate WSDL based on the earlier XSD 1999 working draft, but an ASP.NET Web service would generate WSDL using the final XSD recommendation. Other toolkits handle this conundrum in different ways. The WSDL generated is important primarily because SOAP proxies are created from it.

The Apache SOAP implementation requires that all SOAP (RPC) envelopes be self-describing in terms of types. Apache SOAP does not work without every typed value being explicitly contained in the envelope, using the xsi:type attribute. This is not a SOAP requirement, and many implementations leave out this information.

Many SOAP interoperability issues can be directly correlated to the underlying language used to create and/or read the SOAP message. One example is that Java handles both floating-point numbers and dates differently from SOAP. The SOAP specification states that floating-point numbers can be represented as exponential numbers. Both the Apache SOAP and Axis libraries use Java's toString method to convert floating-point values to java objects. In Java, when a float has an overflow condition, it will output the string as "Infinity." The SOAP specification states that it should appear as "INF."

The decimal data type in SOAP can represent numbers up to 40 digits. In Java, to handle this decimal data type, we would use the BigDecimal class. BigDecimal has an upper limit, based on the underlying platform (Windows, Linux, Solaris, etc.) The current .NET implementation of BigDecimal allows up to 29 digits.

The date type in SOAP allows a `dateTime` type, for centuries, years, months, days, hours, minutes, and seconds. SOAP also allows an arbitrary number of digits to occur after seconds. Many implementations of SOAP on Java use the `java.util.Date` class for date support. Java supports precision only to the nearest millisecond, although .NET can support nanosecond resolutions.

Make sure you also avoid using either HTTP/GET or HTTP/POST bindings in your WSDL. You will typically see these bindings in services generated using Visual Studio. This may cause other toolkits to fail when generating proxies. This can be turned off in the Visual Studio Web service project.

Over the next couple of years, many public UDDI registries will be created on the Internet. The deployment of these registries may follow the same model as search engines, which typically are inconsistent and can point you toward invalid or irrelevant links. Today, no standardized mechanism allows a registry to remove outdated entries. This problem may or may not be solved by a registry's ability to synchronize with others. Synchronization may allow invalid entries to be removed globally but can also compromise registry security. Also, a Web service can appear in multiple registries.

The major interoperability issue in UDDI itself will arise from the nirvana approach to service discovery that many in the industry advocate. Using Web Service Inspection Language (WSIL) or similar approaches to discover a service automatically may be technically possible but not realistic from a business point of view.

The UDDI specification allows for a service to be categorized in a registry using taxonomies to describe its location, service, and product type. This can itself cause a potential interoperability problem, because UDDI is based primarily on self-policing that may prevent dynamic invocation of self-discovered Web services.

Many application servers use the Apache Xerces parser for its JAXP implementation. This parser will fail to read any messages that contain a byte order mark (BOM) for UTF-8–encoded SOAP requests. The BOM is legal in UTF-8–encoded messages and is sent by many non-Java SOAP toolkits.

▶ Pricing Models

Many organizations realize that their current business practices do not fit neatly into a Web services paradigm, and they may need to devise a new pricing model. The elements of the pricing may need to take into account factors such as resources used, number of users, and whatever the market will bear. A typical business-pricing model takes into account supply and demand. Because Web services offerings have not yet reached critical mass, users will need to anticipate which will come first—supply or demand—and plan accordingly. Because most Web services available via the Internet are free, their real value cannot be accurately measured.

To date, the focus on moving to a Web services model has focused primarily on integration within companies. Many large organizations realize the value of using Web services for this. Interoperability between heterogeneous platforms and the applications that run on them, such as mainframes (COBOL), Unix (C++), and Windows (Java), provides an immediate benefit. The primary objective is to reuse existing functionality across lines of business. This translates into reduced IT expenditures, in the form of less duplicated code and increased maintainability.

One of the trends in the industry is toward outsourcing services, sometimes referred to as e-sourcing. E-sourcing is the mechanism to deliver software-based services over the network containing both business and IT features. This automated, pay-as-you-go model is capable of serving multiple consumers and provides capacity on demand.

The older model of being able to give away services in exchange for advertising revenue is no longer relevant, because Web services no longer depend on browsers to render their displays. Web services further complicate accounting in that transactions can cross multiple services. Accounting and metering in a service-oriented architecture is vastly different from current, browser-based scenarios. For one thing, Web services take a higher-level approach than tracking users by IP address, simplistic hit counting, or recording storage use.

In Chapter 15, we discussed the use of digital certificates for signing and non-repudiation. This is especially important for billing purposes. Having a digital signature on hand will prevent inaccurate charges to the service requestor. This may mandate that your service use a digitally signed SOAP message.

The centralization of the digital certificate function should be delegated to an accounting Web service, similar to the trust model discussed in Chapter 15. Its sole responsibility is to act as a resource governor for all Web services. The accounting Web service should appropriately handle the three basic approaches to accounting for Web services use: subscriptions, leasing, and per transaction. It should also handle the following functions if you are going to charge for your service:

- Adding, modifying, suspending, and deleting service requestor accounts on both an ad hoc and as contractual basis

- Recording user start and stop times for the requested service

- Providing reporting capabilities, such as total resource use by user, usage statistics by service, and so on
- Providing a feed to accounts-receivable (billing) and tax-calculation systems
- Using a common billing interface that allows an organization to adjust its rating models dynamically

Defining this service and having all your other services use it from the beginning is important to organizations that charge for their services. In the next section, we will look at the flow of this service.

Accounting Services

Figure 16.1 outlines the flow of our accounting service. Let us walk through the flow, starting with the client after it has discovered the service it wants to use.

1. The client connects to the service provider and executes the service.
2. The requested service binds to the accounting service.
3. The accounting service checks to see if the requested service requires accounting.

Figure 16.1
Accounting
service

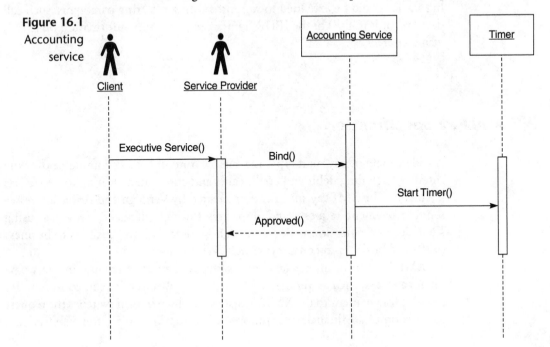

4. If the service requires accounting, the accounting service checks to see if the user is allowed to use the service at the requested time or has exceeded maximum usage.

5. If the above checks pass, the accounting service creates a start-time record using the ID the client used to bind to the initial service.

6. The accounting service lets the requested service know it is okay to execute the requested service. It returns a unique transaction token to the requested service to prevent overlapping messages.

7. When the requested service is finished executing, it calls the accounting service with a stop event, passing in the related token. The accounting service closes the transaction and creates the appropriate billing records.

The ability to dynamically charge for services based on usage provides many organizations with additional pricing capabilities. To further extend the above approach, you could separate accounting from metering. The accounting service could simply become the gatekeeper. The metering service could become a distinct Web service that exists either locally or remotely. The metering service could create the billing records and become outsourced. Furthermore, the metering service could be extended to support existing metering paradigms, such call detail records (CDR) or the IPDR framework. (For more information on IPDR, visit *www.ipdr.org.*)

> XMLPay Specification

A wide variety of payment types is available for conducting commerce over the Internet, including debit and credit cards and automated clearinghouse (ACH) payments. The XMLPay specification, created by VeriSign and Ariba, addresses sending payment requests and responses through financial networks, using XML. The specification is open and can be used in both business-to-business (B2B) and business-to-consumer (B2C) Web services.

XMLPay can communicate requests for payments through intermediary payment gateways, such as VeriSign (Figure 16.2). A Web service can communicate requests for payment to the XMLPay gateway, which in turn switches the request to the appropriate financial institution and returns the result to the Web service.

Figure 16.2
XMLPay flow

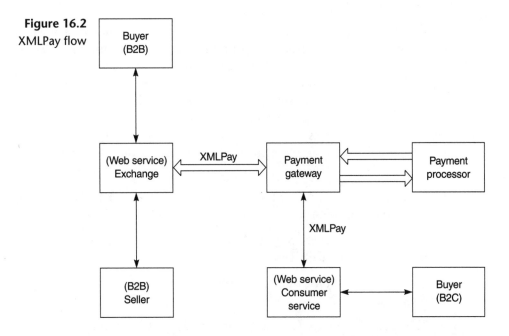

In a B2C scenario, the selling Web service forwards the buyer's payment information to a payment processor. The selling Web service formats an XMLPay request and sends it directly to an XMLPay-compliant payment processor or indirectly via an XMLPay payment gateway. In a B2B scenario, the seller may not initiate payment requests and may use a trading exchange. The trading exchange, in turn, uses XMLPay to communicate purchasing information to the payment gateway. In this manner, payment can be linked to other Web services, such as purchase orders and advance shipping notice delivery.

Services of high importance to an organization are the ones most likely to have charges associated with them. Services such as the weather or stock quotes are most likely to be free. With the advent of a paid Web services model, organizations will also need to consider quality of service guarantees.

> Service Level Agreements

Organizations that employ a Web services approach, especially where they pay for the services, will demand a service level agreement. Service level agreements are formed between two parties and state how services will be used and accounted for and any prerequisites for use. This can become a way for providers of services to distinguish themselves from competition in today's competitive marketplace. Service level agreements in the Web services model can take many forms. The typical written contract has merit for two parties who have prior established relationships. Two parties that are dynamic and learned of the service offering dynamically may agree to handle contractual details through electronically signed contracts and certificates.

A typical (basic) service level agreement covers the following points:

- Starting and ending dates of the contract (e.g., September 10, 2003, through September 10, 2005)

- Availability of the service (e.g., Monday through Friday, 8:00 a.m. to 8:00 p.m., Eastern Standard Time)

- Performance/response time (e.g., 70% of all transactions shall execute within four seconds)

- The type of contract (e.g., unlimited usage, restricted usage during peak times, ad hoc)

- Limitations (e.g., one hundred transactions per day)

- Security (e.g., use of certificates for identity, encryption, and signing)

- Auditing (e.g., monthly reports online at close of last business day)

A detailed service level could include actions the service provider and client would take in case of failure. Providers may also impose limits on the maximum and average response times for notifying a client of downtime or planned outages. Service level agreements may specify penalties if the provider fails to meet defined objectives over the duration of the agreement. An agreement may also provide for the client to terminate for unsatisfactory resolution of problems related to availability, reliability, performance, and security.

To guarantee that your Web service will stand up to whatever service levels you attach to it requires good quality assurance and testing. Table 16.2 is a checklist of Web service features that should be tested. This list is by no means complete but should provide you with a start for offering Web services to paying consumers. In the future, consumers will demand an appropriate service-level agreement before using your Web service. Ideally, your organization will employ automated testing tools, by vendors such as Empirix, PushToTest, and RedAlert, to guarantee ongoing monitoring of compliance to the agreements.

Table 16.2 Web Services Features

Feature	Questions
Security	Can unauthorized users access any function not granted to guests?
	Can authorized users gain access to functions not explicitly assigned to them?
	Does the Web service adequately handle denial-of-service attacks?
Versioning	Does a newer version of your Web service also support older clients?
	Does the new version break any dependent Web services?
Timeout	What happens when a Web service times out?
	Is accounting information accurate when a service exceeds certain thresholds?
Performance	Does the Web service take longer to respond than its stated objective (e.g., five seconds)?
	What happens when the Web service is put under load?
State	Does the Web service respond correctly when you set a value in a stateful request on first and subsequent requests?
Infrastructure failture	Does the Web service dynamically discover new dependent services when a primary service is unavailable?

> Testing Web Services

Like any other application, Web services will require testing. A corporation's Web site goes through several quality assurance and testing scenarios, and a Web service will at minimum require the same level of effort. A Web service, like a corporate Web site, has high visibility, supports unpredictable workloads, and therefore must be robust.

As we have indicated earlier in the book, there are two types of Web services: those that serve internal customers (intranet) and those that serve the general public (Internet). Each poses its own unique difficulties for testing. An internally exposed Web service will not require some forms of testing. For example, it has a theoretical maximum on the number of users. An organization can also enforce policies for an internal Web service's use and make broad, simplistic assumptions about security. A service exposed to the Internet typically means that anyone can access it, which may require additional security, reliability, and scalability.

Many organizations have used testing tools that record macros of a user's action for future playback. This approach will not work with Web services, which have no user interface (UI) to speak of. This will also cause additional difficulty for one-off manual testing scenarios. To successfully test a Web service that does not have a UI may require that the testing team have some programming skills. Simply put, a Web service cannot be tested by monkeys banging on the keyboard.

Types of tests include functional, regression, load/stress, and proof of concept, each with a different goal. Let us look at each type and the best way to realize the goals.

Functional Testing

A functional test ensures that the Web service meets all business requirements and works as expected. Typically, functional tests are based on information contained in a UML use-case diagram or similar notation. A test scenario may look at whether your Web service properly implements authentication, supports multiple communication protocols (e.g., HTTP and messaging), and properly handles alternate scenarios.

This is the introductory form of testing. For Web services, you will need to know how a Web service can be invoked, the information being sent as part of the request, and the appropriate response. Flute Bank may wish to test its stock-trading Web service for multiple data input situations. Let us look at some alternate case scenarios that test for order price:

1. Entering an order price that is not numeric: [five dollars] instead of [5.00]

2. Entering an order price that is valid but awkward: [5 0/32] instead of [5]

3. Entering an order price where the denominator is not evenly divisible: [5 16/33]

4. Entering a negative order price: [–5.25]

5. Entering an order price where 0 is the denominator: [5 3/0]

Functional testing makes sure the system not only works as specified but that it will handle errors appropriately. A complete functional testing plan will include bounds testing and error checking.

As we learned in Chapter 4, a SOAP message is made up of an envelope, a header, and a body. For functional testing, it is useful to trap the SOAP messages sent, because requests and responses are part of interacting with a service. SOAP extensions—code that modifies the contents of a SOAP message and can take actions on it—can be used for this. An extension can compress/decompress, add data, and so on. Sometimes it is useful to have a SOAP extension catch the messages exchanged between services and log them to a text file for analysis.

Flute Bank, in looking at the logs, determined it could gain additional performance by using simple SOAP data types rather than custom data types for its portfolio management service. The bank learned that user-defined types reduce accessibility of the service, because they require special client knowledge to understand the data. Secondarily, the bank determined that it is also taking a performance hit, because the proxy class has more work to do in serializing and deserializing the SOAP messages.

Flute Bank also analyzed its auto-insurance-quote Web service and found additional optimizations. A smart tester, along with help from the architect, noted that a quote from Flute's Web site required two calls to the same Web service. The Web site would pass the vehicle identification number (VIN) once to determine the age of the vehicle and then again to determine the car's owner. Flute decided to optimize its service interface to return both pieces of information in a single method call.

Regression Testing

Regression testing ensures that the target Web service is still working between builds or releases of different versions. Regression testing starts with an assumption that the service worked in the past and checks that it still works as advertised. A regression test is usually a scaled-back version of a functional test and intentionally should not be a full functional test.

A regression test in Flute Bank's stock-trading Web service may look to see if a valid and invalid stock price for purchase generate the appropriate responses. It may also look to see if performance is within normal operating range. Regression tests, by their nature, are repetitive and therefore should be automated.

Load and Stress Testing

The primary goal of load and stress testing is to determine how well a Web service will scale, based on simulated users accessing it. Functional and regression testing prove that a service works with a single user. Load and stress testing prove that it will work with multiple concurrent users.

Flute Bank may want to test each of its Web services with varying numbers of concurrent users, to find the breaking point. This information is useful for capacity planning. The bank may also want to determine whether tripling the number of users will change the response time. The bank may also want to determine whether tripling the capacity of its application server farm will really produce triple the capacity.

Load and stress tests are usually executed in controlled environments. If Flute Bank wants to determine how a particular service responds with increased use, it must isolate or at least stabilize other factors that can skew the results, such as hardware and networking. A successful execution of a load and stress test should result in a statement such as "X Web service will respond within X seconds for up to X clients making X requests per second."

Load and stress testing can also be helpful in creating reasonable service level agreements. You may already know that the service can handle 50 requests a second but need to know what will happen with a massive peak in usage. Will the Web service slow down, crash, or simply return garbage or inaccurate data?

A load and stress testing scenario should preferably capture the metrics in Table 16.3 for further analysis. These are the first steps in measuring your service from the load and stress perspective. The ideal scenario occurs when the number of users can be increased and these numbers stay the same. Likewise, the worst scenario occurs when the numbers increase linearly with the amount of simulated users.

Testing Web services provides unique challenges that are not necessarily encountered in traditional Web-based applications. It becomes more important than ever to validate the capacity, scalability, and reliability of your service-oriented architecture in the design stage as well as to perform a full load and stress test before production release.

Table 16.3 Load Testing Metrics

Metric	Description
Connection time	The time it takes to complete a connection from the client to the Web service. (Lower is better.)
First byte time	The time it takes for the client to receive the first byte of the response from the Web service. This indicates whether the service requires a lot of think time.
Last byte time	The time it takes for the client to receive the last byte of the response from the Web service. This will increase based on the amount of data transmitted.

Proof-of-Concept Testing

One of the biggest mistakes continuously repeated among large and small corporations alike is waiting until it is too late to start testing. One of the basic tenets of Kent Beck's *Extreme Programming Explained* (Addison-Wesley, 1999) and Scott Ambler's *Agile Modeling* (Wiley, 2002) is the need for a test plan before writing a single line of code. Some will argue about the right time to start testing, but the author team recommends at least conducting proof-of-concept testing early in a Web service's development lifecycle.

From the testing perspective, an architect responsible for developing robust Web services will most likely be faced with concerns related to scalability. A realistic scenario is a business sponsor inquiring whether a particular architecture can scale to 1,000 simultaneous users. The smartest thing an architect can do at this stage is to execute a reduced load test (described above). This form of load testing does not need to be run on production-level hardware or provide exact answers. Its sole purpose is to indicate whether you are headed in the right direction.

▷ Performance

Quality of service will become an important attribute in distinguishing your service from others. Quality of service will correlate strongly to your service's overall popularity. Performance is one aspect of quality of service and can be measured by latency and throughput. *Latency* is the roundtrip time, from sending a request to receiving a response. *Throughput* is the number of requests a Web service handles in a specified period.

Over time, many Web services will bump into limitations in the underlying transport protocols, such as HTTP. HTTP is a stateless protocol that only attempts best-effort delivery. This may create many problems for your service, because it does not guarantee that packets will arrive in the order in which they were sent, that all packets will make it to their destination, or that enough bandwidth is available. Several emerging protocols, such as Direct Internet Message Encapsulation (DIME), Reliable HTTP (HTTPR), and Blocks Extensible Exchange Protocol (BEEP), address latency and guaranteed delivery. Adoption of these protocols may take time.

In the meantime, if your service is not response-time sensitive, consider message queuing. Web services can use message queuing implementations based on Java Message Service (described in detail later) for invocations. A messaging approach will provide your service with a reliable, adaptable mechanism for asynchronous exchange of data throughout your enterprise. A message queue can make sure that a message is delivered once and only once. It will also deliver messages to the target as they arrive, without the receiver's having to request them.

One of the biggest slowdowns in performance is related to an XML parser's speed when reading a SOAP message. By its nature, XML does not allow for much size optimization. Because SOAP is based on XML, it has this limitation and more. Unlike regular XML, a SOAP message must include all typing information. Besides parsing this, the XML parser may also need to perform multiple parsing passes to extract the SOAP envelope and body from the SOAP packet.

Many XML parsers are bloated and require significant CPU and memory resources. Some support features such as validating whether a document is well formed, type checking, conversion, and so on. Many of the SOAP stacks are implementations of the Document Object Model (DOM), which is inherently slow to parse large messages. You could consider a nonvalidating, SAX-based SOAP implementation, which will reduce memory overhead and increase throughput.

XML has the side effect of increasing data—in many cases, by five times or more. Because SOAP uses XML as its payload, the best way to increase performance is to consider compressing the XML. In a Java-based Web service, this can be handled easily with a ZippedOutputStream, if your downstream Web services can also use this format. One of the factors to consider when compressing XML is to do it only when the CPU overhead required for compression is less than the network latency.

The best way to determine the performance characteristics of your service is to use a service proxy. Service proxies are used to hide any communications details from a client and are similar to stubs in Java RMI. Service proxies contain code specific to the bindings in the service interface. Listing 16.1 shows the WSDL for a simple timer service that returns the time it took to call another service.

Listing 16.1   WSDL for timer service

```
<?xml version="1.0" encoding="UTF-8"?>
<definitions name="TimerService"
  targetNamespace="http://www.flutebank.com/TimerService"
  xmlns="http://schemas.xmlsoap.org/wsdl/"
  xmlns:soap="http://schemas.xmlsoap.org/wsdl/soap/"
  xmlns:tns="http://www.flutebank.com/TimerService"
    xmlns:xsd="http://www.w3.org/1999/XMLSchema">
<message name="IntimerRequest">
  <part name="meth1_inType1" type="xsd:string"/>
</message>
```

```
<message name="OuttimerResponse">
  <part name="meth1_outType" type="xsd:string"/>
</message>
<portType name="TimerService">
  <operation name="timer">
    <input message="IntimerRequest"/>
    <output message="OuttimerResponse"/>
  </operation>
</portType>
<binding name="TimerServiceBinding" type="TimerService">
  <soap:binding style="rpc" transport="http://schemas.xmlsoap.org/soap/http"/>
  <operation name="time">
    <soap:operation soapAction="urn:timerservice-service"/>
    <input>
      <soap:body
          encodingStyle="http://schemas.xmlsoap.org/soap/encoding/"
          namespace="urn:timerservice-service"
          use="encoded"/>
    </input>
    <output>
      <soap:body
          encodingStyle="http://schemas.xmlsoap.org/soap/encoding/"
          namespace="urn:timerservice-service" use="encoded"/>
    </output>
  </operation>
</binding>
<service
      name="TimerService">
  <documentation>Java Web services Architecture</documentation>
  <port binding="TimerServiceBinding" name="TimerServicePort">
    <soap:address location="http://www.flutebank.com:8080/soap/servlet/rpcrouter"/>
  </port>
</service>
</definitions>
```

Many Web service toolkits will automatically generated a service proxy from WSDL. Creating a timer service requires modifying the generated code. Listing 16.2 contains modified code that simply wraps the call to the Web service through the invoke method.

Listing 16.2   Timer service proxy

```java
import java.net.*;
import java.util.*;
import org.apache.soap.*;
import org.apache.soap.encoding.*;
import org.apache.soap.rpc.*;
import org.apache.soap.util.xml.*;
import com.flutebank.Timer;

public class TimerServiceProxy {

  private Call call = new Call();
  private URL url = null;
  private String SOAPActionURI = "";
  private SOAPMaptimeRegistry smr = call.getSOAPMaptimeRegistry();
   public TimerServiceProxy() throws MalformedURLException {
     call.setTargetObjectURI("urn:timerservice-service");
     call.setEncodingStyleURI("http://schemas.xmlsoap.org/soap/encoding/");
     this.url = new URL("http://www.flutebank.com:8080/soap/servlet/rpcrouter");
     this.SOAPActionURI = "urn:timerservice-service";
   }
   public synchronized void setEndPoint(URL url) {
    this.url = url;
   }
   public synchronized URL getEndPoint() {
    return url;
   }
   public synchronized String time (String meth1_inType1) throws SOAPException {
    if (url == null) {
      throw new SOAPException(Constants.FAULT_CODE_CLIENT, "A URL must be
                                                          specified");
   }
      call.setMethodName("time");
   Vector params = new Vector();
   Parameter meth1_inType1Param = new Parameter("meth1_inType1", String.class,
                                               meth1_inType1, null);

   params.addElement(meth1_inType1Param);
   call.setParams(params);
```

```
// Start an instance of the flutebank Timer
Timer timer = new Timer();
timer.start();

Response res = call.invoke(url, SOAPActionURI);

// Stop the Timer
timer.stop();
    // Calculate the difference in time
System.out.println("Response Time = " + timer.getDifference());

// Check for any errors in the response
if (res.generatedFault()) {
  Fault fault = resp.getFault();
  throw new SOAPException(fault.getFaultCode(), fault.getFaultString());
  }
else
{
  Parameter retValue = res.getReturnValue();
  return (String)retValue.getValue();
  }
}
}
```

Quantifying performance bottlenecks in your service infrastructure will become a necessity. Timing each step in a Web service that uses a chain of Web services could also use the above approach.

> High Availability

Many organizations will initially attempt to deploy Web services for non-mission-critical applications. For others, who are using Web services to generate revenue, making your services highly available becomes mandatory. Before starting the journey to deploying mission-critical systems, you must consider the cost of downtime, lost opportunities, lost revenue, and any stranded fixed cost your organization would need to pay whether productive or not.

Damage is sometimes harder to calculate. Loss of good will with customers, partners, and suppliers affected by unavailable services will give the impression that your organization is poorly run and incapable of fulfilling their needs. If your organization is in the public health or safety area, an unavailable service could potentially cost lives.

An organization must weigh the high cost of downtime. The higher the cost of downtime, the more robust your availability plans must be. Figure 16.3 outlines the relative severity of an impact and its resulting costs. The architects of a Java-based Web service must analyze and document what is affected when a system goes down. Here are some additional thoughts to consider:

- Managers and users may find themselves without information necessary to make intelligent decisions. With lost information, standard activities in an organization may be delayed or incorrectly executed. Downstream systems may also make incorrect decisions based on missing or corrupted information.

- Deadlines may be missed, with catastrophic results. Imagine a Web service that accepts change orders for an expensive, custom-made product. What would happen if a customer could not submit a change before the cutoff time?

- The Internet allows consumers choice. If customers use your service and it does not work, they are unlikely to come back. Consider the effect your service may have on downstream systems, such as order and inventory management, financial reporting, human resources, emergency notification, identification, ATM and other wire transfer facilities, and life-sustaining medical systems.

Figure 16.3
Downtime cost as a function of impact

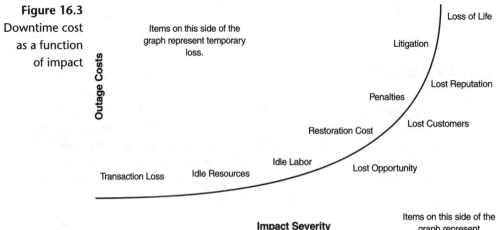

- Consider the impact on morale and legal implications of not being available. Imagine if the military developed a Web service that fed enemy movement information to a central command center, and it was down.

Concepts

Availability refers to the time a service is operational and is expressed as a percentage. High availability usually refers to running for extended periods, exceeding 99.99%, with minimal unplanned outages. . This is referred to as four nines. Similarly, 99.999% is referred to as five nines, which requires all components of your service, including the operating system, network, human errors, and so on to have no more than five minutes of downtime a year (Table 16.4).

To provide a highly available service, every component of your infrastructure must support high availability. The level of availability can be no better than that of the weakest link. Increasing availability requires incremental improvement to each component in your network. This is preferable to seeking 100% availability for a specific component.

Many organizations assume that achieving higher levels of availability is expensive. This is not necessarily true. Availability is not free. It requires executive management attention, hard work, and due diligence to assemble the right people, processes, and tools. It starts with reliable, stable components. Higher levels of availability require methodical system integration and detailed application design.

The real cause of many outages tends to be human error. Many organizations have spent millions of dollars on high-availability solutions, only to have a network administrator accidentally unplug a crucial component. Other outages arise from fixing problems that are not the root cause but appear so because of

Table 16.4 Availability Statistics

Measurement	Number of nines	Time lost in one year
90%	One	36 days (876 hours)
99%	Two	3.6 days (87 hours)
99.9%	Three	8.8 hours
99.99%	Four	53 minutes
99.999%	Five	5 minutes
99.9999%	Six	32 seconds

inadequate documentation. To achieve the highest levels of availability, implement a comprehensive change-management strategy that defines repeatable processes.

Service Design Techniques

To increase the availability of your Web service, include your consumers' requirements for performance, reliability, and availability. Availability is hard to incorporate after the fact and must be included initially in application design. Using a Web service to integrate with legacy systems may require these applications to be redesigned.

Architects and developers alike must be educated about the cost of outages, to make the appropriate tradeoffs. They should also make sure components are suitable for the negotiated availability needs.

The design should keep the scope of a failure small by isolating important processes, such as sessioning, and tightly coupling integration with other components. Those who have worked in mainframe shops may have observed that these machines cannot run a batch cycle while online applications are available. Make sure your service does not depend on other components being available. Also take into account that recovery in case of failure should be fast, intuitive, and should not require a lot of internal or external coordination.

The one step any IT shop can take is to employ standard processes and procedures. Naming conventions help reduce errors and improve communications immensely. By having a standardized process such as naming conventions, compilers can serve as a built-in check for change management and other related activities.

Managing your Web services should take into account the end-to-end view from a business perspective. All resources the Web service uses should be managed within the context of a business process. This allow administrators and the business community to ascertain and understand the business impact on any one resource. It has the additional advantage of allowing administrators to prioritize their next steps in outages, performance slowdowns, and other business-critical situations based on quantifiable business needs.

Another important consideration is a unified view of security. A breach will cause downtime. The main problem is that different roles within an organization, such as architects, developers, security administrators, and operations, typically have their own views of the world. They usually administer security policies on the resources they directly manage. Organizations that don't use single sign-on usually have multiple identities spread across multiple parties. Even the simplest task of disabling a user ID will repeatedly produce inconsistent levels of access throughout the services offered.

Infrastructure Design Techniques

Redundant, reliable components in your infrastructure are the key to availability. Redundancy in components, systems, and data can eliminate single points of failure (Figure 16.4). Consider incorporating clustering (hardware and/or software) into the infrastructure. The essential principle is to present a common addressing scheme to the underlying components.

As an example, a load-balancing appliance (e.g. Alteon, Cisco CSS, F5 Big IP) provides a single IP address for a group of servers. A Web service consumer needs only direct a request to the IP address exposed by the load-balancing appliance.

Figure 16.4
Redundant infrastructure for high availability

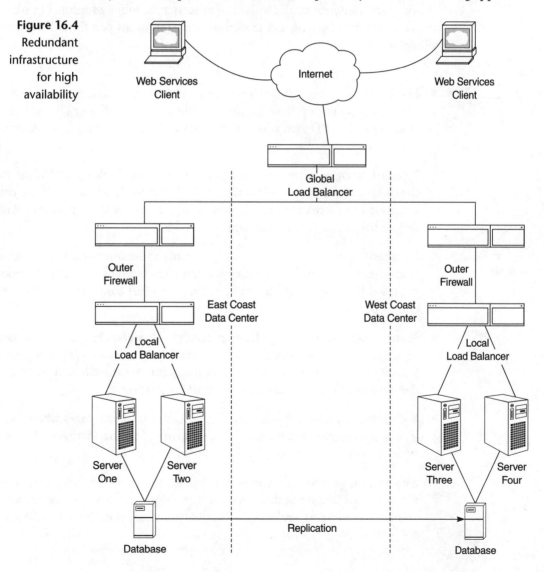

The appliance, in turn, directs the request to the server with the least utilization. The appliance also determines when a server in the cluster is not functioning and routes requests away from it. The added benefit of this approach is the ability to take servers offline one at a time for maintenance without affecting users. Many appliances allow you to implement several algorithms for determining where to direct Web service requests, such as load balancing, server utilization, or application affinity.

Many white papers published by industry analysts such as the Gartner Group and Forrester Research cover the business aspects of high availability and help an organization determine whether it requires "five nines." The technology aspect of high availability especially in Java Web service, requires additional thinking and architectural planning. Let us outline some questions you should ask yourself about each tier:

- **Hardware.** Do the components in your infrastructure (servers, routers, switches, and other appliances) have uninterruptible power supplies or fault tolerant memory or I/O? Do they have redundant disks, controllers, network interfaces, and CPUs?

- **Network.** Is there more than one path (route) to your Web service? What are the characteristics of your network, and do they provide self-healing? Are you connected to more than one Internet service provider? Does your Java Web service have hard-coded host names embedded in it?

- **Database.** Have you consider employing replication, online backup, or other strategies? Does your Java Web service delegate connections to a JDBC pool provided by an application server, so that the J2EE containers can failover connections?

- **Management.** Can your application detect failures and alert the appropriate personnel? Have you turned on SNMP support provided by your application server? Have you built a logging mechanism into your architecture and put the hooks in the appropriate locations of your service?

- **Web servers.** Have you configured appropriate response pages when a service is unavailable? Have you considered using load-balancing appliances, such as those from Cisco, Alteon, Coyote Point, or F5?

- **Application servers.** Are you taking full advantage of the capabilities provided by your Java application server and its support for clustering, hot deployment of components, replicated session state, and a global JNDI namespace?

> Scalability

Before the Internet, many large organizations developed their infrastructures based on monolithic core business functions, such as claims processing systems running on mainframes or large ERP applications running on Sun Enterprise ISK machines. For these types of applications, which placed a CPU-intensive load on the infrastructure, it made good sense to use large, dedicated machines. This approach required a considerable initial investment in infrastructure and personnel. Let us look at developing a scalable Web services infrastructure at a practical cost.

To support efficient scaling, an organization should consider a strategy that allows it to add resources as needed. The recommended approach is to deploy Web services applications in independent server pools that can be joined to provide the appropriate business integration. Applications should be partitioned at a physical level, which has the advantage of providing flexibility of use. Partitioning gives flexibility when deploying multiple workloads on servers. It allows for maximal resource usage and minimal unnecessary resource reallocation.

Larger servers provide high capacity but at a reduction in flexibility of deployment. We prefer using smaller two- or four-way systems that provide the ability to scale quickly and cheaply. This configuration has the added advantage of having a better price/performance ratio than other options. With a lower acquisition cost, it becomes practical to deploy multiple redundant servers throughout your infrastructure. This will guarantee your Web services a higher level of availability.

Before considering this approach, it is important to determine the characteristics of your service. Some Web services are suitable for scaling widely, by deploying them across identically configured servers. Other Web services may be better suited to scaling deeply, into more powerful, large CPU systems. The granularity of control for performance and availability should also become part of your decision.

Also consider taking a multi-tier architectural approach to infrastructure. Partition your infrastructure into at least four distinct tiers for a Web services environment:

- A Web services tier that has an HTTP daemon and application server
- A mid-level business tier for business applications
- An Enterprise Information System (EIS) or database tier that provides a persistence mechanism that could be implemented in either a relational, heirarchical, XML, or object approach
- A potential integration tier that connects the business tier to the EIS resources

Each tier may also provide security, accounting, systems management, and other utility functions. The resource requirements for each tier will be different and can be configured for optimal performance, as opposed to applying generic tuning approaches. As an example, Web services may require fast network throughput and disk caching, while your mid-tier business application may be more CPU intensive. Having the right physical architecture promotes scalability.

The industry trend is away from populating each server with disk drives and toward externalizing all storage onto appliances. This approach is known as Network Attached Storage, which allows for scaling CPU and storage resources independently of each other. This has the added benefit of providing more efficient use of storage resources. Separating storage from processing permits employing redundant storage arrays. This increases availability by eliminating the need to stop server processing during backups and by providing failover capability.

Consolidating the storage function of multiple servers onto a single storage platform provides higher throughput, availability, and scalability. When multiple systems share the same storage platform, applications can be assigned resources in exact quantities, making it a more cost effective solution. Network storage also has the benefit of accelerating backup and replication, because it no longer consumes valuable CPU cycles. Multiple servers can share a single volume, which also helps keep data synchronized without the need to make multiple copies.

The biggest inhibitor to scalability in a J2EE-based Web service is typically at the EJB tier. Many tool vendors provide wizard-like code generation tools that allow you to simply select an EJB and automatically turn it into a Web service. J2EE has helped enterprises build and deploy Web services faster using a standards-based approach but has not helped architects think about the scalability of their applications. Ensuring that your Web service will scale is often a larger challenge that getting it to work in the first place. The typical Web service may update data only 10% of the time and spends most of its time reading and formatting data. It becomes crucial for reading data to be fast and efficient.

Many Java tutorials encourage developers to consider a three-tiered approach to developing applications (Figure 16.5). The presentation tier will be based on servlets or Java Server Pages (JSP) connecting to EJBs for business logic, which in turn connect to a database using JDBC. This approach allows developers to build reusable components and provides for a good separation of concerns. Wizard-style tools that generate Web services also use this model.

The separation of layers in the typical J2EE approach also has the side effect of introducing latency and can be the cause of performance problems. The latency between the client and the Web service are tied to a threading model that uses a thread per request. The allocated thread is blocked until the request re-

Figure 16.5
Typical J2EE
architecture

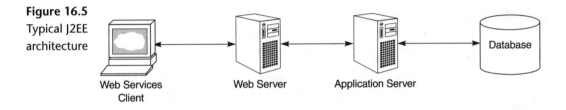

Web Services   Web Server   Application Server   Database
Client

turns. The connection between the presentation tier and the EJB tier typically contains housekeeping information, the majority of which is read-only. The communication between tiers uses Remote Method Invocation (RMI), which has significant overhead. You could consolidate tiers by using local interfaces, but this breaks scalability. The EJB tier also incurs latency overhead, by talking with the database to retrieve what most of the time is unchanged data.

The solution to reducing latency is to implement sound caching strategies and/or defer work that doesn't need to occur in real time and move it to a background process. By using a messaging approach (discussed later), a service has to wait only for the message to be recorded and not completed. This has the effect of removing all blocking. The best approach to avoid continuously rereading data is to employ a cache. Some developers make the mistake of caching frequently-used data in local, static, or global variables but do not exercise control of those variables' lifecycles.

If the majority of your requests are read-only, caching can satisfy the requests for data immediately and eliminate latency. Consider a user who wants to retrieve a stock quote for Sun Microsystems and Univision from the Flute Bank investment Web service. Caching allows the investment Web service to answer the request without connecting a backend quote provider, which allows the infrastructure to handle additional load. A caching strategy for Web services that use other Web services outside their organization may also save transaction fees.

Caching has several issues to consider. When developing your own approach, take into account the points in Table 16.5.

Clustering

A cluster is a logical group of servers that work together to provide more reliability and scalability than a single server could. A cluster will appear to its client as a single server. Scalability is increased because a cluster's capacity is not constrained to a single server. Many application environments support the ability to add

Table 16.5   Caching Considerations

Function	Description
Last image	The ability to snapshot rapidly changing information, such as stock quotes, that will be used for multiple services.
Request	The ability to snapshot dynamically created information that does not change frequently, such as news items for a particular stock.
Delta	The ability to snapshot data that represents changes at the individual message level, such as price upticks.
Events	The ability to allow applications to be notified of changes to underlying cached data.

resources to a cluster dynamically, to increase capacity. A cluster can also provide high availability, because a service deployed on multiple servers insulates a caller from localized failures. Many application servers provide clusterable interfaces to:

- HTTP sessions
- Enterprise Java Beans (EJB)
- Remote Method Invocation (RMI/IIOP)
- Java Messaging Service (JMS)
- JDBC Connections: connection pools and data sources

The typical Java Web service will be deployed on top of an application server. Many application servers themselves provide the ability to cluster instances of services across multiple machines. In this scenario, each instance of a service is referred to as a replica. Typically, the majority of newly developed Java-based services will use the EJB model. Many application servers generate a replica-aware stub. This process happens when an EJB is compiled using the EJB compiler.

Because EJBs use Remote Method Invocation (RMI) for their transport, the replica-aware stub appears as a normal RMI stub. The main difference is that the stub points to a collection of replicas. The stubs may use the Java Naming and Directory Interface (JNDI) to locate instances of objects, because a cluster stores its entire object collection in a replicated JNDI tree. Many stub implementations also contain a load-balancing algorithm that helps them determine the next object to bind to. This form of separation provides a transparent method for the caller to access objects in the cluster. When a stub fails in its operations, it will intercept any exceptions and retry the call using another replica. This provides transparent failover.

When designing a Web service, it is best to avoid making the service stateful. If your service uses a stateless session bean, a replica-aware stub can route the request to any server in the cluster. This is possible because a stateless bean holds zero state for the caller; the stub is free to select any server for which the bean has been deployed. If you must use a stateful bean, the stub may route the request to the original server and, optionally, to a secondary server, but this is application-server dependent.

Capacity planning of a cluster-based implementation also requires understanding the underlying network topology, including routers, switches, load balancers, firewalls, Web servers, and other network appliances. Basic Web service cluster architecture includes elements that handle availability and failover for the various tiers (Web tier, application tier, database tier and so on).

A simplistic implementation will most likely start with reducing failure between clients and the cluster itself, because this is usually where most failures occur. By separating logical tiers, it affords many application servers the ability to load-balance method calls to local EJBs. As previously discussed, in many implementations, a stub will usually bind to an EJB that is local over one that is remote. In a cluster, when a load to any individual server becomes unbalanced, it may sometimes be better to incur a remote method call than a local one, for performance purposes.

The network diagram in Figure 16.6 illustrates an ideal multi-tier cluster architecture. In this architecture, the Web tier may host static HTTP pages, Java Server Pages (JSP), or servlets. Its function is to serve as a client to clustered objects (EJBs) that reside on the application tier. Many application servers may also

Figure 16.6
Cluster
architecture

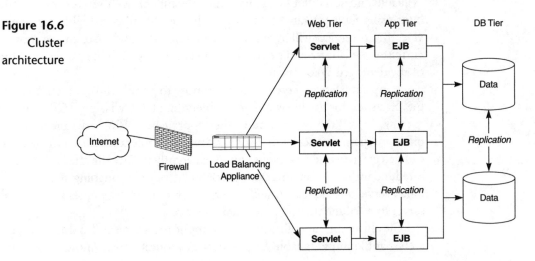

allow you to enable session replication, but this is not necessary in a well-planned Java Web services architecture.

The application tier holds instances of stateless session beans and other clusterable objects and handles the synchronization between servers in the cluster. Separating the Web and application tier provides the ability to load-balance on each method call but may eliminate optimization features of many EJB stub implementations.

This approach affords several advantages, including the potential to reduce hardware and software costs, improved server load balancing, higher availability, and better security. If a client must access a Web service exposed over HTTP, and the request is exclusively satisfied at this tier, you can reduce the number of servers running on the application tier and increase the number on the Web tier, producing better response times.

The above design also uses features built into many application servers, such as WebSphere, iPlanet, and others, to replicate state across members within a cluster. A multi-tier architecture creates fewer points of failure. If a server hosting a particular EJB fails, the servlet/JSP facilities are not affected. Introducing another level of separation also increases security. By providing separation, you can use firewall policies that allow access only to servlets/JSPs via HTTP.

> Fault Tolerance

The business community nowadays expects that a Web service to be not only available and scalable but highly fault tolerant. As Web services evolve, those built using fault tolerant technology will need to support highly complex services. Many services will be expected to handle thousands of clients or more concurrently. Reliability and performance become crucial to the success and brand of the deployed Web services.

Many application server vendors propose to handle this problem by clustering. Each vendor has its own scheme, including DNS aliasing, TCP connection routing, HTTP redirection, and other approaches. While this increases scalability and performance, it does not address fault tolerance for services. Clusters can detect when one server fails and transparently replace the affected server with a redundant one. This increases availability, but any ongoing requests of the failed server will be lost. A fault tolerant server migrates requests on the failed server to a redundant server and starts recovery.

The clustering capabilities of many application servers also do not appropriately handle unpredictable large bursts of requests. Even more important, in high-traffic Web services, requests for low-profit services can overwhelm the request for high-profit services or services for VIP customers. Requests for services, especially highly profitable ones, should remain available, even when the servers are heavily loaded. There is no standard way of providing higher priority for these services over low-profit requests.

To affect these two critical issues, a strategy must be developed that supports request determination and request migration.

Request Determination

A fault tolerant Web service must support two capabilities: checkpointing and recovery. Checkpointing snapshots client requests in an intermediate state and provides for logging. When a Web service fails, the recovery mechanism can read the log of outstanding requests on the failed service and continue processing on an active service.

Capturing the state of all requests could become expensive in terms of performance and therefore should be reserved for mission-critical requests. At minimum, transactional requests should have preference for logging over inquiry requests. Logging and recovery should be transparent to the requestor. The best way to accomplish this is by creating a dispatcher Web service, which takes requests on behalf of other services and dispatches them to the service best suited to handle them. Before sending the request, the dispatcher stores related information about the request and the selected target service in an internal map. The dispatcher also makes routing decisions and could either statically store all service endpoints or maintain its own routing table of services discovered via UDDI.

Request Migration

A Web service requires a mechanism that identifies service overload and/or failure. If the target Web service is inquiry, the dispatcher can send the request to another service for fulfillment. If the target Web service is transactional, the dispatcher may need to participate in a distributed transaction, store the resulting state, and return the results to the client. The client is typically not informed whether a request has committed successfully or of the reason for a failure. Sometimes clients may have to wait for a timeout to occur. Clients that implement retry logic may be charged for submitting the request multiple times, which should be avoided.

Migrating the request to another service requires intimate knowledge of service-specific details, such as the internal state, intermediate parameters, and so on. The intermediate processing state must be replicated to ensure fault tolerance of the service itself.

Fault tolerance assures that no request will be lost because of either server or service failure or overload, but it has a monetary cost and a potential performance cost as well. This approach requires care with implementation details.

> Grid Computing

Grid computing is a collection of computing resources that appear to the end user as one large system and provide a single point of access for performing tasks. Grid computing allows for hundreds, if not thousands, of services and their requests to run concurrently, without being concerned about where they execute.

Grid computing gives enterprises the equivalent of a supercomputer without adding one to their data centers. The ability to use computational power not only within your organization but also from third parties further increases availability.

In a grid, the computational unit of work is a *ticket.* When a service in the grid requests work, computational resources are assigned according to the share entitlement policy. If an administrator assigns 5,000 tickets to a grid, they will be distributed consistent with the entitlements of the share. Grid computing uses tickets to guarantee quality of service in a distributed environment.

Grid resource managers control execution requests submitted by services and schedule them on selected servers, based on resource management policies. Resource management policies are typically determined by a grid system administrator and monitored by the grid resource managers. Currently, four types of policies can be specified: shared, functional, override, and deadline.

Share-based policies allot a percentage of computing resources to all defined users and services in the grid. Share policies also take into consideration prior use of resources. If a service consumes more than its entitlement, the grid manager lowers the entitlement until its use meets the allocation. The grid manager also increases entitlement to compensate for underutilization.

A *functional* policy is analogous to the shared policy but does not penalize a service based on past usage. *Override* policies are typically assigned to a service by the grid administrator and allow for dynamic alteration of resource usage. Override polices are valid until either the administrator removes them or the service executes.

Finally, an administrator allocates a *deadl*ine policy by creating a large number of tickets for the service when it executes. This creates additional opportunities for the service to run ahead of others. The grid manager removes extra tickets from the service after completion.

Web services are about integrating services across distributed heterogeneous infrastructures and creating virtual organizations through resource sharing and service provider relationships. This form of dynamic collaboration should also extend to the infrastructure. The Globus project has defined a grid service that provides the functionality to create, name, and discover transient grid-service instances in a service-oriented manner (with location transparency and support for multiple bindings). This specification is referred to as the Open Grid Services Architecture (OGSA).

OGSA builds on constructs in the WSDL interface and describes lifetime management, change management, and notification. OGSA also supports authentication, authorization, delegation, and reliable invocation. Grid security is based digital certificates. Dynamic service creation is supported through a standard factory interface that all service creation services must implement.

Grid computing also has many fault tolerant characteristics. A distributed infrastructure that uses transient, stateful service instances should provide a method for reclaiming the service itself and the state associated with failed operations. In the Flute Bank example, the portfolio analysis Web service uses both internal and external resources. Unexpected termination of an analysis run also terminates all upstream and downstream services.

Figure 16.7 shows how Flute Bank uses the grid for its infrastructure. The portfolio analysis Web service invokes the create grid service in the second hosting environment. The create grid call likewise creates two factories, one that performs data mining on behalf of the portfolio analysis service and one for the storage reservation used to create the performance statements.

The factory specifies in its service description that mutual authentication of the calling service and the relevant factory must occur. Upon successful authentication, the factory creates a grid service instance. The mining service instance is provided with delegated proxy credentials that allow it to perform remote operations on behalf of the portfolio analysis service.

The mining service uses its proxy credentials to request data from two databases and keeps any intermediate result sets in local storage. The mining service also provides periodic status notifications to its client. The calling client also generates periodic keepalive requests to both grid service instances.

Figure 16.7
Web services using grid computing

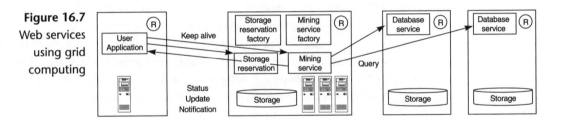

Grid computing may become a solution that will also translate to cheaper infrastructure costs. Unused CPU cycles on idle machines were previously unavailable. The typical infrastructure has more capacity than it uses at any point—it just isn't in the right place at the right time. Many enterprises throw hardware at the problem, filling the data center with bigger and faster servers. Others have upgraded their infrastructures to support Gigabit Ethernet, and some are even looking toward ten Gigabit in the future. Taking such an expensive approach will more than likely lead to expenses higher than the revenue gained.

For enterprises wishing to use Web services for exposing customer relationship management (CRM) systems, grid computing offers some unique solutions. The typical organization that purchases CRM products, such as Siebel or SalesForce.com, hope to integrate data distributed across sales, customer support, billing, shipping, accounts receivable, and other systems. Using a Web service as an integration layer for this has several advantages. Collecting customer data in a single place is a noble goal. Grid computing could massively parallel the customer data analysis and deliver this functionality to every point of customer access in the company. In this scenario, creating a CRM analytics Web service that uses grid computing could be powerful.

The components of the grid service can be used for many higher-level Web services Workflow services can be built, where multiple tasks can be executed on multiple resources. Fraud detection services can be created to analyze data across multiple services. Intrusion detection services can be built to look for use patterns, employing idle resources.

> Enabling Services

The success of Web services requires that many utility services become commoditized, so that each organization is not responsible for developing its own. Service providers will have to have these services in their catalog of offerings and are required for fee-based Web services. Let's say your organization has developed a strong portfolio-management Web service but wants to outsource its infrastructure to a Web services hosting provider. As the owner of the service, you will require the hosting provider to have services that support functionality such as billing, metering, provisioning, and security.

Table 16.6 lists some of the services your service provider should offer, either through local access or by remotely aggregating other providers' services. These enabling services could become business opportunities for the right software vendor. Enabling services are also part of the criteria for developing fee-based

Table 16.6   Enabling Services

Service	Description
Security	User authentication, authorization, encryption, signing, and nonrepudiation services
Key management	Support for digital certificates and other forms of public/private key infrastructures
Logging	A general-use logging service, where activities can be recorded and categorized (e.g. . critical, audit, diagnostic)
Time	The ability to make sure all services used are synchronized
Transformation	The ability to transform incoming and outgoing data between formats such as ebXML, EDI, industry-standard XML, and so on
User management	The ability to add, modify, suspend, and delete users and their attributes
Credit check	The ability to validate a user's creditworthiness
Payment	Support for capturing differing payment instruments (credit cards, checks, Pay Pal, etc.) and reconciling with accounts receivable
Currency	The ability support real-time currency conversion
Provisioning	The ability to associate user accounts with fee-per-use plans for particular services
Order management	Support for tracking service requests. This could include items such as purchase order handling. Should also handle requests that can be fulfilled asynchronously.
Fulfillment	A generic fulfillment service may be required. This could be a simple as delivering an email for electronic products to interfacing with shipping companies such as FedEx or DHL.
Bill presentment	Users of services are moving toward a household model, whereby charges from different parties are aggregated into a single statement. The bill presentment service could also become a fee-based service.

Web services. Fees are necessary to sell software as a service. Enabling services are the foundation of that goal.

> Final Checklist

In closing, we leave you with a checklist to consider when implementing Java-based Web services:

- Implement trust relationships wherever possible. Both the client and server portions of a Web service should be accountable to each other.

- Prefer the use of secure transports wherever possible. SSL or similar protocols can help prevent transaction snooping and are one step toward better security for your application. Client-side certificates with SSL provide encryption and additional security features over the wire, because each side certifies the keys used to encrypt the message.

- Develop secure components. One of the major techniques attackers use is buffer overflow. Make sure your component can handle a message correctly, even when the data is in an unrecognized format, and return an error response to the caller. A user of your Web service who realizes it is secure will most likely move to a new target.

- Consider your encryption, digital signature, and nonrepudiation requirements and take the appropriate steps early to select the right algorithms and approaches that will keep messages secure.

- Use appropriate configuration management practices. There are many great books on this topic. Learn from them and incorporate them into your application lifecycle. Managing configuration information becomes important if your Web service is registered with a public UDDI repository. Make sure appropriate steps have been taken to prevent attackers from changing the public data for your service, because this could also compromise the integrity of other services that rely on it. It could result in lost revenue if an attacker decides to raise your price, so that a competitor looks better. Also, make sure that only services you intend to be publicly accessible are configured in the repository.

- Use Web service proxy capabilities in your firewall. If you are using a robust, corporate-grade firewall, from vendors such as Cisco or Checkpoint, consider also using HTTP proxies with XML parsing capabilities. A proxy with parsing capability can validate each request to your Web service and drop messages that do not conform to the published Web services description.

- Conduct a business exercise on your service availability requirements and let the findings drive your architecture.

- Figure out whether you will charge for your service offerings in advance and establish the appropriate enabling services.

> Summary

We have discussed many topics not typically addressed in other forums. There is, of course, more to cover on high availability and other subjects we have discussed. This chapter covers the fundamentals, to a level sufficient for basic understanding and architecture planning.

Anywhere you turn, you can read articles on Web services and how they are ready for prime time. Web services will be used for a variety of purposes—some to increase the speed and/or quality of information flow, others to make it easier for producers and consumers to locate each other and conduct commerce. We hope this chapter conveys that putting together a robust, scalable Web service is not as easy as it looks. Figure 16.8 summarizes the requirements of Web services.

Figure 16.8
Web services
summary

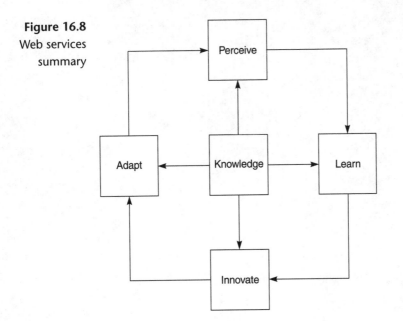

Today's economy requires agile, dynamic enterprises that can:

- *Perceive* what the market demands
- *Learn* from all forms of information, including books such as this
- *Innovate* new services and measure their results
- *Adapt* quickly, to bring solutions to the challenges we face

At the center of this model is *knowledge.* Web services are the empowering technology that will allow organizations to accomplish these goals.

Architects have a long road ahead of them. Keeping up with evolving standards, the balancing act of new technologies contrasted to legacy approaches, and the growing demand by the marketplace for enterprises to become agile require continuous improvement and planning for the next minute. The best way to deal with change is to prepare for it. Hopefully, we have accomplished our goal and made your journey a little easier . . .

Chapter

Future Standards

In Chapter 1, we provided an overview of the Web services technology stack. Subsequent chapters on SOAP, WSDL, and UDDI covered the standard (or de facto standard) technologies and specifications for the service messaging, service description, and service registration layers of the stack. For service security and service transactions layers, consensuses on standards are emerging and those standards were explained in the chapters on security and transactions, respectively. Other areas of the stack either lack standard specifications or have competing standards sponsored by different industry groups. In this chapter, we discuss a few specifications that are possible future standards for Web services.

In Chapter 5, we explained that there are different forms of service definition. WSDL is the specification that details how to describe a Web service's functional interface. It does not cover how the service can be composed into larger applications. Two emerging (and competing) specifications describe the mechanics of service composition: WSCI and BPEL4WS. We will introduce these two specifications in this chapter.

In Chapter 4, we explained that SOAP provides the foundation for Web service messaging and that the SOAP processing model's extensibility features permit more complex message exchange patterns. WS-Routing is a specification that exploits this SOAP feature and proposes the use of standardized SOAP headers to set the path of a SOAP message. We examine WS-Routing and its application in this chapter as well.

In the last section of this chapter, we briefly discuss two JSRs that will have a significant effect on Web services on the Java platform. JSR-181 proposes metadata meant to ease development and deployment of Web services on the J2EE platform. JSR-172 proposes an API for processing XML and conducting XML RPC from J2ME clients.

> **Web Service Composition**

Web service architecture emphasizes loose coupling between constituent services, and a Web service application is often considered a macro Web service—that is, an application formed by wiring together micro Web services. The terms *composition* and *choreography* in the context of Web services refer to wiring services together or wiring together fine-grained operations of a single Web service to create an executable business process. This is not by any means a new technique. "Integration servers" and workflow systems have been doing this for years, though using proprietary wiring languages and proprietary runtime environments.

The Need for Service Composition

Consider the simple example of a travel agency operation. A travel agency allows a consumer to book a travel reservation and then later confirm or cancel the booking. A travel agency Web service therefore must expose two operations: one to allow a consumer to send an itinerary to the service, and the other an operation that instructs the service to confirm the itinerary. As we saw in Chapter 5, WSDL provides an elegant way to describe the set of operations of this travel agency. It also provides a way for a program to invoke these operations by describing the transport (e.g., SOAP) bindings and the service location.

The *business process* of booking a trip involves executing operations in a *sequence*—the consumer first submits an itinerary, then confirms the reservation. But the WSDL description of the service does not provide this sequencing information—it lists the two operations but makes no attempt to describe the order in which they are invoked. WSDL also does not explain how the two operations can be *correlated*—that is, when operations exposed by WSDL are performed in sequence to accomplish a business function, the invocation of multiple operations is essentially stateless. Long-running, asynchronous business operations that involve multiple operations being invoked must somehow be performed as a part of the same conversation (state must be maintained by some mechanism). Correlation between the two operations is necessary, because they must be linked within the same business process context. In this example, the two operations are correlated by using the same itinerary: when confirming an itinerary, the consumer must provide a previously created itinerary ID as the context for confirmation.

Sequencing and correlation of operations to create a business process form the core of service composition. The description of how one or more operations of service(s) are composed to create a business process may not seem useful when considering a human playing the role of a service consumer. A person can infer the sequencing and correlation needs based on common sense and from the meaningful operation names used in WSDL. But what if we wanted machines to understand the business process? In such a situation, we must provide a means to describe the sequence of operations, and the system must provide a mechanism to maintain state across operations invoked.

Adding service composition description to WSDL is not sufficient for a complete description of a Web service. Additional information, such as legal contracts and agreements and quality of service descriptions, are also needed to fully automate the creation of a Web service application from constituent services. This third form of description is commonly called *collaboration* description. Figure 17.1 shows how the three forms of description can be depicted in layers of a service description stack.

At the very bottom of the service description stack is WSDL, which provides the service's entry points—its operations and messages. It also provides details on how the service can be invoked (SOAP bindings, address of the service, etc.) Service composition pertains to a description language used to describe the sequencing and correlation of activities. The collaboration protocol stack describes the legal agreements that must be in place between transacting businesses. Only the ebXML specification suite currently addresses this aspect of the description stack.

Now that we understand the role and position of Web service composition in the Web service description stack, we will examine two competing specifications that provide a language to describe service composition. Neither specification has been accepted as a standard by the industry, so we will describe the approach taken by each, without examining them in detail.

Web Service Choreography Interface (WSCI)

The WSCI (pronounced "whiskey") draft specification was created jointly by Sun Microsystems, BEA, and Intalio in June 2002. WSCI is an XML vocabulary that describes how Web services that participate in long-lived, stateful message exchanges can be wired together. WSCI builds on top of WSDL.

Figure 17.1
The service description stack

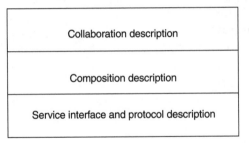

Collaboration description
Composition description
Service interface and protocol description

To illustrate WSCI's major features, we start with a simple example of Flute Bank's loan service. The WSDL document in Listing 17.1 is not complete, because we have not shown the types, message, or service elements. The WSDL shows that the Web service exposes three operations. We define an interface that defines the processes exposed to a Flute customer. The process of helping a customer get a loan is the sequential execution of three steps:

1. The consumer sends a loan application to Flute Bank. Based on the consumer's credit rating and financial worth, the bank returns a list of loan options.

2. Later, from the list of qualified loan options, the consumer sends a selected loan for closing.

3. Because Flute Bank takes five days to process loan closing, the consumer may send a cancel message to Flute to have the loan request canceled within five days of submitting the request.

Listing 17.1 WSDL fragment showing the functional interface for Flute Bank's loan service

```
<definitions>
    ...
    WSDL types, messages etc go here ...
    ...
    <portType name = "consumerLoan">

        <operation name = "applyForLoan">
            <input message = "tns:loanApplication"/>
            <output message = "tns:qualifiedLoans"/>
        </operation>

        <operation name = "selectLoan">
            <input message = "tns:loan"/>
            <output message = "tns:loanConfirmation"/>
        </operation>

        <operation name = "cancelSelectedLoan">
            <input message = "tns:loan"/>
        <output message = "tns:CancelNumber"/>
        </operation>

    </portType>

</definitions>
```

These three steps are exposed as operations in the WSDL for the loan service, but as we mentioned before, the WSDL interface does not provide any sequencing information. Listing 17.2 expands the loan service WSDL and illustrates the WSCI elements that combine the operations in the correct order.

WSCI elements appear within the WSDL definitions (root) element. The WSCI interface element is the container for process definitions. In the example, the Flute Bank loan service interacts with a consumer service and exposes one WSCI interface for the interaction between them. The interface defines a process—the process of requesting a loan. WSCI allows a Web service to have more than one interface element. The intent is to have one interface element contain processes relevant to a particular scenario of interaction.

For example, although not shown here, the loan service will be interacting with an external credit rating service to calculate the consumer's credit rating. The processes used for the interaction between the bank and the credit rating service can be contained in a different interface element.

Listing 17.2 WSDL elements that combine WSDL operations properly

```
<wsdl:definitions>
    <types> ... </types>
    <message> ... </message>
    <portType> ... </portType>
    ... other WSDL elements
    ...
<interface name = "LoanService">
    <process name = "ProcessLoan" instantiation = "message">

        <sequence>
            <action name = "receiveApplication"
                role = "tns:LoanService"
                operation = "tns:consumerLoan/applyForLoan">

                <call process = "tns:CheckCredit" />
            </action>

            <action name = "receiveConfirmation"
                role = "tns:LoanService "
                operation = "tns:consumerLoan/selectLoan">

            <correlate correlation="tns:loanCorrelation"/>
```

```
                </action>
            </sequence>
        </process>

    <process name = "CheckCredit" instantiation = "other">
            <action name = "checkCredit"
              role = "tns:LoanService"
              operation = "tns:CreditAgency/checkConsumerRating">
        </action>

    </process>
</interface>

<correlation name = "loanCorrelation"
    property = "tns:loanRequestNumber">
</correlation>

</wsdl:definitions>
```

A *process* is an activity that establishes a new context of execution. It models the observable behavior of the loan service with respect to a loan request. In the example, ProcessLoan is the process defined in WSCI that models the Web service's behavior for a loan application. Within the process element, we define all relevant information regarding the process: how it is started, which WSDL operations are part of it, the sequence of execution of the operations, and so on. The instantiation = message attribute signifies that the process is instantiated upon receipt of a message—that is, when the first action the process refers to is ready. In this case, the ProcessLoan process will be triggered when the loan service receives the receiveApplication message.

The ProcessLoan process consists of the execution of a set of actions in sequence. The WSCI process uses a sequence element to indicate that activities or actions declared in the element are to be executed in order. The action element identifies an atomic activity—one that performs a single operation. While performing the action, the Web service can represent more than one logical role; the role=loanService attribute specifies that the receiveApplication action is executed on behalf of the loanService role. ▷

Because Flute Bank has to check with an external agency for the consumer's credit rating, the receiveApplication action calls another process that does the credit check. The credit check process is modeled as a separate business process and is declared later in the WSCI as follows:

```
<process name = "CheckCredit" instantiation = "other">
    <action name = "checkCredit"
        role = "tns:LoanService"
        operation = "tns:CreditAgency/checkConsumerRating">
    </action>
</process>
```

In this case, the CheckCredit process has instantiation = "other", signifying that unlike the ProcessLoan process, which is instantiated by the receipt of a message, this process is started by an explicit call. Because receiveApplication is an atomic action, the call to check credit is done within the scope of the action. (Details of the external interface and the CheckCredit process are not shown.)

The second action declared in the ProcessLoan process is receiveConfirmation, which is declared much like the first action. One difference is that the second action declares a correlation element: <correlate correlation="tns:Loan-Correlation"/>. The correlation element provides the mechanism for modeling a conversation in WSCI. The correlation element in this example signifies that the receiveConfirmation action is to be correlated to the previous receive-Application action if the values of the loanRequestNumber fields in the two messages are the same.

The simple example above showed how WSCI proposes to handle sequencing and correlation aspects of Web service business interactions. WSCI can also sequence and correlate message exchanges between two or more Web services. Additionally, it specifies how exceptions (or faults) are to be handled. WSCI supports the Java notion of a recoverable fault (in Java, an application can catch an exception and determine an alternate execution path).

▷   A sequence is one way to represent a complex activity, which consists of multiple subactivities or an activity set. WSCI allows other types of complex activities to be modeled:

- The **all** complex activity can be used where activities in an activity set may be performed in any order.

- **choice** is used where one activity set is selected based on an event and that activity set is performed in order.

- An activity set can be performed for each iteration using the **foreach** complex activity.

- The **switch** complex activity selects an activity set based on a condition and performs that activity set in order.

Although WSCI does not define a mechanism to support transactional processes, it recognizes that activities may need to be processed within the scope of a transaction. In Chapter 14, we explained the BTP and WS-Transaction specifications. WSCI does not endorse any particular transactional specification—it provides support and guidelines for transactional activities within a process. WSCI also supports compensating activities for long-running transactions where locking may not be appropriate to provide transaction isolation (see Chapter 14 for long-running transactional properties).

Business Process Execution Language for Web Services (BPEL4WS)

Submitted jointly by IBM and Microsoft, BPEL4WS, or BPEL, is a specification that unifies and builds on the earlier XLANG (Microsoft) and WSFL (IBM) specifications for Web service composition.

Like WSCI, BPEL is an XML grammar to describe business processes that are a result of composing two or more Web services. BPEL defines two types of business processes: *abstract* and *executable*. Distinguishing between the two requires understanding the BPEL concept of a *business protocol*, which specifies the roles played by interacting businesses and the sequence of messages they must exchange to achieve a business function.

A BPEL process that shows only the details of the business protocol between two parties is called an *abstract business process*, because it does not define the private implementation view of the process. An *executable business process* shows not only the sequence of message exchanges but also the structure of each message, control flow, and so on. An executable business process in BPEL is like a WSCI business process. The BPEL construct that describes an abstract business process is a subset of the BPEL construct needed to describe an executable business process. BPEL, like WSCI, recognizes that WSDL supports only synchronous and uncorrelated asynchronous interactions between Web services. BPEL processes, like WSCI processes, represent long-running stateful (or correlated) conversations between Web services. In BPEL, a process can be conceptually thought of as sitting between interacting Web services (Figure 17.2). To a BPEL process, the participating Web services are partners in the business interaction.

The interaction between a BPEL process and the partner service is usually bilateral and often asynchronous. BPEL uses the notion of a serviceLink to model the peer-to-peer bilateral relationship between a process and its partners. A service link describes the roles played by the partner services and the message and portTypes used in the interactions.

We mentioned before that Web services (with WSDL) inherently do not provide the ability to describe or model long-running stateful message exchanges. In WSCI, correlation elements provide a mechanism to host stateful conversations over multiple WSDL operations. In a business process, messages exchanged be-

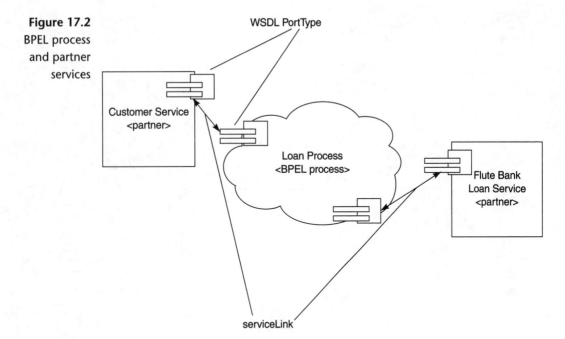

Figure 17.2
BPEL process
and partner
services

tween the partner services (a consumer and a loan service, for example) should provide the illusion of being exchanged directly between the partner services. In reality, the infrastructure that hosts the business process must provide a mechanism to correlate different message exchanges that form a part of the business process.

In WSCI, the correlation element instructs the runtime that activities are to be correlated based on the value of a particular field. In BPEL, a correlation set element correlates activities. Both these methods provide a declarative way to inform the runtime of how a set of activities in a process is to be correlated. Because the process must maintain state, the BPEL runtime must maintain all messages and intermediate data required for business logic. BPEL provides the container element to identify the messages and data that represent state information. All messages exchanged between the process and partners must be WSDL messages and should be identified in the container. Figure 17.3 illustrates the core elements of a BPEL process document.

BPEL also defines primitive and compound activities. Simple activities such as receive (receive input message for an operation), reply (provide a response to an invoked operation), and invoke can be considered steps in the business process. Compound activities are formed by structuring these primitive activities. For example, sequence allows contained activities to be performed in order, flow allows activities to be performed in parallel, and conditional branching is provided for by the switch activity.

Figure 17.3
Core elements
of a BPEL pro-
cess document

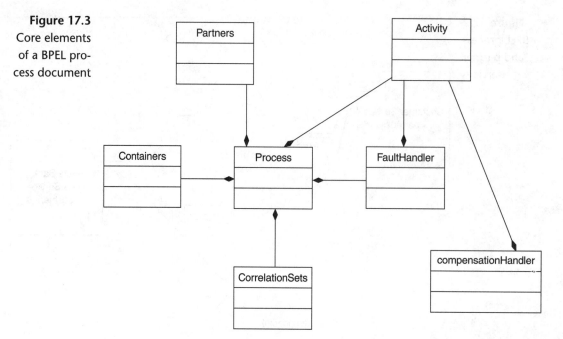

Unexpected errors during the execution of the process are handled by `fault-Handler` declarations. `FaultHandler` elements contain activities performed when declared faults are caught. Long-running processes that do not use locking for concurrency may need to use compensating activities to recover from errors. Compensating activities are an application-specific attempt to undo the partial effects of a business process. BPEL provides the `CompensationHandler` element to list compensating activities.

Figure 17.4 is taken from the BPEL 1.0 specification and illustrates the basic structure of a BPEL document.

Web Service Routing Protocol (WS-Routing) ▷

The WS-Routing protocol uses the SOAP-supplied extensibility mechanisms to define a protocol for guiding a SOAP message through a well-defined path. In

> ▷   The SOAP specification allows intermediary SOAP nodes in the processing path but does not address ordering of SOAP intermediaries in the message path. WS-Routing extends the SOAP intermediary concept by allowing the initial SOAP sender to specify the order in which SOAP intermediaries process the message en route to its destination (see Figure 17.5).

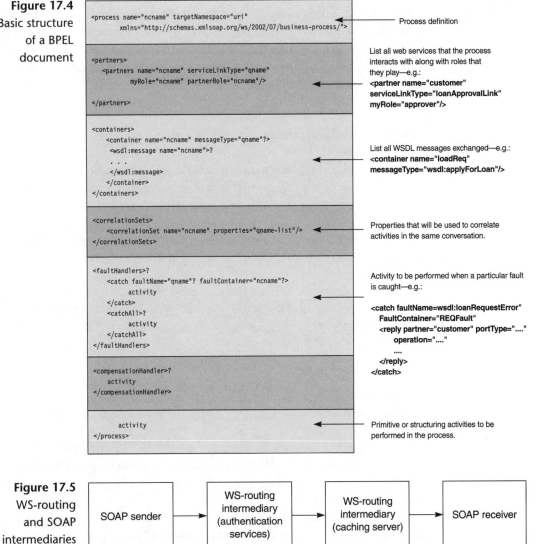

Figure 17.4
Basic structure
of a BPEL
document

```
<process name="ncname" targetNamespace="uri"
        xmlns="http://schemas.xmlsoap.org/ws/2002/07/business-process/">
```
→ Process definition

```
<partners>
   <partners name="ncname" serviceLinkType="qname"
           myRole="ncname" partnerRole="ncname"/>

</partners>
```
→ List all web services that the process
interacts with along with roles that
they play—e.g.:
**<partner name="customer"
serviceLinkType="loanApprovalLink"
myRole="approver"/>**

```
<containers>
   <container name="ncname" messageType="qname"?>
    <wsdl:message name="ncname">?
    . . .
    </wsdl:message>
    </container>
</containers>
```
→ List all WSDL messages exchanged—e.g.:
**<container name="loadReq"
messageType="wsdl:applyForLoan"/>**

```
<correlationSets>
   <correlationSet name="ncname" properties="qname-list"/>
</correlationSets>
```
→ Properties that will be used to correlate
activities in the same conversation.

```
<faultHandlers>?
   <catch faultName="qname"? faultContainer="ncname"?>
         activity
   </catch>
   <catchAll>?
         activity
   </catchAll>
</faultHandlers>
```
→ Activity to be performed when a particular fault
is caught—e.g.:

<catch faultName=wsdl:loanRequestError
 FaultContainer="REQFault"
 <reply partner="customer" portType="...."
   operation="...."
     ....
 </reply>
</catch>

```
<compensationHandler>?
   activity
</compensationHandler>
```

```
      activity
</process>
```
→ Primitive or structuring activities to be
performed in the process.

Figure 17.5
WS-routing
and SOAP
intermediaries

| SOAP sender | → | WS-routing intermediary (authentication services) | → | WS-routing intermediary (caching server) | → | SOAP receiver |

Chapter 4, we explained that the SOAP header, with its actor and mustUnderstand attributes, provides a foundation for vertical extensibility by allowing SOAP message header entries to be addressed to one or more SOAP intermediaries. However, SOAP does not have an inherent mechanism to specify the *order* in which intermediaries are to receive the message—that is, it does not define a message path. WS-Routing builds on top of SOAP and provides a means to specify a path for both one-way and request-response message exchange patterns. WS-Routing also describes the message path independently of the underlying protocol.

WS-Routing defines a single SOAP header entry to describe the forward (usually the SOAP request) message path and, optionally, the reverse (response) message path. Although the message originator may specify a particular path, WS-Routing allows WS-Routing intermediaries to add additional nodes to the path, thereby altering the original path:

```
<env:Envelope
    xmlns:env="http://schemas.xmlsoap.org/soap/envelope/">
    <env:Header>
        <wsr:path xmlns:wsr="http://schemas.xmlsoap.org/rp/">
            <wsr:action>http://www.flute.com/payeeDetails</wsr:action>
            <wsr:to>soap://www.flute.com/billPay</wsr:to>
            <wsr:fwd>
                <wsr:via>soap://www.authenticator.flute.com</wsr:via>
                <wsr:via>soap://www.cache.flute.com</wsr:via>
            </wsr:fwd>
            <wsr:from>mailto:joe@flute.com</wsr:from>
            <mwsr:id>uuid:84b9f5d0-33fb-4a81-b02b-5b760641c1d6</wsr:id>
        </wsr:path>
    </env:Header>
    <env:Body>
        ...
    </env:Body>
</env:Envelope>
```

The above SOAP message fragment shows how WS-Routing proposes to define the message path. A SOAP message may contain only one header entry for WS-Routing. All WS-Routing elements belong to the namespace `http://schemas.xmlsoap.org/rp`.

A WS-Routing entry starts with the `path` element, which is a container for other WS-Routing elements that detail the message path. The `action` element, much like the `SOAPAction` HTTP header, shows the intent of the WS-Routing message. The `action` element is required; its value is a URI. The value of the `action` element is determined by the original SOAP sender and cannot be change en route. If the message is a SOAP fault message, the value of the `action` element must be `http://schemas.xmlsoap.org/soap/fault`. The `to` element identifies the ultimate SOAP receiver. The value of the `to` element is determined by the original sender and cannot be modified en route. ▷

The `fwd` element describes the forward message path and lists the WS-Routing intermediaries in message path order. The forward path can be set by the initial sender and then modified as the message moves along the path. The `via` elements identify soap intermediaries using an absolute URI. In the above example, two intermediaries are identified. First, the message goes to the authenticator (presumably for authentication services), then to the cache server (to short-circuit the path by providing previously cached values of the result).

The from element value is a URI that identifies the original sender. The specification recommends a URI of the form "mailto:...." The id element provides a unique identifier in the form of a URI. The value if the id element may be used to correlate the message with other related messages (e.g., if correlation is needed between a faulty message and the corresponding fault message)

Protocol Bindings

WS-Routing specifies bindings to HTTP, TCP, and UDP. TCP and UDP require DIME (Direct Internet Message Encapsulation), a binary encapsulation mechanism for encapsulating the WS-Routing message. TCP and UDP bindings are not discussed in this section.

When using WS-Routing over HTTP, the mustUnderstand header attribute must be set to true and the SOAP actor attribute must be http://schemas.xmlsoap.org/soap/actor/next, so that all SOAP intermediaries either respect the semantic of the WS-Routing header or are forced to throw a SOAP fault.

When sending a WS-Routing SOAP message, the value of the Request-URI must be the URI of the next node in the message path. That is, if the SOAP message is to be routed via a WS-Routing intermediary, the value of the Request-URI should be the URI of the first intermediary listed in the fwd element. If there are no intermediaries in the path, the Request-URI must have the value of the to element. Also, as mentioned earlier, the value of the SOAPAction header must be the same as the value of the action element.

▷ **The soap URI**

You may have noticed that the URI for the **via** element value in the above example uses a different URI scheme. WS-Routing proposes a new "soap URI" scheme, which has not yet been registered according to the IETF rules for new URI schemes. The default protocol used for retrieving "soap:" URIs is WS-Routing.

The general syntax is

"soap:" "//" host [":" port] [abs_path [";" up] ["?" query]]

where up (underlying protocol) is either "tcp" or "udp" (default is "tcp"). The default port is not specified.

The simple example we used illustrated some of the basic concepts of WS-Routing. A mechanism to specify a message path for both SOAP requests and responses allows us to take advantage of a truly distributed architecture—each SOAP intermediary along the path can use its resources to provide some value-added service.

For example, while the sending and destination SOAP nodes provide the core business functionality, an intermediary can provide automatic authentication and authorization services. SOAP response messages that contain cacheable data can be routed to caching servers that cache responses for faster response to SOAP requests. In this context, WS-Routing is to be looked upon as a building block on which other specifications can rely on for providing value-added messaging patterns. Currently, the WS-Routing specification has not been endorsed or accepted as a routing standard by other industry players—IBM and Sun, for example, do not support WS-Routing.

Web Services Metadata for the Java Platform (JSR-181)

The goal of JSR-181, initiated by BEA and supported by Sun Microsystems, is to simplify the process for developing and deploying Web services on the J2EE platform. JSR-181 builds on JSR-175, which proposes a metadata facility for the Java platform. Development and deployment tools, precompilers, and so on have been using different, nonstandard annotations to classes and methods so that these tools and libraries can provide some special processing to class or source files. In the J2EE platform, XML deployment descriptors, special method-name prefixes and method names, and so on are used to deploy and compile EJBs. JSR-181 is a proposal to create metadata specific to Web services on the J2EE platform. The goal of the metadata is to make it easier for a Java developer to develop and deploy synchronous and asynchronous Web services.

J2ME Web Services Specification (JSR-172)

The JAX* APIs we have discussed in this book provide a Java application the ability to process XML and add the functionality of XML RPC and XML messaging to the Java platform. For J2ME-based applications, additional considerations, such as limited device configurations, memory, and processing power, limit the use of the JAXP and JAXM APIs built for J2SE. Applications running on J2ME-based wireless devices form a large part of the next-generation Web service consumer base, enabling enterprise services to be accessed by consumers who use J2ME devices. JSR-172 proposes two optional packages for J2ME that will add the following functionality:

- XML parsing and processing capabilities
- Accessibility to Web services from CLDC and CDC profiles (i.e., provide J2ME devices the capability to become service consumers)

JSR-172 proposes that a strict subset of JAXP 1.2 be used for XML processing API on J2ME devices. To allow for the maximum number of configurations, the aim of this specification is to use CLDC 1.0 as the lowest common platform for implementation and to limit the size of the JAXP API subset to 25 KB.

JSR-172 JAXP subset differs from the JAXP 1.2 specification in that it requires the subset to support only XML namespaces, predefined XML entity references, UTF-8 and UTF-16 encoding, and SAX 2.0 API. It further requires that the subset not support DOM (neither 1.0 nor 2.0), SAX 1.0 APIs, or XSLT. The subset may optionally support (within the SAX 2.0 API) validation against DTD's.

To provide J2ME device application access to Web services, JSR-172 also proposes a separate download package that provides a subset of the capabilities of the JAX-RPC 1.0 package. The optional package requires that J2ME clients only support the static stub model of invocation (see Chapter 10 for details on client invocation models). The generated stubs must use document-style and literal-use (doc/literal) operation (Chapter 4 explains the use of doc/rpc style and encoded/literal use).

The API subset should support the following data types:

- Boolean
- Byte
- Short
- Int
- Long
- String
- Value types
- Arrays of primitive and value types
- QName
- XML Structs and complex types (mapped to Java Beans as per JAX-RPC mappings, but with a few limitations)

Finally, it must be noted that the J2ME API subset for Web services is meant only for service consumers, not for service providers.

▷ Summary

This chapter provides an overview of a few future standards that affect Web services and the Java platform.

The WSDL-based Web service description does not provide the ability to define asynchronous, long-running interactions between Web services. Web service composition is a means to define business processes that involve Web services. WSCI and BPEL4WS are two competing specifications for Web service composition.

SOAP is designed to be a basic messaging infrastructure protocol for Web services and to be extended so that more complex message exchange patterns can be layered on top of it. One such pattern is message routing, where a SOAP message is directed along a defined path before reaching its destination. WS-Routing takes advantage of the SOAP header processing model and proposes a simple specification that enables SOAP message routing.

Finally, we looked at two JSRs that will prove useful for Web services on the Java platform. AML descriptor files, special method names, and so on are slowly complicating the development and deployment of Web services on the J2EE platform. The Web services metadata JSR (JSR-181) proposes a new annotation for Java classes, so that Web service tools will be able to develop and deploy Java Web services more easily.

Bringing Web services to J2ME is an important step in bringing enterprise services to mobile devices. JSR-172 proposes a lightweight J2ME Web services model that addresses XML processing and XML RPC.

Appendix 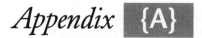 {A}

XML Schema

XML Schema definition language (XSD) is referenced throughout this book. XML Schema is a widely accepted mechanism for defining business rules for XML instance documents. Most Web service specifications—from SOAP to WSDL to BTP—use XML Schema to define their XML message vocabularies. A working knowledge of XML schema is a prerequisite to fully understanding the different Web service specifications. This appendix serves as a quick tutorial and also as a quick reference for the most common XML Schema elements.

The XML used to represent a list of Flute Bank employees' data might look like Listing A.1.

Listing A.1 employeeList XML

```
<?xml version="1.0" encoding="UTF-8"?>
<employeeList>
    <employee type="contract">
        <employee_id>75868</employee_id>
        <name>
            <first_name>John</first_name>
            <last_name>Doe</last_name>
        </name>
        <extn>27304</extn>
        <dept>1104332089</dept>
        <email>john.doe@flute.com</email>
    </employee>
/employeeList>
```

While this XML is well formed—that is, without syntax errors—how does an XML parser at Flute know that this represents an employee, as defined by Flute Bank's business? For example, Flute Bank's business rules may state that

1. A list of Flute Bank employees consists of zero or more employees and that an employee is described fully by providing the employee's ID, name, phone extension, department, and email.

2. All employees must be classified as either "permanent" or "contract."

3. Department numbers within the bank are ten digits and are of the form "999–999–9999".

4. Employee IDs are nonnegative integers between 1 and 100,000.

These rules can be broadly classified into two categories: those that pertain to the XML structure and those that pertain to the datatypes and allowed values of individual elements and attributes. XML Schema is an XML grammar and vocabulary used to define and describe the allowed structure, datatypes, and values of an XML document (often called the XML *instance* document).

A schema is a declarative way to enforce business rules—that is, once declared, the declared rules are enforced not by application code but by standard infrastructure code. Infrastructure elements that parse and validate instance documents against a schema are called *validating parsers.* An organization or business consortium creates a schema and publishes the schema to a known location. The schema then becomes a contract between transacting parties.

For example, an invoice schema between Flute Bank and its suppliers is an agreement on how invoice-related data will be structured and what the contents of an invoice mean. Once the schema is defined and associated with an XML instance document, a validating parser is able to automatically ensure that the XML document is both well formed and valid (conforms to business rules defined in the schema document) (see Figure A.1). Without XML schemas, the conformity of an XML instance document to business rules must be checked programmatically in every application. ▷

XML schemas have other advantages as well: they provide the metadata for automatic GUI generation, and visual editors (e.g., XML Spy) use them to create smart editors for XML documents, allowing only valid values to be input into an XML document.

▷ Although not depicted in the Figure A.1, the XML schema for a Flute Bank employee is also an XML document. The vocabulary and grammar of all schema documents are defined in the "schema of schemas": XMLSchema .xsd. All schemas are validated against the schema of schemas, just as the employee XML instance is validated against the employee XML schema. The "schema of schemas" is further explained in the XML Schema "Namespaces" section later in this chapter.

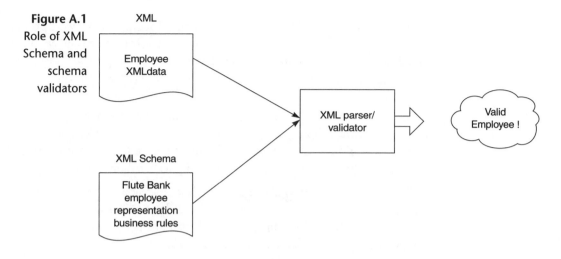

Figure A.1
Role of XML
Schema and
schema
validators

The significance of XML Schema to Web services is this: as you have seen in the chapters on SOAP, transactions, and WSDL, all Web service specifications use XML. XML Schema is the most widely adopted validity-constraint mechanism for XML, and a few (not all) Web-service-related specifications require it as the mechanism. ▷

▷ Document Type Definition

Before XML Schema came into existence in May 2001, XML documents were described using an alternate form: document type definition (DTD). DTD came into existence before XML was used for RPCs and before XML was used to represent

> ▷ From the 0.6 draft of the IETF XML guidelines document *(www.ietf.org/internet-drafts/draft-hollenbeck-ietf-xml-guidelines-06.txt):*
>
> "There is ongoing discussion (and controversy) within the XML community on the use and applicability of various validity constraint mechanisms. The choice of tool depends on the needs for extensibility or for a formal language and mechanism for constraining permissible values and validating adherence to the constraints."
>
> Other popular validity constraint mechanisms are RELAX NG (ISO/IEC Document Schema Definition Language) and Schematron.

complex business data. DTDs were used to describe documents that were primarily for human consumption (as opposed to machine consumption) and are therefore inadequate to describe the complex data structures used in Web services. The main deficiencies of DTDs in comparison to XML Schema are:

- DTDs predated XML namespaces and cannot handle namespaces well. Namespaces are a simple but powerful feature that enable XML documents written by multiple autonomous parties to be combined without the fear of element or attribute name clashes (think of package names in Java).

- DTDs were defined primarily to describe human-readable XML documents and not XML that represents computational data. DTDs therefore lack the ability to describe simple constraints, such as that a person's age should have a nonnegative integer value between 1 and 150, for example. Some specific data type limitations of DTDs are:

  - DTDs support approximately 10 datatypes, whereas XML Schema supports close to 45.
  - DTDs do not support nil values.
  - DTDs cannot express unique value constraints on just any element value (no concept of a "key" element).
  - DTDs are limited in describing the order of child elements.
  - DTDs cannot be used to derive new types (akin to extending a Java class) for a new type definition.

- Unlike the XML documents they describe, DTDs follow an alternate syntax. This makes it unnecessarily difficult for tool vendors to create tools and for programmers to use XML effectively. ▷

A brief introduction to DTD is in order. Figure A.2 shows what the DTD for Listing A.1 looks like.

The DTD for `employeeList` XML starts out by identifying itself as such: the first entry, `!DOCTYPE employeeList`, identifies the document as the DTD (document type) for the root element `employeeList`. Subsequent entries inform the parser that the `employeeList` element may contain zero or more `employee` ele-

▷ **Validating Parsers**

All examples in this appendix were verified using the Apache Xerces validating parser, which comes with Sun's Java Web Service Developer Pack 1.0 (Java WSDP) . Microsoft MSXML is another popular parser. Chapter 9 discusses using Java WSDP for parsing documents.

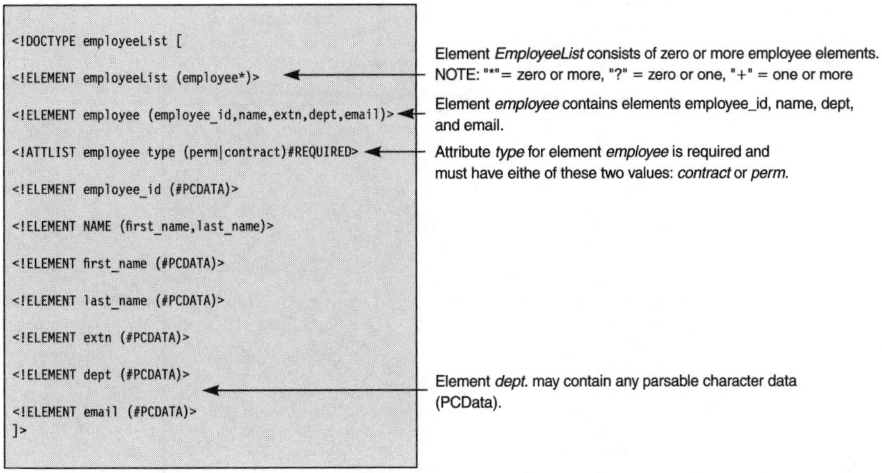

Figure A.2
Simple DTD
for the
employeeList
document

```
<!DOCTYPE employeeList [

<!ELEMENT employeeList (employee*)>

<!ELEMENT employee (employee_id,name,extn,dept,email)>

<!ATTLIST employee type (perm|contract)#REQUIRED>

<!ELEMENT employee_id (#PCDATA)>

<!ELEMENT NAME (first_name,last_name)>

<!ELEMENT first_name (#PCDATA)>

<!ELEMENT last_name (#PCDATA)>

<!ELEMENT extn (#PCDATA)>

<!ELEMENT dept (#PCDATA)>

<!ELEMENT email (#PCDATA)>
]>
```

Element *EmployeeList* consists of zero or more employee elements.
NOTE: "*"= zero or more, "?" = zero or one, "+" = one or more

Element *employee* contains elements employee_id, name, dept, and email.

Attribute *type* for element *employee* is required and must have eithe of these two values: *contract* or *perm.*

Element *dept.* may contain any parsable character data (PCData).

ments and that each employee element must contain the employee_id, name, extn, and dept elements, in that order.

The !ATTLIST statement enforces the rule that the employee element must have a type attribute with only two allowable values, perm or contract. The name element has a description similar to the employee element, in that it consists of two other elements: first_name and last_name. The statement !ELEMENT email (#PCDATA) signifies that the email element can have any parsable character data (a string value) (as explained earlier, DTDs cannot be used to describe many of the datatypes used in programming languages).

While this DTD expresses some of Flute Bank's business rules, it is inadequate to represent more complex business rules. For example, it is inadequate to express that a department number must be the format "XXX-XXX-XXXX", that all valid telephone extensions in Flute Bank are five digits, and that employee IDs range from 1 to 100,000. The limitations of DTDs in the context of describing database and object-oriented programming datatypes and constraints necessitated a new, XML-based description specification: XML Schema definition language.

> XML Schema

Figure A.3 shows the XML schema for the Flute employee list XML from Listing A.1. The first thing you notice is that, compared with the DTD in Figure A.2, the XML schema is much longer. The reason is twofold: First, XML Schema, being XML, is more verbose. Second, XML Schema defines the business rules for a

```
</xml version="1.0" encoding="UTF-8"?>
<xsd:schema xmlns:xsd="http://www.w3.org/2001/XMLSchema          ◄──────  Namespace declaration
       targetNamespace="http://www.flute.com"
       xmlns="http://www.flute.com">

<xsd:element name="employeeList">  ◄───────────────────────────────────  <!Element employeeList (employee*)>
    <xsd:complexType>
      <xsd:sequence>
        <xsd:element ref="employee" minOccurs="1" maxOccurs="unbounded"/>
      </xsd:sequence>
    </xsd:complexType>
</xsd:element>

<xsd:element name="employee">  ◄──────────────────────────────────────  <!ELEMENT employee (employee_id,name,extn,dept, email)>
  <xsd:complexType>
    <xsd:sequence>
      <xsd:element ref="employee_id" minOccurs="1" maxOccurs="1"/>
      <xsd:element ref="name" minOccurs="1" maxOccurs="1"/>
      <xsd:element ref="extn" minOccurs="1" maxOccurs="1"/>
      <xsd:element ref="dept" minOccurs="1" maxOccurs="1"/>
      <xsd:element ref="email" minOccurs="1" maxOccurs="1"/>
    </xsd:sequence>
    <xsd:attributeGroup ref="employeeAttribute"/>
  </xsd:complexType>
</xsd:element>

<xsd:element name="name">  ◄───────────────────────────────────────────  <!ELEMENT name (first_name,last_name)>
  <xsd:complexType>
    <xsd:sequence>
      <xsd:element ref="first_name" minOccurs="1" maxOccurs="1"/>
      <xsd:element ref="last_name" minOccurs="1" maxOccurs="1"/>
    </xsd:sequence>
  </xsd:complexType>
</xsd:element>

<xsd:element name="employee_id">  ◄──────────────────────────────────────  employee_id must be an integer between 1 and
  <xsd:simpleType>                                                          100,000.
  <xsd:restriction base="xsd:int">
    <xsd:minInclusive value="1"/>
    <xsd:maxInclusive value="100000"/>
  </xsd:restriction>
  </xsd:simpleType>
</xsd:element>

<xsd:element name="first_name" type="xsd:string"/>◄──────────────────────  <!ELEMENT first_name (PCDATA)>

<xsd:element name="last_name" type="xsd:string"/>

<xsd:element name="email" type="xsd:string"/>◄───────────────────────────  <!ELEMENT email (PCDATA)>

<xsd:element name="dept" >  ◄─────────────────────────────────────────────  Department must be specified in the form:
  <xsd:simpleType>                                                          "999-999-9999".
    <xsd:restriction base="xsd:string">

      <xsd:pattern value="[0-9]{3}-[0-9]{3}-[0-9]{4}"/>
    </xsd:restriction>
  </xsd:simpleType>
</xsd:element>

<xsd:element name="extn">  ◄──────────────────────────────────────────────  Extension must be specified in the form "99999"
  <xsd:simpleType>                                                          (String consisting of five digits).
  <xsd:restriction base="xsd:string">
      <xsd:pattern value="[0-9]{5}"/>
  </xsd:restriction>
  </xsd:simpleType>
</xsd:element>

<xsd:attributeGroup name="employeeAttribute">◄────────────────────────────  <!ATTLIST employee type (perm|contract)
  <xsd:attribute name="type"  use="required" >                              #REQUIRED>
    <xsd:simpleType>
      <xsd:restriction base="xsd:string">
        <xsd:enumerator value="contract"/>
```

Flute employee much more comprehensively than the DTD. Although it is long, it is easy to understand when broken down into smaller parts. We will introduce the different parts one by one and, where appropriate, map the schema structure to the elements in the `employeeList` DTD.

Namespaces

In the schema for the `employeeList` XML, we used a vocabulary that had particular meaning in the context. The vocabulary used to construct the schema (e.g., element, attribute, restriction, simpleType, complexType, etc.) has specific meanings in an XML Schema document. This vocabulary is defined in a context, or a namespace: `http://www.w3.org/2001/XMLSchema`.

By associating these words with a namespace, we are qualifying the names and, in the process, ensuring no clashes arise between the same words used in different contexts. A Java programmer can think of a namespace as analogous to a package name. The same class name can be used in a piece of Java code, but only if it is qualified by the package name to which it belongs.

Before using a qualified name in a document, a namespace must be declared:

```
xmlns:xsd="http://www.w3.org/2001/XMLSchema"
```

Read this as "XML namespace qualifier 'xsd' represents namespace 'http://www.w3.org/2001/XMLSchema.'" In declaring this namespace, we are essentially saying that all elements and attributes qualified with "xsd" are defined in the namespace *http://www.w3.org/2001/XMLSchema*. A name is qualified by using the declared qualifier as a prefix. For example, the word schema is qualified as `xsd:schema`. This means that the element schema has been defined in the namespace represented by the xsd qualifier. The XML Schema namespace is also called the "schema of schemas," because it defines all schema definition elements and attributes.

The `employeeList` schema also declares a `targetNamespace` and a default namespace. The default namespace is in effect when elements are referred to without a qualifier. The default namespace is declared without a namespace qualifier (which was xsd in the previous example):

```
<xsd:schema  xmlns:xsd="http://www.w3.org/2001/XMLSchema"
            targetNamespace="http://www.flute.com"
            xmlns="http://www.flute.com">
...
<xsd:element  ref="employee" minOccurs="1" maxOccurs="1"/>
```

Figure A.4

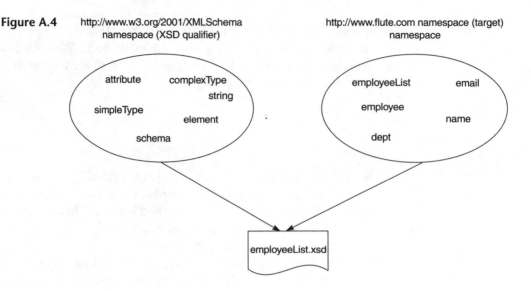

In Figure A.3 the default namespace applies to elements such as employee, employeeList, and dept. In the code above, ref="employee" refers to an employee element declared in the default namespace (http://www.flute.com).

The targetNamespace declaration signifies that the vocabulary defined in this schema document (employee, first_name, email, dept, extn, etc.) belong to the http://www.flute.com namespace (Figure A.4). The target namespace is the one to which the employeeList schema elements are defined. In the example, we have *elected* to associate the default namespace with the target namespace elements—that is, to refer to the target namespace elements without a qualifier. The target namespace value is significant because, when an instance document *uses* the elements *declared* in the schema document, those element declarations must point to the target namespace value. (Figure A.5, in the "Bringing It All Together" section, illustrates this.). ▷

▷ A schema need not define elements in a namespace (i.e., it's okay to have a schema with no targetNamespace attribute). Instance documents that use elements defined without a namespace may use the noNamespace-Schema attribute to provide the process with the schema's location:

xsi:noNamespaceSchemaLocation="employee.xsd"

Simple Types

Elements such as first_name and email have simple datatype values (e.g. strings). These types (string, int, etc.), which are prefixed with the xsd qualifier, are called *built-in* types, because they are defined in the schema of schemas. To declare built-in XML schema simple types in the employeeList XML schema, the schema declaration is straightforward:

```
<xsd:element name="name" type="type" minOccurs="int" maxOccurs="int"/>
```

For example:

```
<xsd:element name="email" type="xsd:string"/ ▷
```

minOccurs and maxOccurs constraints determine how many times that particular element may be repeated in the document. The default value of minOccurs and maxOccurs is "1". A special value of unbounded is used to indicate that a particular element may repeat any number of times. ▷▷

Extending Simple Types

The Flute Bank business rules state that all employee_id values must be between 1 and 100,000. An element declaration such as <xsd:element name="employee_id" type="xsd:int"/> enforces the rule only partially: all employee IDs are integer values. To add further constraints on the declaration, XML Schema allows new types to be defined by extending built-in types, using the simpleType element:

```
<xsd:element name="employee_id">
  <xsd:simpleType>
  <xsd:restriction base="xsd:int">
      <xsd:minInclusive value="1"/>
      <xsd:maxInclusive value="100000"/>
  </xsd:restriction>
```

▷   In a schema, elements and attributes are *declared*, and types are *defined*.

▷▷   Chapter 10 provides mapping between common built-in datatypes and Java types.

```
            </xsd:simpleType>
        </xsd:element>
```

In the above XML fragment, the employee_id element is declared with a new simple type that is a restriction on the base built-in type int. The restrictions are added to the employee_id element on top of the built-in type restriction of integers and are declared using *facets*. In this example, the facets added to the int type are minInclusive and maxInclusive. The general syntax for a simpleType is

```
<xsd:simpleType>
        <xsd:restriction base="simple-type">
              <xsd:facet value="value"/>
              <xsd:facet value="value"/>
              ...
        </xsd:restriction>
    </xsd:simpleType>
```

When a restriction element contains multiple facets, they are ORed if they are enumeration or pattern facets. All other facets are ANDed.

The example below shows how a simple type is created by applying a pattern facet to a string datatype. The pattern expression is a regular expression.

```
<xsd:element name="dept">
  <xsd:simpleType>
    <xsd:restriction base="xsd:string">

        <xsd:pattern value="[0–9]{3}-[0–9]{3}-[0–9]{4}"/>
    </xsd:restriction>
  </xsd:simpleType>
</xsd:element>
```

Table A.1 shows a few facets that can be used with different built-in types to create new simpleTypes.

Complex Types

A complex data structure is modeled with a complexType element. A type created with complexType maps to a Java bean. A complex type can contain other sub-elements and can have attributes (simpleTypes can have neither). In the following code, employee is a complex type consisting of several elements and one attribute:

Table A.1   Facets

Built-in type	Facet
String, all number types	enumeration

Example

```
<xsd:element name=stateCode
<xsd:simpleType>
    <xsd:restriction base="xsd:string">
        <xsd:enumeration value="CA"/>
        <xsd:enumeration value="MA"/>
    </xsd:restriction>
</xsd:simpleType>
</xsd:element name=employeeType
```

stateCode can have only values "CA" or "MA"

Built-in type	Facet
String, token, normalized String	length, minLength, maxLength pattern

Example

```
<xsd:element name=stateCode
<xsd:simpleType>
    <xsd:restriction base="xsd:string">
        <xsd:minLength value="2"/>
        <xsd:maxLength value="2"/>
    </xsd:restriction>
</xsd:simpleType>
</xsd:element name=employeeType
```

stateCode length = 2 characters

```
<xsd:element name="extn">
    <xsd:simpleType>
    <xsd:restriction base="xsd:string">
        <xsd:pattern value="[0–9]{5}"/>
    </xsd:restriction>
    </xsd:simpleType>
</xsd:element>
```

extn is a sequence of five digits. (Any regular expression can be used.)

(continued)

Table A.2   Facets (Cont'd)

Built-in type	Facet
Most numeric types	maxInclusive, minInclusive, maxExclusive, minExclusive

Example

```
<xsd:element name="employee_id">
  <xsd:simpleType>
  <xsd:restriction base="xsd:int">
      <xsd:minInclusive value="1"/>
      <xsd:maxInclusive value="100000"/>
  </xsd:restriction>
  </xsd:simpleType>
</xsd:element>
```

employee_id is an integer between 0 and 100,000.

Built-in type	Facet
Decimal	totalDigits, fractionalDigits

Example

```
<xsd:element name="amount">
  <xsd:simpleType>
  <xsd:restriction base="xsd:decimal">
      <xsd:totalDigits value="10"/>
      <xsd:fractionDigits value="2"/>
  </xsd:restriction>
  </xsd:simpleType>
</xsd:element>
```

```
<xsd:element name="employee">
    <xsd:complexType>
      <xsd:sequence>
          <xsd:element ref="employee_id" minOccurs="1" maxOccurs="1"/>
          <xsd:element ref="name" minOccurs="1" maxOccurs="1"/>
          <xsd:element ref="extn" minOccurs="1" maxOccurs="1"/>
          <xsd:element ref="dept" minOccurs="1" maxOccurs="1"/>
```

```
            <xsd:element ref="email" minOccurs="1" maxOccurs="1"/>
        </xsd:sequence>
        <xsd:attributeGroup ref="employeeAttribute"/>
    </xsd:complexType>
</xsd:element>
```

This example ensures that an employee instance XML will contain elements for employee ID, name, extension, department, and email. You may note that these datatypes of subelements are not defined in the complex type element. Instead, we have chosen to define the subtypes elsewhere in the document and only refer to those definitions here.

For example, `<xsd:element ref="employee_id" minOccurs="1" maxOccurs="1"/>` uses a reference to the `employee_id` element, which is of a `simpleType` defined later in the schema. This is not the only way in which a complex type can be defined. It is also possible to define a `simpleType` inline:

```
<xsd:element name="employee">
    <xsd:complexType>
        <xsd:sequence>
            <xsd:element name="employee_id" minOccurs="1" maxOccurs="1"/>
                <xsd:simpleType>

                    ...

                </ xsd:simpleType>
            <xsd:element>
            <xsd:element ref="name" minOccurs="1" maxOccurs="1"/>
            <xsd:element ref="extn" minOccurs="1" maxOccurs="1"/>
            <xsd:element ref="dept" minOccurs="1" maxOccurs="1"/>
            <xsd:element ref="email" minOccurs="1" maxOccurs="1"/>

        </xsd:sequence>
        <xsd:attributeGroup ref="employeeAttribute"/>
    </xsd:complexType>
</xsd:element>
```

However, defining a `simpleType` with a name and then referring to it wherever it is used lends itself to reuse of types.

sequence *and* all

`sequence` signifies that the order of elements declared in it is important. If the order of the subelements within a `complexType` is not important, the `all` element can be used to convey this:

```
<xsd:complexType>
    <xsd:all>
        <xsd:element ref="employee_id" minOccurs="1" maxOccurs="1"/>
        <xsd:element ref="name" minOccurs="1" maxOccurs="1"/>
        <xsd:element ref="extn" minOccurs="1" maxOccurs="1"/>

    </xsd:all>
</xsd:complexType>
```

choice

What if we want to express that a Flute employee has either a manager_id or an employee_id? (This is not good design, but the point is to illustrate how the XML schema can handle choices.) choices can appear in a sequence:

```
<xsd:element name="employee">
    <xsd:complexType>
        <xsd:sequence>
            <xsd:choice>
                    <xsd:element ref="employee_id" />
                    <xsd:element ref="manager_id" />
            </xsd:choice>
                <xsd:element ref="name" />
            <xsd:element ref="extn" />
            <xsd:element ref="email" />
            <xsd:element ref="dept"/>
        </xsd:sequence>
    </xsd:complexType>
</xsd:element>
```

In the above fragment, employee must have name, extn, email, and dept and either a manager_id or an employee_id.

attributes

In our Flute Bank example, employees can be described by an employee_type attribute indicating whether they are permanent or contract. In an XML Schema document, an element with one or more attributes can be defined only as a complexType. The example below shows how the attribute declaration is made within the employee complexType. In the example, the attribute is allowed only two values (enumeration). This means that using a datatype of xsd:string is insufficient to define the type of the employee_type attribute. Just as we did for employee_id, we must define a new type for this attribute. Just as we created a new simpleType for employee_id, the employee_type attribute defines a new type by restricting the base xsd:string type with enumeration facets:

```
<xsd:element name="employee">
    <xsd:complexType>
        <xsd:sequence>
            <xsd:element ref="employee_id" minOccurs="1" maxOccurs="1"/>
            <xsd:element ref="name" minOccurs="1" maxOccurs="1"/>
            <xsd:element ref="extn" minOccurs="1" maxOccurs="1"/>
            <xsd:element ref="dept" minOccurs="1" maxOccurs="1"/>
            <xsd:element ref="email" minOccurs="1" maxOccurs="1"/>
        </xsd:sequence>
        <xsd:attribute name="empType"  use="required">
            <xsd:simpleType>
                <xsd:restriction base="xsd:string">
                    <xsd:enumeration value="contract"/>
                        <xsd:enumeration value="perm"/>
                </xsd:restriction>
            </xsd:simpleType>
        </xsd:attribute>
    </xsd:complexType>
```

The general syntax for declaring attributes locally is

```
<xsd:attribute name="name" use="required|optional|prohibited" default/fixed="value">
    <xsd:simpleType>
        <xsd:restriction base="built-in type">
            <xsd:facet value="value"/>
            ...
        </xsd:restriction>
    </xsd:simpleType>
</xsd:attribute>
```

or

```
<xsd:attribute name="name" type="built-in type" " use="required|optional|prohibited"
default/fixed="value"/>
```

An attribute can also be defined globally (i.e., not inline within the `complex-Type` element definition) and then referred to within the element. When declaring attributes globally, the use parameter cannot appear within the global declaration; instead, it must be specified in the `complexType` element where it is referenced. The code below shows a global declaration:

```
<xsd:element name="employee">
   <xsd:complexType>
      <xsd:sequence>
         <xsd:element ref="employee_id" minOccurs="1" maxOccurs="1"/>
         ...
         <xsd:element ref="email" minOccurs="1" maxOccurs="1"/>
      </xsd:sequence>
      <xsd:attribute ref="empType" use="required"/>
   </xsd:complexType>
...
   <xsd:attribute name="empType">
      <xsd:simpleType>
         <xsd:restriction base="xsd:string">
            <xsd:enumeration value="contract"/>
            <xsd:enumeration value="perm"/>
         </xsd:restriction>
      </xsd:simpleType>
   </xsd:attribute>
```

attributeGroup

If an element has several attributes, the attribute declarations can be grouped and a single reference made to the attribute group:

```
<xsd:element name="employee">
   <xsd:complexType>
      <xsd:sequence>
         <xsd:element ref="employee_id" minOccurs="1" maxOccurs="1"/>
         <xsd:element ref="name" minOccurs="1" maxOccurs="1"/>
         <xsd:element ref="extn" minOccurs="1" maxOccurs="1"/>
         <xsd:element ref="dept" minOccurs="1" maxOccurs="1"/>
         <xsd:element ref="email" minOccurs="1" maxOccurs="1"/>
      </xsd:sequence>
      <xsd:attributeGroup ref="employeeAttribute">
   </xsd:complexType>
</xsd:element>
```

```
...
<xsd:attributeGroup name="employeeAttribute">
  <xsd:attribute name="USBased" type="xsd:string" use="optional" />
  <xsd:attribute name="empType"  use="required">
      <xsd:simpleType>
         <xsd:restriction base="xsd:string">
             <xsd:enumeration value="contract"/>
             <xsd:enumeration value="perm"/>
         </xsd:restriction>
      </xsd:simpleType>
  </xsd:attribute>
</xsd:attributeGroup>
```

Comments in XML Schema

XML Schema provides the annotation element to document the schema. An annotation element can contain two elements: the documentation element, meant for human consumption, and the appinfo element, for machine consumption:

```
<asd:annotation>
<xsd:documentation xml:lang="en">
 The next appinfo element provides a custom instruction to the processor
</xsd:documentation>

<xsd:appinfo>
        <instruction some instruction </instruction>
  </xsd:appinfo>

</xsd:annotation
```

> ▷   XML Schema cannot handle all types of validations. It cannot handle validations that require complex cross-element or -attribute values (e.g., a rule such as, "If employee_type attribute value is 'contract,' then employee_id value must be between 20,000 and 40,000"). For these types of complex validations, the **appinfo** element can provide instructions to another tool (e.g., an XSLT engine or Schematron) to enforce these complex constraints. An XML schema validator would validate the annotated schema against the instance document, and Schematron would validate the instance document based on the extracted instructions embedded in the **appinfo** elements.

> Bringing It All Together

We have examined the XML schema for the employeeList XML and have explained the various elements that make up the schema definition. In this section, we take a look at how the schema is tied to the employeeList XML instance and briefly describe how a simple JAXP program is used to parse and validate the XML.

The targetNamespace declaration signifies that all elements defined in the schema (employeeList, employee, email, etc.) belong to the www.flute.com namespace. In turn, the XML instance document for Flute employeeList signifies that all elements used in the instance document belong to the www.flute.com namespace. ▷

The instance document also provides a *hint* to the XML processor as to the location of the schema, using the schemaLocation attribute. This attribute contains a pair of values separated by whitespace: The first value (http://www.flute.com) is the namespace, and the second (employee.xsd) is the location of the appropriate schema document. Note that the values provided by this attribute are only a hint and that the processor is free to use other schemas obtained by other means. ▷▷

▷ An XML schema document defines schema elements into the target namespace, and an instance document uses the defined elements from that namespace.

▷▷ **Why the schemaLocation Attribute Value Is Only a Hint**

Acme Manufacturing and Tremont Suppliers, Inc. agree to transact using Web services. Tremont will invoice Acme over the Web, and both parties agree on an invoice schema, invoice.xsd. When Tremont sends an invoice instance document to Acme, it uses the schemaLocation attribute to point to an invoice xsd.

Now, how is Acme to be sure that Tremont is using the agreed-upon schema? Acme has no control over the schema if the only option is to rely on the schemaLocation value set by the sender of the invoice instance document. In the real world, where trust alone is not enough to conduct business, the receiving party must be able to specify the schema to be used.

Acme should use a parser that allows them to override any schemaLocation value specified in the instance document. As an example, see Listing A.2, where the schema location is set as a property to the Xerces parser when it is invoked.

It is not necessary for a schema to define elements in a namespace (i.e., it is acceptable to have a schema with no targetNamespace attribute). Instance documents that use elements defined without a namespace may use the noNamespaceSchema attribute to provide the process with the location of the schema (e.g., **xsi:** noNamespaceSchemaLocation = "employee.xsd").

Figure A.5

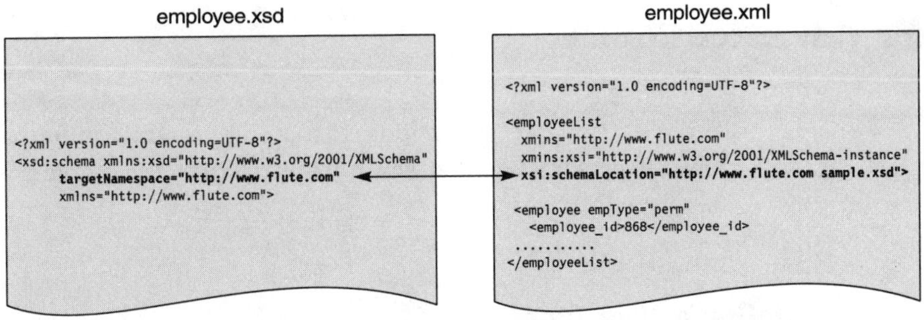

employee.xsd

```
<?xml version="1.0 encoding=UTF-8"?>
<xsd:schema xmlns:xsd="http://www.w3.org/2001/XMLSchema"
    targetNamespace="http://www.flute.com"
    xmlns="http://www.flute.com">
```

employee.xml

```
<?xml version="1.0 encoding=UTF-8"?>

<employeeList
    xmlns="http://www.flute.com"
    xmlns:xsi="http://www.w3.org/2001/XMLSchema-instance"
    xsi:schemaLocation="http://www.flute.com sample.xsd">

  <employee empType="perm">
    <employee_id>868</employee_id>
    ...........
</employeeList>
```

Listing A.2 uses JAXP API to invoke the Apache Xerces validating parser to validate the employee XML with the employee schema. The Xerces parser comes with the JAVA WSDP 1.0 download.

Listing A.2

```
SAXParserFactory factory = SAXParserFactory.newInstance();
factory.setValidating(true);
factory.setNamespaceAware(true);

//apache-specific features to enable XML schema validation
factory.setFeature("http://apache.org/xml/features/validation/schema-full-
checking",true);
    factory.setFeature("http://apache.org/xml/features/validation/schema",true);

SAXParser parser = factory.newSAXParser();

//the schemaLocation attribute is only a hint to the parser. this property
//links the namespace and provides the location of the physical file.
parser.setProperty(
    "http://apache.org/xml/properties/schema/external-schemaLocation",
    "http://www.flute.com employee.xsd");

parser.parse(new File("employee.xml"),this);
```

▷ Advanced Topics

In this section, we take a look at some important features available in XML Schema specifications that were not illustrated by the simple example we picked.

Defining New Types

In previous sections, we looked at how a built-in type could be used as a base type to create new, more restrictive types using facets. For example, the employee_id simpleType is a restriction of the built-in int type. The schema provides other ways to create new types.

Creating New simpleTypes from Other simpleTypes

A simpleType can be used as a base type to create a new, more restrictive type. For example, Flute Bank may assign employee IDs from 1 through 10,000 for U.S.-based employees and 10,001 through 100,000 for non-U.S.-based employees. In such a case, we can create two new types, using the employee_id simple type as a base (instead of a built-in type):

```
<xsd:element name="employee_id">
    <xsd:simpleType>
    <xsd:restriction base="xsd:int">
        <xsd:minInclusive value="1"/>
        <xsd:maxInclusive value="100000"/>
    </xsd:restriction>
    </xsd:simpleType>
</xsd:element>

<xsd:element name="us_employee_id">
    <xsd:simpleType>
    <xsd:restriction base="employee_id">
        <xsd:minInclusive value="1"/>
        <xsd:maxInclusive value="10000"/>
    </xsd:restriction>
    </xsd:simpleType>
</xsd:element>
```

```
<xsd:element name="non_us_employee_id">
    <xsd:simpleType>
    <xsd:restriction base="employee_id">
        <xsd:minInclusive value="10001"/>
        <xsd:maxInclusive value="100000"/>
    </xsd:restriction>
    </xsd:simpleType>
</xsd:element>
```

Given Flute Bank's numbering scheme for employee IDs, it is clear that no employee_id should be less than 1. It makes sense then to restrict new derived types (such as us_employee_id) from breaking this rule. This is achieved by *fixing* the facet value of minInclusive for the employee_id simpleType:

```
<xsd:element name="employee_id">
    <xsd:simpleType>
    <xsd:restriction base="xsd:int">
        <xsd:minInclusive value="1" fixed="true"/>
        <xsd:maxInclusive value="100000"/>
    </xsd:restriction>
    </xsd:simpleType>
</xsd:element>
```

By adding the fixed attribute and setting its value to true, a new simple type cannot be created that changes the minInclusiveValue from 1.

Deriving Types by Extension

We define a Flute employee as below:

```
<xsd:element name="employee">
    <xsd:complexType>
        <xsd:sequence>
            <xsd:element ref="employee_id" minOccurs="1" maxOccurs="1"/>
            <xsd:element ref="name" minOccurs="1" maxOccurs="1"/>
            <xsd:element ref="extn" minOccurs="1" maxOccurs="1"/>
            <xsd:element ref="dept" minOccurs="1" maxOccurs="1"/>
            <xsd:element ref="email" minOccurs="1" maxOccurs="1"/>
        </xsd:sequence>
    </xsd:complexType>
</xsd:element>
```

It is possible to create a new employee type with *additional elements* by extending the above `complexType`. (i.e., derive new complex types by extension). To continue with the example of a Flute employee, assume that a principal-level employee at Flute has two additional subelements: a seniority level (level 1, level 2, etc.) and a specialization (J2EE, security, J2ME, Web services, etc.). A new type called `principalEmployee` can be created, with the new elements added to the base employee:

```
<xsd:complexType name="principalEmployee">
    <xsd:complexContent>
        <xsd: extension base="employee">
            <xsd:sequence>
                <xsd:element name="level" type="xsd:int"/>
                <xsd:element name="specialization" type="xsd:string"/>
            </xsd:sequence>
        </xsd:extension>
    </xsd:complexContent>
</xsd:complexType>
```

In the above example, the content model of the Flute employee type is extended by adding new `complexContent`. The `extension base` is the employee element to which two new subelements are added.

Deriving Types by Restriction

Another way to derive a type is by restriction—that is, derive a new type by *restricting* what the base type represents. Consider this employee definition:

```
<xsd:element name="employee">
    <xsd:complexType>
        <xsd:sequence>
            <xsd:element ref="employee_id" minOccurs="1" maxOccurs="1"/>
            <xsd:element ref="name" minOccurs="0" maxOccurs="1"/>
            <xsd:element ref="extn" maxOccurs="unbounded"/>
            <xsd:element ref="dept" minOccurs="1" maxOccurs="1"/>
            <xsd:element ref="email" minOccurs="0" maxOccurs="1"/>
        </xsd:sequence>
    </xsd:complexType>
</xsd:element>
```

In the above example, an employee may have any number of phone extensions (maxOccurs= unbounded) and may not have any email address (minOccurs=0). It is possible to derive a new employee type by restricting the new type to a maximum of two phone extensions and no email address value:

```
<xsd:complexType name="restrictedEmployee">
    <xsd:complexContent>
        <xsd: restriction base="employee">
            <xsd:sequence>
                <xsd:element ref="employee_id" minOccurs="1" maxOccurs="1"/>
                <xsd:element ref="name" minOccurs="0" maxOccurs="1"/>
                <xsd:element ref="extn" maxOccurs="2"/>
                <xsd:element ref="dept" minOccurs="1" maxOccurs="1"/>

            </xsd:sequence>
        </xsd:restriction>
    </xsd:complexContent>
</xsd:complexType>\
```

In the restricted employee type, we have repeated all subelements that are unchanged (this is a requirement—all subelements must be retyped). The extn element is more restrictive, in that we have changed the maxOccurs value from unbounded to 2. We have also removed the email subelement from the definition of the restricted type.

To restrict the derivation of new types from a base type, the final attribute must be specified:

```
<xsd:complexType name="employee" final=#all|restriction|extension>
```

If final=#all, restriction and extension are prohibited, if final=restriction, derivation by extension is possible; restriction is not.

Unique Values

In the employeeList XML instance, it is possible to list the same employee more than once, because the employeeList schema does not restrict this. One way to ensure that only one employee appears in a list instance is to define that employee_id as a key. When an element is defined as a key, the validating parser will ensure that the instance document contains only unique values for that element.

```
<xsd:element name="employeeList">
    <xsd:complexType>
        <xsd:sequence>
        <xsd:element ref="employee" maxOccurs="unbounded"/>
        </xsd:sequence>
    </xsd:complexType>

    <xsd:key name="emp_key">
        <xsd:selector xpath="fl:employee"/>
        <xsd:field xpath="fl:employee_id"/>
    </xsd:key>
</xsd:element>
```

Note that the selector (which identifies the set of elements to which unique-
ness applies) and the field (which identifies the unique field) are identified using
xpath expressions, which require namespace-qualified names.

Assembling Schemas

Different departments within Flute may define schemas for entities the department primarily owns. For example, the HR department may define the base
schema for all Flute employees, and the marketing department may define what a
Flute customer schema looks like. These schemas can be put into different
schema documents and *included* in another schema that references elements defined in the original schemas. When schemas are included in another schema
document, all schemas must have the same namespace at the including schema.
If one of the included schemas has no targetNamespace, it takes the namespace of
the including schema:

```
<?xml version="1.0"?>
<xsd:schema xmlns:xsd="http://www.w3.org/2001/XMLSchema"
                targetNamespace="http://www.flute.com"
                xmlns="http://www.flute.com">
    <xsd:include schemaLocation="employee.xsd"/>
    <xsd:include schemaLocation="customer.xsd"/>
```

Just as the include element allows you to include schemas from the same
namespace, the import element allows you to import schemas from different
namespaces:

```
<?xml version="1.0"?>
<xsd:schema xmlns:xsd="http://www.w3.org/2001/XMLSchema"
                targetNamespace="http://www.flute.com"
                xmlns="http://www.flute.com">
     <xsd:import namespace = "http://wwww.mktg.flute.com
                schemaLocation="customer.xsd"/>
     <xsd:import namespace = "http://wwww.hr.flute.com
                schemaLocation="employee.xsd"/>
```

Making Schemas Extensible

A sidebar earlier in the chapter discussed one way to extend an XML schema: by providing instructions to another tool, such as Schematron, in an appinfo element, we can get the other tool to provide validations that XML schema parsers cannot handle. The results from the two validations will need to be combined (see Figure A.6).

Extensibility Elements: Creating Schemas That Can Evolve

So far, we have discussed XML schemas that provide a rigid, static structure to instance documents. If Flute Bank wanted to add a new attribute to the employee element or wanted new information in the employee list, the only way to achieve it would be to modify the schema. This might not be a problem if the schema is used and controlled by a single entity. But if a schema for an invoice is published by an industry consortium and is used by many organizations, changing it will

Figure A.6
Extending XML schema using the appinfo element

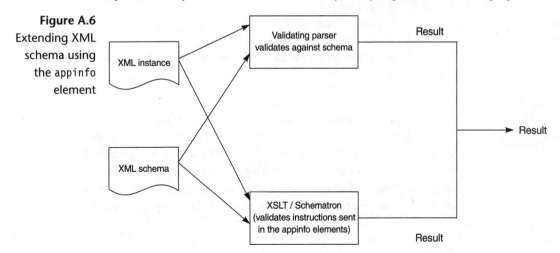

not be easy. XML Schema provides the any and anyAttribute elements to make schemas extensible and open to evolution.

The example below shows the employee schema fragment modified to include the any element:

```
<xsd:element name="employee">
   <xsd:complexType>
     <xsd:sequence>
        <xsd:element ref="employee_id" minOccurs="1" maxOccurs="1"/>
        <xsd:element ref="name" minOccurs="0" maxOccurs="1"/>
        <xsd:element ref="extn" maxOccurs="unbounded"/>
        <xsd:element ref="dept" minOccurs="1" maxOccurs="1"/>
        <xsd:element ref="email" minOccurs="0" maxOccurs="1"/>
        <xsd:any minOccurs=0 />
     </xsd:sequence>
   </xsd:complexType>
</xsd:element>
```

The instance document fragment below is now valid!

```
<employee>
    <employee_id>10000</employee_id>
    <name>
        <first_name>John</first_name>
        <last_name>Doe</last_name>
    </name>
<extn>27304</extn>
<dept>110–433–2089</dept>
    <email>john.doe@acme.com</email>
    <office xmlns="http://www.flute.boston.com"> boston </office>
</employee>
```

In the above example, the instance document added a new subelement to employee. The office element is declared in namespace www.flute.boston.com. It is possible to specify the namespace in which these new elements should be defined. In the above example, we did not restrict the namespace of the new element; by default, the any element without a namespace attribute means that authors of instance documents can add new vocabulary from any namespace. To

restrict the namespace of the new vocabulary, we can specify the any element
with the namespace attribute as follows:

```
<any namespace="http://www.specific.namespace.com"/>
```

Now only elements defined in the http://www.specific.namespace.com
namespace can be added to an instance document.

The following means that new elements in the instance document must not
belong to the targetNamespace (any other namespace is okay):

```
<any namespace="##other"/>
```

The following means that only elements belonging to the target namespace
can be added:

```
<any namespace="##targetNamespace"/>
```

The anyAttribute element allows the author of an instance document to add
one or more attributes:

```
<xsd:element name="employee">
   <xsd:complexType>
      <xsd:sequence>
         <xsd:element ref="employee_id" minOccurs="1" maxOccurs="1"/>
         <xsd:element ref="name" minOccurs="0" maxOccurs="1"/>
         <xsd:element ref="extn" maxOccurs="unbounded"/>
         <xsd:element ref="dept" minOccurs="1" maxOccurs="1"/>
         <xsd:element ref="email" minOccurs="0" maxOccurs="1"/>
         <xsd:any minOccurs=0 />
      </xsd:sequence>
      <xsd:anyAttribute/>
   </xsd:complexType>
</xsd:element>
```

Adding any and anyAttribute elements ensures that schemas can evolve. If a
receiving parser does not know how to handle the extension, it simply ignores it.
That way, new features can be added to an instance document, and processing
nodes can slowly be changed to handle the new changes.

▷ Summary

This appendix provides a quick tutorial on XML schemas, so that the reader can understand the references to them elsewhere in this book. To write schemas for complex enterprises or real-world B2B applications requires a more thorough understanding of their capabilities and best practices.

The XML Schema specifications come in two parts: Part 1, Structures, at *www.w3.org/TR/xmlschema-1,* and Part 2, Datatypes, at *www.w3.org/TR/xmlschema-2.* For a good introduction to XML Schema, see *www.w3.org/TR/xmlschema-0* (the XML Schema primer). A host of best practices for using XML schema in real-world applications can be found at www.xfront.com/BestPracticesHomepage .html.

Appendix  {B}

JSTL

The Java Server Pages Standard Tag Library (JSTL) provides several tag libraries that offer a set of standardized JSP *custom actions* that can be included in pages. This includes tasks such as conditional processing, internationalization, database access, and XML processing. Developers can use this functionality to dramatically reduce development time and scripting elements in their pages. JSTL, like all other Java specifications, has been developed by the community under the JCP as JSR-52 and was finally released in July 2002. The JSTL reference implementation is included in the Java WSDP.

We assume the reader is familiar with JSPs and custom tags, both of which have many good books dedicated to them. We will not cover all JSTL's features and functionality but will limit our discussion to the XML processing tags. These are relevant to developers using Web services who must present a user-facing presentation tier—for example, a console that monitors the number of orders processed by an order-processing Web service.

The advantage of using a standard tag library defined by JSTL is that JSPs using this will be completely portable across all containers. Prior to JSTL, developers had to rely on tag libraries provided by vendors as utilities for common tasks with their respective containers, or on open source code such as the Apache tag libraries. JSTL's standardization lets developers deal with a few tags that can be used on multiple JSP containers. Also, when tags are standardized, the container vendors can work toward optimizing the tag library implementations.

▷ Expression Languages

Before we dive into JSTL, we will examine one of its most important features: expression languages . Expression languages give JSP developers a mechanism for embedding expressions to be evaluated in place of constants or scriptlets.

771

Consider the following example, in which a JSP must display the amount attribute contained in the JavaBean called `PaymentDetail`:

```
<jsp:useBean id="catalog" class="com.officemin.Catalog" scope="application" />
The number of items in the catalog is <%=catalog.getItems().getSize() %>
<!--Other JSP code-->
```

Here, a page author has to use an expression `<%= somevalue %>` to access the properties of the JavaBean component. If the properties are nested, the expression becomes even more complex:

```
<%= catalog.getItems().getItem(0).getName()%>
```

An expression language allows a page author to access an object using a simplified syntax such as `<x:sometag att="${aName}">` for a simple variable or

```
<x:sometag att="${outer.inner.innermost}"> for nested properties.
```

JSTL defines the syntax for such expression languages, based on ECMA-Script and XPath. To be more precise, the JSP 2.0 developed under JSR-152 owns the syntax from which the JSTL expressions are derived. ▷

The expression language defines a set of implicit objects. When an expression references one of these objects by name, the appropriate object is returned instead of the corresponding attribute. For example, `${pageContext}` returns the PageContext object. Most of the implicit objects are modeled as a `java.util.Map` and hold some name value mapping. Table B.1 lists the implicit objects available.

For example, to access the URI from the request, the implicit object request can be used, like `${pageContext.request.requestURI}`. This will obtain the URI of the request, and the container will map this to `HTTPServletRequest.get-RequestURI()`.

To obtain a catalog object from the session, `${sessionScope:catalog}` can be used, and the container will call `pageContext.getAttribute("catalog", Page-Context.SESSION_SCOPE)`.

▷   As result of the confusion and cross-browser compatibility issues of Java-Script, Netscape submitted a proposal to the European Computer Manufacturers Association that was adopted in 1997. The home of the ECMA-Script specification is *www.ecma.ch*.

XPath is used to access different parts of an XML document. It is a W3C specification since 1999 and can be found at *www.w3.org/TR/xpath*.

Table B.1   Implicit objects in JSTL

Implicit Object	Description
pageContext	The PageContext object in JSPs.
pageScope	Maps page-scoped attribute names to their values.
requestScope	Maps request-scoped attribute names to their values. The attributes are available only for the duration of the request.
sessionScope	Maps session-scoped attribute names to their values. Attributes are available until the session is invalidated.
applicationScope	Maps application-scoped attribute names to their values. Attributes are available throughout the application for the life of the container. These map to a ServletContext .getAttribute().
param	Maps parameter names to a single String parameter value using request.getParameter (name).
paramValues	Maps parameter names to a String[] of all values for that parameter using request.getParameter (name).
header	Maps header names to a single String header value using request.getHeader (name).
headerValues	Maps header names to a String[] of all values for the headers.
cookie	Maps cookie names to a single cookie object that is returned using the request.getCookies() method.
initParam	Maps context initialization parameter names to their values using the getInitParameter(name).

> Using JSTL

As mentioned earlier, JSTL includes tags that fit into four areas, each of which is exposed via its own tag library descriptors (TLDs). To use a tag, its corresponding library must be referenced in the JSP. For example, to use the JSTL XML tags in a JSP page, the following taglib directive should be included before the tag is used:

```
<%@ taglib uri="/jstl-x" prefix="x" %>
```

As a result of this *relative* directive, when the JSP is compiled into a servlet, the container will look for the URI in the Web application's WEB-INF file and its corresponding tag library descriptor.

```
<taglib>
  <taglib-uri>/jstl-x</taglib-uri>
  <taglib-location>/WEB-INF/x.tld</taglib-location>
</taglib>
```

Alternatively, the JSP can follow the *absolute* declaration, where the library is referenced by its absolute namespace, in which case the container will resolve this to the appropriate tag library:

```
<%@ taglib uri=" http://java.sun.com/jstl/xml" prefix="x" %>
```

You must have the descriptor (e.g., the x.tld file) and JSTL implementation classes available to the Web application that uses these tags. The TLD and JAR files are packaged with the Java WSDP reference implementation of JSTL. (The JSTL TLD files are in <JWSDP_HOME>/tools/jstl/tlds and the JAR files are in <JWSDP_HOME>/tools/jstl/standard/lib/standard.jar and <JWSDP_HOME>/tools/jstl/jstl.jar). Table B.2 summarizes details of the different actions; Table B.3 gives the absolute URIs for JSTL tags.

▷ XML Support Tags in JSTL

The XML tags provide a way to easily access and manipulate the content of an XML document for JSPs. The custom tags for XML use XPath expressions to perform their actions.

Parsing and Searching

JSTL provides actions that allow a developer to parse and search for data in an XML document that meets certain search criteria.

Table B.2   JSTL tags

Tag	Functional area	Specific tags	TLD	TLD prefix

Core functionality	Expression language support	`catch`
		`out`
		`remove`
		`set`
			`/jstl-c`	`c`

	Flow control	`choose`
		`forEach`
		`forTokens`
		`if`		

	URL management	`import` `url`		

XML specific	Core	`parse`
		`out`
		`set`
			`/jstl-x`	`x`

	Flow control	`choose`
		`forEach`
		`if`		

	Transformation	`Transform`		
Internationalization	Locale	`setLocale`	`/jstl-fmt`	`fmt`

	Message formatting	`bundle`
		`message`
		`setBundle`		

	Number and date formatting	`formatNumber`
		`formatDate`
		`parseDate`
		`parseNumber`
		`setTimeZone`
		`timeZone`		

(continued)

Table B.2 JSTL tags (Cont'd)

Tag	Functional area	Specific tags	TLD	TLD prefix
Database access	SQL	setDataSource	/jstl-sql	sql
		query		
		transaction		
		upate		
		dateParam		
		param		

Table B.3 Absolute URI for JSTL tags

Tag area	Absolute URI in JSP taglib directive
Core	http://java.sun.com/jstl/core
XML	http://java.sun.com/jstl/xml
Internationalization	http://java.sun.com/jstl/fmt
SQL	http://java.sun.com/jstl/sql

x:parse

The parse action parses the content of the XML and stores the contents in a reference that can be used in the JSP. The source can be specified by either the source attribute or the body of the parse tag. The var attribute specifies the JSP scoped attribute in which to save the result. For example, the JSP below parses the items element and stores it in a variable named catalog.

```
<%@ taglib uri=" http://java.sun.com/jstl/xml" prefix="x" %>
<!-other JSP code->
<x:parse var="catalog">
    <items>
        <item>
            <quantity>3</quantity>
            <productnumber>229AXH</productnumber>
                <description>High speed photocopier machine with automatic sensors
                                                        </description>
```

```
            <unitcost>1939.99</unitcost>
        </item>
        <item>
            <quantity>1</quantity>
            <productnumber>1632</productnumber>
            <description>One box of color toner cartridges</description>
            <unitcost>43.95</unitcost>
        </item>
    </items>
</x:parse>
```

The example below shows how a JSP may parse the XML output from another JSP and apply an `org.xml.sax.XMLFilter`, using the filter attribute:

```
<x:parse filter="${olditems}">
    <jsp:include page="xmloutputter.jsp"/>
</x:parse>
```

Another example shows how a JSP can read an XML file containing a catalog,
parse it, and store it in the application context, so that it can be used across the application. The example also shows how XML tags can be combined with other
JSTL tags:

```
<%@ taglib uri="/jstl-c" prefix="c" %>

<%@ taglib uri="/jstl-x" prefix="x" %>

<c:if test="${empty applicationScope.xmlcatalog}" >
  <c:import url="/items.xml" var="xmlfile" />

  <x:parse xml="${xmlfile}" varDom="xmlcatalogDOM"
                  scope="application" />
</c:if>
```

The parse action does not perform any validation against DTD or schemas. If
the var is used to store the processed content, it does not require a specific mechanism. However, the varDOM variable requires that the object be represented as a
`org.w3c.dom.Document` object.

x:out

The out action enables the developer to denote an XPath expression when working with XML documents. The expression specified is applied to the current node, and the result is sent to the JspWriter object for that page. For example, the tag below references the street element in the billingaddress and prints it to the output stream:

```
<%@ taglib uri=" http://java.sun.com/jstl/xml" prefix="x" %>
      <!–other JSP code–>
      <x:out select="${billingaddress/street}" />
```

The action is analogous to the JSP expression `<%= BillingAddress.get-Street() %>`. The out tag can also specify if the special entity characters, such as "<", "&", or "," must be converted to their corresponding entity codes (&lt, &amp, etc.) by including an escapeXml attribute:

```
<x:out select="${billingaddress/street}" escapeXml="true" />
```

x:set

The set action is similar to the out action, but rather than sending the result of the XPath evaluation to the output stream, it stores the results in a variable with a specified scope:

```
<%@ taglib uri=" http://java.sun.com/jstl/xml" prefix="x" %>
      <!–other JSP code–>
      <x:set var="streetaddr" select="${billingaddress/street}" scope="session"/>
```

If the scope is not specified, the default scope of page is assigned to the variable.

XML Flow Control

JSTL includes actions to help iterate over elements in an XML document as well as conditionally process JSP code fragments, depending on the result of an XPath expression.

x:forEach

The forEach action allows developers to iterate over a collection of XML elements that can be specified by the select attribute. The select attribute must contain a valid XPath statement (i.e., XSL statement), which filters the XML. For example, the following JSP segment can be used to iterate over the items element shown earlier:

```
<x:forEach var="item" select="$applicationScope:catalog/items/*">
    Item quantity:      <x:out select="$item/quantity"/>
    Item product number: <x:out select="$item/productnumber"/>
    Item cost:$  <x:out="$item/unitcost"/>
</x:forEach>
```

x:if

The if action is a conditional operator that includes a select attribute. The body of this tag will execute only when the XPath statement in the select attribute evaluates to true at runtime. For example, the following JSP prints out the description if the price is more than $1000:

```
<x:forEach var="item" select="$sessionScope: catalog/items/*">
    <x:if select="$item/unitcost >1000">
      This item has a cost greater than $1000: <x:out select="$item/description"/>
    </x:if>
</x:forEach>
```

x:choose

The choose action acts like a switch statement in Java and, when it evaluates to true, executes its body. The choose action can include multiple when actions that act like the case statement in Java. For example, the choose action can take the following form:

```
<x:choose>
           body content with <x:when> and <x:otherwise> sub tags
      </x:choose>
```

x:when

The when action is a child of the when tag and has a select attribute. The select attribute contains an XPath expression and, when that evaluates to true, the body is executed. For example, the code below can be included in an iteration loop and will execute the two different when blocks in the choose tag:

```
<x:choose>
    <x:when  select="$item/unitcost >1000">
    This item has a cost greater than $1000: $ <x:out select="$item/unitcost"/>
        <br> <x:out select="$item/description"/>
    </x:when>
    <x:when select="$item/unitcost < 100">
        This item has a cost less than $100: $ <x:out select="$item/unitcost"/>
        <br> <x:out select="$item/description"/>
    </x:when>
</x:choose>
```

x:otherwise

The otherwise tag is another child of the choose tag. It is similar to an else statement, in that its body is executed only when all the preceding when actions evaluate to false. For example, the code below can be included in an iteration look
and will execute the otherwise block only if the when condition is not satisfied:

```
<x:choose>
    <x:when select="$item/unitcost < 10">
        This item has a cost less than $10: $ <x:out select="$item/unitcost"/>
        <br> <x:out select="$item/description"/>
    </x:when>
    <x:otherwise>
      This item is more than $10 <x:out select="$item/description"/>
      <br>
    </x:otherwise>
</x:choose>
```

XML Transformation

One of the most common uses of XML in a JSP is to present different views of
the same data by applying different style sheets.

x:transform

The transform action applies an XSL transformation to an XML document. It
can apply the style sheet to either an XML source or the body of the tag itself.
The output can be saved in a variable var, which represents an instance of an
org.w3c.dom.Document class, or can be stored in a javax.xml.transform.Result

object. For example, the tag below applies an XSL to an XML, and the result is sent to the output stream:

```
<x:transform xml="xslinput.xml"xslt="fluteadmin.xsl"/>
```

The following tag applies the transformation and stores the result as a DOM object in the session:

```
<x:transform xml="xslinput.xml"xslt="fluteadmin.xsl"
        result="mydom" scope="sessionScope"/>
```

This example applies the transformation to the body:

```
<x:transform"xslt="fluteadmin.xsl" result="mydom" scope="sessionScope">
        some xml structure here
</transform>
```

▶ Putting It Together

The JSP in Listing B.1 shows some of the XML tags we have discussed, and Figure B.1 shows the corresponding output.

Listing B.1 An example JSP using JSTL XML tags

```
<%@ taglib uri="http://java.sun.com/jstl/xml" prefix="x" %>

<!—other JSP code—>
<x:parse var="catalog" scope="application">
    <items>
        <item>
            <quantity>3</quantity>
            <productnumber>229AXH</productnumber>
            <description>High speed photocopier machine with automatic sensors
                                                        </description>
            <unitcost>1939.99</unitcost>
        </item>
        <item>
            <quantity>1</quantity>
            <productnumber>1632</productnumber>
```

```
                <description>One box of color toner cartridges</description>
                <unitcost>43.95</unitcost>
            </item>
        </items>
</x:parse>
<b> forEach example </b>
c Here is the value stored in the "parseditems" variable
<x:forEach var="item" select="$applicationScope:catalog/items/*">
<br>      Item quantity: <x:out select="$item/quantity"/>
<br>      Item product number: <x:out select="$item/productnumber"/>
<br>      Item product number: <x:out select="$item/productdescription"/>
<br>      Item cost:$  <x:out select="$item/unitcost"/>
<br><br>
</x:forEach>
<hr>


<b> if example </b> <br>
<x:forEach var ="item" select="$applicationScope:catalog/items/*">
    <x: if<D>  select="$item/unitcost >1000">
    This item has a cost greater than $1000: <x:out select="$item/description"/>
    </x:if>
</x:forEach>


<hr>
<b> choose-when example </b><br>
<x:forEach var="item" select="$applicationScope:catalog/items/*">
<x:choose>
    <x:when  select="$item/unitcost >1000">
        This item has a cost greater than $1000: $ <x:out select="$item/unitcost"/>
        <br>  <x:out select="$item/description"/>
    </x:when>


    <x:when  select="$item/unitcost < 100">
        This item has a cost less than $100: $ <x:out select="$item/unitcost"/>
        <br> <x:out select="$item/description"/>
    </x:when>
</x:choose>
</x:forEach>
<hr>
<b> otherwise example </b> <br>
```

Figure B.1
The outout
from the JSTL
example

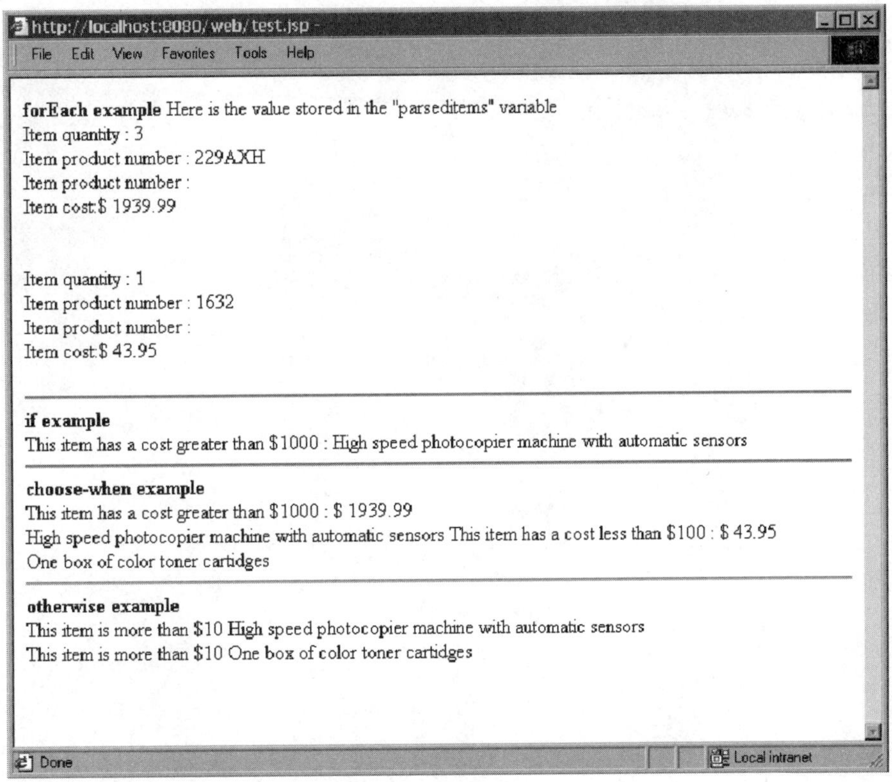

```
<x:forEach var="item" select="$applicationScope:catalog/items/*">
<x:choose>
    <x:when  select="$item/unitcost < 10">
        This item has a cost less than $10: $ <x:out select="$item/unitcost"/>
        <br> <x:out select="$item/description"/>
    </x:when>
    <x:otherwise>
        This item is more than $10 <x:out select="$item/description"/>
        <br>
    </x:otherwise>
</x:choose>
</x:forEach>
```

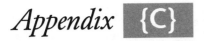

Appendix {C}

The Software Architect's Role

Because this book is about Web services architecture using Java, it is appropriate to include a section on what, exactly, the software architect's role is in developing software and within the organization. The term *software architecture* is only a couple of decades old, and the role of a software architect has only been a distinct role in the past decade or so. The role of the software architect started when software became too complex to be managed by a small team. This led to specializations within software development areas.

> The Architect Manages Stakeholder Expectations

The software architect's primary role is to provide a vision for the development of software products. He or she is involved from the start of a project interacting with all of the stakeholders of the system. Some of the stakeholders are:

- System customers
- Development organizations
- Operations organizations
- Marketing personnel
- End users

The system's customers want the system to be high quality, on budget, and on time. The development organization is looking for the products, frameworks, libraries, and tools from which they can create the system. The operations organization wants the system to be maintainable, configurable, and easily recoverable when something goes wrong. The marketing personnel are interested in how much functionality can be built into the system so they can sell the benefits to their customers. End-users want the system to be easy to use and perform well.

785

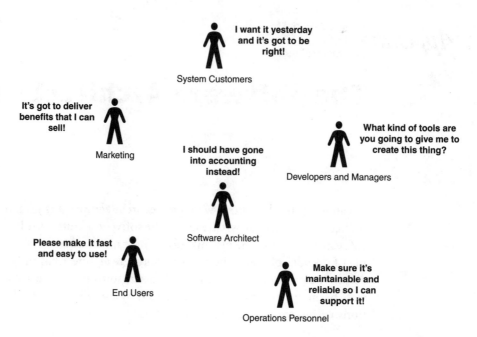

Every stakeholder has their own perspective on the system and it is up to the architect to mediate all of these individual concerns. Tradeoffs have to be made between these concerns. Sometimes, a concern can be easily addressed without affecting anyone else's concern. These are the decisions that the architect must make within the constraints that the project manager places on time and money.

Each concern can be described by the set of quality attributes that a system supports. A system's quality attributes describe the extent to which a system is maintainable, usable, available, portable, interoperable, testable, reliable, functional, and fast (L. Bass, P. Clements, R. Kazman, Software Architecture in Practice, Addison-Wesley 1998). The decisions that the architect makes to enhance one quality attribute often detract from another quality attribute. For instance, to improve maintainability, a configuration file could be used, but that sometimes means that the system will be slower because it has to read from the file.

These decisions are often at odds, and they change throughout the development of the system. Because things change so often, the architect has to be comfortable with ambiguity. Especially at the start of a project, the requirements will be fluid and some design decisions have to wait. But the architect should continue to drive to a solution by continually adding detail to the design. The architect should also be comfortable with changing direction or pulling the plug when it is clear that the current path is a dead end.

As the project moves forward and the details become clearer, the architect advocates the architecture to all of the stakeholders. To successfully advocate and promote the architecture, he or she has to effectively communicate the architecture to each stakeholder based on the stakeholder's perspective. For instance, an architecture presentation to a group of developers will be much different than an architecture presentation to end-users. However, both presentations are dimensions of the same software architecture.

> The Architect Designs the System

To effectively make decisions, advocate for the architecture, mentor developers, and implement key parts of the architecture, the architect must be a technical leader. Although the project manager is responsible for schedule, budget, and resources, the architect is responsible for the technical direction of the project. The architect is involved in interviewing candidates for technical positions, motivating the team, communicating the vision, providing status updates to project management, and generally keeping the development of the system on track. To accomplish this, he or she needs the credibility that comes from mastery of the practice of software development.

The architect advocates consistent practices that improve the software development maturity of the development organization. The architect is a technical expert. He or she came up through the software development ranks. The architect may not have been the top developer in the group, but he or she has the communication, managerial, decision-making, and organizational skills necessary to be successful in a leadership position. However, the architect is the developer's best advocate for promoting technology, process, and sound design and especially for the professional status of the software development practice within the organization.

The architect's skills are broad and deep. The architect should understand the software development lifecycle. He or she should be aware of current best practices and strive to implement them within the organization. The architect should have a deep understanding of the technologies used to implement the project, whether that be Java, C++, or COBOL. The architect should understand what it takes to administer systems from the database, network, and security perspectives. The architect should have a knack for modeling, whether that is UML or another notation. Models are the key artifacts used to communicate the architecture to stakeholders. The architect should be able to identify components and connectors to clearly communicate the design to those with different perspectives on it.

The architect should be skilled at finding the "centers," or those key designs that are cornerstones in the development of the software. In a GUI application, that might be the MVC architectural pattern that provides the metaphor for system construction. In a service-oriented architecture, it might be a model for an open layered service. These centers should be backed up with implementations that give it some concreteness. Some have said that the architect deals in the space where "the rubber meets the sky." These centers are those things that provide the large-grained ideas and structures for the software system. The centers are identified, articulated, communicated, advocated, and implemented. All other aspects of the system must find a place within or adjacent to these centers.

▷ The Architect Implements the Baseline Architecture

The architect implements key parts of the system to demonstrate the architecture he or she is promoting. The architect drives to the baseline architecture for the project. The baseline architecture is an implementation that answers all of the key technical questions for the system. The high-risk areas of the project are implemented in the baseline architecture. Once the baseline architecture has been completed, the architecture is visible and the project can proceed in high gear to deliver the functionality of the system. Once the baseline architecture is completed, the architect also moves from a role of designer and implementer into a role of advocacy and mentoring.

The architect has to be one of the most well-rounded members of the project team. To be effective, he or she has to have an understanding of both people and technology. Because the architect's role is both broad and deep, good architects are hard to find. It is beyond the ability of most to fill the role completely. However, precisely because it is difficult, a career as a software architect is also exciting and rewarding.

Index

abstract business processes, 734
abstract descriptions, 135–137
    illustrated, 139
    messages:, 137
    operations:, 137
    portTypes:, 137
    types:, 137
    See also WSDL; WSDL documents
accessibility, 17–18
accounting services, 695–696
    illustrated, 695
    steps, 695–696
ACID, 583
    atomicity, 584
    consistency, 584
    durability, 585
    isolation, 584–585
    transactions, 597
    WS-Transaction and, 617
Activity Service, 597, 617–618
    defined, 617
    OTS and, 617–618
    specification submission, 617
    See also transaction models; transactions
add publisherAssertions API, 198
addressing, 431
administered objects, 414
annotation element, 567, 568, 769
ANSI X12, 235
Ant, 270–271
    default download, 271
    defined, 27
    samples using, 275

    support, 270–271
    using, 271
    See also Java WSDP (JWSDP)
any element, 768–769
anyAttribute element, 768, 769
Apache
    SOAP, 226, 692
    Xerces parser, 693, 746, 761
    XML project software, 311
    XML security, 639–648
Apache Axis, 267
    digital signature validation with, 645–647
    signer, 640–645
    verifier, 645–647
appinfo element, 759
application architecture, 82–86
    baseline, 82
    business logic, 84–85
    conceptual, 82
    data access layer, 85–86
    framework, 82
    impact, 86
    layered, 82–83
    proxy layer, 83–84
    resource layer, 86
    service façade, 84
    session façade,, 84
    See also architecture
application scenarios, 21–25
    business-to-business, 21–22
    EAI, 22–25
applications
    asynchronous communication, 409

complex messaging, 426
high-level reliability, 409
message trail, 409
MTA, 419
MUA, 419
multiple recipient, 409
security in, 625
store-and-forward, 409
architecture, 81–89
application, 82–86
baseline, 82
conceptual, 82
defined, 81
framework, 82
layered, 82–83
process, 88–89
technical, 86–88
viewpoints, 81
arrays, 122–125
compound types, 123–124, 125
defined, 122
encoding, 122–123
mapping, 326
multidimensional, 124, 326–327
type determination, 326
WSDL specification and, 147, 148
See also compound data types
assertions, 650–658
attribute, 653–654
authentication, 652–653
authorization, 654–657
custom, 657
defined, 651
illustrated, 656–657
publishing, 223–224
response, 657
specification, 651
See also Security Assertions Markup Language
(SAML)
associations
extramural, 489, 491
intramural, 489
registry data, 489–491
XML document options, 293
asymmetric algorithms, 629–630

AsyncClient, 455–464
defined, 455
listing, 456–458
asynchronous invocation, 383–384
asynchronous messaging, 436–439,
451–469
with acknowledgment, 437, 438, 464
AsyncClient, 455–464
CallbackProcessor, 464–469
categories, 436–438
environments, 439
illustrated, 452
inquiry, 437
MessageFactory, 453
one-way, 437, 438
provider roles in, 436
ProviderConnection, 453
ProviderConnectionFactory, 453
PurchaseOrderService, 458, 460–464
requirement, 475
with response, 436–437, 464
self-addressed messages, 455
send message steps, 452
sender, 456–458
service implementation, 461
update, 437
Web components, 465–466
See also JAXM; messaging
asynchronous Web services, 410
atomicity
defined, 584
relaxed, 596
See also ACID
atomicity, consistency, isolation, durability.
See ACID
atoms, 601
application/BTP elements in, 602
coordinator, 601, 603
defined, 600
See also business transactions
attachments, 367–371, 383–384
asynchronous invocation with, 383–384
compound message with, 367–368
JAX-RPC, 367–371
MIME, 367–368

service implementation for processing,
369–370
SOAP, 368
XML, 384
attribute assertion, 653–654
defined, 653–654
request, 654
See also assertions
attributes
declaring, globally, 758
declaring, locally, 757
group, 758–759
values, 756–757
See also XML Schema; XML schemas
authentication
assertion, 652–653
digital signatures, 648
methods, 623
pluggable, 669, 670
support, 687
authorization assertion, 654–657
contents, 656
defined, 654
illustrated, 654–655
response, 655
See also assertions
availability, 707–712
benefit, 30
CBS development, 78–79
concepts, 709–710
damage, 708
defined, 17, 78–79, 709
expense, 709
high, 707–712
infrastructure design techniques, 711–712
questions, 79
redundant infrastructure for, 711
service consumers and, 79
service design techniques, 710
statistics, 709
support, 79

BillPay.java
source file, 352

WSDL, 352–355
billpayservice.wsdl
defined, 508
implementation, 512
schema definition, 511–512
billpayserviceinterface.wsdl
code, 509–511
defined, 580
binding compiler, 551
binding declarations, 555
code generated using, 554
execution, 552
illustrated, 551
interface generation, 560
binding declarations, 555
class, 572–574
component scope, 569
custom, 569, 570–580
definition scope, 569
external, 568
global scope, 568
globalBindings, 570
javadoc, 572
javaType, 575–576
property, 574–575
schema scope, 568
schemaBindings, 570–571
scope, 568–569
typesafeEnum, 576–579
binding element, 154–160
extended, 165, 166
illustrated, 155
name attribute, 156
port elements and, 163
portType, 154
WSDL service interface, 212
binding templates, creating, 183
binding(s)
BTP, 604
default, 555
default, overriding, 580
dynamic, 172
early, 169–171
ebXML registry, 253–254
email, 119

binding(s) (*continued*)
    HTTP, 115–117, 159–160, 693
    Java-XML, 119
    late, 12, 171–173
    MIME, 158–159
    need for, 545–549
    runtime, 12
    SMTP-POP, 117–119
    SOAP, 103, 115, 156–158
    static compile-time, 170–171
    static deploy-time, 171
    static runtime, 171
    WSDL, 156–160
    WSDL operation, 153
bindingTemplate, 187–188
    activity, 201–202
    defined, 187–188
    example, 188
    hostingRedirector, 202
    illustrated, 187
    key to, 188
    See also UDDI informational structural
      model
BizTalk, 470
black box testing. *See* functional testing
Blocks Extensible Exchange Protocol (BEEP),
    703
Blowfish
    defined, 630
    JCE example, 674
    See also encryption algorithms
Body element, 108–109
    defined, 103, 108
    RPC-style, 108
    as special case of header block, 109
    XML document, 108–109
    See also SOAP messages
browse pattern, 200
BTP elements, 599–600
    enroller, 604
    factory, 604
    illustrated, 604
    inferior, 604, 612
    participant, 602, 604, 612
    relationships, 610–612

    roles, 600, 612
    superior, 604, 612
    tree, 611
    See also Business Transaction Protocol (BTP)
BTP transactions, 600
    atoms, 600, 601
    cohesions, 600, 601–603
    locking and, 603
    types of, 600–603
    See also Business Transaction Protocol (BTP)
built-in types, 751–752
business documents validation, 334–335
business entities
    creating, 181
    defined, 178
    deleting, 225
    details, 182
    identifiers, 196–197
    publishing with UDDI4J, 223
    registering divisions as, 223
    registration, 230
    relationships, 198–199, 223
    See also UDDI registries
business logic, 84–85
Business Process Execution Language for Web
    Services (BPEL4WS), 17, 734–736
    CompensationHandler element, 736
    defined, 734
    document structure, 737
    primitive/compound activities, 735
    process and partner services, 735
    process document elements, 735–736
    processes, 734–736
    specification, 736
Business Process Specification Schema (BPSS),
    239–242
    defined, 239
    document generation, 239
    document listing, 240–241
    graphic process modeling and, 240
    See also ebXML
business processes
    abstract, 734
    definition, 237–238
    evolution, 238

executable, 734
execution, 238
management, 238
modeling, 239–240, 242
service composition and, 728
specifications, 238–242
See also processes
business services
creating, 182
defined, 178
updating, 205
See also UDDI registries
Business Transaction Protocol (BTP), 597,
    598–615
abstract message set, 612
actors, 605
BEGIN message, 614
binding, 604
context, 604
CONTEXT message, 613–614
defined, 598
enroller, 604
factory, 604
messages, 598, 604, 605, 612
SOAP bindings and, 612–615
SOAP message pictorially, 615
specification, 599
transaction coordinator, 602
two-phase locking and, 610
two-phase protocol, 606–609
See also BTP elements; BTP transactions;
    transaction models
business transactions, 594, 598–615
atoms, 600, 601
cohesions, 600, 601–603
resource control, 598
See also transactions
businessEntity, 184–186
defined, 184
example, 185–186
in hierarchy, 184
illustrated, 185
See also UDDI informational structural model
BusinessLifeCycleManager interface, 539
defined, 492

as factory, 495
illustrated, 496
obtaining, 500
BusinessQueryManager interface
defined, 492, 497
externalIdentifiers, 498
externalLinks, 498
findQualifiers, 497
illustrated, 497
namePatterns, 497
obtaining, 500
specifications, 498
businessService, 186–187
defined, 186
illustrated, 187
instantiation, 186
unique identifiers, 186
See also UDDI informational structural model
business-to-business (B2B) collaboration, 237
business-to-business transactions, 21–22
byte order mark (BOM), 693

C# client code, 396–397
caching strategies, 715, 716
CallbackProcessor service, 464–469
code, 464–465
defined, 464
See also asynchronous messaging
Canonical XML, 634–635
defined, 634
specification, 634, 635
capability
levels, 481–482
profiles, 481–482
registry, 481
capacity planning, 717
centralized MOM topology, 406
advantages, 406
defined, 406
illustrated, 407
See also message-oriented middleware
    (MOM)
chaining, 373
choreographed messaging, 431

`class` declaration, 572–574
    bindings affected by, 573–574
    defined, 572
    uses, 572
    See also binding declarations
classification, 192–196
    canonical taxonomies, 192–193
    extending, 195
    internal, 193
    UDDI registries, 192–193
    World Geodetic System, 195
    See also UDDI
clients
    choice, 365–367
    EJB, 395
    JAXR, 513–514
    programmatic registration of, 392
    querying registry, 523, 526
    standalone JAXM, 438
    using DII, 359–362
    using dynamic proxies, 362–363
    using stubs, 357–359
    using WSDL, 363–365
client-server computing, 7
client-side handlers
    configuring, 376
    example illustration, 379
    listing, 377–379
    See also handlers
clusters, 715–718
    architecture, 717–718
    capacity, 715
    capacity planning and, 717
    defined, 715
    high availability and, 716
    interfaces, 716
coarse-grained interfaces, 50–59
code inspections, 94
cohesions, 601–603
    application/BTP elements in, 602
    completion, 608
    defined, 600, 603
    scenario, 602
    See also business transactions
cohesive composer, 601, 603

collaboration description, 729
Collaboration-Protocol Agreement (CPA),
    246–250, 261
    defined, 246
    illustrated, 246
    querying, 539
    sample documents, 246–248
    specification, 246
    as XML document, 246
    XML elements, 249–250
    See also ebXML
Collaboration-Protocol Profile (CPP), 242–246
    concept, 243
    defined, 242–243
    document registration, 243
    key elements, 244–245
    organization representation, 245
    querying, 539
    sample document, 243–244
    as XML document, 243, 245
    XML elements, 245
    See also ebXML
collaborations, 239, 242–243, 246
    scenario, 261–262
    use cases mapping to, 239, 242
commission defects, 94
communication
    asynchronous, 409
    document-centric, 475
    fine-grained, 335
    JMS, 411
    in messaging concept, 474
    provider-to-provider, 455, 456, 459
    styles, 474
compilers
    EJB, 716
    schema, 551–552, 554–555
    XML-to-Java, 551
complex elements
    generated binding interface for, 559
    illustrated, 558
    mapping, 558–559
complex types, 752–759
    `all`, 755–756
    `attributeGroup`, 758–759

attributes, 756–758
choice, 756
defined, 752
example, 752–755
sequence, 755–756
component scope, 569
component-based development, 11–12
defined, 11
illustrated, 11
component-based service (CBS)
development, 65–96
architecture, 81–89
availability, 78–79
defined, 65
design, 80–91
functional requirements, 67–68
integrability, 77–78
lifecycle, 66–80
maintenance, 94–95
modifiability, 71–73
nonfunctional requirements, 68–69
performance, 69–71
portability, 80
reliability, 79–80
requirements analysis, 66
reusability, 73–76
security, 71
summary, 95–96
testability, 78
verification and validation, 91–94
components
coordination service, 666
defined, 11
design-time, 239, 250
identity management, 681
interactions, 35
JWSDP, 268–275
protocols accessing, 12
runtime, 239, 250
transaction manager, 594
composability, 59–60
methods, 60
modular structure and, 59
composite service, 25–26
defined, 25

illustrated, 26
See also implementation scenarios
compound data types, 122–125
arrays, 122–125
defined, 122
illustrated, 117–118
structs, 122
See also data types
compound messages
defined, 367
with MIME attachment, 367–368
computer systems
client-server, 7
component-based development, 11–12
deployment transformation, 5
history, 4–13
honey pot, 621
logical evolution, 8–13
monolithic development, 6
N-tier development, 7–8
object-based development, 9–10
physical evolution, 5–8
service-based development, 12–13
structured design, 9
World Wide Web, 8
conceptual service model, 45–47
defined, 45
entity classes, 46
illustrated, 45
manager classes, 46
service layer interfaces, 46
concrete descriptions, 137–138
bindings:, 137
defined, 137
illustrated, 139
services:, 137
See also WSDL; WSDL documents
confirm-set, 607
connections
closing, 500
creating, 500
JAXR and, 493–494
JAXR properties, 493, 495
connectors
defined, 35

connectors (*continued*)
   interoperable, 48
consistency, 584
content trees, 561
coordination service, 666–668
   activation service, 666–667
   components, 666
   coordination context, 667–668
   registration service, 667
CORBA
   analogy, 403
   firewalls and, 8
   implementations, 99
   Web services vs., 3
core assets, 89
counter effect, 603
coupling
   defined, 49
   degree of, 49
   loose, 49, 594–595
create-replace-update-delete (CRUD), 494–496
custom data types
   avoiding, 395
   using, 388–391
   See also data types
custom declarations, 570–579
   class, 572–574
   defined, 569
   example uses, 579–580
   globalBindings, 570
   javadoc, 572
   javaType, 575–576
   property, 574–575
   schemaBindings, 570–571
   typesafeEnum, 576–579
   when to use, 579–580
   See also binding declarations
customer relationship management (CRM)
      system, 23

data access layer, 85–86
   business logic and, 86
   defined, 85
   example, 85–86

data types
   analyzing, 395
   compound, 122–125
   custom, 388–391, 395
   decimal, SOAP, 692
   defining, 146–148
   Java-to-WSDL mapping, 345–351
   Java-to-XML mapping, 321
   simple, 120–122
   XML-to-Java mapping, 322–325
database management system (DBMS), 585
data-centric XML, 277
deadline policies, 720
decentralized MOM topology, 406–408
   advantages, 408
   defined, 406
   illustrated, 407
   See also message-oriented middleware (MOM)
declarative queries, 498–531
DeclarativeQueryManager interface, 539
   defined, 492
   for level 1 providers, 499
decryption, 627
default bindings, 555
defects, 94
definition scope, 569
definitions element
   contents, 145
   extending, 166
   illustrated, 146
   See also WSDL documents
Delivery Status Notification (DSN), 428
denial-of-service attacks, 595
deployment-time publishing, 530
deployment-time security, 622
deserializers, 337
   base, 389
   client-side, 391
   custom, configuring, 391–393
   defined, 388
   illustrated, 388
   portability across implementations and, 390
   specifying, 388
   as utilities by reference implementation, 391
   See also serializers

design, 80–91
   architecture, 81–89
   client code portability and, 395–396
   custom data types and, 395
   data, protocols, encoding schemes
      customization and, 395
   data model analysis and, 394–395
   data types analysis, 395
   interface definition, 89–91
   interoperability testing and, 394
   issues, 89–91
   phase, 80, 81
   proprietary extensions and, 394
   security, 627–628
   transactions, 91
design by contract, 89–91
   defined, 89
   principles, 89–91
Diffie-Hellman, 632
digital certifications
   defined, 623
   players, 625
Digital Signature Algorithm (DSA), 632
digital signatures, 231–232
   advantages, 232–233
   assurance, 232
   authentication, 648
   for non-repudiation, 636
   for publishing entities, 231
   references, 636
   standard, 628
   uses, 636
   validating, 645
   validation check failure, 638
   See also UDDI
direct DII, 360–361
Direct Internet Message Encapsulation
     (DIME), 703
direct mapping, 44–47
   conceptual service model, 45–47
   defined, 44
discrete transactions, 239, 242
Document Object Model. *See* DOM
document type definition (DTD), 745–747
   defined, 745

   example, 746–747
   illustrated, 746
   XML Schema vs., 746
   See also XML documents
document/encoded style, 162–163, 333, 335
   example, 333
   WSDL for, 162–163
   See also styles
document/literal style, 329, 335
   example, 332
   JAX-RPC and, 329
   late binding and, 334
   when to use, 333–335
   WSDL for, 163
   See also styles
documentation element, 759
`DocumentBuilder`, 290, 291
`DocumentBuilderFactory`, 290, 291
document-centric communication, 475
DOM, 704
   core endorsement, 288
   definition, 287
   `DocumentBuilder`, 290, 291
   `DocumentBuilderFactory`, 290, 291
   JAXP and, 290–292
   JDOM vs., 309
   Level 1, 288
   Level 2, 288
   misuse of, 293
   `objectListing` document, 290
   `org.w3c.dom` package, 288, 289
   organization, 288
   parser, 287
   processing, 292
   root elements, 288
   specification, 288
   tree structure, 287
   when not to use, 293
   when to use, 292
Domain Name Service (DNS), 479
domain object models, 480
downtime cost, 708–709
drill-down pattern, 200
Dun & Bradstreet (D&B) Data Universal
     Numbering System (D-U-N-S), 288

durability, 585
dynamic binding
    architectural patterns, 172, 173
    defined, 172
    with known location, 172
    See also binding(s)
dynamic invocation interface (DII)
    advantages, 367
    client using directly, 360–361
    client using indirectly, 361–362
    clients using, 359–362
    defined, 359
    at runtime, 359–360
    support, 359
    WSDL with, 362
dynamic proxies, 84, 172
    clients using, 362–363
    interface implementation, 362
    for type-safe proxy object creation,
      362
    See also proxies

early binding, 169–171
    defined, 169
    example, 169–170
    investigation, 173
    static compile-time, 170–171
    static deploy-time, 171
    static runtime, 171
    variations, 170–171
    See also binding(s)
ebXML, 235–264
    architectural overview, 237–261
    BPSS, 239–242
    business-process model, 237–238, 239
    Collaboration-Protocol Agreement (CPA),
      246–250, 261
    Collaboration-Protocol Profile (CPP),
      242–246
    as community effort, 263
    conventions, 22
    defined, 21
    design-time components, 239, 250
    electronic plug-in, 238

frameworks illustration, 237
    headers, 454
    initiative, 433
    issues, 264
    for message interactions, 22
    message package, 433
    message sent from Flute Bank to OfficeMin,
      466–468
    message sent from OfficeMin to Flute Bank,
      468–469
    Message Service definition, 114–115
    messaging, 433, 454
    messaging service, 256–261
    partner discovery, 238
    partner profiles/agreements, 242–250
    partner sign-up, 238
    power of, 264
    process definition, 237–238
    process evolution, 238
    process execution, 238
    process management, 238
    profiles, 432
    protocol support, 256
    Registry Services Specification, 251–253
    reliable messaging protocol, 260
    RIM, 251, 252
    runtime components, 239, 250
    security, 255
    SOAP headers, 433
    specification status to date, 264
    specifications, 237
    taxonomies, 255
    UDDI vs., 254–256
    understanding, 235
ebXML messaging, 256–261
    header elements, 257–259
    illustrated, 261
    interface, 259
    message illustration, 258
    MSH, 259
    package, 257
    reliable protocol, 261
    SOAP, 256–260
    specifications, 259–261
    system modules, 260

ebXML registries, 250–256, 498
  advantages, 537
  architecture, 251
  bindings, 253–254
  browser, 539
  information model, mapping, 544
  interfaces, 252–253
  JAXR and, 533–544
  publishing content to, 537–539
  publishing example, 539–544
  publishing organizations in, 533–536
  service interface description, 256
  WSDL document publication in, 537
  See also registries
ebXML registry service, 250–256, 533
  abstract description, 254
  concrete description, 254
  definition, 252
  digital certificates and, 533
  specifications, 251–252, 533
EJB, 398
  account management, 590
  clients, 398
  compiler, 716
  deployment, 590
  endpoint for JAX-RPC, 399
  invoking other Web services, 400
  JAXM and, 470–471
  JAX-RPC service implementation as, 400
  as listener, 470
  RMI use, 716
  stateless session, 399
  stub implementations, 716–717
electronic business XML. *See* ebXML
electronic data interchange (EDI), 21, 97, 235
  benefits realization, 236
  business/technical problems, 236
  data/messaging specification, 98
  development of, 235
  focus, 236
  interactions, 235
  standards, 235
  See also ebXML
electronic plug-in, 238
Element interface, 564–565

elliptic-curve algorithms, 632–633
enabling services, 722–724
  defined, 722
  in fee-based Web service criteria, 724
  list of, 723
encoding
  defined, 160, 319
  messages, 160
  SOAP, 119–125, 319–333
encoding schemes, 109
  customizing, 395
  default, 335
  defined, 320
encodingStyle attribute, 120
encryption
  defined, 627
  example, 633–634
  mechanisms, 630
  one-way, 628
  password, 627
  two-way, 628
  XML, 648–650
  See also security
encryption algorithms
  asymmetric, 629–630
  Blowfish, 630
  Diffie-Hellman, 632
  DSA, 632
  elliptic-curve, 632–633
  MD5, 631, 673–674
  Ralph Merkle's Puzzle Protocol, 631–632
  RSA, 632
  S/MIME, 631
  selection, 629–633
  SHA1, 631
  SkipJack, 630
  symmetric, 629, 630
  Triple DES, 631
  Twofish, 631
endpoint interfaces, 399
enterprise application integration (EAI), 22–25
  defined, 22
  hub-and-spoke system, 23
  products, 22
  for protocol/data format translations, 24

enterprise application integration (EAI) (*continued*)
  registries, 230
  solution drawbacks, 23
  Web services approach, 24
  See also application scenarios
enumerations, 555–557
  generated interface for, 556
  mapping, 555–557
  schema with, 556
  typesafe, 556, 557
  See also XML
Envelope element, 105–106
  defined, 102, 105
  See also SOAP messages
error handling, 431
exception handling, 431
exclusive locks, 586
executable business processes, 734
expression languages, 771–772
  defined, 771
  example, 772
  implicit objects, 772, 773
  syntax, 772
extensible elements, 767–769
eXtensible Stylesheet Language (XSL), 298
  defined, 298
  style sheets, 298
  style sheets example, 299–300
  Transformations (XSLT), 298–307
  as W3C specification, 298
extramural associations, 489, 491

facets, 752
  example, 752
  list of, 753–754
  value, fixing, 763
Fault element, 109–111
  detail element, 111
  faultactor element, 110
  faultcode element, 110
  faultstring element, 110
  generation, 110
  subelements, 110–111
  See also SOAP messages

fault element
  defined, 152
  extending, 166
  See also WSDL documents
fault tolerance, 718–720
  assurance, 720
  defined, 718
  request determination, 719
  request migration, 719–720
faultcode element
  defined, 110
  value classes, 111

Federal Deposit Insurance Corporation
    (FDIC), 198
federated identity model, 682–684
  advantages, 684
  defined, 682
  illustrated, 683
  See also Liberty Alliance
federations
  basis, 663
  importance, 663
  security, 679
find operation, 520
find_business method, 222
find_relatedBusinesses API, 198
find_tModel API, 197
fine-grained communication, 335
fine-grained distributed objects, 51
firewalls
  CORBA and, 8
  SOAP and, 668–669
flat transaction model, 589, 594, 619
Flute Bank bill payment service, 140–144
  defined, 140
  Java interface, 140
  operation, 152
  WSDL document, 141–144
  See also WSDL documents
functional policies, 720
functional requirements, 67–68
  developing, 67–68
  example, 67–68
  identifying, 68

See also component-based service (CBS)
  development
functional testing, 700–701
  defined, 92, 700
  plan, 700
  scenarios, 700
  See also testing
future standards, 727–742

get_bindingDetails API, 201
global scope, 568
globalBindings declaration, 570
granularity
  coarse, 50–59
  decision, 54
  degrees, 53
  fine, 51
  multi-grained methods, 55–59
  multi-grained serviced, 53–55
  problem reconciliation, 59
graphical user interface (GUI), 27
grid computing, 720–722
  CRM solutions, 722
  defined, 720
  grid service components, 722
  OGSA, 721
  policies, 720
  solution, 722
  tickets, 720
  Web services using, 721

handler chains
  defined, 373
  handle methods, 374
handlers, 371–384
  advantages, 374–376
  architecture, 372
  asynchronous invocation with, 384
  chained, 373
  client-side, 376, 377–379
  combining, 373
  configuring, 376–383
  for data validation, 375

deployment order, 373
  disadvantages, 383
  fault handling in, 374
  implementations, 372
  in intermediary implementation, 376
  introduction, 383
  last, to process request, 374
  for metadata processing, 375
  multiple, registering, 376
  in performance optimization, 375–376
  programmatic registration of, 377
  for security, 374
  server-side, 376, 380–381
  service configuration, 381–383
  in SOAP attachment processing, 375
  SOAP message, 371
Header element, 106–108
  attributes, 108
  defined, 102, 106
  example, 106–107
  meta-information, 107
  See also SOAP messages
high availability. *See* availability
holder classes, 149, 337, 384–387
  for in parameter, 385
  for inout parameter, 385, 386
  JAX-RPC-defined, 387
  for out parameter, 385, 386
honey pots, 621
horizontal extensibility, 112
HP Web Services Transactions (HP-WST), 615
HTML, XML transformed into, 298, 301
HTTP
  authentication header, 393
  JAX-RPC authentication support, 392–393
  JAX-RPC runtime support, 339
  JMS and, 418
  nodes, 116
  POST request, 116
  response, 116
  SOAP and, 99
  WS-Routing over, 739
HTTP bindings, 115–117, 159–160
  defined, 156
  See also binding(s)

HttpSession object, 340
hub-and-spoke model, 24
human-friendly keys, 232
hybrid MOM topology, 408
Hypertext Transfer Protocol Secure (HTTPS), 392

identifiers, 196–197
    business entity, 196–197
    marking entities with, 196–197
    See also UDDI
identity management, 680–682
    components, 681
    defined, 680
    factors, 680
    features, 686
    implementing, 688
    solution, 681, 686
    Web services and, 681–682
    See also security; SourceID
implementation scenarios, 25–28
    composite service, 25–26
    middleware service, 26
    service bus, 26–28
    simple service, 25
Implementing Enterprise Web Services
    defined, 401
    JAX-RPC and, 401–402
    specification, 398
import element, 164–165
    defined, 164
    use, 164, 176
    See also WSDL documents
include element, 766
independent software vendors (ISVs), 227
indirect DII, 361–362
InfoMosaic SecureXML, 639
information hiding
    contracts and, 47–48
    defined, 9
information models, 480
    creating, 500
    ebXML, mapping to JAXR, 544
    inheritance relationships, 486
    JAXR, 483–491

mapping, 531
UDDI, 506
input element, 152
    extending, 166
    output element before, 152
Inquiry API, 200–201
    browse pattern, 200
    defined, 200
    drill-down pattern, 200
    invocation pattern, 201–202
    See also UDDI
inspections, 94
integrability
    defined, 77
    improving, 77, 78
    questions, 77
    See also component-based service (CBS)
        development
integrity, 18
interface definition, 89–91
intermediaries
    implementing, 376
    SOAP, 113
internationalization, 216–219
    name schemes, 217
    postal address support, 217–218
    time zone support, 217
    UDDI registry support, 217
Internet Message Access Protocol (IMAP), 419
interoperability, 48–49, 690–693
    achieving, 48
    defined, 48
    between heterogeneous platforms, 694
    issues, 690
    JAXM, 472
    JAX-RPC, 393–398
    problems, 393–394
    between security service providers, 628
    as SOAP goal, 690
    testing, 394
    UDDI, 203, 693
intramural associations, 489
invocation pattern, 201–202
    extending, 201–202
    failed invocation of service, 201

implementation, 202
using, 201
See also Inquiry API; UDDI
isolation, 584–585
defined, 584
levels, locking and, 586
read committed, 585
read uncommitted, 585
repeatable read, 585
serializable, 585
See also ACID; transaction management;
    transactions

Java
exceptions, 150
generating WSDL from, 173–174
mapping SOAP-encoded types to, 125
messaging in, 411–428
method declaration, 150
service definition interfaces, 315
Web services and, 20–21
Java 2 Enterprise Edition (J2EE), 21, 33
Activity Service for Extended Transactions,
    618
architecture, 715
blueprints, 201
containers, 401
JAX-RPC and, 398–402
security and, 669–672
servers, 619
Java API for WSDL (JWSDL), 169
Java API for XML Messaging. *See* JAXM
Java API for XML Processing. *See* JAXP
Java API for XML Registries. *See* JAXR
Java API for XML-Based Remote Procedure
    Calls. *See* JAX-RPC
Java Architecture for XML Binding. *See* JAXB
Java Authentication and Authorization Service
    (JAAS), 669–672
APIs, 671
application use, 670
configuration file name, 670
location, 672
LoginModule(s), 670

pluggable authentication, 669, 670
Java classes
generating, 551–552
WSDL and, 173
Java Community Process (JCP), 405
Java Cryptography Extensions (JCE), 672–676
Blowfish example, 674
core classes, 675–676
defined, 672
framework, 672, 675
keystore, 676
MD5 example, 673–674
principle, 672
service support, 673
Java Keystore (JKS), 643
Java Message Service. *See* JMS
Java Naming and Directory Interface (JNDI),
    399, 493, 669, 716
Java Remote Method Protocol (JRMP), 316
Java Server Faces, 275
Java Server Pages (JSP), 275
custom actions, 771
example using JSTL tags, 781–783
multiple containers, 771
as presentation tier basis, 714
Java Server Pages Standard Tag Library. *See* JSTL
Java Transaction API (JTA), 591–593
defined, 591
transaction managers, 592
transaction managers components, 594
transaction managers/application programs
    contract, 591
transaction managers/application services
    contract, 592
transaction managers/transactional resource
    contract, 592
transactions, 401
UserTransaction interface, 618
Java Transaction Service (JTS), 591, 593
defined, 593
transaction manager, 593
Java WSDP (JWSDP), 21, 267–276
Ant, 270–271
availability, 267
components, 268–275

Java WSDP (JWSDP) (*continued*)
    components illustration, 269
    defined, 265, 267
    Java XML APIs, 268–269
    JAXB, 269
    JAXM, 268
    JAXP, 268
    JAXR, 268
    JAX-RPC, 268
    registry browser, 275
    registry server, 270
    SAAJ, 268
    setting up, 268
    summary, 276
    supporting specifications, 275
    Tomcat Web container, 270
    tools, 270–275
    wscompile tool, 273–274
    wsdeploy tool, 271–273
    XML descriptor, 466
    See also JAX APIs
Java XML pack, 267
JavaBeans Activation framework, 368
javadoc declaration, 572
    bindings affected by, 573–574
    defined, 572
    See also binding declarations
JavaMail, 419–428
    advantages, 427–428
    API illustration, 420
    asynchronous B2B messaging with, 426
    for complex messaging applications, 426
    conceptual model, 419
    drawbacks, 428
    implementation cost reduction, 428
    infrastructure leveraging, 427
    Message, 420, 421
    message sorting facilities, 427
    message structure, 421
    messaging MOMs elimination, 427
    multiple recipient delivery support, 427
    notifications support, 427
    packages, 420
    Provider, 420
    receiving mail with, 424

    security support, 427
    sending mail with, 420
    Session, 420
    transaction support and, 428
    Transport, 420
    See also messaging
javaType declaration, 575–576
    annotation result, 576
    defined, 575
    syntax, 575
    See also binding declarations
Java-WSDL mappings, 345–355
    checked expressions, 350–351
    extended interface, 347–348
    interface, 346
    Java identifiers, 351
    method, 347
    method arguments, 348–349
    method returns, 349–350
    package, 346
Java-XML bindings, 119
javax.xml.bind.helper package, 560
javax.xml.bind package, 559–560
javax.xml.bind.util package, 560
javax.xml.bind.Validator interface, 566
javax.xml.messaging, 430
    core interfaces, 452
    defined, 430
javax.xml.messaging.ReqRespListner interface, 447
javax.xml.parsers, 280, 282, 290, 291
    DOM, 290, 291
    SAX, 280, 282
javax.xml.registry.infomodel package, 483
javax.xml.rpc.handler.Handler interface, 372
javax.xml.soap, 430
    JAXM use of, 473
    JAX-RPC use of, 473
    SAAJ model in, 440
javax.xml.soap.SOAPConnectionFactory, 442
javax.xml.soap.SOAPMessage, 372
javax.xml.transform.dom package
    defined, 302
    interfaces, 304
javax.xml.transform package
    defined, 302

interfaces, 304
javax.xml.transform.sax package
  defined, 302
  interfaces, 305
javax.xml.transform.stream package
  defined, 302
  interfaces, 305
JAX APIs
  defined, 265
  JAXB, 266, 545–580
  JAXM, 266, 405–477
  JAXP, 265, 277–312
  JAXR, 266, 479–544
  JAX-RPC, 265, 313–403
  JWSDP, 265, 267–276
  overview, 265–266
JAXB, 545–580
  abstraction layer, 545
  additional mappings, 555
  annotation element, 568
  appInfo element, 568
  application code writing, 552–554
  architecture, 550
  architecture illustration, 550
  business documents, 334–335
  code to read XML documents, 552–553
  context, 560
  customizing, 567–579
  defined, 266, 545
  developing with, 551–554
  goal, 549
  implementations, 551, 560
  Java class generation, 551–552
  JAX-RPC and, 559
  as JWSDP component, 269
  namespace, including, 569–570
  need for, 545–549
  passing techniques, 567
  specifications, 269, 545
  summary, 580
  use scenarios, 549
  validation, 566–567
  validation handler, 562
  when to use, 549
  See also JAX APIs

JAXB API, 550, 553, 559–566
  Element interface, 564–565
  JAXBContext, 560–561
  Marshaller, 562–564
  Unmarshaller, 561–562
  Validator interface, 566–567
JAXBContext, 553, 560, 561
JAXM, 131, 405–477
  API, 430
  API core, 451
  architectural stack, 430
  architecture, 428–433
  choosing, 475
  clients, 472
  conceptual model, 429
  consumers, 429
  defined, 266, 405
  design, 405
  designing with, 434–439
  developing with, 439–472
  EJB and, 470–471
  as interface to JMS, 475
  interoperability, 472, 473
  JAX-RPC decision, 472–476
  as JWSDP component, 268
  with messaging profile, 475
  profiles, 431–433
  provider administration, 455, 460
  providers, 429
  reference implementation, 447
  root in JMS, 418
  services, 472
  SOAP message request sent synchronously,
    443–445
  standalone clients, 438
  summary, 476–477
  uses, 268
  without provider, 475
  See also JAX APIs
JAXP, 277–312
  architecture, 278
  architecture illustration, 279
  bundling, 311
  defined, 265, 277
  development, 278

JAXP (*continued*)
  DOM and, 290–292
  as JWSDP component, 268
  logical architecture, 279
  parsing/validating schemas, 293–294
  RI, 311
  SAX and, 282–287
  schemaLanguage property, 294
  schemaSource property, 294
  summary, 311–312
  uses, 268
  W3C DOM package, 290
  XML schemas and, 293–297
  XSLT and, 301–306
  See also JAX APIs
JAXR, 216, 226, 479–544
  API, 491–530
  API abstraction level, 499
  API illustration, 492
  application connection sequence, 493
  application to publish WSDL, 515–519
  architecture, 480–482
  architecture illustration, 482
  Association interface, 489
  BusinessLifeCycleManager interface, 492, 495,
      496, 500, 539
  BusinessQueryManager interface, 492, 497
  capability profiles, 481–482
  Classification interface, 487
  ClassificationScheme interface, 489
  clients, 513–514
  connection properties, 493, 495
  connections and, 493–494
  CRUD operations and, 494–496
  debugging, 507
  declarative queries and, 498–530
  DeclarativeQueryManager interface, 492, 539
  defined, 266, 268
  ebXML registry and, 533–544
  ExtrinsicObject, 537
  Factory pattern, 493
  get-find operations and, 497–498
  internal taxonomy support, 489
  as JWSDP component, 268
  LifeCycleManager, 494, 496, 539

  mapping ebXML information model to, 544
  providers, 481
  QueryManager interface, 497
  reference implementation, 483
  RegistryObject interface, 487, 491
  summary, 544
  to UDDI mapping, 531–533
  UDDI registry querying with, 520–523
  See also JAX APIs
JAXR information model, 483–491
  core, illustrated, 484
  inheritance relationships, 486
  location, 483
  logical groups of classes, 483
  Organization, 483, 485
  PostalAddress, 483
  Service, 484
  ServiceBinding, 485
  SpecificationLink, 485
  Users, 483
JAX-RPC, 131, 172, 313–403, 359–362
  advanced, 367–393
  attachments, 367–371
  blocking invocation, 474
  choosing, 474–475
  client creation, 274
  clients, 316–317
  client-server interaction, 317
  complex protocols, 315
  compliant implementation, 313
  data type mapping and, 168–169
  defined, 265, 313
  definitions, 316
  DII, 359–362
  document/literal support, 329
  dynamic proxies, 362–363
  handlers, 371–384
  handler-specific API in, 375
  HTTP authentication support, 392–393
  interoperability, 393–398
  J2EE and, 398–402
  JAXB and, 559
  JAXM decision, 472–476
  JSR 153 and, 399–401
  JSR-109 and, 401–402

as JWSDP component, 268
model illustration, 314
need for, 402
non-blocking invocation, 474
pass by reference and, 319
pluggability mechanism, 389–391
portability across, 320
remote object passing and, 319
RPC/encoded support, 329
runtime, 317
runtime information, 317–318
security and, 392–393
server creation, 272
service endpoint, 315
service implementation, 315
service model, 314–315
specifications, 125
stubs, 357
summary, 402
synchronous procedure invocation
    support, 473
uses, 268
in vendor decision, 168–169
vendor standard, 316
See also JAX APIs
JAX-RPC development, 336–367
service consumption, 355–367
service definition, 336–337
service deployment, 339–341
service description, 341–355
service implementation, 337–339
steps, 336
JDOM, 308–311
builder classes, 311
class diagram, 310
classes, 309–311
defined, 308–309
DOM vs., 309
standardization, 311
for transformations, 310–311
JMS, 411–418, 703
administered objects, 414
API illustration, 413
communication, 411
conceptual model, 411

Connection, 414
ConnectionFactory, 414
Destination, 414
destinations, exposing, 475
HTTP and, 418
JAXM as interface to, 475
message consumers, 415
message producers, 415
MessageProducer, 415
messaging illustration, 415
point-to-point messaging, 412
publish-subscribe messaging, 412
receiving messages, 417
sending messages, 416–417
Session, 414
stack, 411
use, 419
vendors, 418
See also messaging
JSRs
JSR-95, 618
JSR-105, 636
JSR-106, 648
JSR-109, 401–402
JSR-153, 399–401
JSR-155, 658
JSR-156, 618
JSR-172, 740–741
JSR-181, 740
JSTL, 275, 771–783
advantages, 771
defined, 771
expression languages and, 771–772
implicit objects, 772, 773
reference implementation, 771
tag library descriptors (TLDs), 773–774
using, 773–774
WSDP reference implementation of, 774
JSTL tags, 774–781
absolute URI for, 776
choose, 779
core functionality, 775
database access, 776
forEach, 778–779
if, 779

JSTL tags (*continued*)
  internationalization, 775
  JSP example using, 781–783
  otherwise, 780
  out, 778
  parse, 776–777
  parsing and searching, 774–778
  set, 778
  transform, 780–781
  when, 779–780
  XML flow control, 778–780
  XML transformation, 780–781
  XML-specific, 775

Kerberos, 623
key agreements, 628
Key Distribution Center (KDC), 678
keyedReference element, 204, 223
keystores, 676

languages
  multiple, 216–219
  supported, 217
  See also internationalization
late binding, 171–173
  defined, 12
  document/literal style and, 334
  dynamic, 172
  dynamic, with known location, 172
  See also binding(s)
latency
  defined, 703
  reduction solution, 715
  See also performance
layered architecture, 82–83
legacy applications, maintaining investment
    in, 30
Liberty Alliance, 682–685
  circles of trust, 683
  defined, 682
  federated identity model, 682–684
  Flute Bank scenario, 684
  local identities, 683

Project Liberty, 682–683
  SourceID and, 685, 686
  specification, 685, 686
LifeCycleManager, 252–253
  defined, 494
  generic methods, 539
  illustrated, 496
lists, mapping, 557–558
load and stress testing, 701–702
  execution, 702
  goal, 701
  metrics, 702
  uses, 702
  See also testing
location transparency, 29
  achieving, 29
  defined, 59
  SOA, 59
locking
  BTP transactions and, 603
  exclusive, 586
  optimistic, 586
  pessimistic, 586
  shared, 586
  update, 586
logical evolution, 8–13
  component-based development, 11–12
  object-based development, 9–10
  service-based development, 12–13
  structured design, 9
long-running transactions, 595, 597
loose coupling, 49, 594–595

Mail Transfer Agent (MTA) applications, 419
Mail User Agent (MUA) applications, 419
maintainability defects, 94
maintenance, 94–95
  cost of, 95
  defined, 94
  goal, 94
  IEEE process activities, 95
management
  business processes, 238
  EJB account, 590

identity, 680–682
importance, 19
reporting, 19
specifications, 31
systems, 689–691
tools, 19
transaction, 583–619
mapping
  arrays, 326
  information model, 531
  Java-to-XML data type, 321
  Java-WSDL, 345–355
  in JAXB, 559
  JAXR to UDDI, 531–533
  in JAX-RPC, 559
  MIME, supported by SAAJ implementation,
    445
  MIME-to-Java data type, 369
  multidimensional arrays, 326–327
  of SOAP simple types to Java, 326
  type, 388, 389
  UDDI Inquiry API to JAXR, 532
  UDDI Publisher API to JAXR, 532
  XML-to-Java, 555–559
  XML-to-Java data type, 322
marketplace registries, 228–229
  authentication token, 229
  hosting, 228
  uses, 229
  See also registries
Marshaller, 562–564
  configuring, 564
  creation, 563
  defined, 562
  event handler registration, 563
  output formatting and, 564
  properties, 564
  UTF-8 default, 564
marshalling, 554
  defined, 315–316
  Java-to-XML, 318–319
  JAX-RPC, 318–319
  object trees to different destinations, 563
  over wire, 316
  parameters, 335

success, 316
  XML, by application code, 554
  See also unmarshalling
matter, subdivisions, 488
MD5
  defined, 631
  JCE example, 673–674
  See also encryption algorithms
message consumers, 415
Message Disposition Notification (MDN), 428
message element, 148–150
  defined, 148
  illustrated, 149
  See also WSDL documents
message handlers. *See* handlers
message packages, 433
message producers, 415
message service handler (MSH), 259
MessageContext object, 340
message-conversation-based services, 262
message-driven beans (MDBs), 470
MessageFactory, 441, 453
message-level security, 625, 627
message-oriented middleware (MOM), 405–409
  for asynchronous communication
    applications, 409
  centralized topology, 406, 407
  decentralized topology, 406–407, 408
  defined, 405
  elimination, 427
  for high-level reliability applications, 409
  hybrid topology, 408
  for message trail applications, 409
  for multiple recipient applications, 409
  popularity, 439
  as postal service messaging technology, 406
  for store-and-forward applications, 409
  topology role, 408
messaging
  addressing and, 431
  asynchronous, 436–439, 451–469
  choreographed, 431
  content processing and, 431
  defined, 406
  ebXML, 433, 454

messaging (*continued*)
   error/exception handling and, 431
   header processing and, 431
   in Java, 411–428
   JavaMail, 419–428
   JMS, 411–418
   MOM-based solutions, 406–409
   point-to-point, 412
   publish-subscribe, 412
   routing and, 431
   security and, 431
   synchronous, 434–436, 439–451
   Web services and, 410–411
   XML, 431–433
Messaging Service, 114–115
metering service, 696
middleware, 26, 474
MIME attachments, 367–368
MIME bindings, 158–159
   defined, 156
   `multipartRelated` element, 159
MIME-to-Java mapping, 369
modifiability, 71–73
   defined, 71
   degrees of, 72
   factors, 72–73
   improving, 76
   questions, 71–72
modularity, 42–44
   composability, 42–43
   continuity, 43–44
   decomposability, 42
   improving, 76
   protection, 44
   understandability, 43
monolithic development, 6
multidimensional arrays, 124
   mapped with SOAP encoding, 326–327
   support, 124
   See also arrays
multi-grained methods, 55–59
   account-holder information and address
      return, 55, 56, 57
   account-holder information or address
      return, 55, 56

   account-holder information return, 55
   requested attributes return, 55, 56–57, 58
multi-grained services, 53–55
   creation, 53–54
   defined, 53
   illustrated, 54
`multipartRelated` element, 159

namespaces
   correspondence, 526
   of included schema, 766
   JAXB, including, 569–570
   restricting, 768–769
   service discovery based on, 527–529
   XML qualifier, 749
   XML Schema, 749
nested transaction model
   defined, 590
   illustrated, 591
   service building, 590
   See also transaction models
Netegrity Siteminder, 687
network-addressable interface, 50
nonblocking RPC invocation, 356
nonfunctional requirements, 68–69
   definition, 68
   QoS, 69
   types of, 69
   usability, 68
   See also component-based service (CBS)
      development
North American Industry Classification System
      (NAICS), 488, 489
notification operation, 152–153
   defined, 152–153
   illustrated, 153
   See also operation element
notifications
   SMTP mechanism, 428
   support, 427
N-tier development, 7–8
   defined, 7
   illustrated, 7
   World Wide Web and, 8

OASIS, 21
    BTP, 597, 598–615
    BTTC, 598
    contributing organizations, 237
    Technical Committee, 659
Object Management Group Interface Definition
    Language (OMG IDL), 288
Object Transaction Service (OTS), 617
object-based development, 9–10
    defined, 9–10
    illustrated, 10
objects
    administered, 414
    definition of, 315
    as service endpoints, 315
    snapshot, 315
    state, 315
OMG Object Request Broker (ORB), 617
omission defects, 94
one-way encryption, 628
one-way operation
    defined, 151
    illustrated, 152
    message, 151
one-way RPC, 356
Open Grid Services Architecture (OGSA), 721
Open System Interconnection (OSI) model, 314
operation element, 150–153
    as container, 150
    defined, 150
    extending, 166
    Java method declaration, 150
    notification operation, 152–153
    one-way operation, 151
    request-response interaction, 151
    schema, 151
    solicit-response operation, 152
    See also WSDL documents
optimistic locking, 586
org.w3c.dom package, 288, 289
org.xml.sax.helpers package, 280, 281
org.xml.sax package, 280, 281
Organization object
    classifying, 500
    defined, 483

    in ebXML registry, 535
    publishing, 485
    querying, 520
    See also JAXR
output element, 152
    before input element, 152
    extending, 166
override policies, 720
overviewURL element, 204, 208

parameterOrder attribute, 149
parsers
    DOM, 287
    SAX, 280
    validating, 744, 746
    Xerces, 693, 746, 761
    XML, 545
parsing, 545
    JAXP schemas, 293–294
    SAX, 284, 285–286
    XML schemas, 293–294
participants, 602, 604, 612
partners
    discovery, 238
    profiles and agreements, 242–250
    sign-up, 238
password encryption, 627
peer-to-peer exchanges, 687
performance, 703–707
    CBS development, 69–71
    defined, 18, 69, 703
    enhancement techniques, 71
    measurement, 703
    optimization, 375–376
    questions, 69
    requirements, 69–70
    scalability and, 70
    strategies, 70, 71
    with stubs, 366
    systems management, 691
pessimistic locking, 586
Phaos XML, 650
physical evolution, 5–8
    client-server, 7

physical evolution (*continued*)
  monolithic, 6
  N-tier development, 7–8
  World Wide Web, 8
pluggable authentication modules (PAMs), 671
point-to-point messaging, 412
POP3 protocol, 419, 423
port element, 163, 166
portability
  component execution environment
      and, 80
  defined, 80
  enhancing, 80
  questions, 80
portal registries, 229–230
  benefits, 230
  defined, 229
  See also registries
PortfolioHolder implementation class, 387
portType element, 154, 155
  binding element, 154
  defined, 154
  illustrated, 155
  name attribute, 154
  See also WSDL documents
Post Office Protocol (POP), 419
postal address support, 217–218
presentation-centric XML, 277
pricing models, 693–696
  accounting services, 695–696
  metering service, 696
  supply and demand, 694
private UDDI registries, 196–197, 227–231
  altering, 228
  auditing capabilities, 227
  benefits, 227
  considerations, 231
  EAI registries support, 230
  extending, 228
  implementation, 227
  implementation availability, 227
  marketplace registries support, 228–229
  portal registries support, 229–230
  recommendations, 231
  See also UDDI registries

procedure-based services, 262
processes, 88–89
  BPEL, 734–736
  business, 237–243
  defined, 732
  OPEN, 88
  product line, 88–89
  RUP, 88
  SCRUM, 88
  XP, 88
processing model, 112–119
  defined, 112
  HTTP binding, 115–117
  SMTP-POP binding, 117–119
  SOAP bindings, 115
  steps, 114
  See also SOAP
product line for services development, 73–76
  commonalities/variations identification, 74
  frameworks and libraries, 75
  infrastructure, 74–75
  organization, 75–76
  patterns, styles, blueprints, 75
  process, 75
profiles, 431–433
  building, 432
  capability, 481–482
  defined, 432
  ebXML, 432
  JAXM use with, 475
  SOAP headers and, 432
  SOAP message structure with, 432
  XML schemes, 432
programmatic registration, 392
proof-of-concept testing, 703
property declaration, 574–575
  defined, 574
  effect, 575
  generateIsSetMethod customization, 574
  syntax, 574
  See also binding declarations
providers
  for ebXML, 535, 536
  JAXR, 481
  publishing with, 539–544

provider-to-provider communication, 455
    block diagram, 456
    defined, 455
    sequence diagram, 456
provisional effect, 603
proxies, 83–84
    dynamic, 84, 172, 362–363
    factory, 88
    service, 83
proxy layer, 83–84
    defined, 83
    functioning, 83–84
public key infrastructure (PKI), 649, 650
public UDDI registries, 227
public/private-key algorithms, 629–630
publisherAssertion API, 198–199
Publishers API, 199–200
publishing
    ability, 213
    business entities, 223
    company information to UDDI registry,
        499–508
    complete WSDL document, 519
    content to ebXML registries, 537–539
    deployment-time, 530
    with JAXR provider, 539–544
    organizations in ebXML registries, 533–536
    service implementation definition, 519
    service information to UDDI registry,
        508–520
    service interface only, 519
    service interface with one service
        implementation, 519
    service interfaces in UDDI, 213–216
    with UDDI4J, 223
    WSDL describing service implementation, 514
    WSDL service interface, 513
publishing assertions
    business entity relationship and, 224
    creating, 223–224
publish-subscribe messaging, 412
purchaseorder.xsd schema, 546–547
PurchaseOrderService, 448–449, 458, 460–464
    asynchronous code, 461–464
    asynchronous version, 460–464

defined, 448, 458, 460
synchronous code, 448–449
synchronous version, 448–449
See also asynchronous messaging; synchronous
    messaging

qualifiers, 224–225
    example, 224–225
    specification, 225
quality of service (QoS), 17–19
    accessibility, 17–18
    availability, 17
    integrity, 18
    multiple services, 134
    parameters, 18
    performance, 18
    regulatory, 18
    reliability, 18
    security, 18
    specification, 17–18
    testing, 92, 93
queries
    CPP/CPA, 539
    declarative, 498–530
    organization information from UDDI,
        521–522
    Organization object, 520
    pattern creation, 520
    registry, 520–523
    service information, 523–526
    SQL, 499
QueryManager interface, 497

Ralph Merkle's Puzzle Protocol, 631–632
redundant infrastructure, 711
references
    defined, 124
    digital signature, 636
    service, 399
    SOAP, 124
registrars, 179
registries, 479–480
    capability, 481–482

registries (*continued*)
    defined, 479
    EAI, 230
    ebXML, 250–256, 498
    heterogeneous, 481
    information model, 480
    marketplace, 228–229
    portal, 229–230
    private UDDI, 196–197, 227–231
    public UDDI, 227
    queries, 497
    querying, 520–523
    RMI, 479–480
    security and, 232
    service, 16, 38
    UDDI, 178–179, 219–220, 224–225,
        227–231, 485, 488, 499–523
    usage, 480
    Web services, 181, 480
    See also UDDI registries
registry browser, 275
registry data
    association of, 489–491
    classification of, 485–489
Registry Information Model (RIM),
        251–252
    defined, 251
    illustrated, 252
    relationships, 251
    UDDI, 255
    See also ebXML
Registry Services Specification,
        251–253
RegistryObject interface, 487, 491
RegistryPackage objects, 538
regression testing
    defined, 93, 701
    example, 701
    See also testing
regulatory, 18
reliability
    CBS development, 79–80
    defects, 94
    defined, 18, 79
    dependence, 61

factors, 79
    measurement, 61
    questions, 79
Reliable HTTP (HTTPR), 703
Remote Method Invocation (RMI), 84
    analogy, 402
    EJB use of, 716
    objects, 140
    registry, 479–480
remote procedure call (RPC), 313
    implementations with SOAP, 317
    nonblocking invocation, 356
    one-way, 356
    performing, 315
    See also JAX-RPC
report-hazard element, 609
reporting, 19
repositories, 479–480
request-response operation, 151
    defined, 151
    illustrated, 152
    See also operation element
request-response processing, 335
requirements analysis, 66
reusability, 28
    CBS development, 73–76
    defined, 73
    improving, 74–76
    questions, 73
Rivest, Shamir, Adelman (RSA), 632
routing, 431
RPC styles, 160, 161
RPC/encoded style, 329, 335
    example, 330
    JAX-RPC and, 329
    when to use, 333–335
    WSDL for, 161
    See also styles
RPC/literal style, 162, 330–331, 335
    example, 330–331
    WSDL for, 162
    See also styles
RSA BSAFE, 639
runtime binding, 12
run-time security, 623–626

S/MIME, 631
save_service API, 204–205
SAX, 278–287
  defined, 278
  details resource, 278
  extensions, 280
  handlers, 280
  helper classes, 280
  interfaces definition, 280
  javax.xml.parsers, 280, 282
org.xml.sax.ext package, 280, 281
  org.xml.sax.helpers package, 280, 281
  org.xml.sax package, 280, 281
  packages, 280–281
  parsers, 280
  parsing code, 284
  parsing handler, 285–286
  processing, 292
  sample XML file parsed with, 283–284
  support, 280
  when not to use, 293
  when to use, 292
SAXParser, 284, 287
SAXParserFactor, 282–283
  configurable properties with, 283
  configuring, 282
  defined, 282
  multi-threading and, 287
  See also SAX
scalability, 713–715
  benefit, 29–30
  cluster capacity and, 715
  infrastructure partitioning, 713–714
  inhibitor, 714
  performance and, 70
schema compiler, 551
  binding declarations, 555
  code generated using, 554
  execution, 552
  illustrated, 551
  interface generation, 560
schema scope, 568
schemaBindings declaration, 570–571
  defined, 570
  nameXmlTransform element, 571

syntax, 570–571
  See also binding declarations
scope, 568–569
  component, 569
  definition, 569
  global, 568
  illustrated, 569
  schema, 568
Secure Sockets Layer (SSL), 626
  basic authentication over, 623
  de facto implementation, 625
  illustrated, 624
  operation, 624
  session establishment, 624–625
  transports using, 625
Securities and Exchange Commission (SEC), 198
security, 621–682
  in applications, 625
  authentication methods, 623
  CBS development, 71
  deployment time, 622
  design, 627–628
  design time, 621–622
  ebXML, 255
  federations, 679
  identity management, 680–682
  implementation scenarios, 676–680
  J2EE and, 669–672
  JavaMail, 427
  JAX-RPC and, 392–393
  message-level, 625, 627
  QoS specification, 18
  registries and, 232
  requirements, 20
  run time, 623–626
  summary, 688
  trust service provider, 679
  unified view, 710
  Web services considerations, 621–626
  Web services initiatives, 626–634
  XML messaging and, 431
Security Assertions Markup Language (SAML),
    628–629, 650–657
  architecture, 652
  assertions, 651–657

Security Assertions Markup Language (SAML)
   (*continued*)
   attribute assertion, 653–664
   authentication assertion, 652–653
   authorization assertion, 654–657
   bindings and profiles, 651, 657
   categories, 651–652
   conformance, 652
   defined, 628, 651
   design, 629
   driving force, 628
   illustrated, 651
   origin, 650–651
   protocol/format definition, 651
   request-response messages, 657
   security and privacy, 652
   SourceID vs., 686
   specification, 650
self-addressed messages, 455
self-healing, 60–61
   architecture, 61
   defined, 60
   reliability, 61
semantic web, 229
serializers, 337
   base, 389
   client-side, 391
   custom, configuring, 391–392
   defined, 388
   illustrated, 388
   portability across implementations and, 390
   porting, 390
   specifying, 388
   as utilities by reference implementation, 391
   See also deserializers
server-side handlers
   configuration, 376
   data encryption/decompression, 379
   listing, 380–383
   request interception, 379
   See also handlers
service bus, 26–28
   defined, 26
   example, 27
   illustrated, 27

   management software, 28
   paradigm, 25
service composition, 16–17, 728–741
   defined, 16–17, 728
   description, 729
   example, 17
   need for, 728–736
service consumers
   availability and, 79
   client-side binding generation, 366
   defined, 38, 355
   discovery, 41–42
   dynamic interaction, 138–139
   WSDL usage, 167
service consumption, 355–367
   client decision, 365–367
   clients using DII, 359–362
   clients using dynamic proxies, 362–363
   clients using stubs, 357–359
   clients using WSDL, 363–365
   invocation modes, 355–356
   nonblocking RPC invocation, 356
   one-way RPC, 355–356
   synchronous request-response, 355
   See also JAX-RPC; JAX-RPC development
service contracts, 12
   defined, 38
   information hiding and, 47–48
service definition, 336–337
   defined, 336
   example, 336–337
   as Java interface, 336
   See also JAX-RPC; JAX-RPC development
service deployment, 339–341
   illustrated, 339
   at runtime, 338
   See also JAX-RPC; JAX-RPC development
service description, 15–16, 341–355
   abstract, 135–137
   collaboration, 729
   concrete, 137–138
   defined, 341
   elements, 134
   functional characteristics, 135–174
   role/position of, 728–729

service aspects, 15
  stack, 729
  use methods, 16
  xrpcc, 341–344
  See also JAX-RPC; JAX-RPC development
service development, 20
service discovery, 41–42
  based on namespace, 527–529
  runtime, 529–530
  support, 41
service element, 164
  defined, 164
  extending, 166
  illustrated, 164
  See also WSDL documents
service endpoints, 315
  defined, 339
  implementation, 339
service façade,, 84
service federation testing, 93
service implementation, 337–339, 369–370
  client-specific state and, 339
  defined, 337
  definition, 508
  definition, publishing, 519
  example, 337–338
  handler configuration, 381–383
  for processing attachments, 369–370
  ServiceLifeCycle interface, 340
  See also JAX-RPC; JAX-RPC development
service information queries
  based on namespace, 527–529
  client-side output, 526
  code, 523–526
service interfaces, 181–184
  abstraction description, 508
  classifying, 513
  defined, 181
  definition, 508
  describing, 181
  documents, 184
  publishing, 513, 519
  publishing, in UDDI, 213–216
  publishing, with one service implementation, 519

  referencing service interface, 211–212
  separated into billpayinterface.wsdl, 509–511
  WSDL, 512
service leases, 40
service level agreements (SLAs), 19, 697–699
  characteristics of, 698
  defined, 697–698
  elements, 698
  feature checklist, 699
service producers, 167–169
service providers, 38
service proxies, 704
  defined, 38–39
  illustrated, 39
  performance enhancement, 39
  provision, 39
service references, 399
service registry, 16, 38
service types, 179
service-based development, 12–13
  defined, 12
  illustrated, 13
  interoperability issue and, 12
ServiceLifeCycle interface, 340
service-oriented architecture (SOA), 35–62
  characteristics, 40–61
  coarse-grained interfaces, 50–59
  composability, 59–60
  defined, 35
  entities, 37–40
  implementation, 37
  interoperability, 48–49
  issues, 35
  location transparency, 59
  loose coupling, 49
  network-addressable interface, 50
  self-contained and modular, 42–48
  self-healing, 60–61
  service consumer, 38
  service contract, 38
  service lease, 40
  service provider, 38
  service proxy, 38–39
  service registry, 38

service-oriented architecture (SOA) (*continued*)
  summary, 61–62
  Web services and, 40
ServletContext object, 340
session façade,, 84
  defined, 84
  illustrated, 85
  See also application architecture
setValidateURI method, 519
SHA1, 631
share-based policies, 720
shared locks, 586
shared secrets, 628
Simple API for XML. *See* SAX
Simple Mail Transfer Protocol (SMTP), 419
  DSN, 428
  MDN, 428
Simple Object Access Protocol. *See* SOAP
simple service, 25
simple types
  defined, 751
  extending, 751–752
  prefix, 751
  See also types
single-phase confirm operation, 609
SkipJack, 630
SMTP-POP binding, 117–119
SOAP, 1, 97–132
  actor roles, 376
  Apache implementations, 692
  with Attachment capability, 99,101
  attachments, 368
  body, 15
  case for, 97–101
  decimal data type, 692
  defined, 97, 99
  envelope structure, 421
  extending, 100–101
  faults, 109
  firewalls and, 668–669
  headers, 15, 691
  horizontal extensibility, 112
  HTTP and, 99
  information definitions, 101
  interoperability goal, 690

interoperability issues, 692
JMS providers using, 476
processing model, 112–119
references, 124
request, 365–366
response, 366
role, 97, 131–132
simplicity, 99, 626
summary, 131–132
toolkits, 692
UDDI business registry access, 203
UDDI relationship, 202–213
versioning, 105
  See also SOAP messages; SOAP nodes
SOAP bindings, 103, 115, 156–158
  BTP and, 612–615
  defined, 156
  extensions, 156
  soap:binding element, 156–157, 161
  soap:body element, 157
  soap:fault element, 158
  soap:header element, 158
  soap:operation element, 157
SOAP encoding, 119–125, 319–333
  compound data types, 122–125
  defined, 320
  literal, 119
  schemes, 320
  "Section 5," 119
  simple data types, 120–122
SOAP messages, 15, 97, 100
  Body element, 103, 108–109
  construction of, 439
  defined, 102
  dumping, 117
  elements, 103–111
  email containing, 117–118
  encoded, 320
  Envelope element, 102, 105–106
  fault, 109–110
  Fault element, 109–111
  guiding, 736
  header, 101, 157
  Header element, 102–103, 106–108
  header insertion, 113

intercepting, 117
modeling, 125
namespaces, 105, 106
one-way message capability, 115
paths, 113
processing steps, 114
request, 104–105, 128
request sent synchronously, 443–445
response, 105, 131
rules, 103
structure, 102–103
structure and content illustration, 104
structure illustration, 102
vertical extensibility, 106
See also SOAP
SOAP nodes
defined, 101
identification, 112–113
illustrated, 101
intermediaries and, 113
intermediate, 100–101
message processing steps, 114
in processing path, 736
roles, 114
SOAP version support, 106
See also SOAP
SOAP with Attachments API for Java (SAAJ),
125–131, 475
abstraction, 125
API, 439
client, 128
for creating/manipulating messages, 418
creation, 125
defined, 125
functioning of, 127–131
as JWSDP component, 268
MessageFactory class, 126
MIME mappings supported by, 445
model in javax.xml.soap package, 440
modeling in, 125
object model, 126
object representation in, 127
SOAP request message, 130
SOAP response message, 131
SOAPConnection class, 126–127

SOAPConnectionFactory class, 127
specifications, 439, 445
uses, 268
See also SOAP
soap:binding element, 156–157, 161
soap:body element, 157
soap:fault element, 158
soap:header element, 158
SoapMailReceiver application, 424–426
SoapMailSender application, 421–423
SOAPMessage message object, 441–443, 447
adding contents to, 442
contents, 441
soap:operation element, 157
solicit-response operation
defined, 152
grammar, 152
illustrated, 153
See also operation element
SourceID, 685–688
authentication/authorization support, 687
defined, 685
delegated administration, 687
focus, 686
goal, 685
identity management features, 686
identity solution, 685
Liberty Alliance and, 685, 686
provisioning/self-service support, 687
SAML vs., 686
SSO kernel, 685
tools, 685–686
specification pointers, 179
SQL queries, 499
standard, 30–33
Standard Generalized Markup Language (SGML),
236
state maintenance, 334
static compile-time binding, 170–171, 529
static deploy-time binding, 171, 530
defined, 530
usefulness, 530
See also binding(s)
static runtime binding, 171
store-and-forward applications, 409

structs, 122
structured design
   defined, 9
   illustrated, 10
stubs
   concept, 357
   configuration, 359
   DII and, 362
   JAX-RPC, 357
   performance with, 366
   reference implementation, 358
   RMI-IIOP, 357
   use code, 358
   use disadvantage, 366
   using, 357
styles, 328–333
   combinations, 328
   document, 161, 328
   document/encoded, 162–163, 333
   document/literal, 163, 329, 332
   RPC, 160, 161, 328
   RPC/encoded, 161, 329, 330
   RPC/literal, 162, 330–331
sub-composers, 610, 612
sub-coordinators, 612
subscriptions, 232–233
subtransactions, 595–597
symmetric algorithms, 629, 630
synchronous messaging, 434–436, 439–451
   with acknowledgment, 435–436
   categories, 434–436
   client-side output, 446–447
   illustrated, 441
   inquiry, 434
   point-to-point, 439–441
   PurchaseOrderService, 448–449
   receivers, 446
   with response, 434–435
   response, 450–451
   senders, 446
   service implementation, 448
   update, 435
   See also JAXM; messaging
synchronous request-response, 355
synchronous Web services, 410

system tests, 93
systems management, 689–691
   backup/recovery, 691
   business problems addressed by, 690
   capacity, 691
   components, 690, 691
   console, 691
   delivery, 691
   efficiency, 690
   network, 691
   performance, 691
   policies/procedures, 690
   scheduling, 691
   service, 691
   service level, 691
   strategy, 689–690
   systems, 691
Systinet WASP, 267

tag library descriptors (TLDs), 773–774
taxonomies
   classification, 192–193
   custom, 193–194
   defined, 192
   ebXML, 255
   external, example, 490
   internal, classification of, 489, 490
   UDDI, 255
TcpMon Java utility, 117
TCPtrace, 117
technical architecture, 86–88
   defined, 86
   impact, 86
   robust, 86–87
   technical services, 87–88
technical services, 87–88
   access, 88
   building, 87
   defined, 87
Templates object, 306
testability, 78
   architecture support, 78
   defined, 78
   requirements, 78

See also component-based service (CBS) development

testing, 699–703
functional, 92, 700–701
load and stress, 701–702
proof-of-concept, 703
QoS, 92, 93
regression, 93, 701
service federation, 93
system, 93
types of, 700
unit, 92
throughput, 703
tickets, 720
time zone support, 217
timer service, 704–707
tModels, 165, 188–192
creating, 183, 192–193
defined, 179, 188
for Flute Bank News service, 191
illustrated, 188
keys, 189
multiple-symbol WSDL document, 209–210
name, 179
overviewURL element, 204
registration, 193
shopping cart configuration, 189
single-symbol WSDL document, 209
in Web services, 189
WSDL service interface representation, 213
See also UDDI; UDDI informational structural model
tool-generated classes, 364
transaction management, 583–619
concepts, 583–593
models, 589–591, 593–597
specifications, 597–618
summary, 619
transaction manager, 585–587
defined, 586
functions, 586–587
JTA, 592
JTS, 593
JTS, components, 594
TP monitor vs., 587

transactional support, 589–591
transaction models, 589–591
business, 598
flat, 589, 594, 619
nested, 590–591
new, 597–598
properties, 598
for Web services, 593–597
transactions
ACID, 597
atomic property, 584
BTP, 600–603
business, 594, 598–615
consistent property, 584
context, 587
context propagation, 401, 597
defined, 583
design, 91
discrete, 239, 242
distributed, 593
durability property, 585
global, 587–589
in-doubt, 589
in-flight, 588–589
isolation property, 584–585
JTA, 401
long-running, 595, 597
nested, 590–591
new specifications, 597–618
scope of, 589
subtransactions, 595–597
two-phase commit and, 587–589
unit of work, 584
Transformation API for XML (TrAX), 302
Triple DES, 631
trust service provider, 679
Trust Services Integration Kit, 650
Twofish, 631
two-phase commit, 587–589
BTP two-phase protocol vs., 609–610
commit phase, 587
defined, 587
global transactions and, 587–589
illustrated, 588
prepare phase, 587

two-phase protocol, 606–609
  illustrated, 606
  participants confirmation, 609–610
  transaction cancellation, 609
  two-phase commit protocol vs., 609–610
  See also Business Transaction Protocol (BTP)
two-way encryption, 628
type mapping
  defined, 388
  system API, 390
  system illustration, 389
types
  base, 762
  built-in, 751–752
  complex, 752–759
  deriving, by extension, 763–764
  deriving, by restriction, 764–765
  new, defining, 762–765
  simple, 51–52
types element, 146–148
  defined, 146
  extending, 166
  illustrated, 146
  See also WSDL documents
typesafe enumeration, 556, 557
typesafeEnum declaration, 576–579
  binding, 578–579
  defined, 576
  syntax, 576
  using, 576
  See also binding declarations

UDDI, 1, 165, 177–233
  add publisherAssertions API, 198
  browse pattern, 200
  as business problem solution, 177
  businessDetail structure, 506
  businessEntity structure, 507
  classification, 192–196
  client API, 255–256
  consortium recommendations, 508
  conversation support, 16
  defined, 16, 177
  deployment-time publishing to, 530

  digital signatures, 231–232
  drill-down pattern, 200
  ebXML vs., 254–256
  "find" aspects, 179
  find_relatedBusinesses API, 198
  founding fathers, 177
  functions, 177
  futures, 231–233
  human-friendly keys, 232
  identifiers, 196–197
  information model, 506
  Inquiry API, 200–201
  interaction illustration, 180
  internationalization, 216–219
  interoperability, 203, 693
  invocation pattern, 201
  JAXR mapping, 531–533
  name schemes, 217
  placeholder, 197
  postal address support, 217–218
  protocol support, 256
  provider, 180–181
  publication to, 507
  Publishers API, 199–200
  publishing WSDL service interfaces in,
    213–216
  querying organization information from,
    521–522
  registration information, 196–197
  Registry Information Model, 255–256
  role in Web services, 179–180
  runtime service discovery from, 529–530
  security, 255
  services information, finding, 523–529
  SOAP interfaces, 199–202
  SOAP/WSDL relationships and, 202–213
  specification, 177, 188–189, 192
  subscriptions, 232–233
  summary, 233
  taxonomies, 255
  time zone support, 217
  tModels, 165, 179
  Version 3.0, 231, 232
  Web interface, 200
  WSDL information published in, 514

WSDL representation in, 513
UDDI informational structural model, 184–192
    bindingTemplate, 187–188
    businessEntity, 184–186
    businessService, 186–187
    tModels, 188–192
UDDI registries, 18, 161, 165, 189, 485, 488
    binding information in, 201
    business entities, 178, 181, 182
    business services, 178, 182
    classification schemes, 192–193
    contents, 178
    defined, 178–179
    deleting information in, 224–225
    extending, 219–220
    Flute Bank as registered in, 499–500
    industry taxonomies, 178
    information types, 178–179
    internationalization support, 216
    maintenance support, 181
    population, 180
    private, 196–197, 227–231
    public, 227
    publishing ability, 213
    publishing company information to, 499–508
    publishing service information to, 508–520
    queries, 255
    querying, with JAXR, 520–523
    service types, 179
    specification pointers, 179
    use, 180
UDDI4J, 216, 221–226
    APIs, 214, 221
    classes, 222
    defined, 221
    development, 221
    goal, 222
    for locating multilingual businesses, 226
    open source, 221
    preferred language identifier, 226
    for publishing business entities, 223
    system properties support, 221–222
UN/CEFACT modeling methodology (UMM), 239
Unique Universal Identifier (UUID) keys, 179

unit testing, 92
Universal Description, Discovery and Integration. *See* UDDI
Unmarshaller, 553, 561–562
    defined, 561
    functions, 561–562
unmarshalling, 554
    defined, 316
    from different sources, 562
    parameters, 335
    requirement, 316
    success, 316
    XML-to-Java, 319
    See also marshalling
update locks, 586
URI, 112, 113
    absolute, for JSTL tags, 776
    identification by, 113
User object
    creating, 500
    defined, 483
    See also JAXR
UserTransaction interface, 618

validating parsers
    defined, 744
    Xerces, 746, 761
validation, 91–94
    digital signatures, 638, 645
    handlers, 562
    JAXB, 566–567
    XML Schema, 759
Validator interface, 566–567
vendor dependence, reduced, 30
vendor tool tasks, 168
verification, 91–94
Verisign XML Signature SDK, 639

Web Service Choreography Interface (WSCI), 729–734
    complex activity modeling, 733
    correlation elements, 734–735
    defined, 729

Web Service Choreography Interface (WSCI)
(*continued*)
elements, 731
interfaces, 731
process definitions, 731–732
sequencing and, 733
specification, 729
Web services
accounting, 694–696
acting as clients to provider, 466
asynchronous, 410
availability, 29–30
benefits, 3, 28–30
categorizing, 192–196
communication stack, 100
composite implementation, 25–26
composition, 29, 728–741
CORBA vs., 3
defined, 4
describing, 134
discovering, 178–192
fault tolerant, 718–720
features, 699
functional characteristics description, 135–174
with grid computing, 721
history, 4–13
implementation checklist, 724–725
as the interoperability standard, 4
invocation order, 134
invoking, 134
Java and, 20–21
location transparency, 29
loose coupling among, 594–595
management, 19
message-conversation-based, 262
messaging and, 410–411
middleware application, 26
multi-grained, 53–55
overview, 3–34
platform independence, 3–4
procedure-based, 262
QoS, 17–19, 134
reduced vendor dependence, 30
registries, 181, 480
reusability, 28

scalability, 29–30
security, 2, 621–626
security initiatives, 626–634
service bus, 26–28
service composition, 16–17
service description, 15–16
service development, 20
service messaging, 14–15
service registry, 16
service transport, 14
simple implementation, 25
SOA and, 40
specifications management, 31
standards, 1
standards bodies, 32
summary, 725–726
synchronous, 410
technical, 87–88
technology, 14–17
technology stack, 14
testing, 699–703
transaction model for, 593–597
UDDI role in, 179–180
Web Services Description Language. *See* WSDL
Web Services Interoperability organization, 394
Web Services Routing Protocol, 454
Web Services Security Assertions, 658
White Mesa, 394
World Geodetic System classification, 195
World Wide Web, 8
World Wide Web Consortium (W3C), 31, 99, 134
wrap and replace, 29
WS-Authorization, 663–666
defined, 660
scenario, 663–665
specification, 663
wscompile tool, 273–274
configuration file, 273–274
defined, 273
invocation syntax, 273
samples using, 275
for server-side ties, 274
xrpcc vs., 345
See also Java WSDP (JWSDP)

WS-Coordination, 616–617, 666–668
  defined, 616
  specification, 666
  WS-Transaction relationship, 616
wsdeploy tool, 271–273
  defined, 271
  illustrated, 273
  samples using, 275
  usage syntax, 271
  See also Java WSDP (JWSDP)
WSDL, 1, 15–16, 133–176
  access point specification, 215
  arrays and, 147, 148
  arrayType attribute, 148
  clients using, 363–365
  defined, 133
  with DII, 362
  for document/encoded style, 162–163
  for document/literal style, 163
  dynamic interactions and, 138–139
  dynamic proxy use, 84
  elements to extend, 166
  extending, 165–166
  extension mechanism, 156
  generating, from Java, 173–174
  importing, 167–168
  information published in UDDI, 514
  JAXR application to publish, 515–519
  for RPC/encoded style, 161
  for RPC/literal style, 162
  server-side Java classes and, 173
  service descriptions, 135
  service implementation, 210–211
  service interface, 512
  specification, 133, 134, 135
  storing in UDDI, 203
  summary, 176
  for timer service, 704–707
  tools/utilities, 165
  UDDI relationship, 202–213
  UDDI representation, 513
  usage patterns, 167–169
WSDL 1.2, 174–175
  clarifications, 175
  description, 174

description components, 175
serviceType, 175
SOAP 1.2 support, 175
specification, 174
Web services description, 174
WSDL bindings
  early, 169–171
  HTTP, 159–160
  late, 171–173
  MIME, 158–159
  service, 212–213
  SOAP, 156–158
  style/use and, 160–163
  types of, 156
  See also binding(s)
WSDL documents
  abstract, 135–137
  allows multiple symbols to be passed, 207–208
  allows single symbol to be passed, 206–207
  binding element, 154–160, 166
  conceptual representation, 136
  conceptually, 174
  concrete descriptions, 137–138
  defined, 135
  definitions element, 145, 166
  elements, 140–144
  fault element, 152, 166
  Flute Bank bill payment service, 141–144
  import element, 164–165
  information organization, 137
  input element, 152, 166
  message element, 148–150
  multiple-symbol, 209–210
  operation element, 150–153, 166
  output element, 152, 166
  overview, 135–139
  parsed, 215
  port element, 163, 166
  portType element, 154, 155
  publishing, 519
  referencing other descriptions, 164–165
  service element, 164, 166
  service interface, 211–212
  single-symbol, 209
  types element, 146–148, 166

WSDL documents (*continued*)
  Web service interface within, 154
  as well-formed XML documents, 139
WSDL messages
  content, 148
  example, 148
  name attribute, 148
  notification, 153
  one-way, 151
  part name, 149
  solicit-response, 153
WSDL operations, 150–153
  bindings, 153
  defined, 150
  Flute Bank bill payment service, 152
  groups, describing, 154
  notification, 152–153
  one-way, 151, 152
  request-response, 151, 152
  schema, 151
  solicit-response, 152
WSDL service interface
  binding element, 212
  document contents, 212
  publishing, in UDDI, 213–216
  referencing another service interface, 211–212
  tModel representation, 213
WSDL4J APIs, 213–214
WSDL-UDDI-SOAP technologies (WUST) stack, 262
WS-Federation, 663
  defined, 660
  use, 663
WS-I organization, 32–33
WS-I specifications, 660–668
  illustrated, 661
  list of, 660
  WS-Authorization, 660, 663–666
  WS-Coordination, 666–668
  WS-Federation, 660, 663
  WS-Policy, 660, 661
  WS-Privacy, 660, 662
  WS-SecureConversation, 660, 662–663
  WS-Security, 660, 661
  WS-Trust, 660, 662

WS-Policy, 661
  defined, 660
  SOAP policy format definition, 661
  specification, 661
WS-Privacy, 662
  defined, 660
  WS-Trust and, 662
WS-Routing protocol, 115, 736–740
  action element, 738
  bindings, 739–740
  defined, 737
  from element, 739
  fwd element, 738
  intermediaries, 738, 739
  over HTTP, 739
  path element, 738
  SOAP header entry, 738
  specification, 740
  via element, 738–739
WS-SecureConversation, 662–663
  defined, 660
  use, 663
WS-Security, 661
  defined, 660
  example, 665–666
  faults, 667
  security-token formats, 661
WS-Transaction, 597, 616–617
  ACID properties and, 617
  atomic transaction coordination pattern, 617
  defined, 616
  specifications, 616, 617
  WS-Coordination relationship, 616
  See also transaction models; transactions
WS-Trust, 662
  defined, 660
  specification, 662
  WS-Privacy and, 662

X.509 certificates
  as checkSignatureValue method argument, 648
  defined, 537
  user sending, 536

working with, 537
in XML D-Sig specifications, 533–535
XML
advantage, 312
attachments, 384
canonical form, 638
CPA elements, 249–250
CPP elements, 244–245
data-centric, 277
descriptors, 466
elements, 564–565
enumerations, 555–557
flow control, 778–780
lists, 557–558
marshalled out by application code, 554
messaging, 431–433
namespaces, 105, 106
parsers, 545
parsing, 545
presentation-centric, 277
representation generation, 549
save_service API, 204–205
support tags in JSTL, 774–781
as test-based protocol, 15
transcoding, into different formats, 302
transformation, 780–781
transformed into HTML, 298, 301
usage, 277
XML Access Control Markup Language
(XACML), 658–659
defined, 629
objects, 658
XML Digital Signature Software Library, 639
XML Digital Signatures, 628, 635–639
implementations, 639
specification, 636
XML Canonical specification and, 638
XML documents
association options, 293
canonical form, 635
configuration file, 173–174
CPA as, 246
CPP, 243, 245
DTD, 745–747
encrypted, 649

instance, 744
JAXB code to read, 552–553
with schema and namespaces, 293–296
schema for, 293–294, 295–297
unencrypted, 648–650
WSDL documents and, 139
XML encryption, 648–650
EncryptedData element, 648
EncryptedKey element, 648
implementations, 650
PKI, 649, 650
using, 649
XML Key Management Specification (XKMS),
626, 659–660
defined, 629, 659
messages, 659
using, 659
XML messaging
definitions, 13
elements, 103–111
envelope, 15
XML Schema, 743–770
annotation element, 567, 759
any element, 768–769
anyAttribute element, 768, 769
appinfo element, 759
defined, 743, 744
documentation element, 759
DTDs vs., 746
namespace, 749
role, 745
significance, 744
specifications, 770
summary, 770
validation types and, 759
XML Schema Definition (XSD), 146, 147, 743
XML schemas, 145–160
assembling, 766–767
complex types, 752–759
derivation support, 220
developer interpretation, 547
for employeeList document, 748
with enumerations, 556
extensible, 767–769
globalBindings declaration, 570

XML schemas (*continued*)
  JAXP and, 293–297
  namespace, 749–750
  new type definition, 762–765
  parsing, 293–294
  preference for, 293
  profiles, 432
  simple types, 751–752
  specifications, 121, 146
  states, 294
  using, 160
  validation, 293–295
  validators, 745
  working knowledge of, 743
  for XML document, 293–294, 295–297
XML Security Library, 650
XML Security Suite, 639, 650
XML Signature Library, 639
XML Transactions for Java (JAXTX), 618
XMLPay, 696–697
  communication, 696, 697
  defined, 696
  flow illustration, 697
  gateway, 696
XMLSpy, 301
XML-to-Java compiler, 551
XML-to-Java mapping, 555–559
  for basic types, 322
  complex types, 558–559
  data types, 323–325
  enumerations, 555–557
  lists, 557–558
  primitives, 555

  simple types, 555
XPath
  defined, 298, 638
  expressions, 658
  transform, 637
XPointer reference, 637
xrpcc, 366, 367
  additional configuration file, 344–345
  artifacts, 341
  configuration for stub and tie generation, 370
  configuration in reference implementation, 342
  handlerChain element, 343–344
  interface element, 343
  internals, 341–344
  namespaceMapping element, 344
  service element, 343
  typeMapping element, 344
  wscompile vs., 345
xsi:type, 121–122
XSL Formatting Objects (XSL-FO), 298
XSL Transformations (XSLT), 298–307
  defined, 298
  importance, 301
  JAXP and, 301–306
  processors, 298
  transformation code, 303–306
  transformation process, 298
XSLTc, 307–308
  architecture, 307
  code to use, 307–308
  defined, 307
  in production applications, 308

About the Authors

James McGovern is currently employed as an enterprise architect for The Hartford Financial Services Group, Inc. and writes the "Ask Doctor Java" column for *Java Developers Journal*. He is the lead author of *XQuery: Rapid Working Knowledge* (Sams Publishing). He is also the lead author of an upcoming book entitled *The Practical Guide to Enterprise Architecture* (Prentice Hall). James has sixteen years of experience in Information Technology. James is member of the Java Community Process and is working on the Performance Metric Instrumentation (JSR 138) specification. He holds industry certifications from Microsoft, Cisco, and Sun, and is a member of the Worldwide Institute of Software Architects. He can be reached at james.mcgovern@thehartford.com.

Sameer Tyagi is coauthor of four recent books on Java technology: *Professional JSP, Professional Java Server Programming J2EE Edition*, and *Core JDO*. He has written numerous magazine articles for *Java World, Java Developers Journal, Java Pro, Java Report*, and *Programmez* (France). He has eight years of experience in Information Technology. He is employed as an enterprise Java architect for Sun Microsystems and works at their Java Center in Burlington, Massachusetts. He can be reached at sameer.tyagi@sun.com.

Michael E. Stevens is employed as an application architect for The Hartford Financial Services Group, Inc. He received his B.S. degree in computer science from Central Connecticut State University and is a candidate for a master's degree in computer science from Rensselaer Polytechnic Institute. He has over fourteen years' experience in information technology and architecting and developing software systems, most recently focusing on J2EE solutions. In addition to having founded a software company that developed solutions for the mailing industry, Michael is a columnist for Developer.com and coauthor of *The Practical Guide to Enterprise Architecture* (Prentice Hall). He is a certified Java programmer and a member of the IEEE Computer Society and the ACM. He can be reached at mike@mestevens.com.

Sunil Mathew has fourteen years of experience in Information Technology and now manages the Java consulting practice for Sun Microsystems in the northeast. He has extensive experience working with senior-level management in defining technical strategy and architecture and in conducting technology evaluations. He can be reached at sunil.mathew@sun.com.

About the CD

This book is accompanied by a CD that contains the authors' example code, as well as evaluation copies of tools provided by industry-leading software vendors such as:

- Altova–XMLSpy
  Description: XML Editor
  Website: http://www.altova.com
  License Expiration: 30 Days

- BEA–Weblogic 7.0
  Description: Application Server
  Website: http://www.bea.com
  License Expiration: 60 Days

- Capeclear–Capeclear Studio
  Description: Web Services Development Tool
  Website: http://www.capeclear.com
  License Expiration: 30 Days

- Collaxa–Scenario Beans
  Description: Workflow
  Website: http://www.collaxa.com
  License Expiration: Never

- Fiorano–Fiorano MQ
  Description: Message Queue
  Website: http://www.fiorano.com

- Iona–XML Bus
  Description: Message Bus for Service-Oriented Architectures
  Website: http://www.iona.com

- Ipedo
  Description: XML Database
  Website: http://www.ipedo.com

- Parasoft–Jtest
  Description: Java Testing Tool
  Website: http://www.parasoft.com

- Popkin–System Architect
  Description: Data Modeling Tool
  Website: http://www.popkin.com
  License Expiration: 30 Days

- Republica–X-Fetch
  Description: XML Service Processor
  Website: http://www.republica.fi

- Sun–Sun One Application Server
  Description: J2EE Application Server
  Website: http://www.sun.com
  License Expiration: Never

- The Mind Electric–GLUE
  Description: Enabler for web services
  Website: http://www.themindelectric.com
  License Expiration: 30 Days

Some of the software contained on the CD may have expiration dates for usage. Please carefully read licensing information at installation time to understand any limitations.

Product features are subject to change and it is recommended that you visit each respective vendor's Web Site for additional information about licensing, pricing, and features.

▷ Requirements and Licenses

Please make sure that you have JDK 1.3.1 or greater installed prior to running any of the installations. To obtain the JDK, visit *http://java.sun.com/getjava/download.html*

Please note that your PC should have at least 256 MB RAM to run the sample products without issues. The software included on this CD is targeted toward users of the Microsoft Windows family of operating systems. If you are a Linux user, please feel free to visit the respective software vendor's site and download a risk-free evaluation copy of their software.

The respective installation files for each of the vendors' products are contained within each respective directory. Please read the ReadMe file in each directory before installing the product.

Each vendor grants you the right to use the software under licensing terms that you will be required to acknowledge upon installation. If there is a license agreement in the directory please read it before installing the product. Some of the products on this CD require a License Key that can be obtained by registering at the respective vendor's Web Site.

BEA has a special URL for registering Weblogic 7.0 and Weblogic workshop: Visit *http://www.bea.com/eval/mcgovern/index.shtml.*